3D AutoCAD® 2002

ONE STEP AT A TIME

3D AutoCAD® 2002

ONE STEP AT A TIME

TIMOTHY SEAN SYKES

www.uneedcad.com

Houston Community College

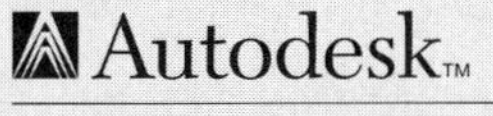

Registered Author/Publisher

PRENTICE HALL, Upper Saddle River, New Jersey, 07458

Library of Congress Cataloging-in-Publication Data

Sykes, Timothy Sean.
3D AutoCAD 2002: one step at a time / Timothy Sean Sykes.
p. cm.
Includes index.
ISBN 0-13-008156-6
1. Computer graphics. 2. AutoCAD. 3. Three-dimensional display systems I. Title.

T385.S875 2002
620'.0042'02855369--dc21

2001058240

Vice President and Editorial Director, ECS: Marcia J. Horton
Executive Editor: Eric Svendsen
Associate Editor: Dee Bernhard
Vice President and Director of Production and Manufacturing, ESM: David W. Riccardi
Executive Managing Editor: Vince O'Brien
Managing Editor: David A. George
Production Editor: Fran Daniele
Director of Creative Services: Paul Belfanti
Creative Director: Carole Anson
Interior Designer: Maureen Eide
Cover Designer: John Christiana
Art Editor: Xiaohong Zhu
Manufacturing Manager: Trudy Pisciotti
Manufacturing Buyer: Lynda Castillo
Marketing Manager: Holly Stark

10 9 8 7 6 5 4 3 2 1

ISBN 0-13-008156-6

Pearson Education Ltd., *London*
Pearson Education Australia Pty. Ltd., *Sydney*
Pearson Education Singapore, Pte. Ltd.
Pearson Education North Asia Ltd., *Hong Kong*
Pearson Education Canada, Inc., *Toronto*
Pearson Educacíon de Mexico, S.A. de C.V.
Pearson Education—Japan, *Tokyo*
Pearson Education Malaysia, Pte. Ltd.
Pearson Education, Inc., *Upper Saddle River, New Jersey*

In Loving Memory of Sue

Brief Contents

Contents

Lesson 12 Three-Dimensional Blocks and Three-Dimensional Plotting Tools 483

Preface

Introduction

3D AutoCAD 2002: One Step at a Time is a great software program, and in writing this text, I have tried to make learning AutoCAD simple and fun. My system of step-by-step instructions, supported by reference material, creates a hands-on approach to which you can refer over and over again. Each lesson includes: explanations of command options, worked examples of each command, and where appropriate, tips on using specific techniques in industry. AutoCAD is a challenging yet powerful program. We developed this package to provide all the support you need to master it.

Integrated, Multimedia Learning System

When you use this book, you are not just using a single text, but an integrated multimedia learning system made up of 2 parts:

1. Book—14 AutoCAD lessons designed to bring you fully up to speed with 2-D drawing, and a first lesson in 3-D. Lessons are clearly marked as to purpose and content, and provide hands-on, step-by-step instructions to help the student master the task. Lessons contain tips and tricks I developed through years of experience as a designer and CAD guru. Each lesson concludes with some extra steps for learning enhancement, several projects from a variety of disciplines and at various levels of mastery, and a list of review questions to validate student accomplishment. All lessons are covered in a clear, friendly, and encouraging writing style to set the student at ease.

WWW

2. World Wide Web—This text makes use of the Web as a self-assessment tool to test your understanding of important concepts at its own Web site **http://www.prenhall.com/sykes/**. It contains sets of questions keyed to approximately half the "Do This" exercises in the text that test your understanding of key concepts. "Do This" exercises that have on-line quiz material are marked with a web icon. Take these quizzes on-line as practice exams, and you will receive immediate feedback to your progress. Instructors can ask students to take these on-line quizzes and submit their results electronically, allowing instructors to easily track the students' progress. Professors may also use the syllabus builder feature of this web page to quickly prepare their own on-line syllabus.

Before You Begin

To complete the "Do This" and end-of-lesson exercises, you will need the reference files. These are available at: **www.prenhall.com/sykes**—simply follow the appropriate text to the download site.

Sometimes a bit of time elapses between publication of the text and availability of the website material. To avoid any hassles, I have provided the same files at my own site as an interim measure. Access the interim site at **www.uneedcad.com/2002/3DFiles**.

All files have been zipped for ease and speed of downloading. If you lack 'unzipping' ability (generally users of Windows 98 or earlier), you can download Winzip from **http://www.winzip.com/ddchomea.htm**. Be sure to unzip the files to "C:"

Winzip will do the rest (place the files in a series of lesson-related subfolders of a folder called Steps3D).

Instructors with text-related questions or students looking for a course may contact the author via the www.uneedcad.com site.

Why I Wrote This Book

Let me repeat some of what I said in *3D AutoCAD 2002: One Step at a Time.*

Some years ago I took my first AutoCAD course. I had been drafting for almost ten years at the time, but I saw that the drawing board would eventually give way to the computer. So I dug deep into the shallow recesses of a draftsman's wallet and came up with the $300 I needed to take the course.

A year or so later, still on the board, I was designing piping systems for one of the big petrochemical companies in Houston. There was one computer on the job, but nobody knew how to use it. I dedicated my lunches and evenings to exploring that old 286—often messing it up badly and having to call the computer support folks to come fix it.

After a few months of this, my immediate supervisor was transferred to an AutoCAD project. He was somewhat lost in the computer world, and I was the only one he knew who could turn one on. So he asked for me to follow him. I was excited by the prospect—until I learned that I was to be in charge of five CAD stations on the new project! Then I was a bit nervous (okay, terrified).

I did what any closet teacher would do—I went right out and bought a book! For the next several weeks, I managed to stay exactly 12 hours ahead of the rest of my crew. That is (it seemed miraculous), what I read one evening was what I was asked about the next day! So my reputation as a guru was established. Later, the questions became more difficult, and I had to buy another book (AutoLISP). But, by the grace of God, I am still staying 12 hours ahead of my students.

So, why am I a guru? Simply because I was the guy who bought (and *read*) a book.

Why this book? *3D AutoCAD 2002: One Step at a Time* continues and concludes the training begun in *AutoCAD 2000: One Step at a Time—Basics*. It does not require familiarity with that text, but it does continue the techniques that readers of *Basics* have come to know.

I have tried, again, to create lessons that are friendly rather than egghead academic. My intent is to teach my students (and readers) how to make a living using AutoCAD—essentially to answer the questions that I faced that first year as a guru and in the years since as an instructor. I will not cover every nook and cranny of this marvelous tool, but let's face it, it's not an encyclopedia. (I tend to shy away from people who promise it all.)

I am not "just a teacher" or "just a writer" or "just a designer." I have made a good living using AutoCAD for several years. I am a trained and experienced instructor (I have a degree in Secondary Education and instructor certifications from both Autodesk and Microsoft), a trained and experienced writer (my third and fourth teaching fields are English and English Language Arts), and I was a Senior Piping

Designer when I finally left the petrochemical industry for greener pastures. (I have also designed furniture, architectural structures, and "those nifty little houses that Santa sits in down at the mall." And my fifth teaching field is industrial Education.)

Why this book? Because here I bring all of this together to help my students and readers conquer their goal of making a living using AutoCAD.

Who Should Use This Book

I have written this book for draftsmen who have already achieved competence in basic AutoCAD operation.

As with the *Basics* book, I make no attempt to teach drafting here, but you should have some education or background in drafting, or at least in reading blueprints, *before attempting to learn AutoCAD*. For more on the basics of drafting, I highly recommend Frederick E. Giesecke's *Technical Drawing* (Prentice Hall). Now in its eleventh edition, it has been the basic drafting text of choice at least since I studied the subject more than 20 years ago.

Likewise, I do not attempt to instruct the user on how to use Windows or any other computer operating system. However, you should be familiar with a computer and its operating system before attempting to master any complex software like AutoCAD. If you are not comfortable with Windows, please precede your AutoCAD attempts with an appropriate computer ops course. If there are no courses available or convenient, I suggest picking up a copy of Microsoft's *Windows 95* [98] *Step by Step*. All of Microsoft's *Step by Step* books are remarkably good course material—simple to follow and easy to understand.

Expertise with other software is also not required, but some experience with MS Access (or some other database program) as well as any graphics program can be quite beneficial.

People are still asking me who my target audience is. I find the question a bit confusing since the training is the same regardless of whom is being trained. I have designed these texts to stand alone or as classroom guides. Therefore, anyone can use it—from high school students through college or professional development instructors.

Shaded boxes provide useful tips or tricks for making 3D AutoCAD 2002: One Step at a Time easy.

Sykes' engaging writing style is easy to follow.

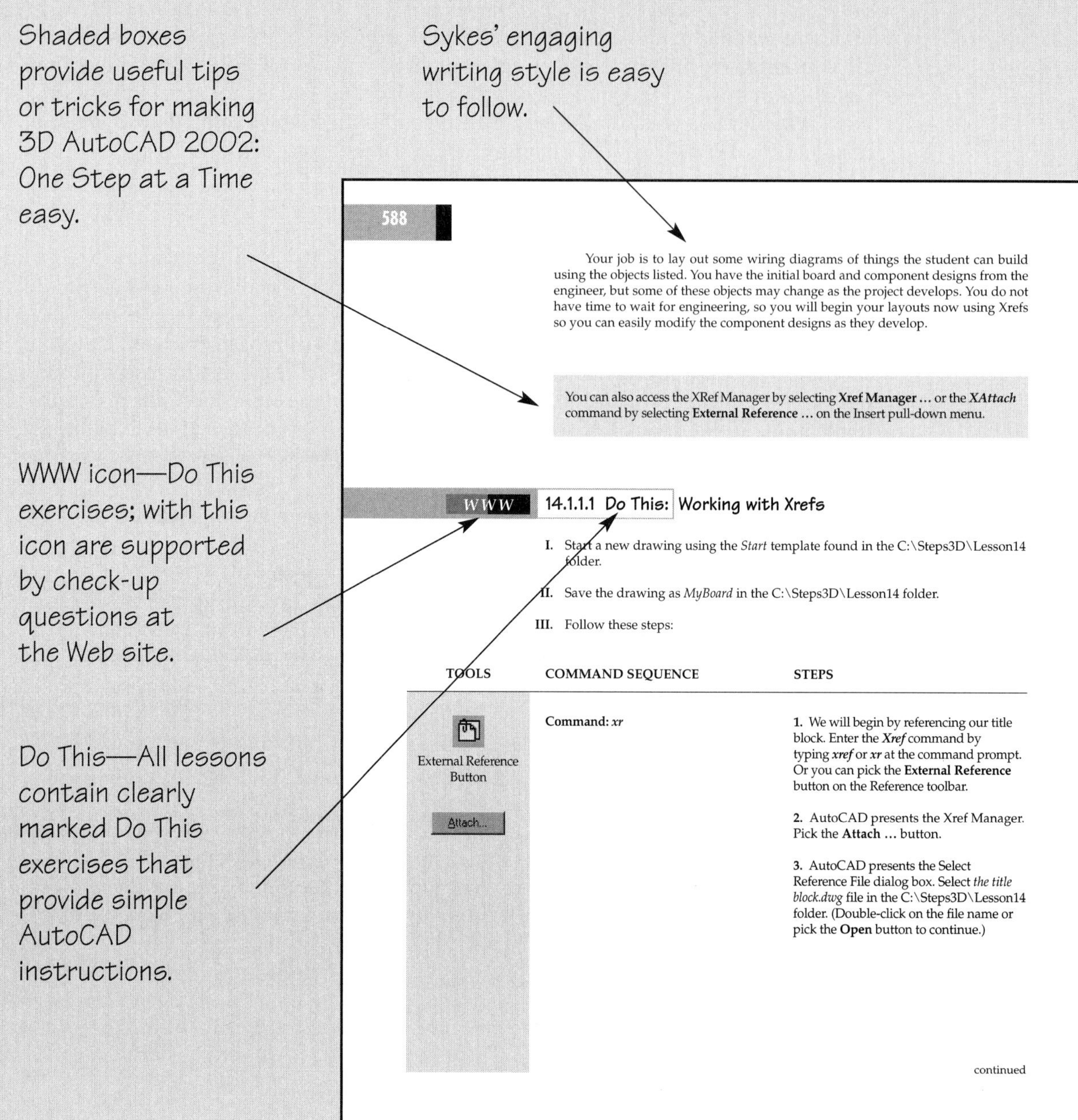

588
Your job is to lay out some wiring diagrams of things the student can build using the objects listed. You have the initial board and component designs from the engineer, but some of these objects may change as the project develops. You do not have time to wait for engineering, so you will begin your layouts now using Xrefs so you can easily modify the component designs as they develop.
You can also access the XRef Manager by selecting Xref Manager ... or the XAttach command by selecting External Reference ... on the Insert pull-down menu.
WWW
14.1.1.1 Do This: Working with Xrefs
I. Start a new drawing using the Start template found in the C:\Steps3D\Lesson14 folder.
II. Save the drawing as MyBoard in the C:\Steps3D\Lesson14 folder.
III. Follow these steps:
TOOLS
COMMAND SEQUENCE
STEPS
External Reference Button
Attach...
Command: xr
1. We will begin by referencing our title block. Enter the Xref command by typing xref or xr at the command prompt. Or you can pick the External Reference button on the Reference toolbar.
2. AutoCAD presents the Xref Manager. Pick the Attach ... button.
3. AutoCAD presents the Select Reference File dialog box. Select the title block.dwg file in the C:\Steps3D\Lesson14 folder. (Double-click on the file name or pick the Open button to continue.)
continued

WWW icon—Do This exercises; with this icon are supported by check-up questions at the Web site.

Do This—All lessons contain clearly marked Do This exercises that provide simple AutoCAD instructions.

Pages not sequential

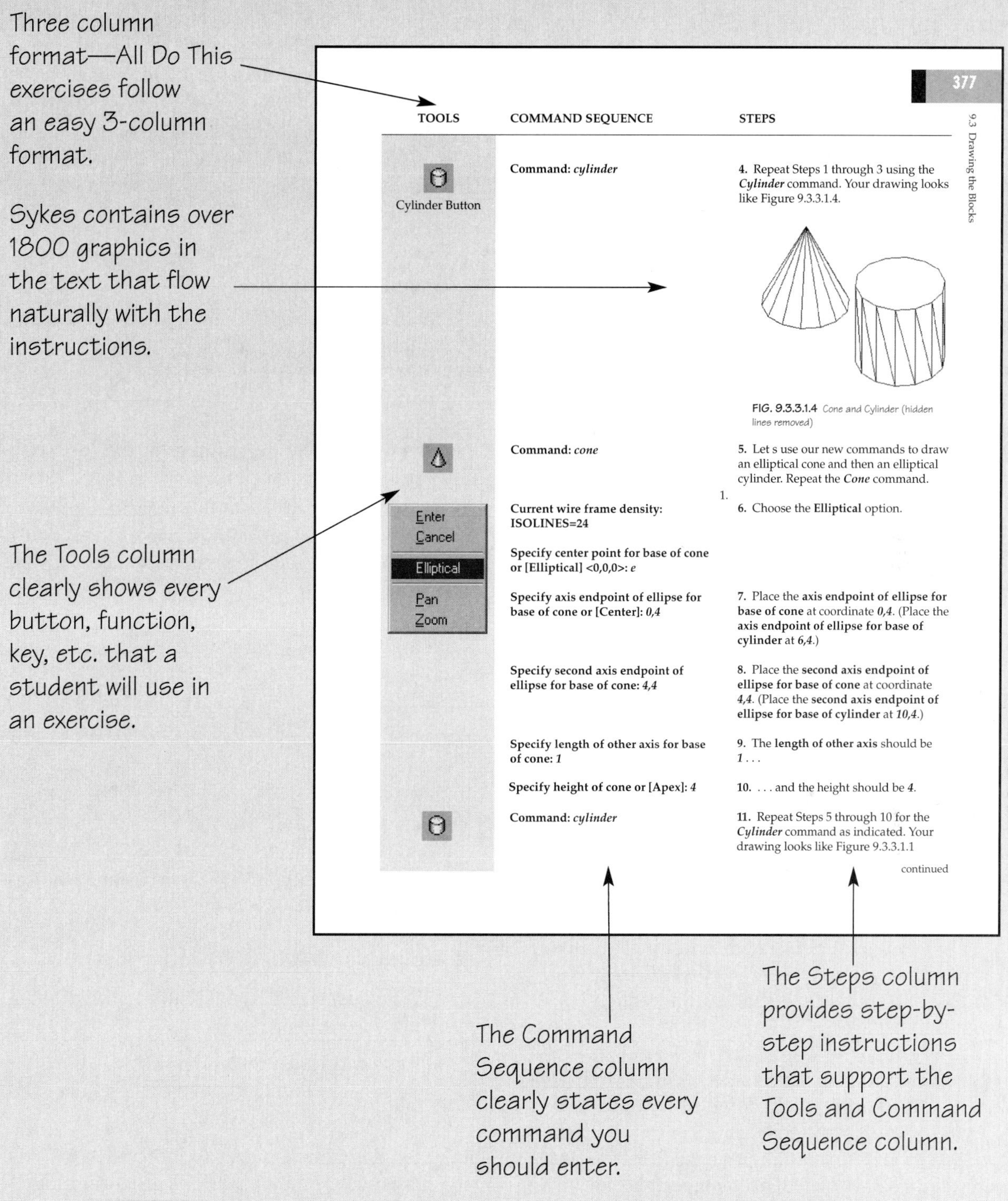

Three column format—All Do This exercises follow an easy 3-column format.
Sykes contains over 1800 graphics in the text that flow naturally with the instructions.
The Tools column clearly shows every button, function, key, etc. that a student will use in an exercise.
The Command Sequence column clearly states every command you should enter.
The Steps column provides step-by-step instructions that support the Tools and Command Sequence column.

377

9.3 Drawing the Blocks

TOOLS	COMMAND SEQUENCE	STEPS
Cylinder Button	**Command:** ***cylinder***	**4.** Repeat Steps 1 through 3 using the ***Cylinder*** command. Your drawing looks like Figure 9.3.3.1.4.
		FIG. 9.3.3.1.4 Cone and Cylinder (hidden lines removed)
	Command: ***cone***	**5.** Let s use our new commands to draw an elliptical cone and then an elliptical cylinder. Repeat the ***Cone*** command.
Enter Cancel Elliptical Pan Zoom	**Current wire frame density: ISOLINES=24**	1. **6.** Choose the **Elliptical** option.
	Specify center point for base of cone or [Elliptical] <0,0,0>: *e*	
	Specify axis endpoint of ellipse for base of cone or [Center]: ***0,4***	**7.** Place the **axis endpoint of ellipse for base of cone** at coordinate ***0,4***. (Place the **axis endpoint of ellipse for base of cylinder** at ***6,4***.)
	Specify second axis endpoint of ellipse for base of cone: ***4,4***	**8.** Place the **second axis endpoint of ellipse for base of cone** at coordinate ***4,4***. (Place the **second axis endpoint of ellipse for base of cylinder** at ***10,4***.)
	Specify length of other axis for base of cone: ***1***	**9.** The **length of other axis** should be ***1*** . . .
	Specify height of cone or [Apex]: ***4***	**10.** . . . and the height should be ***4***.
	Command: ***cylinder***	**11.** Repeat Steps 5 through 10 for the ***Cylinder*** command as indicated. Your drawing looks like Figure 9.3.3.1.1

continued

How to Use This Book

Each lesson follows that old saw I learned back in "teacher school": Tell 'em what you're gonna tell 'em; tell 'em; tell 'em what you told 'em.

So we begin each lesson with a set of goals stated simply as ***Following this lesson, you will:***. This page gives you some idea of what you will cover in the lesson.

Next, we cover the material. This occurs in three steps.

- First we discuss a topic—generally a command or procedure. This discussion includes the purpose of the command or procedure and a sample and explanation of either the command sequence or the dialog box. Refer to this section to answer questions concerning what a command or option does.
- Second we have a guided exercise called **Do This**. These exercises act as an instructor telling you what to do *one step at a time*.

  The exercises are generally divided into three columns. The **Steps** column *tells* you what to do. The **Command Sequence** column *shows* you what to do. The **Tools** column generally gives you a button or drop-down box option to the keyboard approach shown in the **Command Sequence** column.

  Refer to this section to answer questions concerning how to do something.
- Last we have an independent project (or several). This occurs in the **Exercises** section at the end of each lesson. Here you find a project that you must do on your own. Setup information will be provided, but you must refer to previous lessons as needed to complete the project independently.

Throughout the lesson, you will find inserts that provide additional information or tricks to help in your understanding of the topic.

After covering the material, there is an **Extra Steps** section in each lesson. These are full of added features, tidbits of knowledge, or suggestions for further study.

The *tell 'em what you told 'em* part (found in the **What Have We Learned?** section) does just that. In this section, I also try to give you some idea of what will come next.

I finish each lesson with some review questions to reinforce what we have covered.

Apparently, my system for identifying graphics has caused some confusion among reviewers. Because of the number of graphics involved in all of the *3D AutoCAD 2002: One Step at a Time* books, tracking them became quite a challenge. Here is what I did.

Each graphic

- begins with the word *FIG.* to identify it as a graphic.
- bears the number of the section or exercise in which it resides (i.e., 14.2.1).

Graphics in a stepped exercise

- are identified by the number of the step with which they are associated.
- may contain a letter after the numbering (*a*, *b*, *c*, etc.) if there are more than one of them—this helps identify each graphic associated with a specific step.

Graphics not in a stepped exercise

- conclude with a letter to track them within a particular section of the book.

Style Notes

I have followed several conventions in creating this text. Understanding them will make it easier to follow:

- Throughout the text:
  - I use *italics* for emphasis and to indicate the names of files
  - I use **bold** to indicate AutoCAD prompts, buttons and names of buttons, system variables, and dialog box tabs
  - I use ***bold and italics*** to indicate AutoCAD command names, hotkeys, and user input
  - I CAPITALIZE names of dialog boxes and pull-down menus
  - I use bullets and graduated indention to organize explanations of command options

Art

I wrote this text to be the most visual book on the market. Whenever possible, I tried to illustrate how to create drawings through generous use of detailed screen shots, and actual drawings. In teaching, I have found that my students really appreciate a visual approach to learning. This text contains over 1800 graphics!

Supplements

We are also supporting the text with the Sykes Web site—**http://www.prenhall.com/sykes/**, and qualified instructors using this text may order an instructor's solutions disk. To order this disk, either contact your local Prentice Hall sales rep, order online at **http://www.prenhall.com**, or call 1-800-922-0579.

Bundling Options

To make the cost of purchasing several books for one course more manageable for students, Prentice Hall offers discounts when you purchase this book with several other Prentice Hall textbooks. Discounts range from 10 to 20% off the price of the two books separately. At press time, you may bundle this text for discounts with any core Prentice Hall graphics text by Giesecke, Earle, Lockhart/Johnson, or Sorby. You may also bundle this text with the Advanced version when it is published for a discount. To request more specific pricing information, get isbn's for ordering bundles, and learn more about Prentice Hall's offerings in graphics and CAD, either contact your Prentice Hall Sales rep, or go to **http://www.prenhall.com/cadgraphics/**. For the name and number of your sales representative, please contact Prentice Hall Faculty Services at 1-800-526-0485.

About the Author

Timothy Sean Sykes has been an instructor at Houston Community College in Houston, TX, for the past 6 years. Tim has a degree in secondary education from Lamar University. Prior to teaching, he spent 16 years as a designer in the Piping, Furniture, Structural, and Display fields. Tim has extensive writing experience; he has worked as a freelance writer, published two cookbooks, written a newsletter, published two field guides for edible wild plants, and has written assembly instructions for modular and furniture construction articles.

Acknowledgments

This book would not have been possible except for the help, patience, and support of a great many people. I'd like to name a few who merit special attention.

- My mother—Elizabeth Sykes—(the Comma Queen) who patiently read every word and explained (again and again) the difference between affect and effect!
- My father—Walter P. Sykes—who gave me a free country in which to live, work, and raise my family.
- My wife—Barbara—who has stood by me through the writing of each of my books—prodding me when I got lazy and encouraging me when I got downhearted.
- My kids for their quiet patience and encouragement—a father has never produced finer children.
- Eric Svendson—Prentice Hall editor—for believing in me enough to launch another book from the strength (and weaknesses) of three rough chapters.
- Our Lord for making me who and what I am, and for providing me with so much.

PART

Important Review

This part of our text contains these lessons:

1. Space for a New Beginning
2. After the Setup

LESSON 1

Space for a New Beginning

Following this lesson, you will:

- Be familiar with Viewports
- Know the difference between Model Space and Paper Space
- Know how to set up a drawing in the Paper Space environment—the **MView** command

Have you ever tried to print (or plot) a drawing in Model Space? If you have, then you understand the complexity of the mathematics involved—How large is the area to plot? How large is the paper? At what scale will I want to plot? And a host of other questions that must be answered. And then there is the question of text and dimensions—plotted size × drawing scale factor. Does it have to be that difficult? The answer is a resounding *NO*!

We begin this section of our text by simplifying these tasks with a remarkable tool called *Paper Space*.

When it comes to drawing display and arrangement, there exist two distinct groups of CAD operators—those who have used Paper Space and would never use anything else, and those who (generally for lack of training) have not used Paper Space.

This lesson will familiarize you (painlessly) to the wonders of *Paper Space* and *Viewports* so that you may join the ranks of enlightened operators! To keep it simple, we will remain in the two-dimensional world throughout this lesson.

Let's begin by answering the basic questions.

1.1 Understanding the Terminology

1. What Is a Viewport?

My *New American Dictionary* defines a port as a window in the side of a ship. Similarly, a viewport is a window into your drawing.

If you imagine viewing an object that is resting in the center of a box through holes in the sides, top, and bottom of the box, you will get a fairly good idea of what viewports are. Essentially, viewports are openings into your drawing, each presenting a different view of the drawn object(s).

There are two types of viewports—simple *tiled* viewports and more complex *floating* (or untiled) viewports. We will look at each of these.

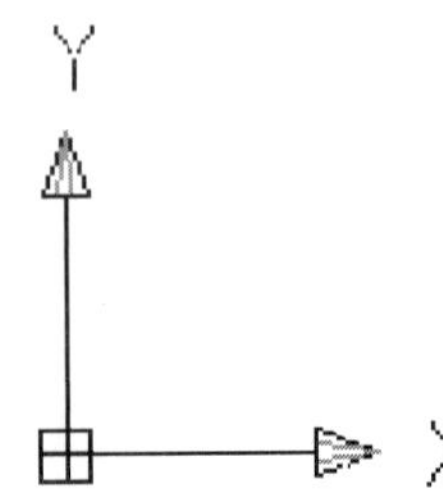

FIG. 1.1a Model Space UCS Icon

2. What Is Paper Space?

Paper Space is a plotting tool. It provides the operator with a method for creating a finished drawing that uses more than one scale and/or view of a drawing. In other words, this is how you can create a drawing with separate details shown at larger scales for ease in viewing (and dimensioning).

You will create the drawing as you always have—in *Model Space* (the *space* where you create your drawing, or three-dimensional *model*). But before you plot, you will place the drawing and details in their own spaces on an imaginary sheet of *paper*.

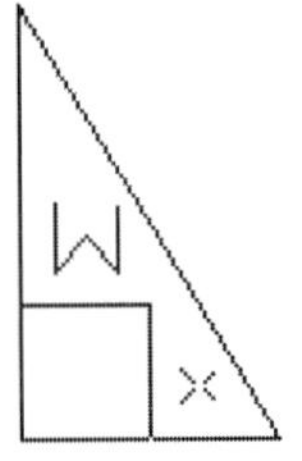

FIG. 1.1b Paper Space UCS Icon

3. How Do I Know Which Space I Am Using?

There are a couple of ways to know.

First, look at the UCS icon. The standard X-Y icon (Figure 1.1a) indicates Model Space; the triangular icon (Figure 1.1b) indicates Paper Space.

If you have the UCS icon turned off, you can look at the **Model/Paper** toggle on the status bar. If **MODEL** appears, you are in Model Space. Conversely, if **PAPER** appears, you are in Paper Space.

4. How Do I Switch Between Model Space and Paper Space?

Again, there are a couple of ways to do this.

The keyboard approach is simply to type ***MSpace*** (or ***MS***) for Model Space or ***PSpace*** (or ***PS***) for Paper Space at the command prompt.

Or you can pick the toggle on the status bar.

All of this will become clearer as we proceed

1.2 Using Tiled Viewports

Use Tiled Viewports in Model Space (what you might consider "normal" drawing space) to enhance your ability to see several parts of the drawing at once. This ability will become particularly important when drawing in three dimensions. You can place a three-dimensional view of the object in one viewport while drawing on a single two-dimensional plane (one side of the object) in another.

Create Tiled Viewports using the Viewports dialog box (Figure 1.2a). Access the dialog box using the ***Viewports*** command (or the ***VPorts*** hotkey).

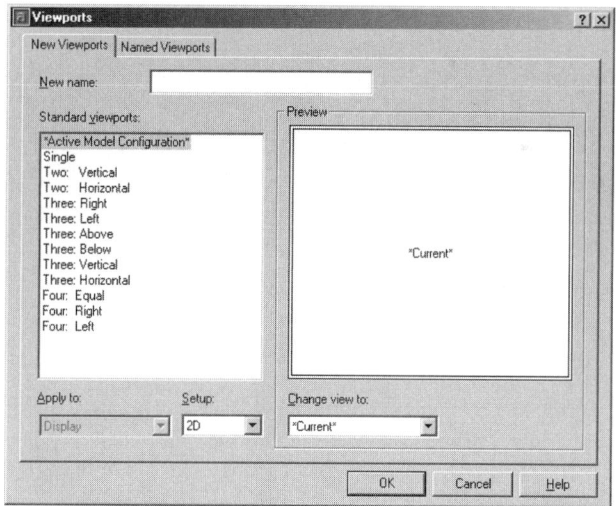

FIG. 1.2a *Viewports Dialog Box*

Let's take a look at our options.

The names of the two tabs indicate their function: Use **New Viewports** to create new viewports and **Named Viewports** to activate (or set current) a saved viewport configuration. We will begin with the **New Viewports** tab.

- The **New Viewports** tab presents several options.
  - Place a name or title in the **New name:** text box at the top if you wish to save a current configuration. (Do not use a name if you will not need to save the configuration.) You will be able to recall your configuration later using the **Change view to:** control box (lower-right center of the dialog box) or the **Named Viewports** tab.
  - The **Standard viewports:** list box provides a list of the more common viewport setups. Select each and see the configuration in the **Preview** frame.
  - Once you have selected a viewport configuration, you may choose to apply your selection to the **Display** or the **Current Viewport** using the **Apply to:** control box. Using the **Display** option will replace the drawing's current configuration with the new selection. Using the **Current Viewport** option will place the new configuration inside the currently active viewport. This is how you customize your viewports.
  - The **Setup** control box offers two choices: **2D** or **3D.**
    - The **2D** option will place the drawing's current view in each of the viewports.
    - The **3D** option will create the viewports using standard 3D views (top, front, side, isometric).

    Once selected, you can adjust the view using display commands (***Zoom, Pan, View***).

- The **Named Viewports** tab (Figure 1.2b) presents the **Named viewports:** list box and a **Preview** frame.

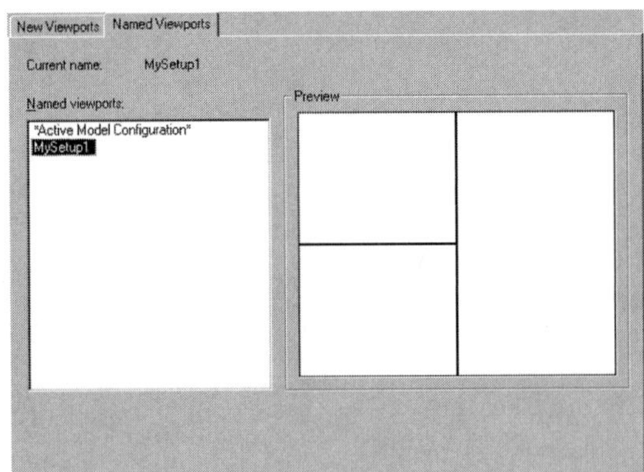

FIG. 1.2b Named Viewports Tab

  - The **Named viewports:** list box offers the names of any viewport configurations that have been saved. The user can set a viewport configuration current by selecting its name and picking the **OK** button.

- The **Preview** frame allows the user to see the setup of the selected viewport configuration.

Let's experiment a bit.

> You can also access the Viewports dialog box by selecting it from the pull-down menus. Follow this path:
>
> *View—Viewports—New Viewports . . .*

WWW 1.2.1 Do This: Working with Tiled Viewports

I. Open the *flr-pln1a.dwg* file located in the C:\Steps3D\Lesson01 folder. The drawing appears in Figure 1.2.1a.

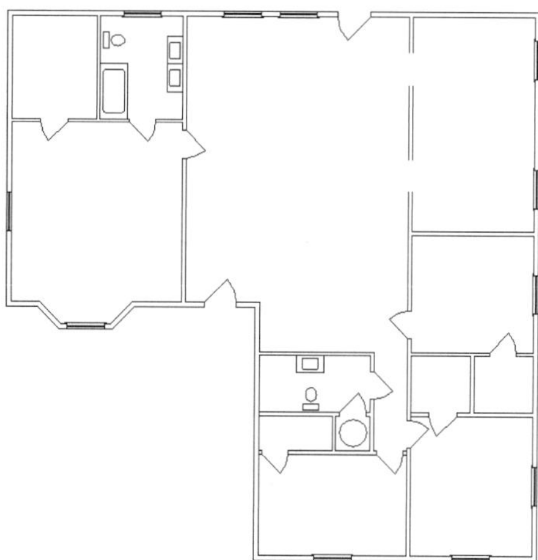

FIG. 1.2.1a *flr-pln1a.dwg*

II. Follow these steps:

TOOLS	COMMAND SEQUENCE	STEPS
 Display Viewports Dialog Button	**Command:** *vports*	**1.** We will begin by creating some viewports. Enter the ***Viewports*** command by typing ***Viewports*** or ***vports*** at the command prompt. You can also pick the **Display Viewports Dialog** button on the Layouts toolbar.

continued

TOOLS	COMMAND SEQUENCE	STEPS
		2. Select the **Three: Right** configuration. Notice the **Preview** screen (Figure 1.2.1.2).

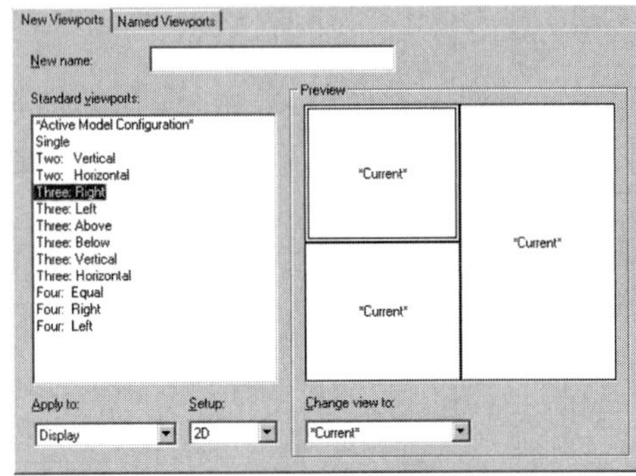

FIG. 1.2.1.2 Select the Configuration

TOOLS	COMMAND SEQUENCE	STEPS
OK		**3.** Pick the **OK** button to continue. Your drawing looks like Figure 1.2.1.3.

FIG. 1.2.1.3 Set Up Viewports

continued

TOOLS	COMMAND SEQUENCE	STEPS

Place your cursor into each of the viewports. Notice that only the right (active) viewport presents crosshairs. Other (inactive) viewports present a cursor arrow. Activate a viewport by placing the cursor in the desired viewport and picking once with the left mouse button. Notice that you can activate only one viewport at a time.

Notice also that each viewport contains the UCS icon. You can manipulate each viewport separately as though it were your entire drawing screen.

4. Be sure the right viewport is active. (Place the cursor in the right viewport and pick once with the left mouse button.)

Zoom Extents Button

Command: *z*

5. ***Zoom*** extents. Notice that the ***Zoom*** command affects only the active viewport. Then ***Pan*** (if necessary) to center the floor plan in the viewport.

6. Pick anywhere in the upper left viewport to activate it.

Zoom Window Button

Command: *z*

7. Zoom in around the master bath. The viewport will look like Figure 1.2.1.7.

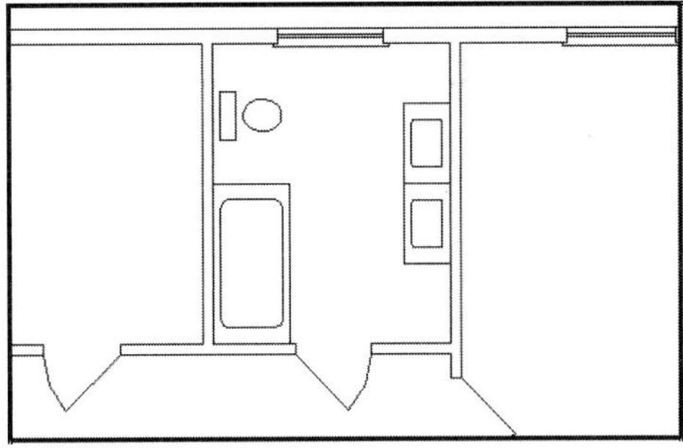

FIG. 1.2.1.7 Upper Left Viewport Showing Master Bath (UCS icon removed for clarity)

8. Now activate the lower left viewport.

continued

TOOLS	COMMAND SEQUENCE	STEPS
	**Command:** *z*	**9.** Zoom in around the common bath. The viewport will look like Figure 1.2.1.9.
		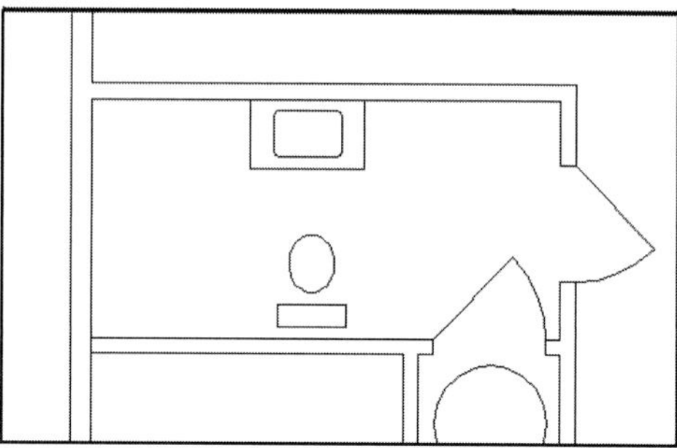 FIG. 1.2.1.9 Lower Left Viewport Showing Common Bath
 Copy Button	**Command:** *co*	**10.** Let's place a tub in the common bath. Enter the ***Copy*** command.
	Select objects: 1 found **Select objects:** *[enter]* **Specify base point or displacement, or [Multiple]: _endp of**	**11.** Pick once in the upper left viewport to activate it; then select the bathtub. Select the lower left endpoint of the tub as your base point.

continued

TOOLS	COMMAND SEQUENCE	STEPS
	Specify second point of displacement or <use first point as displacement>: _endp of	**12.** Pick once in the lower left viewport to activate it, then place the tub in the lower left corner of the bathroom. Your screen now looks like Figure 1.2.1.12. Notice that the changes are reflected in the right viewport as well as the lower left.

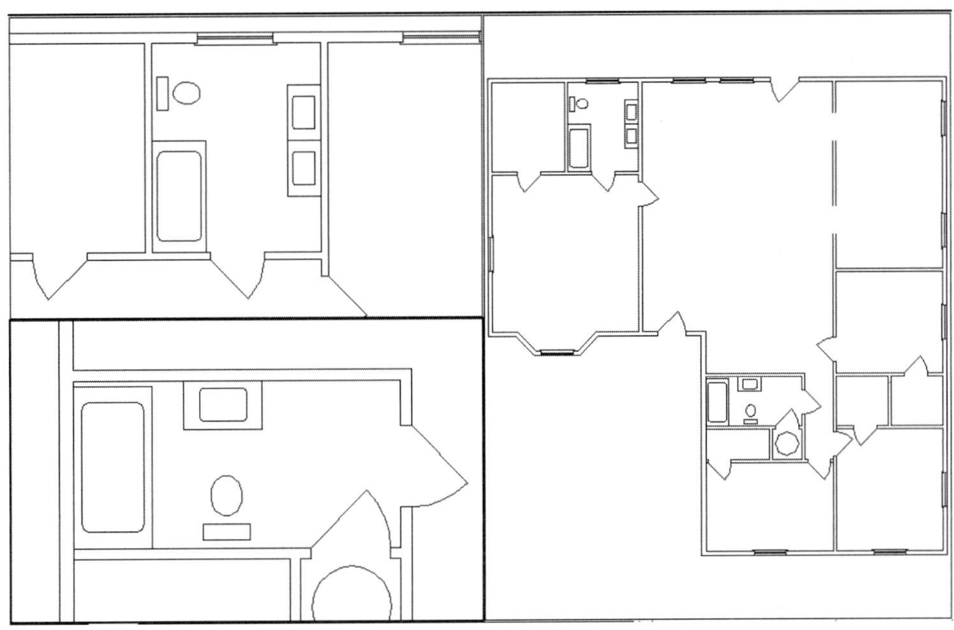

FIG. 1.2.1.12 Viewports After Copying the Tub

TOOLS	COMMAND SEQUENCE	STEPS
 Save Button	**Command:** ***qsave***	**13.** Remember to save the drawing occasionally.
	Command: ***vports***	**14.** Now let's save our viewport configuration. Enter the ***Viewports*** command.
	New name: Baths	**15.** Enter the name *Baths* in the **New Name:** text box.
OK		**16.** Pick the **OK** button to complete the procedure.
	Command: ***vports***	**17.** Now let's reset the screen to a **Single** viewport. Repeat the ***Viewports*** command.

continued

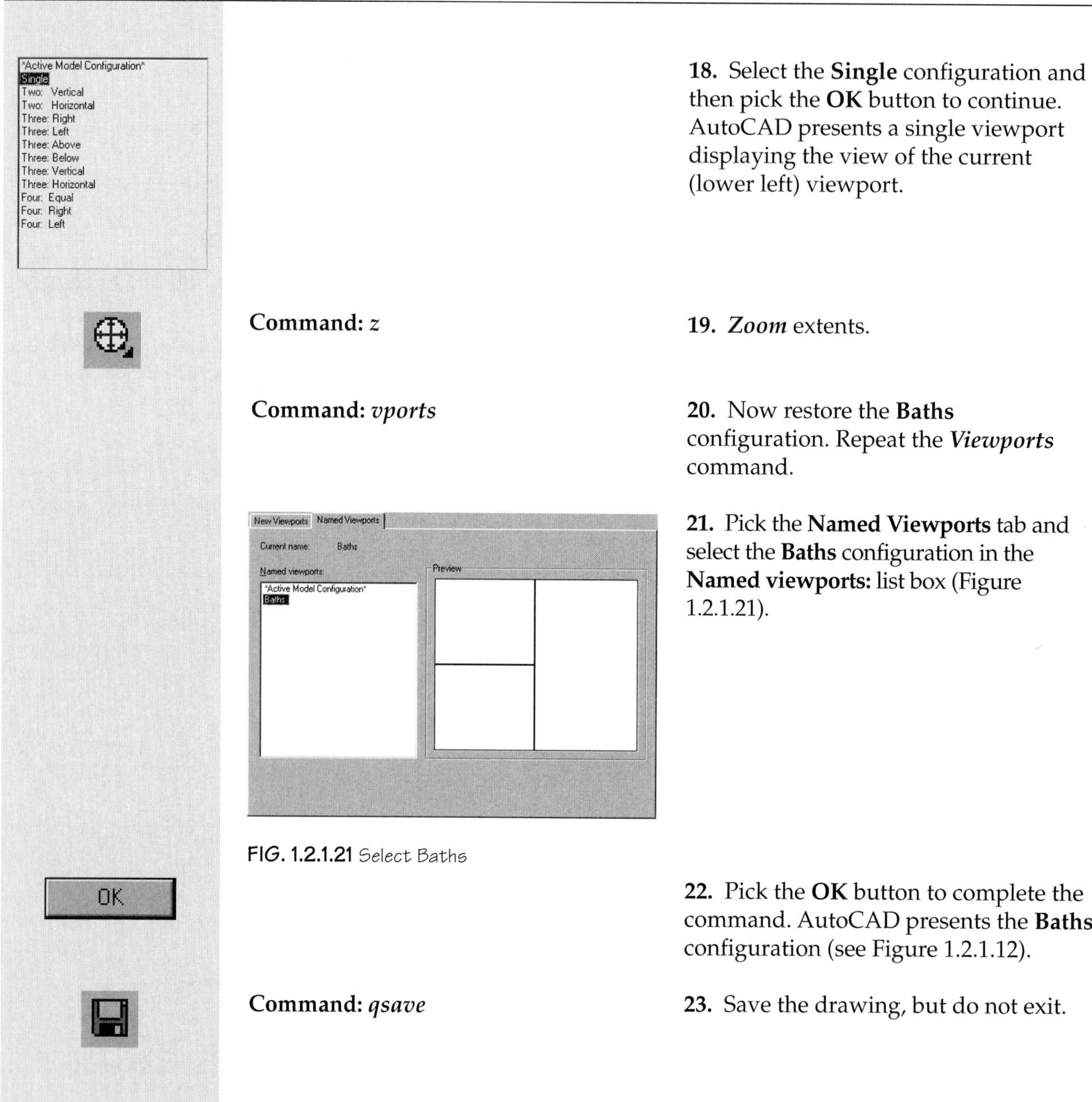

TOOLS	COMMAND SEQUENCE	STEPS
		18. Select the **Single** configuration and then pick the **OK** button to continue. AutoCAD presents a single viewport displaying the view of the current (lower left) viewport.
	Command: *z*	**19.** *Zoom* extents.
	Command: *vports*	**20.** Now restore the **Baths** configuration. Repeat the ***Viewports*** command.
		21. Pick the **Named Viewports** tab and select the **Baths** configuration in the **Named viewports:** list box (Figure 1.2.1.21).
	FIG. 1.2.1.21 Select Baths	
		22. Pick the **OK** button to complete the command. AutoCAD presents the **Baths** configuration (see Figure 1.2.1.12).
	Command: *qsave*	**23.** Save the drawing, but do not exit.

You can see the benefits of using viewports when manipulating several smaller parts of your drawing at one time. But when we consider the limitations of Tiled Viewports, we can see that they were designed as drawing aids—not plotting tools.

Some things to remember about Tiled Viewports include:

- Tiled Viewports were designed for use in Model Space.
- Tiled Viewports are not objects and will not plot. Your plot will show only the view in the *active* viewport.

- Only one viewport is *active* at a time. This means that you can draw only in one viewport at a time, but you can activate a new viewport transparently (or while using another command).
- The active viewport will show crosshairs while inactive viewports will show a cursor. Place the cursor in the viewport you wish to activate and click once to activate it.
- Layers behave universally in Tiled Viewports. You cannot freeze or thaw a layer just for one viewport as you can with Floating Viewports. (You will see how to use layers in Floating Viewports in Lesson 2.)
- While you can control the number and position of Tiled Viewports, you cannot easily control the size. You cannot control the shape at all (all Tiled Viewports are rectangular.)
- You can create viewports within viewports, but you should consider the size of the viewports and the size of your monitor before attempting this.
- Manipulation of viewports does not affect the actual drawing.

To see how you can use viewports to assist in plotting a drawing that uses multiple scales, we will take a look at Floating Viewports in Section 1.4. But first, we must set up our Paper Space environment.

1.3 Setting Up a Paper Space Environment

Entering Paper Space is as easy as picking a **Layout** tab just above the command line. When you select a **Layout** tab for the first time, AutoCAD will present the Page Setup dialog box with the **Layout Settings** tab on top (Figure 1.3a). (*Note:* If you make a mistake during the page setup or cancel before you have finished, you can access the Page Setup dialog box with the ***Pagesetup*** command.)

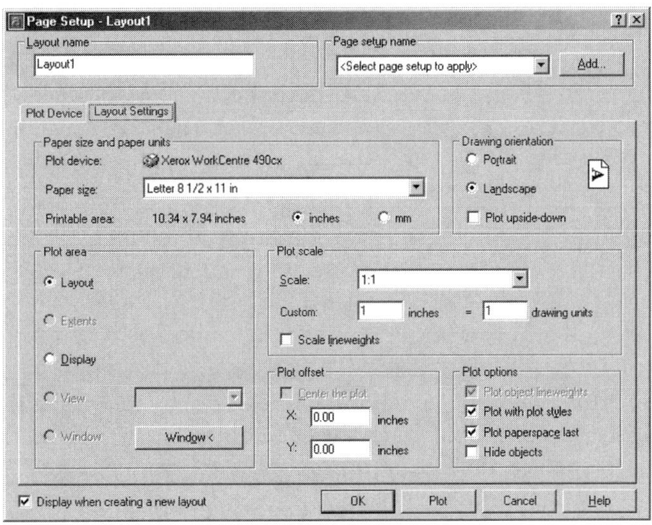

FIG. 1.3a Page Setup Dialog Box

You will often see the term *Paper Space* written as *paperspace*. Both refer to the same thing, though *paperspace* is generally a programmer's term.

Like Model Space, Paper Space must be set up. But it is quite a bit easier with Paper Space. Let's take a look at the **Layout Settings** tab.

The tab closely resembles the **Plot Settings** tab of the Plot dialog box, but let me repeat the pertinent information here.

- At the top of the dialog box, you will find two frames: **Layout name** and **Page setup name**.
  - The **Layout name** identifies which tab you will plot.

You can rename the space tabs to make it easier to keep track of them. Simply right-click on the tab, select **Rename** from the cursor menu, and enter the new name in the dialog box that appears.

  - Once we make our selections on the **Layout Settings** tab, we should add a new name (in the **Page setup name** box) to save our new settings.
- Below the frames, AutoCAD provides two tabs: **Plot Device** and **Layout Settings**.
- The **Layout Settings** tab contains the bulk of the information required to set up the layout.
  - The **Paper size and paper units** frame contains:
    - Which device you will be using (you can change this on the **Plot Device** tab, if necessary).
    - A control box for the user to select the size of the sheet of paper.
    - The amount of area on the sheet (given in inches or millimeters) that the drawing will actually occupy.
    - Option buttons to set up the layout in inches or millimeters.
  - The **Drawing orientation** frame allows the user to orient the drawing on the paper. Use the sample page (at the right side of the frame) as a guide. Generally, you will want to use a **Landscape** orientation. Use **Portrait** for $8\frac{1}{2}$" × 11" detail sheets.
  - In the **Plot area** frame, the user determines the area of the drawing to plot.
    - A bullet in the **Layout** option tells AutoCAD to set the plot area according to the paper size. Use this default setting for plotting Paper Space layouts.
    - A bullet in the **Display** option tells AutoCAD to plot the drawing in Model Space (no Paper Space objects will be plotted).

- Pick the **Window** < button to place a window around the objects in the drawing to be plotted. AutoCAD will automatically place the bullet in the **Window** option.

- In the **Plot scale** frame, the user tells AutoCAD at what scale to plot the drawing. Use the **Scale** control box to select a scale or to select **Custom**. When **Custom** is selected, AutoCAD uses the scale defined in the **Custom** text boxes. Leave the numbers in the **Scale** control box at their default setting of 1:1 to plot a Paper Space drawing.
- The **Plot offset** frame offers X and Y text boxes to help locate the drawing on the page.
- The last frame—**Plot options**—provides the user with four check boxes:
  - **Plot with lineweights**—check here to use the lineweights defined in the drawing.
  - **Plot with plot styles**—check here to use plot styles defined in the drawing.
  - **Plot paper space last**—in earlier releases of AutoCAD, paper space geometry (objects drawn in Paper Space) was always drawn (plotted) first. In more recent releases, you have a choice of which to plot first.
  - **Hide objects**—check this only when you are using the third dimension and you wish to avoid plotting objects that are hidden behind other objects.

Let's set up a Paper Space layout for our floor plan.

> *Note:* This procedure will utilize my printer—a Xerox Work Centre 490cx. You may have to adjust the settings to match your printer's or plotter's setup.

WWW 1.3.1 Do This: Creating a Paper Space Layout

I. Be sure you are still in the *flr-pln1a.dwg* file located in the C:\Steps3D\Lesson01 folder. If not, open it now.

II. Set **VPORTS** as the current layer.

III. Follow these steps:

TOOLS	COMMAND SEQUENCE	STEPS
	Model Layout1 ←	**1.** Pick on the **Layout1** tab just above the command line. AutoCAD presents the Page Setup—Layout 1 dialog box (see Figure 1.3a). This may take a few seconds. If the **Layout Settings** tab is not on top, pick it now.

continued

TOOLS	COMMAND SEQUENCE	STEPS
OK		**2.** I will use the default settings—AutoCAD sets these to print with a single Floating Viewport on the page. Pick the **OK** button. Your drawing looks like Figure 1.3.1.2.

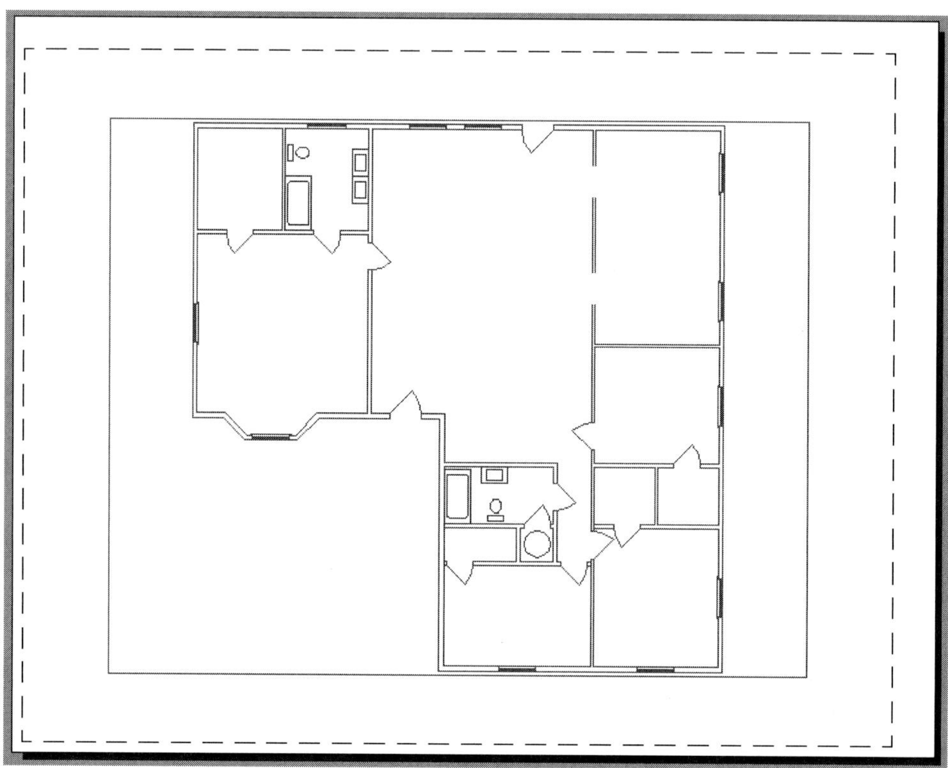

FIG. 1.3.1.2 New Layout

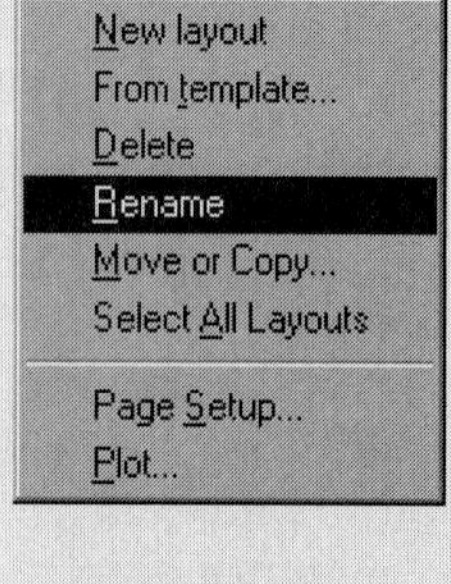

3. Let's rename the tab for better understanding. Right-click on the **Layout1** tab and select **Rename** from the cursor menu.

continued

TOOLS	COMMAND SEQUENCE	STEPS
 OK		**4.** Call the layout *My First House* (Figure 1.3.1.4) and then pick the **OK** button to continue. Notice the new name on the tab.

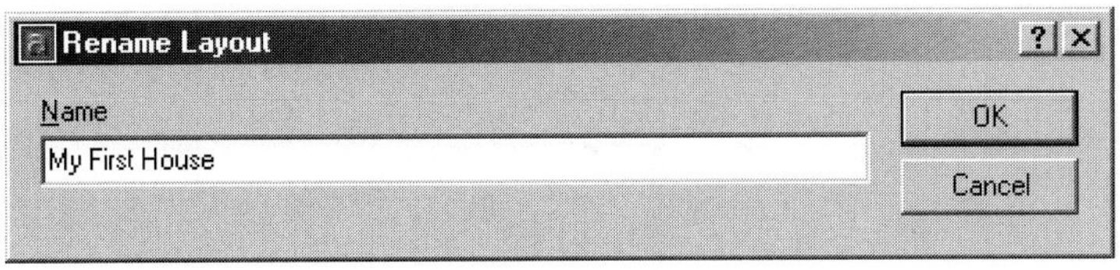

Rename Layout

Name

My First House

OK

Cancel

FIG. 1.3.1.4 Rename Layout Dialog Box with My First House Entered

TOOLS	COMMAND SEQUENCE	STEPS
	**Command:** *qsave*	**5.** Save the drawing.
 Erase Button	**Command:** *e* **Select objects:**	**6.** Try erasing different parts of the drawing. Notice that only the frame around the floor plan (the Floating Viewport) is selectable. It is the only thing that exists in Paper Space. Erase the Floating Viewport. Notice that the entire floor plan disappears. There is no longer a hole (a viewport) in the paper through which to see the model (your drawing).
	**Command:** *qsave*	**7.** Save the drawing, but do not exit.

You have seen how to start a Paper Space layout—go to the **Layout** tab, define the page (we accepted the $8\frac{1}{2}" \times 11"$ default size), and let AutoCAD do the rest. AutoCAD presents a sheet of paper with a floating viewport (a hole in the page) that is the only thing that exists on the page. (The dashed outline shows the margins of the working area on the page.)

You can have more than one layout in your drawing—each set up differently for different printing needs. Use the ***Layout*** command to add, remove, or copy layout tabs. It presents the following options:

> **Enter layout option [Copy/Delete/New/Template/Rename/SAveas/Set/?] <set>:**

Most of these options are self-explanatory. However, the **Save** option might not do what you expect. It replaces the default layout with the current setup (all future layouts will begin with the current setup).

An easier approach than the command line is simply to right-click on a tab and select the desired option from the cursor menu (Figure 1.3.1a).

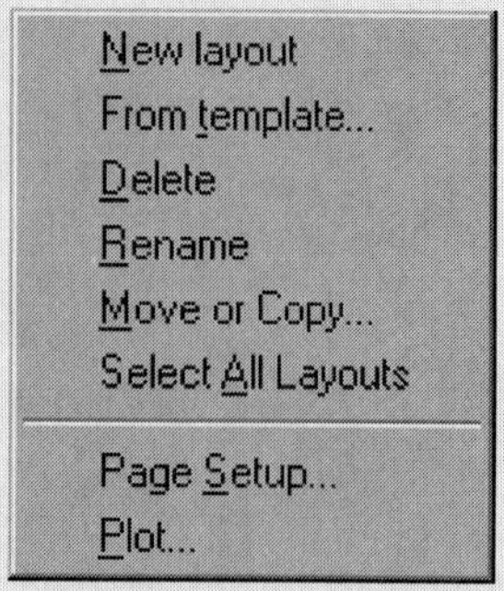

New layout
From template...
Delete
Rename
Move or Copy...
Select All Layouts
Page Setup...
Plot...

FIG. 1.3.1a Cursor Menu

You can place objects on the paper that will not affect the model (title block, text, and so forth). Or you can return to Model Space to work on the model. (You can work on the Model through the viewport by entering the ***MSpace*** command.) We will look at this in more detail in later sections of this lesson. But first, let's examine Floating Viewports.

1.4 Using Floating Viewports

Floating (or Untiled) Viewports, although more complex than Tiled Viewports, offer considerably more flexibility. But how are Floating Viewports different from Tiled Viewports? Let's take a look.

As we saw in Section 1.2, AutoCAD designed Tiled Viewports as *drawing* tools for a Model Space environment. Tiled Viewports act like holes in an imaginary box through which you view different parts of your drawing. The location and size of the hole determine what you *see*, how much you see, and at what angle you see the drawing objects. Tiled Viewports do not affect how the drawing will be plotted.

Floating Viewports were designed as *plotting* tools in a Paper Space environment. Floating Viewports also act like holes, but this time they are holes in a sheet of paper covering the drawing objects. The location and size of Floating Viewport holes determine what will be *plotted*, how much will be plotted, and at what angle the drawing objects will be plotted.

Some things to remember about Floating Viewports include:

- Floating Viewports are objects and can be moved, stretched, and erased like any other object on a drawing. Consequently, the user may place them on a separate layer that can be frozen at plot time.
- Unlike Tiled Viewports, Floating Viewports do not have to be rectangular.
- Floating Viewports may overlap.
- The user can control layers within each viewport independently of the rest of the drawing. This is a key benefit since the user often will not want details shown in one viewport reflected in another.
- Use Floating Viewports to show different views of one or more objects on a single plot.

- Like Tiled Viewports, only one Floating Viewport is active at a time.
- Floating Viewports live in Paper Space (on a **Layout** tab). Although they are not available in Model Space, the user can work in Model Space through a Floating Viewport (much as a doctor works on a kidney or gall bladder through a hole in the skin).
- Sizing text in Paper Space is really quite easy. Since you are working on the actual plotted page, simply enter the text at the desired plotted size. No need for scale factors!

1.4.1 Creating Floating Viewports Using MView

Creating Floating Viewports using the *MView* command appears more daunting than it actually is. The command sequence looks like this:

Command: *mview* **(or** *mv***)**

Specify corner of viewport or

[ON/OFF/Fit/Hideplot/Lock/Object/Polygonal/Restore/2/3/4] <Fit>: *[begin a window]*

Other corner: *[complete the window]*

Let's look at each option.

- The **ON/OFF** options allow the user to "open" or "close" the viewport through which he sees the drawing. If the viewport is **OFF**, it is closed and the user cannot see through it. Thus, that part of the drawing is hidden.

  When one of these options is chosen, AutoCAD will prompt the user to select the viewport to turn **ON** or **OFF.**
- The **Fit** option will create a single, maximum-size Floating Viewport within the display area.
- When **ON**, **Hideplot** allows the user to remove hidden lines from the selected viewport during plotting. (These are not lines drawn using a hidden linetype but lines "hidden" or behind other lines or objects in three-dimensional space.)
- The **Lock** option allows the user to lock a viewport. It prompts

  Viewport View Locking [ON/OFF]: *[enter On or Off]*

  Select objects: [*select the viewport to lock or unlock*]

- The **Object** option was new to AutoCAD 2000 and was long awaited. Using this option, the user may select any existing closed polyline, ellipse, spline, region, or circle and turn it into a Floating Viewport. (The object selected must exist in Paper Space.)
- The **Polygonal** option allows the user to create a Floating Viewport with any number of sizes and in any shape. It prompts

  Specify start point: [*pick a start point*]

  Specify next point or [Arc/Length/Undo]: [*create the shape just as you would a polyline*]

- The **2/3/4** options tell AutoCAD to create two, three, or four viewports. AutoCAD will prompt the user to locate the viewports.
- **Restore** is a very useful tool. It allows the user to translate Tiled Viewports into Floating Viewport objects. When selected, AutoCAD allows the user to enter the name of a saved tiled configuration or to translate the current tiled configuration into Floating Viewports.
- Of course the default option—**Specify corner of viewport**—allows the user to manually create viewports one at a time.

Let's insert a title block into our drawing and then set up some Floating Viewports.

WWW 1.4.1.1 Do This: Creating Floating Viewports

I. Be sure you are still in the *flr-pln1a.dwg* file located in the C:\Steps3D\Lesson01 folder. If not, open it now.

II. Follow these steps:

TOOLS	COMMAND SEQUENCE	STEPS
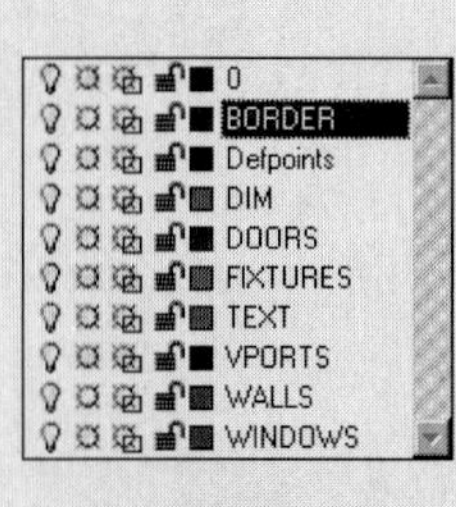	**Command:** *la*	**1.** Set the **Border** layer current.
 Insert Button	**Command:** *i*	**2.** Insert the *ANSI-A title block* drawing that came with AutoCAD. (Find it in the \AutoCAD 2002\Template folder.) Put it at the 0,0 coordinates.
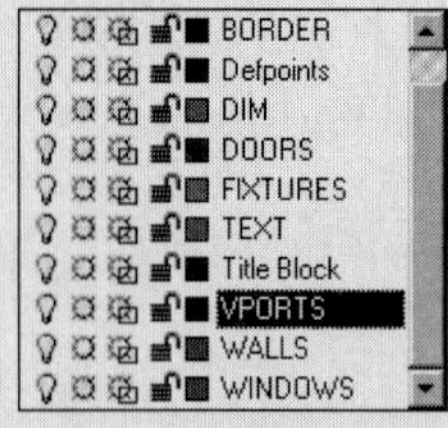		**3.** Set the **VPorts** layer current.
	Command: *mv*	**4.** Enter the ***MView*** command by typing ***mview*** or ***mv*** at the command line.

continued

TOOLS	COMMAND SEQUENCE	STEPS
	Specify corner of viewport or [ON/OFF/Fit Hideplot/Lock/Object/ Polygonal/Restore/2/3/4] <Fit>: *.5,7.5* **Specify opposite corner:** *4.75,4.25*	**5.** Place the first Floating Viewport as indicated.
	Command: *[enter]* **Specify corner of viewport or [ON/OFF/Fit/Hideplot/Lock/Object/ Polygonal/Restore/2/3/4] <Fit>:** *5,6.5* **Specify opposite corner:** *10,2.5*	**6.** Place a second Floating Viewport as indicated. Your drawing now looks like Figure 1.4.1.1.6.

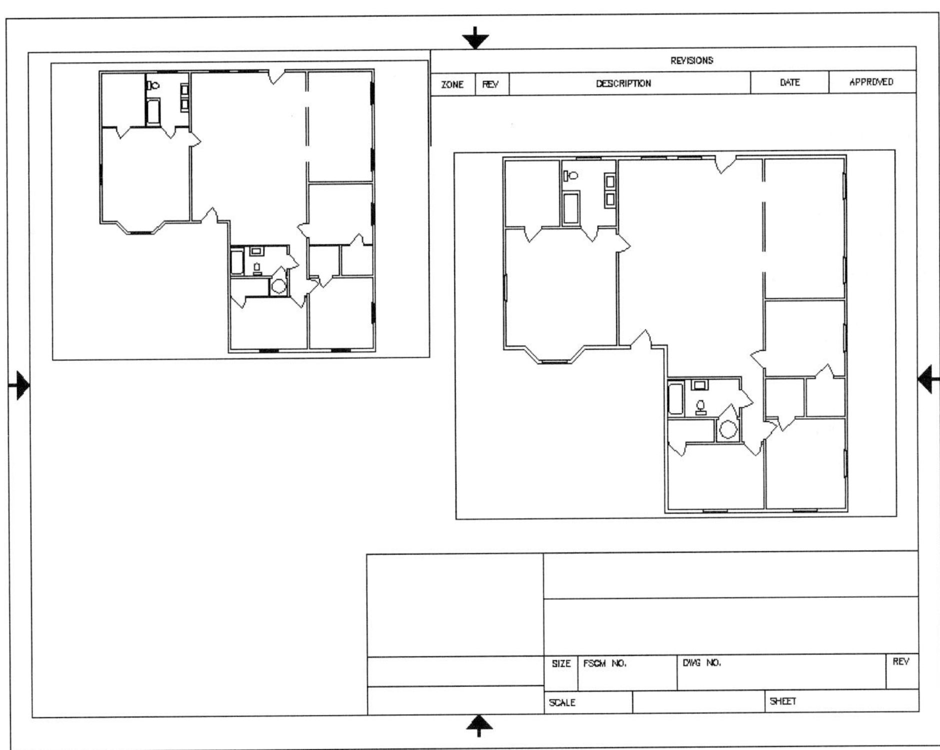

FIG. 1.4.1.1.6 Two Floating Viewports

continued

TOOLS	COMMAND SEQUENCE	STEPS
 Circle Button	**Command:** *c* **Specify center point for circle or [3P/2P/Ttr (tan tan radius)]:** *2.25,2.25* **Specify radius of circle or [Diameter]:** *1.75*	**7.** Now let's make a nonrectangular viewport—the easy way. Draw a circle as indicated.
	Command: *mv*	**8.** Now we will use the *MView* command to convert the circle to a Floating Viewport. Enter the *MView* command. (We will look at the buttons on the Viewports toolbar in a moment.)
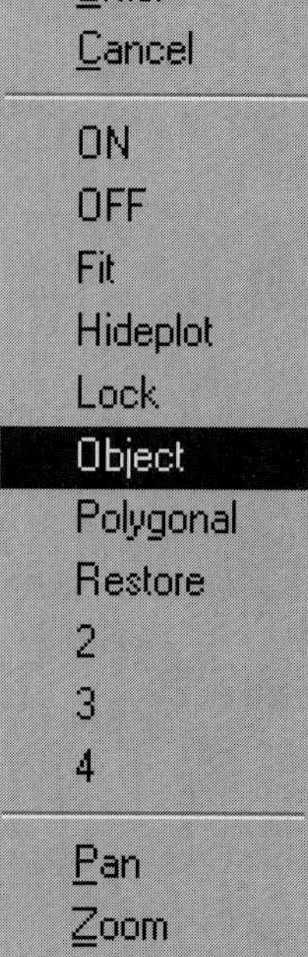	**Specify corner of viewport or [ON/OFF/Fit/Hideplot/Lock/Object/Polygonal/Restore/2/3/4] <Fit>:** *o*	**9.** Use the **Object** option.

continued

TOOLS	COMMAND SEQUENCE	STEPS
	Select object to clip viewport:	**10.** Select the circle. Your drawing now looks like Figure 1.4.1.1.10. Notice that the round viewport shows only part of the drawing. It began with the full drawing and then *clipped* away the part that did not fit into the circle.

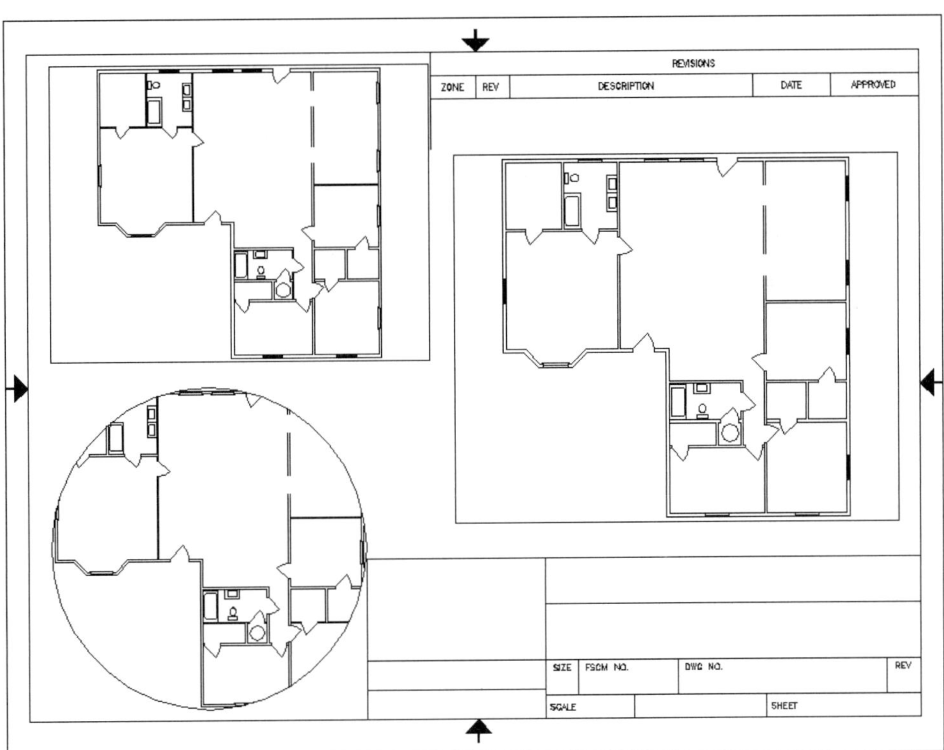

FIG. 1.4.1.1.10 Completed Floating Viewports

TOOLS	COMMAND SEQUENCE	STEPS
	**Command:** *qsave*	**11.** Save the drawing, but do not exit.

1.4.2 The Viewports Toolbar

We have made a good start with Paper Space and Floating Viewports. But have you *discovered* the Viewports toolbar yet (Figure 1.4.2a)?

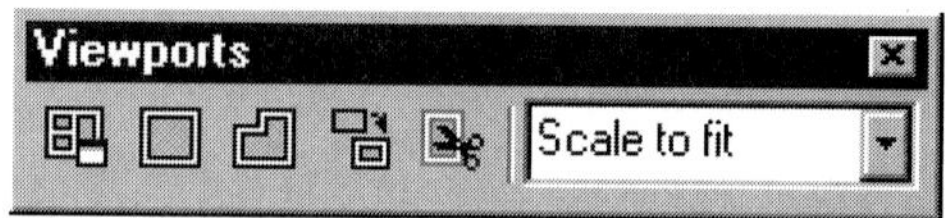

FIG. 1.4.2a The Viewports Toolbar

> *The one common thread that permeates the thrills of life—your first kiss, your first child, your first paycheck—is that each results from the* ***discovery*** *of something new and wonderful.*
>
> *Never miss an opportunity to explore or you may miss an opportunity to discover.*
>
> *Anonymous*

This handy item provides single-button selection of some of the ***MView*** options as well as some other tools.

Let's take a look.

- The first button—**Display Viewports Dialog**—does just that. It displays the Viewports dialog box that we used to create Tiled Viewports in Section 1.2 of this lesson. You may also use this dialog box to create *Floating* Viewports in Paper Space! Simply follow the same procedures you learned for Tiled Viewports. (Notice that the Viewports dialog box presented when in Paper Space does not have the **New name:** text box. Floating Viewport configurations are saved as layouts.)
- The second button—**Single Viewport**—executes the **Fit** option of the ***MView*** command.
- The third button—**Polygonal Viewport**—allows the user to create a viewport with any number of sizes and in any shape by executing the **Polygon** option of the ***MView*** command.
- The fourth button—**Convert Object to Viewport**—does just that (as we did with the circle in our last exercise). It executes the **Object** option of the ***MView*** command.
- The last button—**Clip Existing Viewport**—is a modifying tool used to redefine viewport boundaries. We will learn more about it in Lesson 2.
- On the right end of the toolbar, you will find the **Viewport Scale Control** box. You will use this to set the scale of the image seen through the Floating Viewport. We will look at this procedure next.

1.4.3 Adjusting the Views in Floating Viewports

Once Floating Viewports have been created, you will need to adjust what you see through them. This means adjusting the scale and then panning to achieve the appropriate view for your plot. Before we do either, we must tell AutoCAD to allow us to work in the Model Space we see through the Floating Viewport. Do this by simply entering ***MSpace*** or ***MS*** at the command prompt and then selecting the viewport you wish to use.

> To toggle between Paper Space and Model Space, simply type ***PSpace*** (or ***ps***) or ***MSpace*** (or ***ms***) at the command prompt. Or you may pick on **PAPER** or **MODEL** on the status bar. You may also double-click in a Paper Space area to activate Paper Space, or in a viewport to activate Model Space (simultaneously making that viewport current).

We will begin by setting the scale for the viewport. AutoCAD provides two methods of doing this—the **XP** option of the ***Zoom*** command or the **Viewport Scale control** box on the Viewports toolbar.

- The **Zoom Approach**: While at the ***Zoom*** prompt, simply type ***1/[SF]xp*** (where ***SF*** is the scale factor for the scale you wish to use in this particular viewport—refer to Appendix A).
- The **Control Box Approach**: Pick the down arrow and select the appropriate scale. Or you can type a scale into the box. (*Note:* A 1:1 scale often returns a value in the control box as 1" = 1'. This programming glitch does not affect the actual 1:1 scale of the viewport, although it can be confusing.)

Let's try it.

1.4.3.1 Do This: Scaling Floating Viewports

I. Be sure you are still in the *flr-pln1a.dwg* file located in the C:\Steps3D\Lesson01 folder. If not, open it now.

II. Follow these steps:

TOOLS	COMMAND SEQUENCE	STEPS
PAPER Paper/Model Space Toggle	**Command:** *ms*	**1.** Open Model Space by typing ***mspace*** or ***ms*** at the command prompt. Or you may pick **PAPER** on the status bar.

continued

TOOLS	COMMAND SEQUENCE	STEPS
		2. Select anywhere in the upper left viewport to activate it. Notice that the boundary darkens to indicate that it is active.
 Pan Button	**Command:** ***p***	**3.** Use the ***Pan*** command to center the master bath in the viewport.
	Command: ***z***	**4.** Now we will set the scale for this viewport. Enter the ***Zoom*** command.
	Specify corner of window, enter a scale factor (nX or nXP), or [All/Center/Dynamic/Extents/ Previous/Scale/Window] <real time>: ***1/48xp***	**5.** We wish to set the scale of this viewport to $\frac{1}{4}$" = 1' – 0". The scale factor for this scale is 48 (see Appendix A). So enter the scale factor, as shown, using the ***xp*** suffix to indicate that you are scaling Paper Space.

AutoCAD scales the viewport. (You may have to pan slightly to center the view again.) This viewport now looks like Figure 1.4.3.1.5.

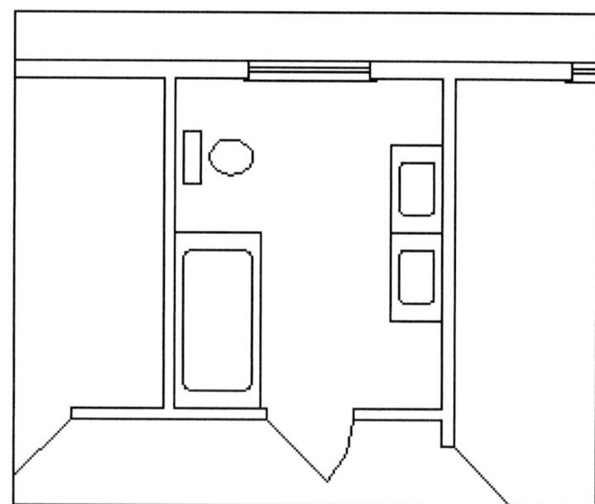

FIG. 1.4.3.1.5 Scaled Viewport Showing Master Bath (USC Icon removed for clarity)

continued

TOOLS	COMMAND SEQUENCE	STEPS

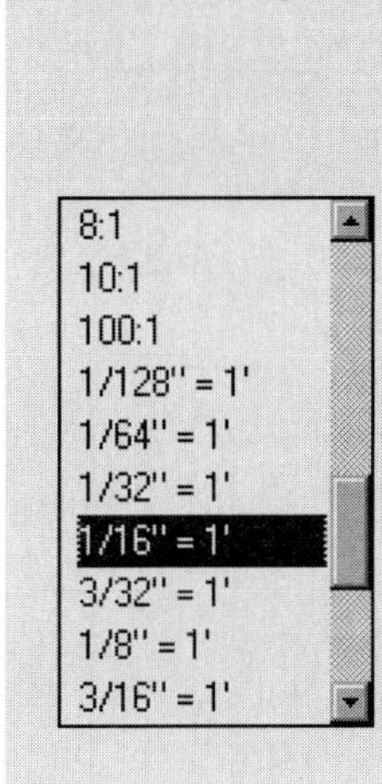

6. Now let's use the control box method. Pick anywhere in the right viewport to activate it.

7. Pick the down arrow in the **Viewport Scale Control** box, and then scroll down until you can see the $\frac{1}{16}$**" = 1'** selection. Pick that one.

Easy? This viewport now looks like Figure 1.4.3.1.7.

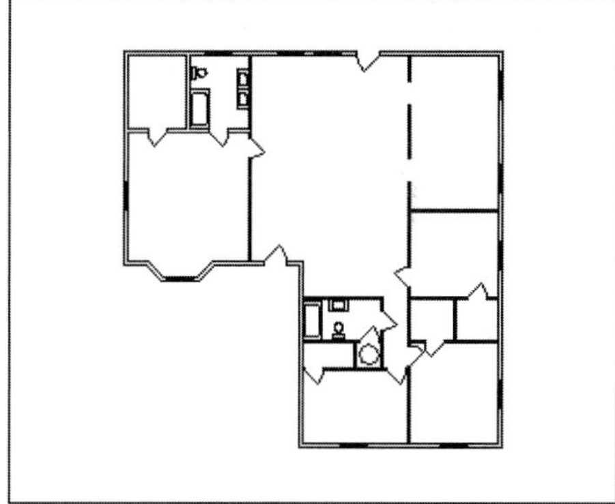

FIG. 1.4.3.1.7 *Scaled Viewport*

Command: *p*

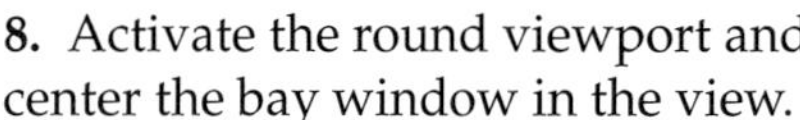

8. Activate the round viewport and center the bay window in the view.

9. Use either of the methods we have discussed to set the scale in this viewport to $\frac{1}{4}$" = 1' – 0".

Command: *ps*

10. Return to Paper Space.

continued

TOOLS	COMMAND SEQUENCE	STEPS
		11. On the **Text** layer, add the geometry shown in Figure 1.4.3.1.11.

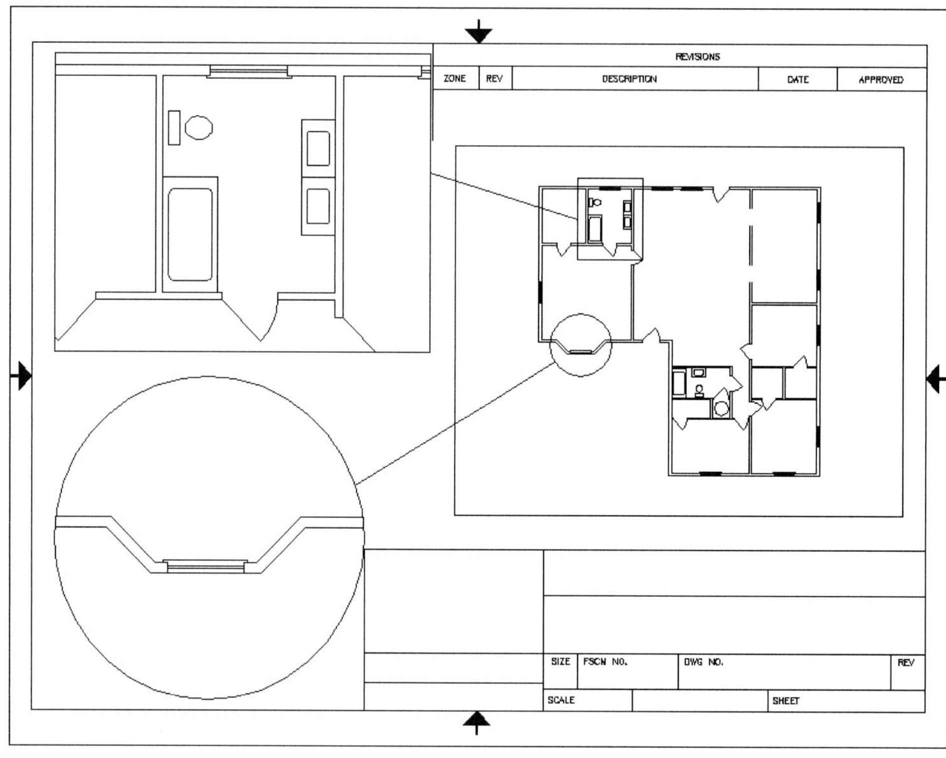

FIG. 1.4.3.1.11 Completed Exercise

TOOLS	COMMAND SEQUENCE	STEPS
	Command: ***saveas***	**12.** Save the drawing as *MyFlr-pln2a* in the C:\Steps3D\Lesson02 folder. Close the drawing.

The drawing now shows the full plan at a $\frac{1}{16}$" = 1' − 0" scale and the common bathroom and bay window at a $\frac{1}{4}$" = 1' − 0" scale.

We have completed the Paper Space setup of our drawing. Let's review what we have accomplished.

- We began with a floor plan drawn in Model Space. The limits of Model Space had been set to produce a $\frac{1}{4}$" = 1' − 0" drawing on a C-size sheet of paper.
- We opened the layout tab of our drawing and set it up to print our Model Space drawing on an A-size sheet (11" × 8$\frac{1}{2}$"). We used an AutoCAD title block designed for this page size and added three Floating Viewports—two rectangular and one converted object (circle).
- We set different views of the same model in each of the Floating Viewports—each viewport having its own scale.

1.5 And Now the Easy Way—The *LayoutWizard* Command

We have explored several steps in creating and setting up a Paper Space layout. But I always save the best for last.

I briefly discussed the ***Layout*** command in Section 1.3. That command allowed the user to create new layouts. But AutoCAD's **Layout Wizard** does the same thing and more!

Using the ***LayoutWizard*** command, the user can create a new layout and set it up as well.

Let's take a look at the wizard.

> Why learn the tedious method first?
>
> The reason for this is quite simple—once a student learns the easy way of doing something, there is little desire to learn any other method. This often means missing out on some valuable options.

WWW

1.5.1 Do This: Using the Layout Wizard

I. Open the *flr-pln1b.dwg* file located in the C:\Steps3D\Lesson01 folder. This is the same file as *flr-pln1a* but has not had the layout set up yet.

II. Set the **VPorts** layer current.

III. Follow these steps:

TOOLS	COMMAND SEQUENCE	STEPS
No Button Available	**Command:** ***layoutwizard***	**1.** Enter the ***LayoutWizard*** command by typing ***layoutwizard*** at the command prompt. Or you can use the pull-down menus. Follow this path: *Tools—Wizards—Create Layout . . .*

continued

TOOLS	COMMAND SEQUENCE	STEPS

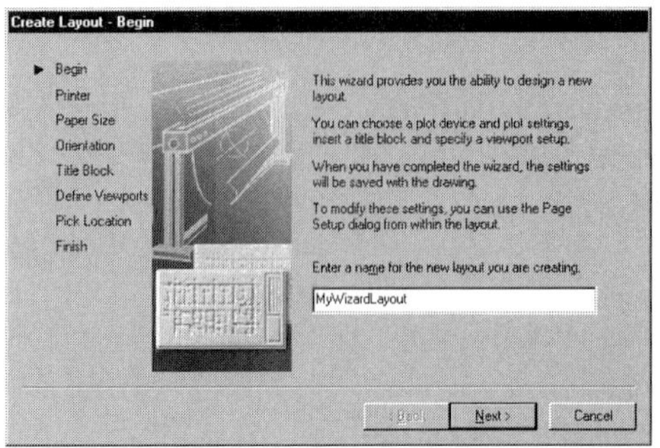

2. AutoCAD presents the **Create Layout—Begin** dialog box. Enter the name *MyWizardLayout* in the text box as shown.

Pick the **Next** button to continue.

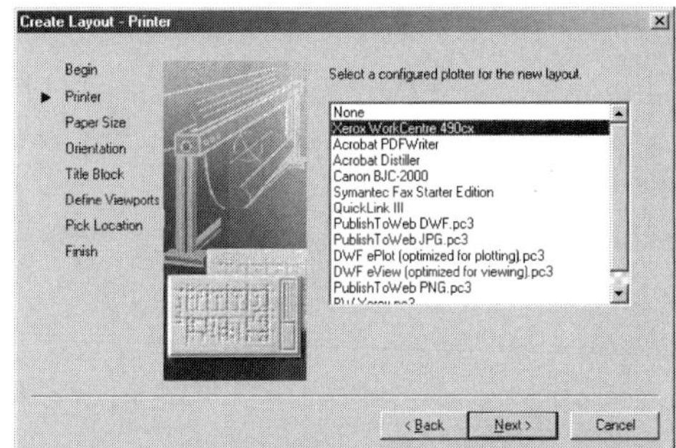

3. Select the printer or plotter you wish to use. (Your options may differ from mine.)

Pick the **Next** button to continue.

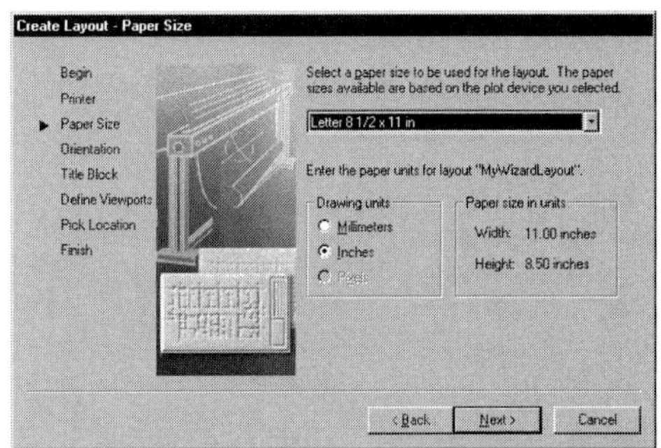

4. Select a paper size for the layout (I will use the **8 $\frac{1}{2}$" × 11"** size). Remember to tell AutoCAD to set up the layout in **Inches** or **Millimeters**. Here we will use **Inches**.

Pick the **Next** button to continue.

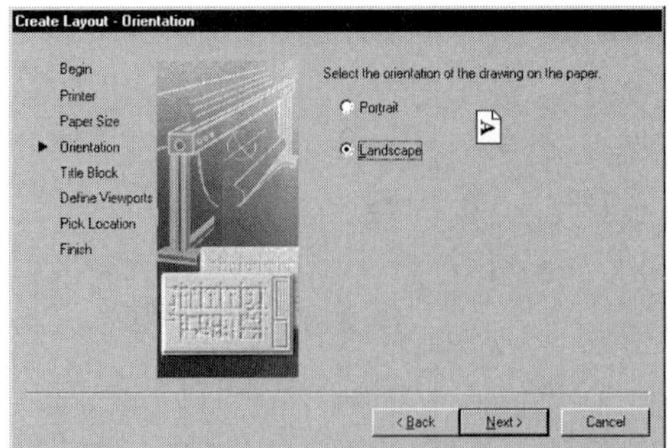

5. You will probably want to leave the layout set to **Landscape** as we will here. Use **Portrait** when you wish to print to an upright sheet of paper (the longer dimension vertical rather than horizontal).

Pick the **Next** button to continue.

continued

TOOLS	COMMAND SEQUENCE	STEPS

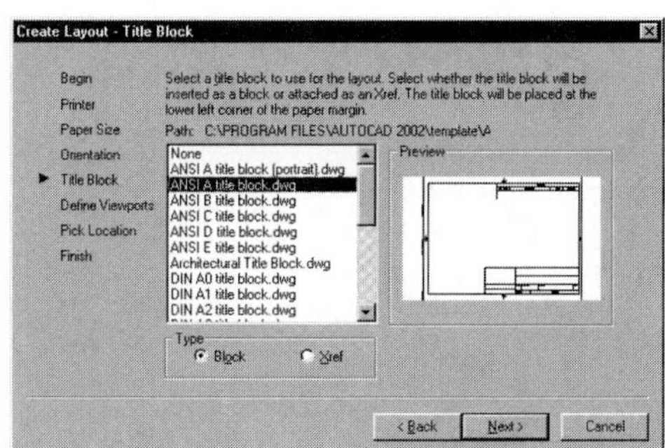

6. Select the title block you wish to use or choose **None** if you want none or wish to insert one later. I will use **ANSI A title block**.

Below the list box you will find a **Type** frame. Tell AutoCAD you wish to insert the title block as a **Block**. (We will discuss **Xrefs** later in this text.)

Pick the **Next** button to continue.

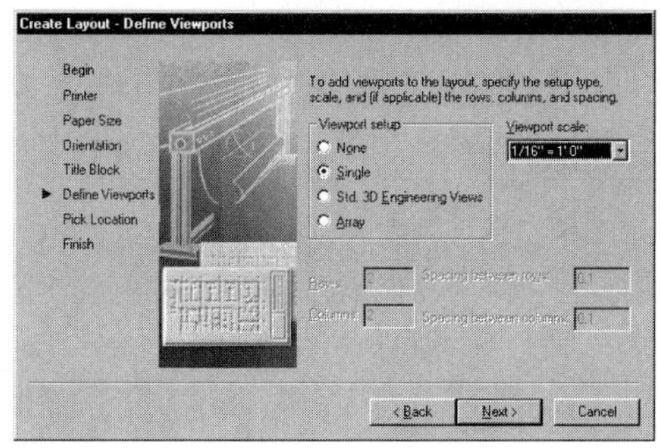

7. Now we can create a rough setup for our viewports.

In the **Viewport setup** frame, select the **Single** option to create a single viewport. You may use the other options to create the standard three-dimensional engineering views (four viewports—three with orthographic views and one three-dimensional view) or an **Array** of viewports. The **Array** option displays the **Rows/Columns** and **Spacing** boxes below the **Viewport setup** frame.

In the **Viewport scale:** control box, set the scale for our single viewport at $\frac{1}{16}$" = 1' − 0".

Pick the **Next** button to continue.

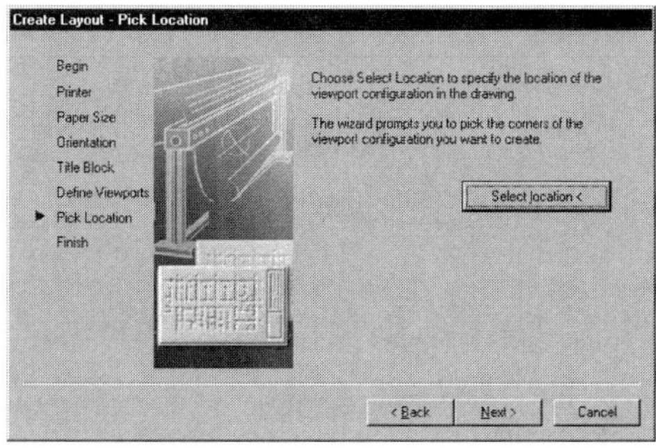

8. Pick the **Select Location<** button on the next screen to locate the viewport.

Specify first corner: ***4.75,6.5***

Specify opposite corner: ***10,2.25***

9. AutoCAD takes you to the graphics screen of your new layout, shows you the title block you selected, and prompts for the corners of the viewport. Enter the coordinates indicated.

continued

TOOLS	COMMAND SEQUENCE	STEPS
	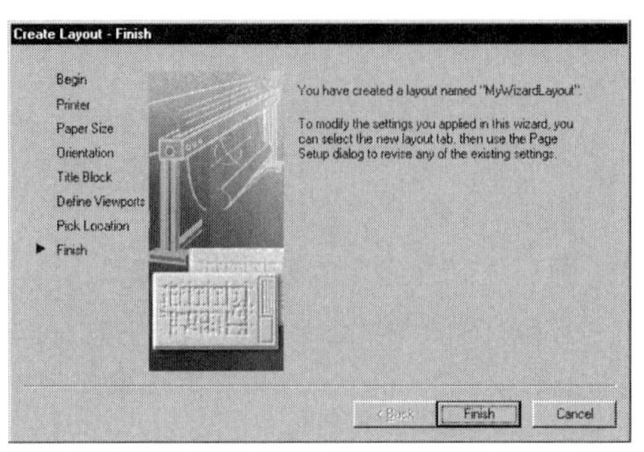 	**10.** AutoCAD returns to the wizard. Pick the **Finish** button to complete the command. AutoCAD returns to the graphics screen with the new layout visible.
	Command: *qsave*	**11.** Save the drawing.

Was that not easier than our previous exercises? You can use the ***MView*** command to add additional viewports as desired, but the bulk of the work has been accomplished in fewer steps and with less effort.

How will you set up your layouts?

We have set up our page using the ***Pagesetup*** command (or AutoCAD's automatic access to the Page Setup dialog box). And we have used the ***MView*** command to set up our Floating Viewports. We have also seen an easier approach to creating layouts—using the ***Layoutwizard*** command. But wait! There is another approach.

AutoCAD provides a method that incorporates all aspects of Paper Space setup into a single command—the ***MVSetup*** command. You may experiment with this command if you like, but be warned that consolidation does not always make a task easier! We will explore ***MVSetup*** as an editing tool in Lesson 2.

Although we have accomplished quite a lot in this short lesson, we have not finished learning the basics of Paper Space. We must consider how dimensions, layers, text, and plotting relate to Paper Space, as well as some methods of editing our layout. We will look at these in Lesson 2, but for now, let's take time for some projects.

1.6 Extra Steps

If you have access to a printer or plotter, try to plot the results of the last exercise. Do not worry if you have problems; we will cover plotting in Paper Space in Lesson 2. This is just a preview.

Some important things to remember when plotting include:

- Be sure to plot the **My First House** tab.
- Plot to a 1=1 scale.
- Use an A-size sheet of paper (ANSI-A is 11" × $8\frac{1}{2}$").

Examine the scale. Designers use Paper Space to create drawings at industry standard scales while showing details at whatever scale is necessary for clarity.

1.7 What Have We Learned?

Items covered in this lesson include:

- *Tiled viewports (Model Space)*
- *Floating viewports (Paper Space)*
- *The **PSpace** and **MSpace** commands*
- *The **Pagesetup** command*
- *The **Viewports** command and command options*
- *The **MView** command and command options*
- *The Layout Wizard*
- *The **MVSetup** command*

We have seen the basic setup of Paper Space in two-dimensional drawings.

While the setup may seem somewhat confusing at first, the benefits of practice cannot be overemphasized. In the two-dimensional world, Paper Space provides convenience when using multiple drawing scales and details. In the three-dimensional world, you will find Paper Space an essential tool for printing the same object from different angles simultaneously!

Try some of the exercises at the end of this lesson to make yourself more comfortable with Paper Space. Then move on to the next lesson where you will discover more about how to work in Paper Space.

1.8 EXERCISES

1. Open the *Needle.dwg* file in the C:\Steps3D\Lesson01 folder. Create the drawing configuration for plotting found in Figure 1.8.1. Some helpful information includes:
   1.1. The page size is A4 (metric—10 mm × 297 mm).
   1.2. The title block is the *ISO-A4* file found in AutoCAD's Template folder. (You may need to adjust its position on the sheet.)
   1.3. The title block text is attributed.
   1.4. Watch your layers (place viewports on the **VPorts** layer).
   1.5. The radius of the large circle is 60 mm; the radius of the smaller circle is 36 mm.

1.6. Remember that Floating Viewports can overlap.
1.7. The scale of each viewport (from top to bottom) is 10:1, 8:1, 2:1.
1.8. Fill in the title block as desired.
1.9. Save the drawing as *MyNeedle* in the C:\Steps3D\Lesson02 folder.

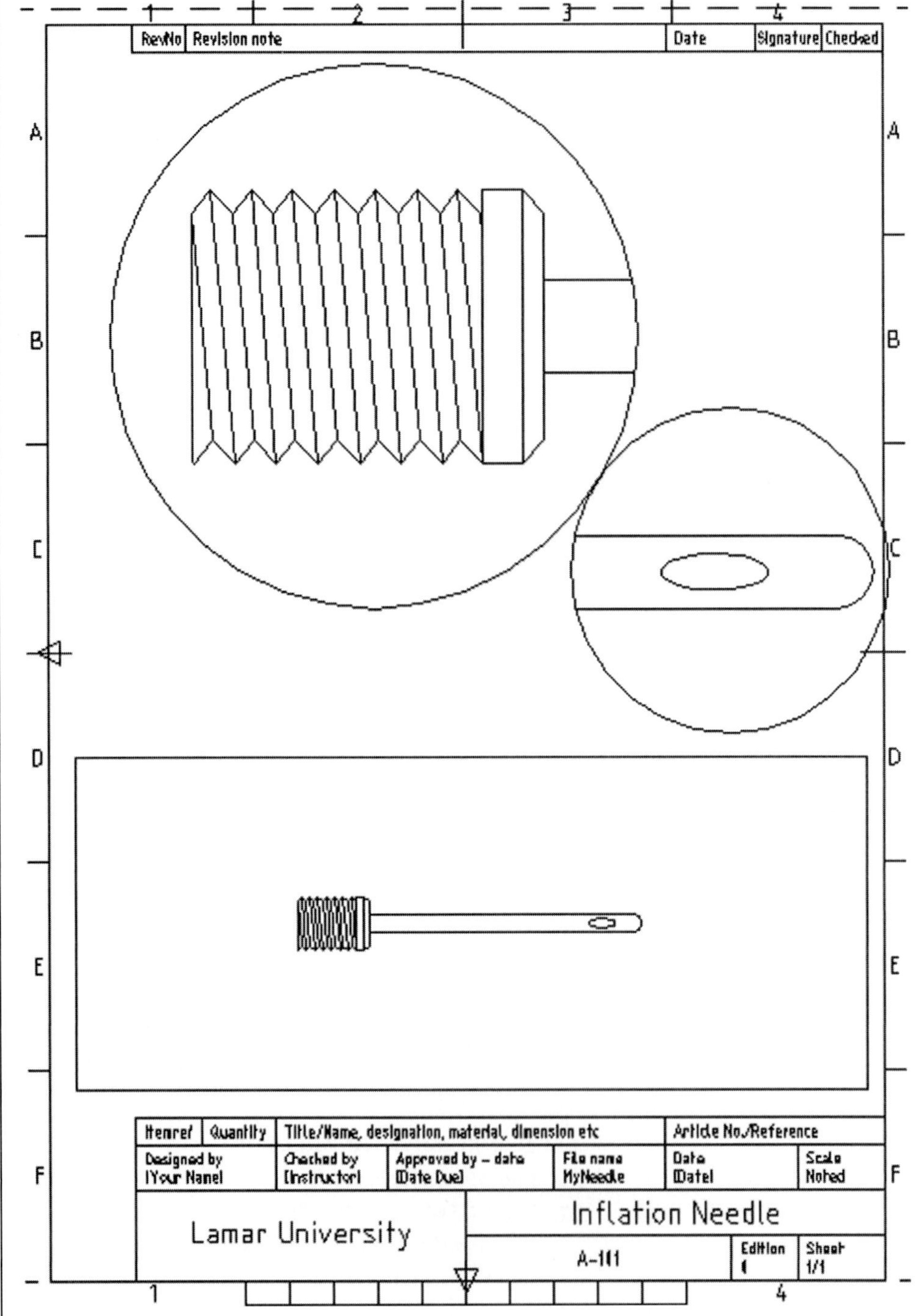

FIG. 1.8.1 Inflation Needle

2. Open the *cable splitter.dwg* file in the C:\Steps3D\Lesson01 folder. Create the drawing configuration for plotting found in Figure 1.8.2. Some helpful information includes:
   - **2.1.** The page size is 11" × $8\frac{1}{2}$".
   - **2.2.** Watch your layers (place viewports on the **VPorts** layer).
   - **2.3.** The radius of the circle is 1.75".
   - **2.4.** The title block is the *ANSI A title block* file found in AutoCAD's Template folder. (You may need to adjust its position on the sheet.)
   - **2.5.** The scale of each viewport is 4:1 (upper left), 4:1 (lower left), and 1:1 (right).
   - **2.6.** Fill in the title block as desired.
   - **2.7.** Save the drawing as *MySplitter* in the C:\Steps3D\Lesson02 folder.

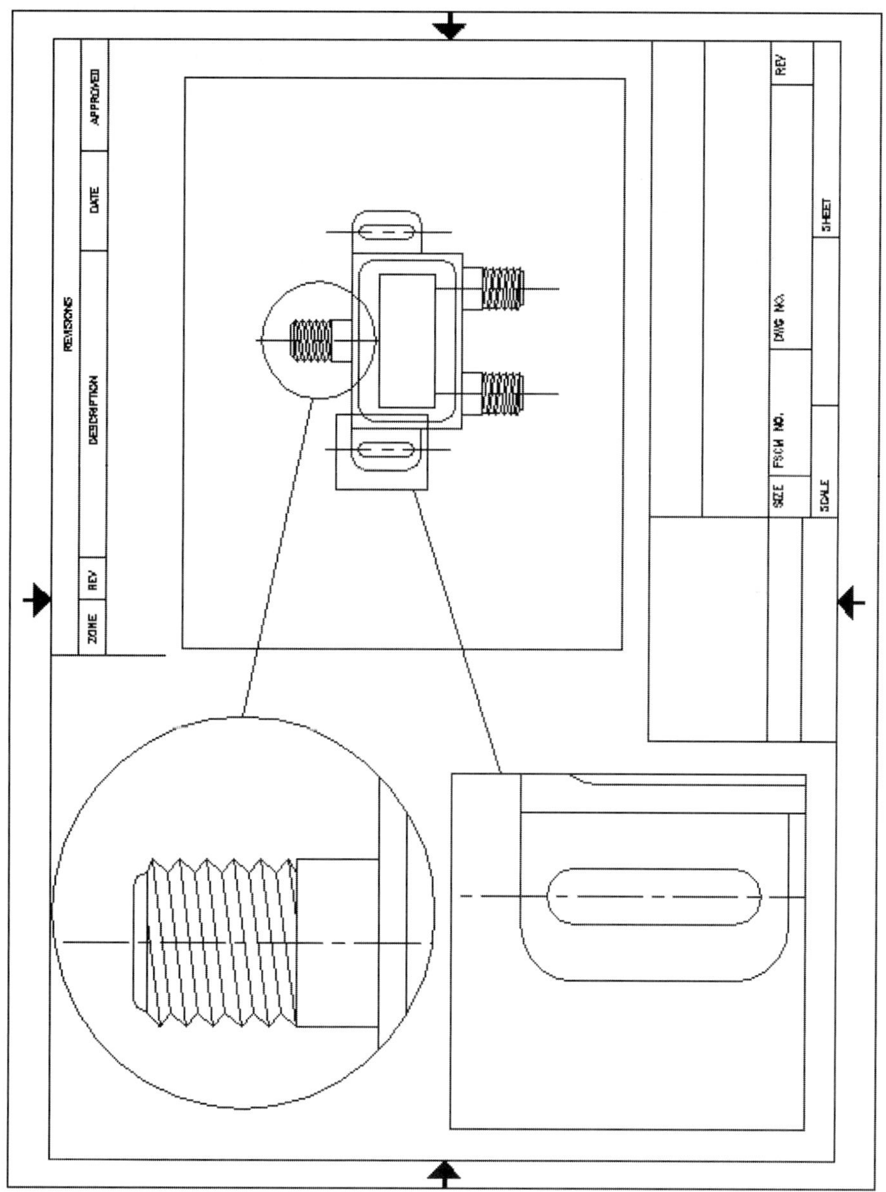

FIG. 1.8.2 Cable Splitter.dwg

3. Open the *glass cutter.dwg* file in the C:\Steps3D\Lesson01 folder. Create the drawing configuration for plotting found in Figure 1.8.3. Some helpful information includes:
   - **3.1.** The page size is 11" × $8\frac{1}{2}$".
   - **3.2.** Watch your layers (place viewports on the **VPorts** layer).
   - **3.3.** The radius of the circle is 1.25".
   - **3.4.** The title block is the *ANSI A title block* file found in AutoCAD's Template folder.
   - **3.5.** The scale of each viewport is 4:1 (upper left), 2:1 (upper right), and 1:2 (lower).
   - **3.6.** Fill in the title block as desired.
   - **3.7.** Save the drawing as *MyCutter* in the C:\Steps3D\Lesson02 folder.

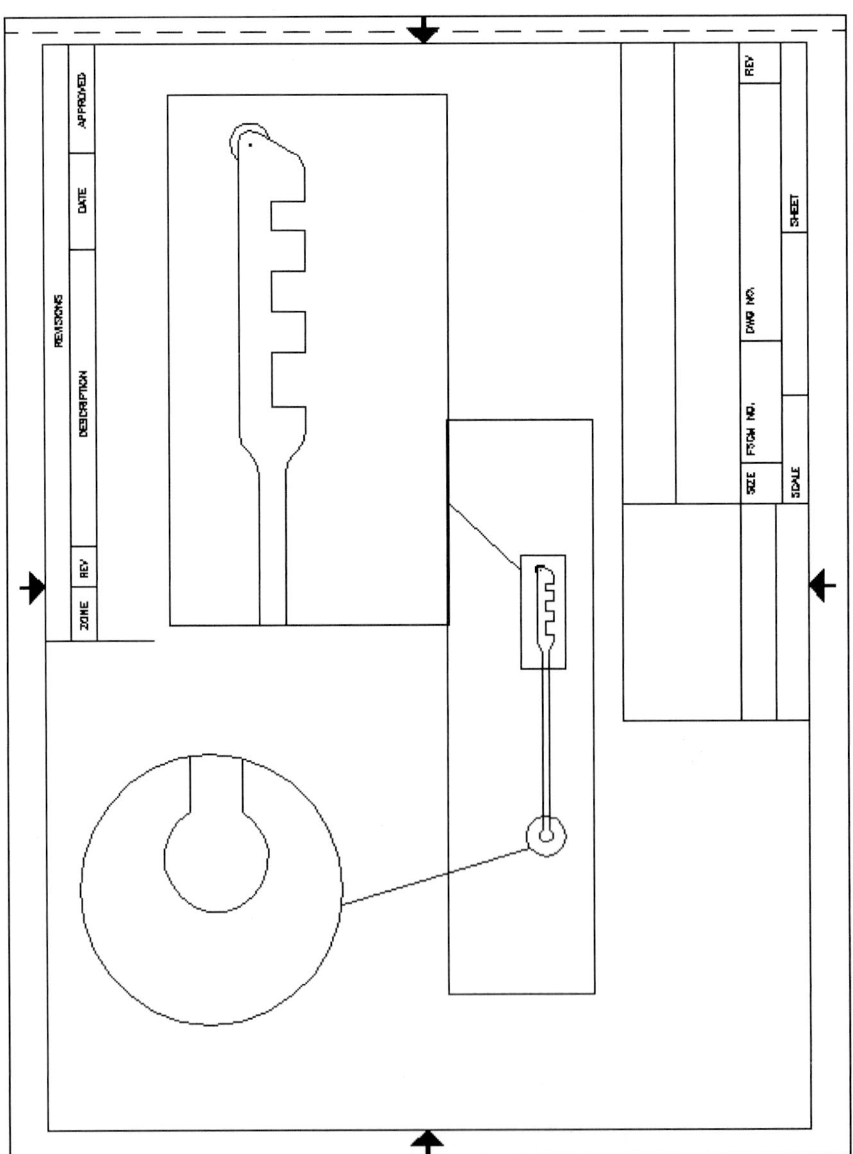

FIG. 1.8.3 Glass Cutter

4. Open the *Spice Rack.dwg* file in the C:\Steps3D\Lesson01 folder. Create the drawing configuration for plotting found in Figure 1.8.4. Some helpful information includes:
   - **4.1.** The page size is 11" × $8\frac{1}{2}$".
   - **4.2.** Watch your layers (place viewports on the **VPorts** layer).
   - **4.3.** The title block is the *ANSI A title block* file found in AutoCAD's Template folder.
   - **4.4.** The scale of each viewport is 1:1 (upper left), 1:1 (lower left), and 6" = 1' (right).
   - **4.5.** Fill in the title block as desired.
   - **4.6.** Save the drawing as *My Spice Rack* in the C:\Steps3D\Lesson02 folder.

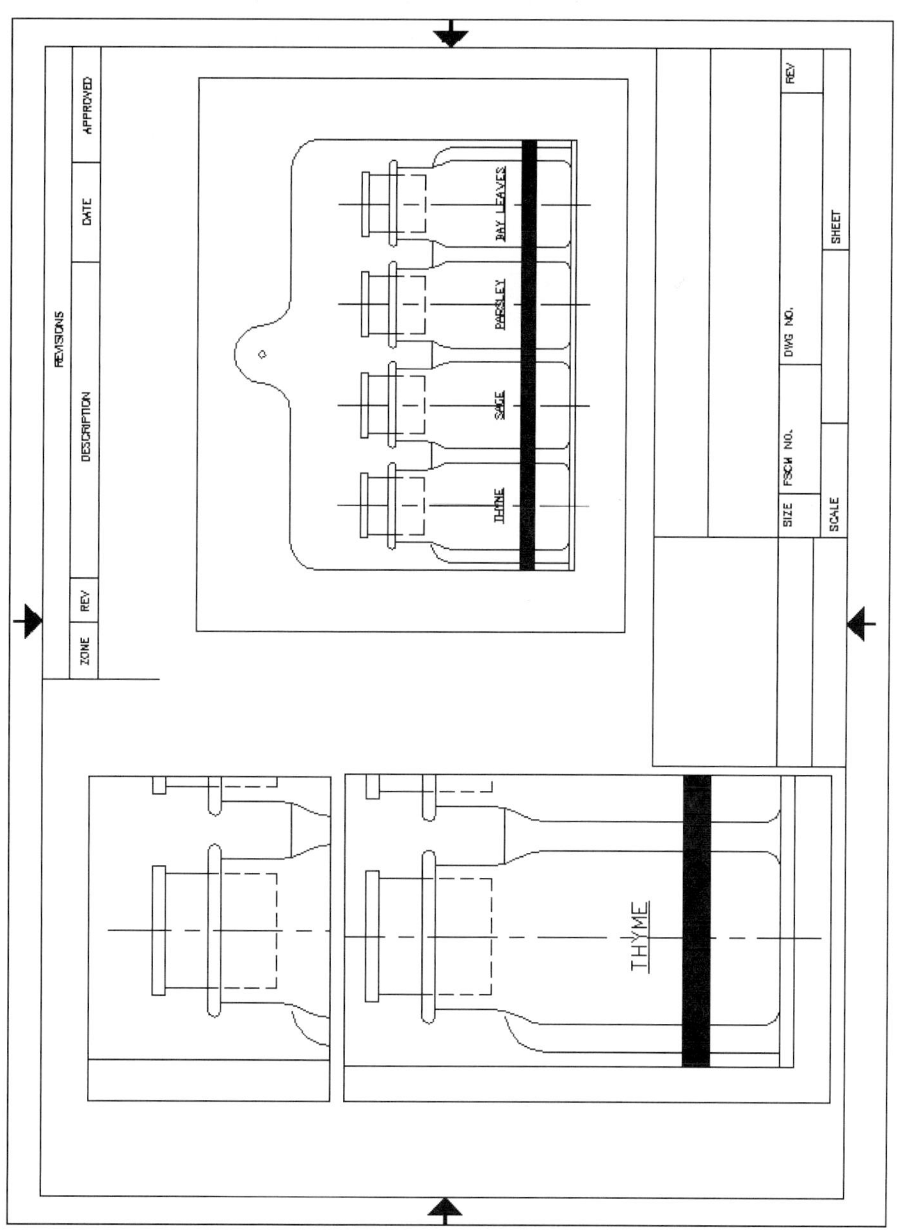

FIG. 1.8.4 Spice Rack

5. Open the *motor-assbly.dwg* file in the C:\Steps3D\Lesson01 folder. Create the drawing configuration for plotting found in Figure 1.8.5. Some helpful information includes:
   - **5.1.** The page size is 17" × 11". (*Hint:* If your printer will not support this sheet size, set up the page using **NONE** as the printer. AutoCAD will then make all of the sheet sizes available to you.)
   - **5.2.** Watch your layers (place viewports on the **VPorts** layer).
   - **5.3.** The title block is the *ANSI B title block* file found in AutoCAD's Template folder.
   - **5.4.** The scale of each viewport is 1:4 (upper left), 1:2 (lower left), and 1:2 (right).
   - **5.5.** Fill in the title block as desired.
   - **5.6.** Save the drawing as *MyAssbly* in the C:\Steps3D\Lesson02 folder.

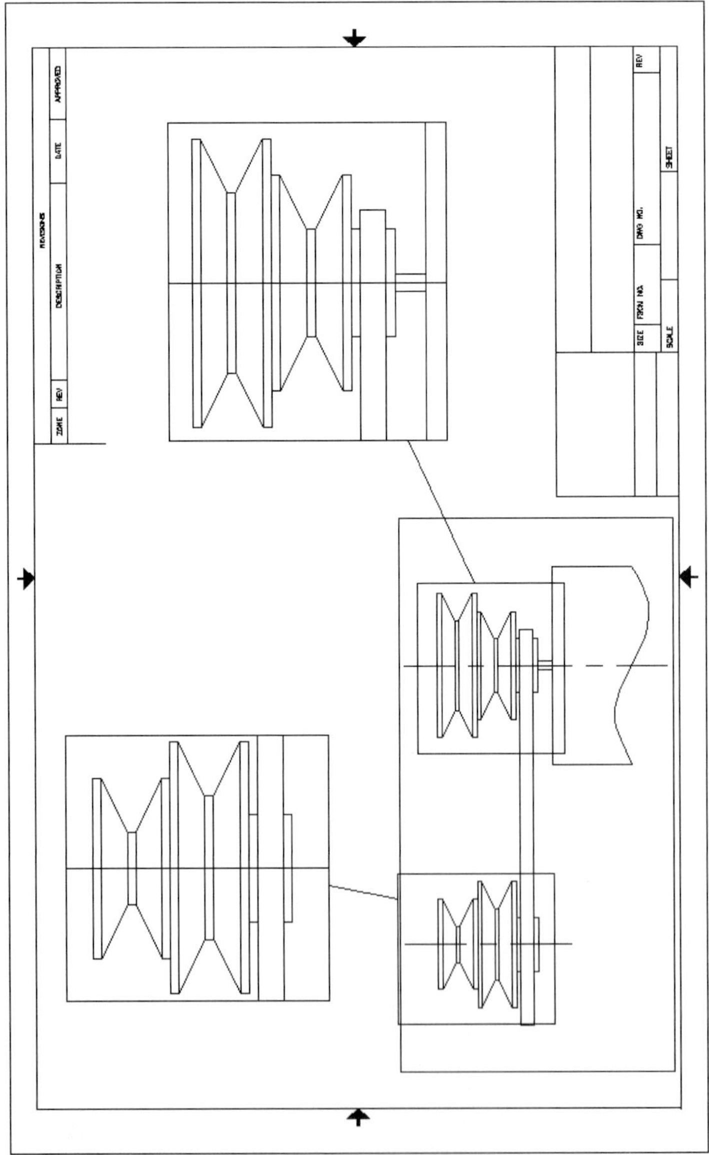

FIG. 1.8.5 Motor Assembly

6. Open the *remote1.dwg* file in the C:\Steps3D\Lesson01 folder. Create the drawing configuration for plotting found in Figure 1.8.6. Some helpful information includes:
   - **6.1.** The page size is 11" × $8\frac{1}{2}$".
   - **6.2.** Watch your layers (place viewports on the **VPorts** layer).
   - **6.3.** The title block is the *ANSI A title block* file found in AutoCAD's Template folder.
   - **6.4.** The scale of each viewport is 1:1 (upper left, center left, lower left), and 1:2 (right).
   - **6.5.** Fill in the title block as desired.
   - **6.6.** Save the drawing as *MyRemote* in the C:\Steps3D\Lesson02 folder.

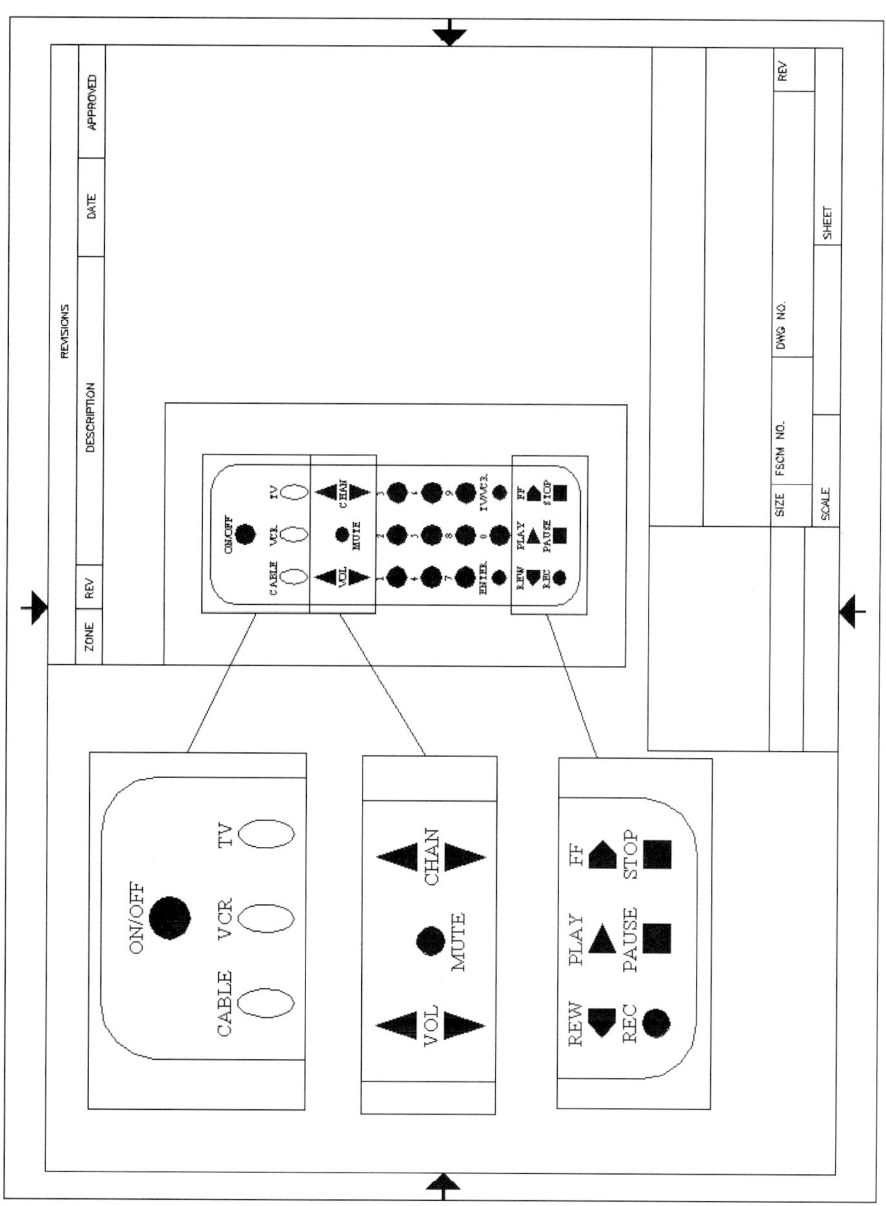

FIG. 1.8.6 Remote

7. Open the *Cabin.dwg* file in the C:\Steps3D\Lesson01 folder. Create the drawing configuration for plotting found in Figure 1.8.7. Some helpful information includes:
   7.1. The page size is 34" × 22".
   7.2. Watch your layers (place viewports on the **VPorts** layer).
   7.3. The title block is the *ANSI D title block* file found in AutoCAD's Template folder.
   7.4. The scale of each viewport is 1:1 (upper left and upper right), and 6" = 1' (lower left and lower right).
   7.5. Fill in the title block as desired.
   7.6. Save the drawing as *MyCabin* in the C:\Steps3D\Lesson02 folder.

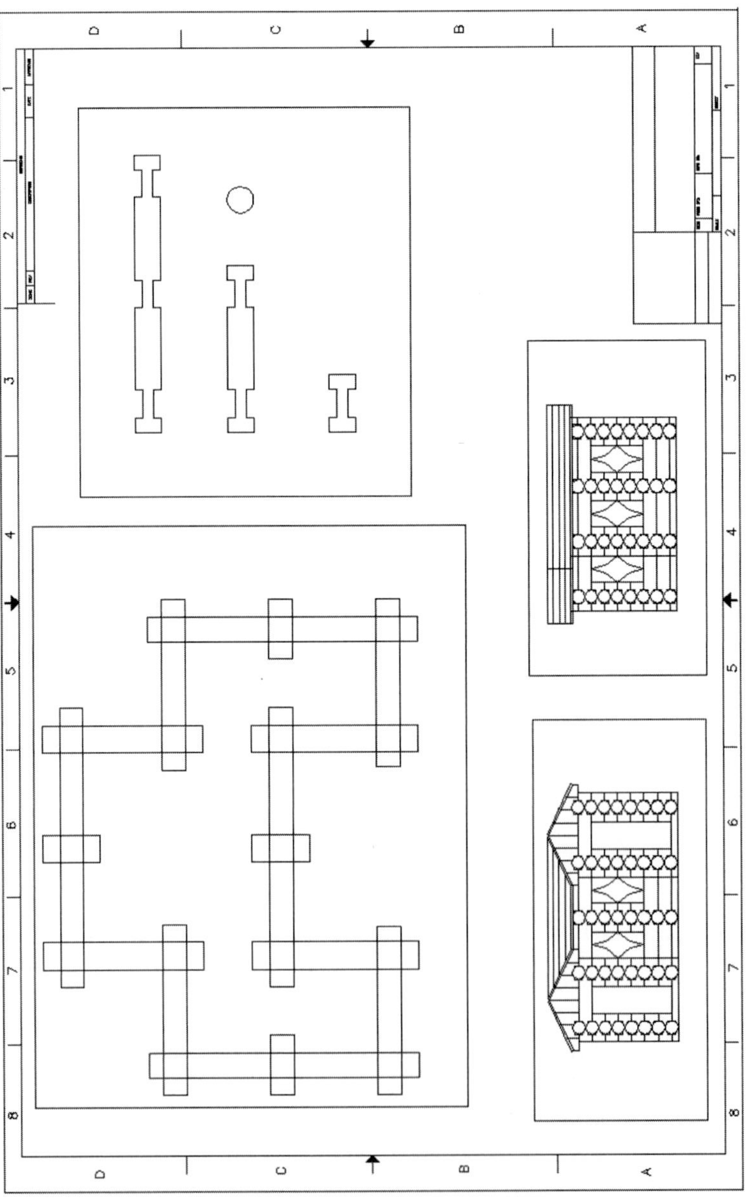

FIG. 1.8.7 Cabin

8. Open the *Piping plan 1.dwg* file in the C:\Steps3D\Lesson01 folder. Create the drawing configuration for plotting found in Figure 1.8.8. Some helpful information includes:
   - **8.1.** The page size is 34" × 22".
   - **8.2.** Watch your layers (place viewports on the **VPorts** layer).
   - **8.3.** The title block is the *ANSI D title block* file found in AutoCAD's Template folder.
   - **8.4.** The scale of each viewport is $\frac{3}{8}$" = 1' (main) and $\frac{3}{4}$" = 1' (detail).
   - **8.5.** Fill in the title block as desired.
   - **8.6.** Save the drawing as *My Piping Plan* in the C:\Steps3D\Lesson02 folder.

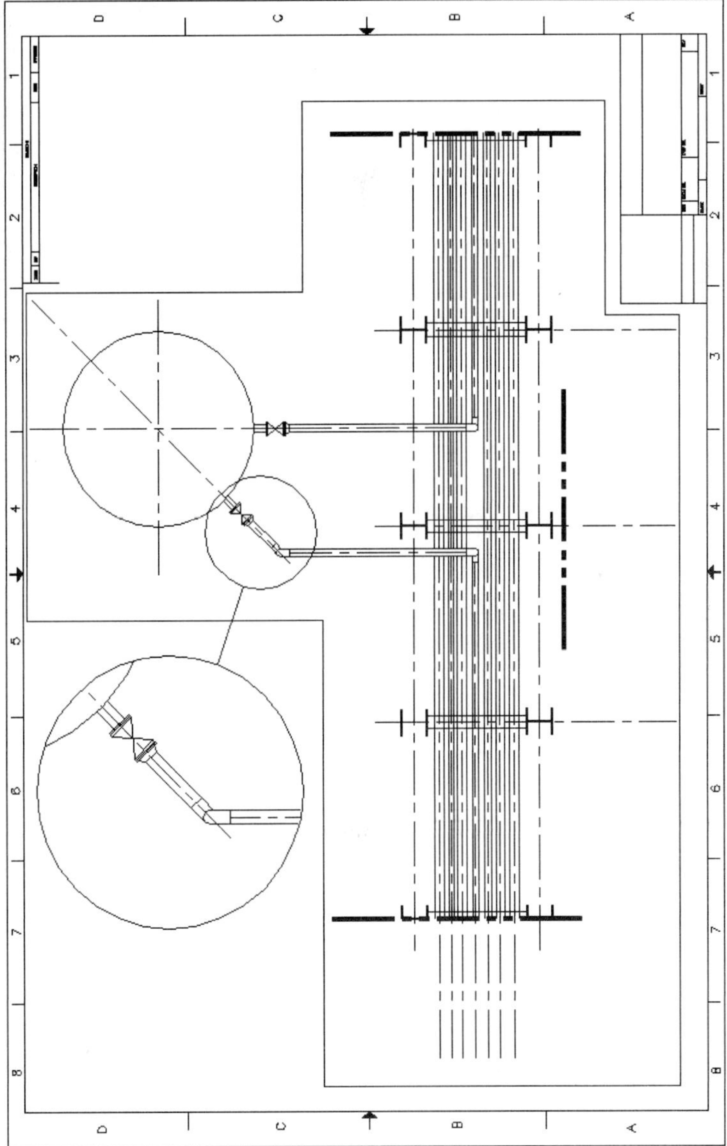

FIG. 1.8.8 Piping Plan 1

1.9 REVIEW QUESTIONS

Please write your answers on a separate sheet of paper.

1. A __________ can be considered a window into your drawing.

2 and 3. The two types of viewports are __________ and __________.

4 and 5. The two ways to tell which space you are using are __________ and __________.

6 and 7. The keyboard approach to switching between Model Space and Paper Space is by using the commands __________ (or its hotkey "ms") or __________ (or its hotkey "ps").

8. Use __________ viewports in Model Space.

9. Access the Viewports dialog box using the __________ command.

10. (T or F) It is possible to place a viewport configuration into a single active viewport.

11 and 12. It is easy to tell the difference between active and inactive viewports. Active viewports present __________ while inactive viewports present a __________.

13. To activate a viewport, place the cursor in it and click once with the __________.

14. (T or F) Tiled viewports will plot, so it is important to have them set up properly.

15. Layers behave __________ in tiled viewports.

16. If you need to reenter the Page Setup dialog box, use the __________ command.

17. (T or F) You can rename a space tab to help keep track of what is on it.

18. Paper Space drawings should be plotted at a scale of __________.

19. The UCS icon becomes a __________ when in Paper Space.

20. (Floating, Tiled) viewports are objects that can be moved.

21. (T or F) Floating viewports must be rectangular.

22. (T or F) Unlike tiled viewports, more than one floating viewport can be active at a time.

23. (T or F) You can work in Model Space from a Layout tab.

24. Use the __________ command to create floating viewports.

25. Use the __________ command to convert tiled viewports to floating viewports.

26. (T or F) Once a viewport has been created, it cannot be modified.

27. Set a $\frac{1}{4}$" = 1' – 0" scale in a floating viewport by using the __________ command.

28. If you do not want to use the command in Question 27, you can use the __________ on the Viewports toolbar.

LESSON 2

After the Setup

Following this lesson, you will:

- Know how to work with a Paper Space drawing
  - Know how to use layers in Paper Space
  - Know how to use text in Paper Space
  - Know how to dimension in Paper Space
  - Know how to plot a Paper Space drawing
- Know how to use ***MVSetup*** as a Floating Viewport editor
- Know how to use ***Regenall*** and ***Redrawall*** to refresh viewports

You have seen how to show a drawing (a *model*) at different scales on the same page. But what will happen to text and dimensions when the scale changes? What will happen when you need to show information in a detail that you do not want to see on the plan? (After all, that is why we use details.)

Up until now you have determined text and dimension sizes using a mathematical formula based on the desired size at plot time and the drawing scale factor. An undiscovered error in your math might have wreaked havoc when you went to plot the drawing and discovered that all the text and dimension elements had to be resized.

In creating Paper Space, AutoCAD took these problems into consideration and provided some clever solutions. In Lesson 2, we will investigate these solutions as well as some tricks to control the display both inside and outside of your viewports.

Let's begin.

2.1 Dimensioning and Paper Space

AutoCAD has two ways to create dimensions when Paper Space is involved—the *Olde Way* and the *New Way*. The Olde Way takes considerably more work and will, no doubt, eventually pass the way of Beta VCRs and the two-dollar bill. Still, you will probably find yourself editing older drawings from time to time; knowledge of how it was done "in olden times" will be beneficial. You will almost certainly prefer the New Way.

Let's take a look at both.

2.1.1 Dimensioning and Paper Space—The Olde Way

The Olde Way of setting up dimensioning for a Paper Space drawing was almost identical to setting up dimensioning for Model Space. The subtle difference involved the scale factor on the **Fit** tab of the Dimension Style Manager. For Model Space dimensioning, you must enter the scale factor, but for Paper Space dimensioning, you had to put a check in the **Scale dimensions to layout (paperspace)** check box. AutoCAD would scale the arrowheads, text, and other dimension objects accordingly.

The confusing part was answering the question of just where to place the dimensions. When thinking about dimensioning and Paper Space, it helped to remember that old adage: *Dance with the one what brung you*. In other words, if you drew it in Model Space, you placed your dimensions in Model Space; if you drew it in Paper Space, you placed your dimensions in Paper Space.

This will become clearer with an example. Let's step back in time, play some Beatles tunes on the 8-track, and try one.

WWW

2.1.1.1 Do This: Adding Paper Space Dimensions—The Olde Way

I. Open the *MyFlr-pln2a.dwg* file located in the C:\Steps3D\Lesson02 folder. (If this drawing was not completed in the last exercise, open the *flr-pln2a.dwg* file instead.)

II. Follow these steps:

TOOLS	COMMAND SEQUENCE	STEPS
PAPER	**Command:** ***ms***	**1.** Open Model Space by typing ***mspace*** or ***ms*** at the command prompt. Or you can pick the **Paper** toggle on the status bar.
		2. Activate the upper left viewport.
Dimension Style Button	**Command:** ***ddim***	**3.** Call the Dimension Style Manager.
ARCH Angular STANDARD		**4.** Select the **Arch** parent style . . .
Modify...		**5.** . . . and pick the **Modify** button.
	Scale for Dimension Features Use overall scale of: 0.0000 Scale dimensions to layout (paperspace)	**6.** In the **Scale for dimension features** frame of the **Fit** tab, place a bullet next to **Scale dimensions to layout (paperspace)**.
OK Close		**7.** Pick the **OK** button and then the **Close** button to continue. (The rest of the setup has been done for you.)
BORDER Defpoints DIM DOORS FIXTURES TEXT Title Block VPORTS WALLS WINDOWS		**8.** Set the **Dim** layer current.

continued

TOOLS	COMMAND SEQUENCE	STEPS

9. Place the dimensions shown in Figure 2.1.1.1.9. (Use grips or the ***Stretch*** command to adjust the size and shape of the viewport as necessary.)

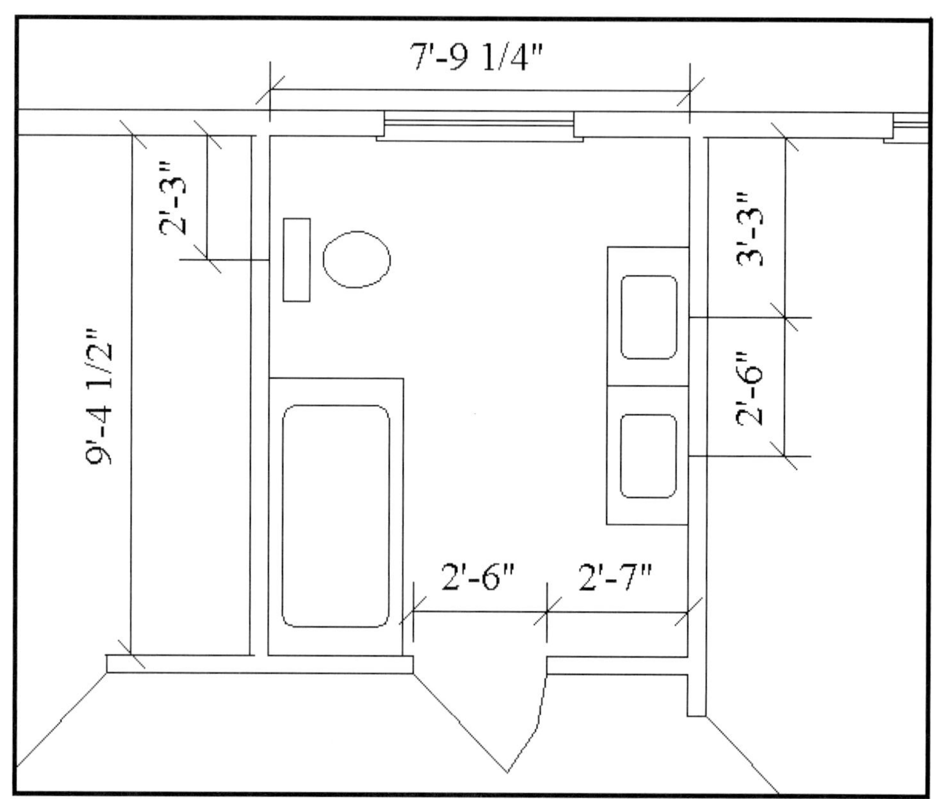

FIG. 2.1.1.1.9 Dimensioned Viewport

10. Now place the dimensions in the round viewport as shown in Figure 2.1.1.1.10. (*Hint:* You may have to use ***DimTedit*** to help you.)

continued

TOOLS	COMMAND SEQUENCE	STEPS
		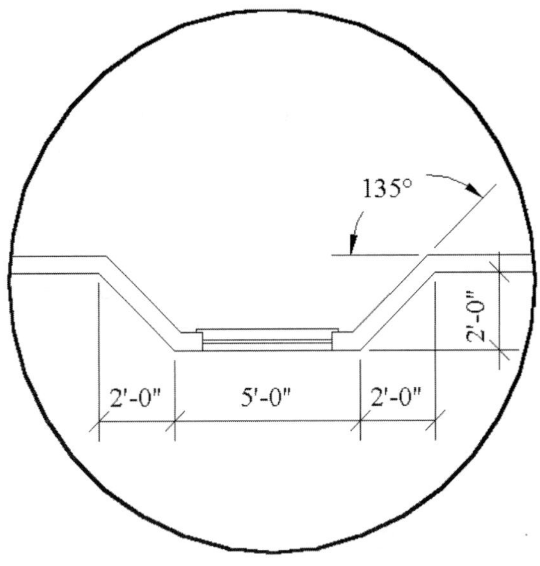 FIG. 2.1.1.1.10 Dimensioned Bay Window
MODEL	**Command:** *ps*	**11.** Return to Paper Space by double-clicking outside the viewports. Or you can use the **MODEL** toggle on the status bar.
	**Command:** *qsave*	**12.** Save the drawing as *Myflr-pln2a*, but do not exit.

As you can see, the only problem presented by dimensioning in Paper Space was one of room. But if dimensions didn't fit into the viewport, you could use standard modifying tools (grips or the ***Stretch*** command) to resize it. (Remember that the viewport exists in Paper Space. So any modifying on the viewport itself must be done there.)

Did you notice that the dimensions appeared not only in the active viewport but also in the other viewports as well? (Look in the large viewport where you can see both the bath and bay window.) This presented a problem that users of older AutoCAD releases would fix with careful manipulation of layers. Regardless of how you place dimensions, the techniques used to manipulate those layers are still quite useful today for a host of other reasons. You will learn the how-to's of layers in Paper Space in Section 2.2, but first let's take a look at the modern approach to Paper Space dimensioning.

2.1.2 Dimensioning and Paper Space—The New Way

Despite the name, the New Way of Paper Space dimensioning really involves no new techniques at all. With some programming adjustments that appeared with the 2002 release, the user simply places dimensions in Paper Space rather than Model Space (regardless of where the objects to be dimensioned reside). AutoCAD automatically interprets in which space the objects exist and adjusts the dimension accordingly. Using this new program, all dimensions exist in Paper Space—even if the object dimensioned exists in Model Space.

You should remember some general rules when using this new approach:

- The **Dimassoc** system variable must be set to **2**. Since this is the default for new drawings in AutoCAD 2002, you will not have a problem with them. However, if you are working with a drawing created in an earlier release, you will have to change the variable setting.
- The new programming may have a problem recognizing multilines. If this occurs, you will find it necessary to either explode the multilines or use the Olde Way as detailed in Section 2.1.1.

2.1.2.1 Do This: Adding Paper Space Dimensions—The New Way

I. Open the *flrpln2a-new.dwg* file located in the C:\Steps3D\Lesson02 folder. This file is the same as the *flr-pln2a.dwg* file but hasn't been modified yet.

II. Be sure the **Dimassoc** system variable is set to **2**.

III. Be sure you are in Paper Space (the toggle on the status bar should read **PAPER**).

IV. Follow these steps:

TOOLS	COMMAND SEQUENCE	STEPS
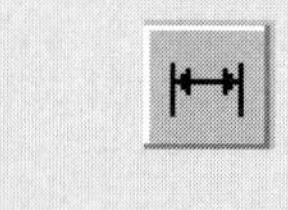	**Command:** ***dli*** 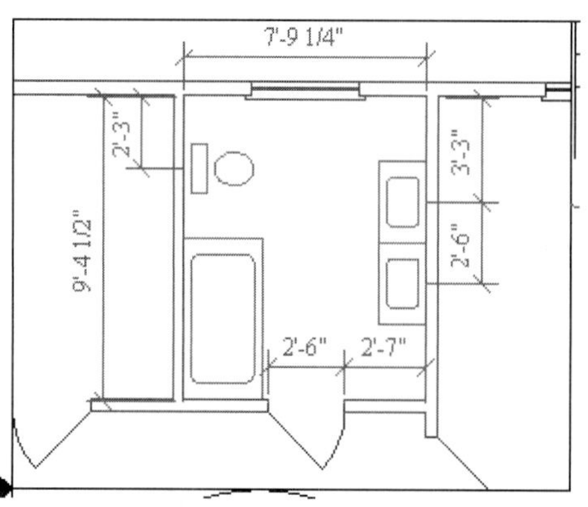	**1.** Place the dimensions indicated in Figure 2.1.2.1.1 for the upper left viewport. Do *not* change to Model Space except to make adjustments in the display as needed. Use grips to resize the viewport as needed. (Put the dimensions on the **Dim** layer) FIG. 2.1.2.1.1 Dimensions in Paper Space for Upper Left Viewport

continued

TOOLS	COMMAND SEQUENCE	STEPS

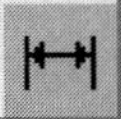

Command: *dli*

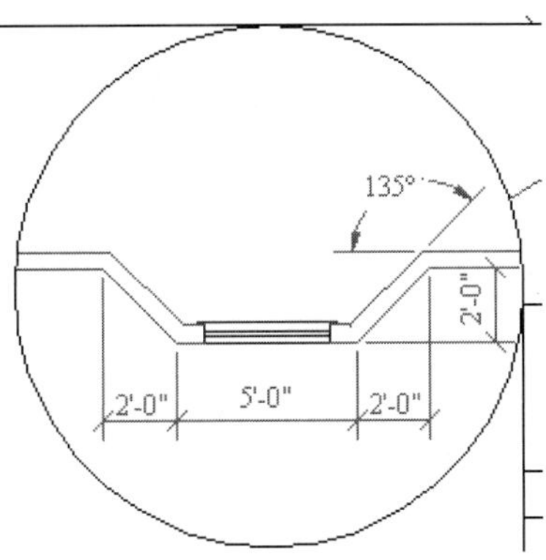

2. Now dimension the bay window as shown in Figure 2.1.2.1.2. Again, do not change to Model Space except to make adjustments in the display.

FIG. 2.1.2.1.2 Dimensions in Paper Space for Lower Left Viewport

Command: *z*

3. Now Zoom All and look at the drawing. Compare it to the drawing you did in the last exercise (open that drawing if necessary and view the two side by side).

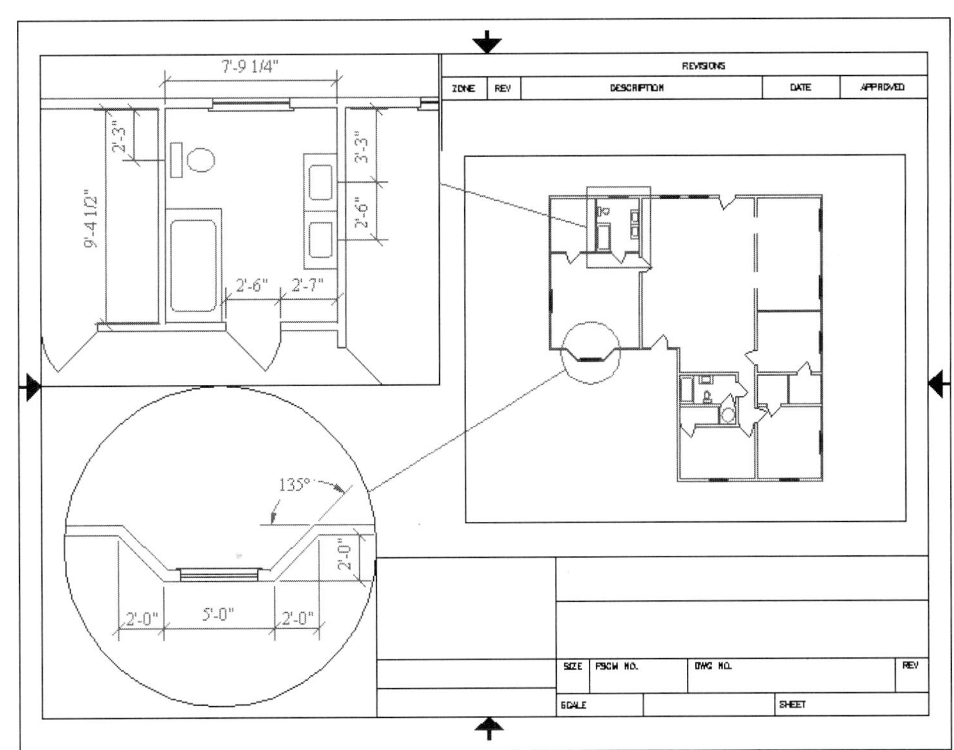

FIG. 2.1.2.1.3 Completed Drawing

Command: *qsave*

4. Save the drawing and exit.

Did you notice the difference between the two drawings?

You should have seen that the dimensions placed in the first exercise appeared both in the viewport being dimensioned and in the full viewport at right. This happens because the dimensions exist in Model Space, which appears through the viewports. In the drawing you created in the second exercise, the dimensions appear only at the viewports where you created them. These dimensions, although detailing objects that live in Model Space, exist in Paper Space.

It will not be necessary to manipulate layers to hide dimensions in the second drawing, but you will have to do so in the first. You'll see how in our next section.

2.2 The Benefits of Layers in Paper Space

FIG. 2.2a Thawed Layer in Current Viewport

FIG. 2.2b Frozen Layer in Current Viewport

One of the real wonders of Paper Space has to be the user's ability to manipulate layers in a single viewport independently of other viewports. In other words, you can freeze (or thaw) layers in one viewport while leaving them thawed (or frozen) in another! The trick lies in using the ***VPLayer*** command instead of the ***Layer*** command in your manipulations. Or you can use the **Freeze or Thaw in Current Viewport** column on the **Layer Control** box. The symbols for frozen or thawed layers in the current viewport can be seen in Figures 2.2a and 2.2b.

> A layer must be turned on and thawed globally before the ***Vplayer*** command will affect it.

The ***VPLayer*** command sequence goes like this:

Command: ***vplayer***

Enter an option [?/Freeze/Thaw/Reset/Newfrz/Vpvisdflt]:
[tell AutoCAD what you want to do]

Let's look at each option:

- The **?** option prompts the user to select a viewport. Then AutoCAD shows the layers that are frozen in that particular viewport. If the command is given from Model Space, AutoCAD will switch to Paper Space just long enough to complete the procedure.
- The **Freeze/Thaw** options allow the user to enter the name(s) of a layer(s) and then prompts the user to select the viewports in which the layer(s) will be frozen or thawed. The command sequence looks like this:

Enter layer name(s) to freeze:

Enter an option [All/Select/Current] <Current>: ***[tell AutoCAD to freeze/thaw the layer in All the viewports, Selected viewports, or the Current viewport]***

- The **Reset** option sets layers to their default settings. Use the **Vpvisdflt** option to create the default settings. The **Vpvisdflt** option will prompt as follows:

  Enter layer name(s) to change viewport visibility: *[name the layer(s)—use commas to separate several layer names]*

  Enter a viewport visibility option [Frozen/Thawed] <Thawed>: *[tell AutoCAD how you wish this layer to behave by default]*

- The **Newfrz** option will create a new layer that is frozen in all viewports.

Let's take a look at how layers interact with viewports.

WWW 2.2.1 Do This: Manipulating Layers in Floating Viewports

I. Go back to the *Myflr-pln2a.dwg* in the C:\Steps3D\Lesson02 folder. Reopen it if necessary.

II. Be sure you are in Paper Space.

III. Follow these steps:

TOOLS	COMMAND SEQUENCE	STEPS
No Button Available	**Command:** *vplayer*	**1.** Enter the ***VPLayer*** command by typing ***vplayer*** at the command prompt. There is no hotkey, button, or pull-down menu selection for the ***VPLayer*** command.
	Enter an option [?/Freeze/Thaw/Reset/ Newfrz/Vpvisdflt]: *f*	**2.** Tell AutoCAD you wish to freeze the **Dim** and **fixtures** layers.
	Enter layer name(s) to freeze: *dim,fixtures*	
	Enter an option [All/Select/Current] <Current>: *s* **Select objects:** *[select the right viewport]*	**3.** AutoCAD asks you to identify the viewport in which you want the layer frozen. Tell it that you will select one. Then select the right viewport.
	Select objects: *[enter]* **Enter an option [?/Freeze/Thaw/Reset/ Newfrz/Vpvisdflt]:** *[enter]*	**4.** Hit *enter* to confirm the selection and again to complete the command. The drawing now looks like Figure 2.2.1.4.

continued

TOOLS	COMMAND SEQUENCE	STEPS

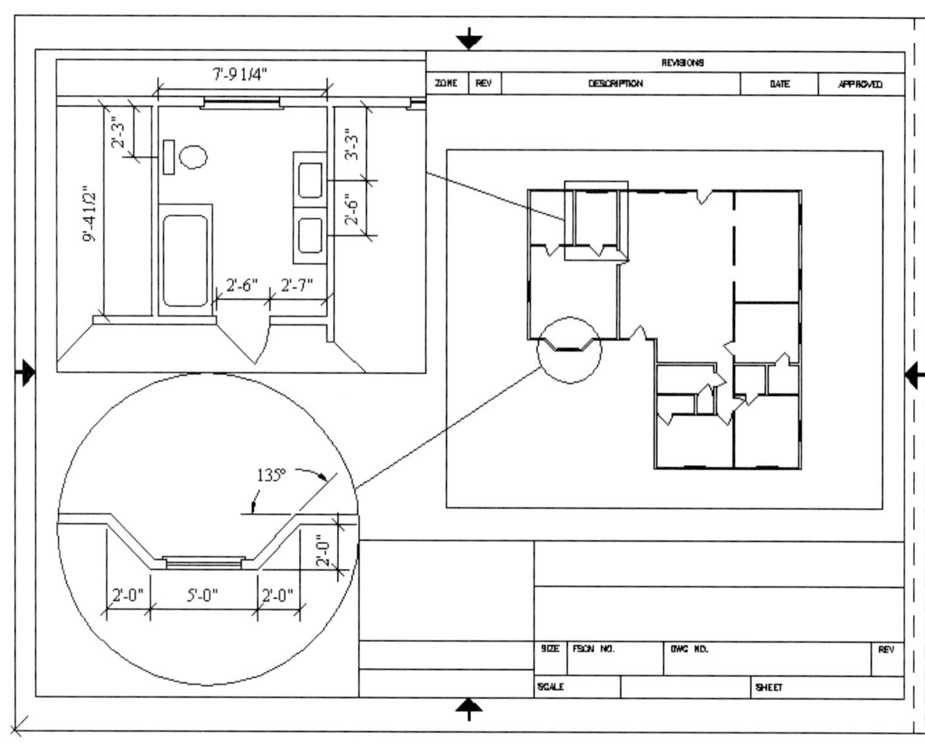

FIG. 2.2.1.4 Layers Frozen in One Viewport

Layer Button

Command: ***la***

5. Let's crosshatch the master bath area (the area shown in the detail) in the right viewport. First, create a layer called **Hatch**. Make it a dark color, and make it current.

Command: ***ms***

6. Return to Model Space and activate the right viewport.

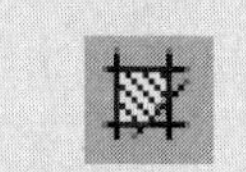
Hatch Button

Command: ***h***

7. Now enter the ***BHatch*** command.

continued

TOOLS	COMMAND SEQUENCE	STEPS
	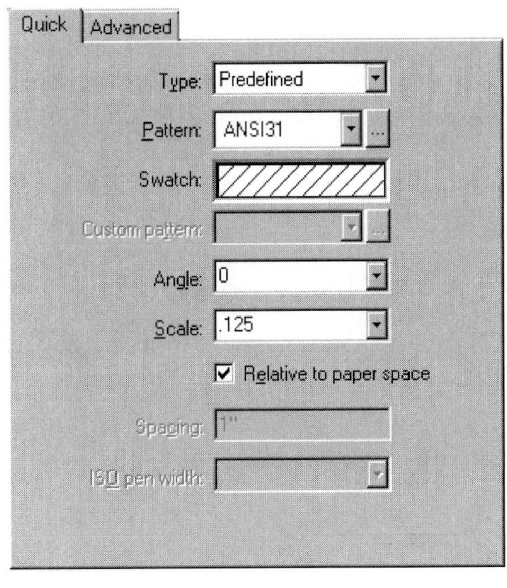	**8.** On the **Quick** tab, set the **Scale** to $\frac{1}{8}$" and place a check in the **Relative to paper space** box. AutoCAD will adjust the hatch spacing according to the scale of the viewport.
 Pick Points Button	**Select objects:** **Select objects:** *[enter]*	**9.** Pick the **Pick Points** button and select a point inside the master bath. Hit *enter* to return to the dialog box.
		**10.** Pick the **OK** button to continue. Notice that the hatch pattern appears in both viewports that show the master bath.
		11. Let's try an easier way to freeze layers. Make the upper left viewport current.

continued

TOOLS	COMMAND SEQUENCE	STEPS

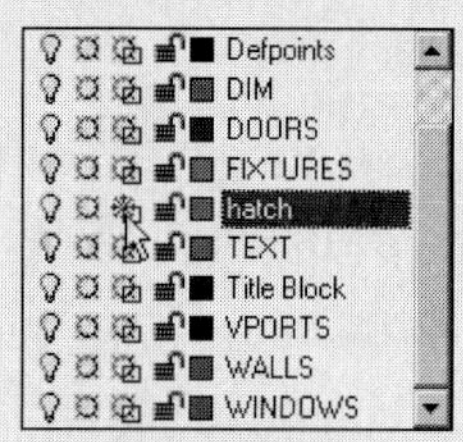

12. Now use the toggle in the **Layer Control** box to freeze the **hatch** layer in the current viewport. Your drawing looks like Figure 2.2.1.12.

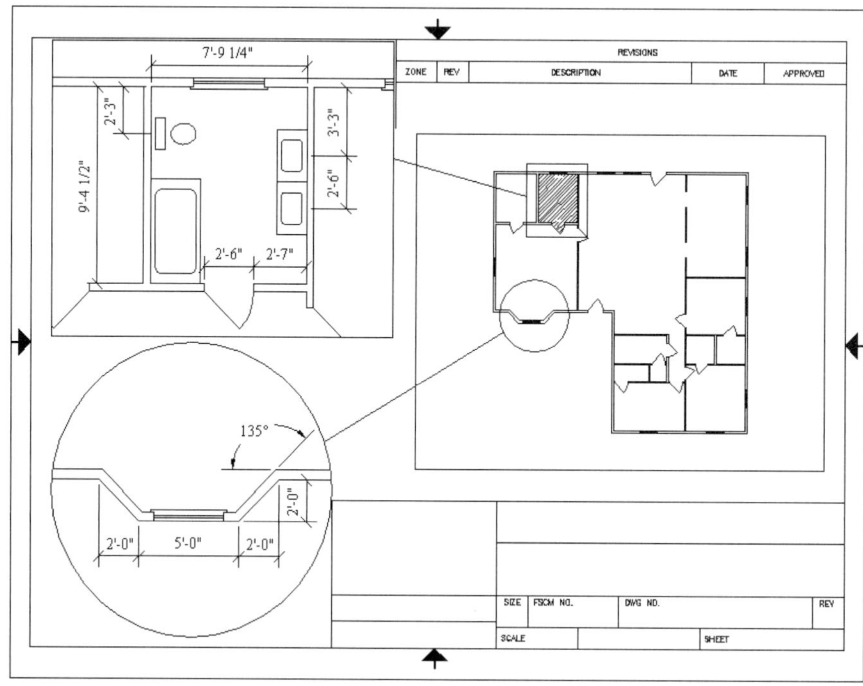

FIG. 2.2.1.12 Hatched Bath in a Single Viewport

Command: *ps*

13. Return to Paper Space.

Command: *props*

14. Change the two viewports on the left to the **Text** layer.

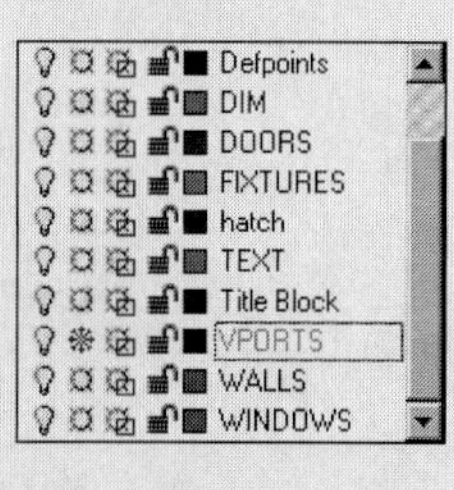

Command: *la*

15. Now freeze the **VPorts** layer. Your drawing now looks like Figure 2.2.1.15.

continued

TOOLS	COMMAND SEQUENCE	STEPS

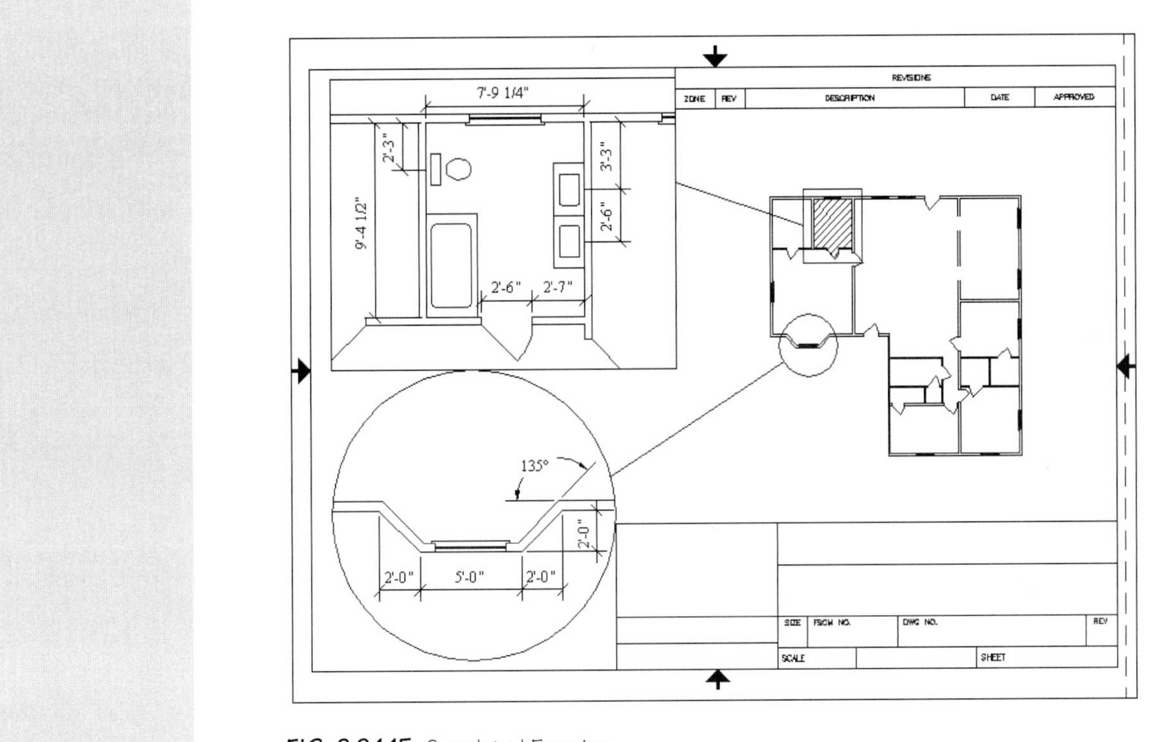

FIG. 2.2.1.15 Completed Exercise

TOOLS	COMMAND SEQUENCE	STEPS
	Command: *qsave*	**16.** Save the drawing, but do not exit.

This is a much finer image for plotting, but there is still more to do. We must add some callouts to the drawing before we plot it.

2.3 Using Text in Paper Space

In a drawing that uses Paper Space, place all text in Paper Space unless it is part of the model. The reasoning behind this general rule is this: Placing text in Paper Space is considerably easier than placing text in Model Space.

Let me explain.

Remember how difficult you found sizing text in Model Space? You had to consider the size that you wanted the text to be at plot time and the scale at which you would plot. Then you had to work some mathematical wizardry to determine the size of the text to use in your drawing. You had to do all of this before placing any text.

Try this formula to determine text height in Paper Space: The height you want the text to be when you plot equals the height you make your text. It just cannot get any simpler than that!

But wait! AutoCAD has included a new tool with its 2002 release that greatly simplifies the Paper Space to Model Space (and vice versa) translation of text sizes. When you determine that text simply must go into Model Space, use the ***SpaceTrans*** command to help you determine its size. This transparent command works anytime AutoCAD asks you for a size. Look at its sequence here:

Command: *dt*

Current text style: "TIMES" Text height: 0'−6"

Specify start point of text or [Justify/Style]:

Specify height <0'−6">: *'spacetrans*

>>Specify paper space distance <1'>: 1/4

Resuming DTEXT command.

Specify height <0'−6">: 12.0000000

Specify rotation angle of text <0>:

Enter text:

Enter text:

Spacetrans determines the appropriate Model Space size for the text and responds to the **Specify height** prompt for you!

You will see this in action in our next exercise.

> Use either of AutoCAD's text commands—***Text*** or ***MTText***—to place the text in Paper Space.

Let's add a bit of text to our drawing.

2.3.1 Do This: Adding Text in Paper Space

I. Open the *flr-pln2b-new.dwg* file located in the C:\Steps3D\Lesson02 folder.

II. Be sure you are in Paper Space.

III. Follow these steps:

TOOLS	COMMAND SEQUENCE	STEPS
AI	**Command:** *dt*	**1.** On the **Text** layer, add the callouts shown in Figure 2.3.1.1. Larger text is $\frac{3}{16}$" and smaller text is $\frac{1}{8}$". (Use the **Times** text style that has already been set up for you.)

continued

TOOLS | COMMAND SEQUENCE | STEPS

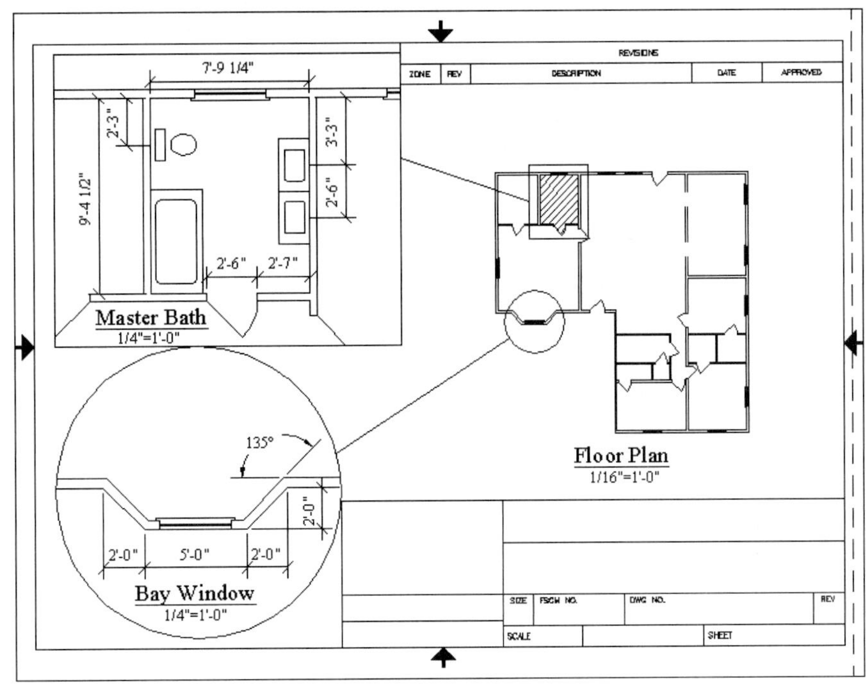

FIG. 2.3.1.1 Master Bath Callout

2. Now fill out the title block as shown in Figure 2.3.1.2. Text sizes are $\frac{1}{4}$", $\frac{3}{16}$", and $\frac{1}{8}$". Feel free to use your own school's name.

FIG. 2.3.1.2 Completed Title Block

Command: ***qsave***

3. Save the drawing, but do not exit.

PAPER

Command: ***ms***

4. Now let's add some text to Model Space. We'll have AutoCAD size it for us. First, activate Model Space and make the right viewport current.

continued

TOOLS	COMMAND SEQUENCE	STEPS
	Command: *dt* **Current text style: "TIMES"** **Text height: 0'–0 1/8"** **Specify start point of text or [Justify/Style]:** *c*	**5.** Begin the ***Text*** command and center the text in the den (refer to Figure 2.3.1.8).
	Specify center point of text: **Specify height <0'–0 1/8>:** *'spacetrans*	**6.** Now enter the ***SpaceTrans*** command transparently.
	>> Specify paper space distance <1">: *3/32*	**7.** Tell AutoCAD to make the text height $\frac{3}{32}$".
	Resuming TEXT command. **Specify height <0'–0 1/8>:** **18.00000000000000** **Specify rotation angle of text <0>:** *[enter]* **Enter text:** *Den* **Enter text:** *[enter]*	**8.** AutoCAD resumes the ***Text*** command and provides the appropriate text height. Complete the command, entering the text *Den* as shown in Figure 2.3.1.8.

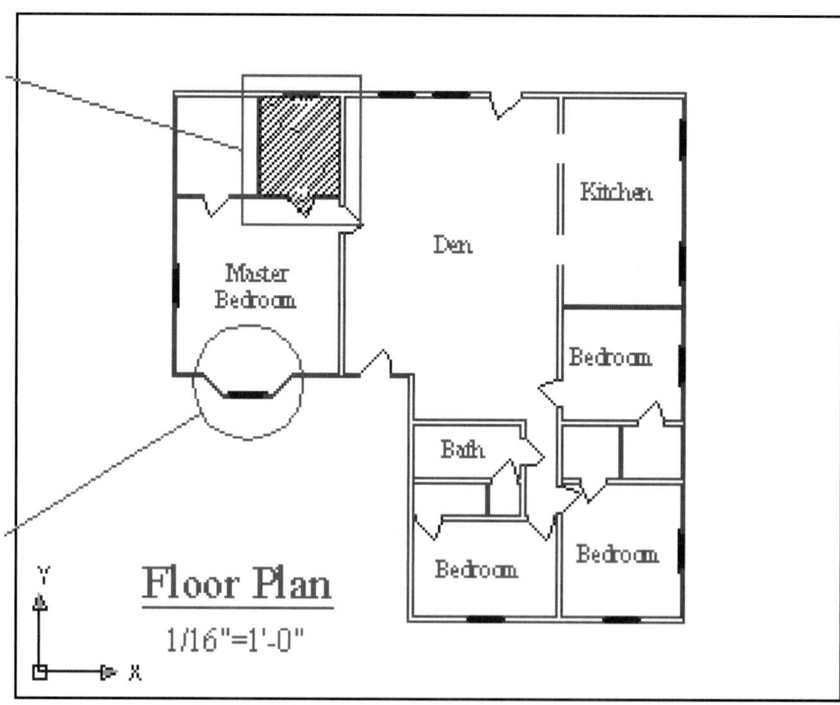

FIG. 2.3.1.8 Model Space Text

TOOLS	COMMAND SEQUENCE	STEPS
	Command: *qsave*	**9.** Save the drawing.

Take a moment and toggle between the **Model** tab and the Layout (**My First House**) tab of your drawing. Notice which objects exist as part of the model and which do not. Only those objects that you created through the viewports in Model Space exist on the **Model** tab. Everything else exists as part of the paper on which you will plot your model.

Once the dimensions are drawn and the text placed—the *i*'s dotted and the *t*'s crossed—it is time to plot the drawing. Let's look at that next.

2.4 Plotting the Layout

It is funny that, after all the setting up, creating, and manipulating, it always comes back to getting it on paper. Perhaps that is why AutoCAD has put so much time and money into making printing as user friendly as possible.

Printing a layout is not very different from printing Model Space (although it is a bit easier). Let's print our floor plan layout.

2.4.1 Do This: Plotting the Layout

I. Be sure you are still in the *flr-pln2b-new.dwg* file located in the C:\Steps3D\Lesson02 folder. If not, open it now.

II. Follow these steps:

TOOLS	COMMAND SEQUENCE	STEPS
	Command: ***plot***	**1.** Enter the ***Plot*** command by typing ***plot*** at the command line. Or you can pick the **Plot** button on the Standard toolbar. AutoCAD presents the Plot dialog box.
	Layout name My First House ☑ Save changes to layout	**2.** At the top of the dialog box, you will find a frame called ***Layout name***. If the name shown is not the name of your layout (as it appears on the tab), **Cancel** the plot and pick the layout tab you wish to plot. Then you can restart. Place a check in the **Save changes to layout** box so that you will not have to repeat the plot setup later.

continued

TOOLS	COMMAND SEQUENCE	STEPS
 Plot Device		**3.** We will begin by selecting the plotting device we wish to use. Pick on the **Plot Device** tab.
		4. In the **Plotter configuration** frame, use the **Name** control box to select the plotter or printer you wish to use.
		5. Be sure you plot one copy of the **Current tab**. [These should be defaults in the **What to plot** frame (lower left corner of the dialog box).]
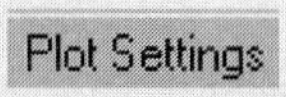 Plot Settings		**6.** Return to the **Plot Settings** tab.
		7. The **Paper size and paper units** frame now shows the printer or plotter you selected as the **Plot device**. Select the ***Letter*** **Paper size** from the control box and be sure you are using **inches**.
		8. Be sure you are plotting **Landscape . . .**
		9. . . . your **Plot area** is set to **Layout . . .**
		10. . . . and your **Plot scale** is set to ***1:1***. [Yes, you can plot to **Fit** a layout. If you have set up your page to a larger sheet (say, a D-size), you can still plot working drawings on smaller pages (A- or B-size).]

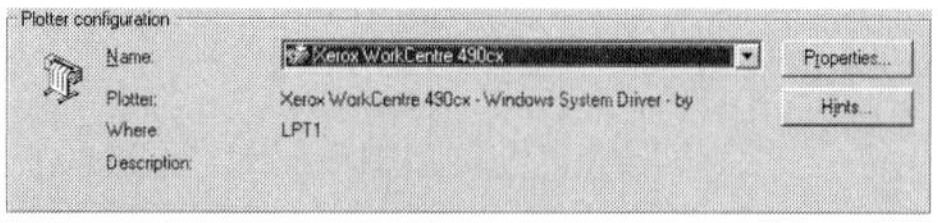

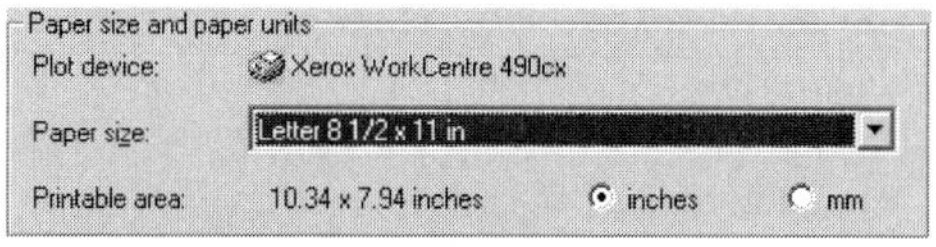

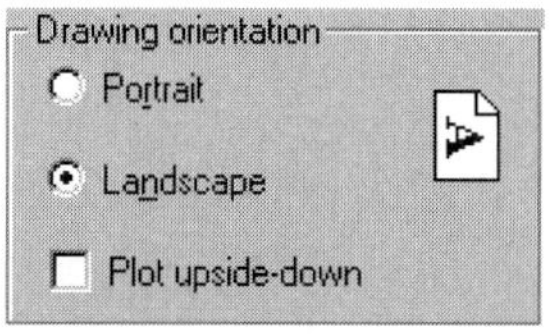

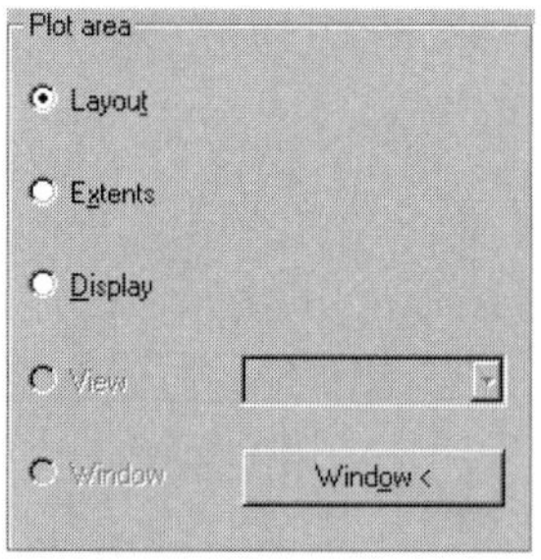

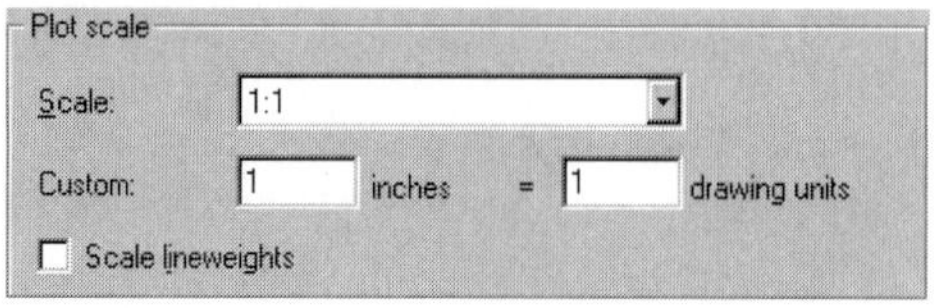

continued

TOOLS	COMMAND SEQUENCE	STEPS
	Plot offset Center the plot X: -0.12 inches Y: -0.25 inches	**11.** Use the **Preview** buttons to help set the **Plot offset** to properly center your drawing on the page. (Your numbers may vary from mine.)
OK		**12.** When you are satisfied with the offset, pick the **OK** button to print the drawing.
	Command: *qsave*	**13.** Save the drawing.

Use a draftsman's scale to check the dimensions on your plot. How did you do?

As with any print job, it is inevitable that something must be modified after the plot. Despite the ability to preview a drawing before plotting, some things simply do not show up until you see it on paper.

You can make changes in Model Space through the viewports or on the **Model** tab. You can make changes in Paper Space on the **Layout** tab. However, changes to the viewports themselves may require some additional tools. We will look at these next.

2.5 Tweaking the Layout

Generally speaking, modifying the layout is as easy as modifying any other part of a drawing. The basic modifying tools—***Move***, ***Copy***, ***Stretch***, and so forth—will work in Paper Space as well as Model Space. However, adjusting the view through a viewport or adjusting the shape or scale of a viewport will require some new modifying procedures. These include two commands: ***MVSetup*** and ***VPClip***.

Let's look at these now.

2.5.1 Modifying Viewports with the *MVSetup* Command

AutoCAD originally designed the ***MVSetup*** command to perform the same function as the **Layout Wizard**. Using the single ***MVSetup*** command, we can insert the title block, and create/scale the viewports just as we did with the wizard. But the wizard is so much easier to use than ***MVSetup***'s command line approach that ***MVSetup*** might have been removed. But AutoCAD chose to leave it (it is so hard to lose a good tool) because of its use as a *modifying* tool.

We will look at all parts of the *MVSetup* command, but we will use the command as a modifying tool.

The command sequence looks like this:

Command: *mvsetup*

Initializing . . .

Enable paper space? [No/Yes] <Y>:

When entered while on the **Model** tab, the *MVSetup* command initially asks if you wish to enable Paper Space. What follows depends on your answer.

- If you respond *No*, you will set up the drawing for Model Space. AutoCAD prompts as follows:

  Enter units type [Scientific/Decimal/Engineering/Architectural/Metric]:

  Tell AutoCAD which type of units you wish to use. AutoCAD will respond with a list of scale factors available. Select one. Then AutoCAD will ask for the width and height of the sheet of paper to which you will plot. When it has all the information, it will place a polyline border around the limits of the drawing.

  This approach is a bit quicker for someone who is comfortable with AutoCAD and the keyboard, but an AutoCAD novice might wish to use the **Setup Wizard** in lieu of the command line.

- If you respond *Yes* to the **Enable Paper Space** prompt (or if you enter the command while on a layout tab), AutoCAD flips to the first tab, creates a single viewport (if none currently exists), and then prompts as follows:

  Regenerating layout.
  Regenerating model. (These lines appear only when executing the *MvSetup* command from the **Model** tab.)

  Enter an option [Align/Create/Scale viewports/Options/Title block/Undo]:

  The first two lines simply let you know what AutoCAD is doing.

  The last line presents several options. These include:

  - The **Align** option allows the user to align a view in one viewport with the view in another.
  - **Create** allows the user to create (or delete) Floating Viewports. It will prompt:

    Enter option [Delete objects/Create viewports/Undo] <Create>:

    - The **Delete** option, of course, allows the user to remove a viewport.
    - The default option—**Create**—offers these choices:
      - Available layout options . . .

        0: None *[for no viewports]*

        1: Single *[for a single viewport]*

2: **Std. Engineering** *[This option creates four viewports with standard three-dimensional views (plan, front, side, isometric).]*

3: **Array of Viewports** *[This option allows the user to create a rectangular array of viewports—the user defining the number of rows and columns to use and the spacing between them.]*

- **Enter layout number to load or [Redisplay]:** *[Make your selection or hit enter to return to MVSetup's first option line.]*

- **Scaling** the **viewports** can be done one at a time or uniformly. Setting the scale one viewport at a time is more easily accomplished using the **Viewports Scale Control** box on the Viewports toolbar or the ***Zoom*** command. If you select more than one viewport to scale, AutoCAD will prompt as follows:

  Set zoom scale factors for viewports. Interactively/<Uniform>:

  Set the ratio of paper space units to model space units . . .

  Enter the number of paper space units <1.0>: *[usually hit enter]*

  Enter the number of model space units <1.0>: *[enter a scale factor]*

- The **Options** prompt allows the user to set the following:

  Enter an option [Layer/LImits/Units/Xref] <exit>:

  Most of these are obvious. You can set the current layer and Paper Space units, or you can allow AutoCAD to set the limits according to the drawing you have created. We will look at Xrefs later in this text.

- The **Title Block** option allows the user to insert a title block in Paper Space.

Let's change the scale in one of our viewports. We will use the ***MVSetup*** command to change the actual scale. Then we will use more conventional commands to adjust the viewport.

2.5.1.1 Do This: Using MVSetup as a Modifying Tool

I. Be sure you are in the *flr-pln2b-new.dwg* file located in the C:\Steps3D\Lesson02 folder.

II. Follow these steps:

TOOLS	COMMAND SEQUENCE	STEPS
No Button Available	**Command:** *mvsetup*	1. Enter the *MVSetup* command.

continued

TOOLS	COMMAND SEQUENCE	STEPS
Enter Cancel Align Create Scale viewports Options Title block Undo Pan Zoom	**Enter an option [Align/Create/ Scale viewports/Options/ Title block/Undo]:** *s* **Select the viewports to scale . . .** **Select objects:** *[select the upper left viewport]* **Select objects:** *[enter]*	**2.** Choose the **Scale viewports** option and select the upper left viewport (the master bath). Hit ***enter*** to complete the selection.
	Set the ratio of paper space units to model space units . . . **Enter the number of paper space units <1.0>:** *[enter]*	**3.** Now you will set the ratio of Paper Space to Model Space. Accept ***1*** as the number of Paper Space units.
	Enter the number of model space units <1.0>: *64*	**4.** We will change the scale from $\frac{1}{4}$" = 1' − 0" to $\frac{3}{16}$" = 1 − 0". Enter the scale factor for the $\frac{3}{16}$" scale (***64***). Notice how everything in Model Space is rescaled.
	Enter an option [Align/Create/Scale viewports/Options/Title block/Undo]: *[enter]*	**5.** Complete the command. Notice that the dimensions automatically update—even though they are in Paper Space!
MODEL	**Command:** *ps*	**6.** Return to Paper Space. (Use ***DimTedit*** to adjust the locations of the dimensions as needed.)
		7. Using Grips or other modifying tools, resize and reposition the viewport. Then edit the text as shown in Figure 2.5.1.1.7.

continued

TOOLS	COMMAND SEQUENCE	STEPS

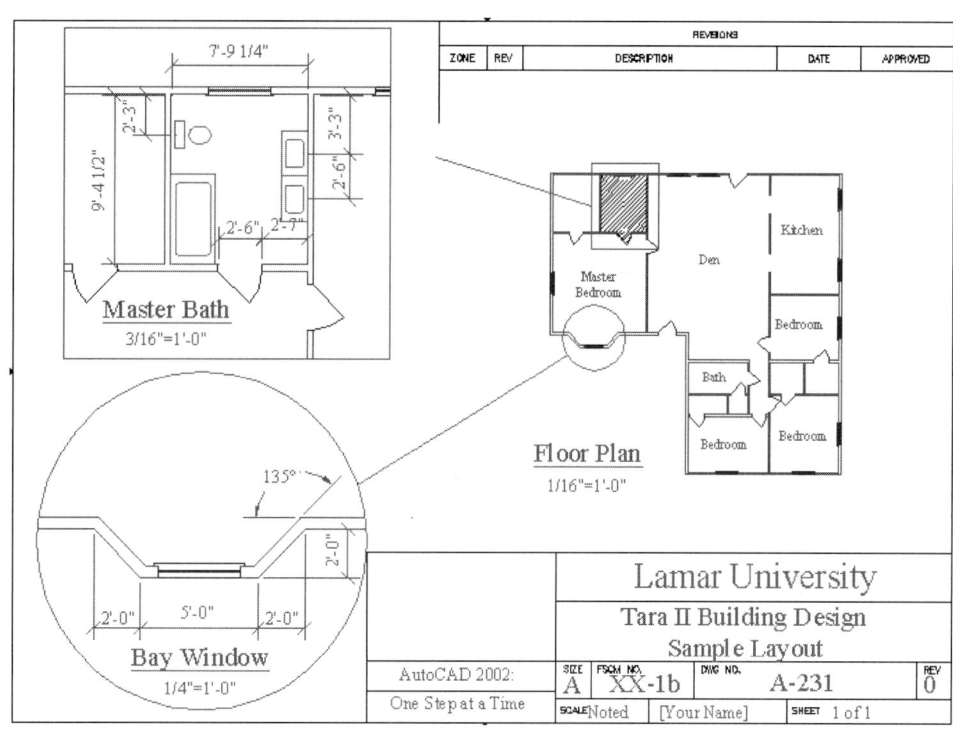

FIG. 2.5.1.1.7 Completed Drawing

Command: ***qsave***

8. Save the drawing, but do not exit.

When working with several viewports, you may notice that the ***Redraw*** and ***Regen*** commands only affect the one that is currently active. To use these commands to refresh all of the viewports simultaneously, use the ***Redrawall*** and ***Regenall*** commands.

Now that our viewports have been created and Paper Space is set up, let's see what comes next.

2.5.2 Changing the Shape of a Viewport with the *VPClip* Command

Occasionally you will discover that the shape you chose for your viewport does not satisfy the needs of that particular view. If you created the viewport using the **Object** option of the ***MView*** command to convert a polygon, closed polyline, or spline to a viewport, you can use the ***Pedit*** or ***Splinedit*** commands to reshape the viewport. If you used any other method to create the viewport, modifying the shape will not be so easy.

Fortunately, AutoCAD has provided the ***VPClip*** command. You can use this to reshape the view in a standard rectangular viewport. The command sequence looks like this:

Command: *VPClip*

Select viewport to clip: *[pick the viewport you wish to reshape (clip)]*

Select clipping object or [Polygonal] <Polygonal>: *[enter]*

Specify start point:

Specify next point or [Arc/Close/Length/Undo]: *[this line operates like the PLine command and repeats until the polyline is closed]*

Command:

Let's look at each of the prompts.

- The first line is simple enough. It asks which viewport you wish to clip. Select one.
- The next line appears as shown if the viewport has not been previously clipped. If it has been clipped, the line appears with an additional option, like this:

  Select clipping object or [Polygonal/Delete] <Polygonal>:

  - The default option—**Polygonal**—allows the user to place the clipping border manually. If the user responds with a ***P*** (or hits ***enter*** to accept the default), it prompts:

    Specify start point:

    Specify next point or [Arc/Close/Length/Undo]:

    Respond to these prompts as if you were drawing a polyline.
  - The **Delete** option allows the user to remove a clipping border. It will return the view to its original shape.
  - Enter **S** to use the **Select clipping object** option if you have created a new boundary around the view using a polyline, spline, and so forth. It prompts:

    Select object to clip viewport:

    Simply select the object you wish to use as the new viewport.

You can also access the ***VPCLip*** command by selecting the viewport to clip, opening the cursor menu, and selecting **Viewport Clip.**

Let's clip the round viewport in our drawing.

2.5.2.1 Do This: Reshaping a Viewport

I. Be sure you are still in the *flr-pln2b-new.dwg* file located in the C:\Steps3D\Lesson02 folder. If not, open it now.

II. Thaw the **VPorts** layer and set it current.

III. Follow these steps:

TOOLS	COMMAND SEQUENCE	STEPS
	Command: *ps*	**1.** Be sure you are in Paper Space.
	Command: *pl*	**2.** Draw a closed polyline around the bay window similar to the one shown in Figure 2.5.2.1.2.

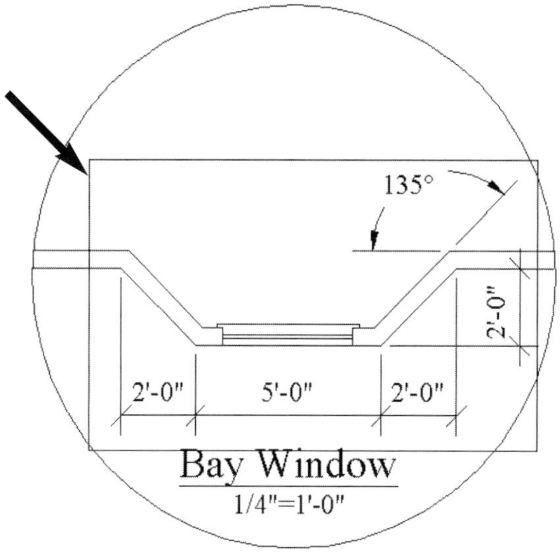

FIG. 2.5.2.1.2 Draw a Closed Polyline

continued

TOOLS	COMMAND SEQUENCE	STEPS
	**Command:** ***vpclip***	**3.** Enter the ***VPClip*** command or pick the **Clip Existing Viewport** button on the Viewports toolbar.
	Select viewport to clip:	**4.** Select the viewport (the circle).
	Select clipping object or [Polygonal/Delete] <Polygonal>:	**5.** Select the polyline. AutoCAD replaces the circle with a new viewport based on the shape of the polyline.
DefPoints DIM DOORS FIXTURES hatch TEXT Title Block VPORTS WALLS WINDOWS	**Command:** ***la***	**6.** Set **Text** as the current layer and freeze the **VPorts** layer.
	**Command:** ***c***	**7.** Redraw a circle around the viewport. Your drawing looks like Figure 2.5.2.1.7.

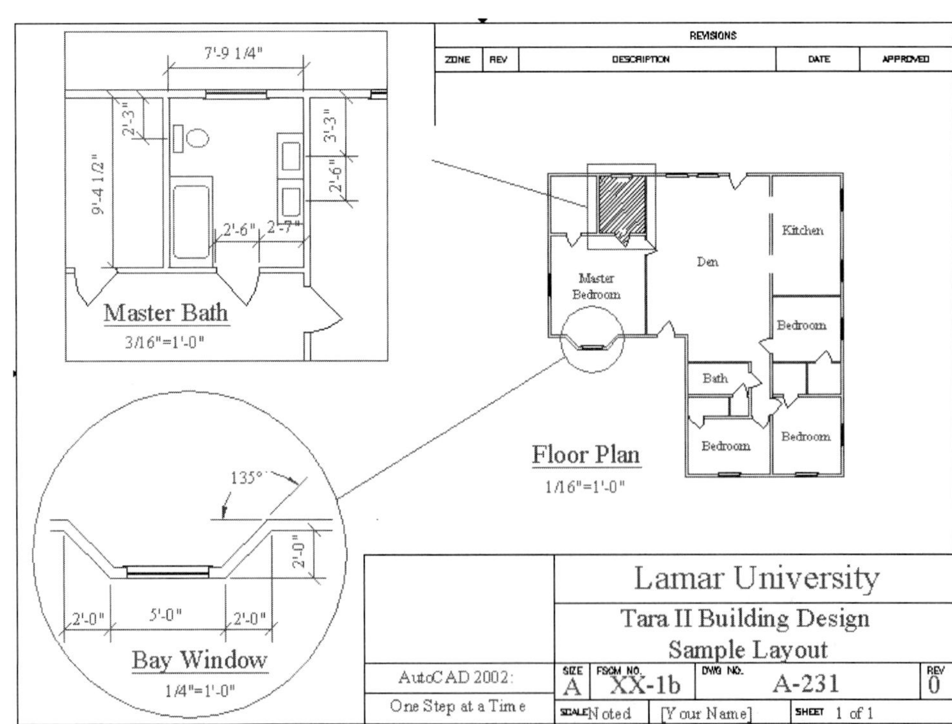

FIG. 2.5.2.1.7 Completed Drawing

continued

TOOLS	COMMAND SEQUENCE	STEPS
	Command: *qsave*	**8.** Save and close the drawing.

2.6 Putting It All Together—A Project

We have learned quite a bit about Paper Space and viewports. Let's try a project from the beginning (well, almost the beginning—I will provide the drawing).

2.6.1 Do This: From Setup to Plot—A Project

I. Open the *table saw.dwg* file in the C:\Steps3D\Lesson02 folder. The drawing looks like Figure 2.6.1a.

FIG. 2.6.1a Table Saw.dwg

II. Set **VPorts** as the current layer.

III. Follow these steps:

TOOLS	COMMAND SEQUENCE	STEPS
No Button Available	**Command:** ***layoutwizard***	**1.** Let's start the easy way. Enter the ***LayoutWizard*** command.
	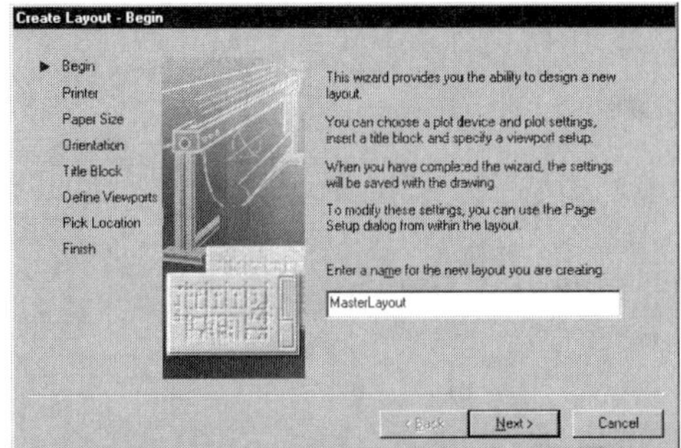	**2.** Call the layout *MasterLayout*. Pick the **Next** button to continue.
	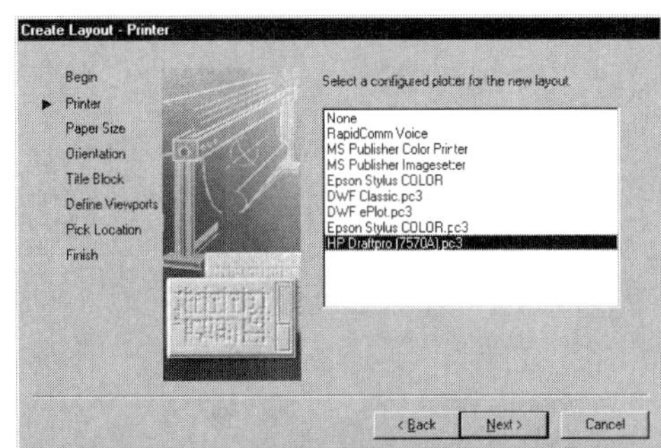	**3.** Select a plotter if one is available. Otherwise, select **None**. Pick the **Next** button to continue.
	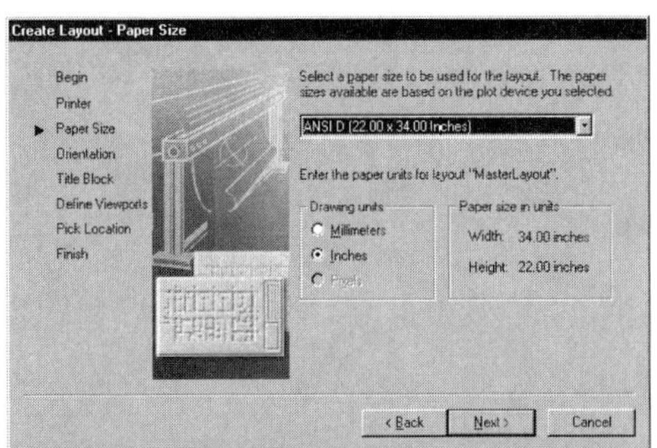	**4.** Select an **ANSI D** size sheet. Pick the **Next** button to continue.
	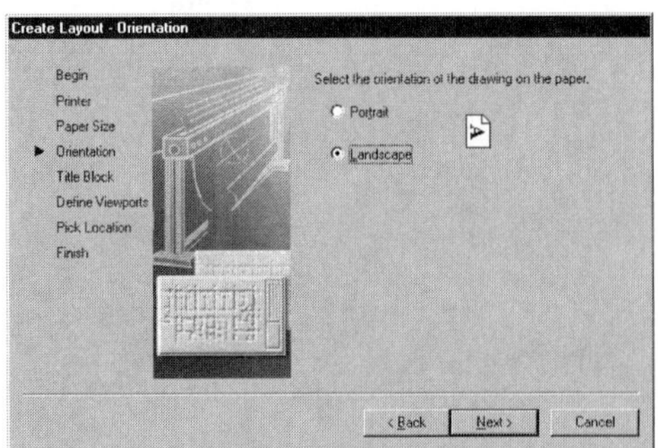	**5.** Tell AutoCAD to plot a **Landscape** drawing. Pick the **Next** button to continue.

continued

TOOLS	COMMAND SEQUENCE	STEPS

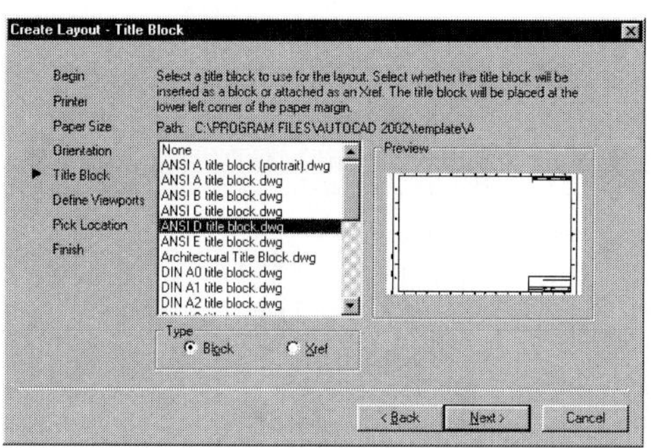

6. Select an appropriate title block for the size sheet of paper you selected in Step 4.

Pick the **Next** button to continue.

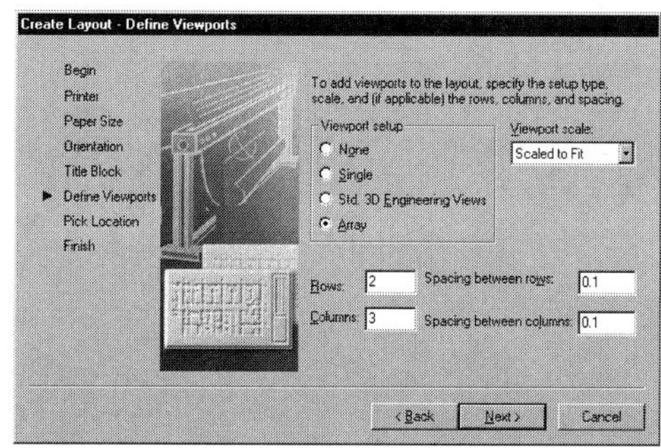

7. Define the viewports by **Array**. Use **2** rows and **3** columns and accept the default spacing.

Pick the **Next** button to continue.

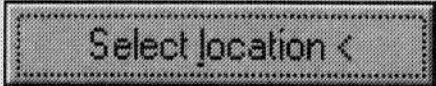

8. Pick the **Select location <** button.

Specify first corner: ***1.5,19***

Specify opposite corner: ***31,3***

9. Specify the area for the viewports (the indicated area is for the D-size title block we specified earlier).

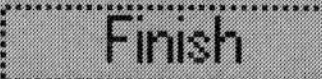

10. Pick the **Finish** button to complete the command.

continued

TOOLS	COMMAND SEQUENCE	STEPS
	**Command:** ***qsave***	**11.** Remember to save occasionally. Your drawing looks like Figure 2.6.1.11.

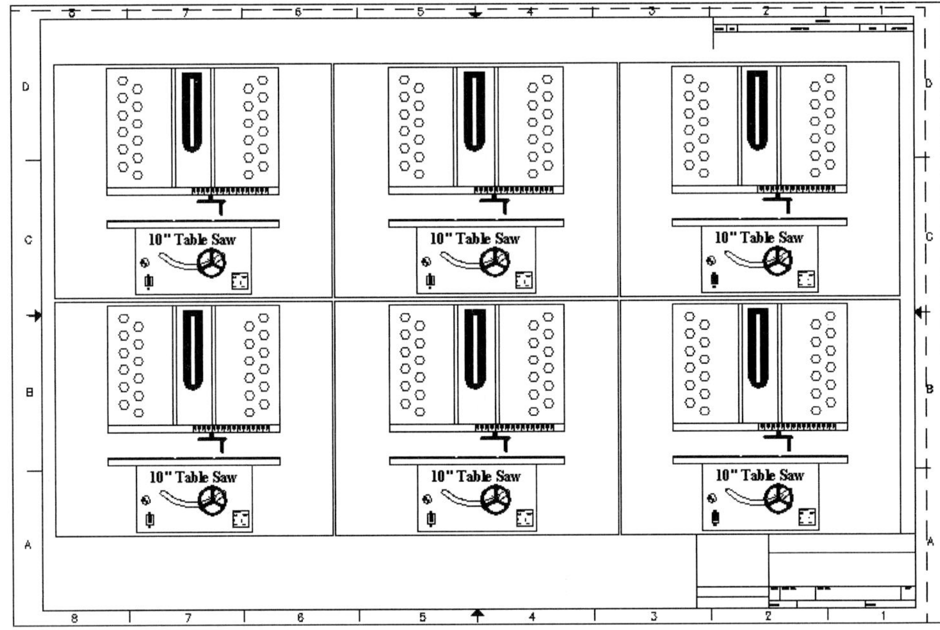

FIG. 2.6.1.11 Paper Space Setup

TOOLS	COMMAND SEQUENCE	STEPS
No Button Available	**Command:** ***ucsicon***	**12.** For aesthetics, let's turn the UCS icon off in all of the viewports. Enter the ***UCSIcon*** command.
	Enter an option [ON/OFF/All/ Noorigin/ORigin] <ON>: ***a***	**13.** Use the **All** option . . .
	Enter an option [ON/OFF/ Noorigin/ORigin] <ON>: ***off***	**14.** . . . and turn the icon **Off**.
		15. Set the scale in each viewport as follows (use either the Viewport Scale control box on the Viewports toolbar or the ***MVSetup*** command): First row: 1:1, 1:2, 2:1 Second row: 1:1, 1:2, NTS

continued

TOOLS	COMMAND SEQUENCE	STEPS

In Model Space, pan each viewport to look like Figure 2.6.1.15.

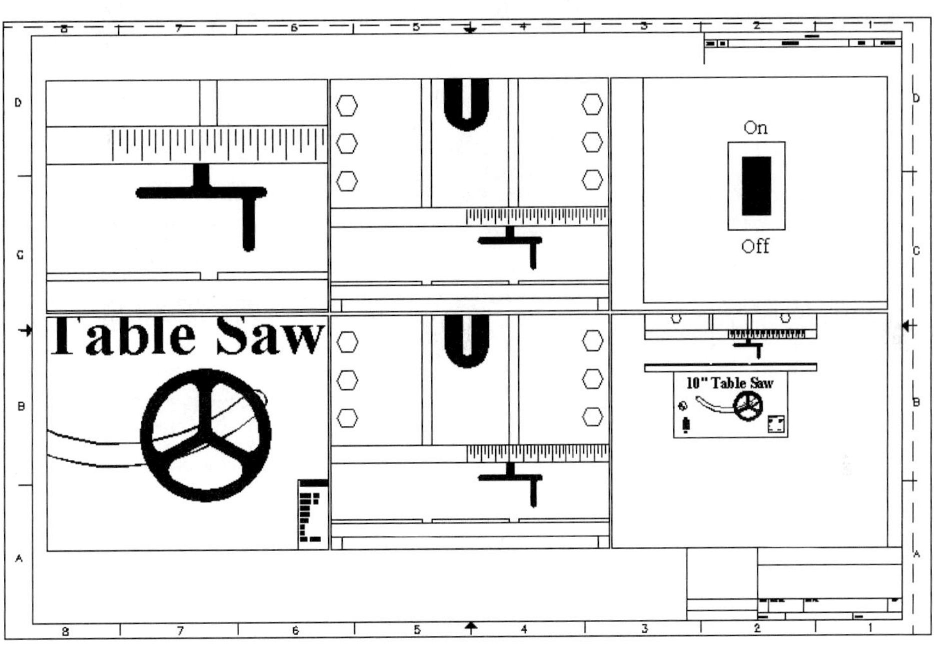

FIG. 2.6.1.15 *Scaled Viewports*

16. Resize and relocate each viewport using grips and/or the ***Stretch*** and ***Move*** commands. (*Readjust the views in each port as shown in Figure 2.6.1.16.*) The lower left and upper right coordinates for each viewport follow. (*Hint:* Grips and absolute coordinates make this job much easier.)

VIEWPORT (ROW/COLUMN)	HANDWHEEL PLAN (1/1)	SAW PLAN (1/2)	SWITCH (1/3)	HANDWHEEL ELEV. (2/1)	SAW ELEV. (2/2)	SPEC. PLATE (2/3)
Lower left coordinate	1.5,15.1	7.25,8.25	2,1.75	1.5,10	7.25,1	22.75,4
Upper right coordinate	7.75,19	23.5,20	5.75,7.75	7.75,15	23.5,11	31,11.75

continued

TOOLS	COMMAND SEQUENCE	STEPS

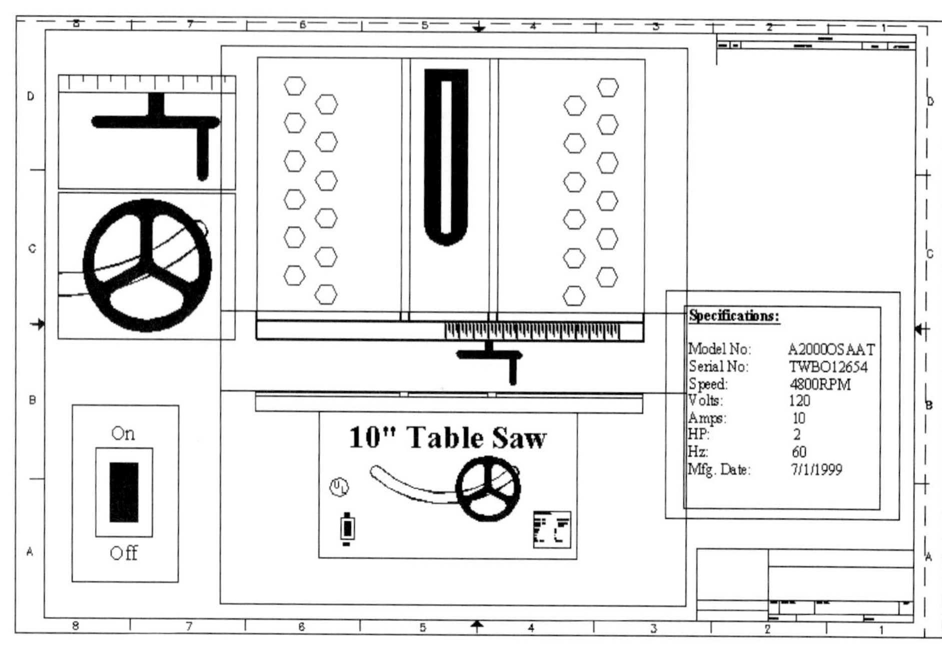

FIG. 2.6.1.16 Resized and Relocated Viewports

17. Use the ***VPLayer*** command to freeze unwanted layers as follows. (*Hint:* It might be faster to freeze all layers with the * and then thaw the few you wish to be visible.)

VIEWPORT	HANDWHEEL—PLAN & ELEVATION	SWITCH	SAW—PLAN & ELEVATION	SPECS
Freeze All Layers Except:	Obj3 Obj3a	Obj2 Obj2a Obj3 Text	(Do not freeze any layers)	Text

continued

TOOLS	COMMAND SEQUENCE	STEPS
	Command: ***qsave***	**18.** Remember to save occasionally. Your drawing looks like Figure 2.6.1.18.

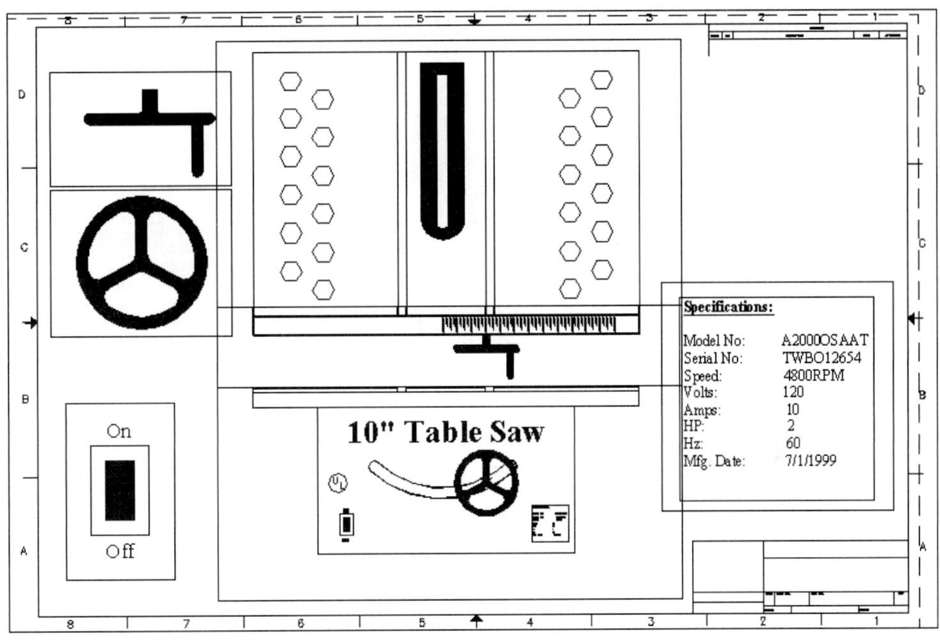

FIG. 2.6.1.18 Frozen Layers

TOOLS	COMMAND SEQUENCE	STEPS
No Button Available	**Command:** ***mvsetup***	**19.** Now use the ***MVSetup*** command to align the views in the handwheel plan and elevation. Begin by entering the command.
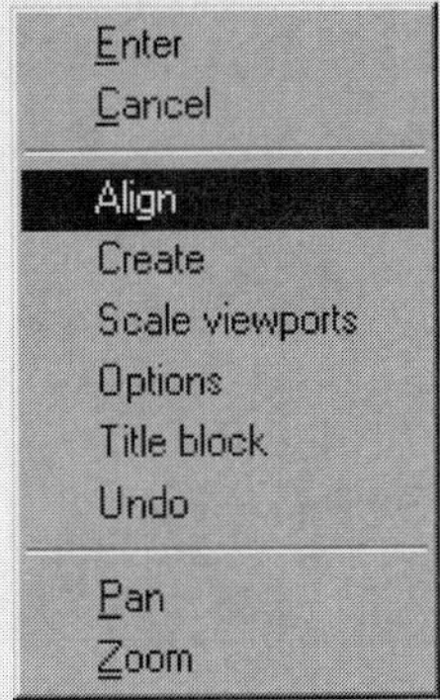	**Enter an option [Align/Create/Scale viewports/Options/Title block/ Undo]:** ***a***	**20.** Select the **Align** option.

continued

TOOLS	COMMAND SEQUENCE	STEPS
Enter Cancel Angled Horizontal Vertical alignment Rotate view Undo Pan Zoom	**Enter an option [Angled/Horizontal/ Vertical alignment/Rotate view/ Undo]:** *v*	**21.** We will align the objects vertically.
	Specify basepoint: _qua of	**22.** Select the leftmost quadrant of the handwheel in the plan view . . .
	Specify point in viewport to be panned: _qua of	**23.** . . . and the corresponding quadrant in the elevation view.
	Enter an option [Angled/Horizontal/ Vertical alignment/Rotate view/ Undo]: *[enter]* **Enter an option [Align/Create/Scale viewports/Options/Title block/ Undo]:** *[enter]*	**24.** Hit *enter* twice to complete the command.
No Button Available	**Command:** *mvsetup*	**25.** Repeat Steps 19 through 24 to align the plan and elevation of the saw.
		26. Use the ***VPClip*** command to set the saw plan and elevation viewports so that all you see is the plan in the plan viewport and the elevation in the elevation viewport.

continued

TOOLS	COMMAND SEQUENCE	STEPS
	**Command:** ***pl***	Begin by drawing a polyline around the elevation in the bottom viewport as seen in Figure 2.6.1.26. (Be sure you are in Paper Space and that the **VPorts** layer is current.)

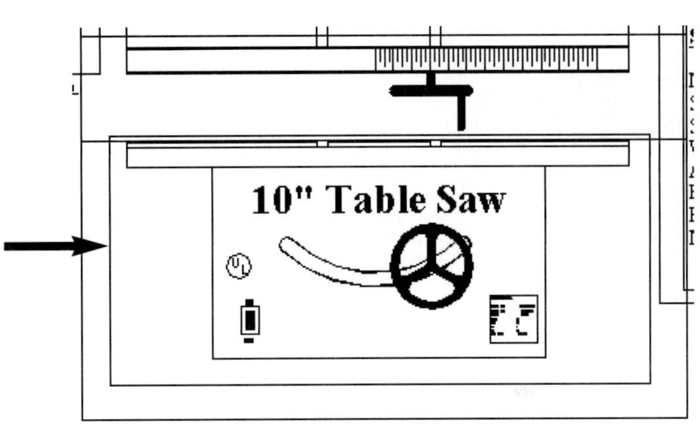

FIG. 2.6.1.26 Draw a Rectangle

TOOLS	COMMAND SEQUENCE	STEPS
	**Command:** ***vpclip***	**27.** Enter the ***VPClip*** command.
	Select viewport to clip:	**28.** Select the viewport with the saw elevation in it.
	Select clipping object or [Polygonal] <Polygonal>: ***s***	**29.** Tell AutoCAD you wish to **Select clipping object** . . .
	Select object to clip viewport:	**30.** . . . and then select the polyline you drew in Step 26.
	**Command:** ***la***	**31.** Move the title block to the **Title Block** layer. Set the **Text** layer current and freeze the **VPorts** layer.

continued

TOOLS	COMMAND SEQUENCE	STEPS
	**Command:** *qsave*	**32.** Remember to save occasionally. Your drawing looks like Figure 2.6.1.32.

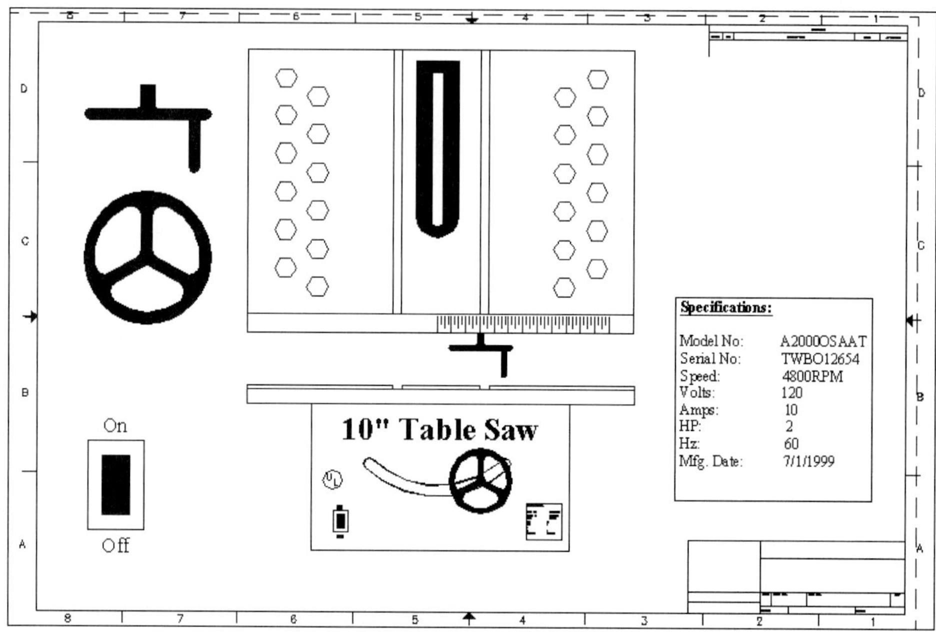

FIG. 2.6.1.32 Frozen VPorts Layer

33. Add the text and detail markings as shown in Figure 2.6.1.33. Text heights are $\frac{1}{4}$" and $\frac{3}{16}$". The text style is *Simple*. (Place the detail markings on the **details** layer.)

continued

TOOLS	COMMAND SEQUENCE	STEPS

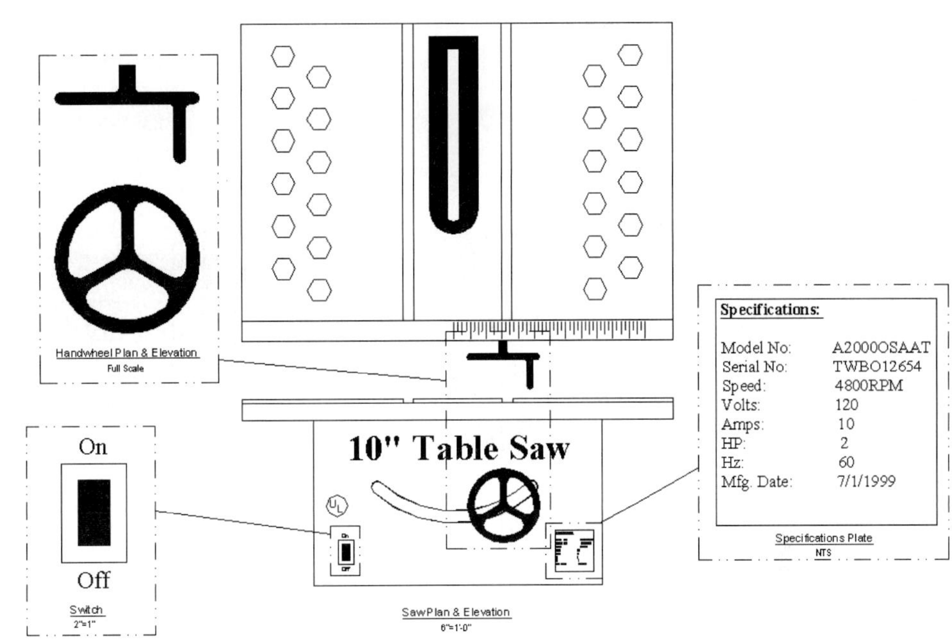

FIG. 2.6.1.33 Text Added to Table Saw Windows

Command: ***dt***

34. Fill in the title block as shown in Figure 2.6.1.34. Text size is $\frac{1}{4}$", $\frac{3}{16}$", and $\frac{1}{8}$". Styles are *Timesbold* and *Times*.

	Garage Tools University			
	Tim's Table Saw Sample Paper Space Plot			
AutoCAD 2002:	SIZE D	FSCM NO. XX-123	DWG NO. D-261	REV 0
One Step at a Time	SCALE Noted	[Your Name]	SHEET 1 of 1	

FIG. 2.6.1.34 Title Block Text

Command: ***qsave***

35. Remember to save occasionally.

Command: ***plot***

36. Now we must plot the drawing. Begin by entering the ***Plot*** command. You may also select the **Plot** button on the Standard toolbar.

continued

TOOLS	COMMAND SEQUENCE	STEPS
		37. Your Plot dialog box should resemble the one in Figure 2.6.1.37. Your plotter may vary and the **Plot offset** may vary. Use the **Full Preview** button to be sure you have set up the plot correctly and then plot the drawing.

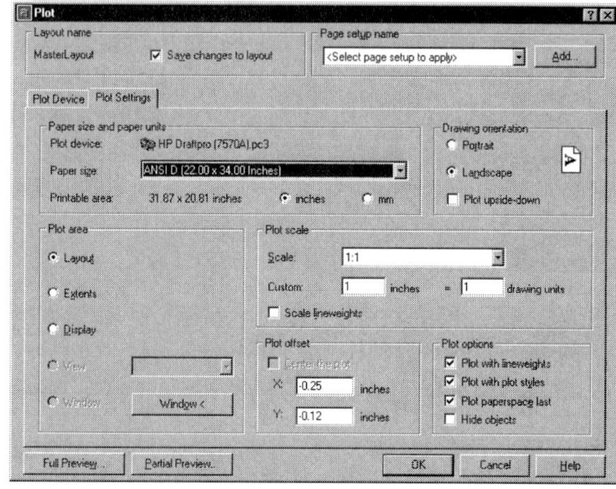

FIG. 2.6.1.37 Plot Dialog Box

TOOLS	COMMAND SEQUENCE	STEPS
[save icon]	**Command:** *qsave*	**38.** Save the drawing and exit.

How was that? Just 38 easy steps to completion!

I know what that sounds like, but most of these steps will become second nature in time. Where it probably took 45 minutes to complete the exercise, with experience it will take about 15 minutes to complete a similar project on the job. This text can help you acquire some of that experience. Try some of the projects at the end of this lesson!

2.7 Extra Steps

- Try setting up and plotting some of your own drawings in a Paper Space environment.
- Try plotting the drawing from Exercise 2.6.1 to **Fit** on an 11" x $8\frac{1}{2}$" sheet of paper.

2.8 What Have We Learned?

Items covered in this lesson include:

- *Using layers in Paper Space*
- *How to use text in Paper Space*
- *How to dimension in Paper Space*
- *How to plot a Paper Space drawing*
- *Commands*
  - ***MVSetup***
  - ***VPLayer***
  - ***VPClip***
  - ***Regenall***
  - ***Redrawall***

Remember the first paragraphs of Lesson 1? You may now step into that group of CAD operators who have used Paper Space and would never use anything else!

In Paper Space, you have taken your first steps into a whole new AutoCAD world! With experience, you will soon wonder why we do not teach Paper Space from the beginning. But think back to what you knew when you began your first AutoCAD class. So much of what you learned in the last two lessons requires that you already have a foundation in the basics. And now, with Paper Space (and Viewports) under your belt, you have a foundation for what comes next.

2.9 EXERCISES

1. Open the *MyNeedle.dwg* file in the C:\Steps3D\Lesson02 folder. (If that drawing is not there, use the *needle 2.dwg* file in the same folder.) Complete the drawing configuration found in Figure 2.9.1. Some helpful information includes:
   1.1. The text height is 5mm and 2.5mm; the font is Times New Roman.
   1.2. The title block text is attributed.
   1.3. I used two dimension layers (create new layers as required).
   1.4. Dimension text is 3mm.
   1.5. Save the drawing as *MyNeedle2.dwg* in the C:\Steps3D\Lesson02 folder.

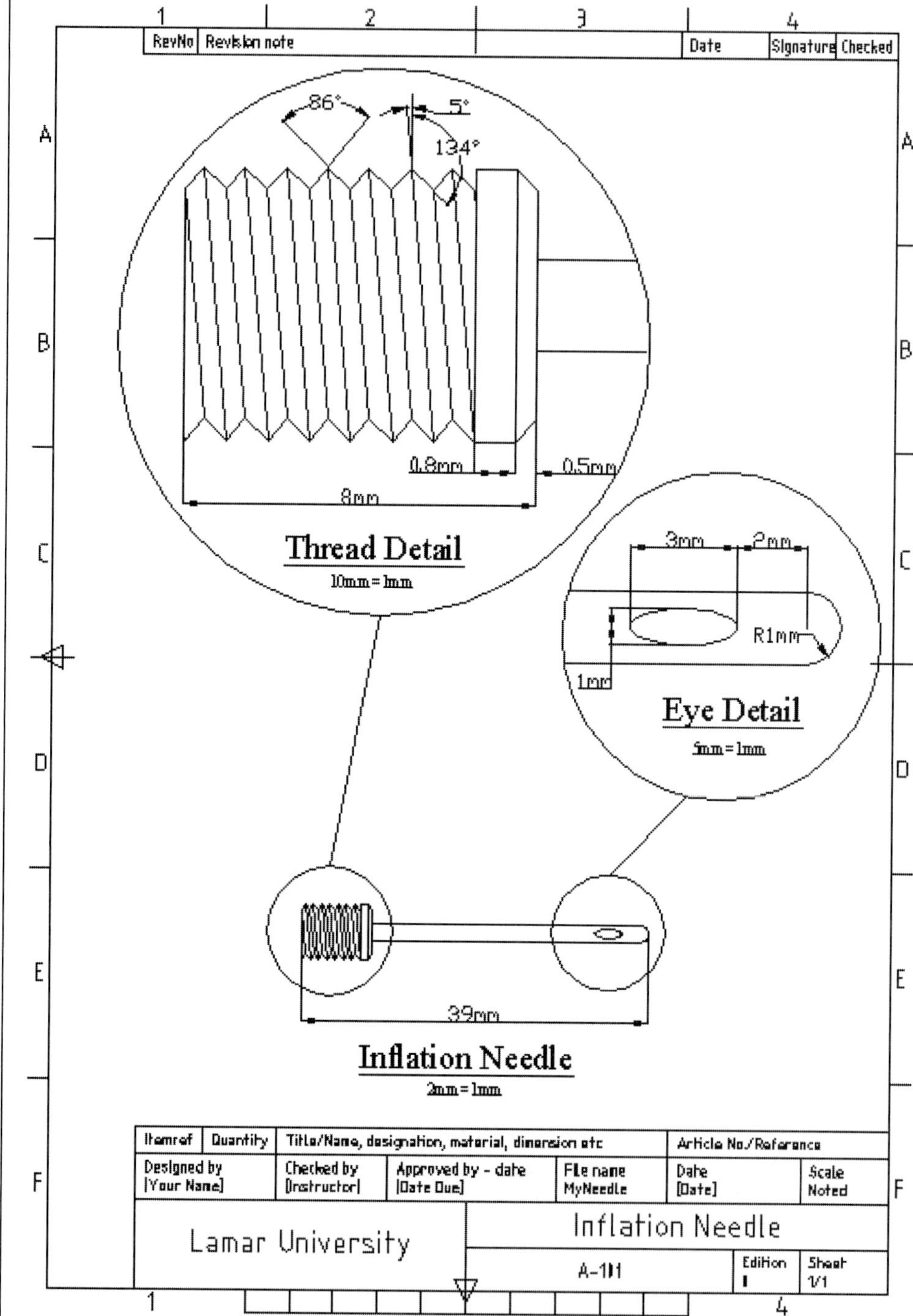

FIG. 2.9.1 *Needle.dwg*

2. Open the *MySplitter.dwg* file in the C:\Steps3D\Lesson02 folder. (If this drawing is not there, open the *Cable Splitter 2.dwg* file instead.) Complete the drawing configuration found in Figure 2.9.2. Some helpful information includes:
   2.1. The text height is $\frac{3}{16}$" and $\frac{1}{8}$"; the font is Times New Roman.
   2.2. The title block text is $\frac{1}{4}$", $\frac{3}{16}$", and $\frac{1}{8}$"; the font is Times New Roman.

2.3. I used two dimension layers (create new layers as required).

2.4. Dimension text is $\frac{1}{8}$".

2.5. Save the drawing as *MySplitter2.dwg* in the C:\Steps3D\Lesson02 folder.

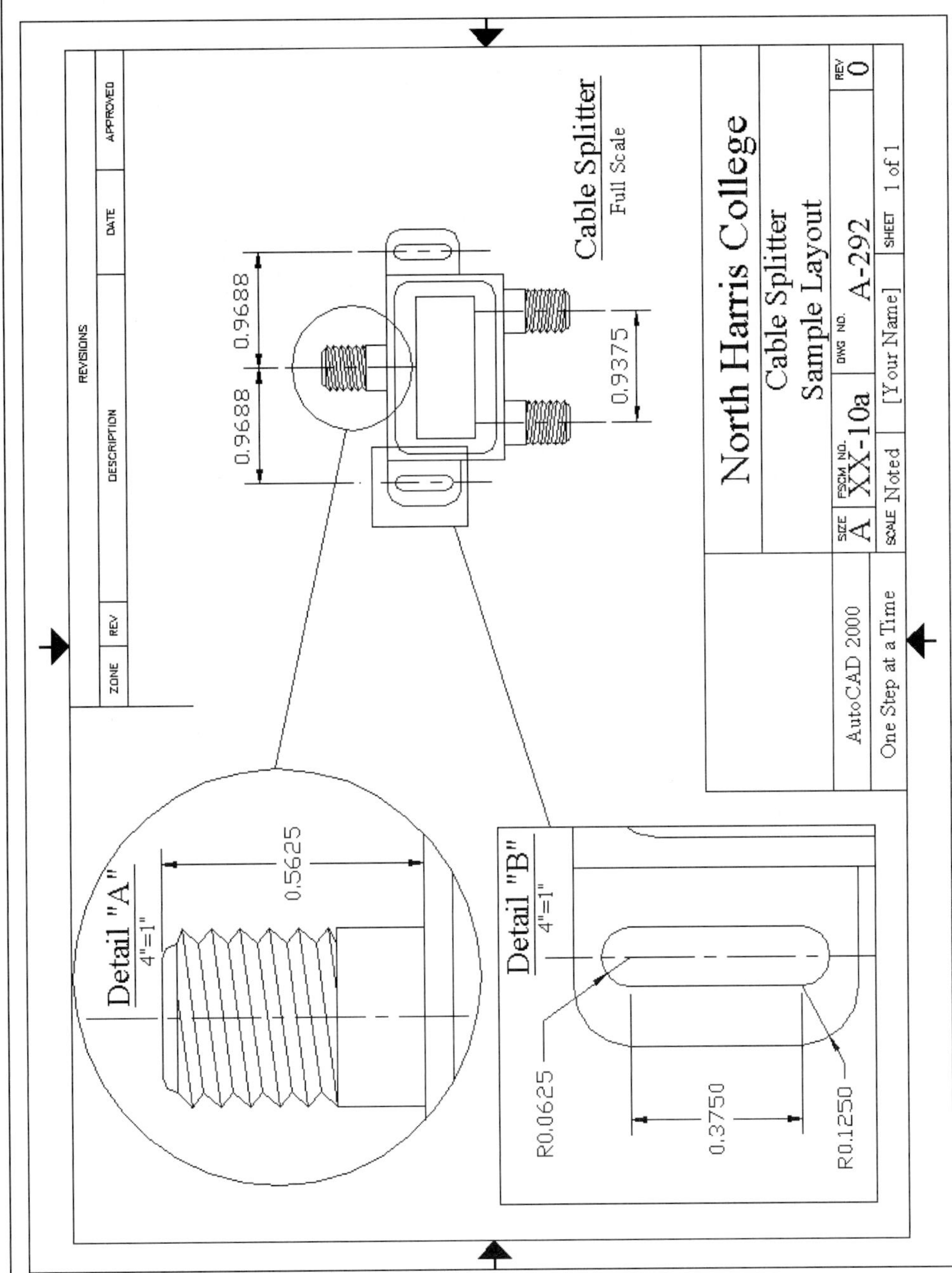

FIG. 2.9.2 Cable Splitter.dwg

3. Open the *MyCutter.dwg* file in the C:\Steps3D\Lesson02 folder. (If this drawing is not there, open the *Glass Cutter 2.dwg* file instead.) Complete the drawing configuration found in Figure 2.9.3. Some helpful information includes:
   3.1. The text height is $\frac{3}{16}$" and $\frac{1}{8}$"; the font is Times New Roman.
   3.2. The title block text is $\frac{1}{4}$", $\frac{3}{16}$", and $\frac{1}{8}$"; the font is Times New Roman.
   3.3. I used two dimension layers (create new layers as required).
   3.4. Dimension text is $\frac{1}{8}$".
   3.5. Save the drawing as *MyCutter2.dwg* in the C:\Steps3D\Lesson02 folder.

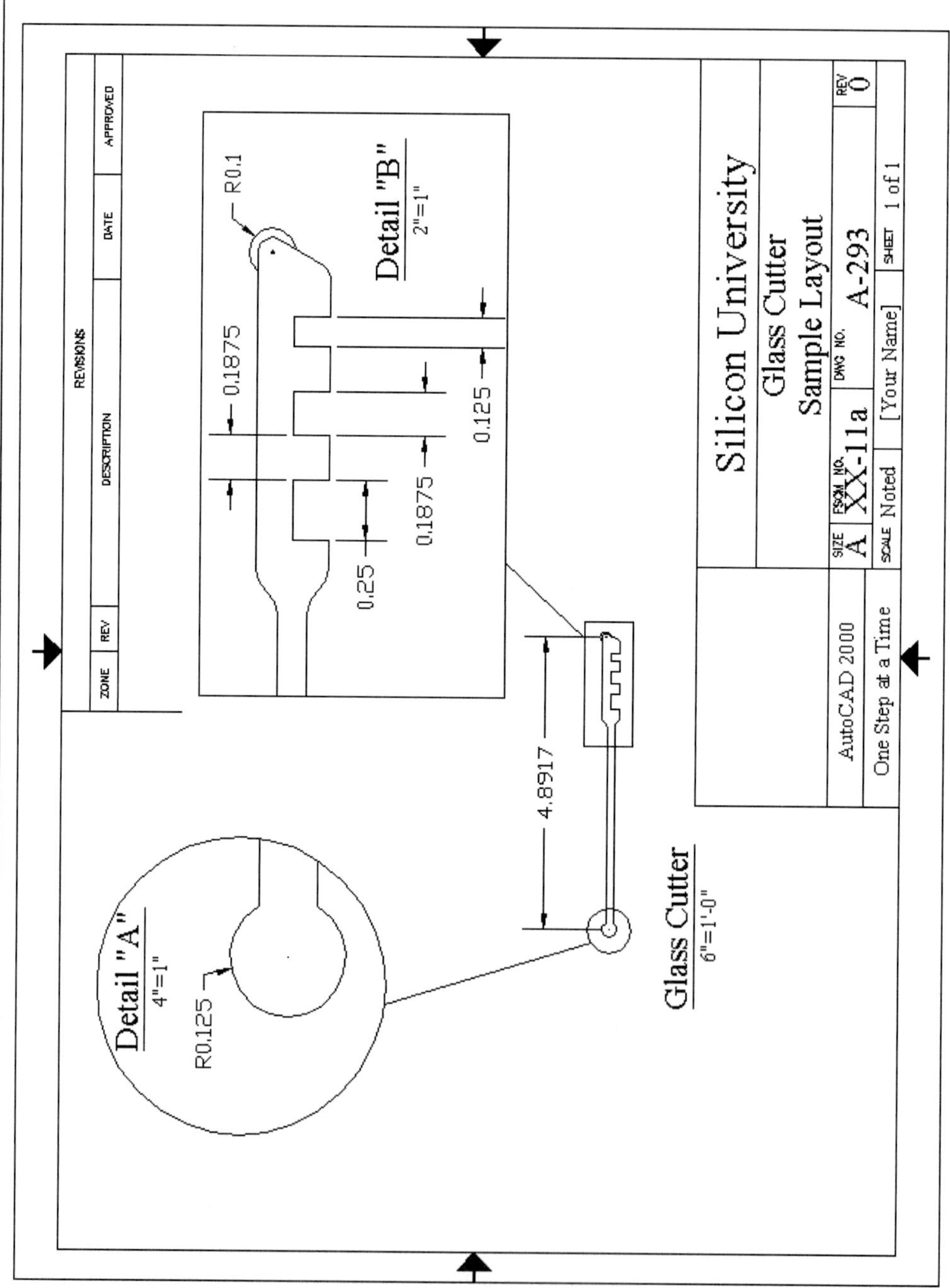

FIG. 2.9.3 Glass Cutter.dwg

4. Open the *My Spice Rack.dwg* file in the C:\Steps3D\Lesson02 folder. (If this drawing is not there, open the *Spice Rack 2.dwg* file instead.) Complete the drawing configuration found in Figure 2.9.4. Some helpful information includes:
   - **4.1.** The text height is $\frac{3}{16}$" and $\frac{1}{8}$"; the font is **Txt.**
   - **4.2.** The title block text is $\frac{1}{4}$", $\frac{3}{16}$", and $\frac{1}{8}$"; the font is Times New Roman.
   - **4.3.** I used three dimension layers (create new layers as required).
   - **4.4.** Dimension text is $\frac{1}{8}$".
   - **4.5.** Align the bottle and cap.
   - **4.6.** Save the drawing as *My Spice Rack 2.dwg* in the C:\Steps3D\Lesson02 folder.

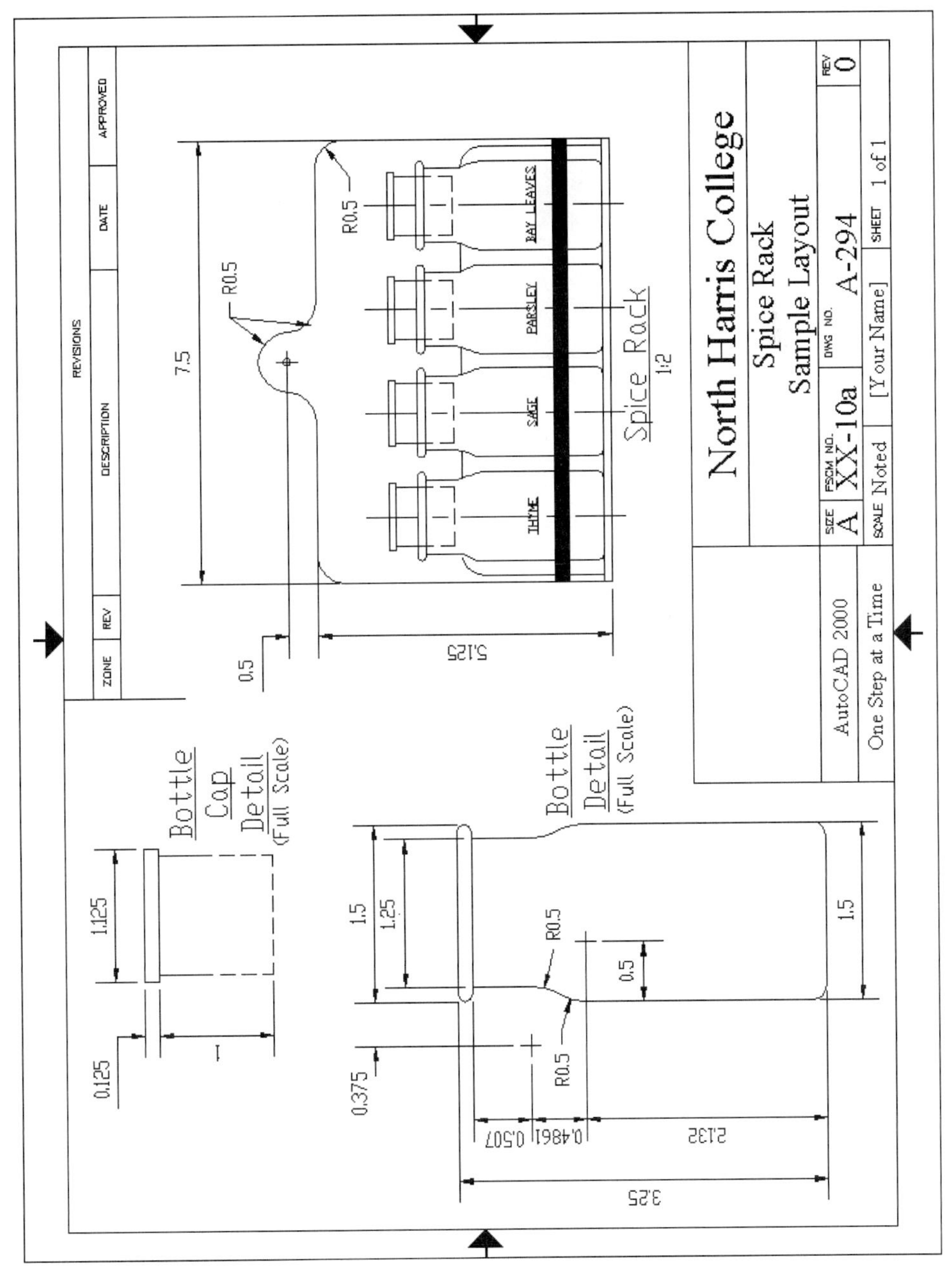

FIG. 2.9.4 Spice Rack

5. Open the *MyAssbly.dwg* file in the C:\Steps3D\Lesson02 folder. (If this drawing is not there, open the *motor assbly 2.dwg* file instead.) Complete the drawing configuration found in Figure 2.9.5. Some helpful information includes:
   - **5.1.** The text height is $\frac{3}{16}$" and $\frac{1}{8}$"; the font is Times New Roman.
   - **5.2.** The title block text is $\frac{1}{4}$", $\frac{3}{16}$", and $\frac{1}{8}$"; the font is Times New Roman.
   - **5.3.** I used three dimension layers (create new layers as required).
   - **5.4.** Dimension text is $\frac{1}{8}$".
   - **5.5.** Save the drawing as *MyAssbly2.dwg* in the C:\Steps3D\Lesson02 folder.

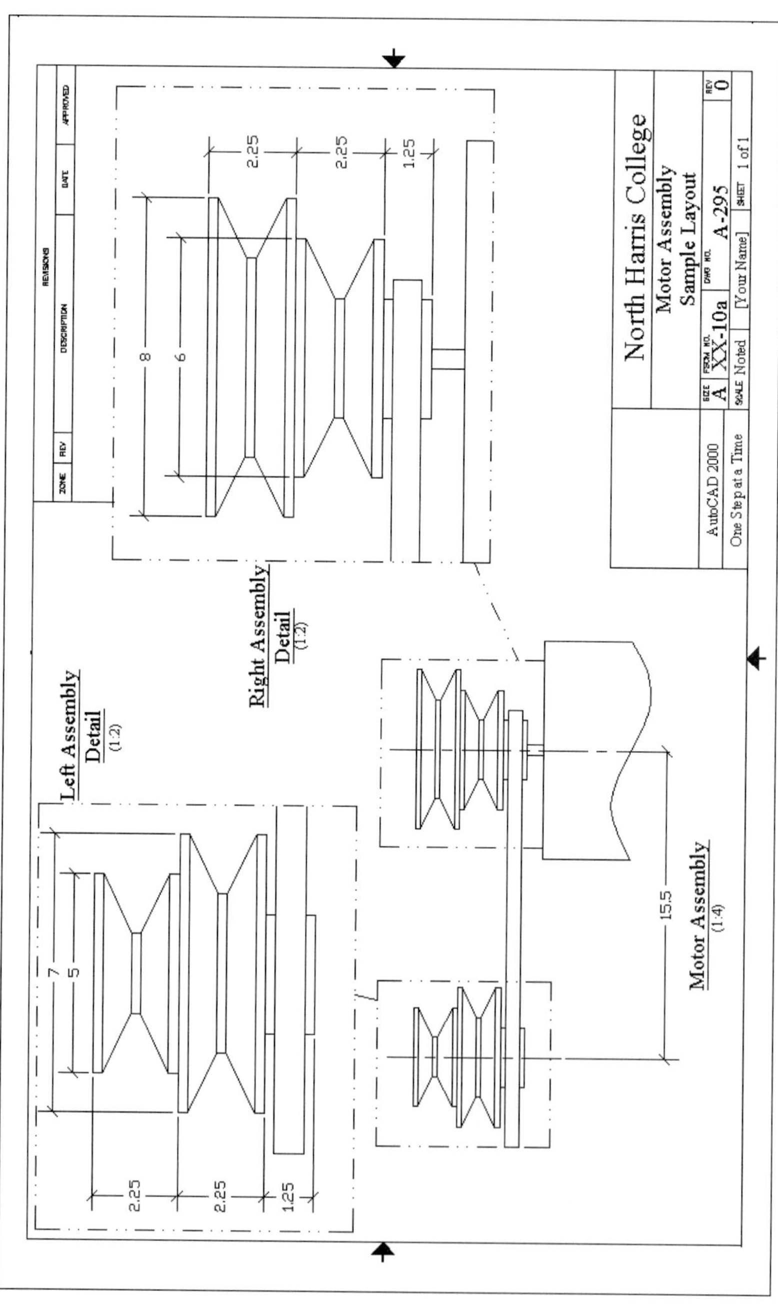

FIG. 2.9.5 Motor Assembly

6. Open the *My Piping Plan.dwg* file in the C:\Steps3D\Lesson02 folder. (If this drawing is not there, open the *Piping plan 2.dwg* file instead.) Complete the drawing configuration found in Figure 2.9.6. Some helpful information includes:
   - **6.1.** The text height is $\frac{3}{16}$" and $\frac{1}{8}$"; the font is Times New Roman.
   - **6.2.** The title block text is $\frac{1}{4}$", $\frac{3}{16}$", and $\frac{1}{8}$"; the font is Times New Roman.
   - **6.3.** I used two dimension layers (create new layers as required).
   - **6.4.** Dimension text is $\frac{1}{8}$".
   - **6.5.** Save the drawing as *My Piping Plan2.dwg* in the C:\Steps3D\Lesson02 folder.

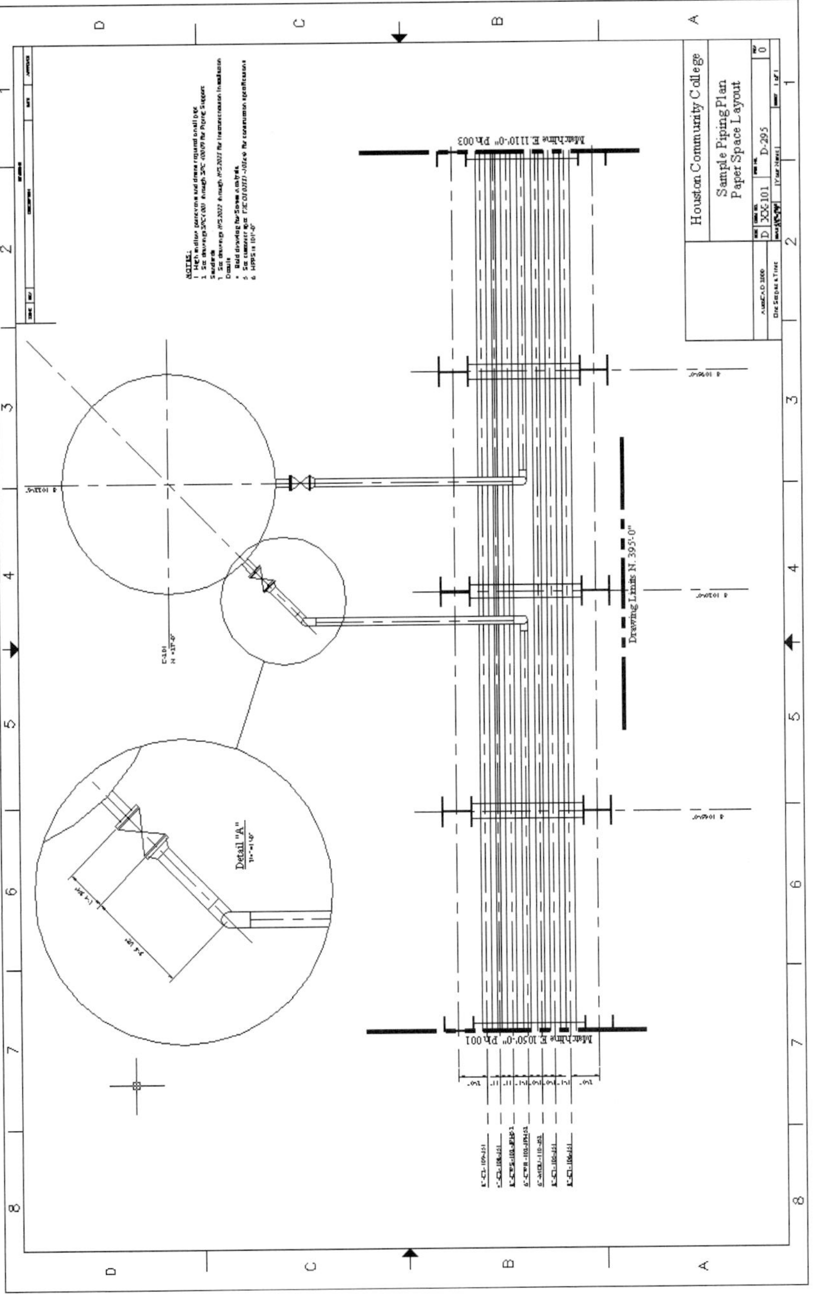

FIG. 2.9.6 Piping Plan

7. Open the *drillguide 2.dwg* file in the C:\Steps3D\Lesson02 folder. Create the drawing configuration found in Figure 2.9.7. Some helpful information includes:
   - **7.1.** The title block is the *ANSI B title block* file found in AutoCAD's Template folder.
   - **7.2.** The text height is $\frac{3}{16}$" and $\frac{1}{8}$"; the font is Times New Roman.
   - **7.3.** The title block text is $\frac{1}{4}$", $\frac{3}{16}$", and $\frac{1}{8}$"; the font is Times New Roman.
   - **7.4.** I used three dimension layers (create new layers as required).
   - **7.5.** Dimension text is $\frac{1}{8}$".
   - **7.6.** Save the drawing as *MyDrillGuide.dwg* in the C:\Steps3D\Lesson02 folder.

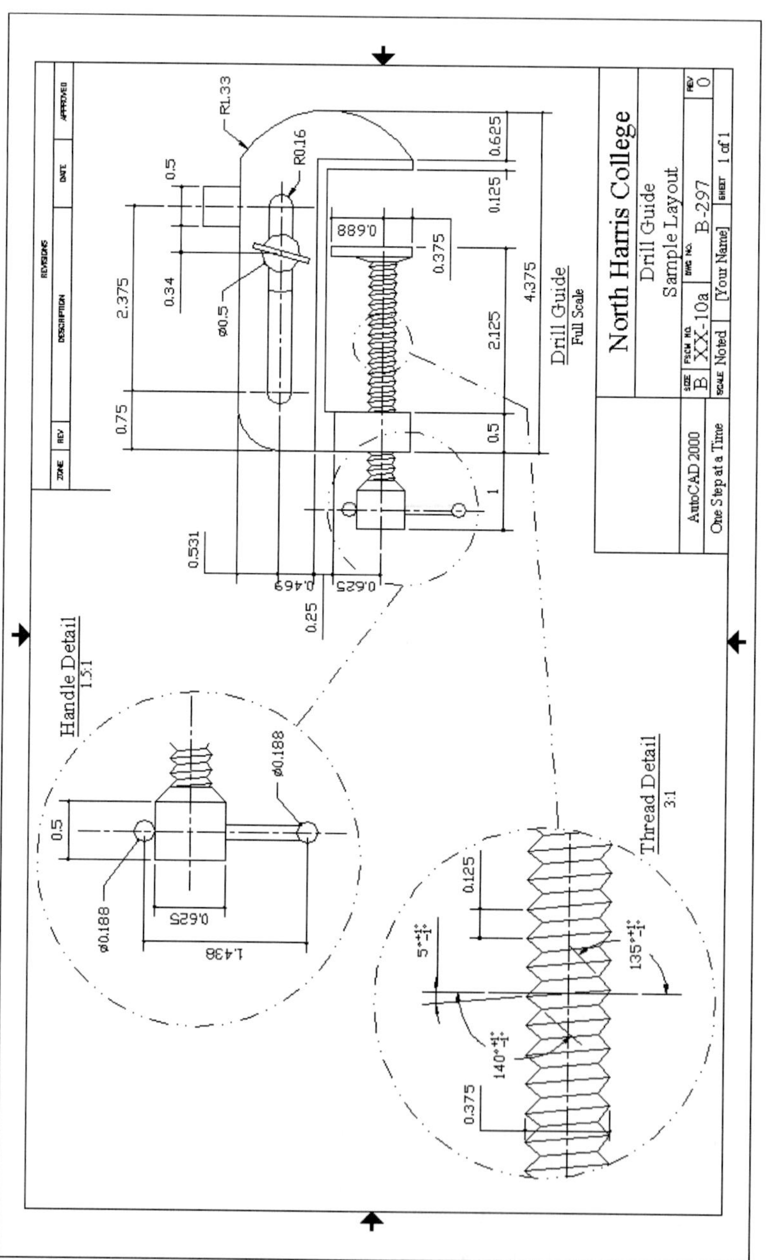

FIG. 2.9.7 Drill Guide

8. Open the *Sawed Joint.dwg* file in the C:\Steps3D\Lesson02 folder. Create the drawing configuration found in Figure 2.9.8. Some helpful information includes:
   - **8.1.** The title block is the *ANSI A title block (portrait)* file found in AutoCAD's Template folder.
   - **8.2.** The text height is $\frac{3}{16}$" and $\frac{1}{8}$"; the font is Times New Roman.
   - **8.3.** The title block text is $\frac{1}{4}$", $\frac{3}{16}$", and $\frac{1}{8}$"; the font is Times New Roman.
   - **8.4.** I used two dimension layers (create new layers as required).
   - **8.5.** Dimension text is $\frac{1}{8}$".
   - **8.6.** Save the drawing as *MyJoint.dwg* in the C:\Steps3D\Lesson02 folder.

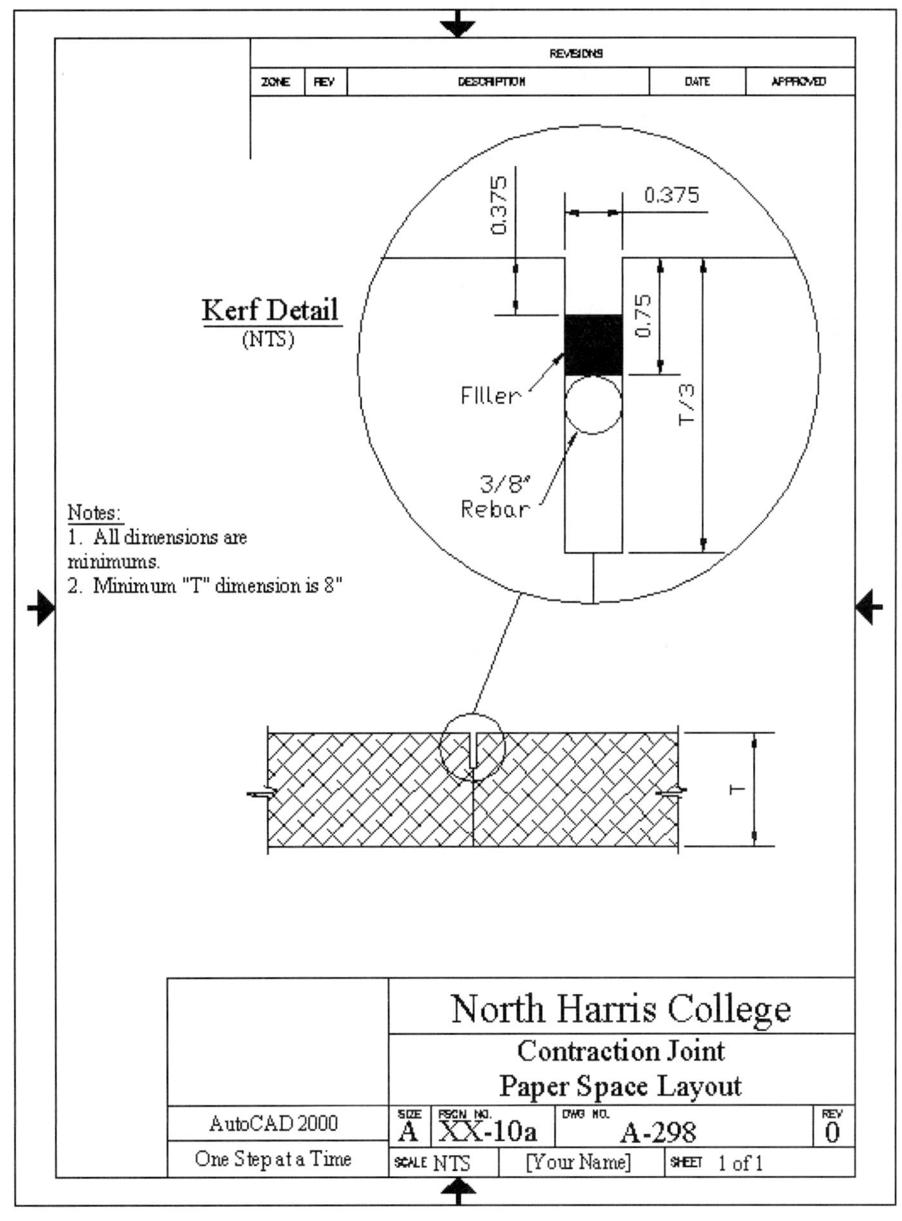

FIG. 2.9.8 Contraction Joint

2.10 REVIEW QUESTIONS

Please write your answers on a separate sheet of paper.

1. Explain the difference between dimensioning in Model Space and dimensioning in Paper Space.

2. If you drew it in Model Space, place your dimensions in (Model Space, Paper Space).

3. Any modifications to a viewport must be done in __________ space.

4. Use the __________ command to freeze a layer in one viewport only.

5. and 6. Change the default settings of layers in a specific viewport using the __________ option of the __________ command.

7. and 8. To scale hatch patterns to a viewport's scale, place a check in the __________ box of the __________ dialog box.

9. In a drawing that uses Paper Space, place all the text in Paper Space unless __________.

10. Write the formula you would use to size text in Paper Space.

11. Use the __________ command to print or plot a Paper Space layout.

12. (T or F) You cannot work in Model Space on a layout tab.

13. (T or F) Most basic modifying tools will work in Paper Space as they do in Model Space.

14. Thanks to the Layout Wizard, the MVSetup command is more useful today as a __________ tool.

15. (T or F) MVSetup can be used to set up Model Space.

16 and 17. To refresh or regenerate all of the viewports at one time, use the __________ or the __________ command.

18. Use the __________ command to reshape a viewport that was created by converting a closed polygon to a viewport.

19. Reshape a standard rectangular viewport using the __________ command.

PART

Welcome to the Third Dimension

This part of our text contains these lessons:

LESSON 3

"Z" Basics

Following this lesson, you will

- Know how to maneuver in three-dimensional space
  - Understand the ***VPoint*** and ***DDVPoint*** commands
  - Understand the Right-Hand Rule
  - Know how to use the ***Plan*** command
- Know how to draw simple three-dimensional objects
  - Know how to use **Elevation** and **Thickness** in your drawings
- Know some of the basic tricks used to view a three-dimensional drawing
  - Know how to use the ***Hide*** and ***Shademode*** commands

Does anyone not remember Mr. Woopie's coveted 3D BB? How many times did he pull that tiny block from his closet, stretch it into a full-size blackboard, and help Tennessee Tuxedo devise yet another wonderful scheme?

Who would have thought—way back in those simple cartoon days—that one day you would be learning to use your own 3D BB?

You are about to go where no board draftsman has gone before. You are about to enter Z-Space. Z-Space is that area defined by the Z-axis. Remember the X- and Y-axes? They travel left to right and top to bottom on a sheet of paper (or drafting board). The Z-axis rises and falls into the space above and below the paper. It takes all three axes to create a three-dimensional object.

But oh, the wonders you will see!

3.1 The UCS Icon and the Right-Hand Rule

Before entering Z-Space (the third dimension), you must learn to keep your bearings. That is, you must learn to tell up from down, top from bottom, and left from right, regardless of your orientation within the drawing. Sound simple enough? Place your hand over Figure 3.1b and then look carefully at the drawing in Figure 3.1a. Are you looking at the top or bottom of the object? Now look at Figure 3.1b. How did you do?

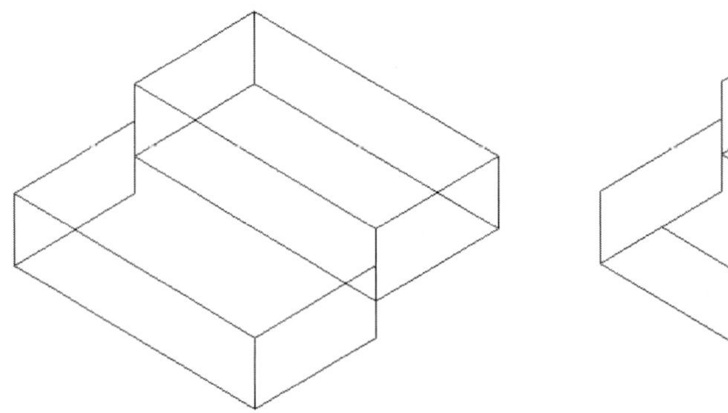

FIG. 3.1a Look Carefully

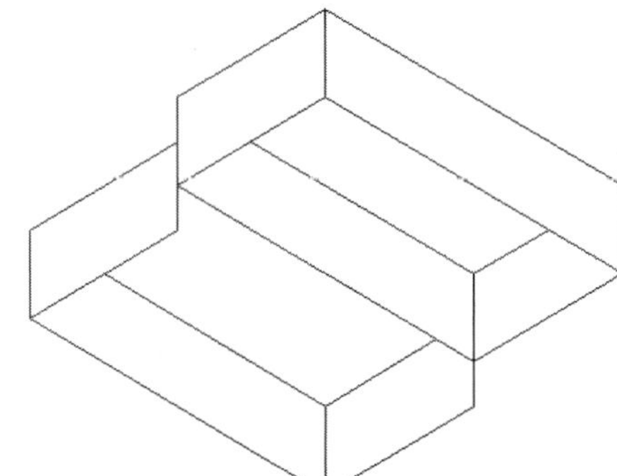

FIG. 3.1b Better?

I have removed the hidden lines in Figure 3.1b (more on that in Section 3.4.1). However, it is not always practical to do that, so AutoCAD has provided a method to determine your orientation at any time and at any place in the drawing. We will use the UCS icon (Figure 3.1.1a).

3.1.1 The UCS Icon

In our basic text, I told you how to turn off the UCS icon. In two-dimensional space it has little use. However, to operate in three-dimensional space, you must activate the UCS icon or risk being forever lost. (The icon acts like a lighthouse on a dark and stormy night—giving the mariner a reference point from which to navigate.) Use the ***UCSIcon*** command to control the UCS icon. It works like this:

Command: ***ucsicon***

Enter an option [ON/OFF/All/Noorigin/ORigin/Properties] <ON>:

This simple command provides options that will prove indispensable in a three-dimensional drawing:

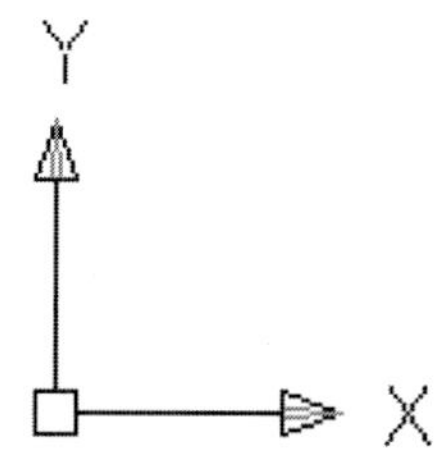

FIG. 3.1.1a The UCS Icon

- The **ON/OFF** options are self-explanatory. They turn the icon **On** or **Off**. They work only in the current viewport in Model Space or on the Paper Space icon in Paper Space.
- The **All** option prompts as follows:

  Enter an option [ON/OFF/Noorigin/ORigin/Properties] <OFF>:

  These options perform the same function as the first tier of options—but operate on *all* the viewports.
- The UCS icon remains in the lower-left part of the graphics screen by default. It is unaffected by normal display manipulation (zooms and pans). Using the **ORigin** option attaches the UCS icon to the 0,0,0 coordinate where it remains regardless of the display (as long as the 0,0,0 coordinate is on the screen). This provides a fixed point in space from which the draftsman can navigate (the mariner's lighthouse). If the 0,0,0 coordinate leaves the graphics area (through zooming or panning), the UCS icon returns to the lower-left corner of the screen.
- **Noorigin** disables the **ORigin** setting.
- The **Properties** option calls the UCS icon dialog box shown in Figure 3.1.1b. Here you can set up the icon's physical properties to suit your preferences.

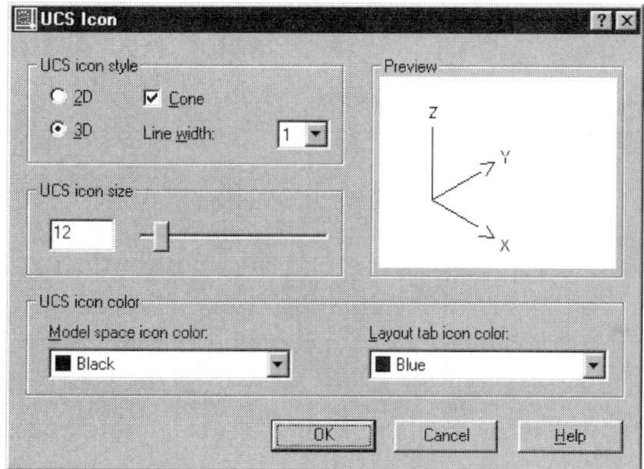

FIG. 3.1.1b The UCS Icon Dialog Box

- In the **UCS icon style** frame, you can tell AutoCAD to use a two-dimensional (**2D**) or three-dimensional (**3D**) icon. AutoCAD will use the 3D icon by default. (We used the 2D icon in earlier releases of AutoCAD. It is considerably more complicated to understand, so we will welcome the 3D icon and ignore its ancestry.)

  You can use conical pointers at the ends of the icon arrows (the default setting) or remove them in favor of simple arrowheads by removing the check next to **Cone**. You can also control the **Line width:** of the icon using the selection box in the lower right corner of the frame.
- The **UCS icon size** frame presents two tools—a text box and a slider bar—which allow you to control the size of the icon. The default works well, but some operators prefer something a bit smaller and less obtrusive. Three-dimensional novices might prefer something larger until they become accustomed to Z-Space.
- The **UCS icon color** frame allows the user more control over the color of the icon. Most people leave this at its default, although an occasional change in color does tend to relieve the monotony.

Let's experiment a bit with the UCS icon.

> You can access the various options of the ***UCSIcon*** command using the View pull-down menu. Follow this path:
>
> *View—Display—USC Icon—[option]*

WWW 3.1.1.1 Do This: Manipulating the UCS Icon

I. Open the *ucs Practice.dwg* in the C:\Steps3D\Lesson03 folder. The drawing looks like Figure 3.1.1.1a. [Do not let the funny angle of the crosshairs or UCS icon bother you—you are viewing the model from an angle in Z-Space. More on this setup in Section 3.2.]

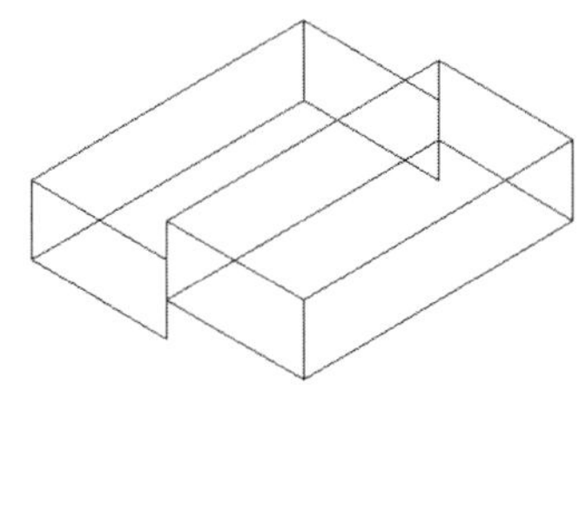

FIG. 3.1.1.1a UCS practice.dwg

II. Follow these steps:

TOOLS	COMMAND SEQUENCE	STEPS
No Button Available	**Command:** ***ucsicon***	**1.** Enter the ***UCSIcon*** command. There is no button or hotkey available. [*Note:* There are two UCS toolbars but neither will help in this exercise. We will look at those tools in Lesson 4.]
Enter Cancel ON OFF All Noorigin ORigin Properties Pan Zoom	**Enter an option [ON/OFF/All/ Noorigin/ORigin/Properties] <ON>:** ***or***	**2.** Use the **ORigin** option (Enter ***or*** at the prompt or select it from the cursor menu.) Notice that the icon moves to the 0,0,0 coordinates.

continued

TOOLS	COMMAND SEQUENCE	STEPS

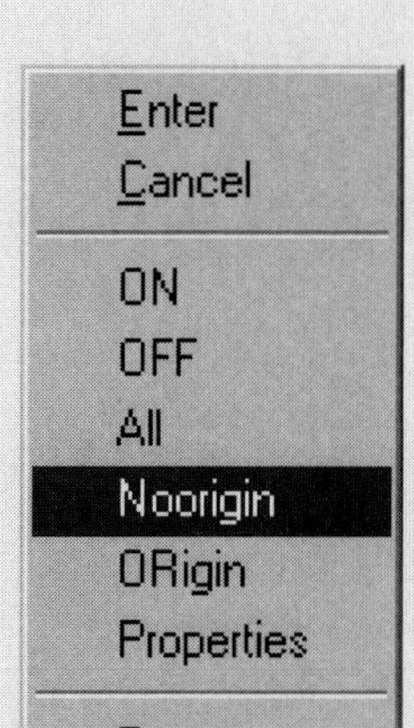

Command: *ucsicon*

Enter an option [ON/OFF/All/ Noorigin/ORigin/Properties] <ON>: *n*

3. Disable the **ORigin** option as indicated. The icon returns to the lower-left quadrant of the screen.

Named Views Button

Command: *v*

4. Use the *View* command to change the view to **negative z-space** (already created for you). The view changes to that shown in Figure 3.1.1.1.4. Notice the UCS icon. The Z-axis appears dashed. This indicates that you are seeing the model from underneath.

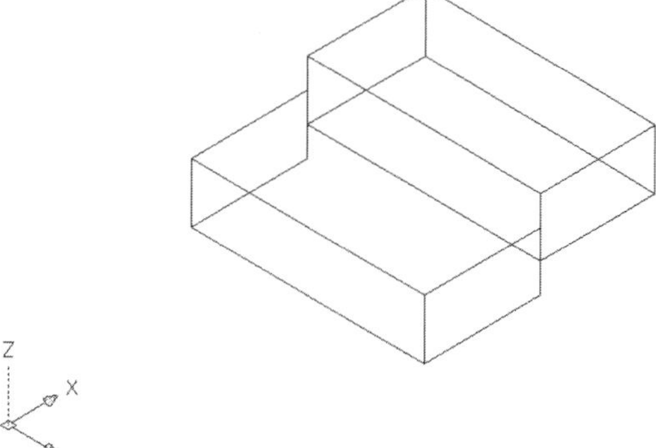

FIG. 3.1.1.1.4 Negative Z-Space View

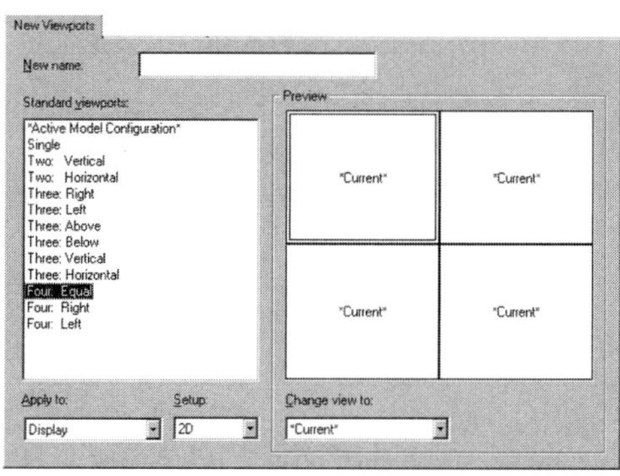

5. Use the *VPorts* command to set up **Four: Equal** viewports. Notice that each viewport has a UCS icon.

continued

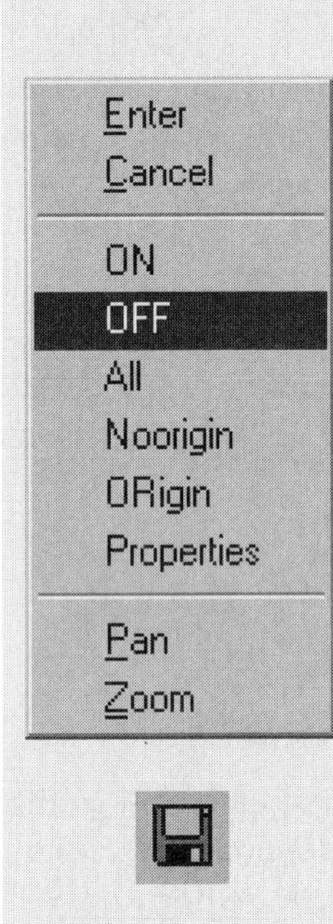

TOOLS	COMMAND SEQUENCE	STEPS
	Command: *ucsicon* **Enter an option [ON/OFF/All/ Noorigin/ORigin/Properties] <ON>:** *off*	**6.** Use the ***UCSIcon*** command to turn **OFF** the icon. Notice that only the icon in the currently active viewport (lower right) disappears.
	Command: *ucsicon* **Enter an option [ON/OFF/All/ Noorigin/ORigin/Properties] <OFF>:** *a* **Enter an option [ON/OFF/Noorigin/ ORigin/Properties] <OFF>:** *[enter]*	**7.** Now use the ***UCSIcon*** command to turn **OFF** the icon in **All** the viewports. Notice the difference.
	Command: *qsave*	**8.** Save the drawing and exit.

These simple tricks to manipulate and read the UCS icon will become second nature with experience. But there is another tool you can use to ease the learning curve—the Right-Hand Rule.

3.1.2 The Right-Hand Rule

The Right-Hand Rule provides another means of navigating Z-space. It works very much like the UCS icon but is a bit more "handy." It works like this (refer to Figure 3.1.2a):

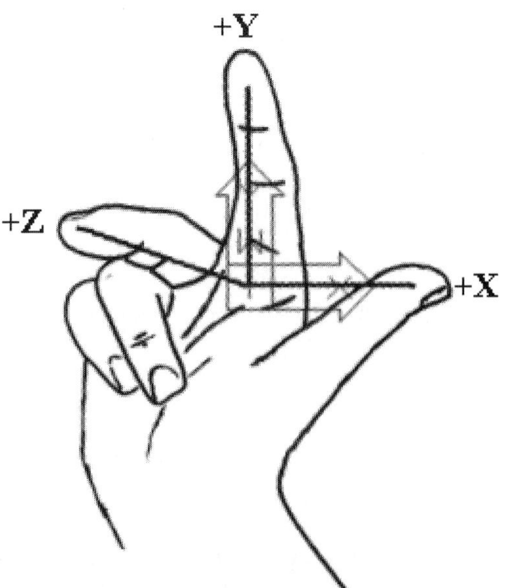

FIG. 3.1.2a Right-Hand Rule

1. Make a fist with your right hand.
2. Extend the index finger upward.
3. Extend the thumb at a right angle to the index finger.
4. Extend the middle finger at a right angle to the index finger (pointing outward).

How is that for feeling really awkward?

Each finger serves a purpose; each indicates the positive direction of one of the XYZ axes as indicated in Figure 3.1.2a. See how it correlates with the UCS icon? Using the right hand in this fashion, you will always be able to determine the third axis if you know the other two. Simply orient your right hand with the appropriate fingers pointing along the known axes and the location of the unknown axis becomes clear!

3.2 Maneuvering Through Z-Space with the *VPoint* Command

So now you know how to determine your own orientation in Z-Space, but how do you reorient the model itself? In other words, how do you turn the model this way and that in order to work on all sides of it? AutoCAD has provided a simple but powerful tool to help you—the ***VPoint*** command.

It might help your understanding if I begin by telling you that the model will not actually move or rotate. Using the ***VPoint*** command, the model holds still while you change position.

Let's use an airplane as an example. The airplane is a three-dimensional object (it has length, width, and height or thickness). To draw the top of the airplane, we will climb into a helicopter and hover above it for a better view. To draw the front, we must fly to the front of the airplane. Side and bottom views will also require us to fly to a better vantage point.

AutoCAD's helicopter is the ***VPoint*** command.

There are three approaches to using the ***VPoint*** command: coordinate input, compass, and dialog box. Let's look at each.

3.2.1 Using Coordinates to Assign a Viewpoint

The ***VPoint*** command prompt looks like this:

Command: ***vpoint*** **(or** ***−vp*****)**

Current view direction: VIEWDIR=0.0000,0.0000,1.0000

Specify a view point or [Rotate] <display compass and tripod>: *[enter a coordinate]*

- The default response to this prompt requires the user to enter the coordinates from which he wishes to view the model. Does that sound simple? It is actually easier than that! AutoCAD will not read the XYZ coordinates entered as actual coordinates but rather as a ratio. That is (let's keep this simple), a coordinate of 1,−1,1 tells AutoCAD that you wish to stand—in relation to the model—a bit to the right (+1 on the X-axis), back a bit (−1 on the Y-axis), and above (+1 on the Z-axis).

The default viewpoint for new or two-dimensional drawings is 0,0,1. This means that the user views the drawing from above (+1 on the Z-axis). Draftsmen generally refer to this view as the *Plan* view.

Remembering the simple ratio approach, what do you think a coordinate a 4,−2,1 will mean?*

When the absolute value of all three axes entries is the same (as in 1,1,1 or 1,−1,1), you have an *isometric* view of the drawing. [*Iso* means one—you are using the same absolute value on each axis.]

When only two of the absolute values are the same (as in 2,2,1 or −2,2,1), you have a *dimetric* view. [*Di* means two.]

What do you suppose you have when all three of the absolute values are different? Of course—it is a *trimetric* view.

Why the ratio approach? When you change your vantage or viewpoint (your VPoint), AutoCAD will automatically zoom to the drawing's extents (move as close as possible while showing you everything on the model)!

You already know that a plan view is achieved when the VPoint coordinates are 0,0,1. These coordinates allow you to view the model from a step up (+Z). What do you suppose happens when you set the coordinates to 1,0,0 or 0,−1,0? These coordinates provide elevations of the model—1,0,0 provides a right elevation (a step to the right or +X) and 0,−1,0 provides a front elevation (a step back or −Y). Which coordinates would provide a back or left elevation?*

AutoCAD lets you know when you are in an elevation view by changing the appropriate axis on the UCS icon to a small circle (Figure 3.2.1a).

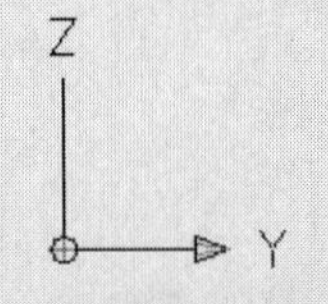

FIG. 3.2.1a
UCS Icon

*Back elevation coordinates = 0,1,0; left elevation coordinates = −1,0,0.

- The **Rotate** option of the ***VPoint*** command allows the user to specify his vantage point by the angle at which he wishes to see the model. The prompts look like this:

Specify a view point or [Rotate] <display compass and tripod>: ***r [tell AutoCAD you wish to use the Rotate option]***

Enter angle in XY plane from X axis <[xx]>: ***[indicate the two-dimensional angle (the angle along the ground) at which you wish to see the model]***

*It means: I want to stand twice as far to the right as I am standing back, and twice as far back as I am standing above the model.

Enter angle from XY plane <xx>: ***[indicate the three-dimensional angle (the upward angle—like the angle of the sun in the sky) at which you wish to see the model]***

This will become clearer in our next exercise.

> You can access several preset viewpoints using buttons on the View toolbar or by selecting the view from the View pull-down menu. Follow this path:
>
> *View—3D Views—[selection]*

We will look at the compass and tripod in Section 3.2.2, but first let's try the coordinate approach to the ***VPoint*** command.

3.2.1.1 Do This: The Coordinate Approach to Setting the Viewpoint

I. Open the *VPoint practice.dwg* in the C:\Steps3D\Lesson03 folder. The drawing looks like Figure 3.2.1.1a. The drawing is currently in the plan view.

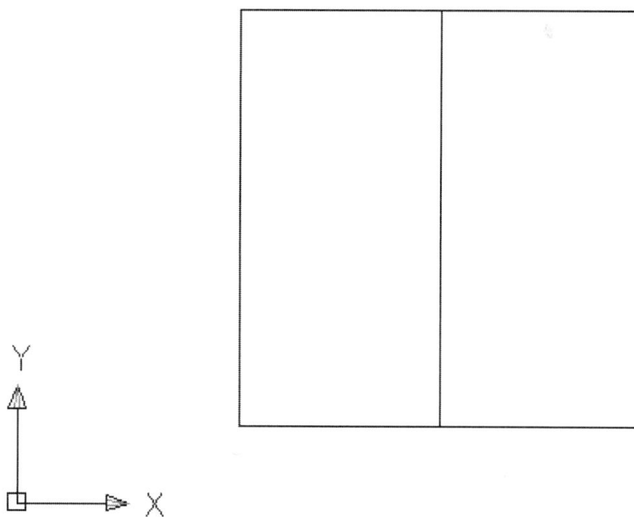

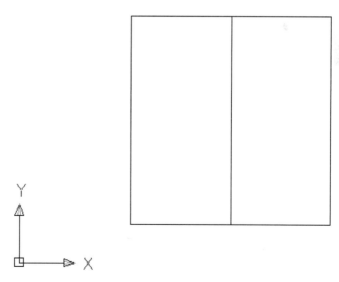

FIG. 3.2.1.1a *Vpoint Practice.dwg*

II. Follow these steps:

TOOLS	COMMAND SEQUENCE	STEPS
	Command: ***−vp***	**1.** Enter the ***VPoint*** command by typing ***vpoint*** or ***−vp*** at the command prompt.
	Current view direction: VIEWDIR=0.0000,0.0000,1.0000 **Specify a view point or [Rotate] <display compass and tripod>:** ***1,−1,1***	**2.** AutoCAD tells you the current coordinate setting and prompts you to either **Specify a view point** or to **Rotate**. Let's use the first option. Tell AutoCAD to move to the right, back, and up as indicated (the SE Isometric View). Your drawing looks like Figure 3.2.1.1.2.
SE Isometric View Button		(You can achieve the same results as Steps 1 and 2 using the **SE Isometric View** button on the View toolbar.)

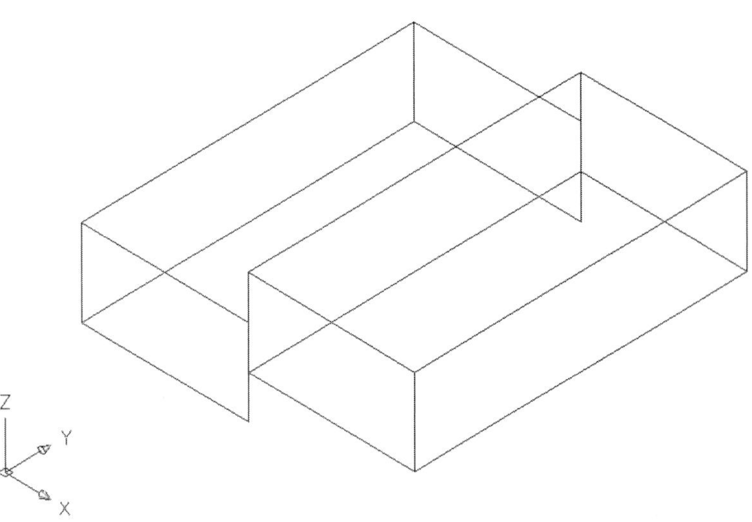

FIG. 3.2.1.1.2 Viewpoint 1,-1,1 (Using the UCS Icon, you can see that you are above the drawing, below zero on the Y-axis, and to the right of zero on the X-axis.)

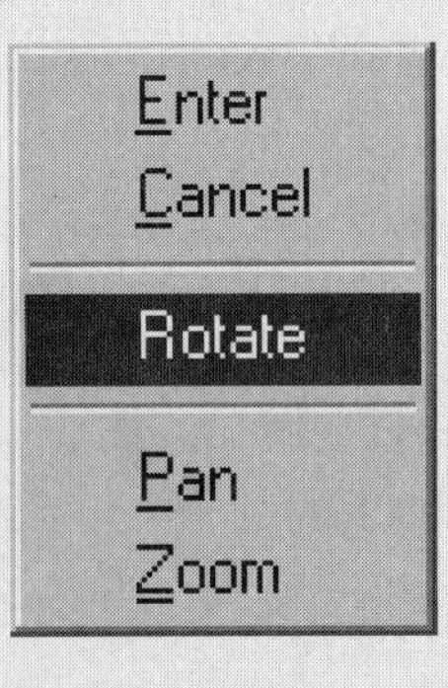

TOOLS	COMMAND SEQUENCE	STEPS
	Command: ***[enter]*** **Current view direction: VIEWDIR=1.0000,−1.0000,1.0000** **Specify a view point or [Rotate] <display compass and tripod>:** ***r***	**3.** Let's try the **Rotate** option. Repeat the ***VPoint*** command and select the **Rotate** option.

continued

TOOLS	COMMAND SEQUENCE	STEPS
	Enter angle in XY plane from X axis <315>: *225*	**4.** AutoCAD asks for a two-dimensional angle. We will stand in the −X,−Y quadrant. Enter the angle indicated.
	Enter angle from XY plane <35>: *45*	**5.** Now AutoCAD asks for a three-dimensional angle (the angle up or down in Z-Space). We will stand above the model. Enter the angle indicated. Your drawing now looks like Figure 3.2.1.1.5.

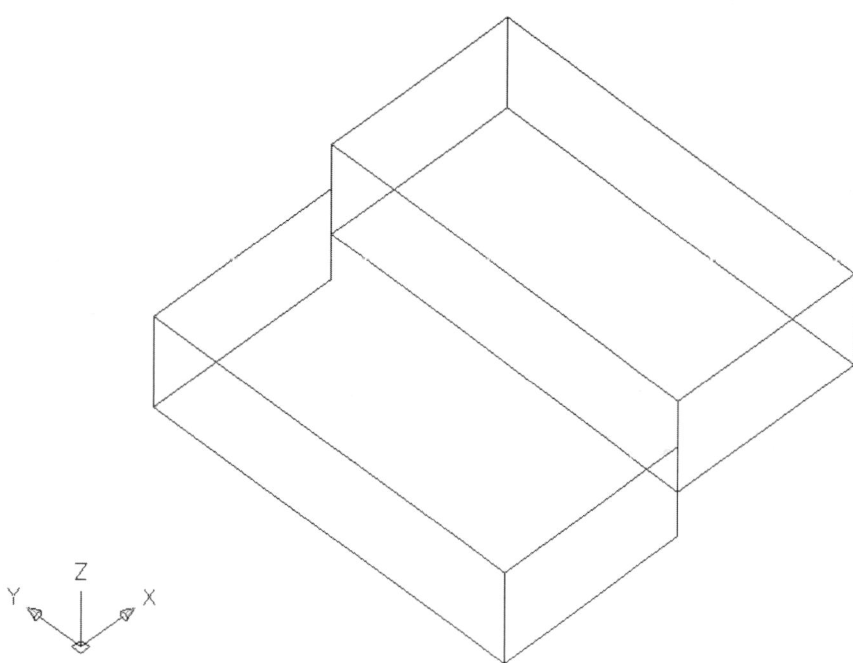

FIG. 3.2.1.1.5 Model at 225° in the XY Plane and 45° from the XY Plane

continued

TOOLS	COMMAND SEQUENCE	STEPS
	Command: *[enter]* **Current view direction: VIEWDIR=−0.8660,−0.8660,1.2247** **Specify a view point or [Rotate] <display compass and tripod>:** ***0,−1,0***	**6.** Repeat the ***VPoint*** command. This time enter coordinates for a front elevation as indicated. Your drawing looks like Figure 3.2.1.1.6. Notice the **UCS** icon. (*Caution:* Do *not* use the **Front View** button on the View toolbar because it will also change the UCS.)

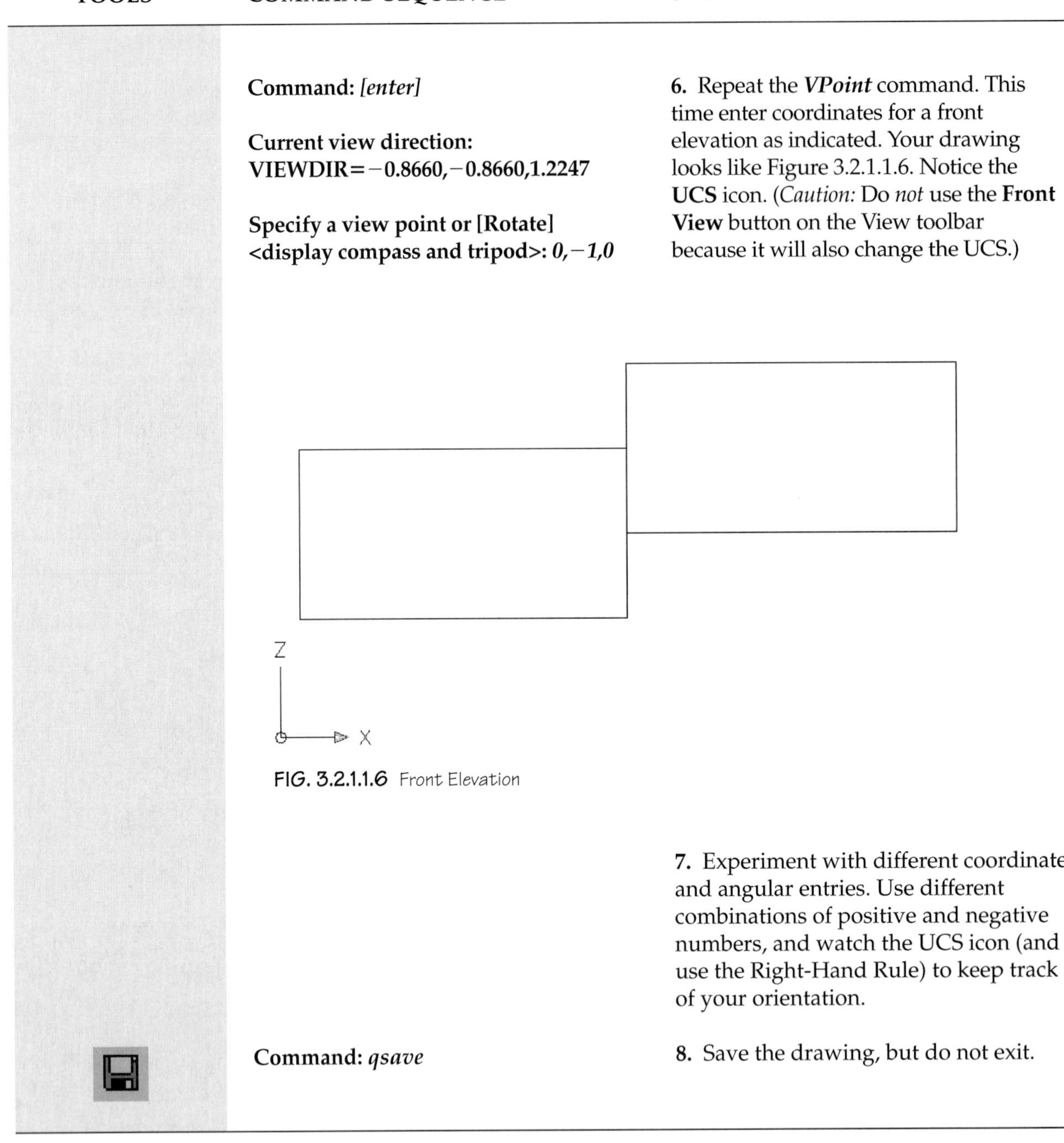

FIG. 3.2.1.1.6 Front Elevation

TOOLS	COMMAND SEQUENCE	STEPS
		7. Experiment with different coordinate and angular entries. Use different combinations of positive and negative numbers, and watch the UCS icon (and use the Right-Hand Rule) to keep track of your orientation.
	Command: *qsave*	**8.** Save the drawing, but do not exit.

3.2.2 Using the Compass to Assign a Viewpoint

Often the precise coordinate or angle from which you view the model will not be all that important. You will be in a hurry, know the general area in which you wish to stand, and want to go there quickly. For these times, AutoCAD provides the **compass and tripod** option of the ***VPoint*** command.

Access the compass and tripod by hitting **enter** at the **Specify a view point or [Rotate] <display compass and tripod>:** prompt. AutoCAD presents the tripod and compass screen (Figure 3.2.2a).

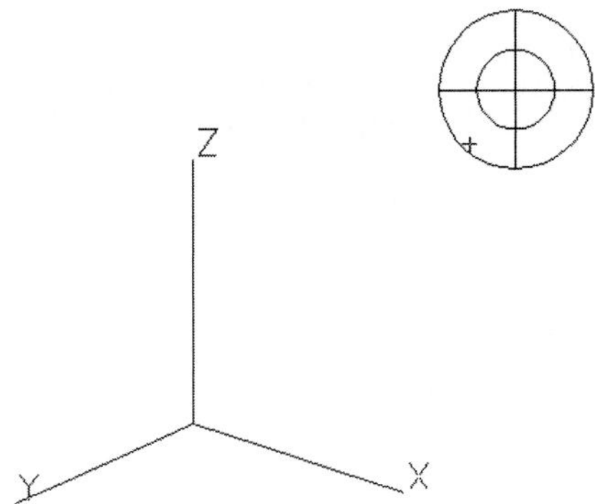

FIG. 3.2.2a Tripod and Compass

- Although it is fast, the tripod is difficult to use. Imagine your drawing resting at the vertex (center) of the tripod. Use the mouse to maneuver the XYZ-axes as desired. When you are happy with the orientation, left-click to return to the graphics screen.
- The compass in the upper-right quadrant of the screen is much easier to use than the tripod. This ingenious tool represents the positive and negative regions of a model. Refer to Figure 3.2.2b.

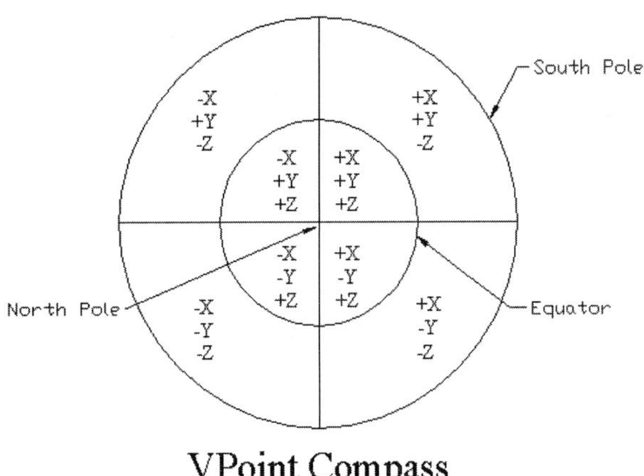

FIG. 3.2.2b Compass Values

Imagine that your model exists at the core of a globe. Where you stand on the globe determines your view of the model. The VPoint Compass is a two-dimensional representation of that globe. Use it to show AutoCAD where you wish to stand.

Inside the inner circle of the compass represents the upper (or northern) hemisphere of the globe. Since this is the upper part of the globe, we see the model from the top so the area inside the inner circle is on the +Z-axis. The four quadrants of the inner circle represent the positive and negative X- and Y-axes as shown.

Between the inner and outer circles of the compass is the lower (or southern) hemisphere of the globe. Since this is the lower part of the globe, we see the model from the bottom so this area is on the −Z-axis. The four outer quadrants represent the positive and negative X- and Y-axes as shown.

The compass may seem confusing at first, but (except for the toolbar) it is considerably faster than any other method of VPoint selection once you get used to it.

> You can create a series of viewpoints by saving each, using the same ***View*** command that was so beneficial in two-dimensional AutoCAD.

Let's try the compass approach to the ***VPoint*** command.

WWW 3.2.2.1 Do This: Using the VPoint Compass

I. Be sure you are still in the *VPoint practice.dwg* in the C:\Steps3D\Lesson03 folder. If not, open it now.

II. Follow these steps:

TOOLS	COMMAND SEQUENCE	STEPS
	Command: −*vp*	**1.** Begin the ***VPoint*** command.
	Current view direction: VIEWDIR=−0.8660,−0.8660,1.2247	**2.** Hit ***enter*** at the first prompt to access the tripod and compass.
	Specify a view point or [Rotate] <display compass and tripod>: *[enter]*	

continued

TOOLS	COMMAND SEQUENCE	STEPS
		3. Place the compass cursor in the +X+Y+Z coordinate as indicated in Figure 3.2.2.1.3a and pick once with the left mouse button to return to the graphics screen. Your drawing looks something like Figure 3.2.2.1.3b.

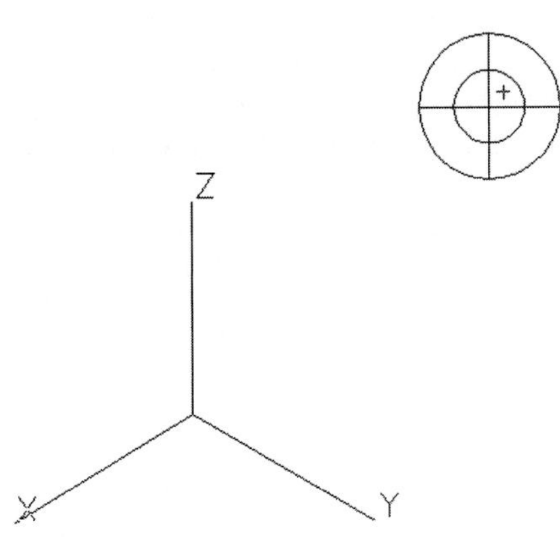

FIG. 3.2.2.1.3a Compass Cursor

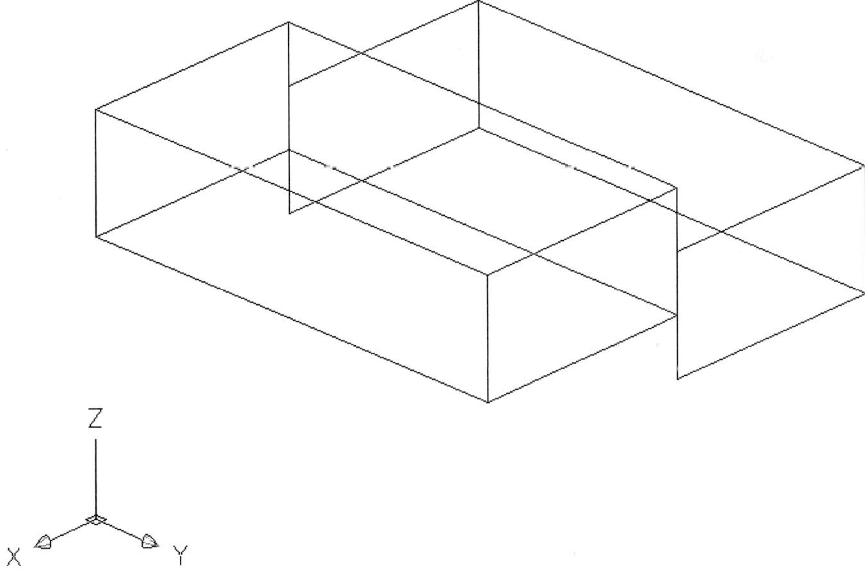

FIG. 3.2.2.1.3b New View

TOOLS	COMMAND SEQUENCE	STEPS
	Command: *−vp*	**4.** Experiment using different quadrants (and locations within quadrants) of the compass. Try using the tripod instead of the compass. Which is easier?
	**Command:** *qsave*	**5.** Save the drawing, but do not exit.

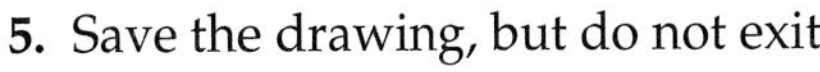

3.2.3 Setting Viewpoints Using a Dialog Box

Setting viewpoints using a dialog box is very similar to setting viewpoints using the **Rotate** option of the ***VPoint*** command.

Access the Viewpoint Presets dialog box (Figure 3.2.3a) with the ***DDVPoint*** command or the ***VP*** hotkey. [You can also access the dialog box using the View pull-down menu. Follow this path: *View—3dViews—Viewpoint Presets*.]

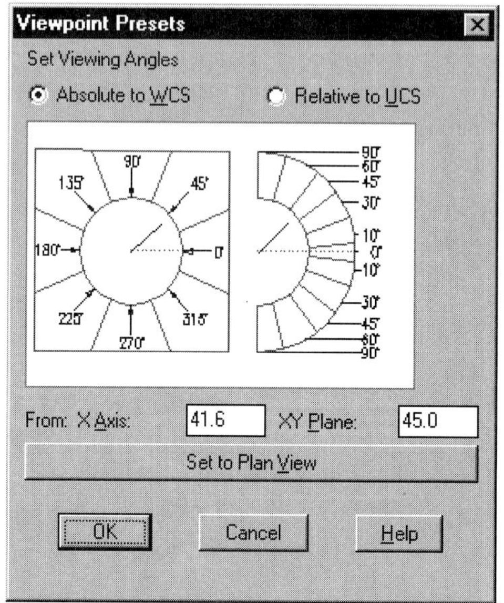

FIG. 3.2.3a Viewpoint Presets Dialog Box

The first things you will notice on the dialog box are the two large drawings in the center. The first (on the left) looks something like a compass, and the second looks like half a compass. Use the compass on the left to set the two-dimensional angle (*in* the XY-plane); use the compass on the right to set the three-dimensional angle (up or down *from* the XY plane).

You can set the angles in two ways—by keyboard entry in the text boxes below the compasses or by mouse selection on the compasses themselves.

At the top of the dialog box, AutoCAD asks the user to identify the angle in **Absolute to WCS** or **Relative to UCS** terms. We will learn more about the WCS (World Coordinate System) and UCS (User Coordinate System) in Lesson 4. For now, leave the viewing angles set to **Absolute to WCS**.

The long button across the bottom of the dialog box is our first "Hail Mary" button for this text. If you read the basic text, you know to use a Hail Mary button in an emergency. AutoCAD designed this button to return the drawing to the plan view from anywhere. Set the **Absolute to WCS** option at the top of the dialog box and then pick the **Set to Plan View** button to return to a "normal" two-dimensional view of your model. This is quite handy when you become lost in Z-Space.

The keyboard equivalent of the **Set to Plan View** "Hail Mary" button is the ***Plan*** command. It looks like this:

> **Command:** ***plan***
>
> **Enter an option [Current ucs/Ucs/World] <Current>:**

Again, we will look at the WCS and UCS in Lesson 4. Enter *w* for the **World** option and hit enter to do what the **Set to Plan View** button does—return to a normal two-dimensional view of your model.

Let's try the dialog box.

WWW 3.2.3.1 Do This: Using the Viewpoint Presets Dialog Box

I. Be sure you are still in the *VPoint practice.dwg* in the C:\Steps3D\Lesson03 folder. If not, open it now.

II. Follow these steps:

TOOLS	COMMAND SEQUENCE	STEPS
No Button Available	**Command:** ***vp***	**1.** Enter the ***DDVPoint*** command by typing ***ddvpoint*** or ***vp*** at the command line. AutoCAD presents the Viewpoint Presets dialog box (Figure 3.2.3a).
	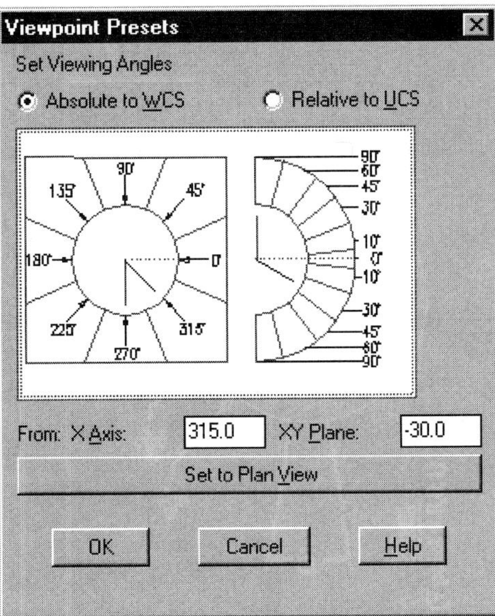	**2.** Set the viewpoint to 315° on the left compass. Set the viewpoint to −30° on the right compass. (You can do this by typing the numbers into their respective text boxes or by picking on the numbers on the compasses themselves.)

continued

TOOLS	COMMAND SEQUENCE	STEPS
OK		3. Pick the **OK** button to complete the command. Your drawing looks like Figure 3.2.3.1.3. Notice the UCS icon.

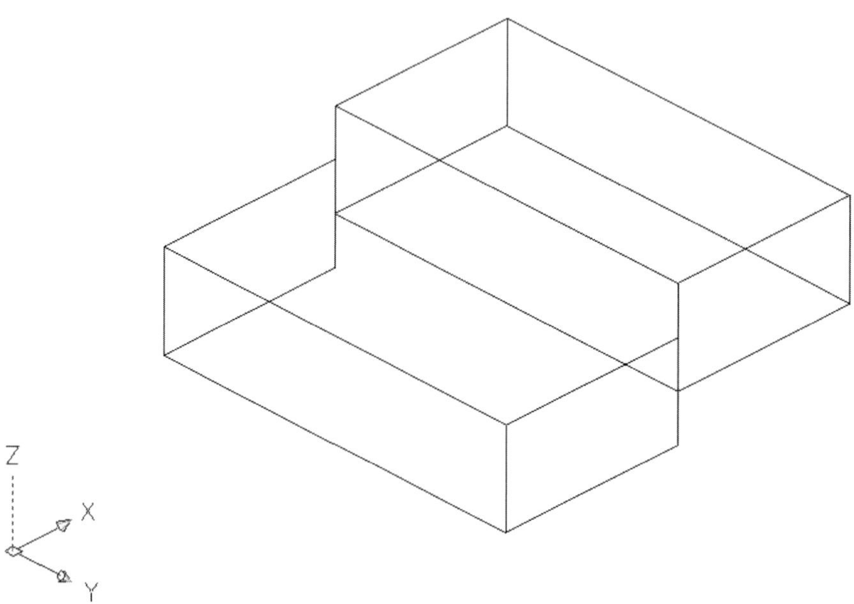

FIG. 3.2.3.1.3 New View

TOOLS	COMMAND SEQUENCE	STEPS
	Command: ***[enter]***	4. Repeat the ***DDVPoint*** command.
	Set to Plan View	5. Pick the **Set to Plan View** button.

continued

TOOLS	COMMAND SEQUENCE	STEPS
OK		**6.** Pick the **OK** button to complete the command. Your drawing looks like Figure 3.2.3.1.6.

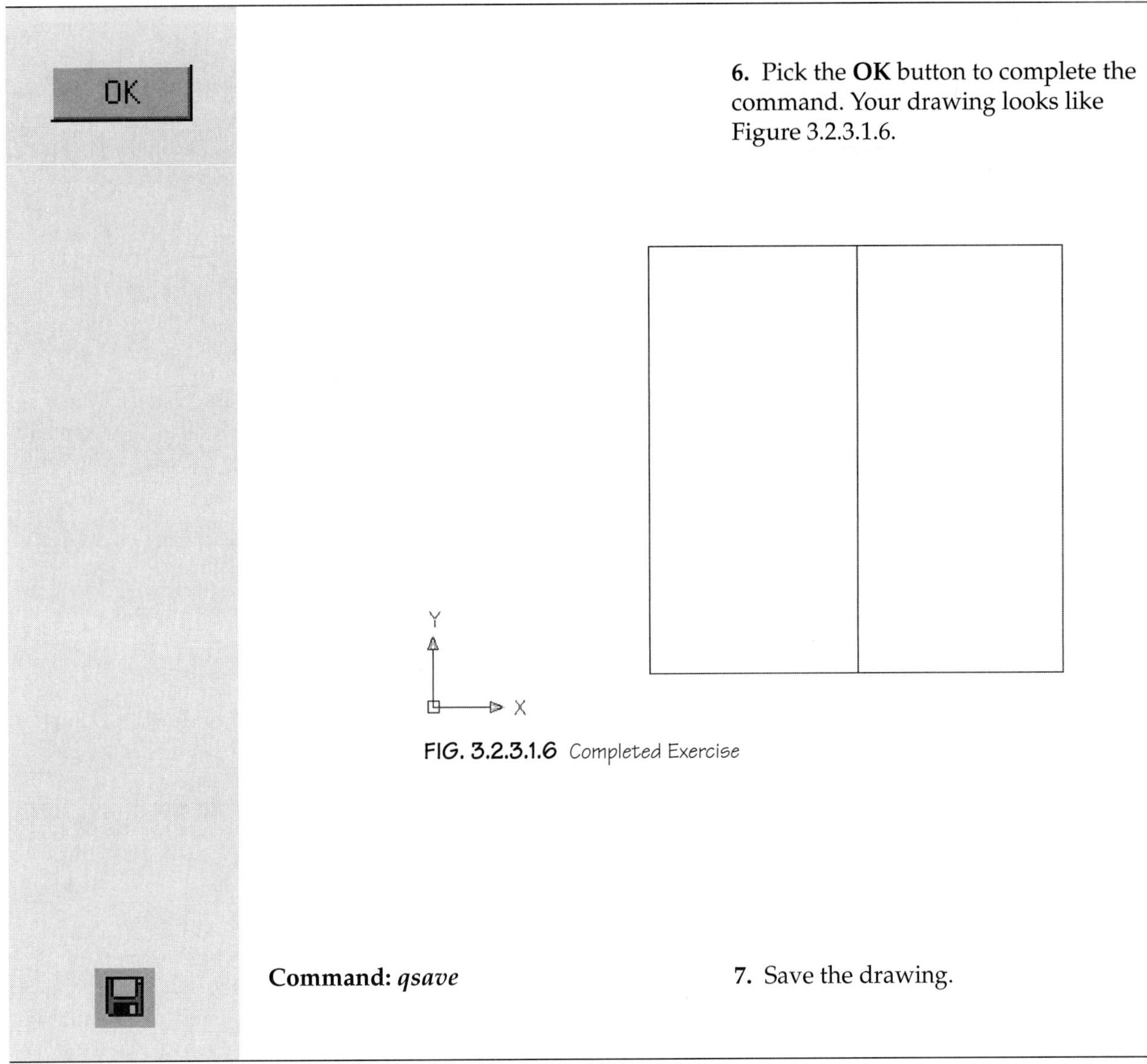

FIG. 3.2.3.1.6 Completed Exercise

TOOLS	COMMAND SEQUENCE	STEPS
	Command: *qsave*	**7.** Save the drawing.

We have spent a great deal of time in this lesson on a single aspect of Z-Space—viewpoints. I cannot overemphasize the importance of being comfortable with viewpoints. Consider the astronaut floating in space. A basic understanding of geography will tell him where he is in terms of continent, nation, or even city (XY-Space). But if he does not understand his altitude (his Z-Space position), he cannot know if he is coming or going. He might wind up on the wrong planet altogether!

If necessary, repeat this lesson to this point to get comfortable with viewpoints and the ***VPoint*** command (the astronaut's navigator). Experiment with viewpoints in different viewports (each viewport can have its own viewpoint). Then proceed to the next section where we will take our first tender steps in creating three-dimensional objects.

3.3 Drawing with the Z-Axis

I wish I could begin this section of our text by saying that three dimensional drafting is no different from two-dimensional drafting. However, that is simply not the case. You have already seen that more navigation tools are required. Additionally, there are two other basic items you must consider that had no meaning in a two-dimensional drawing—the Z-coordinate (or elevation) and the thickness of the object you are drawing.

Let's look at these.

3.3.1 Three-Dimensional Coordinate Entry

We began our basic text with a study of the Cartesian Coordinate System. Likewise, we must begin our study of three-dimensional drafting with a look at the Cartesian Coordinate System and how it works with the Z-axis. Consider the following table.

SYSTEM	ABSOLUTE	RELATIVE	POLAR
2D Entry	X,Y	@X,Y	@Dist<Angle
3D Entry	X,Y,Z	@X,Y,Z	@truedist<XYangle<Zangle *or* @dist<2Dangle,Z-dist

The Absolute and Relative systems are easy enough to understand. Simply add the location on the Z-axis to the X and Y locations to have an XYZ-coordinate. But Polar Coordinate entry might need some explaining.

The first formula for 3D entry of Polar coordinates looks like this:

@truedist<XYangle<Zangle

(Read as *at a true distance of ___ . . . at an XY angle of ___ . . . and a Z angle of ___.*) We call this type of coordinate entry *Spherical*. (Refer to Figure 3.3.1a.) Begin Spherical coordinate entry with the true three-dimensional length of the line (or other object). Follow with the same two-dimensional (XY) angle you have always used for Polar Coordinates. Follow that with the three-dimensional angle (above or below the XY-plane).

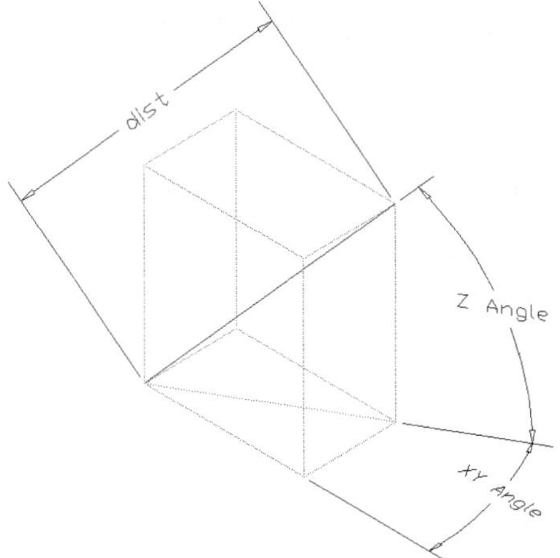

FIG. 3.3.1a Spherical Coordinate Entry

The other formula for 3D entry of Polar coordinates looks like this:

@dist<XYangle,Z-dist

(Read as *at a distance of* ___ . . . *and an XY angle of* ___ . . . *at a Z distance of* ___.) We call this type of coordinate entry *Cylindrical*. (Refer to Figure 3.3.1b.) Like the Spherical Coordinate entry method, begin Cylindrical Coordinate entry with the distance of the line *but this time, use only the XY distance*. Follow with the two-dimensional angle but conclude with the distance *along the Z-axis* (perpendicular to the XY-plane).

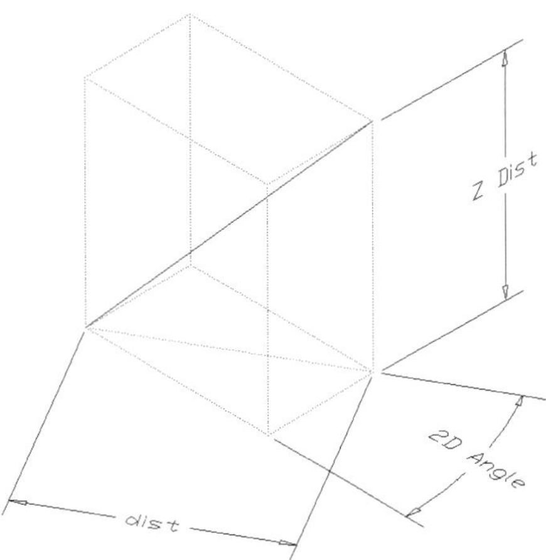

FIG. 3.3.1b Cylindrical Coordinate Entry

We will use these methods to draw the stick figure of a house in our next exercise.

3.3.1.1 Do This: Three-Dimensional Coordinate Entry

I. Open the *3-3D-1.dwg* file in the C:\Steps3D\Lesson03 folder. This drawing has been set up with a viewpoint of 1,−2,1, and layers have been created.

II. Be sure that layer **Obj1** is current.

III. Follow these steps:

TOOLS	COMMAND SEQUENCE	STEPS
	Command: ***l***	**1.** We will begin using Absolute Coordinates. Draw a line as indicated. Do not exit the command. Notice that a Z-coordinate entry is not required if the value is **0**.
	Specify first point: ***1,1***	
	Specify next point or [Undo]: ***4,1***	
	Specify next point or [Undo]: ***4,1,2***	**2.** Now draw a line straight up into Z-Space.
	Specify next point or [Undo]: ***1,1,2***	**3.** Continue the line to complete the first side of the house.
	Specify next point or [Close/Undo]: ***c***	
	Command: ***l***	**4.** We will use Relative Coordinates as indicated to draw the other side.
	Specify first point: ***1,3***	
	Specify next point or [Undo]: ***@3,0***	
	Specify next point or [Undo]: ***@0,0,2***	
	Specify next point or [Close/Undo]: **@−3,0,0**	
	Specify next point or [Close/Undo]: ***c***	

continued

TOOLS | **COMMAND SEQUENCE** | **STEPS**

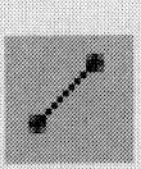

Command: ***l***

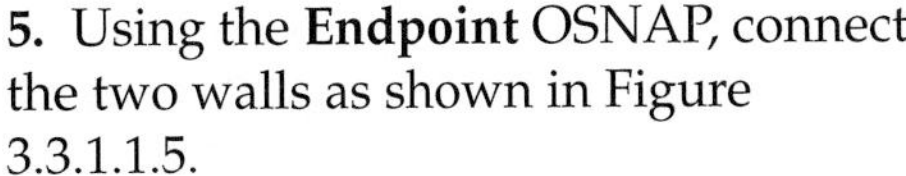

5. Using the **Endpoint** OSNAP, connect the two walls as shown in Figure 3.3.1.1.5.

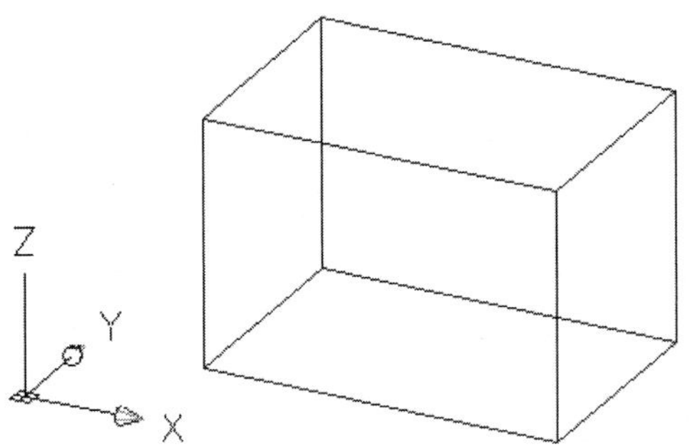

FIG. 3.3.1.1.5 Completed Stick Walls

Command: ***saveas***

6. Remember to save occasionally. Save the drawing as *My Stick House* in the C:\Steps3D\Lesson03 folder.

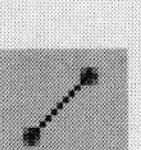

Command: ***l***

Specify first point: ***mid***

7. Now use Spherical Coordinates as indicated to locate the peak of the roof. Begin at the midpoint of the upper line marking the west side of the house.

Specify next point or [Undo]: ***@1.5<0<60***

8. We will want a 1.5″ line at 0° on the XY-plane and 60° upward.

Specify next point or [Undo]: ***[enter]***

continued

TOOLS	COMMAND SEQUENCE	STEPS
	**Command:** *[enter]* **LINE Specify first point:** *mid* **Specify next point or [Undo]:** *@1.5<180<60* **Specify next point or [Undo]:** *[enter]*	**9.** Repeat Steps 7 and 8 to locate the roof peak on the opposite wall. Your drawing looks like Figure 3.3.1.1.9. **FIG. 3.3.1.1.9** Roof Peak Locators
	**Command:** *[enter]*	**10.** Using the **Endpoint** OSNAP, draw the roof as shown in Figure 3.3.1.1.10. Erase the roof peak locators. **FIG. 3.3.1.1.10** Completed Stick House
	**Command:** *qsave*	**11.** Save the drawing, but do not exit.
	Command: *vp*	**12.** Take a few moments and examine the model using different viewpoints. Return to a location of 1,−2, 1 when you have finished.

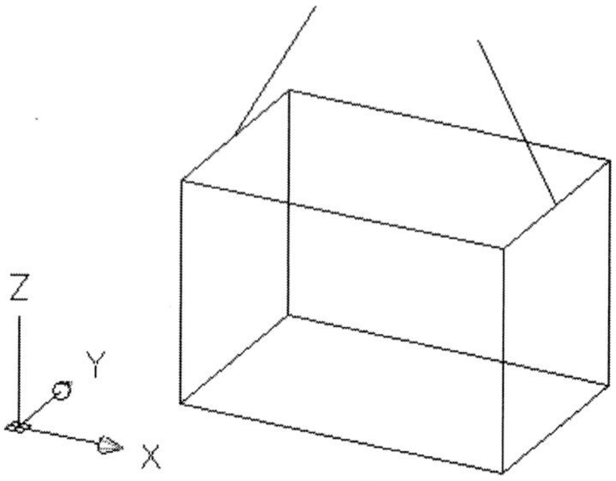

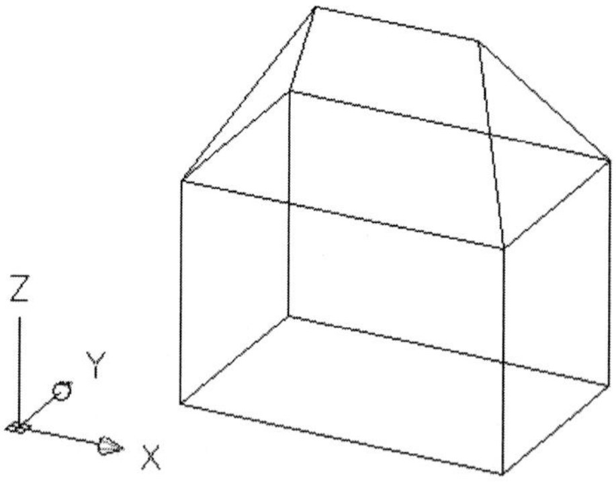

Congratulations! You have created your first three-dimensional drawing.

You may have noticed some three-dimensional idiosyncrasies. If not, let me list a few.

- Ortho works only on the XY-plane.
- Object and Polar Tracking work only on the XY-plane.
- OSNAPs work on most objects regardless of their XYZ-coordinate.
- It is impossible to locate a point in a three-dimensional drawing by arbitrarily picking a point on the screen. Remember that your screen is two dimensional. An arbitrary point lacks a definition on one of the X-, Y-, or Z-axes, so there is no guarantee where it may actually be. *Always identify a three-dimensional point using a coordinate entry method or an OSNAP!* (Now you see why we put so much emphasis on coordinates and OSNAPs in the basic book!)
- Use three-dimensional coordinates just as you did two-dimensional coordinates when modifying the drawing (copying, moving, etc).
- Only very rarely will you want to create a three-dimensional object using a simple line command. (After all, how often does your boss request stick figure drawings?)

> Point filters are also very useful in Z-Space. Refer to Section 4.5.1 in *AutoCAD 2002: One Step at a Time* for details on the use of point filters.

Let's look next at adding a new dimension to our objects. We will call our new dimension *Thickness* and do marvelous things with it.

3.3.2 Using the Thickness and Elevation System Variables

Thickness is that property of an object that takes it from a stick figure to a true three-dimensional object. Until now, all the objects you have drawn have been stick figures. That is, they have all existed in a single two-dimensional plane. Even the lines we used to create our stick house in the last exercise existed in two-dimensional planes (although they crossed three-dimensional space). Clear as milk? Let me help.

Consider each line created in our stick house. (Consider each line individually—not as it relates to other lines or coordinates.) Describe each in terms of length, width, and height. In each case, you can describe the line using two of the three terms mentioned. In no case can you use all three terms. Consider the first line you drew. It has a length of 3 units and a width (or lineweight) of 0.01″ (AutoCAD's default). But it has no height—no *thickness*.

Drawing with thickness is as easy as setting the system variable, like this:

Command: *thickness* (or *th*)

Enter new value for THICKNESS <0.0000>: *.25*

All objects drawn while the **Thickness** system variable is set to **.25** will have a thickness of .25. This brings up another very important point: *Always remember to reset the* ***Thickness*** *system variable to* ***0*** *when finished drawing an object.*

You can access the ***Thickness*** command from the Format pull-down menu. Follow this path:

Format—Thickness

Let's redraw our walls using **Thickness**.

3.3.2.1 Do This: Drawing with Thickness

I. Be sure you are still in the *My Stick House.dwg* file in the C:\Steps3D\Lesson03 folder. If not, open it now.

II. Follow these steps:

TOOLS	COMMAND SEQUENCE	STEPS
No Button Available	**Command:** *th*	**1.** Set the **Thickness** system variable to 2.
	Enter new value for THICKNESS <0.0000>: 2	
	Command: *l*	**2.** Draw the walls as indicated.
	LINE Specify first point: *6,1*	
	Specify next point or [Undo]: *@3<0*	
	Specify next point or [Undo]: *@2<90*	
	Specify next point or [Close/Undo]: *@3<180*	
	Specify next point or [Close/Undo]: *c*	
	Command: *th*	**3.** Reset the **Thickness** to *0*.
	Enter new value for THICKNESS <2.0000>: *0*	

Notice that we used simple two-dimensional coordinate entry. The thickness system variable took care of the Z requirements.

Another very useful tool to employ in three-dimensional drafting is the **Elevation** system variable. When we drew our original house, we had to enter a location on the Z-axis as part of the coordinate whenever the value of Z was not zero (whenever it was above or below zero-z). The **Elevation** system variable is designed to minimize the need for entering that third number. The command looks like this:

Command: *elevation*

Enter new value for ELEVATION <0.0000>: *[enter the desired elevation]*

Once set, AutoCAD draws all objects at the identified elevation.

> Use the *Elev* command to set both the **Elevation** and **Thickness** system variables at once. The command looks like this:
>
> **Command:** *elev*
>
> **Specify new default elevation <0.0000>:** *[enter the elevation]*
>
> **Specify new default thickness <0.0000>:** *[enter the thickness]*

Let's try using elevation.

WWW 3.3.2.2 Do This: Drawing with Thickness and Elevation

I. Be sure you are still in the *My Stick House.dwg* file in the C:\Steps3D\Lesson03 folder. If not, open it now.

II. Follow these steps:

TOOLS	COMMAND SEQUENCE	STEPS
No Button Available	**Command:** *elev* **Specify new default elevation <0.0000>:** 2 **Specify new default thickness <0.0000>:** *1.299*	**1.** Set the **Elevation** to 2 and the **Thickness** system variable to ***1.299***.

continued

TOOLS	COMMAND SEQUENCE	STEPS

Command: *l*

Specify first point: *6.75,2*

Specify next point or [Undo]: *8.25,2*

Specify next point or [Undo]: *[enter]*

2. Draw a line as indicated. Notice that, although no Z-axis location is given, AutoCAD assumes an elevation of 2.

Command: *th*

Enter new value for THICKNESS <1.2990>: *0*

3. Reset the **Thickness** to ***0***.

Command: *l*

4. Draw the roof as shown in Figure 3.3.2.2.4.

FIG. 3.3.2.2.4 Roof and Walls

Properties Button

Command: *props*

5. And now let's use the Property Manager to modify the roof locator to make it the peak line of the roof. Select the roof locator line and then enter the ***Properties*** command.

Geometry	
Start X	6.7500
Start Y	2.0000
Start Z	2.0000
End X	8.2500
End Y	2.0000
End Z	2.0000
Delta X	1.5000
Delta Y	0.0000
Delta Z	0.0000
Length	1.5000
Angle	0

6. In the **Geometry** section of the Properties Manager, pick on **Start Z**. Notice that a **Pick** button appears to the right.

continued

TOOLS	COMMAND SEQUENCE	STEPS
		**7.** Pick on the **Pick** button. AutoCAD highlights that location and allows you to redefine it by picking another point on the screen. Using the **Endpoint** OSNAP, pick the upper point of that same line (the western point of the roof peak).
		8. Repeat Steps 6 and 7 to relocate the **End Z** point. Your drawing looks like Figure 3.3.2.2.8.

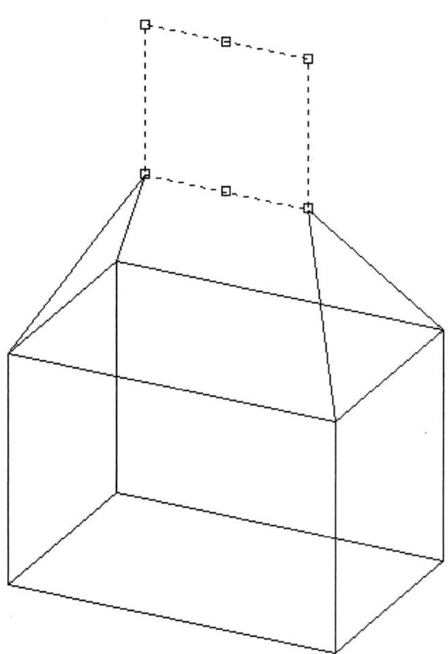

FIG. 3.3.2.2.8 Relocated Roof Locator

continued

TOOLS	COMMAND SEQUENCE	STEPS
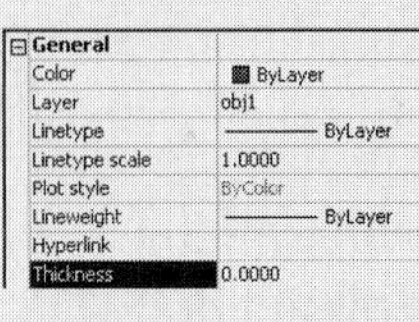		**9.** Now change the thickness of the line to ***0***. The **Thickness** property is located in the **General** section of the Property Manager. Clear the grips. Your drawing now looks like Figure 3.3.2.2.9. 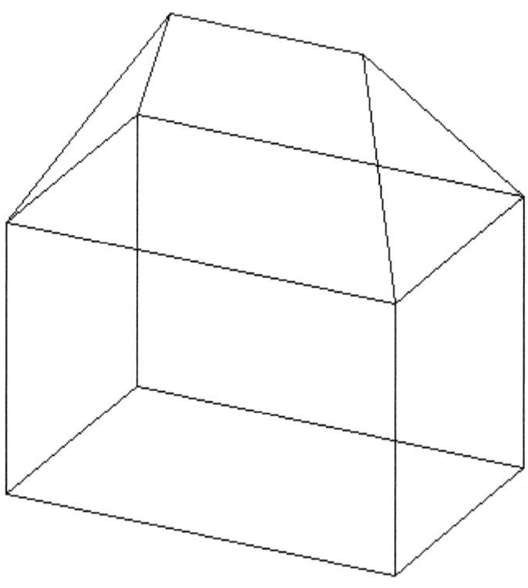 **FIG. 3.3.2.2.9** Completed Drawing
	**Command:** *qsave*	**10.** Save the drawing.

Do the two houses look the same? They should. But don't let that fool you. There are subtle (and remarkable) differences. We will look at those in a few moments. First, let me list some things to remember about drawing with thickness and elevation.

- Always remember to reset **Thickness** and **Elevation** to zero when you have finished drawing an object. Otherwise, you may have to redo the next object when it is drawn with incorrect properties.
- Use the Object Properties Manager to change the thickness and elevation of drawn objects.
- The user can enter positive or negative values for **Elevation** and **Thickness**.
- Closed objects behave differently from opened objects when drawn with thickness. We will see this in our next section.

3.4 Three-Dimensional Viewing Made Easy

Have you tried to view your houses from different viewpoints yet? Is it difficult to tell up from down in your drawing? Look back at Figures 3.1a and 3.1b. Remember how we needed the UCS icon to tell where we were?

Our next two commands will help us to see our drawings more clearly. The first—***Hide***—is simple and fast. The second—***Shademode***—is slower but more colorful.

3.4.1 The Hide Command

The ***Hide*** command removes "hidden" lines. That is, it removes lines that will normally not be seen because they are behind other objects in the drawing. (It does not remove lines drawn with the **Hidden** line type.) It looks like this:

Command: ***hide***
Regenerating model.

It is just that simple. But the results are like a light in a dark tunnel. Give it a try in your *My Stick House* drawing. Your drawing will look like Figures 3.4.1a and 3.4.1b. Notice the difference between the two houses. The first (western) is unaffected by the command. This house was drawn with lines only (like the little piggy's house that was made of sticks). There is nothing to hide behind. The second (eastern) house, however, looks quite different. This house has solid walls (like the little piggy's brick house) with a stick roof. You used lines with *thickness*—or three-dimensional objects—to draw the walls.

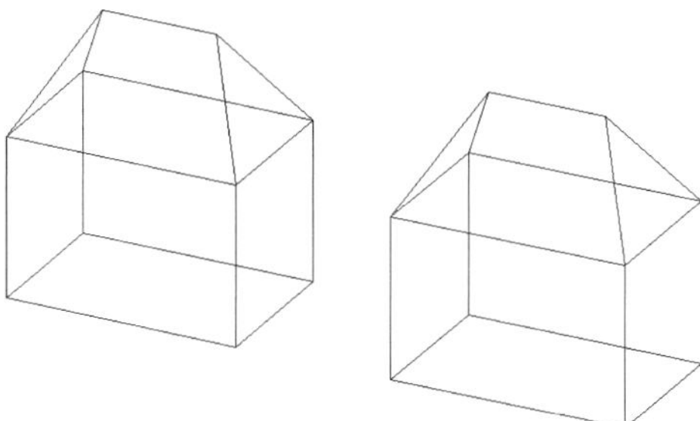

FIG. 3.4.1a Before the ***Hide*** Command

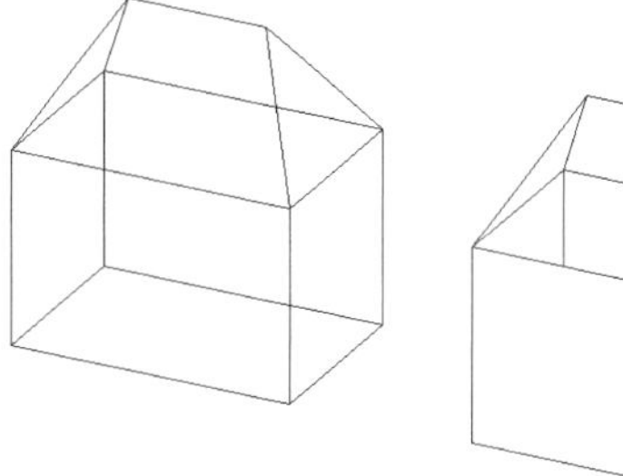

FIG. 3.4.1b After the ***Hide*** Command

You can change the viewpoint (and use modifying tools such as **Move** and **Copy**) while hidden lines are removed, but the commands will cause hidden lines to be visible again. Repeat the ***Hide*** command after the modifying procedure or change in view to again remove hidden lines. Try using the ***Hide*** command from different viewpoints.

To restore all hidden lines to view, regenerate the drawing (use the ***Regen*** command).

This might be a good time to examine how thickness affects closed objects.

3.4.1.1 Do This: Thickness and Closed Objects

I. Open the *Closed Objects.dwg* file in the C:\Steps3D\Lesson03 folder. The drawing looks like Figure 3.4.1.1a. (Each object has been drawn with a thickness of ***1***.)

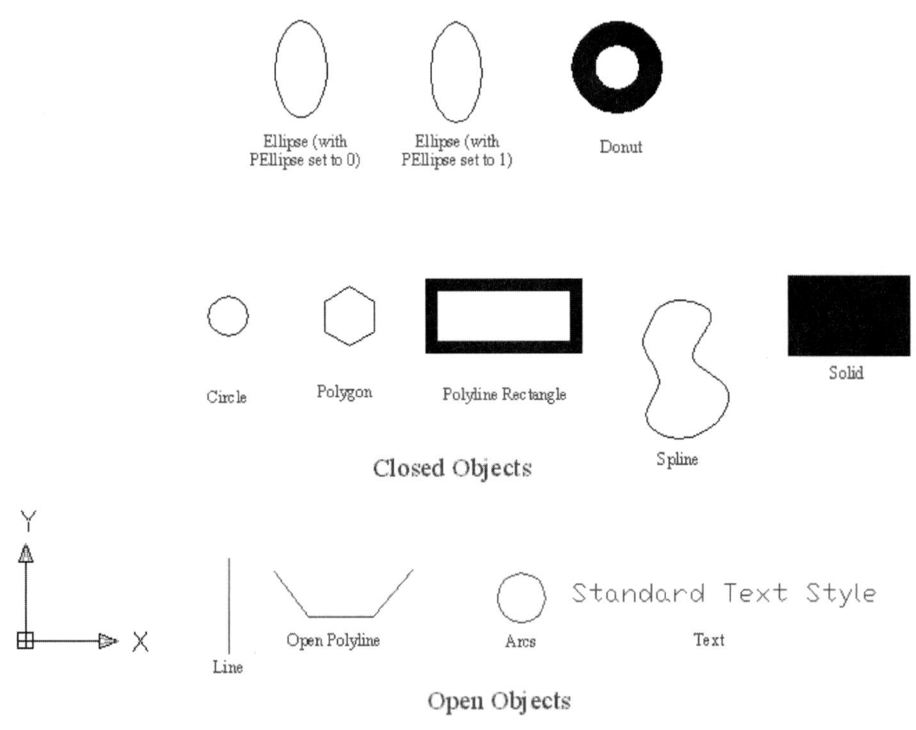

FIG. 3.4.1.1a *Closed Objects.dwg*

II. Follow these steps:

TOOLS	COMMAND SEQUENCE	STEPS
	**Command:** ***−vp***	**1.** Set the viewpoint to 1,−1,1.
No Button Available	**Command:** ***hide***	**2.** Enter the ***Hide*** command at the command line or select **Hide** from the **View** pull-down menu. Your drawing looks like Figure 3.4.1.1.2.

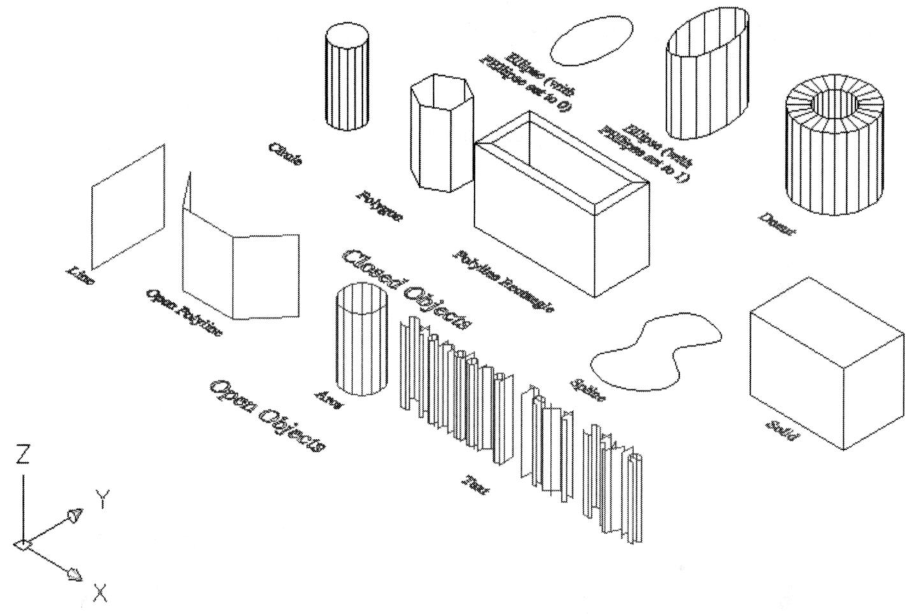

FIG. 3.4.1.1.2 Hidden Lines

Let's consider each item.

- Closed objects:
  - **Circles** become cylinders with solid cores.
  - **Polygons** and **Closed Polylines** contain length, width, and height as shown, but the area enclosed by the polyline is unaffected by thickness.
  - **Splines** cannot contain thickness.
  - **Solids** become solid blocks.
  - **Ellipses** drawn with the **Pellipse** system variable set to 0 cannot contain thickness.
  - **Ellipses** drawn with the **Pellipse** system variable set to 1 behave like polylines.
  - **Donuts** behave like polylines.
- **Open objects:**
  - **Lines** contain length, width, and height as shown.
  - **Open Polylines** contain length, width, and height as shown.

- **Arcs** contain length, width, and height. Closed arcs (shown here) look like circles but have no solid core. Use these to create ***holes.***
- AutoCAD standard text contains length, width, and height as shown. Notice, however, that the callouts (drawn using a true-type font) cannot contain thickness.

3.4.2 The Shademode Command

AutoCAD revamped the ***Shade*** command considerably for AutoCAD 2000. In fact, it received a new name—***Shademode***—and became quite easy to use.

So what is ***Shademode*** (or ***Shade***)?

Well, where the ***Hide*** command served to remove hidden lines and make it easier for the user to tell up from down in a drawing, the ***Shademode*** command actually fills in a solid object or three-dimensional face and gives it more of a *real* appearance. Compare Figure 3.4.2a with Figure 3.4.1b (p. 123). Shading gives the model a fuller, more complete look.

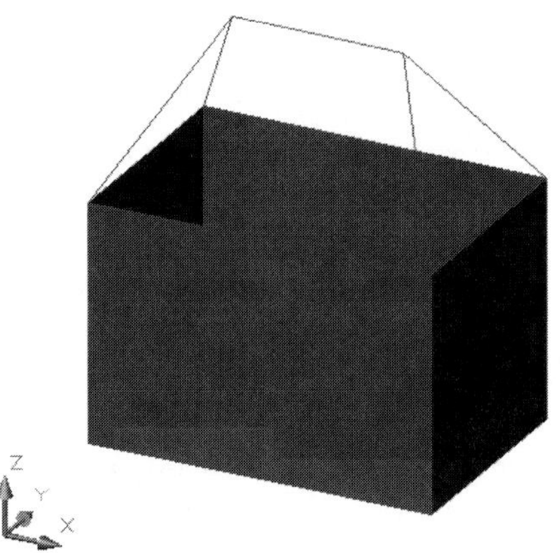

FIG. 3.4.2a Shaded House with Stick Roof

Notice that the UCS Icon has changed. This colorful tool is the Shademode icon. It provides directional information just as the UCS icon does, but its presence lets you know that you are in one of the Shademode options.

But the comparison with the ***Hide*** command does not end here. Whereas modification, regeneration, or changes in view will make hidden lines visible again, ***Shademode*** causes no such trauma to your model. Once active, Shademode will remain active until reset to **2D wireframe** by the user.

Some surfaces on a shaded model appear to have shadows. This helps distinguish one surface from another. The light source for this shadow comes from behind the user's left shoulder. We will discuss assigning other light sources in Lesson 13.

The *Shademode* command sequence looks like this:

Command: ***shademode***

Current mode: 2D wireframe

Enter option [2D wireframe/3D wireframe/Hidden/Flat/Gouraud/ fLat+edges/gOuraud+edges] <2D wireframe>: ***[enter your choice of shading modes]***

Let's look at each option.

- Remember the **2D wireframe** option! It is your ticket out of Shademode. Use it to clear any shading in the model and replace the Shademode icon with the UCS icon.
- At first, the **3D wireframe** option appears the same as the previous option. But the **3D wireframe** option will not display raster images, linetypes, and lineweights (the **2D wireframe** option will).
- The **Hidden** option is similar to the ***Hide*** command (it removes hidden lines). However, the line will remain hidden using this option, even during regeneration or modification. As with the **3D wireframe** option, raster images, linetypes, and lineweights will disappear when you activate the **Hidden** option.
- The **Flat** option shades the faces but does not show (or highlight) the edges. The appearance is like that resulting from a flat paint. Materials assigned to the object will show (more on materials in Lesson 13).
- **Gouraud** presents the best image of all. This option shades faces and smoothes edges for a more realistic appearance. Materials assigned to the object will show.
- The other two options—**fLat+edges** and **gOuraud+edges**—work the same as the **Flat** and **Gouraud** options except that edges will be highlighted.

The older ***Shade*** command is still available but provides no options. Using the ***Shade*** command is faster—much like the ***Hide*** command—and provides the same shading as the last, non-2D wireframe option of the ***Shademode*** command that you used.

Let's experiment.

Shademode options can also be accessed by (right-click) cursor menu once the ***Shademode*** has been entered. Or the user can select the option from the View pull-down menu. Follow the path:

View—Shade—[option]

WWW 3.4.2.1 Do This: Shading Objects

I. Reopen the *My Stick House.dwg* file in the C:\Steps3D\Lesson03 folder.

II. Zoom in around the house on the right (the one with the walls drawn with thickness).

III. Follow these steps:

TOOLS	COMMAND SEQUENCE	STEPS
	**Command:** *props*	**1.** Change the linetype of the rooflines to **Dashed**. (You will need to load the **Dashed** linetype first.) Your drawing looks like Figure 3.4.2.1.1. 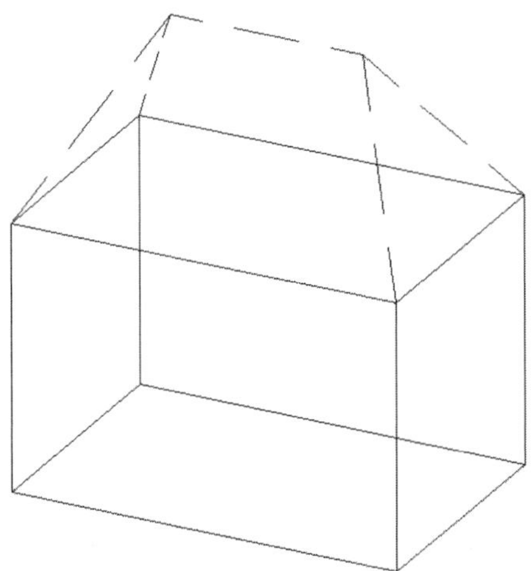 **FIG. 3.4.2.1.1** Changed Roof Lines
No Button Available	**Command:** *shademode*	**2.** Enter the ***Shademode*** command. There is no button or hotkey; however, there is a Shade toolbar that provides buttons for each of the ***Shademode*** options. (*Note:* It is not necessary to enter the command at the command line if you are going to use the buttons on the Shade toolbar.)

continued

TOOLS	COMMAND SEQUENCE	STEPS
 3D Wireframe Button (on the Shade Toolbar)	**Current mode: 2D wireframe** **Enter option [2D wireframe/ 3D wireframe/Hidden/Flat/Gouraud/ fLat+edges/gOuraud+edges] <2D wireframe>:** *3*	**3.** Tell AutoCAD you wish to use the **3D wireframe** option. The UCS icon changes to the Shademode icon and the hidden lines become solid (Figure 3.4.2.1.3).

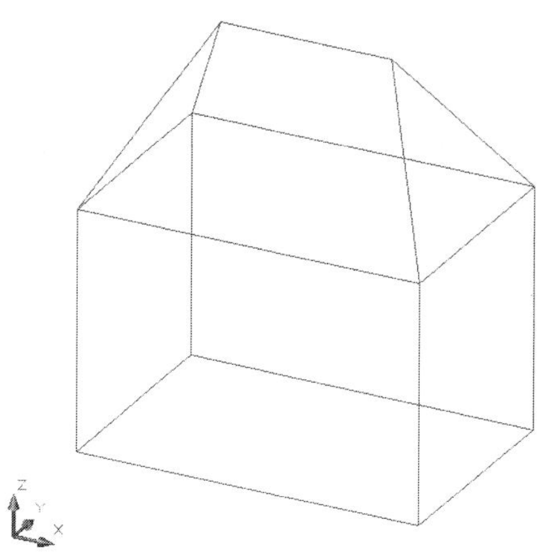

FIG. 3.4.2.1.3 3D Wireframe Shading

TOOLS	COMMAND SEQUENCE	STEPS
 Hidden Button	**Command:** *[enter]* **Current mode: 3D wireframe** **Enter option [2D wireframe/3D wireframe/Hidden/Flat/Gouraud/ fLat+edges/gOuraud+edges] <3D wireframe>:** *h*	**4.** Try the **Hidden** option. AutoCAD removes hidden lines (just as the ***Hide*** command did).

continued

TOOLS	COMMAND SEQUENCE	STEPS
 Flat Shaded Button	**Command:** *[enter]* **Current mode: Hidden** **Enter option [2D wireframe/3D wireframe/Hidden/Flat/Gouraud/ fLat+edges/gOuraud+edges] <Hidden>:** *f*	**5.** Now **Flat** shade the house. Your drawing looks like Figure 3.4.2.1.5. 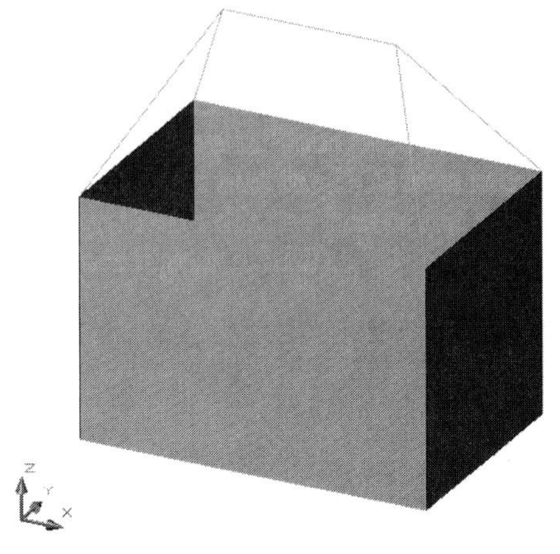 **FIG. 3.4.2.1.5** Flat Shading
 Flat Shaded Edges on Button	**Command:** *[enter]* **Current mode: Flat** **Enter option [2D wireframe/3D wireframe/Hidden/Flat/Gouraud/ fLat+edges/gOuraud+edges]<Flat>:** *l*	**6.** Compare the **fLat+edges** option (Figure 3.4.2.1.6) to the **Flat** option you used in Step 5. 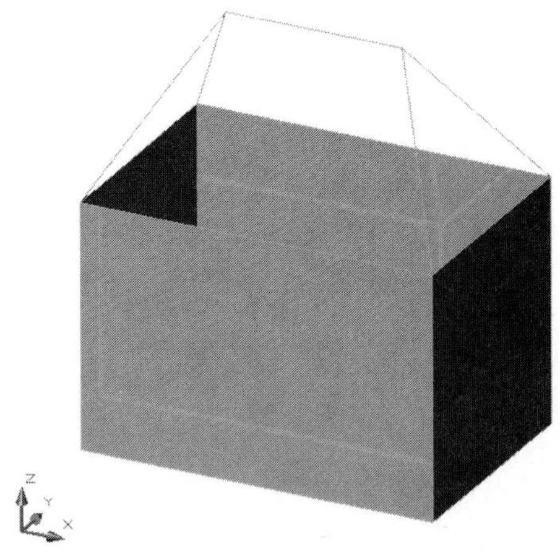 **FIG. 3.4.2.1.6** Flat Shading with Edges Shown

continued

TOOLS	COMMAND SEQUENCE	STEPS
		7. Return to the *Closed Objects.dwg* file.
 Gouraud Shaded Button	**Command:** ***shademode*** **Current mode: Flat+Edges** **Enter option [2D wireframe/3D wireframe/Hidden/Flat/Gouraud/ fLat+edges/gOuraud+edges] <Flat+Edges>:** ***g***	**8.** Now try the **Gouraud** option. Your drawing looks like Figure 3.4.2.1.8.

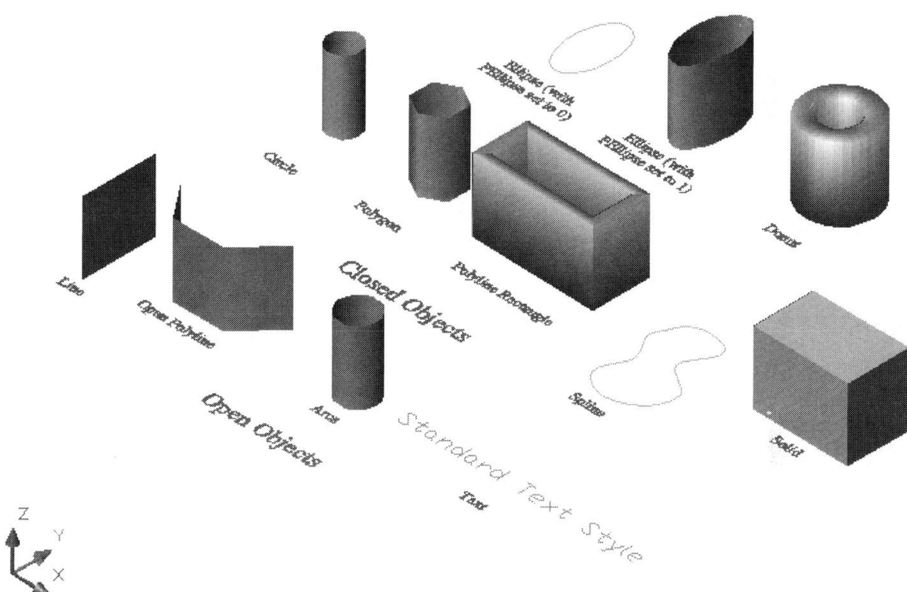

FIG. 3.4.2.1.8 Gouraud Shading

continued

TOOLS	COMMAND SEQUENCE	STEPS
 Gouraud Shaded Edges on Button	**Command:** *[enter]* **Current mode: Gouraud** **Enter option [2D wireframe/ 3D wireframe/Hidden/Flat/Gouraud/ fLat+edges/gOuraud+edges] <Gouraud>:** *o*	**9.** Compare the **gOuraud+edges** option (Figure 3.4.2.1.9) to the **Gouraud** option you used in Step 8.

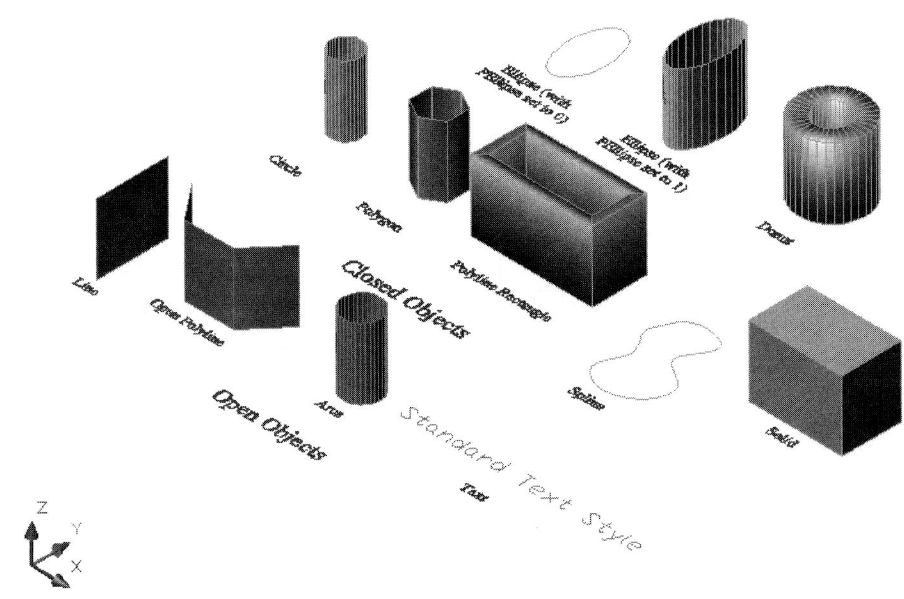

FIG. 3.4.2.1.9 Gouraud Shading with Edges Shown

TOOLS	COMMAND SEQUENCE	STEPS
 2D Wireframe Button	**Command:** *[enter]* **Current mode: Gouraud+Edges** **Enter option [2D wireframe/3D wireframe/Hidden/Flat/Gouraud/ fLat+edges/gOuraud+edges] <Gouraud+Edges>: 2**	**10.** Restore the drawing to a 2D wireframe and the Shademode icon to the UCS icon.
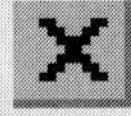	**Command:** *quit*	**11.** Exit both drawings without saving.

AutoCAD has hidden an extremely useful tool called **Display Order** in the Tools pull-down menu. When shading objects, occassionally one object may hide another (regardless of which is actually on top). Using the Display Order options (**Bring to Front, Send to Back, Bring Above Object, and Send Under Object**), the user can change the *display* of the objects without actually changing their positions. (For more on **Display Order**, see Section 24.2.3 of *AutoCAD 2002: One Step at a Time.*)

3.5 Extra Steps

Repeat all of Exercise 3.4.2.1 using the *Closed Objects.dwg* file in the C:\Steps3D\Lesson03 folder to see how shading affects the different objects. View each Shademode option from at least five different viewpoints.

Open some of the three-dimensional sample files that ship with AutoCAD (look in the \Sample subfolder of the Acad2002 folder). Practice your viewpoint manipulation and shading options. I recommend at least two of the following files: *Campus.dwg*, *EXPO Headquarters model.dwg*, *Truck model.dwg*, or *Watch.dwg*.

Plot a drawing or two using Paper Space and shading.

3.6 What Have We Learned?

Items covered in this lesson include:

- *The UCS Icon and the Right-Hand Rule*
- *Adjusting the user's view of the model*
  - *Isometric view*
  - *Dimetric views*
  - *Trimetric views*
  - *Plan view*
  - *Coordinate approach*
  - *Compass and tripod approaches*
  - *Dialog box approach*
- *Coordinates in a three-dimensional drawing*
  - *Cartesian Coordinate entry*
  - *Spherical and Cylindrical Coordinate entry*
- *Commands:*
  - ***Ucsicon***
  - ***VPoint***
  - ***DDVPoint***
  - ***Thickness***
  - ***Elevation***
  - ***Elev***
  - ***Hide***
  - ***Shade and Shademode***

What a list! Stop and catch your breath.

We covered a tremendous amount of new material in this lesson. But it is all fundamental to three-dimensional drafting. After some practice, you will find this material as easy as two-dimensional work.

I must caution you, however, about just how *fundamental* this material is. You must achieve at least a small degree of expertise with these methods and those in Lesson 4 to be able to function effectively in Z-Space. But that is the benefit of a good textbook! You can repeat the lesson(s) until you are comfortable.

We have seen how to maneuver around a three-dimensional model, how to improve our view for better navigation (and aesthetics), and some fundamentals of creating three-dimensional objects. But there is much more to consider! How do I draw a three-dimensional object at an angle—such as creating a solid roof instead of the stick figure outline on our stick house? Is there an easier way to rotate our viewpoint in Z-Space for a better view?

We will continue our study of Z-Basics in Lesson 4 where we will answer some of these questions (and present some others). But, first, we should practice what we have learned so far.

3.7 EXERCISES

1. **through 8.** Create the "w" drawings in Appendix B. (Refer to the "su" drawings for a clearer image.) Follow these guidelines.
   - **1.1.** Do not try to create the dimensions yet.
   - **1.2.** Start each drawing from scratch and use the default settings.
   - **1.3.** Adjust the viewpoint as needed to help your drawing.
   - **1.4.** Save each drawing as *My [title].dwg* (as in: *MyB−1w.dwg*) in the C:\Steps3D\Lesson03 folder.
9. Create the drawing in Figure 3.7.9 according to the following parameters:
   - **9.1.** Start the drawing from scratch and use the default settings.
   - **9.2.** Set the viewpoint to 8.5,11,5.75.
   - **9.3.** Do not attempt to draw the dimensions yet.
   - **9.4.** Use a thickness setting of ***0***.
   - **9.5.** The depth of the piece is $\frac{1}{2}$".
   - **9.6.** Save the drawing as *My Twisted Y.dwg* in the C:\Steps3D\Lesson03 folder.

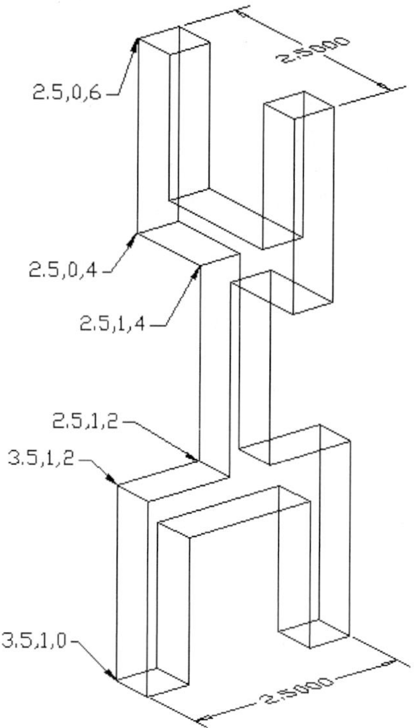

FIG. 3.7.9 My Twisted Y

10. Create the drawing in Figure 3.7.10 according to the following parameters:
    10.1. Start the drawing from scratch and use the default settings.
    10.2. Do not attempt to draw the dimensions yet.
    10.3. Text is in Paper Space and is $\frac{3}{16}''$ and $\frac{1}{8}''$.
    10.4. Title block text is $\frac{1}{4}''$, $\frac{3}{16}''$, and $\frac{1}{8}''$.
    10.5. The viewpoint for each viewport is indicated.
    10.6. Use lines with thickness.
    10.7. Use the ***Hide*** command to achieve the dimetric view.
    10.8. Save the drawing as *My Block.dwg* in the C:\Steps3D\Lesson03 folder.

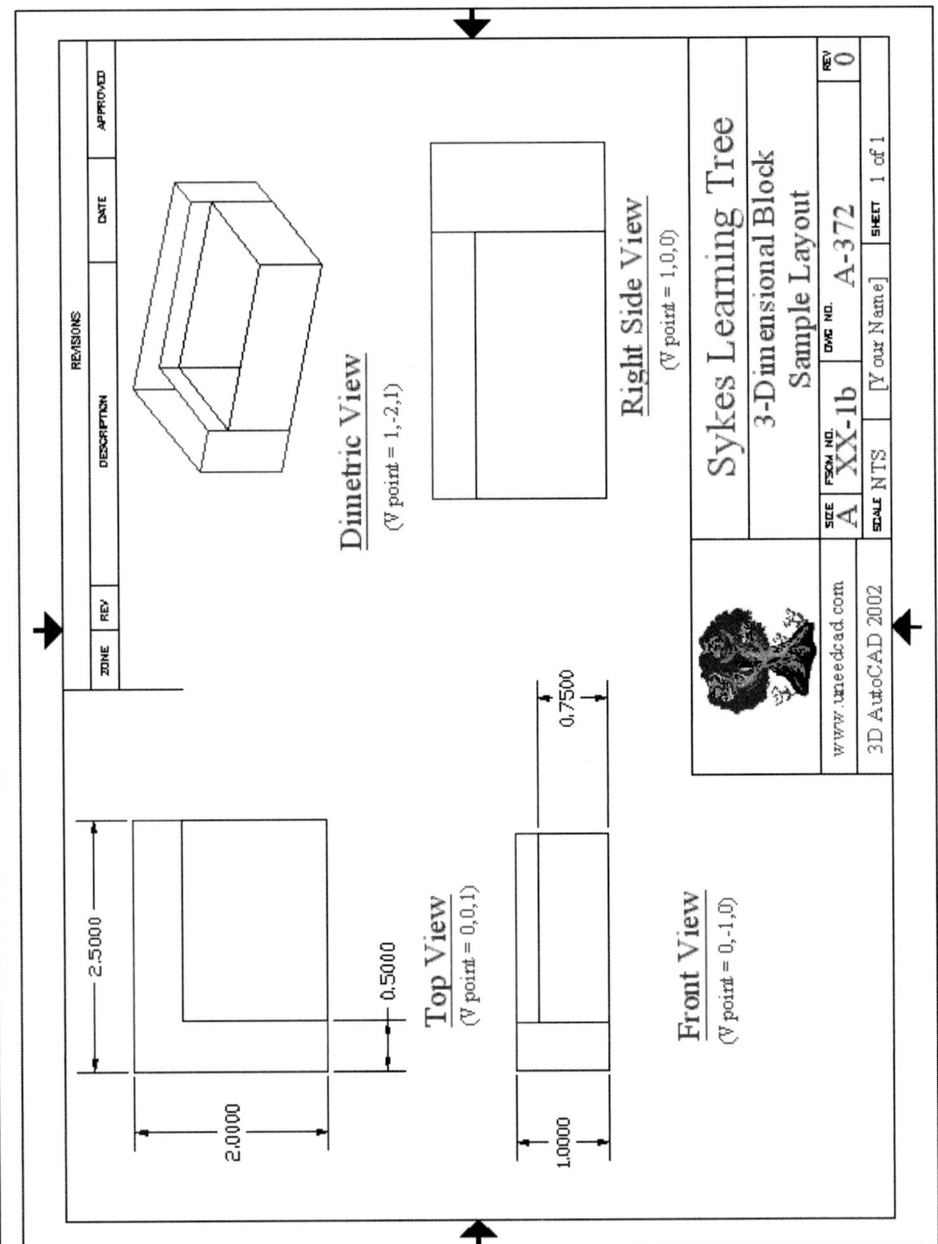

FIG. 3.7.10 Three-Dimensional Block

11. Create the drawing in Figure 3.7.11 according to the following parameters:

- **11.1.** Start the drawing from scratch and use the default settings.
- **11.2.** Use polylines with $\frac{1}{16}$″ width for everything except the handle.
- **11.3.** Use a thickness of $\frac{1}{16}$″ for all objects.
- **11.4.** I used a scale of 1:4 in the plan and elevation views but no scale in the isometric.
- **11.5.** Do not attempt to draw the dimensions yet.
- **11.6.** Use the *Logo-mini.gif* file in the title block as shown.

11.7. Text is in Paper Space and is $\frac{3}{16}''$ and $\frac{1}{8}''$.

11.8. Title block text is $\frac{1}{4}''$, $\frac{3}{16}''$, and $\frac{1}{8}''$.

11.9. Save the drawing as *MyGrill.dwg* in the C:\Steps3D\Lesson03 folder.

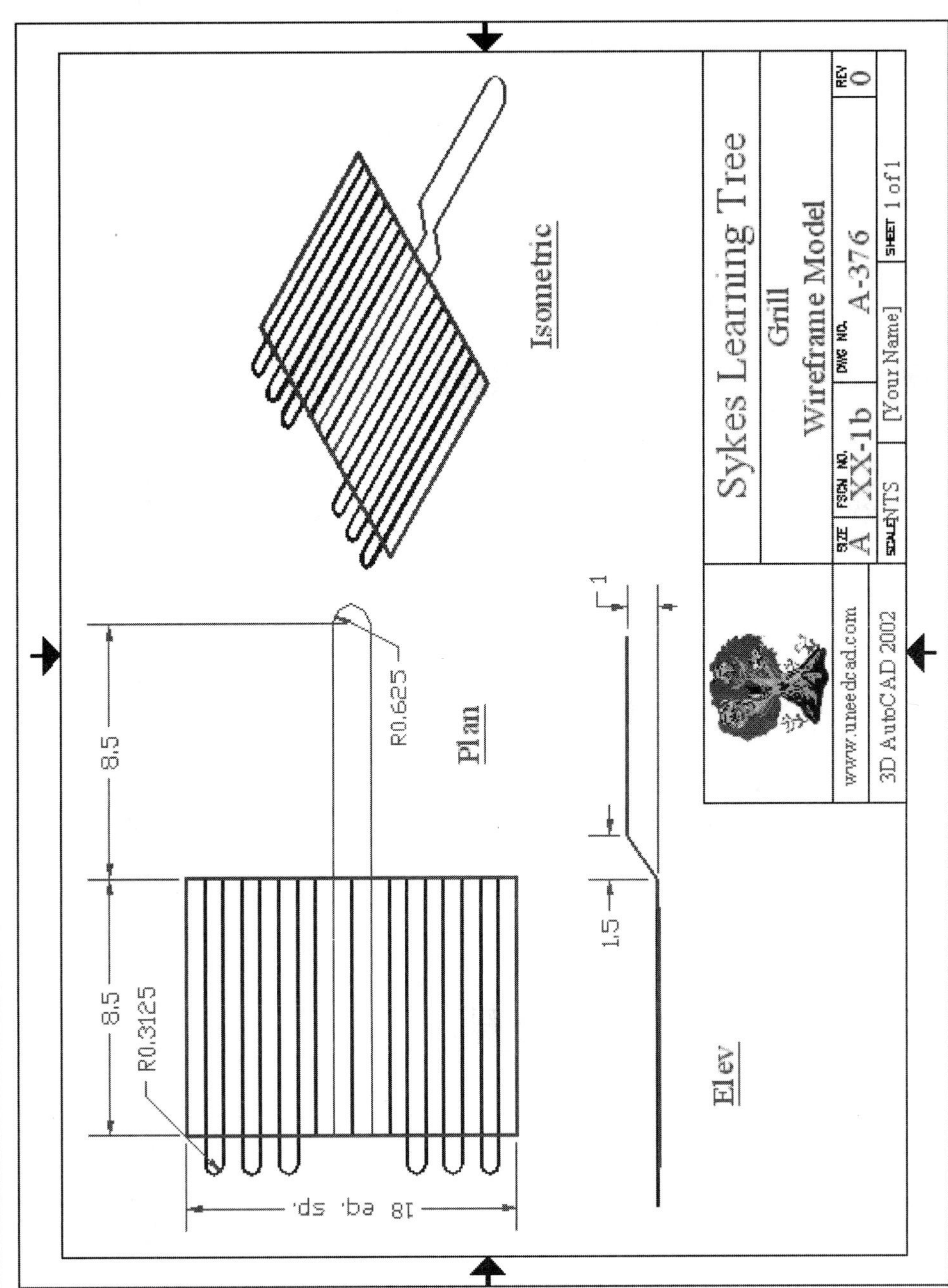

FIG. 3.7.11 *Grill*

12. Create the drawing in Figure 3.7.12 according to the following parameters:

12.1. Start the drawing from scratch and use the default settings.

12.2. I used a scale of 1:2 for all views.

12.3. Do not attempt to draw the dimensions yet.

12.4. Text is in Paper Space and is $\frac{3}{16}$" and $\frac{1}{8}$".
12.5. Title block text is $\frac{1}{4}$", $\frac{3}{16}$", and $\frac{1}{8}$".
12.6. You will find it easier to fillet the corners rather than drawing arcs.
12.7. Use the *Logo-mini.gif* file in the title block as shown.
12.8. Save the drawing as *MyBookEnd.dwg* in the C:\Steps3D\Lesson03 folder.

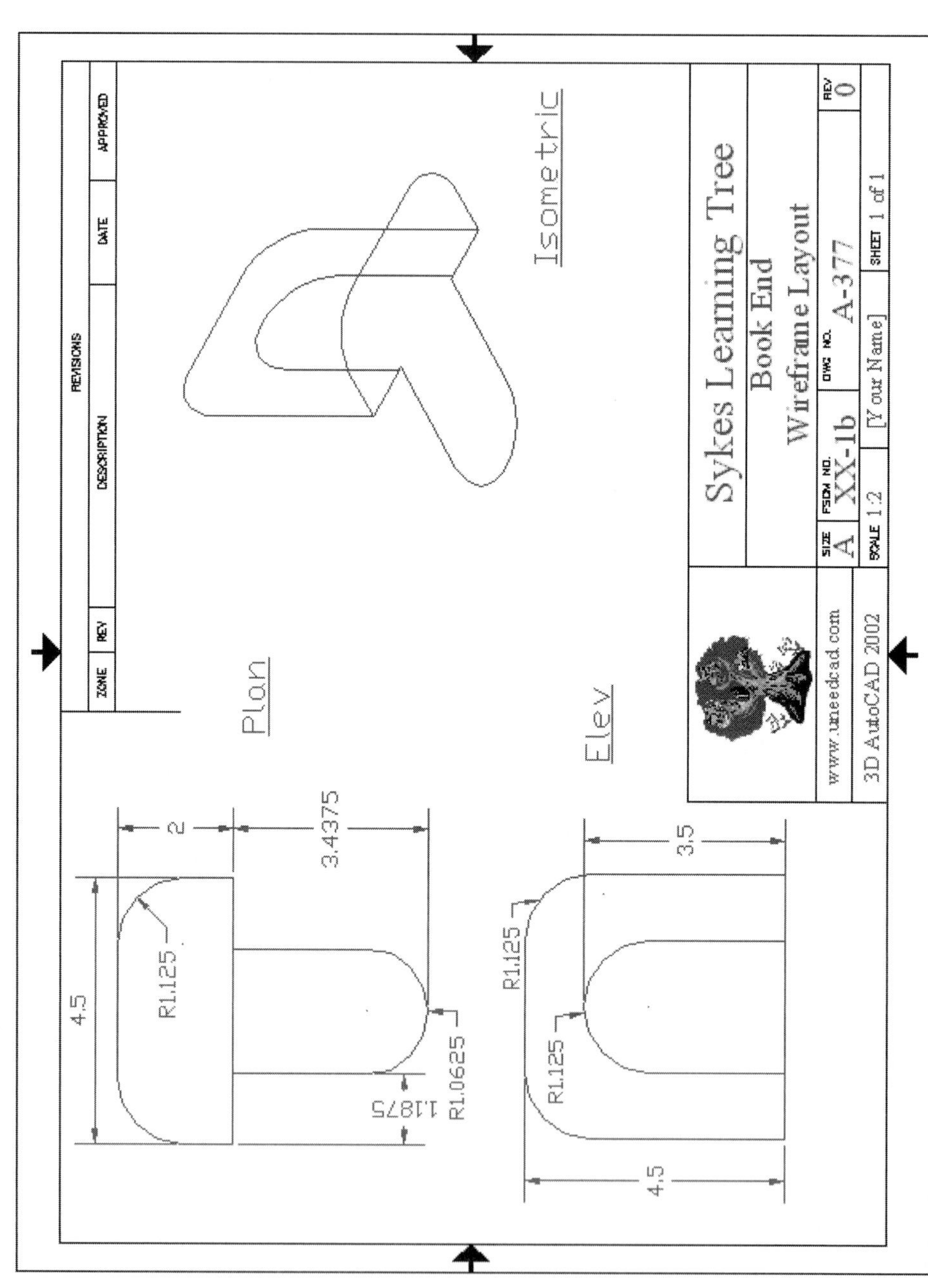

FIG. 3.7.12 Book End

13. Create the drawing in Figure 3.7.13 according to the following parameters:
    13.1. Start the drawing from scratch and use the default settings.
    13.2. Use 0.6-mm lineweights for all lines.
    13.3. Do not attempt to draw the dimensions yet.
    13.4. Text is in Paper Space and is $\frac{3}{16}''$ and $\frac{1}{8}''$.
    13.5. Title block text is $\frac{1}{4}''$, $\frac{3}{16}''$, and $\frac{1}{8}''$.
    13.6. I used $\frac{1}{2}''$-diameter circles with $\frac{1}{2}''$ thickness for the legs.
    13.7. Save the drawing as *MyMagRack.dwg* in the C:\Steps3D\Lesson03 folder.

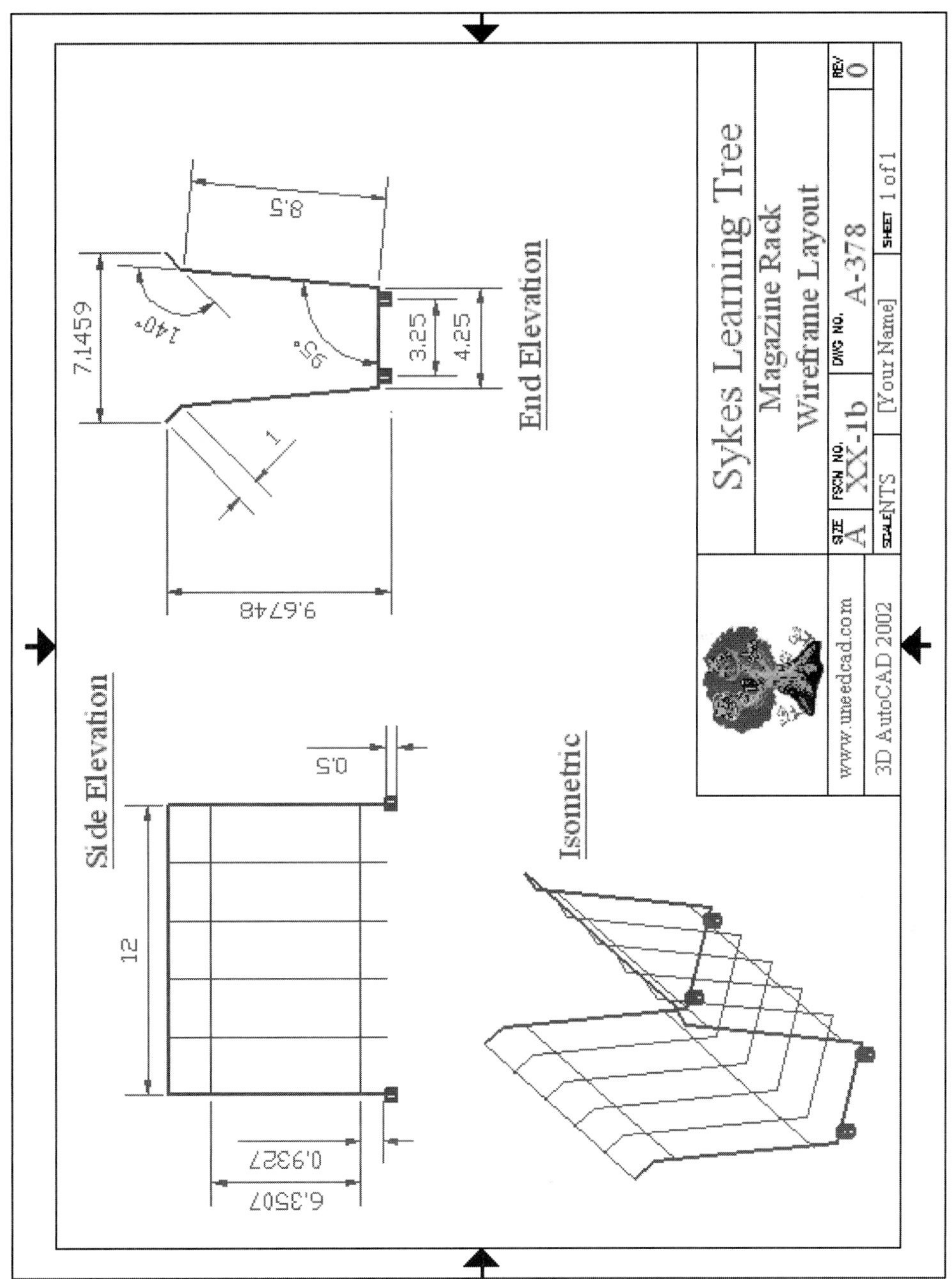

FIG. 3.7.13 Magazine Rack

14. Create the drawing in Figure 3.7.14 according to the following parameters:

14.1. Start the drawing from scratch and use the default settings.

14.2. Do not attempt to draw the dimensions yet.

14.3. Text is in Paper Space and is $\frac{3}{16}''$ and $\frac{1}{8}''$.

14.4. Title block text is $\frac{1}{4}''$, $\frac{3}{16}''$, and $\frac{1}{8}''$.

14.5. The viewpoint for each viewport is indicated.

14.6. Use lines without thickness except when drawing the slot.

14.7. Save the drawing as *My Anchor Stop.dwg* in the C:\Steps3D\Lesson03 folder.

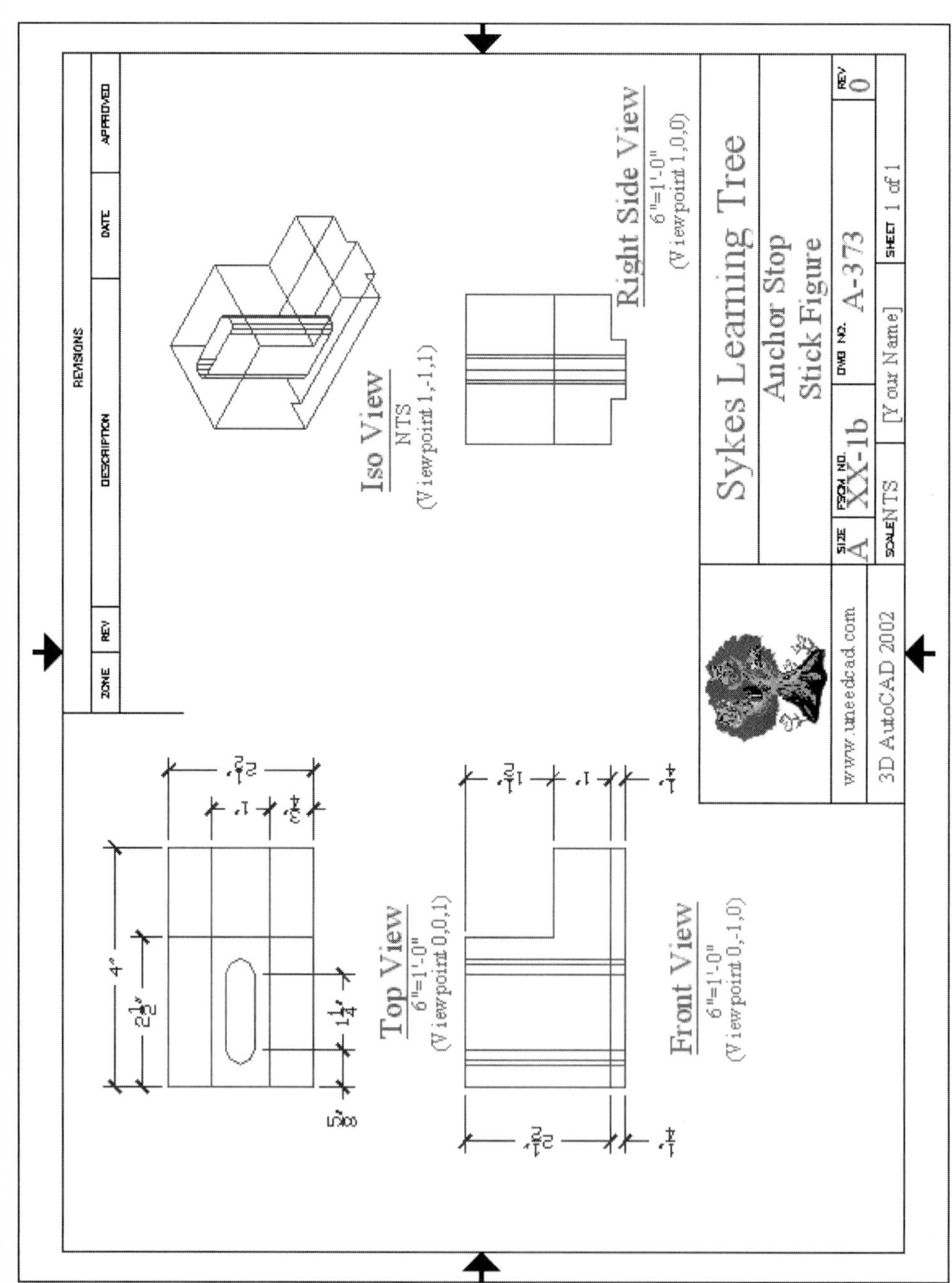

FIG. 3.7.14 Three-Anchor Stop

15. Create the drawing in Figure 3.7.15 according to the following parameters:

- **15.1.** Start the drawing using the *template #1* template file found in the C:\Steps3D\Lesson03 folder.
- **15.2.** Do not attempt to draw the dimensions yet.
- **15.3.** Text is in Paper Space and is $\frac{3}{16}''$ and $\frac{1}{8}''$.
- **15.4.** Title block text is $\frac{1}{4}''$, $\frac{3}{16}''$, and $\frac{1}{8}''$.
- **15.5.** The crown is made up of solids drawn with thickness.
- **15.6.** The round pieces are donuts drawn with thickness.
- **15.7.** The dimetric view has been Gouraud shaded.
- **15.8.** Save the drawing as *My Queen.dwg* in the C:\Steps3D\Lesson03 folder.

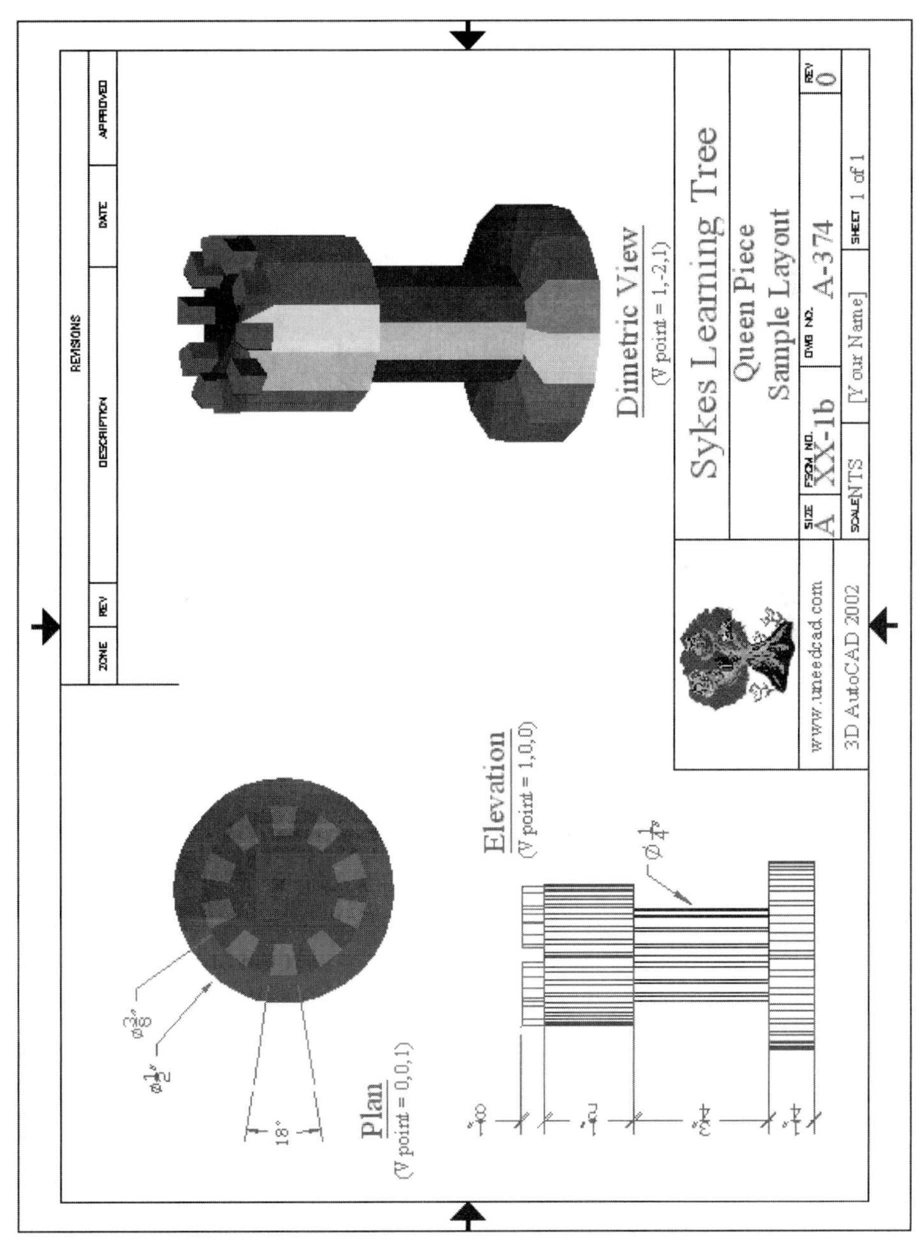

FIG. 3.7.15 *Queen Piece*

16. Create the drawing in Figure 3.7.16 according to the following parameters:
    - **16.1.** Start the drawing using the *template #1* template file found in the C:\Steps3D\Lesson03 folder.
    - **16.2.** Do not attempt to draw the dimensions yet.
    - **16.3.** Text is in Paper Space and is $\frac{3}{16}$″ and $\frac{1}{8}$″.
    - **16.4.** Title block text is $\frac{1}{4}$″, $\frac{3}{16}$″, and $\frac{1}{8}$″.
    - **16.5.** Polylines have a width of $\frac{1}{16}$″.
    - **16.6.** Anchors are donuts with an outer diameter of $\frac{9}{16}$″ and an inner diameter of $\frac{3}{16}$″.
    - **16.7.** The washer is a donut with an outer diameter of 1″ and an inner diameter of $\frac{1}{4}$″; its thickness is $\frac{1}{16}$″.
    - **16.8.** The nut is a six-sided polygon inscribed in a radius of $\frac{1}{4}$″; its width is $\frac{1}{16}$″.
    - **16.9.** The isometric view has been Gouraud shaded.
    - **16.10.** Save the drawing as *My Ring Stand.dwg* in the C:\Steps3D\Lesson03 folder.

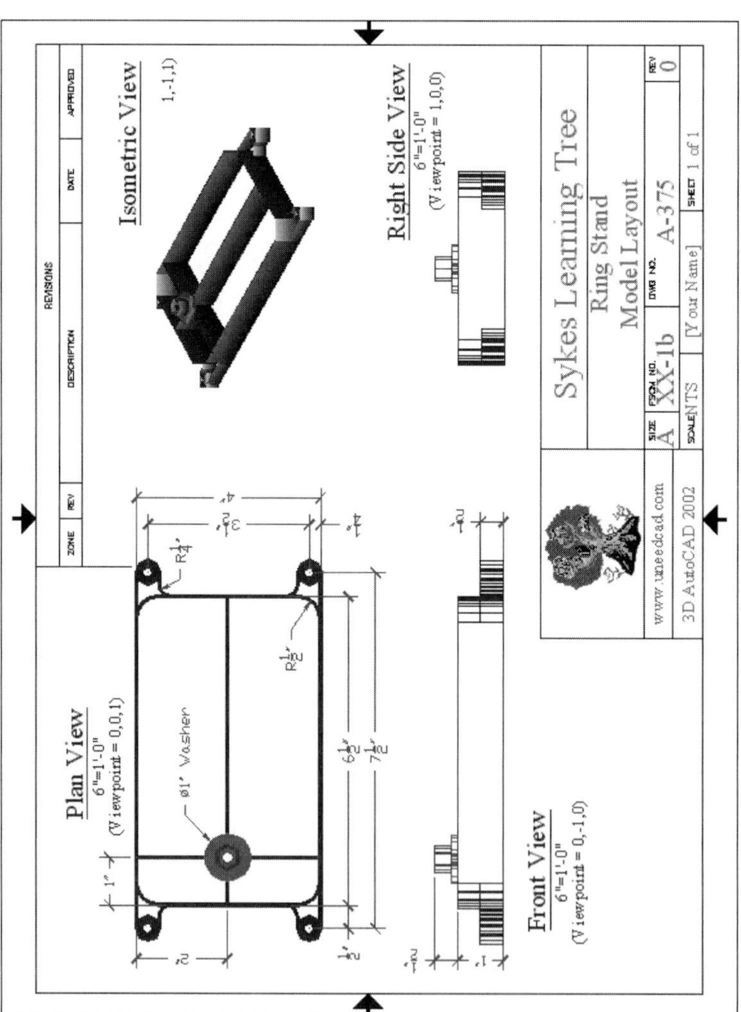

FIG. 3.7.16 Ring Stand

3.8 REVIEW QUESTIONS

Please write your answers on a separate sheet of paper.

1. Who was Mr. Woopie?

2. __________ refers to the area above and below a drawing board.

3. Use the __________ icon to help determine where you are in a three-dimensional drawing.

4 and 5. Use the __________ option of the __________ command to require the UCS icon to remain at the 0,0,0 coordinate regardless of the display.

6. To turn the UCS icon off in all viewports, you must first select the __________ option of the UCSIcon command.

7. Use the __________ as you would use the UCS icon to identify the location of the X-,Y-, and Z-axes.

8. Use the __________ command to change your positional view of the model.

9. An __________ view is when the absolute value of the all three axes is the same.

10. What type of view results from a viewpoint ratio of 1,−2,1?

11. What is the viewpoint ratio in a plan view?

12. Write the coordinate ratio for a rear elevation.

13. AutoCAD lets you know when you are in an elevation view by changing the UCS icon to a __________.

14. through 16. List three ways to reset the viewpoint.

17. When resetting your viewpoint, the __________ provides a visual representation of your view.

18. Use the __________ command to return to a viewpoint of 0,0,1 (a plan view) from anywhere in Z-Space.

19. Write the formula for entering spherical coordinates.

20. Write the formula for entering cylindrical coordinates.

21. through 31. Identify *X, Y,* and *Z* as + or − in Figure 3.8.21. Identify the poles and equators as well.

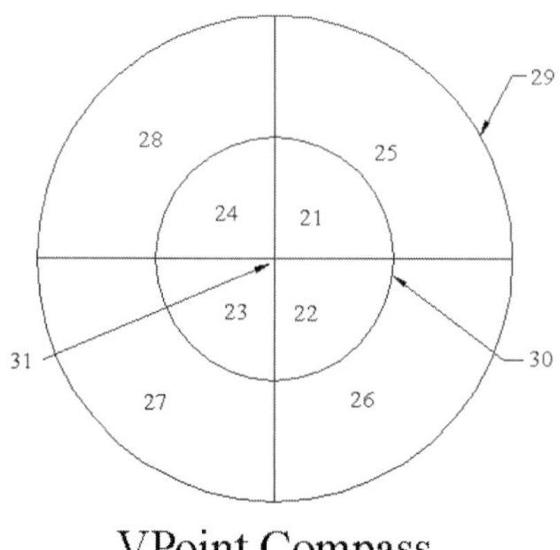

FIG. 3.8.21 *VPoint Compass*

32. (T or F) Ortho works only on the XY-plane.

33. (T or F) Object and Polar Tracking work only on the XY-plane.

34. (T or F) OSNAPs work only on the XY-plane.

35. __________ is that property of an object that takes it from stick figure to model object.

36. The __________ enables the user to set the thickness and elevation system variables at one time.

37. Use the CHProp command or the __________ manager to change the thickness or elevation of an existing object.

38. (T or F) The Hide command removes lines drawn using the hidden line type.

39. The __________ command fills in a solid object and gives it a real appearance.

40. By default, the light source in a shaded model comes from __________.

41. Use the __________ option of the Shademode command to clear any shading in the model.

LESSON 4

More of Z Basics

Following this lesson, you will

- ➥ Understand the differences between the UCS and the WCS
  - Know how to use the ***UCS*** command to create working planes
  - Know how to use the UCS Manager
  - Know how to dimension a three-dimensional drawing
- ➥ Be familiar with some advanced viewing techniques
  - Be able to use the ***3DOrbit*** and ***3DCOrbit*** commands
  - Be able to use the ***3DPan*** and ***3DZoom*** commands

When we first drew our three-dimensional stick figure house, it had no walls and only sticks for a roof. Later we saw that, by using the *Thickness* and *Elevation* system variables, we could make our walls solid. But what about the roof? There must be an AutoCAD tool for making it solid as well.

We also discussed the need for point entry precision in Z-Space. What about text and dimensions? Must we use coordinates to place them? (Have you tried to dimension a three-dimensional drawing yet?) And what if I want to place text along a slope (like the roof)?

Believe it or not, all of these questions have the same answer! The answer is a tool called the User Coordinate System—the UCS.

In Lesson 3, you learned how to create simple three-dimensional objects and how to view those objects from different angles. In Lesson 4, we will discuss the tools with which you will work on the different faces of your three-dimensional objects. Then we will look at some more advanced viewing tools.

Let's begin with the UCS.

4.1 WCS vs. UCS

Although you may not be aware of it, you are already familiar with the UCS. You have been using it since you began your study of AutoCAD. However, it has always been aligned with the World Coordinate System—the WCS—so you never noticed it. So what is the difference? You need to understand a little about how AutoCAD works to really understand the UCS.

In the basic text, we learned that all objects in an AutoCAD drawing are defined by information stored in that drawing's *database.* When you regenerate a drawing, AutoCAD reads this information and restores the drawing accordingly. When you create an attributed block, the attribute information is also stored in the database.

Part of the information stored in a drawing's database are the location and orientation of each object. For consistency (and to avoid a programming nightmare), AutoCAD developed a coordinate system that remains the same throughout the life of the drawing. Thus, the definition of point 0,0,0 will remain the same, and the point will always be in the same place. The X, Y, and Z directions will never change. This coordinate system is the WCS.

> To avoid any chance of damage to the WCS, AutoCAD placed it out of reach to the AutoCAD user.

AutoCAD uses the WCS point 0,0,0 much as a mariner uses the North Star. Unchanging in the night sky, Polaris shows the sailor the way home. Unchanging in the WCS, point 0,0,0 shows AutoCAD how to orient any object in the drawing.

The User Coordinate System—or UCS—is what the CAD operator uses to determine up from down and left from right for the immediate task at hand. Until now, the UCS has always been aligned with the WCS—our mariner's ship has always been pointed toward the North Star. Until now, the front of our ship has always been north; the masts have always pointed upward. With a compass, our sailor could find anything on the ship. Until now, we had only two dimensions with which to create a drawing—our sailor had only a single deck on which to work. Until now, the CAD operator had no need to know about the UCS or WCS. Until now . . .

Now our ship has changed directions and acquired new decks. Our sailor with the compass is completely lost. To make it easier for him to understand where things are on the ship, he must change his reference point from the North Star to something on the ship itself. This way, he can always find his way regardless of the direction in which the ship is sailing.

He will use the mainsail as his reference point (0,0,0). His compass directions will now reference points on the ship—the bow becomes north, the stern becomes south, starboard and port become east and west. The mainsail will always point upward from the main deck (regardless of how violently the sea rocks the ship). So now, using the North Star, our mariner's ship will never be lost, and using his new Mariner's Coordinate System, he will never be lost on the ship.

CAD operators must adjust for Z-Space as our mariner adjusted for a change in the ship's direction. Using the 0,0,0 coordinate of the WCS as our North Star, we can always find our way home. And using the User Coordinate System as our sailor used his Mariner's Coordinate System, we can work on any surface—or working plane—of a three-dimensional model (as our mariner could work on any deck of his ship).

So how do you use the UCS? Where do you begin?

Let's begin by accessing the ***UCS*** command. What do you suppose the command would be?

To keep it simple, AutoCAD called the command ***UCS***! The command-line approach looks like this:

Command: *ucs*

Current ucs name: *WORLD*

Enter an option [New/Move/orthoGraphic/Prev/Restore/Save/Del/Apply/?/World]
<World>: [*enter an option*]

Let's look at each option.

- The **New** option, of course, allows the user to create a new UCS—that is, the user can define a new 0,0,0 and new orientations for the X-, Y- and Z-axes. He can do this in one of several ways depending on the option he selects at the prompt:

  Specify origin of new UCS or [ZAxis/3point/OBject/Face/View/X/Y/Z] <0,0,0>:

  - Using the **ZAxis** option, the user defines the new UCS by identifying a location for 0,0,0 and then a point on the Z-axis.
  - The **3point** option allows the user to define the new UCS by identifying a location for 0,0,0 and then points on the X- and Y-axes.
  - The **OBject** option allows the user to define the new UCS by selecting an existing three-dimensional object. AutoCAD aligns the new UCS with that object.

- The **Face** option allows the user to define the new UCS by selecting a face on an existing three-dimensional solid object.
- The **View** option sets the UCS flat against the screen (the +X-axis parallel to the bottom of the screen and the +Y-axis parallel to the left side of the screen). The 0,0,0 coordinate remains where it is currently located.
- The **X/Y/Z** options allow the user to rotate the UCS around the selected axis. It prompts

  Specify rotation angle about X *[or* Y *or* Z*]* axis <90>:

- **Move** allows the user to move the UCS without changing its orientation. It prompts:

  Specify new origin point or [Zdepth]<0,0,0>:

  The user responds by picking a new origin point or typing **Z** for the **Zdepth** option. The **Zdepth** option allows the user to move the origin along the Z-axis.
- The **orthoGraphic** option is quite handy. It offers a quick way to change the UCS to one of the standard orthographic projections without moving 0,0,0 from the WCS location. It prompts

  Enter an option [Top/Bottom/Front/BAck/Left/Right]<Top>:

- **Prev**, of course, restores the previous UCS.
- **Save** allows the user to save a current UCS for later retrieval. **Restore** allows the user to restore a previously saved UCS.
- **Del** allows the user to delete a stored UCS.
- The **Apply** option allows the user to apply the current UCS setting to another viewport(s).
- The **World** option may be the most important. It tells AutoCAD to restore the UCS to match the WCS's orientation. In other words, when you get lost, use the **World** option to reorient yourself.

Most of this will become clearer with practice. Let's try a get-acquainted exercise.

AutoCAD provides several methods of accessing the ***UCS*** command and its options. Easiest, perhaps, is the **UCS** toolbar. But you can also access the options by right-click cursor menu once the ***UCS*** command has been entered or by selecting from the Tools pull-down menu.

4.1.1 Do This: Manipulating the UCS

I. Open the *ucs practice 4.dwg* in the C:\Steps3D\Lesson04 folder. The drawing looks like Figure 4.1.1a.

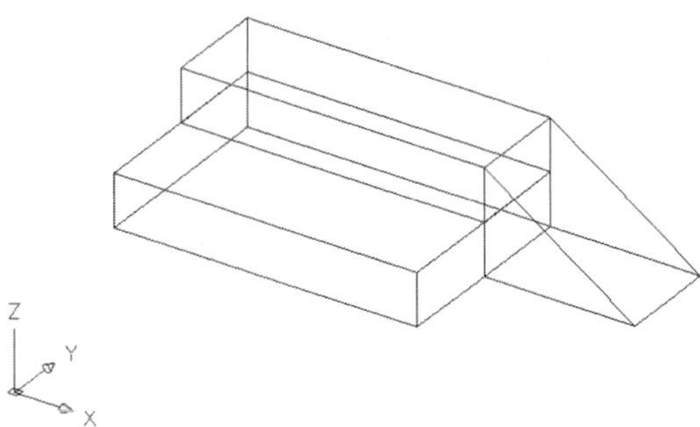

FIG. 4.1.1a UCS Practice 4.dwg

II. Follow these steps:

TOOLS	COMMAND SEQUENCE	STEPS
No Button Available	**Command:** *ucsicon* **Enter an option [ON/OFF/All/ Noorigin/ORigin/Properties] <ON>:** *or*	**1.** Our first step is one of the most important steps to remember when manipulating the UCS. Set the UCS icon to **ORigin.** This way, you will always know where 0,0,0 is.
UCS Button	**Command:** *ucs*	**2.** Now we will tell AutoCAD to use the UCS (our mariner must navigate *within* the ship). Enter the ***UCS*** command or pick the **UCS** button on the UCS toolbar.
Enter Cancel New Move orthoGraphic Prev Restore Save Del Apply ? World Pan Zoom	**Current ucs name: *WORLD*** **Enter an option [New/Move/ orthoGraphic/Prev/Restore/Save/ Del/Apply/?/World]<World>:** *n*	**3.** AutoCAD responds by asking what you would like to do. We will create a new UCS. Select the **New** option.
	Specify origin of new UCS or [ZAxis/ 3point/OBject/Face/View/X/Y/Z] <0,0,0>: *za*	**4.** Our first UCS will simply relocate 0,0,0. We will use the **ZAxis** option.

continued

TOOLS	COMMAND SEQUENCE	STEPS
	Specify new origin point <0,0,0>: **Specify point on positive portion of Z-axis <1.000,1.000,1.000>:** *[enter]*	**5.** Specify the bottom-left corner of the object and accept the default Z-axis point. Notice that the UCS icon moves as shown in Figure 4.1.1.5. It is locating 0,0,0 as we told it to do in Step 1. **FIG. 4.1.1.5** New UCS with 0,0,0 Located by the UCS Icon
	Command: *[enter]*	**6.** Now we will save this UCS for later retrieval. Repeat the ***UCS*** command.
	Current ucs name: *NO NAME* **Enter an option [New/Move/orthoGraphic/Prev/Restore/Save/Del/Apply/?/World]<World>:** *s*	**7.** Tell AutoCAD you wish to **Save** the UCS by typing *s* or by selecting **Save** on the cursor menu . . .
	Enter name to save current UCS or [?]: *lower left base*	**8.** . . . and call it something appropriate.

continued

TOOLS	COMMAND SEQUENCE	STEPS
	Command: *[enter]* **Current ucs name: *WORLD*** **Enter an option [New/Move/ orthoGraphic/Prev/Restore/Save/ Del/Apply/?/World]<World>:** *n*	**9.** Now let's create another UCS. Repeat the command and tell AutoCAD to create a new UCS.
3 Point UCS Button	**Specify origin of new UCS or [ZAxis/ 3point/OBject/Face/View/X/Y/Z] <0,0,0>:** *3*	**10.** This time we will use the **3point** method. (You can skip Step 9 by using the **3 Point UCS** button.)
	Specify new origin point <0,0,0>: *[select point 1]* **Specify point on positive portion of X-axis <1.0000,0.0000,0.0000>:** *[select point 2]* **Specify point on positive-Y portion of the UCS XY plane <0.0000,1.0000,0.0000>:** *[select point 3]*	**11.** Select the points indicated in Figure 4.1.1.11.

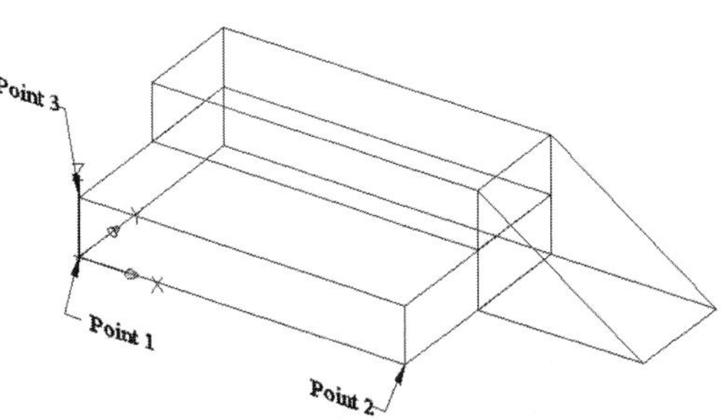

FIG. 4.1.1.11 Select These Points

12. The UCS icon now appears like Figure 4.1.1.12.

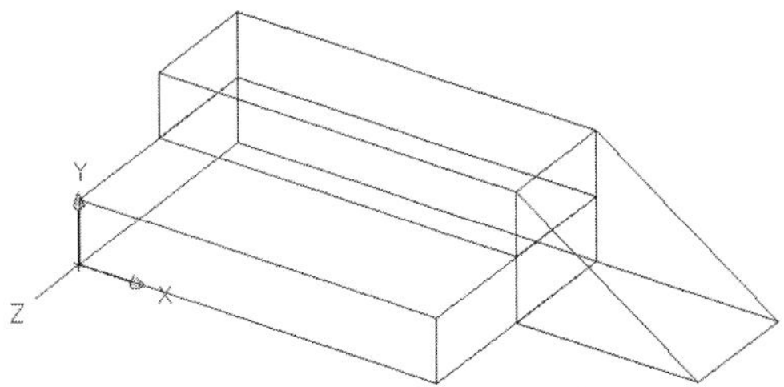

FIG. 4.1.1.12 New UCS

Before continuing, stop and ask yourself where the X-, Y-, and Z-axes are located. Use the UCS icon and the Right-Hand Rule to help answer that question.*

* The UCS Icon indicates the X- and Y-axes. The Z-axis extends outward from the screen.

continued

TOOLS	COMMAND SEQUENCE	STEPS
	**Command:** *[enter]*	**13.** Repeat Steps 6 through 8 to save this UCS as ***myFront.***
 Object UCS Button	**Command:** *ucs* **Current ucs name: *myFront*** **Enter an option [New/Move/ orthoGraphic/Prev/Restore/Save/Del/ Apply/?/World]<World>:***n* **Specify origin of new UCS or [ZAxis/ 3point/OBject/Face/View/X/Y/Z] <0,0,0>:** *ob*	**14.** Now let's look at some other ways to set the UCS. You can select the **New** option of the ***UCS*** command for the next few steps, or you can simply pick the button indicated. Let's begin with the **Object** option. Enter the sequence shown or pick the **Object UCS** button on the UCS toolbar.
	Select object to align UCS:	**15.** Select the north–south line closest to the lower-left corner of the screen. The UCS icon now looks like Figure 4.1.1.15. The 0,0,0 coordinate of the UCS matches the first point in the line's definition (the point I entered at the **From point** prompt when I drew the line). The Y- and Z-axes also line up according to the line's definition. 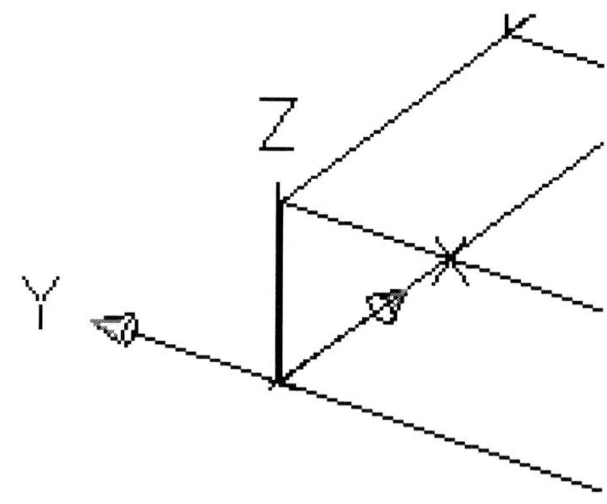 **FIG. 4.1.1.15** *Object UCS*
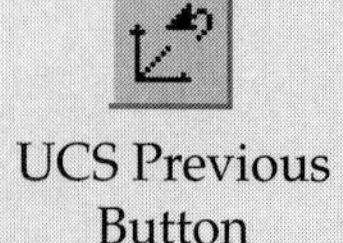 UCS Previous Button	**Command:** *ucs* **Current ucs name: *NO NAME*** **Enter an option [New/Move/ orthoGraphic/Prev/Restore/Save/Del/ Apply/?/World]<World>:***p*	**16.** Restore the **Previous** UCS.

continued

TOOLS	COMMAND SEQUENCE	STEPS
 Face UCS Button	**Command:** *ucs* **Current ucs name: *NO NAME*** **Enter an option [New/Move/orthoGraphic/Prev/Restore/Save/Del/Apply/?/World]<World>:***n* **Specify origin of new UCS or [ZAxis/3point/OBject/Face/View/X/Y/Z] <0,0,0>:** *f*	**17.** Now we will use the **Face** option. (The wedge piece is a three-dimensional solid—an item we will discuss in Lesson 9. It was necessary to include it here for demonstration purposes.) Enter the sequence shown or pick the **Face UCS** button on the UCS toolbar.
	Select face of solid object: **Enter an option [Next/XFlip/YFlip] <accept>:** *[enter]*	**18.** Select the lower-left corner of the front of the wedge. Notice that you can adjust the UCS after selecting the solid. When yours looks like Figure 4.1.1.18, accept it.

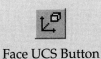

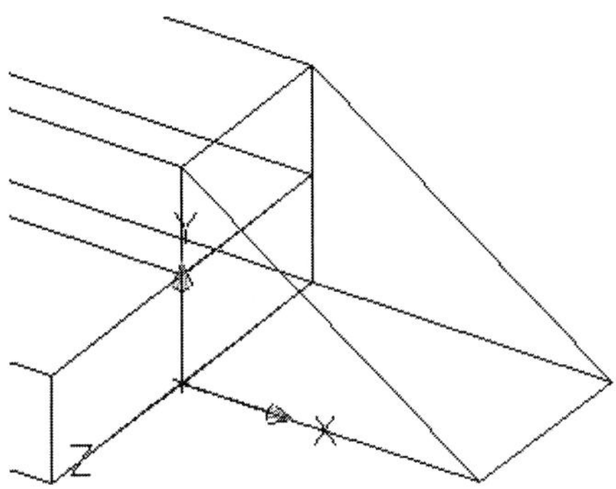

FIG. 4.1.1.18 *Face UCS*

continued

TOOLS	COMMAND SEQUENCE	STEPS

View UCS Button

Command: *ucs*

Current ucs name: *NO NAME*

Enter an option [New/Move/orthoGraphic/Prev/Restore/Save/Del/Apply/?/World]<World>:*n*

Specify origin of new UCS or [ZAxis/3point/OBject/Face/View/X/Y/Z] <0,0,0>: *v*

19. Now set the UCS according to the current view. Enter the sequence shown or pick the **View UCS** button. Notice the new orientation of the UCS icon. Notice also that, although it changes orientation, it does not change position.

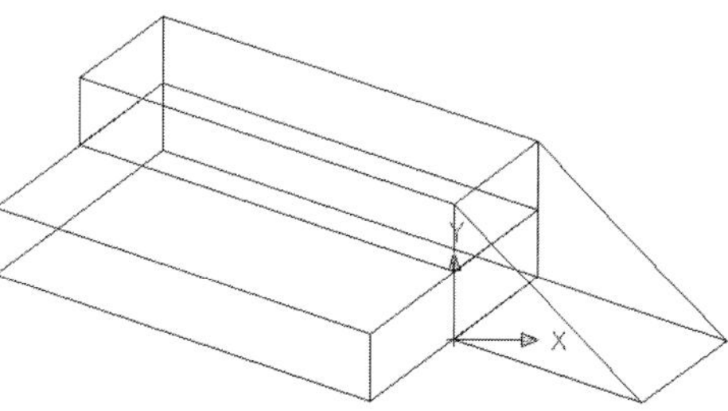

FIG. 4.1.1.19 UCS Aligned with the View

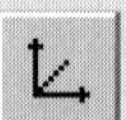

Command: *UCS*

Current ucs name: *NO NAME*

Enter an option [New/Move/orthoGraphic/Prev/Restore/Save/Del/Apply/?/World]<World>:*r*

Enter name of UCS to restore or [?]: *myfront*

20. Restore the *myFront* UCS. Notice that the UCS icon returns to the location defined by the *myFront* UCS.

X Axis Rotate UCS

Command: *UCS*

Current ucs name: myFront

Enter an option [New/Move/orthoGraphic/Prev/Restore/Save/Del/Apply/?/World]<World>:*n*

Specify origin of new UCS or [ZAxis/3point/OBject/Face/View/X/Y/Z] <0,0,0>: *x*

21. Let's experiment with the **X/Y/Z** options. Watch the UCS icon as we rotate the UCS.

Enter the sequence shown or select the **X Axis Rotate UCS** button.

continued

TOOLS	COMMAND SEQUENCE	STEPS
	Specify rotation angle about X axis <90>: *[enter]*	**22.** Accept the 90° default and watch the UCS icon (Figure 4.1.1.22). It can be difficult to follow axial rotations, but here is where the Right-Hand Rule comes in "handy." Here is how it works: Point the finger that represents the axis about which you are rotating (in this case the thumb) directly at your nose. Now rotate your hand 90° (or the desired angle of rotation) counterclockwise. This configuration will match the UCS icon and show you the orientation of your UCS.

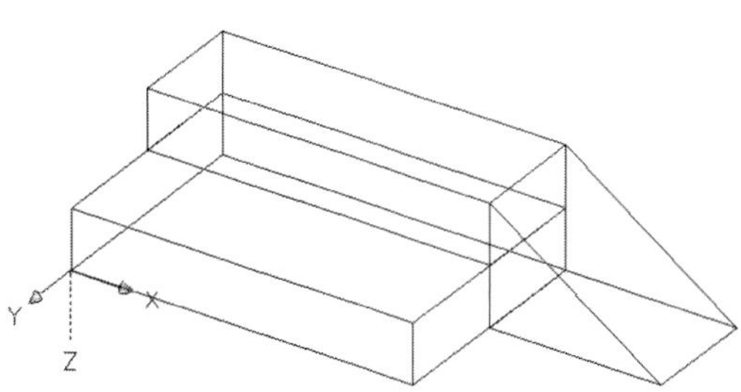

FIG. 4.1.1.22 Rotated UCS

TOOLS	COMMAND SEQUENCE	STEPS
	Command: *[enter]*	**23.** Repeat Step 22 for the **Y** and **Z** options.

continued

TOOLS	COMMAND SEQUENCE	STEPS
		24. Using any of the tools just discussed, create the new UCS setups identified in Figures 4.1.1.24a through 4.1.1.24f. Save the setups as indicated.

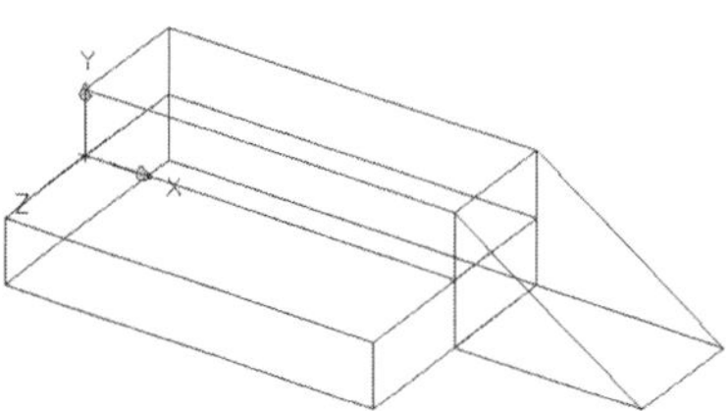

FIG. 4.1.1.24a *myFront-1*

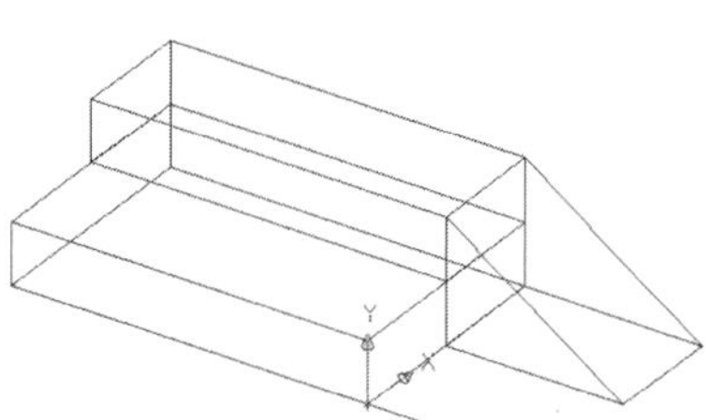

FIG. 4.1.1.24b *myRight*

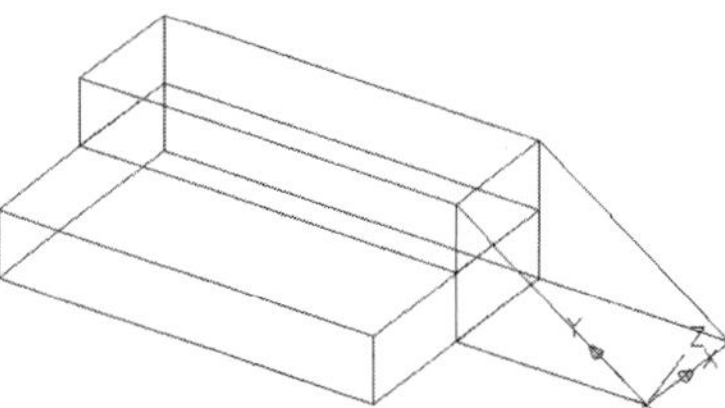

FIG. 4.1.1.24c *Inclined*

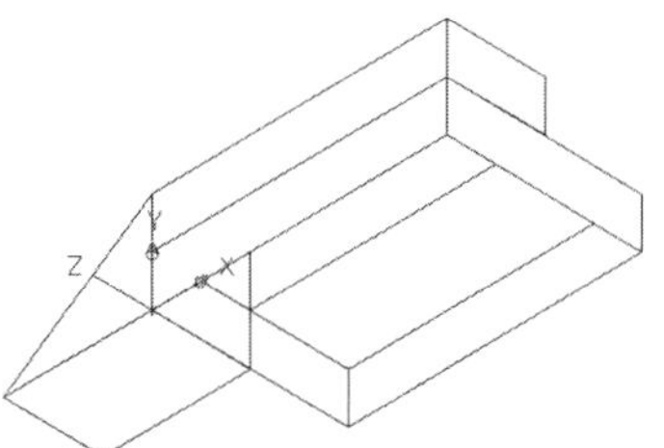

FIG. 4.1.1.24d *myBack*

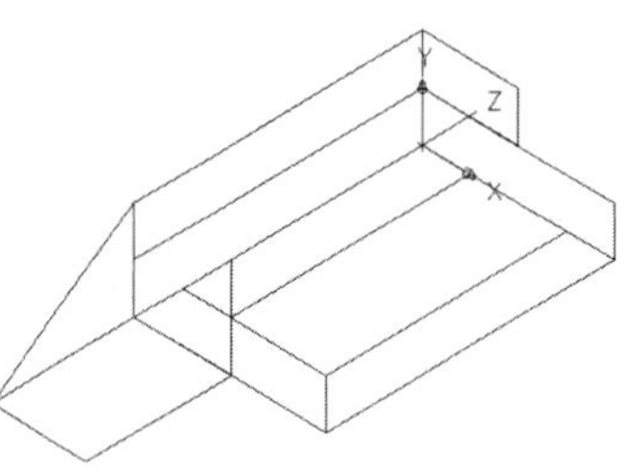

FIG. 4.1.1.24e *myLeft*

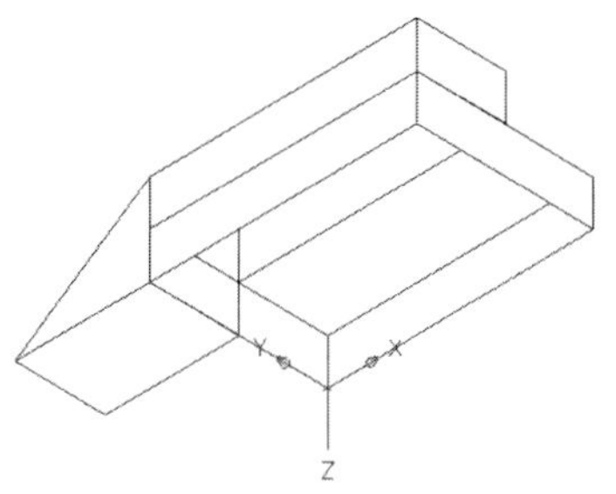

FIG. 4.1.1.24f *myBottom*

TOOLS	COMMAND SEQUENCE	STEPS
	**Command:** *qsave*	**25.** Save the drawing.

You have created several UCS setups using a variety of methods. It is okay to be a bit confused at this point. Let's pause for a moment, catch our breath, and review what we have learned. Here are some important things to remember.

- Despite their similarities, Viewpoints, Viewports, and the UCS are three *different* things. Remember:
  - Viewpoints are *points* (where you stand) *from* which you *view* the model.

- Viewports are like *port*holes in a ship *through* which you *view* the model.
- The UCS orients the user *on* the model itself.

- Points used to define Viewpoints will always reference the World Coordinate System (*not* the UCS). This will make it easier for you to get your bearings.
- The ***View*** command will save viewpoints.
- Each viewport can have a unique viewpoint and/or UCS assigned to it.
- Each—Viewpoint, Viewport, and UCS—works independently of the other two but should be considered as a team to assist the CAD operator working on a three-dimensional model.

Let's take a moment to look at a tool that might make UCS management easier. Then we will use the working planes to create some lines, text, and dimensions on our stick house.

4.2 The UCS Manager

Over the course of creating a drawing—particularly a larger drawing—you may find it necessary to create several UCSs. You have already seen how to save these setups for later retrieval—but where do you keep the list of names you have assigned the UCSs?

AutoCAD makes it simple with the UCS Manager (Figure 4.2a)—a dialog box approach to keeping track of the various setups as well as some additional tools. Access the UCS Manager by entering the ***UCSMan*** command (or the older ***DDUCS*** command).

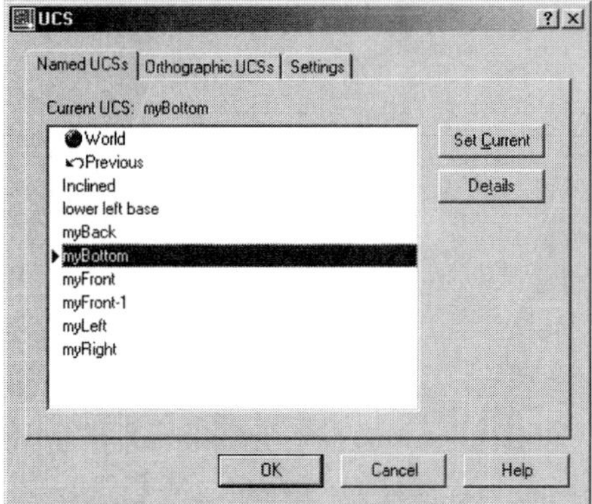

FIG. 4.2a The UCS Manager

Let's take a look.

- The first tab presents a list of **Named UCSs** as well as **World** and **Previous** options. To set a UCS current, either double-click on its name or select the name and pick the **Set Current** button. Then pick the **OK** button to complete the procedure. It is that simple—no need to remember or to store a list of names! (But it is always a good idea when assigning the name to make it something obvious.)

  The **Details** button presents a dialog box (Figure 4.2b) that indicates the origin location, as well as the orientation of the X-, Y-, and Z-axes for the currently selected UCS. You can view the data in relation to the WCS or any other existing UCS by selecting the coordinate system from the **Relative to:** control box.

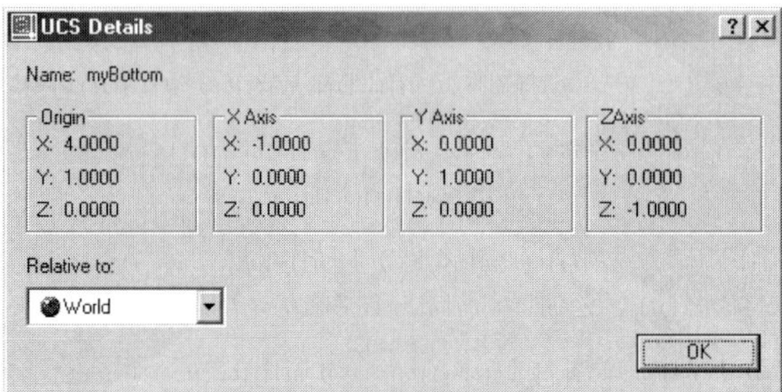

FIG. 4.2b Relative to: Control box

- The middle tab (Figure 4.2c)—**Orthographic UCSs**—lists several standard UCSs (the same ones available using the **orthoGraphic** option of the ***UCS*** command). Use the same procedure you used on the **Named UCSs** to set one current.

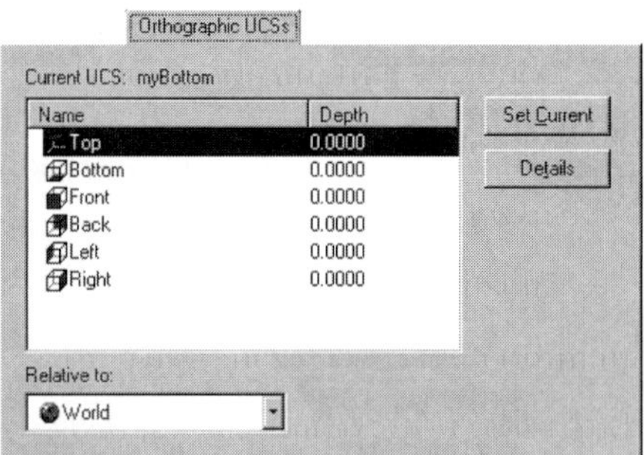

FIG. 4.2c Orthographic UCSs Tab

  Notice the **Relative to:** control box on this tab. You can set one of the orthographic UCSs relative to the WCS or relative to one of the user-defined UCSs. I suggest leaving this control set relative to the WCS—at least for now. Any other setting might make it difficult to orient yourself.

- The **UCS icon settings** frame of the **Settings** tab (Figure 4.2d) is a visual replacement for the ***UCSIcon*** command.

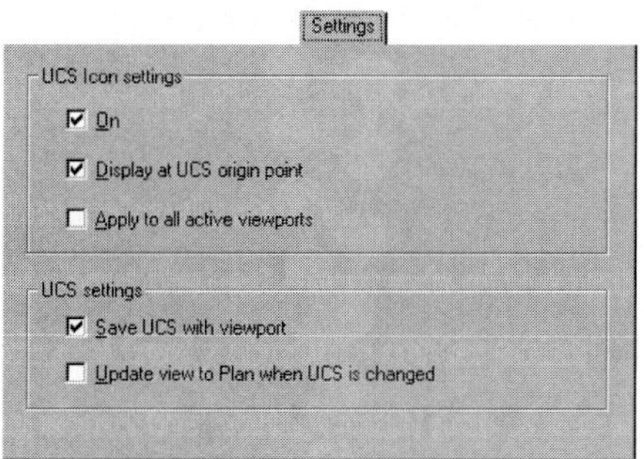

FIG. 4.2d Settings Tab

Use the **UCS settings** frame to **Save UCS with viewport** (the default). This means that each viewport can have its own UCS settings. Clear this check, and each viewport will reflect the UCS settings of the current viewport.

A check in the **Update view to Plan when UCS is changed** will regenerate the viewport in a plan view of the current UCS whenever the UCS settings are changed. I suggest leaving this box clear since you are more likely to want to keep the view even if you change the UCS.

We will use the UCS Manager in our next exercise to help us see how using different UCS settings can benefit us.

4.3 Using Working Planes

We have spent many pages learning to set up User Coordinate Systems. But as yet, we have not seen how to use the UCS once it is set up. We have not seen the answers to the questions with which we began our lesson—How do we make a solid roof? How do we place text and dimensions in a three-dimensional drawing?

Let's do an exercise to put our UCSs to practical use.

WWW 4.3.1 Do This: Working Planes

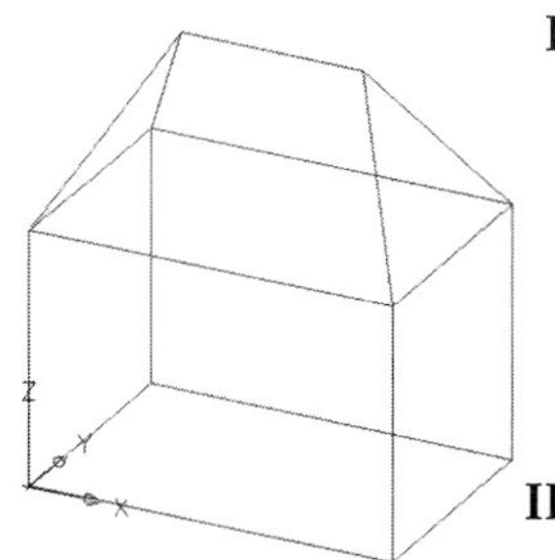

FIG. 4.3.1a *Stick House 4.dwg*

I. Open the *Stick House 4.dwg* in the C:\Steps3D\Lesson04 folder. The drawing looks like Figure 4.3.1a.

This drawing has already been set up for you with several UCSs and Paper Space viewports. The house is a stick figure (wireframe) structure. We will recreate the house using lines with thickness. And we will create a solid roof. Then we will add a few dimensions.

II. Be sure **Obj2** is the current layer.

III. Follow these steps:

TOOLS	COMMAND SEQUENCE	STEPS
	**Command:** ***th***	**1.** Begin by drawing the walls with 8″ thickness. Trace the bottom lines using lines with 8″ thickness. You will not need to change the UCS for this step.
	Enter new value for THICKNESS <0.0000>: ***8***	
	Command: ***l***	
	Command: ***hide***	**2.** Remove the hidden lines to help see what you have done. Your drawing looks like Figure 4.3.1.2.

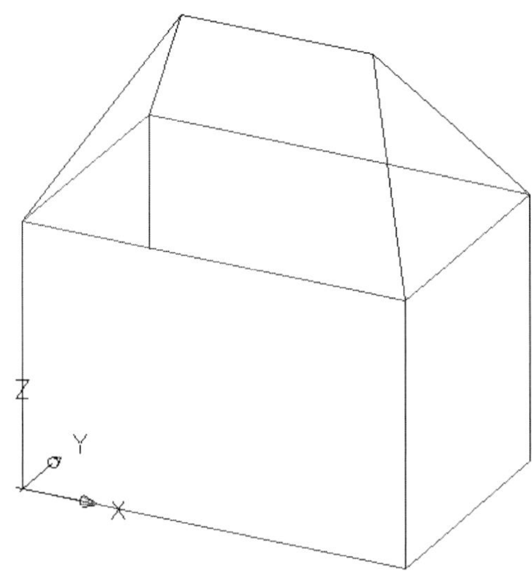

FIG. 4.3.1.2 Solid Walls with Hidden Lines Removed

TOOLS	COMMAND SEQUENCE	STEPS
	Command: ***th***	**3.** Set the thickness back to ***0.***
	Enter new value for THICKNESS <8.0000>: ***0***	

continued

TOOLS	COMMAND SEQUENCE	STEPS
	 **Command:** *so*	**4.** Try drawing a solid using the points indicated in Figure 4.3.1.4.
	**Command:** *e*	**5.** Notice that the solid was drawn two dimensionally in the current UCS (Figure 4.3.1.5). To use a solid to form the roof, the UCS must be aligned to the side of the roof you are drawing. Erase the solid.

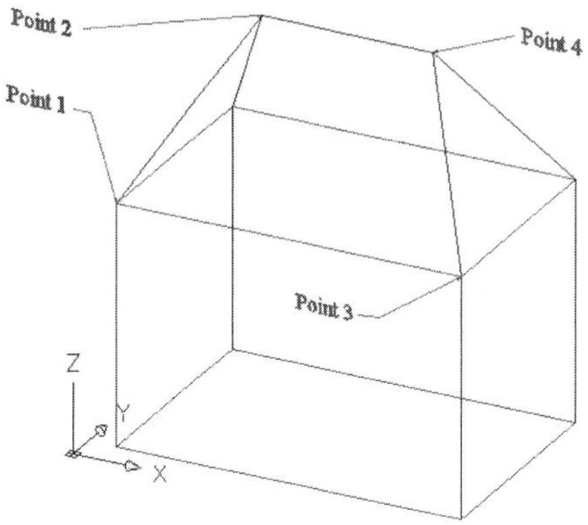

FIG. 4.3.1.4 Draw a Solid Using These Points

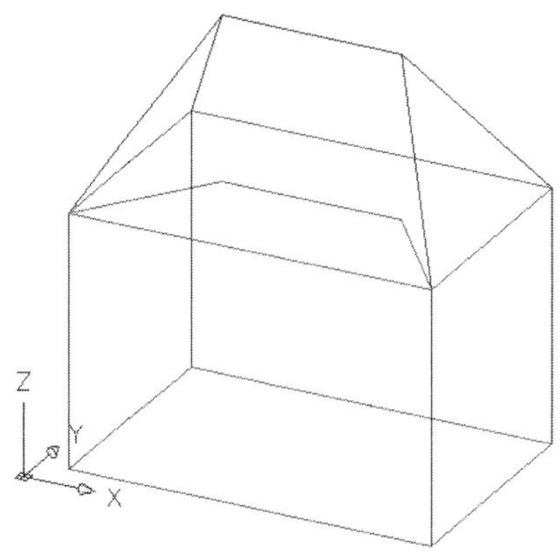

FIG. 4.3.1.5 Two-Dimensional Solid in the Wrong UCS

continued

TOOLS	COMMAND SEQUENCE	STEPS
 Display UCS Dialog Button	**Command:** ***ucsman***	**6.** Call the UCS Manager.
	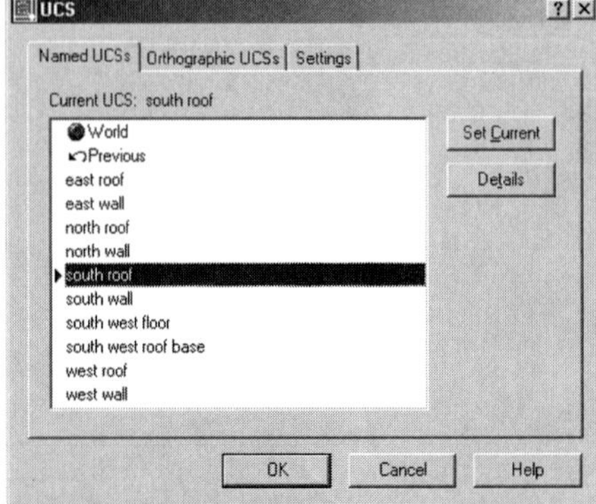	**7.** Double-click on the **south roof** UCS to make it current. Then pick the **OK** button. Notice that the UCS icon moves to align itself with the face of the south roof (see Figure 4.3.1.8).
	Command: ***so***	**8.** Now that the UCS has been properly set, repeat Step 4. Use the ***Hide*** command to see the results (Figure 4.3.1.8).

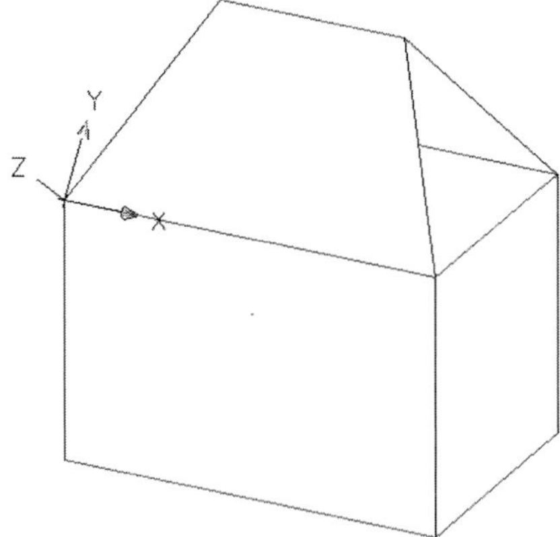

FIG. 4.3.1.8 Solid Roof (south side only)

continued

TOOLS	COMMAND SEQUENCE	STEPS
		9. Using the techniques seen in this exercise, complete the roof using solids (adjust the viewpoint as necessary, then return to the current setting of 1,−2,1). Your drawing looks like Figure 4.3.1.9.

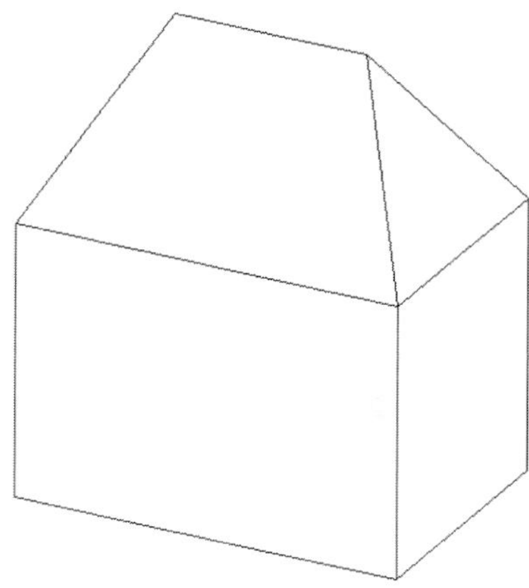

FIG. 4.3.1.9 Completed House (hidden lines removed and Obj1 layer frozen for clarity)

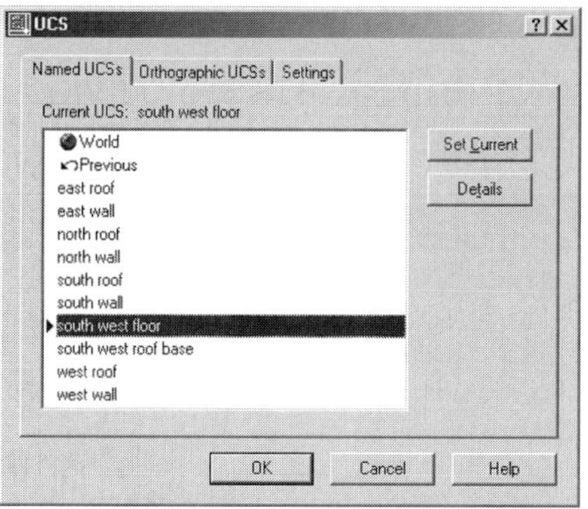

10. Set the current UCS to **south west floor.**

11. We will now add some dimensions, but we need to use viewports to do this properly. Activate the **Layout1** tab.

PAPER

Command: *ms*

12. Open Model Space. (Refer to Figure 4.3.1.17 for Steps 12–17.)

continued

TOOLS	COMMAND SEQUENCE	STEPS

13. Activate the upper-left viewport and do the following:

(a) Create a WCS plan view (set the viewpoint to 0,0,1).

(b) Set the scale for this viewport to 1:8.

14. Activate the lower-left viewport and do the following:

(a) Create a WCS front view (set the viewpoint to 0,−1,0).

(b) Set the scale for this viewport to 1:8.

(c) Adjust the size of the viewport and the position of the house as necessary to see the entire house.

15. Activate the lower-right viewport and do the following:

(a) Create a WCS right side view (set the viewpoint to 1,0,0).

(b) Set the scale for this viewport to 1:8.

(c) Adjust the size of the viewport and the position of the house as necessary to see the entire house.

16. Activate the upper-right viewport and do the following:

(a) Set the scale to 1:8.

(b) Adjust the size of the viewport and the position of the house as necessary to see the entire house.

continued

TOOLS	COMMAND SEQUENCE	STEPS

Command: ***mvsetup***

17. Use the ***MVSetup*** command to align the plan, front, and side views. Adjust the position of the viewports as necessary for aesthetics. Your drawing looks something like Figure 4.3.1.17.

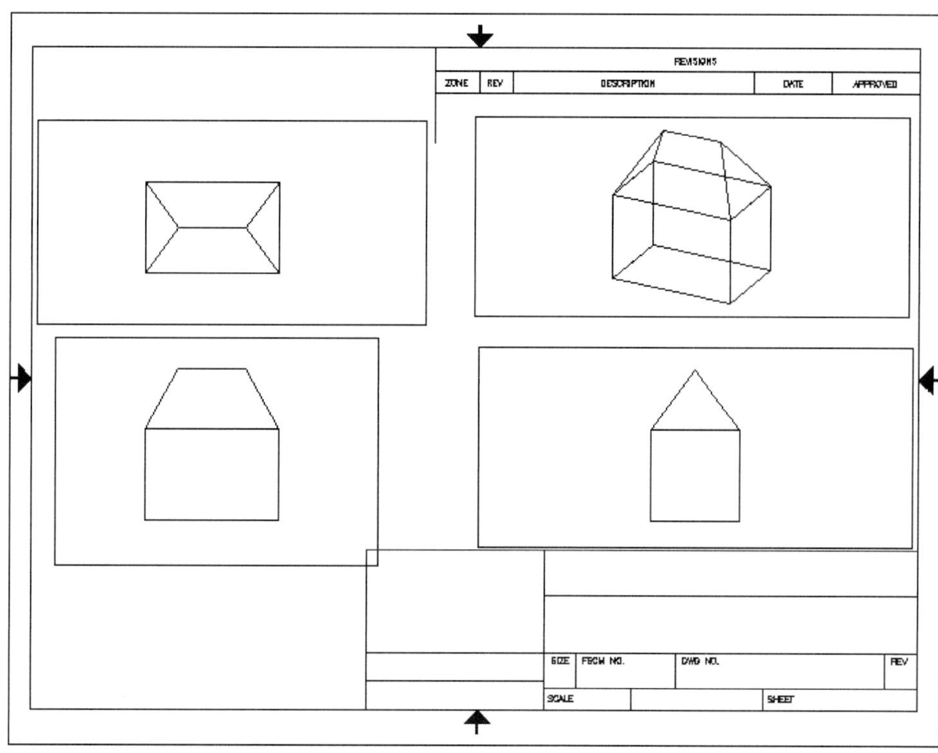

FIG. 4.3.1.17 Layout

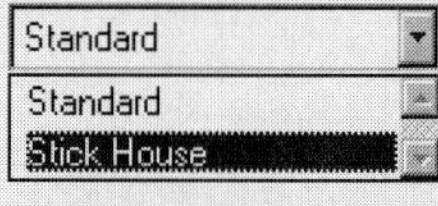

Command: ***ddim***

18. Be sure the **Stick House** dimstyle is current. (This style has been set up to work in Paper Space.)

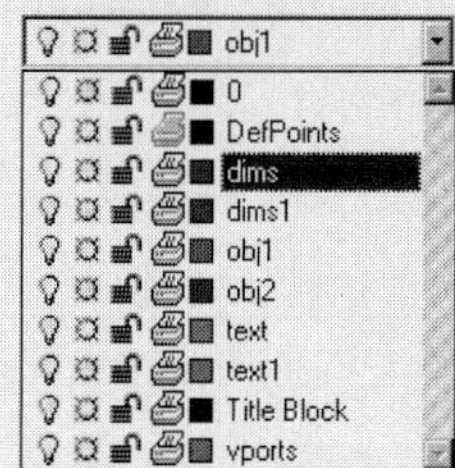

Command: ***la***

19. Set **dims** as the current layer.

continued

TOOLS	COMMAND SEQUENCE	STEPS
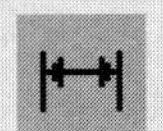	**Command:** *dli*	**20.** Add the dimensions shown in the upper-left viewport (Figure 4.3.1.20). (*Note:* Freeze the **Obj2** layer and then **Obj1** to make this easier.)

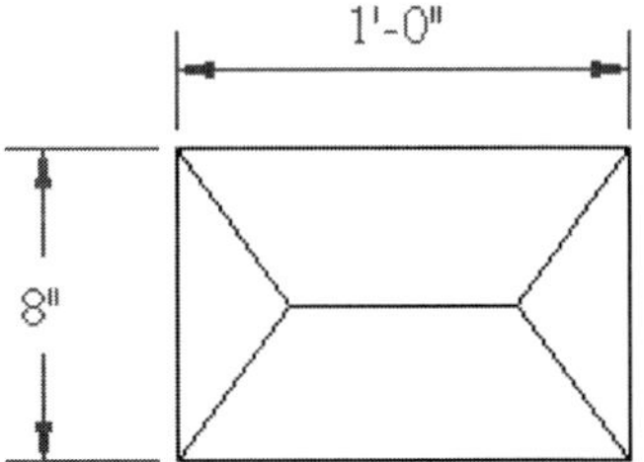

FIG. 4.3.1.20 Dimensioned Viewport

21. Activate the lower-left viewport.

TOOLS	COMMAND SEQUENCE	STEPS
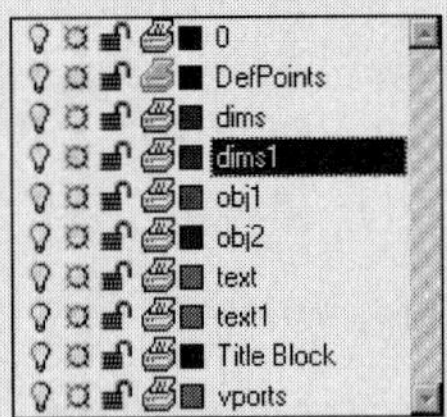	**Command:** *la*	**22.** Set **dims1** as the current layer.

23. Try to draw the dimensions shown in Figure 4.3.1.23. (You cannot do it because the UCS is not set up for it.)

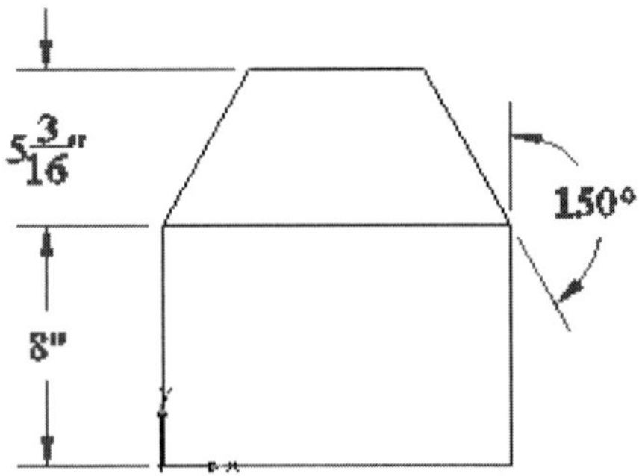

FIG. 4.3.1.23 Dimensioning in Front View

continued

TOOLS | **COMMAND SEQUENCE** | **STEPS**

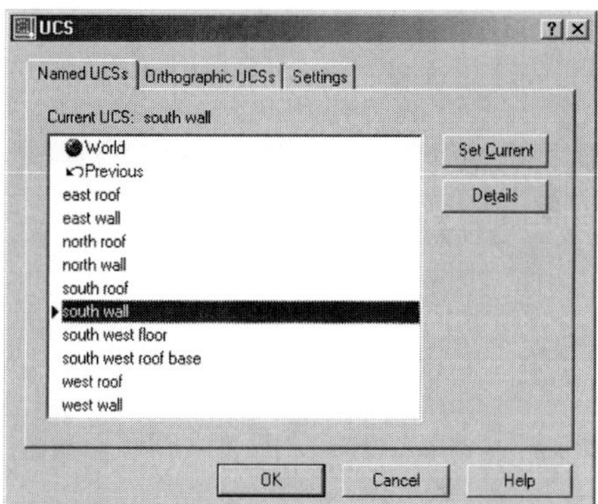

24. Use the UCS Manager to make **south wall** the current UCS.

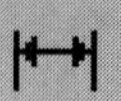

Command: *dli*

25. Now place the dimensions shown in Figure 4.3.1.23. (*Hint:* Freeze the **Obj2** layer when dimensioning the angle.)

Command: *vplayer*

26. Use the ***VPLayer*** command to freeze the **Dims** layer in all but the upper-left viewport and the **Dims1** layer in all but the lower-left viewport.

Command: *ucsicon*

Enter an option [ON/OFF/All/Noorigin/ORigin] <OFF>: *a*

Enter an option [ON/OFF/Noorigin/ORigin] <OFF>: *off*

27. Turn off the UCS icon in all viewports.

continued

TOOLS	COMMAND SEQUENCE	STEPS
		28. Complete the drawing as shown in Figure 4.3.1.27. Here are some hints.

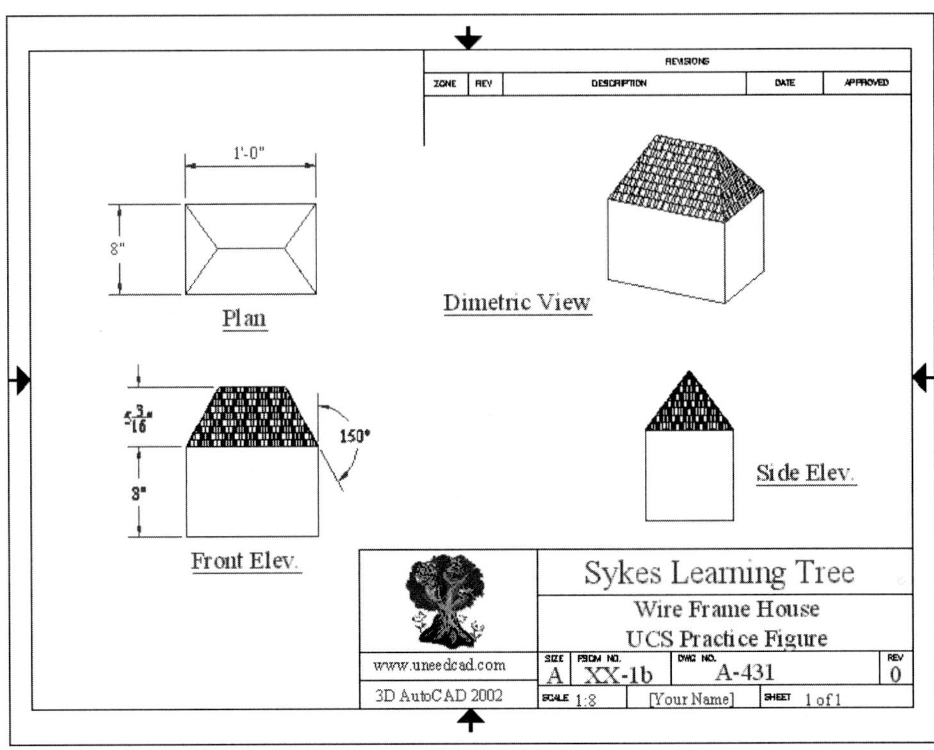

FIG. 4.3.1.28 Completed Drawing

- Try to hatch a shingle pattern onto the roof—I used the *AR-RSHKE* pattern at a $\frac{1}{16}$″ scale. (You must use the direct hatch option.)
- Like dimensioning, you can only hatch in the current UCS.
- Use the **Hidden** option of the ***Shademode*** command in the Dimetric View.

continued

TOOLS	COMMAND SEQUENCE	STEPS
		■ You may notice that the Shademode used in the **Dimetric View** hides the text if you use the Times New Roman font. This is because true type fonts sometimes disappear when the ***Shademode*** command is used in a Paper Space viewport. If this happens to you, resize the viewport and place the text outside of it.
	Command: ***saveas***	**29.** Save the drawing as *My Wire Frame House* in the C:\Steps3D\Lesson04 folder.

4.4 Advanced Viewing Techniques

We discovered some very useful viewing tools and procedures in our last lesson and have used some of them in this lesson. Indeed, we will continue to use them throughout our text and our computer-drafting career. But consider this scenario.

A builder is creating an object—we will use the figure we saw in our *UCS Practice 4* drawing (Exercise 4.1.1) as an example. As he adds a piece here or trims a piece there, he holds the object in his hand and rotates it this way and that to get a better understanding—a better feel for its shape. How can you do the same thing with the computer model *before* our builder creates it?

You can use the Viewpoint tool we have been using. You can even speed it up slightly by using preset viewpoints on the View toolbar. But let's face it—at best, this tool is too slow and cumbersome for the scenario just discussed. It will not provide the insights our builder will get by rotating the object at different angles.

For this reason, AutoCAD has provided two extraordinary tools—***3DOrbit*** and ***3DCOrbit*** (3D Continuous Orbit). Let's take a look at each.

4.4.1 3DOrbit

The ***3DOrbit*** command allows the user to rotate a model on the computer screen just as the builder did in his hand.

Hands are marvels of engineering. We use them without a second thought—forgetting the time our infant minds struggled to control them.

3DOrbit is also quite a marvel—and it will also take some time to learn to control it. But we will soon come to appreciate it almost as much as a builder appreciates his hands!

Access the 3D Orbit screen with the ***3DOrbit*** command like this:

Command: ***3dorbit*** **(or** ***orbit*****)**

3DORBIT Press ESC or ENTER to exit, or right-click to display shortcut-menu.

AutoCAD displays a sort of three-dimensional compass over the screen (in the current viewport). The compass is called an **Arcball** and will help you control your movements while using the orbiter. Let's examine how it works (refer to Figure 4.4.1a).

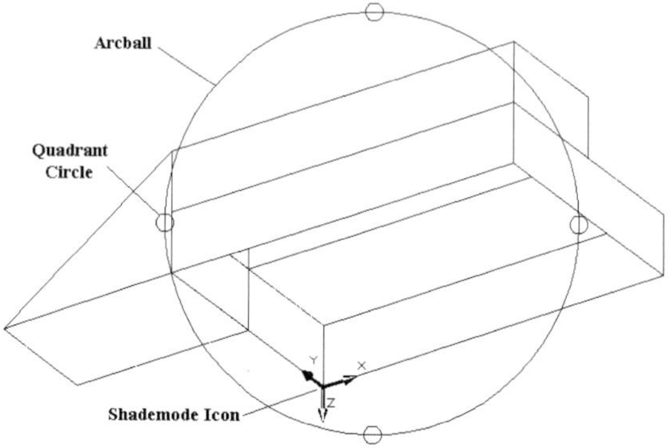

FIG. 4.4.1a Arcball Shown in the *UCS Practice 4* Drawing

- When you enter the orbiter screen, the UCS icon will be replaced with the Shademode icon. Here you see it located at the 0,0,0 UCS point identified in Exercise 4.1.1.
- The arcball and smaller quadrant circles allow the user to determine how to manipulate the model. It works like this.

WHEN THE CURSOR BEGINS:	DRAGGING THE CURSOR WILL:	THE CURSOR WILL BE A:
Inside the arcball	Manipulate the model freely about its center point.	
Outside the arcball	Perform a two-dimensional rotation (called a *roll*) about an axis extending through the center of the arcball (and outward from the screen).	
Inside the east or west quadrant circle	Rotate the model about the north/south axis of the arcball.	
Inside the north or south quadrant circle	Rotate the model about the east/west axis of the arcball.	

To reset the original view, right-click and select **Reset View** from the cursor menu. (More on the cursor menu after the next exercise.)

Most of this will become clearer with practice. Let's try an exercise.

WWW 4.4.1.1 Do This: Three-Dimensional Orbiting

I. Reopen the *UCS Practice 4.dwg* in the C:\Steps3D\Lesson04 folder. The drawing should look like Figure 4.4.1.1a. If not, restore the *MyBottom* UCS and set the viewpoint to −1,1.5,−1. (If you did not save your changes in this drawing, open *UCS Practice 4a.dwg* instead.)

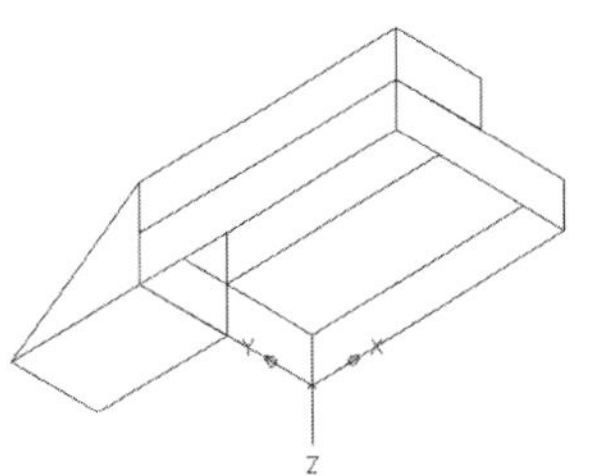

FIG. 4.4.1.1a UCS Practice 4a.dwg (shown with hidden lines removed)

II. Follow these steps:

TOOLS	COMMAND SEQENCE	STEPS
 Hidden Button (Shade Toolbar)	**Command:** ***shademode*** **Current mode: 2D wireframe** **Enter option [2D wireframe/ 3Dwireframe/Hidden/Flat/Gouraud/ fLat+edges/gOuraud+edges] <2D wireframe>:** ***h***	**1.** Use the **Hidden** option of the ***Shademode*** command to remove the hidden lines.
 3D Orbit Button	**Command:** ***orbit***	**2.** Enter the ***3DOrbit*** command by typing ***3dorbit*** or ***orbit*** at the command prompt. You may also select **3D Orbit** from the View pull-down menu or the **3D Orbit** button on the 3D Orbit toolbar. (The **3D Orbit** button is also located on the Standard toolbar next to the **Zoom** and **Pan** buttons.)
 Cursor Icon	**Press ESC or ENTER to exit, or right-click to display shortcut-menu.**	**3.** Place your cursor in the western quadrant circle (refer to Figure 4.4.1a).

continued

TOOLS	COMMAND SEQUENCE	STEPS

4. With the left mouse button, click and drag to the opposite quadrant circle. Notice how the model rotates. Release the mouse button.

Your drawing now looks like Figure 4.4.1.1.4.

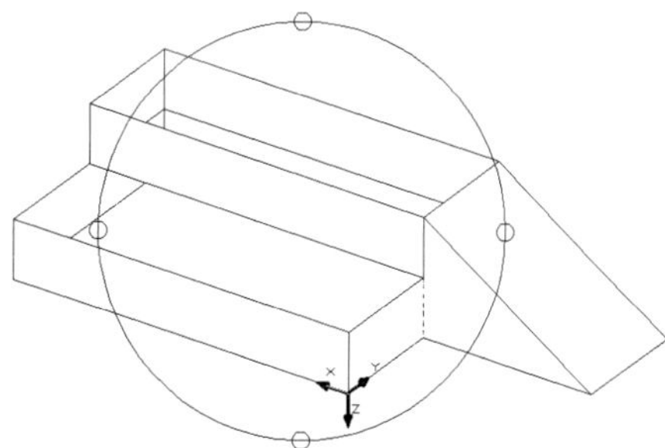

FIG. 4.4.1.1.4 Rotated Left to Right

Cursor Icon

5. Repeat Steps 3 and 4, but this time begin in the upper quadrant circle and end in the lower quadrant circle. Your drawing looks like Figure 4.4.1.1.5. (Notice that the UCS icon continues to orient the model for you.)

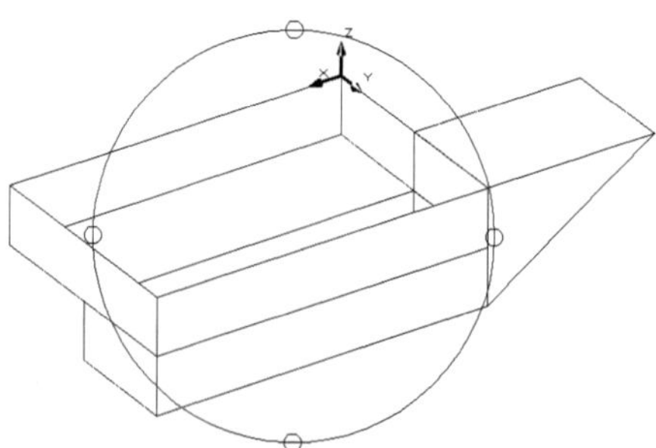

FIG. 4.4.1.1.5 Rotated Top to Bottom

continued

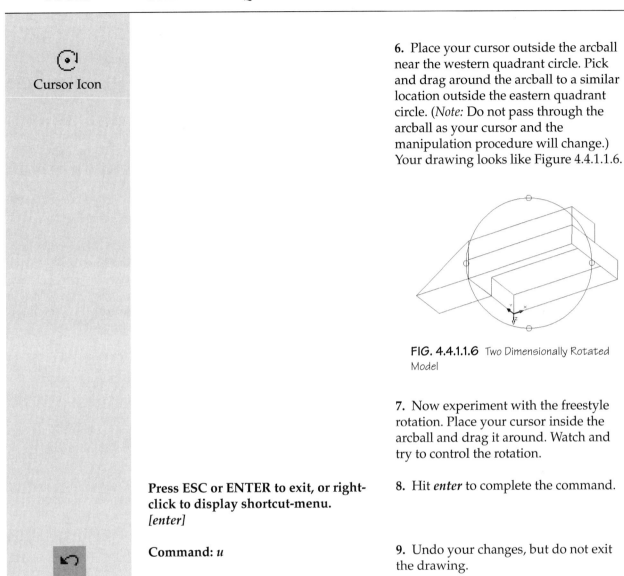

TOOLS	COMMAND SEQUENCE	STEPS
Cursor Icon		**6.** Place your cursor outside the arcball near the western quadrant circle. Pick and drag around the arcball to a similar location outside the eastern quadrant circle. (*Note:* Do not pass through the arcball as your cursor and the manipulation procedure will change.) Your drawing looks like Figure 4.4.1.1.6.
		FIG. 4.4.1.1.6 Two Dimensionally Rotated Model
		7. Now experiment with the freestyle rotation. Place your cursor inside the arcball and drag it around. Watch and try to control the rotation.
	Press ESC or ENTER to exit, or right-click to display shortcut-menu. *[enter]*	**8.** Hit ***enter*** to complete the command.
	Command: *u*	**9.** Undo your changes, but do not exit the drawing.

Of course, you do not have to drag from quadrant circle to quadrant circle. We just used these as guides. Feel free to rotate as much or as little as you like.

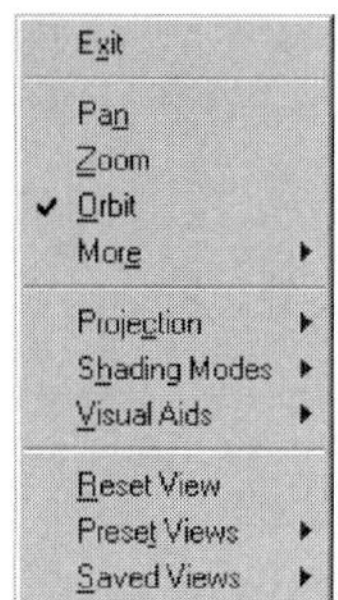

FIG. 4.4.1f Orbiter Cursor Menu

As if these options alone would not make this a priceless tool in a three-dimensional world, notice that the command line instructs you to **right-click to display shortcut-menu.** There is more! Let's take a look at the cursor menu (refer to Figure 4.4.1f).

- The top frame contains only one option. Select **Exit** to leave the orbiter.
- The first two options in the next frame probably look familiar. But these are not the **Pan** and **Zoom** commands you already know and love.
  - Selecting ***Pan*** is the equivalent of entering the ***3DPan*** command at the command line. The ***3DPan*** command is very similar to the ***Pan*** command (it even uses the same cursor) except that, with ***3DPan***, the user can pan using a single object (or a few objects) as a reference. AutoCAD removes all other objects from the display until the user exits the command.

    The trick is to select the objects you wish to view *before* entering the ***3DOrbit*** or ***3DPan*** command. AutoCAD then removes all but the selected objects from view during the Pan or Orbit procedure.
  - Selecting **Zoom** is the equivalent of entering the ***3DZoom*** command at the command line. Like the ***Pan*** and ***3DPan*** commands, ***Zoom Realtime*** and ***3DZoom*** also share the same cursor. Also like ***3DPan***, ***3DZoom*** may view only selected objects (again, if they were selected before entering the command). ***3DZoom*** may cause some distortion in the image the way a zoom lens distorts an image.

    We will get a chance to use ***3DPan*** and ***3DZoom*** in our next exercise.
  - The **Orbit** option is the one we examined in our last exercise.
  - **More** calls another menu (Figure 4.4.1g).

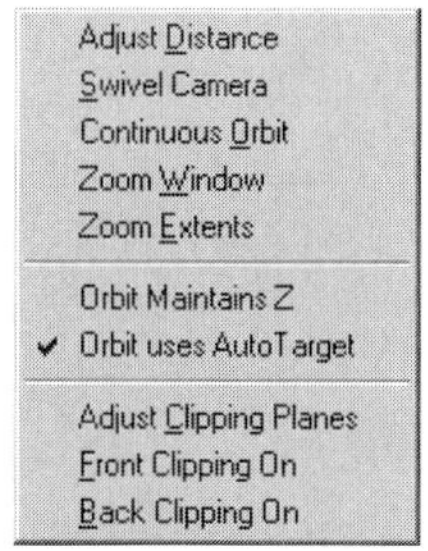

FIG. 4.4.1g More Options

- The **Adjust Distance** option of the **More** cursor menu appears to do the same thing that the ***3DZoom*** command did. The difference is that this option calls the ***3DDistance*** command, which actually changes the distance between the user and the model. No distortion results from the ***3DDistance*** command as it may from the ***3DZoom*** command. The ***3DDistance*** command even has its own cursor (Figure 4.4.1h).

FIG. 4.4.1h 3D Distance Cursor

- The **Swivel Camera** option calls the ***3DSwivel*** command. This adjusts the view as though the camera, although stationary, is revolving on its tripod. (See Figure 4.4.1i for the ***3DSwivel*** command's cursor icon.) This tool comes in handy when viewing an architectural, structural, or piping drawing from inside the model.

FIG. 4.4.1i 3D Swivel Cursor

- The **Continuous Orbit** option calls the ***3DCOrbit*** command. We will discuss this command in Section 4.4.2.
- **Zoom Window** and **Zoom Extents** are the standard ***Zoom*** options but allow the command to take place transparently—without leaving the orbiter.
  - When checked, **Orbit Maintains Z** forces the 3D orbiter to hold the Z-axis when rotating objects horizontally. The user must use the left/right quadrant circles when dragging. This handy setting will save you a lot of grief by preventing the model from accidentally rotating off the screen.
  - I suggest keeping the **Orbit Uses AutoTarget** option checked (default setting). This ensures that rotations will be about the target point on the objects you are viewing (instead of the center of the viewport). Removing this may cause some undesirable effects.
- **Adjust Clipping Planes** calls the ***3DClip*** command. This command presents a separate window with the model shown at 90° to the current 3D Orbital display (Figure 4.4.1j). The lines through the center of the window

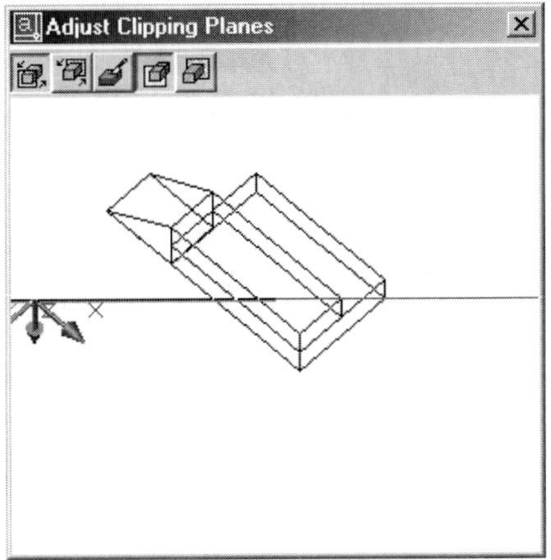

FIG. 4.4.1j 3DClip Window

(although you can only see one, there are actually two of them) are the Clipping Planes. Pick and drag to adjust their locations.

Control what you see with the five buttons along the top of the window. These are (from the left):

- **Adjust Front Clipping** allows the user to move the front clipping plane up or down.
- **Adjust Back Clipping** allows the user to move the back clipping plane up or down.
- **Create Slice** allows the user to move both clipping planes together.
- **Front Clipping On/Off** toggles front clipping on or off. When **On** (the button is depressed as shown in Figure 4.4.1j), AutoCAD will not display anything in front of (below) the front clipping plane.
- **Back Clipping On/Off** toggles back clipping on or off. When **On**, AutoCAD will not display anything behind (above) the clipping plane.
- Toggle both clippings off to view the entire model.

➠ **Front Clipping On** and **Back Clipping On** are toggles that work the same as the buttons in the Clipping Window.

(We will see more on clipping planes in our next exercise.)

- The third frame of the Orbiter's cursor menu contains three options—**Projection**, **Shading Modes,** and **Visual Aids.** Each calls a separate menu, but these are much simpler than the **More** menu.

➠ The **Projection** option allows the user to select either a **Parallel** or a **Perspective** view. In engineering drafting, you will almost always wish to keep the default **Parallel** view. A **Perspective** is more artistic but also more difficult to use when creating dimensionally correct drawings.

➠ The **Shading Modes** option lists the same options available in the ***Shademode*** command.

➠ **Visual Aids** include the UCS Icon, a two-dimensional grid, or a three-dimensional compass. Although you can use any or all of the tools, I recommend using the UCS Icon. The two-dimensional grid is distracting in three-dimensional space and the compass does not display well.

- The bottom frame of the Orbiter's cursor menu also presents three options—**Reset View**, **Preset Views,** or **Saved Views.**
  - **Reset View** behaves like an undo or previous command within the orbiter. It restores the view that was current when the orbiter was displayed.
  - **Preset Views** presents a list of AutoCAD's preset viewpoints.
  - **Saved Views** presents a list of user created views.

Let's look more closely at the Orbiter's clipping planes.

4.4.1.2 Do This: Using the Orbiter's Clipping Planes

I. Be sure you are still in the *UCS Practice 4.dwg* file in the C:\Steps3D\Lesson04 folder.

II. Be sure the **Hidden** option of the Shademode is active.

III. Follow these steps:

TOOLS	COMMAND SEQUENCE	STEPS
	**Command:** ***orbit***	**1.** Open the Orbiter.
		2. Right-click in the graphics screen to call the cursor menu.
	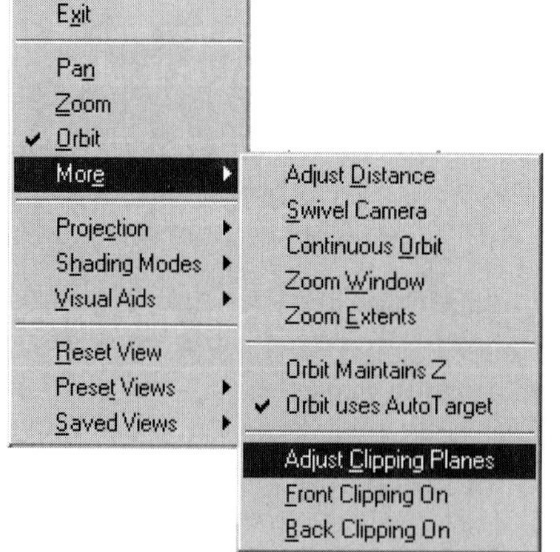	**3.** Select the **More** option and then the **Adjust Clipping Planes** option.
Adjust Front Clipping On/Off Button		**4.** AutoCAD presents the **Adjust Clipping Planes** window with **Front Clipping** toggled **On** (refer to Figure 4.4.1j). If the **Adjust Front Clipping** button is not depressed, pick it now.
		5. Move the front clipping plane up and down (pick and drag). Watch the display in the orbiter as you move the clipping plane.

continued

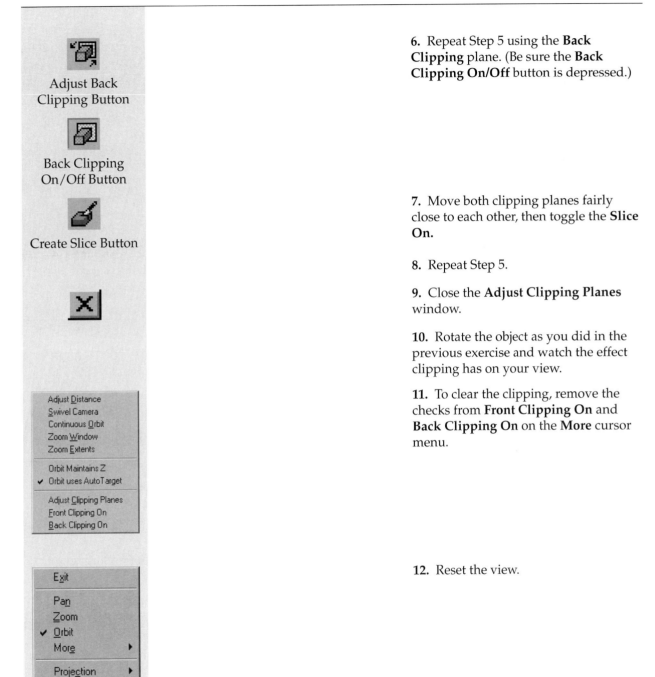

TOOLS	COMMAND SEQUENCE	STEPS
 Adjust Back Clipping Button  Back Clipping On/Off Button		**6.** Repeat Step 5 using the **Back Clipping** plane. (Be sure the **Back Clipping On/Off** button is depressed.)
 Create Slice Button		**7.** Move both clipping planes fairly close to each other, then toggle the **Slice On.**
		8. Repeat Step 5.
		**9.** Close the **Adjust Clipping Planes** window.
		10. Rotate the object as you did in the previous exercise and watch the effect clipping has on your view.
Adjust Distance Swivel Camera Continuous Orbit Zoom Window Zoom Extents Orbit Maintains Z ✔ Orbit uses AutoTarget Adjust Clipping Planes Front Clipping On Back Clipping On		**11.** To clear the clipping, remove the checks from **Front Clipping On** and **Back Clipping On** on the **More** cursor menu.
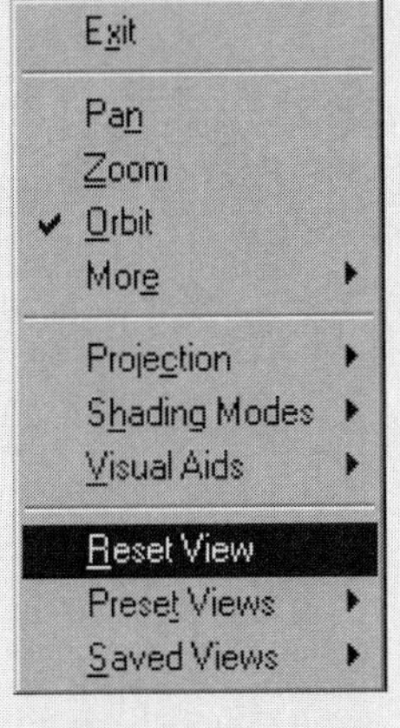		**12.** Reset the view.

continued

TOOLS	COMMAND SEQUENCE	STEPS
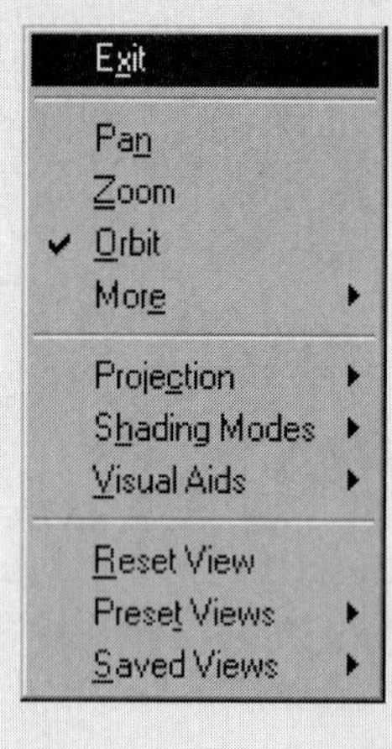	Command: *−vp*	**13.** Exit the orbiter, and set the vpoint to 1,−1.5,1.
		14. Without entering a command, select the inclined solid on the east end of the object (Figure 4.4.1.2.14).
 3D Pan Button	**Command:** *3dpan*	**15.** Enter the ***3DPan*** command at the command prompt or pick the **3D Pan** button on the Orbit toolbar. Notice that only the selected objects appear on your screen.
		16. Hold down the left mouse button and move the object around the screen.
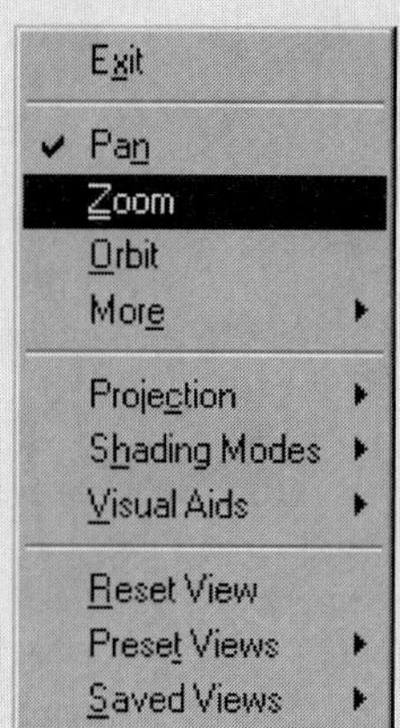		**17.** Right-click and select **Zoom** from the cursor menu. (If you were at the command prompt, you could pick the **3D Zoom** button on the Orbit toolbar.)

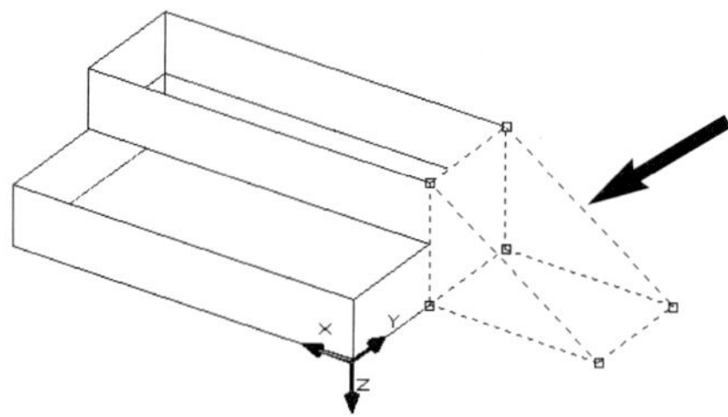

FIG. 4.4.1.2.14 *Select the Inclined Object*

continued

TOOLS	COMMAND SEQUENCE	STEPS
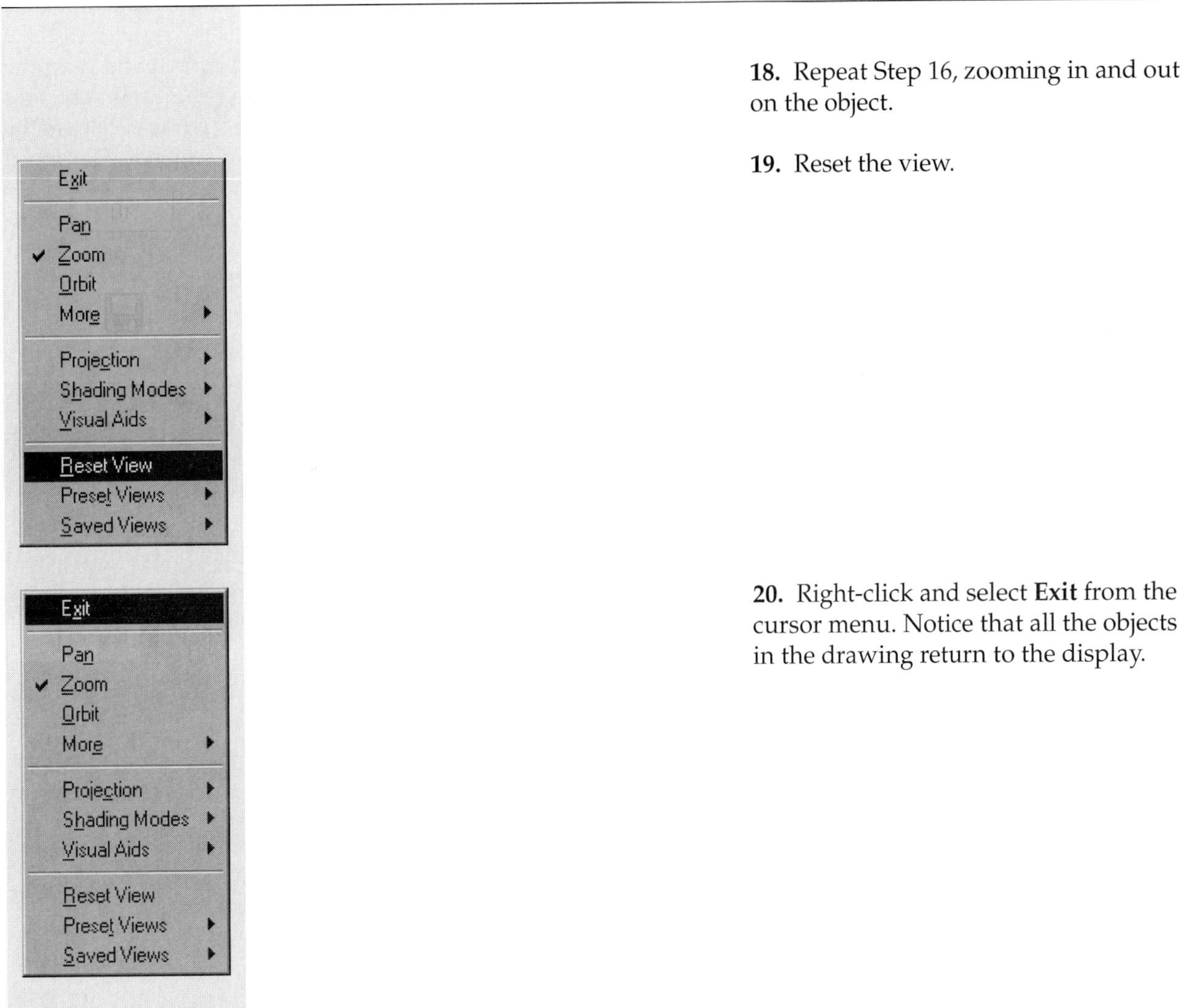		**18.** Repeat Step 16, zooming in and out on the object.
		19. Reset the view.
		20. Right-click and select **Exit** from the cursor menu. Notice that all the objects in the drawing return to the display.

4.4.2 A Continuous Three-Dimensional Orbit—3DCOrbit

This tool is guaranteed to razzle-dazzle friends and co-workers (and employers) alike! The ***3DCOrbit*** command (3D Continuous Orbit) allows the user to begin a rotation—and then remove his hands from the keyboard/mouse and watch as AutoCAD continuously rotates the model on the screen.

To use the ***3DCOrbit*** command, first enter the command or select it from the 3DOrbit toolbar. AutoCAD prompts

Command: *3dcorbit*

Press ESC or ENTER to exit, or right-click to display shortcut-menu.

Notice that the prompt is the same as the *3DOrbit* command prompt. By right-clicking at any time during the 3D Continuous Orbit, you can access the same cursor menu available through any of the ***3DOrbit*** commands. Or you can begin a continual orbit of the model. To do this, pick any point on the screen and drag the cursor in the direction you would like the model to spin. Notice the cursor changes to one of the 3DOrbit cursors (depending on which direction you drag). Release the mouse button and the model continues to spin on its axis—like a planet. The speed at which you drag the cursor determines the speed of the spin.

To stop the spinning, hit either the **Enter** or **Escape** key on the keyboard or right-click and select **Exit** from the cursor menu. The model stops spinning where it is. Use the ***Undo*** command to return to the orientation it had before the command.

Give it a try.

4.4.2.1 Do This: Creating a Continuous Orbit

I. Be sure you are still in the *UCS Practice 4.dwg* file in the C:\Steps3D\Lesson04 folder.

II. Follow these steps:

TOOLS	COMMAND SEQUENCE	STEPS
3D Continuous Orbit Button	**Command:** *3dcorbit*	**1.** Enter the ***3DCOrbit*** command at the command line or pick the **3D Continuous Orbit** button on the 3DOrbit toolbar.
	Press ESC or ENTER to exit, or right-click to display shortcut-menu.	**2.** Pick a point on the right side of the screen and drag to the left. Release the mouse button about halfway across the screen but continue the mouse movement (use some follow-through as though you are hitting a golf ball).
		3. Watch the model spin before your eyes.
	Press ESC or ENTER to exit, or right-click to display shortcut-menu. *[enter]*	**4.** Hit ***enter*** to stop the rotation.
	Command: *u*	**5.** Undo the rotation by entering ***U*** at the command line or picking the **Undo** button on the Standard toolbar.

4.5 Extra Steps

It may take some practice to get the feel of the ***3DCOrbit*** command. Take a few minutes now and repeat the last exercise until you feel comfortable. For a real treat, shade the model (use the Gouraud Shademode) before starting the 3D Continuous Orbit. Change some of the colors for a flashier show. Try different speeds of rotation.

Can you see how this tool might be useful?

4.6 What Have We Learned?

Items covered in this lesson include

- *The differences between the UCS and the WCS*
- *How to use the UCS and different working planes*
- *How to use the UCS Manager*
- *How to dimension a three-dimensional drawing*
- *How to use AutoCAD's orbiting tools*
- *Commands*
    - ***UCS***
    - ***UCSMan / DDUCS***
    - ***3DOrbit***
    - ***3DPan***
    - ***3DZoom***
    - ***3DDistance***
    - ***3DSwivel***
    - ***3DClip***
    - ***3DCOrbit***

My chief Grammar and Usage Editor will say this was another *full* lesson!

But pat yourself on the back! Having made it to this point is no slight accomplishment. In these few lessons, you have mastered the basics for working in Z-Space. Let's take a minute and think about what you can do now that you could not do before beginning this text.

- You can maneuver in a drawing from front to back, side to side, and *up and down* (Spherical and Cylindrical Coordinate Systems, Point Filters).
- You can see your drawing from any point in the universe (***VPoint*** and ***Plan***).
- You can work on any surface as though it were lying flat on your desk (***UCS***).
- You have a host of new viewing tools to help you see your model from any angle or several angles at a time (***VPoint***, ***VPorts***, 3DOrbit tools, ***Shademode***).
- You can create three-dimensional stick figures (wireframes) and even draw with thickness and elevation.

You have come a long way in a short period of time, but there is still far to go. Most of what you learn about Z-Space from here will be tools and techniques to make three-dimensional drawing easier and faster.

As always, we should practice what we have learned before continuing our study. Do the exercises and answer the questions. Then proceed to our study of Wireframe and Surface Modeling techniques.

4.7 EXERCISES

1. through 8. Dimension the drawings you created in Exercises 1 through 8 of Section 3.7 (in Lesson 3). Refer to the drawings in Appendix B as a guide. If these drawings are not available, use the corresponding drawing in the C:\Steps3D\Lesson04 folder.

9. (Refer to Section 3.7 of Lesson 3—Exercise 9.) Open the *My Twisted Y.dwg* file in the C:\Steps3D\Lesson03 folder. (If the *My Twisted Y.dwg* file is not available, use the *Twisted Y.dwg* file found in the C:\Steps3D\Lesson04 folder.)

9.1. Place the dimensions shown in Figure 3.7.9.

9.2. Save the drawing to the C:\Steps3D\Lesson04 folder.

10. (Refer to Section 3.7 of Lesson 3—Exercise 10.) Open the *My Block.dwg* file in the C:\Steps3D\Lesson03 folder. (If the *My Block.dwg* file is not available, use the *Block.dwg* file found in the C:\Steps3D\Lesson04 folder.)

10.1. Place the dimensions shown in Figure 3.7.10.

10.2. Save the drawing to the C:\Steps3D\Lesson04 folder.

11. (Refer to Section 3.7 of Lesson 3—Exercise 11.) Open the *MyGrill.dwg* file in the C:\Steps3D\Lesson03 folder. (If the *My Grill.dwg* file is not available, use the *Grill.dwg* file found in the C:\Steps3D\Lesson04 folder.)

11.1. Place the dimensions shown in Figure 3.7.11.

11.2. Save the drawing to the C:\Steps3D\Lesson04 folder.

12. (Refer to Section 3.7 of Lesson 3—Exercise 12.) Open the *MyBookEnd.dwg* file in the C:\Steps3D\Lesson03 folder. (If the *MyBookEnd.dwg* file is not available, use the *BookEnd.dwg* file found in the C:\Steps3D\Lesson04 folder.)

12.1. Place the dimensions shown in Figure 3.7.12.

12.2. Save the drawing to the C:\Steps3D\Lesson04 folder.

13. (Refer to Section 3.7 of Lesson 3—Exercise 13.) Open the *MyMagRack.dwg* file in the C:\Steps3D\Lesson03 folder. (If the *MyMagRack.dwg* file is not available, use the *MagRack.dwg* file found in the C:\Steps3D\Lesson04 folder.)

13.1. Place the dimensions shown in Figure 3.7.13.

13.2. Save the drawing to the C:\Steps3D\Lesson04 folder.

14. (Refer to Section 3.7 of Lesson 3—Exercise 14.) Open the *My Anchor Stop.dwg* file in the C:\Steps3D\Lesson03 folder. (If the *My Anchor Stop.dwg* file is not available, use the *Anchor Stop.dwg* file found in the C:\Steps3D\Lesson04 folder.)

14.1. Place the dimensions shown in Figure 3.7.14.

14.2. Save the drawing to the C:\Steps3D\Lesson04 folder.

15. (Refer to Section 3.7 of Lesson 3—Exercise 15.) Open the *My Queen.dwg* file in the C:\Steps3D\Lesson03 folder. (If the *My Queen.dwg* file is not available, use the *Queen.dwg* file found in the C:\Steps3D\Lesson04 folder.)

15.1. Place the dimensions shown in Figure 3.7.15.

15.2. Save the drawing to the C:\Steps3D\Lesson04 folder.

16. (Refer to Section 3.7 of Lesson 3—Exercise 16.) Open the *My Ring Stand.dwg* file in the C:\Steps3D\Lesson03 folder. (If the *My Ring Stand.dwg* file is not available, use the *Ring Stand.dwg* file found in the C:\Steps3D\Lesson04 folder.)
    - **16.1.** Place the dimensions shown in Figure 3.7.16.
    - **16.2.** Save the drawing to the C:\Steps3D\Lesson04 folder.
17. Create the drawing in Figure 4.7.17 according to the following parameters:
    - **17.1.** Start the drawing using the *template #2* file found in the C:\Steps3D\Lesson04 folder.
    - **17.2.** The Paper Space text is $\frac{3}{16}''$ and $\frac{1}{8}''$.
    - **17.3.** Title block text is $\frac{1}{4}''$, $\frac{3}{16}''$, and $\frac{1}{8}''$.
    - **17.4.** Use the **Hidden** option of the ***Shademode*** command where necessary to achieve the views shown.
    - **17.5.** Text on the blocks uses either AutoCAD's standard text style or a style using the Times New Roman font. Text heights are $\frac{1}{4}''$.
    - **17.6.** Save the drawing as *My Angled Blocks.dwg* in the C:\Steps3D\Lesson04 folder.

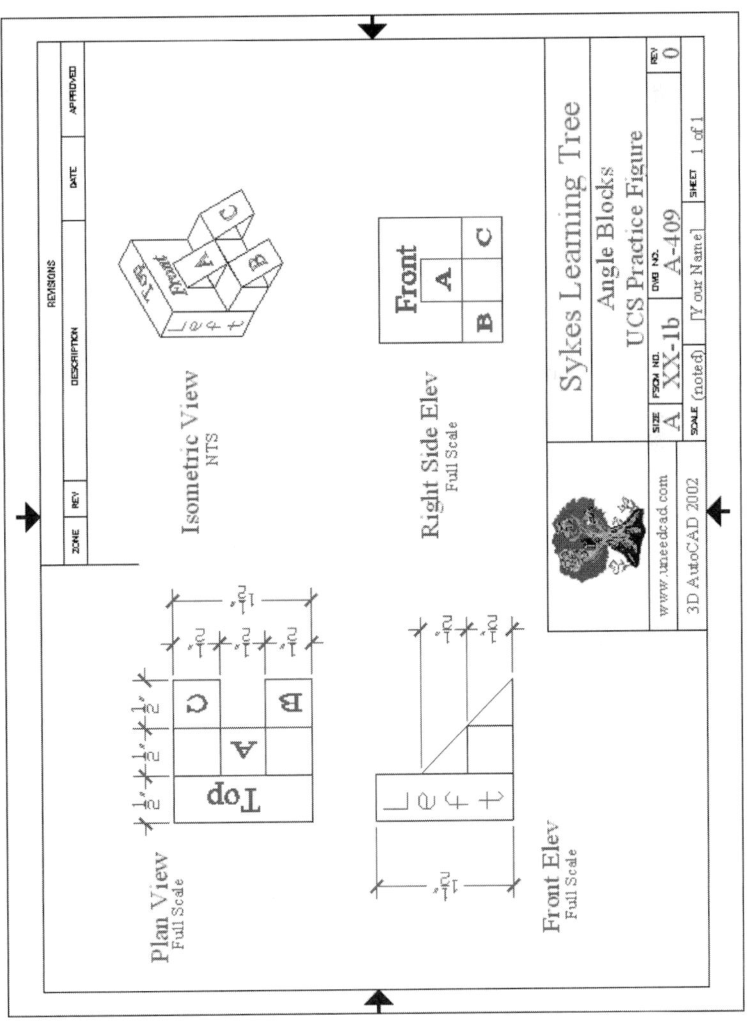

FIG. 4.7.17 My Angled Blocks

18. Create the drawing in Figure 4.7.18 according to the following parameters:
    - **18.1.** Start the drawing using the *template #1* file found in the C:\Steps3D\Lesson03 folder.
    - **18.2.** The Paper Space text is $\frac{3}{16}''$ and $\frac{1}{8}''$.
    - **18.3.** Title block text is $\frac{1}{4}''$, $\frac{3}{16}''$, and $\frac{1}{8}''$. The font is Times New Roman.
    - **18.4.** Use the **Hidden** option of the ***Shademode*** command where necessary to achieve the views shown.
    - **18.5.** Text on the blocks uses AutoCAD's standard text style. Text heights are $\frac{3}{16}''$.
    - **18.6.** Save the drawing as *My Corner Steps.dwg* in the C:\Steps3D\Lesson04 folder.

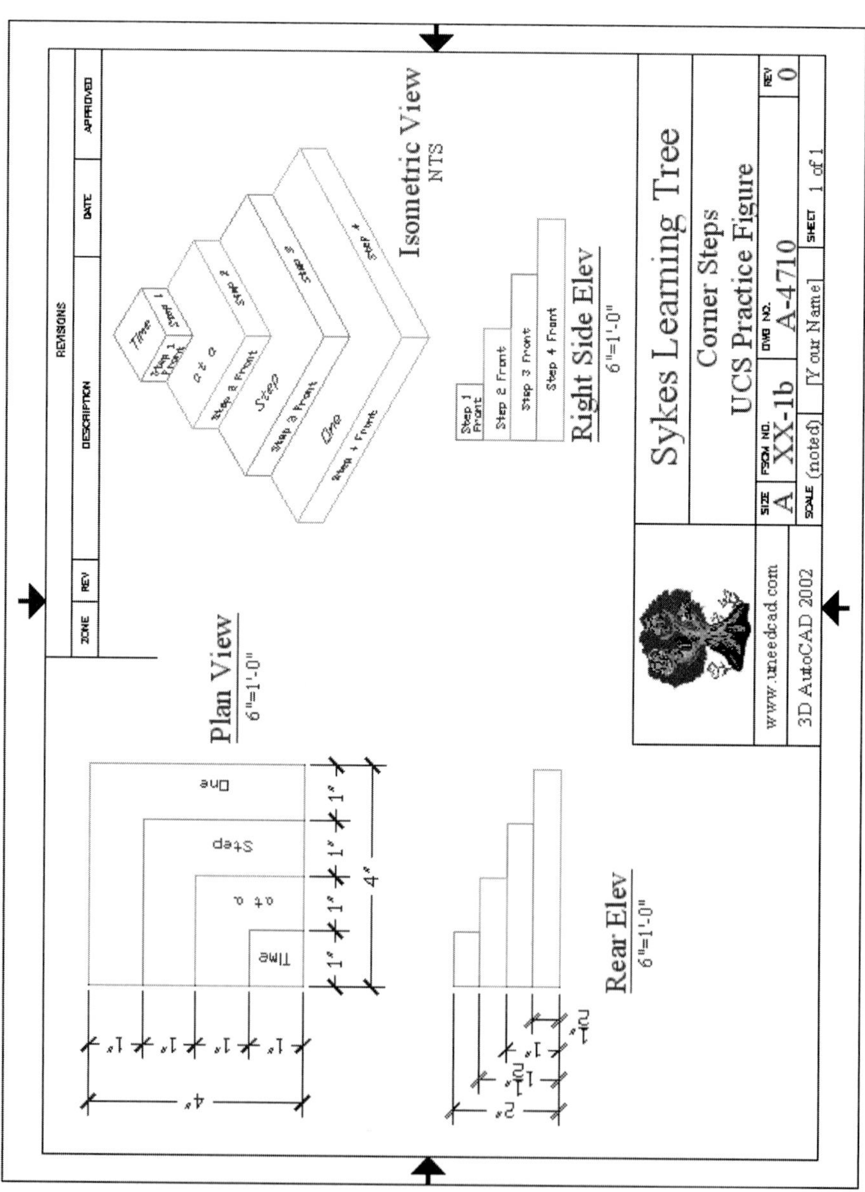

FIG. 4.7.18 My Corner Steps

19. The drawing in Figure 4.7.19 is a game of UCS manipulation and the ***Array*** and ***Mirror*** commands. Create it according to the following parameters:

19.1. The table top is a 5″ wide × 5″ long polyline drawn with a $\frac{1}{2}$″ thickness.

19.2. Each of the eight legs is made up of eight lines. Each line is 5″ long. The original was drawn at 30° in the XY-plane and 60° from the XY-plane. The lines were then arrayed in a $\frac{1}{16}$″ circle.

19.3. The eight "feet" are $\frac{1}{4}$″ radius circles. Again, they were arrayed (eight circles in each array).

19.4. The center ball is also an arrayed circle (eight in all)—this one with a $\frac{1}{2}$″ radius.

19.5. The upper legs are mirrored from the bottom.

19.6. Have fun!

19.7. Save the drawing as *My Table.dwg* in the C:\Steps3D\Lesson04 folder.

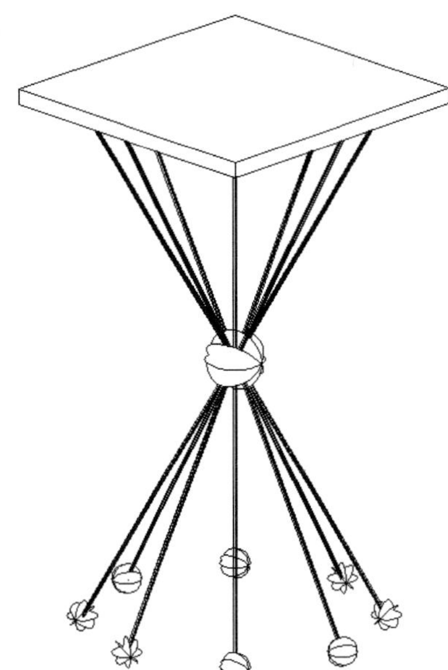

FIG. 4.7.19 Table

20. Create the drawing in Figure 4.7.20 according to the following parameters:

20.1. This is a B-size (17″ × 11″) layout. Use the appropriate AutoCAD title block/border.

20.2. The Paper Space text is $\frac{3}{16}$″ and $\frac{1}{8}$″.

20.3. Title block text is $\frac{1}{4}$″, $\frac{3}{16}$″, and $\frac{1}{8}$″. The font is Times New Roman.

20.4. The top is a single polyline drawn with $\frac{1}{2}$″ thickness.

20.5. *Hint:* Use the **TTR** option of the ***Circle*** command to draw the leg curves.

20.6. Save the drawing as *My Other Table.dwg* in the C:\Steps3D\Lesson04 folder.

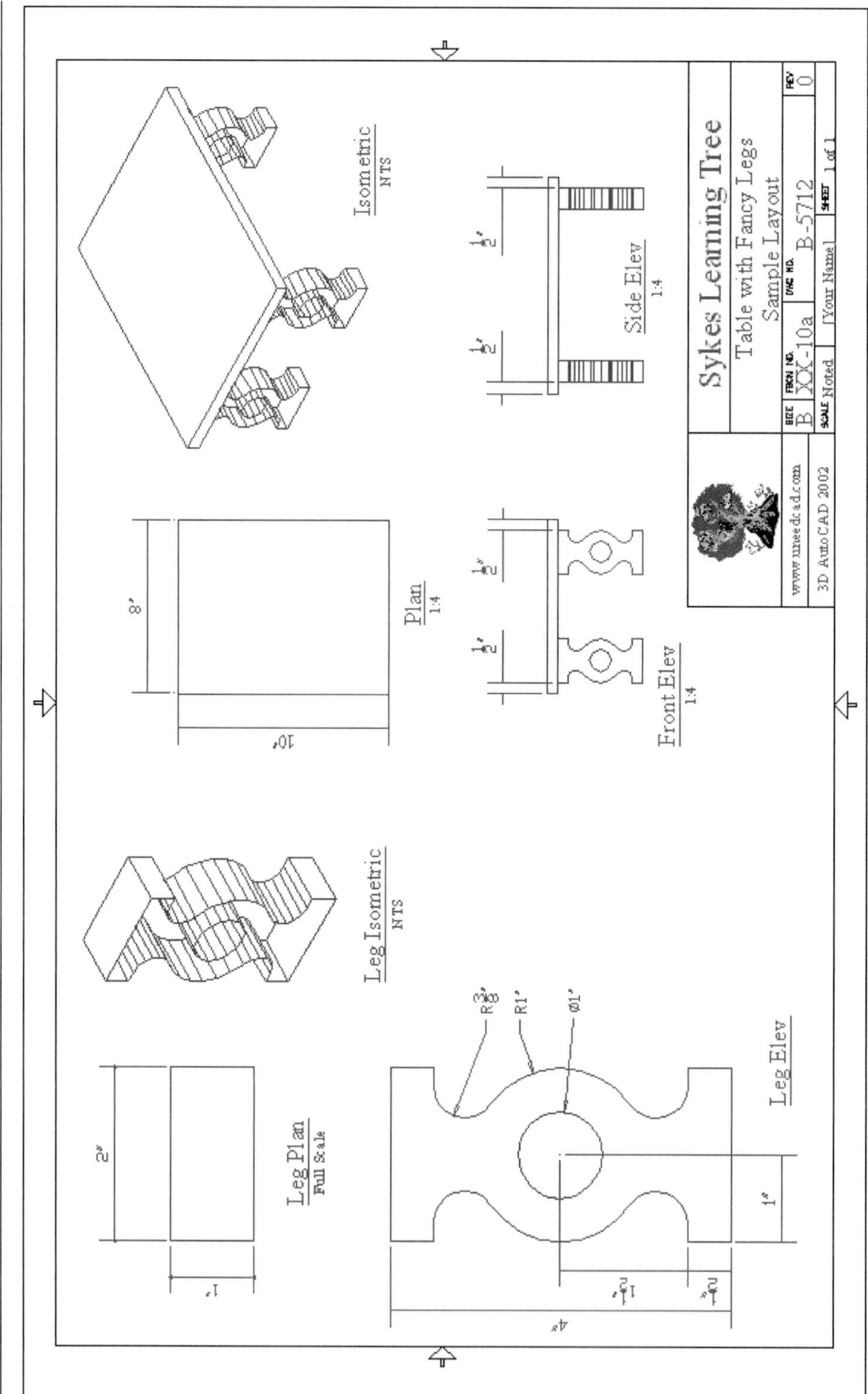

FIG. 4.7.20 Other Table

21. Create the drawing in Figure 4.7.21 according to the following parameters:

21.1. This is a B-size (17″ × 11″) layout. Use the appropriate AutoCAD title block/border.

21.2. The Paper Space text is $\frac{3}{16}$″ and $\frac{1}{8}$″.

21.3. Title block text is $\frac{1}{4}$″, $\frac{3}{16}$″, and $\frac{1}{8}$″. The font is Times New Roman.

21.4. This is a wireframe drawing—use thickness only on the arcs/circles.

21.5. Save the drawing as *My Corner Bracket.dwg* in the C:\Steps3D\Lesson04 folder.

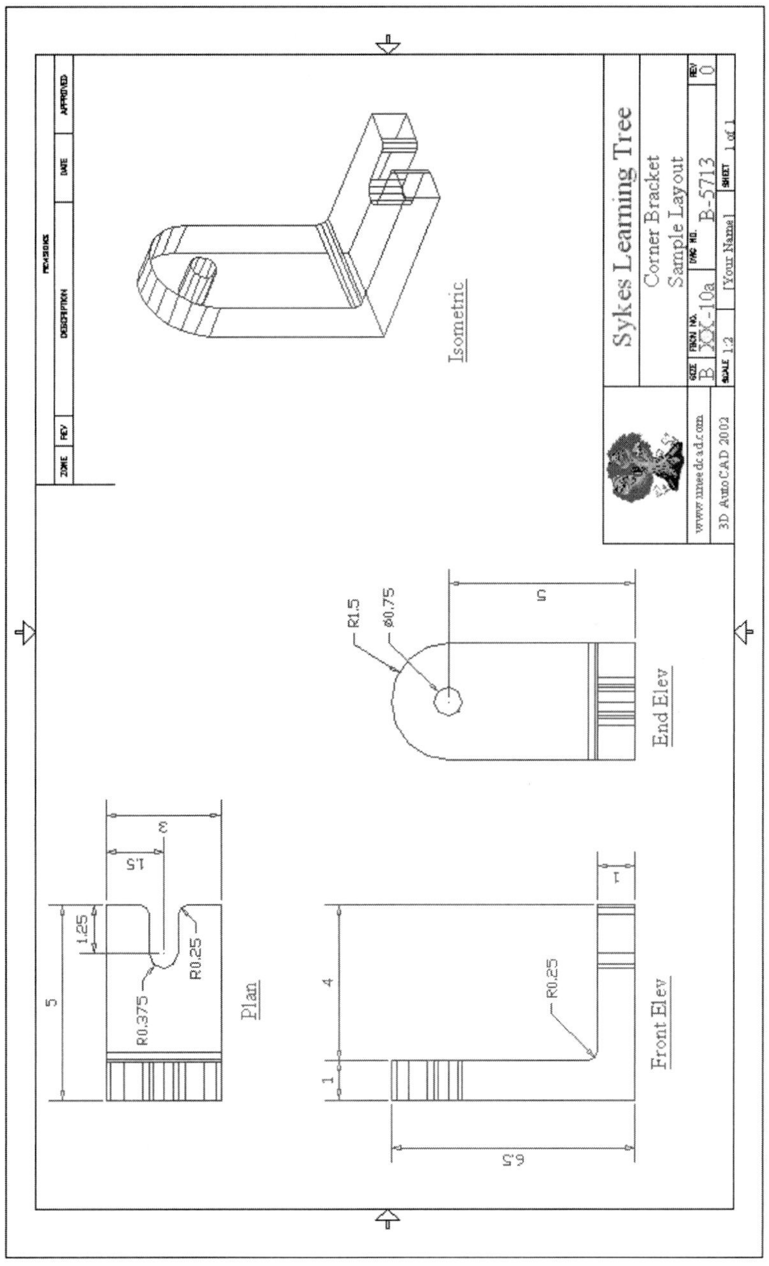

FIG. 4.7.21 Corner Bracket

22. Create the drawing in Figure 4.7.22 according to the following parameters:
    22.1. This is an A-size (11″ × $8\frac{1}{2}$″) layout. Use the appropriate AutoCAD title block/border.
    22.2. The Paper Space text is $\frac{3}{16}$″ and $\frac{1}{8}$″.
    22.3. Title block text is $\frac{1}{4}$″, $\frac{3}{16}$″, and $\frac{1}{8}$″. The font is Times New Roman.
    22.4. This is a wireframe drawing—do not use thickness.
    22.5. You will need to use the ***3DClip*** procedures to clean up the views.
    22.6. Save the drawing as *My Phone Plug.dwg* in the C:\Steps3D\Lesson04 folder.

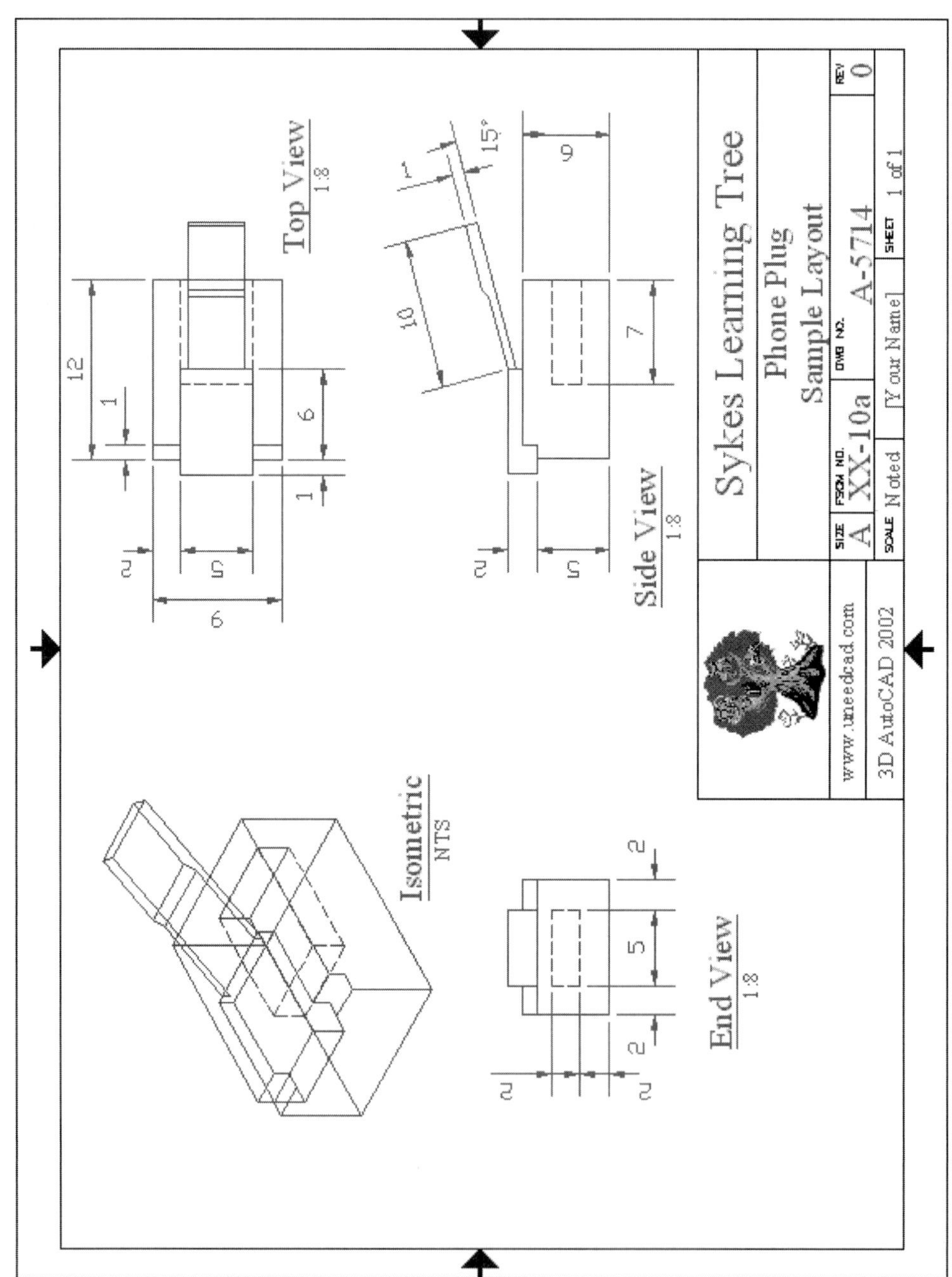

FIG. 4.7.22 Phone Plug

23. Create the drawing in Figure 4.7.23 according to the following parameters:

23.1. This is a B-size (17″ × 11″) layout. Use the appropriate AutoCAD title block/border.

23.2. The Paper Space text is $\frac{3}{16}$″ and $\frac{1}{8}$″.

23.3. Title block text is $\frac{1}{4}$″, $\frac{3}{16}$″, and $\frac{1}{8}$″. The font is Times New Roman.

23.4. This is a wireframe drawing—use thickness only on the arcs/circles.

23.5. You will need to use the ***3DClip*** procedures to clean up the views.

23.6. Save the drawing as *My Other Corner Bracket.dwg* in the C:\Steps3D\Lesson04 folder.

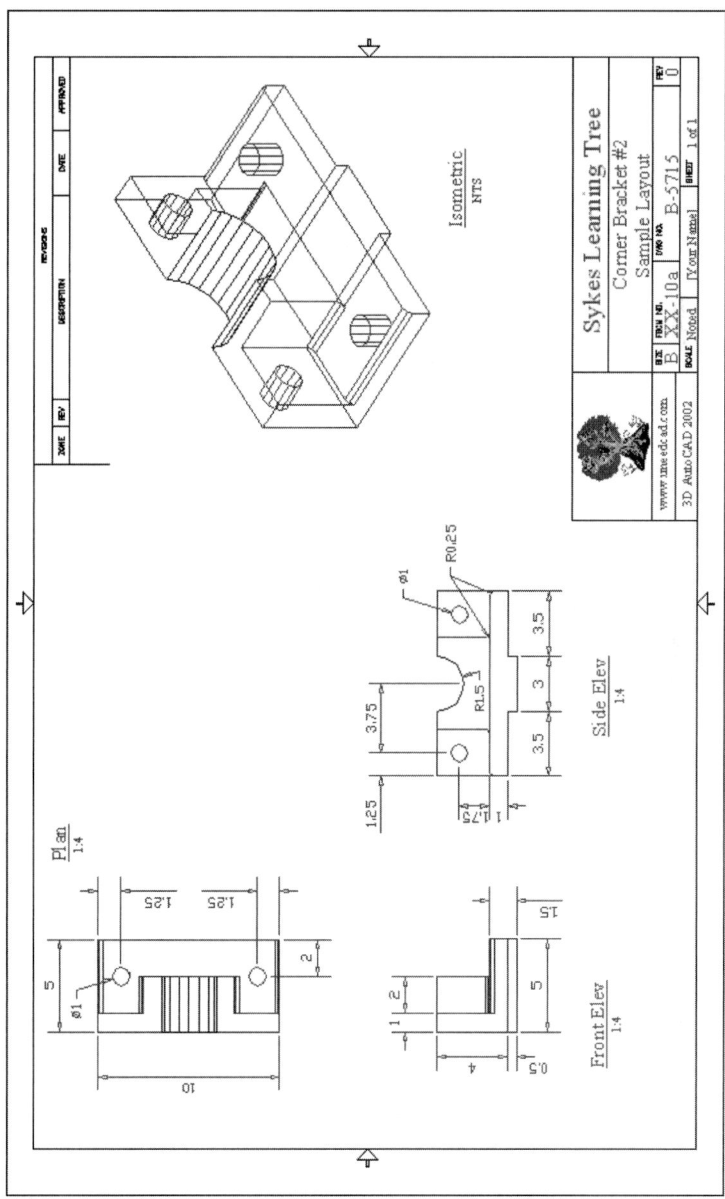

FIG. 4.7.23 Other Corner Bracket

4.8 REVIEW QUESTIONS

Please write your answers on a separate sheet of paper.

1. through 10. Identify the button and the toolbar on which you will find it.

IMAGE					
Button	1	3	5	7	9
Toolbar	2	4	6	8	10

11. Access the UCS from the command line with the __________ command.

12. Use the __________ option of the UCS-New prompt to define a new UCS by identifying the 0,0,0 point and a point on the Z-axis.

13. Use the __________ option of the UCS-New prompt to define a new UCS by identifying the 0,0,0 point and a point on each of the X- and Y-axes.

14. Use the __________ option of the UCS prompt to move the UCS 0,0,0 point without changing its orientation.

15. The best way to set the UCS according to a standard orthographic front view of the model is to use the __________ option of the UCS command.

16. Use the __________ option of the UCS command to restore the UCS to match the WCS's orientation.

17. and 18. One of the first things you should do when working with the UCS is to set the __________ to __________. This way, you will always know where 0,0,0 is.

19. (T or F) Viewpoints and viewports are the same thing.

20. __________ are points from which you view the drawing.

21. __________ are like portholes in a ship through which you view the model.

22. The __________ orients the user on the model itself.

23. Save viewpoint views by using the __________ command.

24. (T or F) Each viewport can have a unique viewpoint and/or UCS assigned to it.

25. Use the __________ to keep track of the UCSs you have created.

26. How would I find the origin in WCS coordinates, as well as the X-, Y-, and Z-axes of a defined UCS?

27. (T or F) When drawing a two-dimensional solid, the UCS must be aligned with the plane on which you wish to draw.

28. (T or F) When placing dimensions, the UCS must be aligned with the object you are dimensioning.

29. Making dimensions visible in one viewport but not others is accomplished by careful manipulation of __________.

30. Use the __________ command to turn the model (as a builder turns the object for examination in his hands).

31. The arcball is associated with what command?

32. through 39. Use the answers provided to identify the cursor with its location and function.

(a) Perform a two-dimensional rotation

(b) Rotate the model about the east/west axis of the arcball

(c) Manipulate the model freely about its center point

(d) Rotate the model about the north/south axis of the arcball

(e) **(f)** **(g)** **(h)**

WHEN THE CURSOR IS	DRAGGING THE CURSOR WILL:	THE CURSOR WILL BE A:
Inside the arcball	**32.**	**33.**
Outside the arcball	**34.**	**35.**
Inside the east or west quadrant circle	**36.**	**37.**
Inside the north or south quadrant circle	**38.**	**39.**

40. If you wish to return to the view you had when you began the 3DOrbiter, select __________ from the cursor menu.

41. The __________ command allows the user to continually rotate the model without using the mouse or keyboard.

42. 3D Continuous Orbit spins the model like (a) a planet on its axis or (b) a planet around the sun.

PART

Simple Modeling

This part of our text contains these lessons:

5. Wireframes and Surface Modeling
6. Predefined Surface Models
7. Complex Surface Models

LESSON 5

Wireframes and Surface Modeling

Following this lesson, you will

- Know the differences between a polyline and a three-dimensional polyline
- Know how to project a curved surface in three dimensions
- Know how to create a three-dimensional face (***3DFace***)
    - Know how to make the edges of a face visible or invisible
- Know the differences between Solids and Regions
    - Know how to create a Region with the **Region** command
    - Know how to create a Region with the **Boundary** command
    - Know how to use the ***Subtract*** command to remove one Region from another

Most textbooks separate Wireframe Modeling and Surface Modeling into two distinct chapters. But the inevitable result is confusion. The two are so closely related that distinguishing between them often causes more bewilderment than just teaching them as they are—two sides of the same coin.

Let me make the distinction as simple as possible.

A Wireframe Model (what we have called a stick figure up until now) is a skeleton drawing. It has all the necessary parts—but no flesh. Drawing a Wireframe Model is relatively fast (compared to a Surface Model), but it provides little more than an outline of the model. When used, wireframes generally lead the three-dimensional design process (in the layout stage). Fleshing out the wireframe—turning it into a Surface Model—comes when the layout is accepted, and you want to turn the skeleton into a production or display drawing.

A Surface Model essentially stretches some skin over the skeleton. We have seen that the *Shademode* and *Hide* commands have no effect on wireframe models. Fleshing out the skeleton makes it possible to see surfaces (hence, the name *Surface Modeling*).

In this lesson, we will learn how to create more complex Wireframe Models. Then we will look at some ways to create surfaces on them.

5.1 3DPoly vs. PLine

Now that you are working with Z-coordinates, you may have noticed a certain limitation in polylines—polylines are two-dimensional creatures. True, you can give a polyline thickness and elevation, but you cannot draw a polyline using different points on the Z-axis. That is, when prompted to **Specify next point**, your selection will use the same point on the Z-axis as the first point you identified—regardless of any three-dimensional coordinate you give it!

But that does not mean that you must sacrifice the benefits of a polyline . . . well, not all the benefits anyway. AutoCAD provides a three-dimensional version of the polyline called the 3DPoly. When you need a multisegmented polyline drawn in Z-Space, simply use the ***3DPoly*** command instead of the ***PLine*** command.

There are, however, some restrictions to the 3DPoly. Chief among these is that a 3D polyline cannot contain width. AutoCAD has not added this useful property yet. Additionally, you cannot draw a 3D polyline using arcs or linetypes other than continuous.

Bear in mind that, while use of the polyline is restricted in Z-Space, use of the spline is not. You can use the ***Spline*** command when you wish to draw curved lines in three dimensions. However, most surfaces created for a Surface Model will have flat edges and will not be able to lie flat against a spline.

The benefits of the 3DPoly include the ability to draw it in three dimensions, to edit it with the ***Pedit*** command, and to spline it.

We will use the ***3DPoly*** command in our first exercise.

5.2 Drawing in Three Directions at Once—Point Projection

You may be thinking that Wireframe Modeling is a fairly easy thing to do. After all, a Wireframe Model is just stick figures, right?

Of course, you are absolutely right. Stick figures are quite simple to draw—as long as the model you want to draw uses nice straight sticks. But consider the curved panel roof in Figure 5.2a. Using the UCS procedures you learned in Lesson 4, you can easily draw the arcs and roof lines. But how would you draw the joint between the roofs?

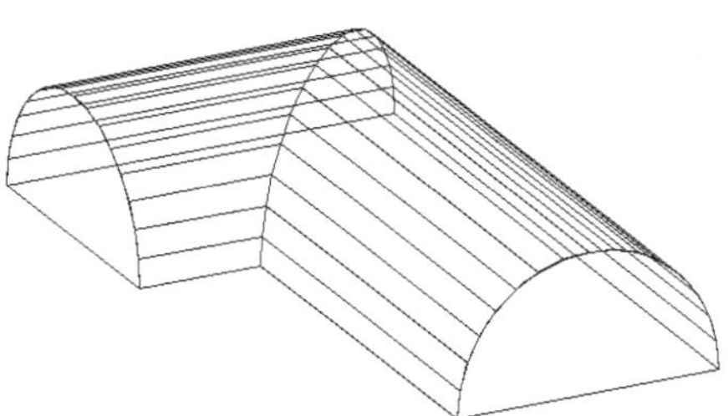

FIG. 5.2a Wireframe Model of a Curved Panel Roof

To draw in three directions at once as this joint requires—(front to back, side to side, and up and down)—means that the user must identify a series of points where the two roofs intersect. To do this, you must project points—or identify points by intersection of lines in Z-Space.

Remember that all three-dimensional drafting requires precise point identification using one of the methods we have already discussed. You cannot pick an "about here" point and get away with it as you could in two-dimensional drafting.

This is not as difficult as it sounds. In fact, it is a lot like duck hunting (or skeet shooting for those with weaker stomachs). To hit a moving target, you must *lead* it a bit so that your bullet and the bird (or clay pigeon) arrive at the same place at the same time. What you do when you project points is simply identify where the bird and the bullet will meet. You do this by projecting one line along the bird's flight path and another along the barrel of your rifle. The intersection of the two lines is your actual target—or in drafting terms, your projection point.

Let's see how this works. We will use our projection technique to identify the intersecting arc of the two roofs and then draw the arc using a 3DPolyline.

WWW 5.2.1 Do This: Projections and 3D Polylines

I. Open the *Cabin.dwg* file located in the C:\Steps3D\Lesson05 folder. The drawing appears in Figure 5.2.1a.

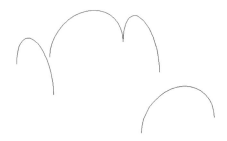

FIG. 5.2.1a *Cabin.dwg*

II. Follow these steps:

TOOLS	COMMAND SEQUENCE	STEPS
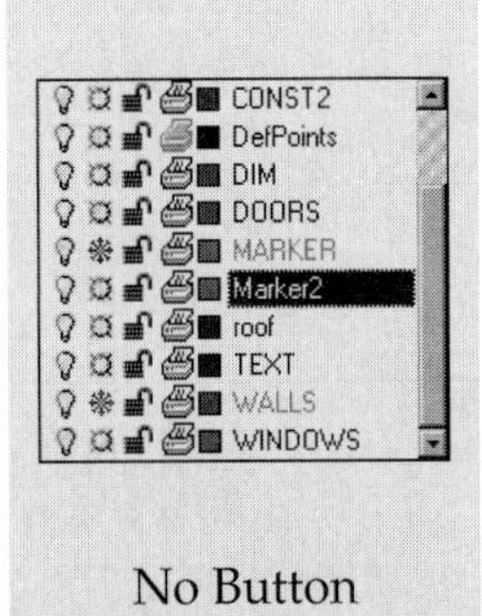	**Command:** ***la***	**1.** Create a **Marker2** layer and set it current.
No Button Available	**Command:** ***div*** **Select object to divide:** **Enter the number of segments or [Block]:** ***16***	**2.** Use the ***Divide*** command to divide each of the arcs into 16 segments. (If the divisions are not marked clearly, set the **PDMode** system variable to ***3*** and regen the drawing.) Notice that the nodes appeared in the UCS that was current when the arcs were drawn.

continued

TOOLS	COMMAND SEQUENCE	STEPS
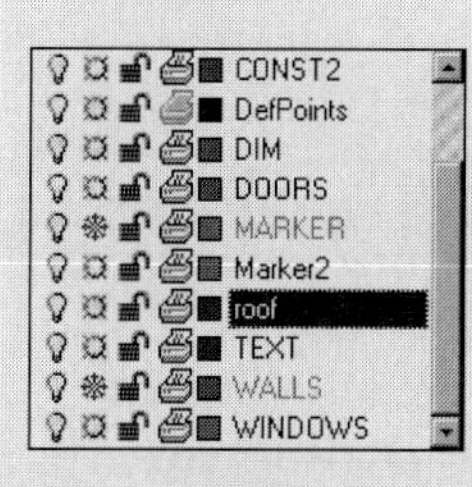	**Command:** *la*	**3.** Set the **Roof** layer current.
	**Command:** *l*	**4.** Draw lines between the corresponding nodes and endpoints as shown in Figure 5.2.1.4. (The lines represent the duck's flight path and the barrel of our rifle.) (*Hint:* You may find it easier to draw one line in each direction and then copy it to each of the nodes/endpoints.)

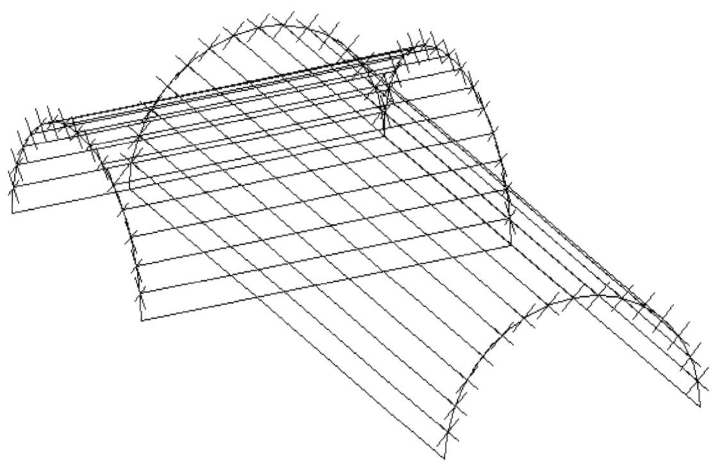

FIG. 5.2.1.4 Projected Roof Lines

TOOLS	COMMAND SEQUENCE	STEPS
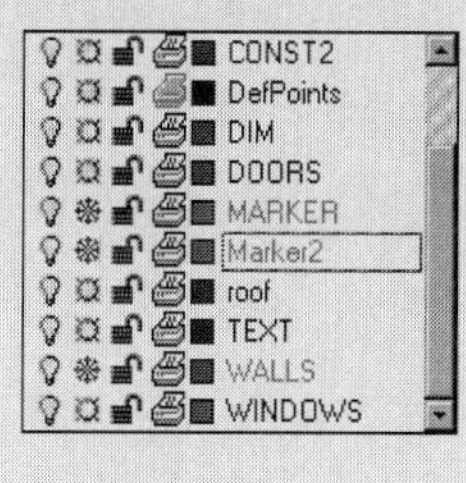	**Command:** *la*	**5.** Freeze the **Marker2** layer.

continued

TOOLS	COMMAND SEQUENCE	STEPS
	**Command:** *tr*	**6.** *Carefully* trim the extra portions of the lines. Start with the nearest intersection —lowest north–south line with lowest east–west line—and work back. (*Hint:* You may find it easier to do this from the plan view. But watch the first and last endpoints.) Return to this view (VPoint 2,−1,1) when you are finished. Your drawing looks like Figure 5.2.1.6.

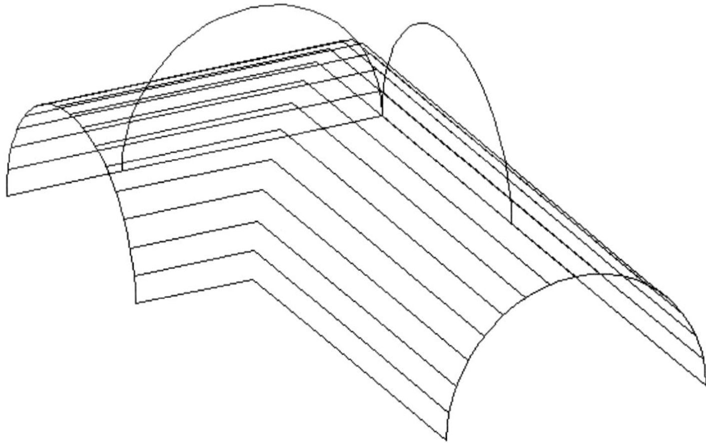

FIG. 5.2.1.6 When Trimmed, Projection Lines Become Roof Lines

TOOLS	COMMAND SEQUENCE	STEPS
	**Command:** *e*	**7.** Erase the arcs in the back.

continued

TOOLS	COMMAND SEQUENCE	STEPS
No Button Available	**Command:** ***3dpoly***	**8.** Draw a 3D Polyline connecting the intersections of the extension lines as shown in Figure 5.2.1.8. Use OSNAPs! (It might be easier to do this in plan view.)

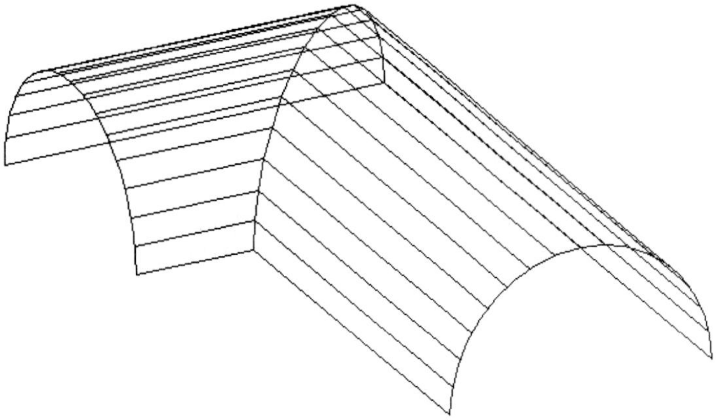

FIG. 5.2.1.8 Completed Wireframe Roof

TOOLS	COMMAND SEQUENCE	STEPS
	**Command:** ***qsave***	**9.** Save the drawing, but do not exit.

Did you try the ***Hide*** or ***Shademode*** commands on the drawing? If you did, you noticed that they have no effect. Remember that we have created a *Wireframe Model*—a skeleton of the roof we want.

Look closely at the 3D Polyline you created. Notice that it is a series of straight lines, not curved like the roof. We might have used a spline instead of a 3D Polyline and achieved a nice soft curve, but the tool we will use to "stretch the skin around our skeleton" does not allow for curves. So we are better off using the straighter 3D Polyline (as we will soon see).

5.3 Adding Surfaces—Regions, Solids, or 3D Faces

AutoCAD provides three methods for creating Surface Models—the ***Region***, ***Solid***, and ***3DFace*** commands. The three are so closely related that it is often difficult to tell the difference:

- Each is drawn as a two-dimensional object.
- Each becomes a 3D Solid when extruded (more on the ***Extrude*** command in Lesson 9).
- Each creates an opaque (or solid) surface.

But despite their similarities, each has its place.

- The ***Region*** command *converts* a closed object (polygon, circle, two-dimensional spline, etc.) into a surface. A Region cannot have thickness.
- The ***Solid*** command fills an area only in the current UCS, but it can have thickness.
- The ***3DFace*** command draws a true three-dimensional surface (in all of the X-, Y-, and Z-planes). A 3D Face cannot have thickness.

When would you use one instead of the other two? Let's take a look at each and see.

5.3.1 3D Face

Of the three surfacing methods, the ***3DFace*** command is the most versatile. However, it is also more difficult to use when cutouts are involved. The ***3DFace*** command makes no allowance for removal of part of the surface (as the ***Trim*** command allows the user to remove part of a line or circle). The user can, however, draw a 3D Face without concern for the current UCS (provided coordinate entry is precise).

The command sequence looks like this:

Command: *3DFace*

Specify first point or [Invisible]: *[select the first point]*

Specify second point or [Invisible]: *[select the second point]*

Specify third point or [Invisible] <exit>: *[select the third point]*

Specify fourth point or [Invisible] <create three-sided face>: *[select the fourth point or hit enter to create a 3D Face from the three points already selected]*

Specify third point or [Invisible] <exit>: *[you may continue selecting points or hit enter to exit the command]*

The only option available—**Invisible**—is not one you really want to use. When creating 3D Faces, it will occasionally be necessary to hide one of the edges (or make it invisible). This will become apparent in the next exercise. The command line procedure for doing this involves typing an ***I*** before the first point selection that defines the edge to be hidden. The edge drawn between the two points that follow the ***I*** will be invisible. This becomes a real chore when two or more edges must be hidden. We will look at an easier approach to hiding the edges of 3D Faces following the next exercise.

First, let's use the ***3DFace*** command to place a surface—with a window in it—on one of the walls of our cabin.

You can also access the ***3DFace*** command by using the **3D Face** button on the Surfaces toolbar or by selecting it from the Draw pull-down menu. Follow this path:

Draw—Surfaces—3D Face

WWW 5.3.1.1 Do This: *Surfaces with 3D Face*

I. Be sure you are still in the *Cabin.dwg* file located in the C:\Steps3D\Lesson05 folder. If not, open it now.

II. Set UCS = WCS.

III. Follow these steps:

TOOLS	COMMAND SEQUENCE	STEPS
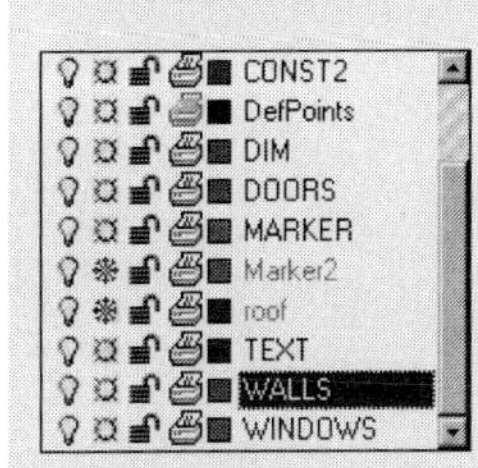	**Command:** ***la***	**1.** Thaw layers **Walls** and **Marker**. Set **Walls** current and freeze the **Roof** layer. The drawing looks like Figure 5.3.1.1.1.

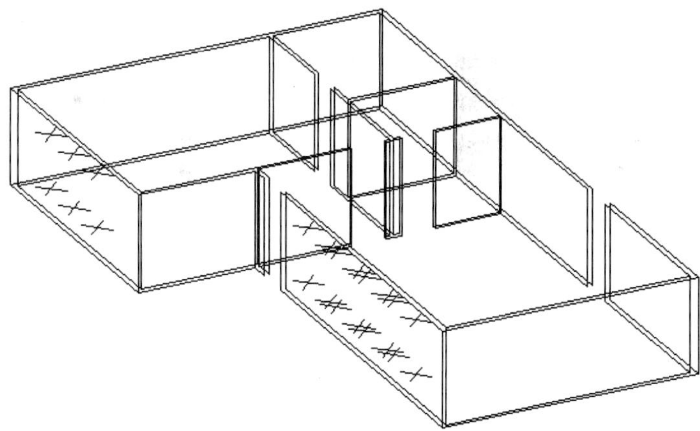

FIG. 5.3.1.1.1 Walls Shown

TOOLS	COMMAND SEQUENCE	STEPS
	**Command:** ***z***	**2.** Zoom in around the protruding part of the cabin—the wall with six nodes (refer to Figure 5.3.1.1.4).

continued

TOOLS	COMMAND SEQUENCE	STEPS
 Properties Button	**Command:** *props*	**3.** The front wall consists of two lines drawn with thickness. We cannot put a window in these objects, so we will remove the thickness and replace the lines with 3D Faces. Begin by changing the thickness of both lines (inner and outer walls) to ***0***. (Use the Properties Manager.)
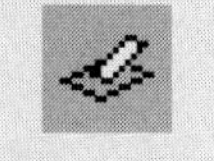 3D Face Button	**Command:** *3dface* **Specify first point or [Invisible]:** *[select Point 1]*	**4.** (Refer to Figure 5.3.1.1.4) Begin the ***3DFace*** command by typing ***3dface*** at the command prompt or picking the **3D Face** button on the Surfaces toolbar. Pick Point 1 as your first point.

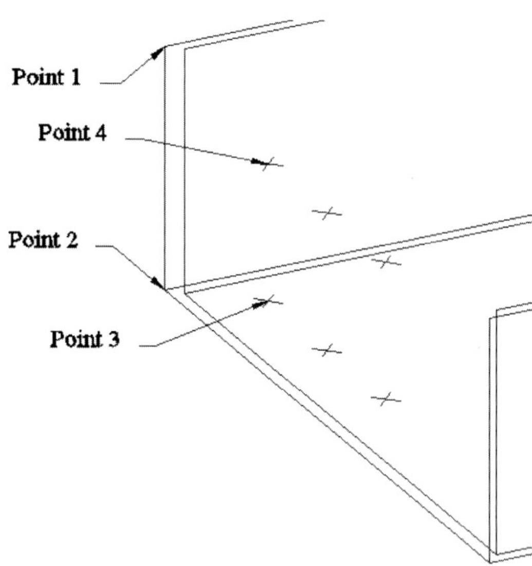

FIG. 5.3.1.1.4 Refer to These Points

TOOLS	COMMAND SEQUENCE	STEPS
	Specify second point or [Invisible]: *[select Point 2]*	**5.** Pick Point 2 as the second point.
	Specify third point or [Invisible] <exit>: *.xy* **of** *[select Point 3]*	**6.** We will use point filters to locate the third point. Tell AutoCAD to use the X and Y values of Point 3 . . .

continued

TOOLS	COMMAND SEQUENCE	STEPS
	(need Z): ***[select Point 2]***	**7.** . . . and the Z value of Point 2.
	Specify fourth point or [Invisible] <create three-sided face>: ***.xy***	**8.** Again, we will use point filters to locate the fourth point. Tell AutoCAD to use the X and Y values of Point 4 . . .
	of ***[select Point 4]***	
	(need Z): ***[select Point 1]***	**9.** . . . and the Z value of Point 1.
	Specify third point or [Invisible] <exit>: ***[enter]***	**10.** Hit ***enter*** to complete the command. Your drawing looks like Figure 5.3.1.1.10.

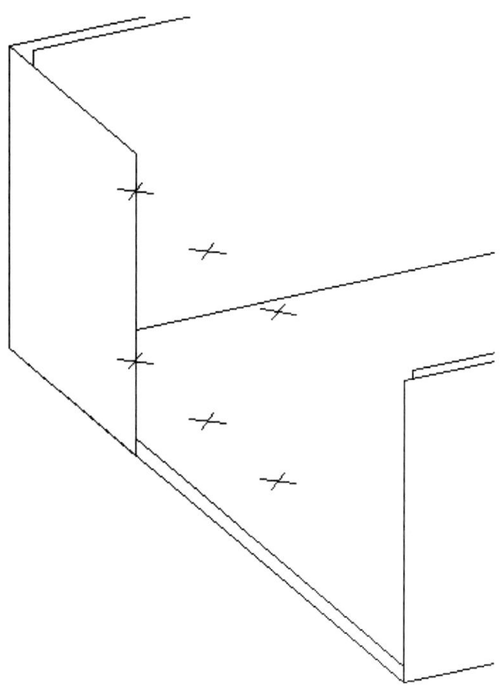

FIG. 5.3.1.1.10 Your First 3D Face (hidden lines removed)

continued

TOOLS	COMMAND SEQUENCE	STEPS
	Command: *3dface*	**11.** Repeat Steps 4 through 10 to draw the other end of the wall and the walls above and below the window. Your drawing will look like Figure 5.3.1.1.11.
		FIG. 5.3.1.1.11 Completed 3D Faces (hidden lines removed)
	**Command:** *qsave*	**12.** Save the drawing, but do not exit.

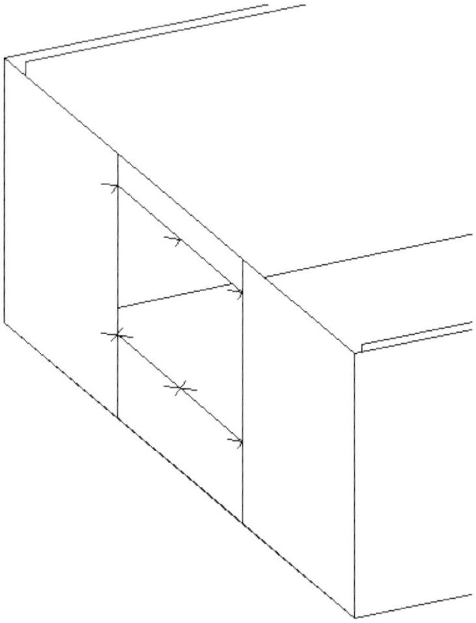

You should have noticed three things about the last exercise.

- Although quite useful, the skeleton (Wireframe Model) is not required when drawing a Surface Model.
- The *3DFace* command has left lines (edges) above and below the window that do not normally appear on a model (or a wall).
- The current UCS did not affect placement of the 3D Face.

Let's take a look at those edges.

5.3.2 Invisible Edges in 3D Faces—SPLFrame and the Edge Command

Although you can make 3D Face edges invisible as you draw them, it is a tedious, time-consuming, and error-prone task. You will find it much easier to draw the 3D Face and then use the ***Edge*** command to hide the edges that you do not want to see.

The command sequence looks like this:

Command: *edge*

Specify edge of 3dface to toggle visibility or [Display]:

Simply select the edge you wish to make invisible. How much easier can they make it?

The **Display** option prompts like this:

Enter selection method for display of hidden edges [Select/All] <All>:

Respond by selecting a 3D Face whose invisible edges you would like to see or by hitting enter to accept the **All** option. The **All** option means that AutoCAD will show all the invisible edges in the display.

Use of the **Display** option allows the user to *temporarily* display all invisible edges. Once the command ends, invisible edges are once again invisible.

To display all the 3D Face edges in a drawing, whether visible or not, set the **SPLFrame** system variable to ***1***.

Let's make the necessary edges invisible on our new surfaces.

> You can also access the ***Edge*** command by using the **Edge** button on the Surfaces toolbar or by selecting it from the Draw pull-down menu. Follow this path:
>
> *Draw—Surfaces—Edge*

WWW 5.3.2.1 Do This: Invisible Edges

I. Be sure you are still in the *Cabin.dwg* file located in the C:\Steps3D\Lesson05 folder. If not, open it now.

II. Follow these steps:

TOOLS	COMMAND SEQUENCE	STEPS
 Edge Button	**Command:** *edge*	**1.** Enter the ***Edge*** command by typing ***edge*** at the command line or by selecting the **Edge** button on the Surfaces toolbar.

continued

TOOLS	COMMAND SEQUENCE	STEPS

Specify edge of 3dface to toggle visibility or [Display]:

2. Select the two edges below the window and the two edges above the window. Also select the upper and lower window edges.

Specify edge of 3dface to toggle visibility or [Display]: *[enter]*

3. Complete the command.

CONST2
DefPoints
DIM
DOORS
MARKER
Marker2
roof
TEXT
WALLS
WINDOWS

Command: *hide*

4. Freeze the **Marker** layer and use the ***Hide*** command to remove hidden lines. Your drawing looks like Figure 5.3.2.1.4.

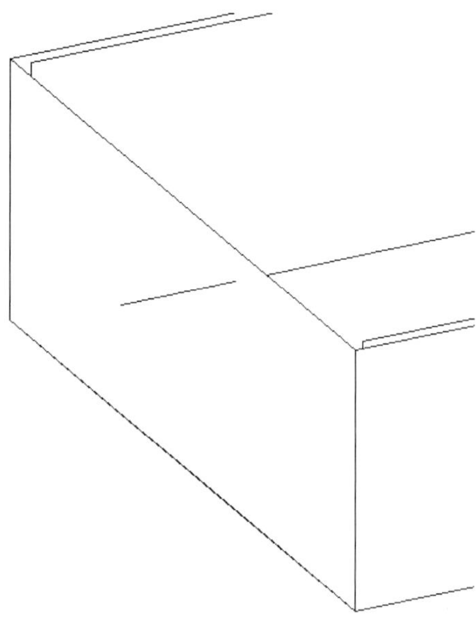

FIG. 5.3.2.1.4 Invisible Edges

No Button Available

Command: *splframe*

Enter new value for SPLFRAME <0>: ***1***

5. Now we will draw the actual window. First we need to find the edges of our 3D Face. Do this by setting the **SPLFrame** system variable to ***1***. (Regen the drawing to see the results.)

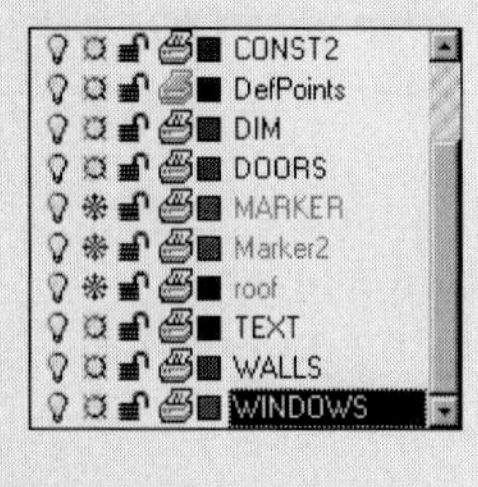

Command: *la*

6. Set **Windows** as the current layer.

continued

TOOLS	COMMAND SEQUENCE	STEPS
	Command: ***ucs***	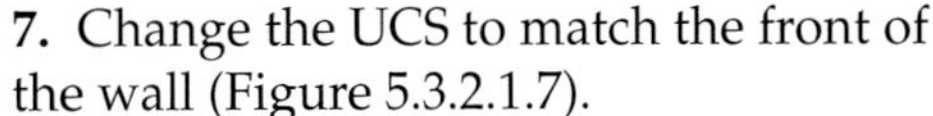 **7.** Change the UCS to match the front of the wall (Figure 5.3.2.1.7).

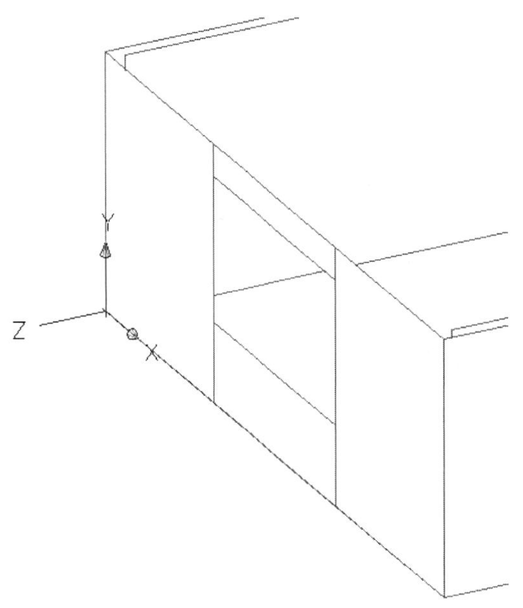

FIG. 5.3.2.1.7 New UCS

TOOLS	COMMAND SEQUENCE	STEPS
	Command: ***th***	**8.** Set Thickness to −5.5.
	Enter new value for THICKNESS <0′−0″>: −5.5	
	**Command:** ***l***	**9.** Draw the window frame. (Trace the opening.)

continued

TOOLS	COMMAND SEQUENCE	STEPS
	Command: *splframe* **Enter new value for SPLFRAME <1>:** *0*	**10.** Return the **SPLFrame** system variable to zero and enter the ***Hide*** command. Your drawing looks like Figure 5.3.2.1.10.

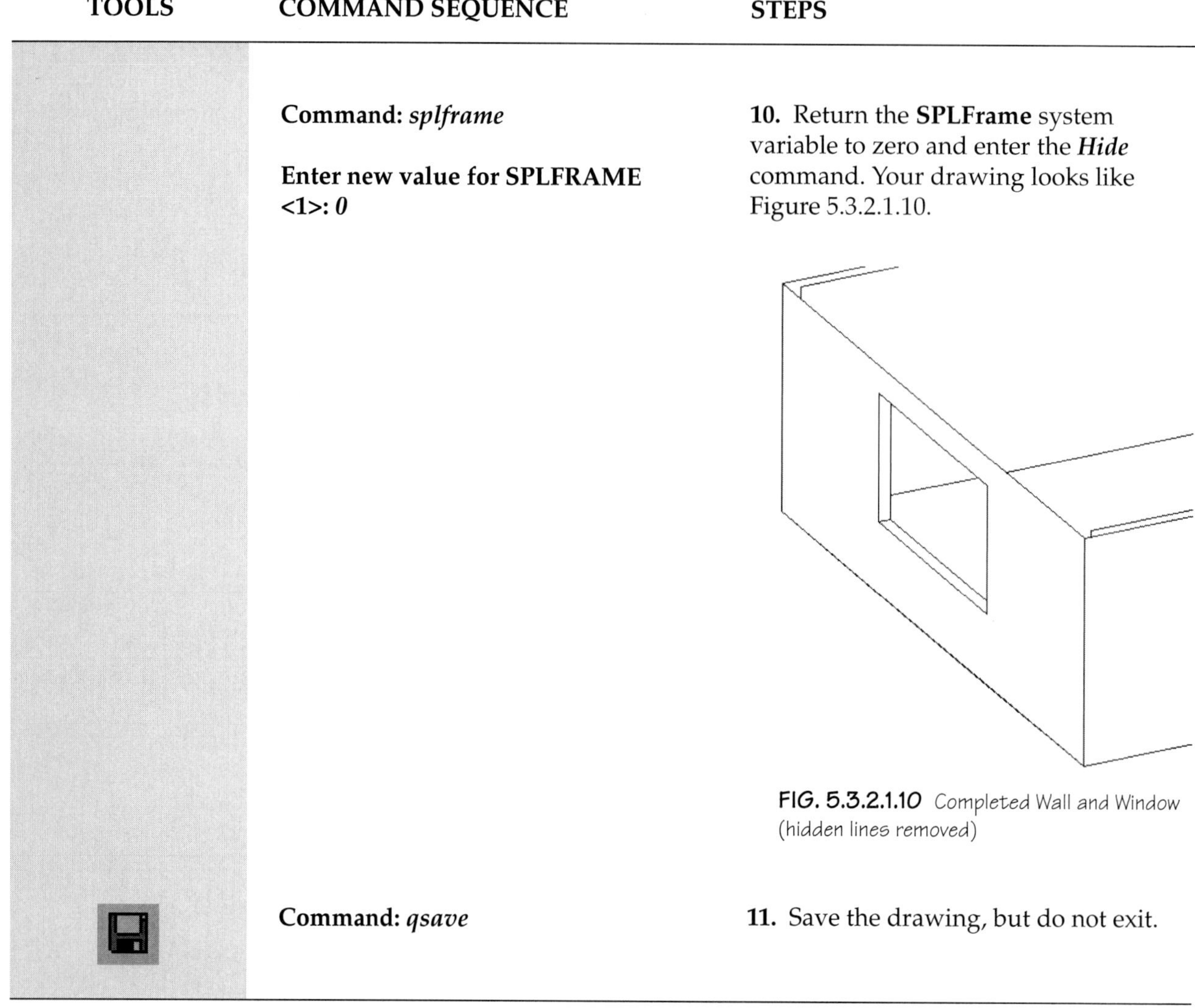

FIG. 5.3.2.1.10 Completed Wall and Window (hidden lines removed)

TOOLS	COMMAND SEQUENCE	STEPS
	Command: *qsave*	**11.** Save the drawing, but do not exit.

Of course, you have only drawn the outer surface of the wall. If you would like, you may repeat the exercise to draw the inner surface as well. Then we can look at another method of Surface Modeling—Regions.

5.3.3 Solids and Regions

There are two real differences between Solids and Regions. The first is that a Solid is a filled two-dimensional polygon (although it can have thickness) while a Region is an actual surface. The second is that you can create a Solid from scratch while creating a Region requires an existing object.

A general rule of thumb to follow when considering Solids and Regions is this: Use a Region for a surface and a Solid to fill in a two-dimensional object.

Since we looked at Solids in the basic text and will spend several lessons on Solid Modeling, we will concentrate here on Regions.

Some confusion inevitably arises between the terms *Solid* and *3D Solid*. Let me clarify the distinction.

A *Solid* is a two-dimensional, filled polygon. Use Solids when you need to highlight a particular object, building, or area on a drawing. Create a Solid using the ***Solid*** command.

AutoCAD has no ***3DSolid*** command. The term *3D Solid* refers to a family of objects (including spheres, cones, boxes, and more). Although similar objects can be created using Surface Modeling techniques, those techniques will not create *solid* objects. We will discuss techniques to create 3D Solid objects in Lessons 9 and 10.

What is a Region? Without getting too technical, a Region is a two-dimensional surface. It looks very much like a 3D Face, but you do not have to hide the edges. You would use a Region anywhere an arc, circle, or hole is required. (Imagine trying to show a hole with the ***3DFace*** command. Remember that you are restricted to straight edges!)

Let's compare 3D Faces with Regions.

3D Face	REGION
Can be drawn in three dimensions.	Selected objects must be coplanar (share the same UCS). The ***boundary*** command will only create Regions with current UCS.
Cannot use to show curves or arcs.	Can use to show curves and arcs.
May need to make some edges invisible.	No need to worry about edges.
Can be extruded into a 3D Solid.	Can be extruded into a 3D Solid.
Create using the ***3DFace*** command.	Create using either the ***Region*** command or the ***Boundary*** command.

There are two ways to create a Region. Let's consider both.

- The ***Region*** command converts an existing closed object into a Region. The objects you can convert include closed lines, polylines, or curves (arcs, circles, splines, and ellipses). Once converted, the original object(s) exists as a Region—it is no longer a line, polyline, or curve. AutoCAD will create a Region from a selected object regardless of the object's relation to the current UCS.
- The ***Region*** command looks like this:

Command: ***region*** **(or** ***reg*****)**
Select objects: ***[select the closed object you wish to convert]***
Select objects: ***[hit enter to complete the selection]***
1 Region created. ***[AutoCAD tells you how many Regions have been created]***

- The ***Boundary*** command uses boundaries to create a Region. (We discussed boundaries as part of Boundary Hatching in Section 18.2 of the basic text.) No objects are lost or converted with the boundary approach and AutoCAD uses a dialog box to assist you. For the ***Boundary*** command to work properly, the objects forming the boundary must be on the zero coordinate of the Z-axis in the current UCS.

We will use both of these methods to add some more windows in our cabin.

You can also access the ***Region*** command by using the **Region** button on the Draw toolbar. Or you can access both the ***Region*** and ***Boundary*** commands by selecting them from the Draw pull-down menu.

5.3.3.1 Do This: Creating Regions

I. Be sure you are still in the *Cabin.dwg* file located in the C:\Steps3D\Lesson05 folder. If not, open it now.

II. Set the viewpoint to 1,−1,1 (the SE Isometric view).

III. Follow these steps:

TOOLS	COMMAND SEQUENCE	STEPS
	**Command:** *z*	**1.** Zoom in around the other front wall as shown in Figure 5.3.3.1.1.

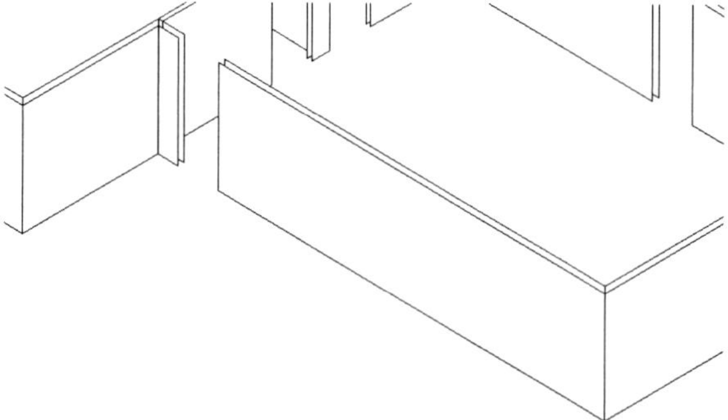

FIG. 5.3.3.1.1 Current Display (hidden lines removed)

continued

TOOLS	COMMAND SEQUENCE	STEPS
	Command: *props*	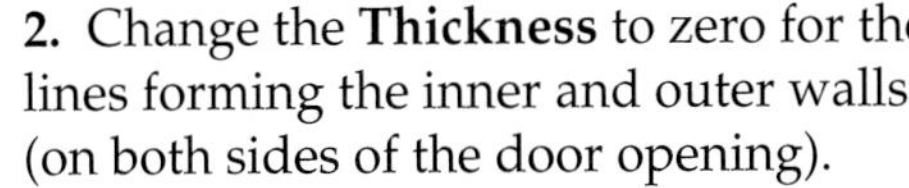 **2.** Change the **Thickness** to zero for the lines forming the inner and outer walls (on both sides of the door opening).
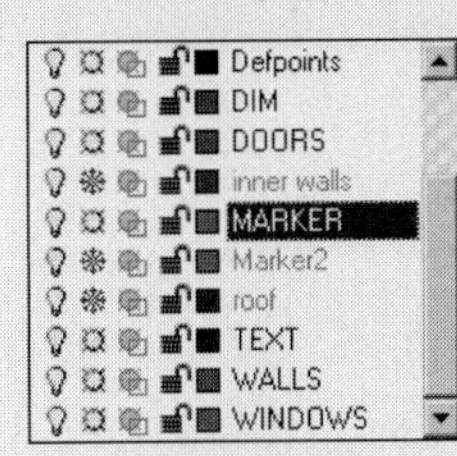	Command: *la*	**3.** Thaw the **Marker** layer. A group of nodes appears on your screen.
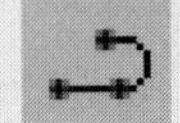	Command: *pl*	**4.** Use the nodes as a guide to draw four closed-polyline windows as shown in Figure 5.3.3.1.4. (The thickness should set be set to −5.5. If not, you will need to set it before drawing the polylines.)

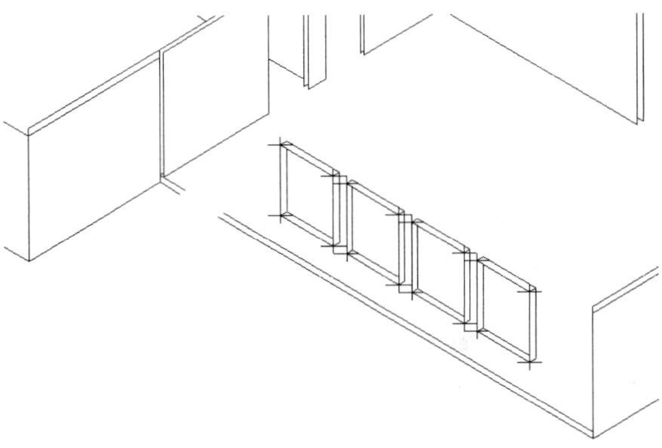

FIG. 5.3.3.1.4 Draw Four Windows

TOOLS	COMMAND SEQUENCE	STEPS
	Command: *th*	**5.** Set Thickness to zero.
	Enter new value for THICKNESS <−0′−5 1/2″>: *0*	
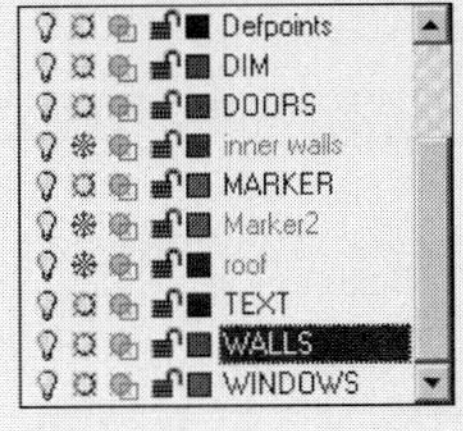	Command: *la*	**6.** Set the **Walls** layer current.

continued

TOOLS	COMMAND SEQUENCE	STEPS
	**Command:** ***pl***	**7.** Use a polyline to draw the outline of the outer wall as shown in Figure 5.3.3.1.7 (the height of the door opening is 6′–8″). Be sure to close the polyline.

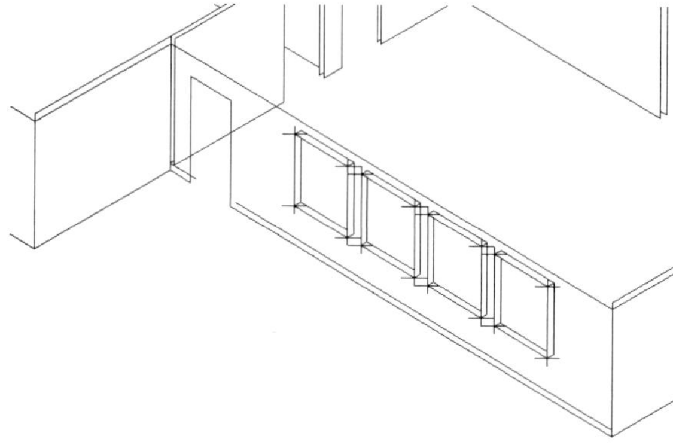

FIG. 5.3.3.1.7 Draw the Outer Wall

TOOLS	COMMAND SEQUENCE	STEPS
 Region Button	**Command:** ***reg***	**8.** Now we will create our first Region. Enter the ***Region*** command by typing ***region*** or ***reg*** at the command prompt. Or you can pick the **Region** button on the Draw toolbar. (If you have not entered the command previously, it may take a moment to load.)
	Select objects: **Select objects:** ***[enter]*** **1 loop extracted.** **1 Region created.**	**9.** Select the polyline that defines the wall and then hit enter to complete the command. AutoCAD tells you that it has created a Region.

continued

TOOLS	COMMAND SEQUENCE	STEPS
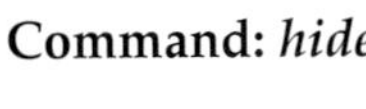	Command: *hide*	**10.** Freeze the **Marker** layer and then remove hidden lines. Your drawing looks like Figure 5.3.3.1.10.

Notice that you cannot see through the windows. This is because the wall is a Region and there are, as yet, no openings for the windows. We will deal with that now, first by creating window Regions and then removing the window Regions from the wall Region.

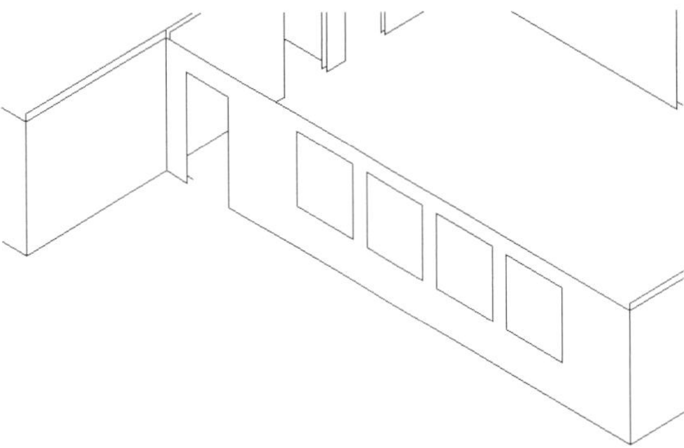

FIG. 5.3.3.1.10 Region Created and Hidden Lines Removed

continued

TOOLS	COMMAND SEQUENCE	STEPS

Origin UCS Button (UCS Toolbar)

Command: *ucs*

Current ucs name: *NO NAME*

Enter an option [New/Move/ orthoGraphic/Prev/Restore/Save/Del/ Apply/?/World]<World>:*m*

Specify new origin point or [Zdepth] <0,0,0>: *[pick the lower left corner of the wall]*

11. Move the current UCS to the lower left corner of the wall as shown in Figure 5.3.3.1.11.

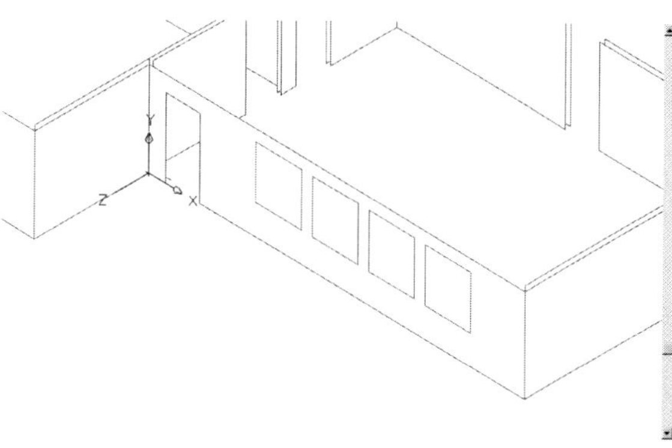

FIG. 5.3.3.1.11 Move the UCS

No Button Available

Command: *bo*

12. Enter the ***Boundary*** command by typing ***boundary*** or ***bo*** at the command line. AutoCAD presents the Boundary Creation dialog box. (You are familiar with it from your study of hatching in the basic text.)

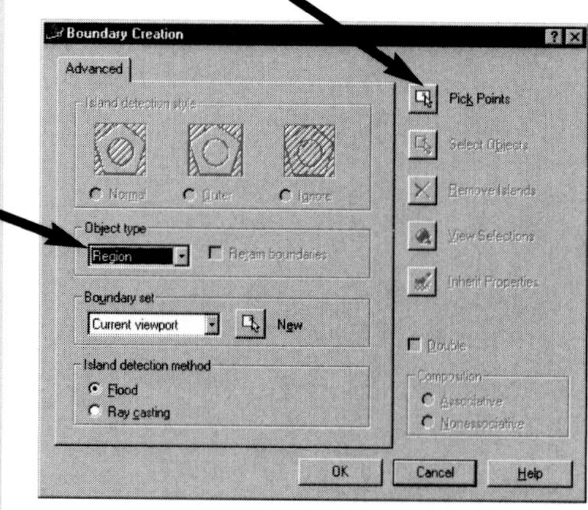

FIG. 5.3.3.1.13t

13. (Refer to Figure 5.3.3.1.13t.) Set the control box in the **Object type** frame to **Region** as indicated by the lower-left arrow. Then pick the **Pick Points** button indicated by the upper-right arrow. AutoCAD returns to the graphics screen.

continued

TOOLS	COMMAND SEQUENCE	STEPS
	Select internal point:	**14.** Select points inside each of the four windows as shown in Figure 5.3.3.1.14.

FIG. 5.3.3.1.14 Select the Windows

TOOLS	COMMAND SEQUENCE	STEPS
	Select internal point: ***[enter]*** **4 loops extracted.** **4 Regions created.** **BOUNDARY created 4 Regions**	**15.** Hit ***enter*** to complete the command. You can see that the new Regions were created without converting the polylines (Regions are on the **Walls** layer while the polylines are still on the **Windows** layer).
	Command: *qsave*	**16.** Save the drawing, but do not exit.

You have used two methods to create your Regions. The first—the ***Region*** command—converted the polyline outlining the wall to a Region. That polyline does not exist anymore. The second—the ***Boundary*** command—created Regions within the defined boundaries without changing the boundaries themselves (the polylines defining the windows).

But what you have not done is use the Regions created with your window boundaries to cut holes in the wall for the windows. Right now, you simply have four window Regions sitting on top of a wall Region. Let's take a look at how we can cut those holes.

We will use a tool with which we will become considerably more familiar when we study Solid Modeling. In fact, the tool is one of several modifying tools shared by Regions and Solid Models. The tool we will use here is the ***Subtract*** command. It looks like this:

Command: *subtract* **(or** *su***)**

Select solids and Regions to subtract from . . .

Select objects: *[select the Region (or solid) from which you will subtract—in our exercise this would be the wall]*

Select objects: *[hit enter to complete the selection]*

Select solids and Regions to subtract . . .

Select objects: *[select the Regions you wish to remove]*

Select objects: *[hit enter to complete the selection]*

Let's finish our wall.

You can also begin the ***Subtract*** command by using the **Subtract** button on the Solids Editing toolbar, or you can access the ***Subtract*** command (and explore other tools shared by Regions and Solid Models) by selecting it from the Modify pull-down menu. Follow this path:

Modify—Solids Editing—Subtract

5.3.3.2 Do This: Using Regions to Create Holes

I. Be sure you are still in the *Cabin.dwg* file located in the C:\Steps3D\Lesson05 folder. If not, open it now.

II. Follow these steps:

TOOLS	COMMAND SEQUENCE	STEPS
Subtract Button	**Command:** *su*	**1.** Enter the ***Subtract*** command by typing ***subtract*** or ***su*** at the command prompt. Or you may pick the **Subtract** button on the Solids Editing toolbar.
	Select solids and Regions to subtract from . . .	**2.** AutoCAD needs to know from which surface you will subtract. Select the wall.
	Select objects: *[select the wall]*	
	Select objects: *[enter]*	

continued

TOOLS	COMMAND SEQUENCE	STEPS
	Select solids and Regions to subtract . . . **Select objects:** *[select the windows]* **Select objects:** *[enter]*	**3.** Now AutoCAD needs to know what to subtract. Select the windows. (Be sure to select the Regions—not the polylines.)
	Command: *hide*	**4.** Remove the hidden lines. Your drawing looks like Figure 5.3.3.2.4.

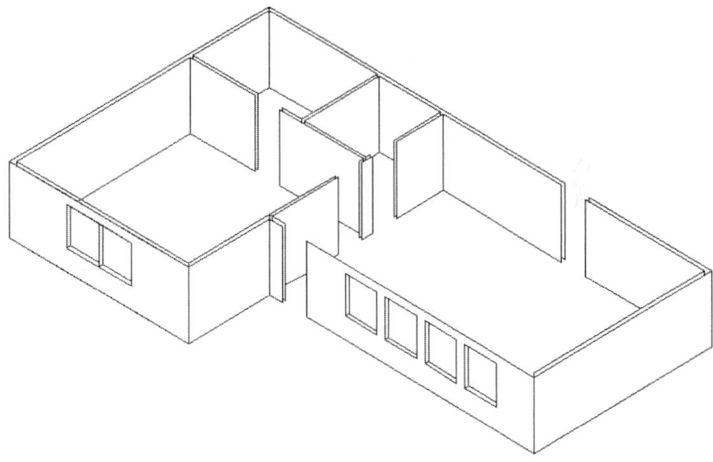

FIG. 5.3.3.2.4 Completed Wall

TOOLS	COMMAND SEQUENCE	STEPS
	**Command:** *qsave*	**5.** Save the drawing.

5.3.4 Which Method Should I Use?

Which method of Surface Modeling do you prefer—3D Face or Regions? Believe it or not, you will need both.

Consider the model in Figure 5.3.4a. Take a moment to consider each surface. Ask yourself which method of Surface Modeling you would use to create it. Then (more importantly) ask yourself why you would use that method.

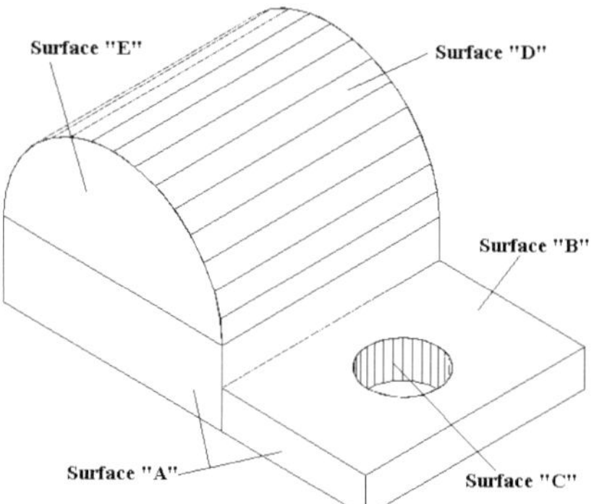

FIG. 5.3.4a Model

Once you have examined each surface, you may continue to the following explanations.

- You can easily draw Surface "A" using lines with thickness. This brings us to the first rule of three-dimensional work: *Never draw a surface when a line will do.* Surfaces are complex objects and take up more drawing memory than simple lines.
- Surface "B" has a round hole in it. 3D Faces create flat edges so they will not work here. A Region will serve best, but which method should you use? Using the Boundary method to create a Region, you can pick a point inside the rectangular area (but outside the circle) and let AutoCAD do the rest. This is the best approach.
- Surface "C" is the inside surface of the hole. The only method we have seen to create this surface is **Thickness**. But you cannot use a circle to create a hole (refer to Figure 3.4.1.1.2 in Lesson 3, p. 125). That will result in a closed cylinder (a drum). You must use two arcs with thickness to create the hole.
- Surface "D" looks very much like the roof of our cabin. Indeed it is the same type of construction. You may use a Region or solid to create the surfaces over the wireframe, but that would involve setting the UCS flat against the surface to be created for each roof section. There are 16 sections, so you would have to set the UCS and then draw the surface 16 times, or you can draw 16 3D Faces. So the ***3DFace*** command would be most efficient.

  (An alternative to drawing surfaces on the roof might be to use an arc with thickness in the proper UCS. This has the benefit of creating a true rounded shape. You would not, however, be able to do much with the object once it was drawn. For example, you could not create a jointed roof as we did in our first exercise.)
- Surface "E" has an odd shape to it. Like Surface "B," the odd shape gives away the answer. Another rule of three-dimensional surface work is: *When faced with an unusual shape or holes in a surface, use the Boundary approach to create a Region.*

Use Figure 5.3.4a as a guide in your first steps toward creating three-dimensional Surface Models. (We'll draw Figure 5.3.4a in our exercises. Then you can plot it and hang it on your monitor!) Memorize the explanation of each surface and consider each point when determining how to draw a surface on your model.

5.4 Extra Steps

Did you use the **Subtract** button on the Solids Editing toolbar in Exercise 5.3.3.2? If you did, you might have noticed that it was grouped with two other buttons—**Union** and **Intersect**. These three buttons work on Regions as well as 3D Solids. Can you tell from their symbols what they will do?

We will discuss them in more detail in Lesson 11, but that does not mean that you cannot experiment with them now.

Open the *Solids & Regions.dwg* file in the C:\Steps3D\Lesson05 folder. (It looks like Figure 5.4a.) Experiment with each of these commands on the objects shown. When you have finished, see Figure 5.4b for the results.

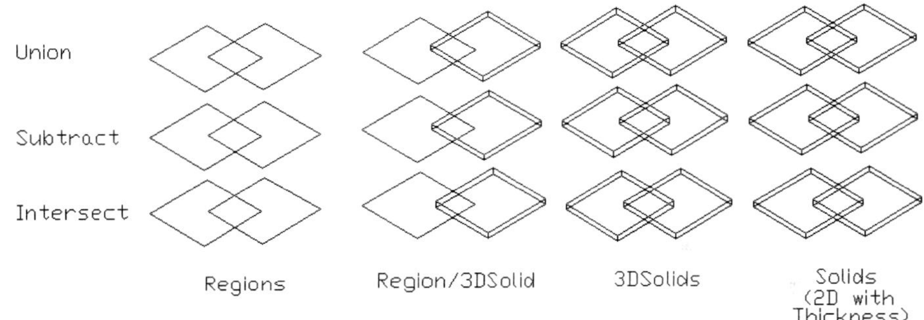

FIG. 5.4a *Solid & Regions.dwg*

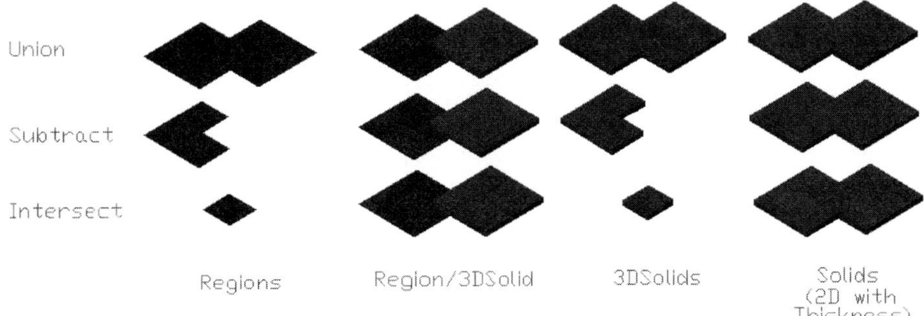

FIG. 5.4b *Solid & Regions.dwg* after the Exercise

You will notice that these commands work on Regions or 3D Solids. You cannot, however, use them to subtract, join, and so forth different types of objects with each other. Additionally, you will notice that they do not work at all on simple Solids. This is why you should generally use Regions and 3D Faces when creating Surface Models!

Let's do one more thing while we are still in the *Solids & Regions.dwg* file. Use the Gouraud Shademode to shade the drawing. Now use the ***3DOrbit*** command to flip the view (from bottom to top). Notice anything (Figure 5.4c)?

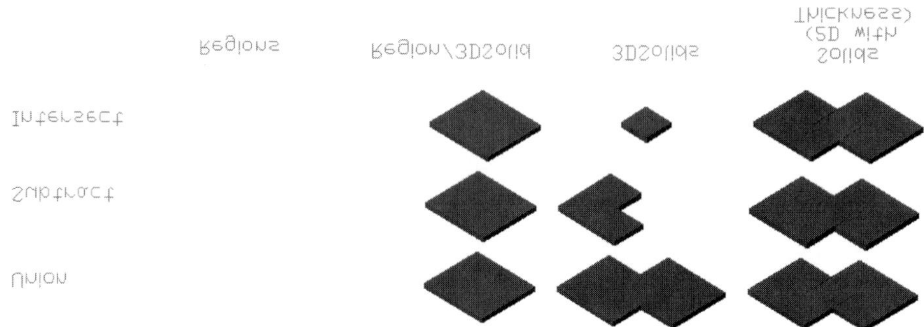

FIG. 5.4c View from Below

You should notice that all of the objects shaded nicely on top and bottom—*except* the Regions. This brings up an interesting quirk about Regions—you can see the shading on a Region only from the top! Does that mean that you cannot use a Region for a bottom surface?

No! It means that you must draw the bottom Region of an object *upside down*. How will you do that? Well, you will not actually draw upside down. You will use the ***UCS*** command to tell AutoCAD that down is up. In other words, use the UCS command to flip the positive and negative directions of the Z-axis. (Remember this when drawing the cinder block in Exercise 5.6.18.)

5.5 What Have We Learned?

Items covered in this lesson include:

- *The differences between 3D Faces, Solids, 3D Solids, and Regions*
- *The differences between Polylines and 3D Polylines*
- *Projecting points in three dimensions*
- *The two approaches to creating Regions*
  - *Region*
  - *Boundary*
- *Commands*
  - ***3DPoly***
  - ***3DFace***
  - ***Region***
  - ***Edge***

- *SPLFrame*
- *Boundary*
- *Subtract*

It has taken a few lessons to get comfortable with the basics of Z-Space Wireframe and Surface Modeling. At this point, you are either anxious to continue or feeling somewhat overwhelmed by it all (probably a little of both).

I cannot overemphasize the importance of practice—if you are uncomfortable with the material thus far, go back and do it again. You should not feel that you are the only person who ever found Z-Space difficult to master. But that is the benefit of computer labs and a good textbook! (If you have already changed the files that came from the Web, just reload them to start over!)

Are you ready for an easy lesson? Our next chapter—"Predefined Surface Models"—will show you how to create some more complex objects easily. So do the problems that follow . . . review as necessary to get comfortable . . . then forward—ever forward!

5.6 EXERCISES

1. **through 8.** Add surfaces to the drawings you created in Exercises 1 through 8 of Section 3.7 (in Lesson 3). Refer to the drawings in Appendix B as a guide. If these drawings are not available, use the corresponding drawing in the C:\Steps3D\Lesson05 folder.
9. Open the *My Twisted Y.dwg* file you created in Section 4.7—Exercise 9 (C:\Steps3D\Lesson04 folder). (If that file is not available, use the *Twisted Y-5.dwg* file in the C:\Steps3D\Lesson05 folder.) Convert the drawing into a Surface Model by placing Thickness, 3D Faces, or Regions on the necessary surfaces. See Figure 5.6.9 for the completed drawing.

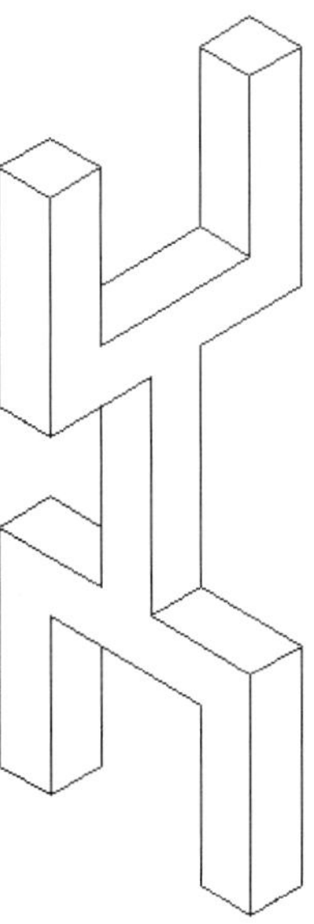

FIG. 5.6.9 Completed Twisted Y

10. Open the *My Block.dwg* file you created in Section 4.7— Exercise 10 (C:\Steps3D\Lesson04 folder). (If that file is not available, use the *Block-5.dwg* file in the C:\Steps3D\Lesson05 folder.) Convert the drawing into a Surface Model by placing Thickness, 3D Faces, or Regions on the necessary surfaces. See Figure 5.6.10 for the completed drawing.

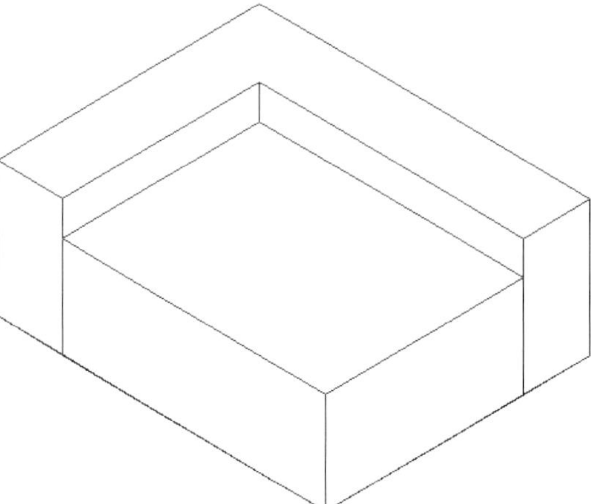

FIG. 5.6.10 Completed Block

11. Open the *MyBookEnd.dwg* file you created in Section 4.7— Exercise 12 (C:\Steps3D\Lesson04 folder). (If that file is not available, use the *Book End-5.dwg* file in the C:\Steps3D\Lesson05 folder.) Convert the drawing into a Surface Model by placing Thickness, 3D Faces, or Regions on the necessary surfaces. See Figure 5.6.11 for the completed drawing.

FIG. 5.6.11 Completed Bookend (Gouraud shading)

12. Open the *My Anchor Stop.dwg* file you created in Section 4.7— Exercise 14 (C:\Steps3D\Lesson04 folder). (If that file is not available, use the *Anchor Stop-5.dwg* file in the C:\Steps3D\Lesson05 folder.) Convert the drawing into a Surface Model by placing 3D Faces or Regions on the necessary surfaces. See Figure 5.6.12 for the completed drawing.

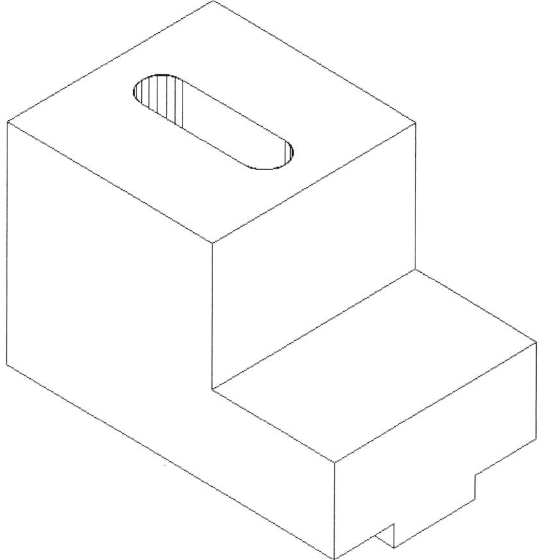

FIG. 5.6.12 Completed Anchor Stop

13. Open the *My Other Table.dwg* file you created in Section 4.7— Exercise 20 (C:\Steps3D\Lesson04 folder). (If that file is not available, use the *Other Table-5.dwg* file in the C:\Steps3D\Lesson05 folder.) Convert the drawing into a Surface Model by placing 3D Faces or Regions on the necessary surfaces. See Figure 5.6.13 for the completed drawing.

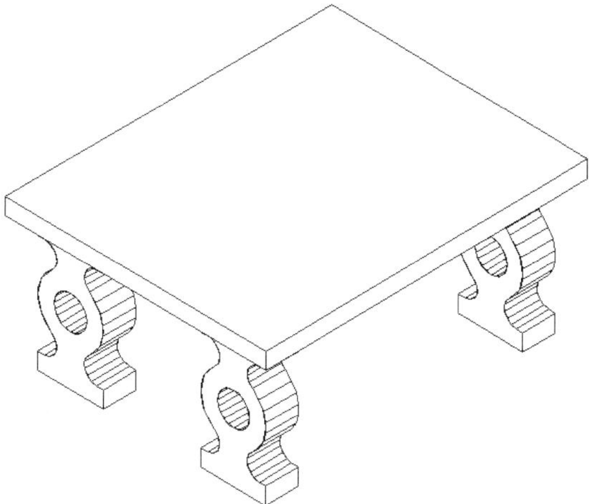

FIG. 5.6.13 Completed Other Table

14. Open the *My Corner Bracket.dwg* file you created in Section 4.7— Exercise 21 (C:\Steps3D\Lesson04 folder). (If that file is not available, use the *corner bracket-5.dwg* file in the C:\Steps3D\Lesson05 folder.) Convert the drawing into a Surface Model by placing 3D Faces or Regions on the necessary surfaces. See Figure 5.6.14 for the completed drawing.

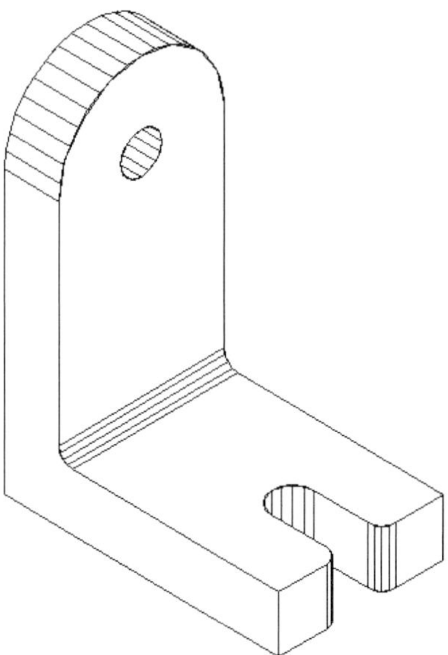

FIG. 5.6.14 Completed Corner Bracket

15. Open the *My Phone Plug.dwg* file you created in Section 4.7— Exercise 22 (C:\Steps3D\Lesson04 folder). (If that file is not available, use the *phone plug-5.dwg* file in the C:\Steps3D\Lesson05 folder.) Convert the drawing into a Surface Model by placing 3D Faces or Regions on the necessary surfaces. See Figure 5.6.15 for the completed drawing.

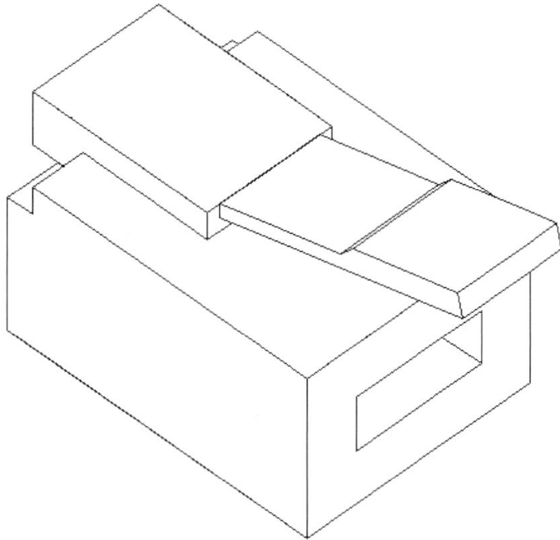

FIG. 5.6.15 Completed Phone Plug

16. Open the *My Other Corner Bracket.dwg* file you created in Section 4.7— Exercise 23 (C:\Steps3D\Lesson04 folder). (If that file is not available, use the *other corner bracket-5.dwg* file in the C:\Steps3D\Lesson05 folder.) Convert the drawing into a Surface Model by placing 3D Faces or Regions on the necessary surfaces. See Figure 5.6.16 for the completed drawing.

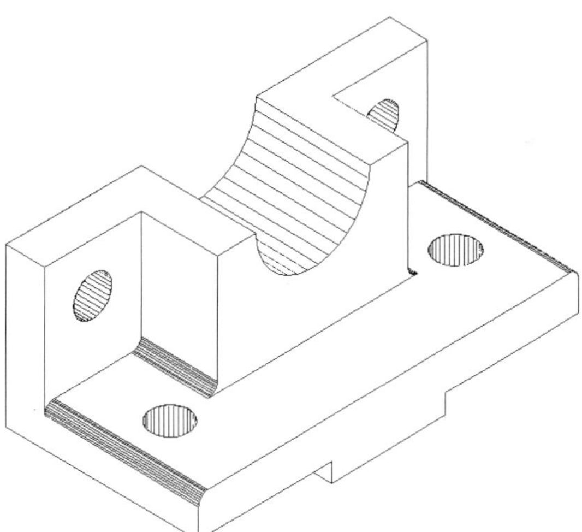

FIG. 5.6.16 Completed Other Corner Bracket

17. Open the *projection.dwg* file in the C:\Steps3D\Lesson05 folder. Create the saddle tee shown in Figure 5.6.17. Save the drawing as *My Saddle Tee.dwg* in the C:\Steps3D\ Lesson05 folder.

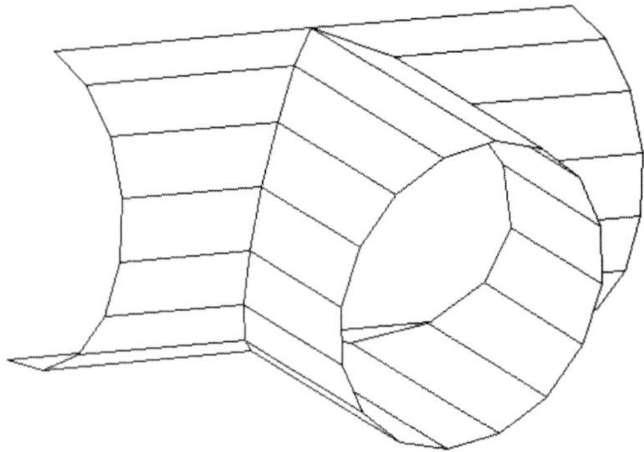

FIG. 5.6.17 My Saddle Tee

18. Create the cinder block shown in Figure 5.6.18. The following details will help.

18.1. The overall dimensions of a cinder block are 8″ × 8″ × 16″.

18.2. The holes are 7″ × $6\frac{1}{2}$″ and are evenly spaced.

18.3. The fillets in the holes have a 1″ radius.

18.4. Color 164 looks like a cinder block.

18.5. Remember that a Region can only be seen from what was the positive Z-axis direction at the time of its creation.

18.6. Save the drawing as *My Cinder Block.dwg* in the C:\Steps3D\Lesson05 folder.

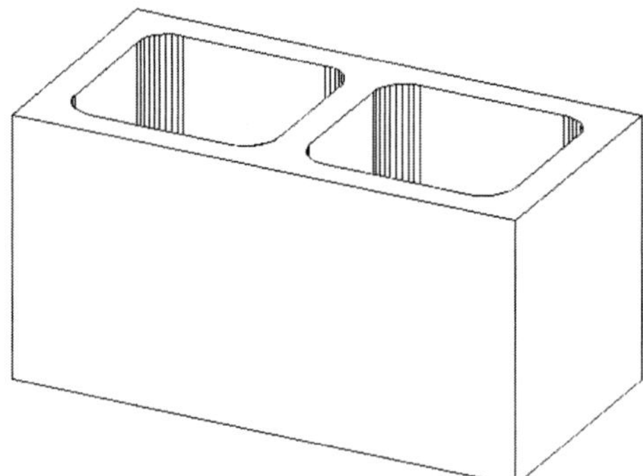

FIG. 5.6.18 My Cinder Block

19. Draw the demo model in Figure 5.3.4a (refer to Figure 5.6.19). Use the following details as a guide.

19.1. Label the types of surfaces as explained in Section 5.3.4.

19.2. Save the drawing as *Surfaces Model.dwg* in the C:\Steps3D\Lesson05 folder.

19.3. Plot the drawing to fit on about one quarter of a standard $8\frac{1}{2}$″ × 11″ sheet of paper. Cut it out and tape it to the side of your monitor as a reference.

19.4. You do not have to dimension the drawing.

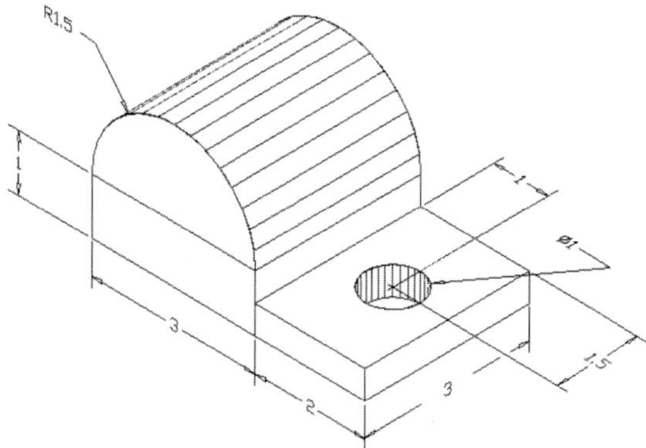

FIG. 5.6.19 Surfaces Model Dimensions

20. Finish the *Cabin.dwg* we started in this lesson. The final drawing is shown in Figure 5.6.20. Use these details as a guide.
    20.1. All windows are the same size.
    20.2. All windows are 12″ from the top of the walls.
    20.3. Spaced windows are 12″ apart.
    20.4. Change the layer for all inner walls to a new Inner Walls layer. Then freeze the layer for clarity.
    20.5. Use the ***3dClip*** command for clarity on the elevations.
    20.6. The scale in each viewport is $\frac{1}{16}''$ = 1′−0″ (this layout is set up for an $8\frac{1}{2}''$ × 11″ sheet).
    20.7. Use the title block of your choice, and plot the drawing.
    20.8. Save the drawing in the C:\Steps3D\Lesson05 folder.

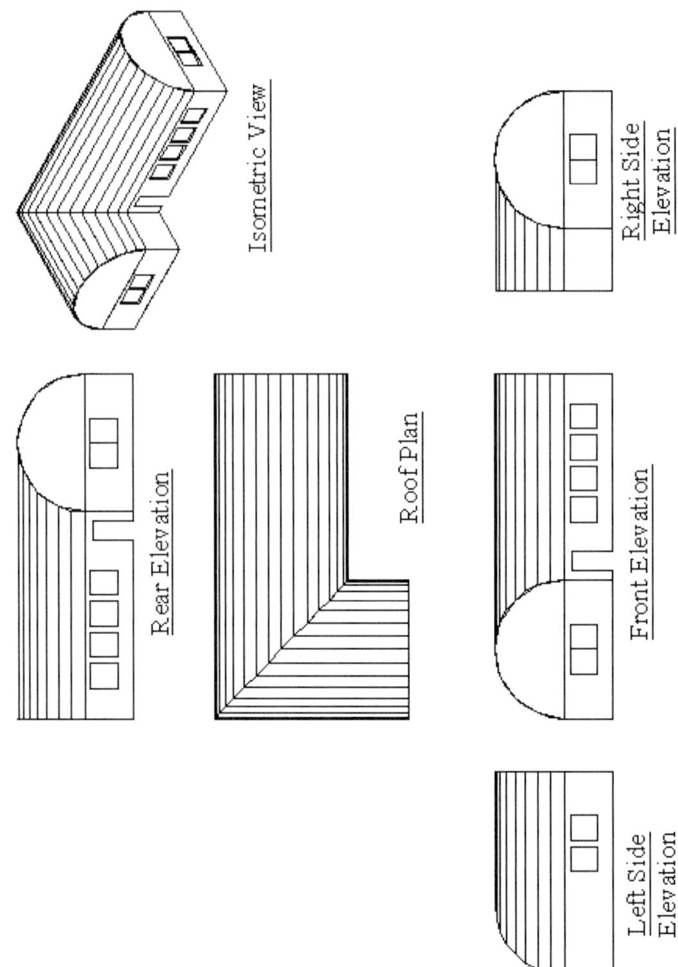

FIG. 5.6.20 Completed Cabin Drawing

21. Reopen the *Cabin.dwg* you completed in Exercise 20. We will add a different roof and a chimney. Follow these guidelines. (The final drawing is shown in Figure 5.6.21).

- **21.1.** Freeze the **Roof** layer.
- **21.2.** Add two new layers—**Roof 2** and **Chimney**.
- **21.3.** On the **Roof** 2 layer, add hexagons at the end walls of the roofs (in the same location where the arcs were found in Exercise 5.2.1).
- **21.4.** Add the 3D Polyline and 3D Faces to complete the roof.
- **21.5.** Place a 4′ × 2′ rectangle, with a thickness of 24′, at coordinates 33′,22′,0.
- **21.6.** Use construction lines and UCS manipulation to locate where the chimney penetrates the roof. Draw a polyline around the penetration.
- **21.7.** Finish drawing the chimney using wireframe techniques. Erase the rectangle.
- **21.8.** Add 3D Faces to the chimney.
- **21.9.** Hatch everything as shown.
- **21.10.** Save and plot the drawing.

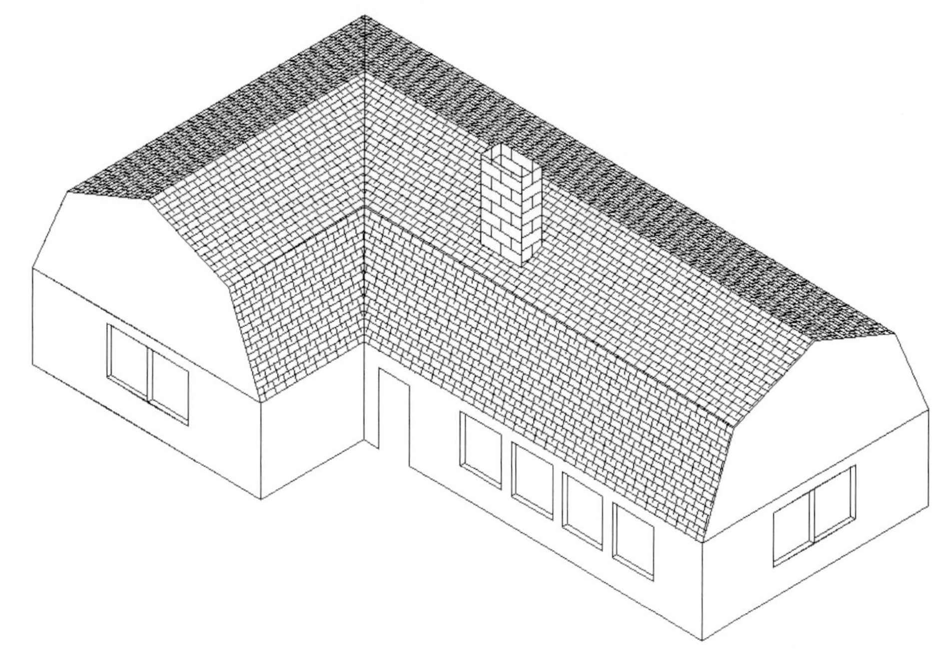

FIG. 5.6.21 Cabin with a New Roof

5.7 REVIEW QUESTIONS

Please write your answers on a separate sheet of paper.

1. A __________ Model is a skeleton drawing (a stick figure).

2. A __________ Model stretches some skin over the skeleton.

3. Use the (pline, 3DPoly) command to draw a polyline with different z-coordinates.

4. (T or F) A 3DPoly has no width property.

5. Use the __________ command to create a curved line in Z-Space.

6. Use the __________ technique to identify points by intersecting lines in Z-Space.

7. When you cannot see points on a drawing, reset the __________ system variable.

8. (T or F) Hide and Shademode commands have no affect on a Wireframe Model.

9. through 11. Name the three types of surfaces used in Surface Modeling.

12. Which of the above allows for removal of part of the surface?

13. Which converts an existing object into a Region?

14. Which can be drawn without concern for the current UCS?

15. and 16. You can use the __________ option of the 3DFace command to hide some edges, or you can wait and use the __________ command to remove them after the 3D Face has been drawn.

17. (T or F) A Wireframe Model is required when drawing a Surface Model (over which you will stretch the "skin").

18. To temporarily view invisible edges of a 3D Face, use the __________ option of the Edge command.

19. To keep invisible edges of a 3D Face visible, set the __________ system variable to 1.

20. A __________ is a filled, two-dimensional polygon.

21. and 22. In surfaces, a __________ can be created from scratch, but a __________ requires an existing closed object.

23. The term __________ refers to a family of solid objects including spheres, cones, and boxes.

24. Use a (Region, 3D Face) anywhere an arc, circle, or hole is required.

25. A (Region, 3D Face) can be drawn in three dimensions.

26. There are no edge concerns when drawing a (Region, 3D Face).

27. The __________ command uses boundaries to create a Region.

28. For the Boundary command to work properly, the objects forming the boundary must be on the __________ of the Z-Axis in the current UCS.

29. To create a Region using the Boundary command, the Object type (in the Boundary Creation dialog box) must be set to __________.

30. through 32. List the three modifying tools we discussed that are shared between Regions and 3D Solids.

33. through 37. Refer to Figure 5.7.33. Identify what type of surface you would use and explain why.

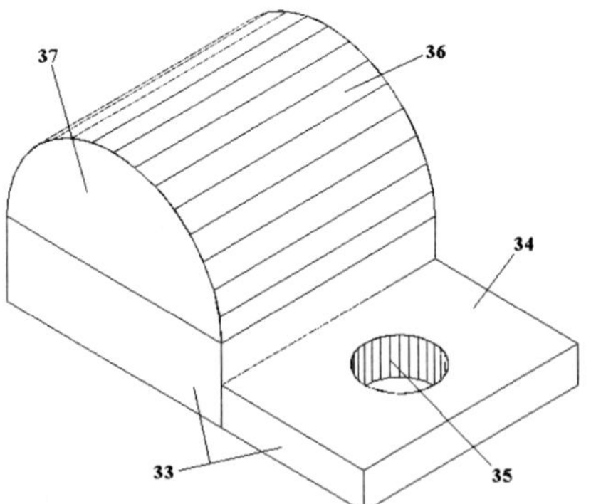

FIG. 5.7.33 Surfaces

LESSON 6

Predefined Surface Models

Following this lesson, you will

➥ Know how to build AutoCAD's predefined Surface Models
- **Box**
- **Wedge**
- **Pyramid**
- **Cone**
- **Sphere**
- **Dome**
- **Dish**
- **Torus**

➥ Know how to use the ***3D*** command

In our next two lessons, we will look at some tools that will greatly simplify your work with Surface Models.

First, in this lesson, we will learn to use AutoCAD's predefined Surface Models. Draftsmen at all levels of development can quickly and easily learn to use these remarkable timesaving devices. In fact, I would be surprised if you had not discovered them in your three-dimensional explorations already.

Then in Lesson 7, you will discover some surprisingly simple tools that can be used to create elaborate, nonuniform Surface Models.

Let's begin with an overview of the predefined Surface Modeling tools AutoCAD has provided.

6.1 What Are Predefined Surface Models?

Simply put, predefined Surface Models are standard geometric shapes that AutoCAD creates for you with a minimal amount of user input. The shapes include a box (Figure 6.1a), a wedge (6.1b), four types of pyramid (6.1c–6.1f), two types of cone (6.1g and 6.1h), a dome (6.1i), a dish (6.1j), a sphere (6.1k), and a torus (6.1l). User input for each commonly includes length, width, height, radius, and rotation angle definitions.

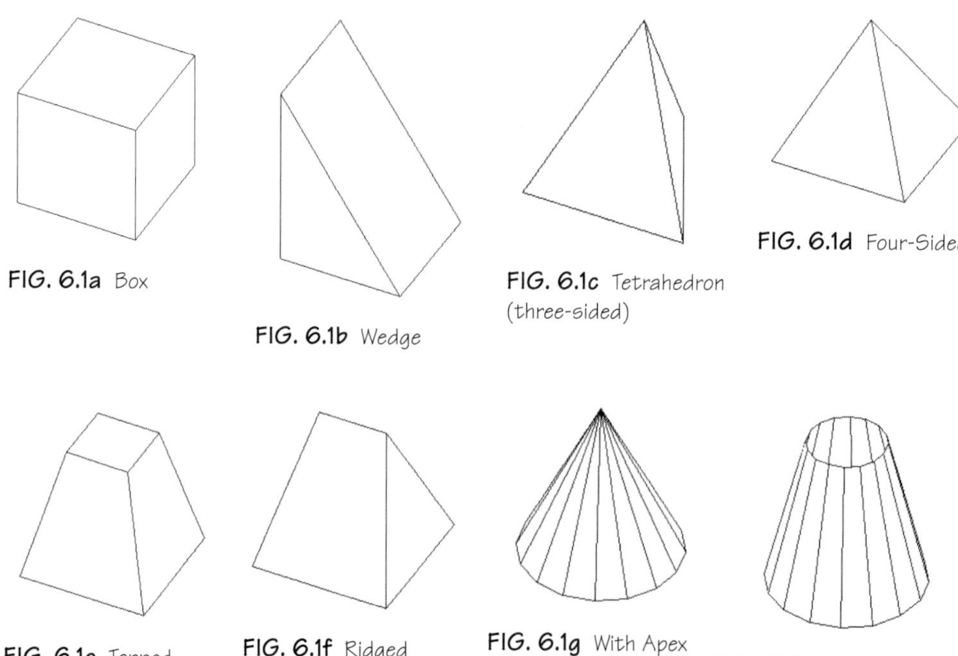

FIG. 6.1a Box

FIG. 6.1b Wedge

FIG. 6.1c Tetrahedron (three-sided)

FIG. 6.1d Four-Sided

FIG. 6.1e Topped

FIG. 6.1f Ridged

FIG. 6.1g With Apex

FIG. 6.1h With Top Radius

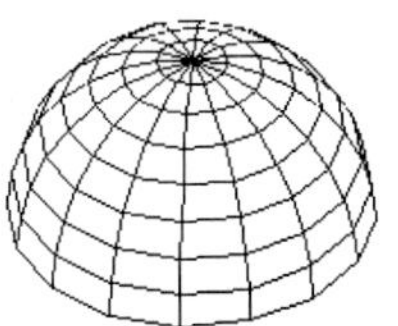

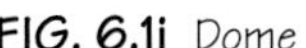

FIG. 6.1i Dome

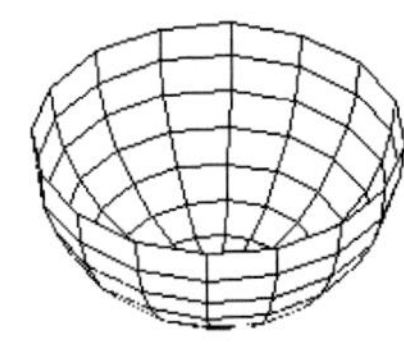

FIG. 6.1j Dish

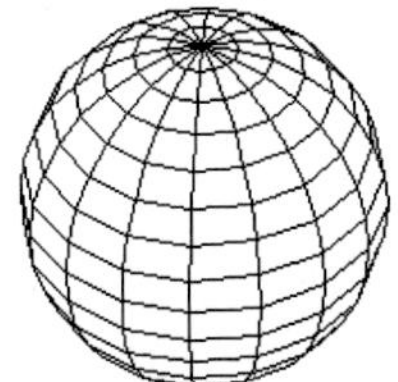

FIG. 6.1k Sphere

FIG. 6.1l Torus

You can create each of these models with little effort—simply follow AutoCAD's prompts.

AutoCAD creates each Surface Model as a 3D Mesh (more on 3D Meshes in Lesson 7). You can then edit a 3D Mesh with the ***Pedit*** command (as we will see in Lesson 8). Additionally, the user can explode the model into a series of 3D Faces. This enables him to remove part of the model (with the ***Erase*** command) or hide some of the edges (with the ***Edge*** command) without affecting the rest of the faces.

6.2 Drawing Predefined Surface Models

Commands used to create predefined Surface Models must be preceded with the characters: ***AI_***. This is necessary for two reasons: The ***AI_*** differentiates the command from a similar command that will create a predefined 3D Solid Model, and it tells AutoCAD to call an *Autodesk Incorporated* lisp routine (a program included with but not actually part of the AutoCAD program).

However, AutoCAD has included a command that enables the user to access predefined Surface Models without difficulty. The command is (simply enough) ***3D***. Its sequence looks like this:

> *Command:* **3d**
>
> **Enter an option**
>
> **[Box/Cone/DIsh/DOme/Mesh/Pyramid/Sphere/Torus/Wedge]:**

The user responds with the type of object he wants to draw. But if the keyboard is too much trouble, AutoCAD provides a toolbar—Surfaces—to make accessing its predefined Surface Modeling tools even easier.

> You can also select a predefined Surface Model from an image slide using the **3D Surfaces** . . . selection on the Draw pull-down menu. Follow this path:
>
> *Draw—Surfaces—3D Surfaces . . .*

> We will discuss predefined Solid Models and compare them with predefined Surface Models in Lesson 9.

Let's examine the procedures for drawing each of the predefined Surface Models.

6.2.1 Box

Use the *AI_Box* command to draw any six-sided box whose sides, top, and bottom are parallel or perpendicular to the current UCS. The command sequence looks like this:

> **Command:** *ai_box*
>
> **Specify corner point of box:** *[identify the first corner of the box]*
>
> **Specify length of box:** *[tell AutoCAD how long to make the box]*
>
> **Specify width of box or [Cube]:** *[tell AutoCAD how wide to make the box or type C for a cube]*
>
> **Specify height of box:** *[tell AutoCAD how tall to make the box—this prompt is skipped if the Cube option is selected at the last prompt]*
>
> **Specify rotation angle of box about the Z axis or [Reference]:** *[tell AutoCAD the desired rotation angle or type R for a reference angle]*
>
> **Command:**

The main option in this sequence is whether or not to create a cube. A cube is a box whose sides, top, and bottom are all equal. Consequently, when the user selects the **Cube** option, AutoCAD uses the length value as the value for the width and height as well.

Let's try one.

6.2.1.1 Do This: Creating a 3D Surfaced Box

I. Start a new drawing using the *lesson 06 template* file located in the C:\Steps3D\Lesson06 folder.

II. Follow these steps:

TOOLS	COMMAND SEQUENCE	STEPS
Box Button	**Command:** *ai_box*	**1.** Enter the *AI_Box* command by typing ***ai_box*** at the command line or by picking the **Box** button on the Surfaces toolbar.

continued

TOOLS	COMMAND SEQUENCE	STEPS
	Initializing . . . 3D Objects loaded.	**2.** If this is the first time you have drawn the Surfaced Box in this drawing session, AutoCAD will initialize the AI material.
	Specify corner point of box: ***1,1***	Specify the start point of the box as indicated.
	Specify length of box: ***4***	**3.** Specify the **length** of the box.
	Specify width of box or [Cube]: ***2***	**4.** We will not draw a cube this time, so enter the **width** and **height** as indicated.
	Specify height of box: ***1***	
	Specify rotation angle of box about the ***Z*** **axis or [Reference]:** ***0***	**5.** And give the box a zero rotation angle. Your box looks like Figure 6.2.1.1.5.
		FIG. 6.2.1.1.5 Box
	Command: ***[enter]***	**6.** Let's place a cube atop the box. Repeat the ***AI_Box*** command.
	Specify corner point of box: ***1,1,1***	**7.** Place the first corner atop the first corner of the box.
	Specify length of box: 2	**8.** Give our cube a length of 2 . . .
Enter Cancel Cube Pan Zoom	**Specify width of box or [Cube]:** ***c***	**9.** . . . and tell AutoCAD to use the length dimension for the width and height as well by selecting the **Cube** option.

continued

TOOLS	COMMAND SEQUENCE	STEPS
	Specify rotation angle of box about the Z axis or [Reference]: *0*	**10.** Give the cube the same rotation angle as our first box. Your drawing looks like Figure 6.2.1.1.10.

FIG. 6.2.1.1.10 Cube and Box (hidden lines removed)

TOOLS	COMMAND SEQUENCE	STEPS
	Command: *save*	**11.** Save the drawing as *MyBoxes* in the C:\Steps3D\Lesson06 folder.
	Command: *li*	**12.** Perform the ***List*** command on the upper box. Notice that each vertex is identified as a polyline *mesh* (Figure 6.2.1.1.12).

```
    POLYLINE  Layer: "obj1"
              Space: Model space
     Handle = C0
     6x3 mesh

    VERTEX    Layer: "obj1"
              Space: Model space
     Handle = C1
Mesh
  at point, X=   3.0000  Y=   1.0000  Z=   3.0000
```

FIG. 6.2.1.1.12 Partial Listing of the Upper Box

TOOLS	COMMAND SEQUENCE	STEPS
	Command: *ex*	**13.** Explode the upper box.

continued

TOOLS	COMMAND SEQUENCE	STEPS
	Command: *li*	**14.** Repeat Step 12. Notice the difference (Figure 6.2.1.1.14). Now you can use the *Edge* command to hide edges.

```
3D FACE    Layer: "obj1"
           Space: Model space
    Handle = DD
 first point, X=   3.0000  Y=   3.0000  Z=   1.0000
second point, X=   3.0000  Y=   1.0000  Z=   1.0000
 third point, X=   3.0000  Y=   1.0000  Z=   3.0000
fourth point, X=   3.0000  Y=   3.0000  Z=   3.0000
```

FIG. 6.2.1.1.14 Completed Listing of One Face of the Upper Box

TOOLS	COMMAND SEQUENCE	STEPS
	Command: *qsave*	**15.** Save the drawing.

Was that not easier than drawing a stick figure and stretching skin around it? (I love it when it's easy!)

Let's try another predefined Surface Model.

6.2.2 Wedge

You will not find many differences between the ***AI_Wedge*** command and the ***AI_Box*** command. In fact, without the **Cube** option, the ***AI_Wedge*** command is actually easier! It looks like this:

Command: ***ai_wedge***

Specify corner point of wedge: ***[identify the first corner of the wedge]***

Specify length of wedge: ***[tell AutoCAD how long to make the wedge]***

Specify width of wedge: ***[tell AutoCAD how wide to make the wedge]***

Specify height of wedge: ***[tell AutoCAD how tall to make the wedge]***

Specify rotation angle of wedge about the Z axis: ***[tell AutoCAD the desired rotation angle]***

Command:

Does that look familiar? Let's draw one for practice.

6.2.2.1 Do This: Creating a 3D Surfaces Wedge

I. Start a new drawing using the *Lesson 06 Template* file located in the C:\Steps3D\Lesson06 folder.

II. Follow these steps:

TOOLS	COMMAND SEQUENCE	STEPS
Wedge Button	**Command:** *ai_wedge*	**1.** Enter the *AI_Wedge* command by typing ***ai_wedge*** at the command line or by picking the **Wedge** button on the Surfaces toolbar.
	Specify corner point of wedge: *1,1*	**2.** Identify the starting point of the wedge as indicated.
	Specify length of wedge: *4* **Specify width of wedge:** *2* **Specify height of wedge:** *1* **Specify rotation angle of wedge about the** ***Z*** **axis:** *0*	**3.** Specify the **length, width, height,** and **rotation angle** of the wedge as indicated. Your drawing looks like Figure 6.2.2.1.3. FIG. 6.2.2.1.3 Wedge
	Command: *save*	**4.** Save the drawing as *MyWedge* in the C:\Steps3D\Lesson06 folder.

Remember that you can change the UCS prior to creating the wedge to help control the direction of the slope. You cannot, however, use negative numbers.

Let's look at something more complex than simple boxes and wedges. Let's look at the ***AI_Pyramid*** command.

■ 6.2.3 Pyramid

Did you know that there is more than one kind of pyramid?

Technically speaking, a pyramid is a polyhedron, or multitriangular structure. The common idea of a pyramid comes from the Egyptian model with a rectangular base (or four triangular sides on a rectangular base). Most of the Egyptian pyramids come to a point at the top.

But there are other pyramids. In fact, the largest pyramid in the world is not Egyptian at all. Look for it just outside Mexico City. And it has a flat top!

Some pyramids even have triangular bases—or three triangular sides on a triangular base. These are called tetrahedrons.

You probably did not realize how complicated the world of pyramids was! But not to worry—AutoCAD provides for drawing each within one simple command—*AI_Pyramid*. Its command sequence looks like this:

Command: ***ai_pyramid***

Specify first corner point for base of pyramid: *{specify the corners of the}*

Specify second corner point for base of pyramid: *{pyramid's base}*

Specify third corner point for base of pyramid:

Specify fourth corner point for base of pyramid or [Tetrahedron]: ***[if the base has four corners, enter the fourth point; otherwise enter* T *for a three-sided base (tetrahedron)]***

Specify apex point of pyramid or [Ridge/Top]: ***[enter a point in Z-Space to identify the point at the top of the pyramid, or tell AutoCAD you wish to create a ridge (2-point) or top (3 or 4 point depending on the base)]***

It is really not as complicated as it looks. Let's draw some pyramids and see.

6.2.3.1 Do This: Creating 3D Surfaced Pyramids

I. Start a new drawing using the *Lesson 06 Template* file located in the C:\Steps3D\Lesson06 folder.

II. Follow these steps:

TOOLS	COMMAND SEQUENCE	STEPS
 Pyramid Button	**Command:** ***ai_pyramid***	**1.** Enter the ***AI_Pyramid*** command by typing ***ai_pyramid*** at the command prompt or picking the **Pyramid** button on the Surfaces toolbar.

continued

TOOLS	COMMAND SEQUENCE	STEPS
	Specify first corner point for base of pyramid: *1,1* **Specify second corner point for base of pyramid:** *5,1* **Specify third corner point for base of pyramid:** *5,5* **Specify fourth corner point for base of pyramid or [Tetrahedron]:** *1,5*	**2.** We will start with a simple, four-sided pyramid that comes to a point at the top. Enter the base coordinates indicated.
	Specify apex point of pyramid or [Ridge/Top]: *3,3,4*	**3.** An apex point (sharp point at the top) is the default, so enter the three-dimensional coordinate indicated. Your first pyramid looks like Figure 6.2.3.1.3. **FIG. 6.2.3.1.3** Four-Sided Pyramid with Apex Point (hidden lines removed)
	Command: *[enter]*	**4.** Let's draw a three-sided pyramid—a tetrahedron. Repeat the command.
	Specify first corner point for base of pyramid: *11,1* **Specify second corner point for base of pyramid:** *11,5* **Specify third corner point for base of pyramid:** *7,3*	**5.** We will draw this one next to the first. Enter the coordinates indicated for the three corners of the base.

continued

TOOLS	COMMAND SEQUENCE	STEPS
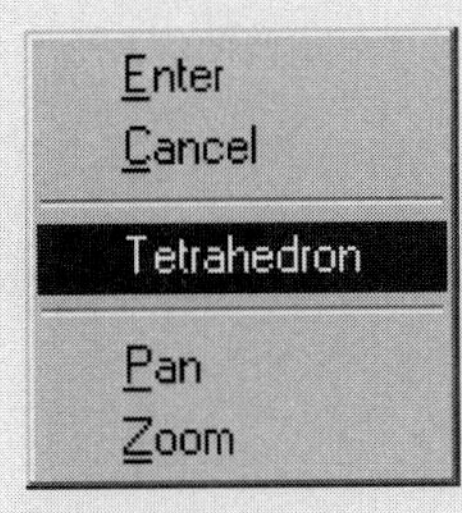	**Specify fourth corner point for base of pyramid or [Tetrahedron]:** *t*	**6.** When AutoCAD asks for a fourth corner, type ***T*** to tell it to draw a tetrahedron.
	Specify apex point of tetrahedron or [Top]: *9,3,4*	**7.** And place the apex point as indicated. Your drawing looks like Figure 6.2.3.1.7. 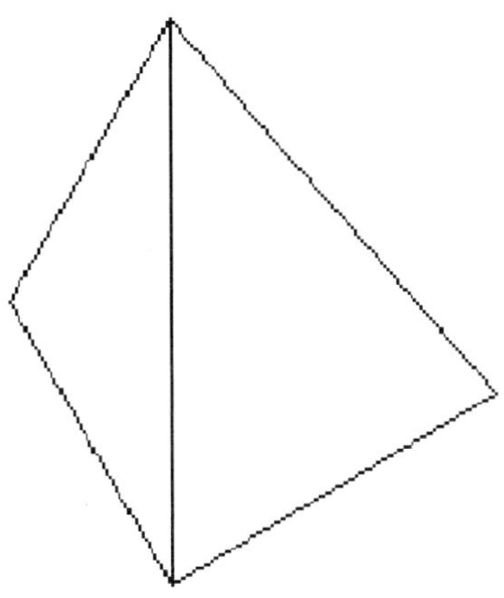 **FIG. 6.2.3.1.7** Tetrahedron (hidden lines removed)
	**Command:** *ai_pyramid*	**8.** Now let's draw a four-sided pyramid with a flat top. (Erase the previous pyramids or freeze their layer and set a different one current.) Repeat the command.
	Specify first corner point for base of pyramid: *1,1* **Specify second corner point for base of pyramid:** *1,5* **Specify third corner point for base of pyramid:** *5,5* **Specify fourth corner point for base of pyramid or [Tetrahedron]:** *5,1*	**9.** First, draw the base just as you did for the first pyramid.

continued

TOOLS	COMMAND SEQUENCE	STEPS
	**Specify apex point of pyramid or [Ridge/Top]:** *t*	**10.** But instead of identifying an apex point, tell AutoCAD to draw a **Top** on the pyramid.
	Specify first corner point for top of pyramid: *2,2,4* **Specify second corner point for top of pyramid:** *2,4,4* **Specify third corner point for top of pyramid:** *4,4,4* **Specify fourth corner point for top of pyramid:** *4,2,4*	**11.** Identifying the points for the top is just like identifying the points for the base—except that the top points must be three-dimensional coordinates. Enter these as indicated. Your drawing looks like Figure 6.2.3.1.11. 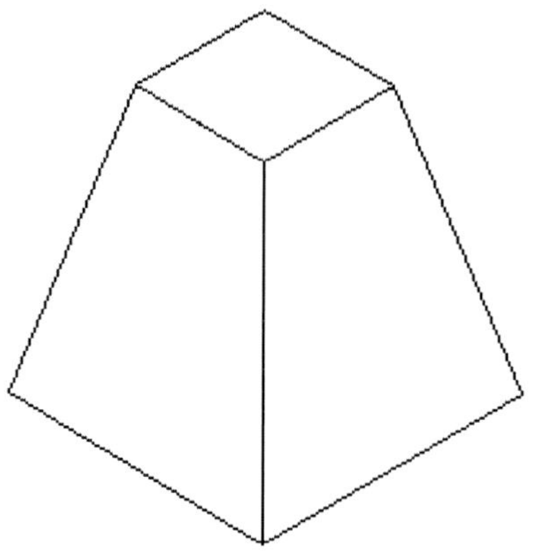 **FIG. 6.2.3.1.11** Four-Sided Pyramid with Top I am not sure that our next pyramid would qualify as a true pyramid—it only has two triangles, but it also has two quadrilaterals and a rectangular base. Still, it fits better with the pyramid command than any other, and an ***AI_Triangles_Quadrilaterals_Rectangle*** command might be too much to type! Let's draw a ridge.
	**Command:** *ai_pyramid*	**12.** Repeat the command.

continued

TOOLS	COMMAND SEQUENCE	STEPS
	Specify first corner point for base of pyramid: *7,1*	**13.** Draw the base as indicated.
	Specify second corner point for base of pyramid: *11,1*	
	Specify third corner point for base of pyramid: *11,5*	
	Specify fourth corner point for base of pyramid or [Tetrahedron]: *7,5*	
Enter Cancel Ridge Top Pan Zoom	**Specify apex point of pyramid or [Ridge/Top]:** *r*	**14.** But tell AutoCAD to draw a **Ridge** rather than an apex point.
	Specify first ridge end point of pyramid: *8,3,4*	**15.** Then identify the points on the ridge. Notice that the ridge is parallel to the first base line you drew (Figure 6.2.3.1.15).
	Specify second ridge end point of pyramid: *10,3,4*	
		FIG. 6.2.3.1.15 Four-Sided Pyramid with Ridge
	Command: *save*	**16.** Save the drawing as *MyPyramids* in the C:\Steps3D\Lesson06 folder.

Now let's look at pyramids with round bottoms—let's look at cones.

6.2.4 Cone

Like pyramids, cones are smaller on the top than on the bottom (generally speaking). The top can be pointed like the pyramid's apex point, or it can be flat. But the similarities end there.

The smaller-top/larger-base definition is simply to help in user recognition. It is possible, and at times desirable, to have a pyramid or cone with a larger top than base, or a cone with equal top and base.

The predefined Surface Models we have examined so far have all had sides that loaned themselves easily to 3D Faces. Beginning with cones, we will look at several predefined shapes that incorporate circles or arcs in their structures. Because these structures are 3D Meshes (and will convert to 3D Faces when exploded), we must tell AutoCAD how many faces to use when creating the surfaces of the circles or arcs.

The command sequence for cones is:

Command: *ai_cone*

Specify center point for base of cone: *[identify the center point for the base of the cone]*

Specify radius for base of cone or [Diameter]: *[identify the radius of the cone or type D to specify a diameter]*

Specify radius for top of cone or [Diameter] <0>: *[hit enter to accept zero as the top radius—AutoCAD will draw a cone with a point at the top; or identify the radius for the top and AutoCAD will draw an open top]*

Specify height of cone: *[specify the height of the cone]*

Enter number of segments for surface of cone <16>: *[tell AutoCAD how many faces to use to create the surface of the cone. Remember that 3D Faces are flat, so the more faces you use, the rounder the cone will appear. Remember also that the more faces you use, the larger your drawing becomes. Go for a healthy compromise between appearance and size.]*

Command:

Use the ***AI_Cone*** command to draw a cylinder. Simply make the top and base radii the same.

We will draw a couple of cones for practice.

6.2.4.1 Do This: Creating 3D Surfaced Cones

I. Start a new drawing using the *Lesson 06 Template* file located in the C:\Steps3D\Lesson06 folder.

II. Follow these steps:

TOOLS	COMMAND SEQUENCE	STEPS
 Cone Button	**Command:** *ai_cone*	**1.** Enter the *AI_Cone* command by typing ***ai_cone*** at the command prompt or picking the **Cone** button on the Surfaces toolbar.
	Specify center point for base of cone: *3,3*	**2.** Identify the **center point** and the **radius** of the base as indicated.
	Specify radius for base of cone or [Diameter]: *2*	
	Specify radius for top of cone or [Diameter] <0>: *[enter]*	**3.** We will draw a pointed cone first. Accept the default **radius** of zero for the top of the cone.
	Specify height of cone: *4*	**4.** Specify the **height** of the cone. The height must be a positive number.
	Enter number of segments for surface of cone <16>: *[enter]*	**5.** Remember—more surface segments mean a rounder appearance; fewer mean a less pronounced curve. Let's accept the default. Your drawing looks like Figure 6.2.4.1.5. 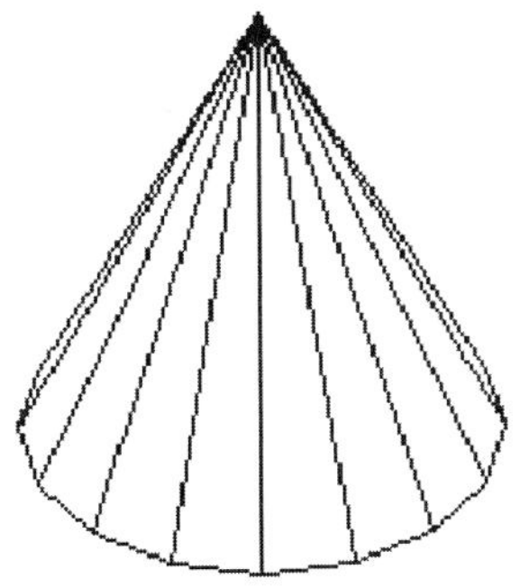 **FIG. 6.2.4.1.5** Pointed Cone (hidden lines removed)

continued

TOOLS	COMMAND SEQUENCE	STEPS
	Command: ***[enter]***	**6.** Now let's draw a cone with an opening at the top as well as the bottom. Repeat the command.
	Specify center point for base of cone: *9,3*	**7.** Locate the **base** and specify the **radius** as you did in Step 2.
	Specify radius for base of cone or [Diameter]: 2	
	Specify radius for top of cone or [Diameter] <0>: ***1***	**8.** But this time, identify a **radius** for the top as well.
	Specify height of cone: ***4***	**9.** Specify the **height** as you did in Step 4.
	Enter number of segments for surface of cone <16>: 32	**10.** Let's see what the cone will look like with more surface segments (Figure 6.2.4.1.10).
		FIG. 6.2.4.1.10 Cone with Open Top and Bottom
	Command: ***save***	**11.** Save the drawing as *MyCones* in the C:\Steps3D\Lesson06 folder.

6.2.5 Sphere

Spheres also require the user to identify the number of faces required to make up the arc. But with spheres, the user must identify the number of latitudinal *and* longitudinal faces. In other words, into how many pieces will you divide the sphere from top to bottom (latitude) and side to side (longitude)?

Again, it is not as difficult as it sounds. The prompts look like this:

Command: *ai_sphere*

Specify center point of sphere: *[specify the center point of the sphere; unless you want half the sphere to be underground, use a three-dimensional coordinate to do this]*

Specify radius of sphere or [Diameter]: *[specify the radius or diameter of the sphere]*

Enter number of longitudinal segments for surface of sphere <16>: *[how many divisions will you want from side to side]*

Enter number of latitudinal segments for surface of sphere <16>: *[how many divisions will you want from top to bottom]*

Let's draw one.

6.2.5.1 Do This: Creating 3D Surfaced Spheres

I. Start a new drawing using the *lesson 06 template* file located in the C:\Steps3D\Lesson06 folder.

II. Follow these steps:

TOOLS	COMMAND SEQUENCE	STEPS
Sphere Button	**Command:** *ai_sphere*	**1.** Enter the *AI_Sphere* command by typing ***ai_sphere*** at the command prompt or picking the **Sphere** button on the Surfaces toolbar.
	Specify center point of sphere: *3,3,3*	**2.** Specify the **center point** of the sphere. Be sure to use a three-dimensional coordinate as indicated.
	Specify radius of sphere or [Diameter]: 2	**3.** Identify the **radius** as indicated.

continued

TOOLS	COMMAND SEQUENCE	STEPS
	Enter number of longitudinal segments for surface of sphere <16>: *[enter]* **Enter number of latitudinal segments for surface of sphere <16>:** *32*	**4.** Accept the default number of **longitudinal segments** but increase the number of **latitudinal segments** as indicated (this way you can see the difference). Your drawing looks like Figure 6.2.5.1.4.

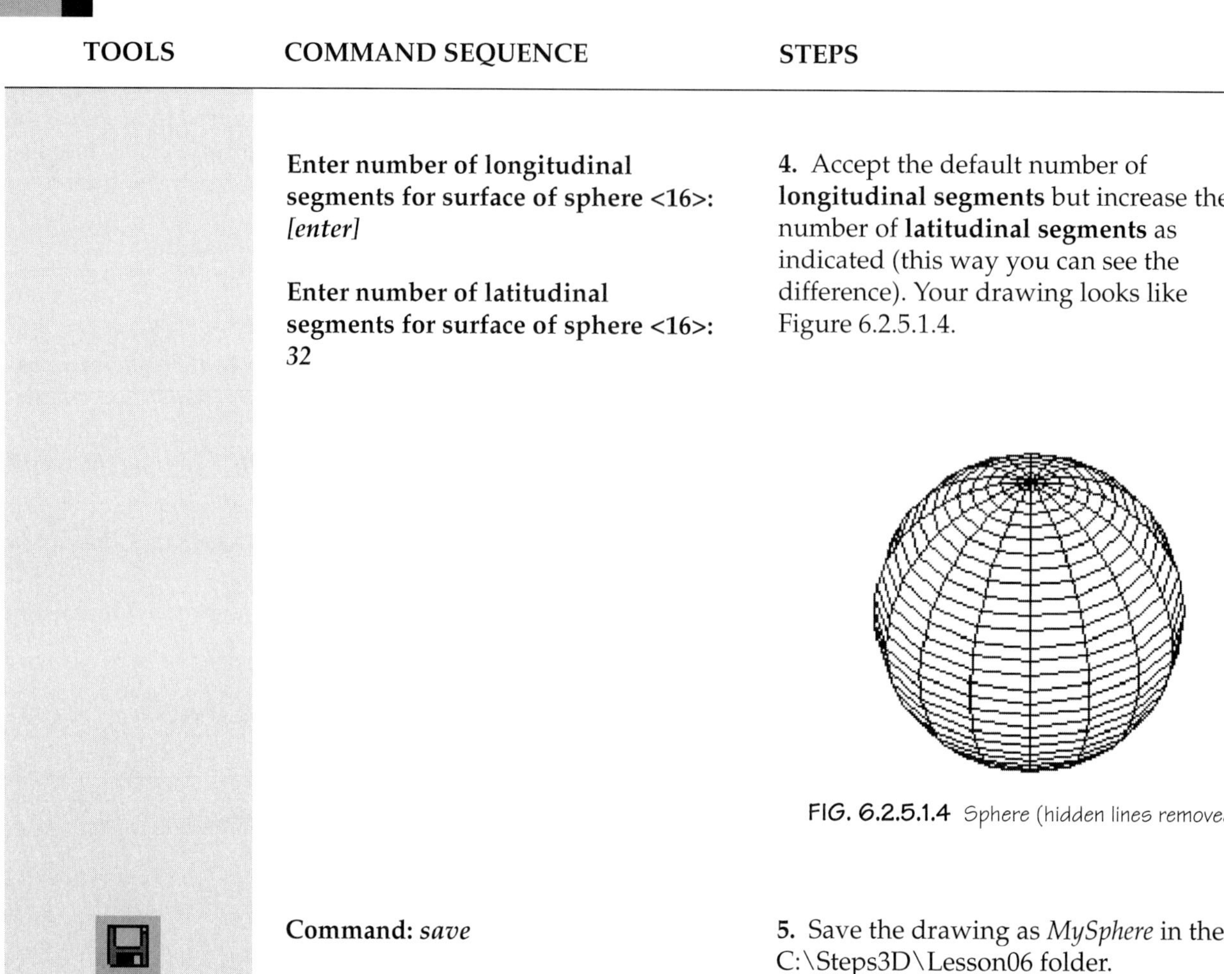

FIG. 6.2.5.1.4 Sphere (hidden lines removed)

TOOLS	COMMAND SEQUENCE	STEPS
	Command: *save*	**5.** Save the drawing as *MySphere* in the C:\Steps3D\Lesson06 folder.

6.2.6 Domes and Dishes

A dome is simply the upper half of a sphere; a dish is the lower half. The command sequences for both *AI_Dome* and *AI_Dish* are identical to the sphere's sequence but result in only half a sphere being drawn.

> **Command:** *_ai_dome* **(or** *ai_dish***)**
>
> **Specify center point of dome:** *[specify the center point of the open face of the dome; unless you want the dome to rest on the ground, use a three-dimensional coordinate to do this]*
>
> **Specify radius of dome or [Diameter]:** *[specify the radius or diameter of the dome]*
>
> **Enter number of longitudinal segments for surface of dome <16>:** *[how many divisions will you want from side to side]*

Enter number of latitudinal segments for surface of dome <8>: *[how many divisions will you want from top to bottom]*
Command:

Let's draw one of each.

6.2.6.1 Do This: Creating 3D Surfaced Domes and Dishes

I. Start a new drawing using the *lesson 06 template* file located in the C:\Steps3D\Lesson06 folder.

II. Follow these steps:

TOOLS	COMMAND SEQUENCE	STEPS
Dome Button	**Command:** *ai_dome*	**1.** Enter the *AI_Dome* command by typing ***ai_dome*** at the command prompt or picking the **Dome** button on the Surfaces toolbar.
	Specify center point of dome: *3,3,5*	**2.** Use a three-dimensional coordinate for the **center point** as indicated.
	Specify radius of dome or [Diameter]: 2	**3.** Specify the **radius**.
	Enter number of longitudinal segments for surface of dome <16>: *[enter]*	**4.** Accept the default number of **longitudinal** and **latitudinal segments**. Your drawing looks like Figure 6.2.6.1.4.
	Enter number of latitudinal segments for surface of dome <8>: *[enter]*	FIG. 6.2.6.1.4 Dome (hidden lines removed)

continued

TOOLS	COMMAND SEQUENCE	STEPS
 Dish Button	**Command:** *ai_dish*	**5.** We will draw the dish below the dome. Enter the ***AI_Dish*** command by typing ***ai_dish*** at the command prompt or picking the **Dish** button on the Surfaces toolbar.
	Specify center point of dish: 3,3,2 **Specify radius of dish or [Diameter]:** 2 **Enter number of longitudinal segments for surface of dish <16>:** *[enter]* **Enter number of latitudinal segments for surface of dish <8>:** *[enter]*	**6.** Follow the sequence indicated. Your drawing looks like Figure 6.2.6.1.6. 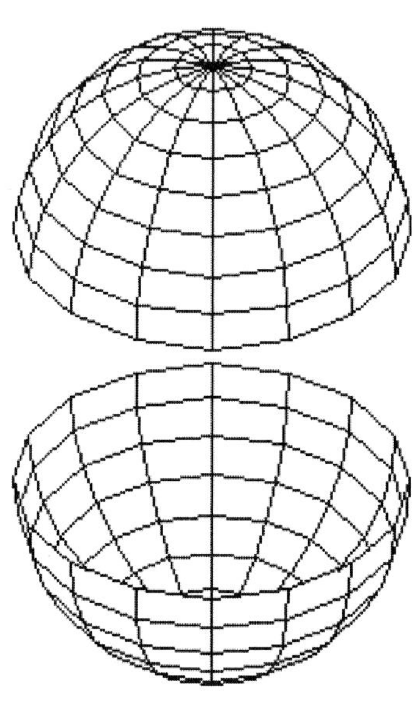 **FIG. 6.2.6.1.6** Dish and Dome (hidden lines removed)
	Command: *save*	**7.** Save the drawing as *MyDome* in the C:\Steps3D\Lesson06 folder.

6.2.7 Torus

A torus looks like the inner tube you used at the beach or lake when you were younger. Like the sphere and dome/dish objects, you will be required to identify the number of segments or faces, as well as the radius. But when drawing a torus, you must identify not only the radius of the torus but also the radius of the tube.

The command sequence looks like this:

Command: *_ai_torus*

Specify center point of torus: *[specify the center point of the torus; unless you want half of the torus to be underground, use a three-dimensional coordinate and move it upward on the Z-axis]*

Specify radius of torus or [Diameter]: *[specify the radius or diameter of the torus—this is the distance from the center of your inner tube to the outer edge of the tube]*

Specify radius of tube or [Diameter]: *[specify the radius or diameter of the tube—this is how big to make the tube itself]*

Enter number of segments around tube circumference <16>: *[how many divisions will you want around the circumference of the tube]*

Enter number of segments around torus circumference <16>: *[how many divisions will you want along the circumference of the inner tube]*

Command:

Manipulating the various radii of a torus can lead to some startling results as you will discover when working with 3D Solids in Lesson 9.

Let's give it a try.

6.2.7.1 Do This: Creating a 3D Surfaced Torus

I. Start a new drawing using the *lesson 06 template* file located in the C:\Steps3D\Lesson06 folder.

II. Follow these steps:

TOOLS	COMMAND SEQUENCE	STEPS
Torus Button	**Command:** *ai_torus*	**1.** Enter the *AI_Torus* command by typing ***ai_torus*** at the command prompt or picking the **Torus** button on the Surfaces toolbar.
	Specify center point of torus: *5,5,.5*	**2.** Locate the torus using a three-dimensional coordinate.

continued

TOOLS	COMMAND SEQUENCE	STEPS
	Specify radius of torus or [Diameter]: *4*	**3.** Specify the radii of the torus and the tube as indicated.
	Specify radius of tube or [Diameter]: *1*	
	Enter number of segments around tube circumference <16>: *[enter]*	**4.** Accept the default **number of segments** around the tube . . .
	Enter number of segments around torus circumference <16>: 32	**5.** . . . but increase the **number of segments** around the torus. This way you can see the difference. Your drawing looks like Figure 6.2.7.1.5. Notice the number of segments in each direction.

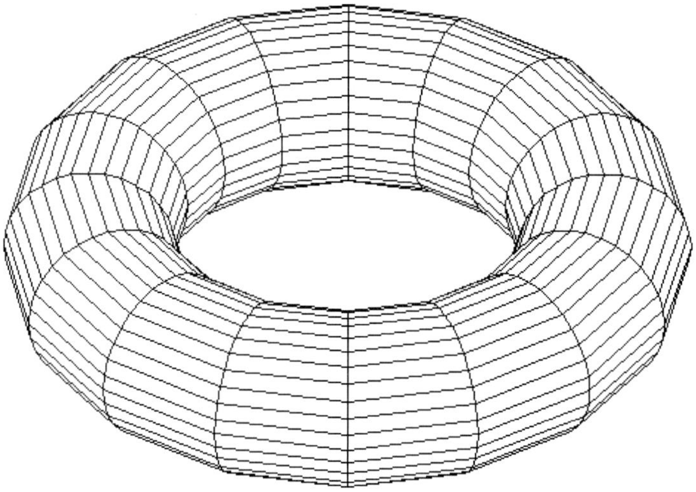

FIG. 6.2.7.1.5 Torus (hidden lines removed)

TOOLS	COMMAND SEQUENCE	STEPS
	**Command:** *save*	**6.** Save the drawing as *MyTorus* in the C:\Steps3D\Lesson06 folder.

6.3 Understanding the Limitations of Predefined Surface Models

By now you may be thinking how wonderful predefined Surface Models are. And you are right to think so. But remember that you have yet to consider their limitations. Let's look at some of these now.

- The Surface Models discussed in this lesson are objects. Although you can explode them into 3D Faces, neither the original objects nor the 3D Faces can be modified easily. You cannot trim or extend these objects. Nor can you fillet, chamfer, break, lengthen, or offset these objects. (But you can stretch, mirror, array, rotate, and copy them.)
- Neither 3D Faces nor 3D Meshes have wall thickness. They are, essentially, two-dimensional objects existing in three-dimensional space.
- While you can use these predefined shapes to build many things, you cannot combine them as you can solids. (The ***Union***, ***Subtract***, and ***Intersect*** commands will not work on Surface Models.)
- Not all OSNAPs will work on predefined Surface Models.

But take heart, AutoCAD has several other commands (that you will see in our next lesson) to enable you to draw shapes that are not predefined. Then in Lesson 8, we will look at some editing tools that do work!

6.4 Extra Steps

You have probably noticed that there are two toolbars listing similar predefined models—the Surfaces toolbar and the Solids toolbar. We have spent this lesson studying the predefined objects on the Surfaces toolbar. Take a few minutes and compare the two. Are they the same? What are the differences? Do they make the same types of models available?

In a new drawing created with the *Lesson 06 Template*, open both toolbars. Create a box using the Surface approach, and then create another box using the Solid approach. Notice the differences in the command sequences. Repeat this procedure for each of the predefined models.

It is early to be studying Solid Modeling, yet the similarities between Solids and Surfaces are too tempting to ignore. As you continue your study of Surface Modeling, bear in mind that each procedure probably has a Solid Modeling equivalent. Then, when we get to Solid Modeling, you will be a step ahead of the game!

6.5 What Have We Learned?

Items covered in this lesson include

- *AutoCAD's predefined Surface Models*
  - *Box*
  - *Wedge*
  - *Pyramid*
  - *Cone*
  - *Sphere*
  - *Dome*
  - *Dish*

This has been a fun lesson. It's nice to know that they aren't all difficult!

We have seen several predefined objects designed by AutoCAD to make three-dimensional drafting move more quickly. But you should not limit these objects to their obvious uses. Whenever you have a complex object to build with Surface Models, think about these predefined tools as basic—and often elastic—building blocks. For example, when you need a cylinder, consider using a cone with equal radii at both ends. Or when you need a ramp and the wedge is too straight, try using a pyramid with an offset ridge.

Practice the exercises at the end of this lesson for experience. Remember to use the ***UCS*** and ***Shademode*** commands to assist you. Then try to draw different objects around your desk—how about your mouse or the keyboard?

Our next lesson will cover more complex, user-defined shapes created as Surface Models. So what you cannot draw yet, you soon will be able to draw!

6.6 EXERCISES

1. through 8. Recreate the "su" drawings found in Appendix B using the tools found in this lesson to help you. You will need to explode many of the primitives to get 3D Faces to manipulate, but the drawing should be faster. Use cylinders rather than arcs to line the holes.

9. Create the flying saucer drawing shown in Figure 6.6.9. The following hints will help.
   - **9.1.** Use the *lesson 06 template* to begin.
   - **9.2.** Change the layer colors as needed.
   - **9.3.** Use these tools: cone, dish, dome, and torus.
   - **9.4.** Use clipping planes to create the section.
   - **9.5.** Use the direct hatch approach to hatch the section.
   - **9.6.** While you are still in Model Space, use the continuous orbit tool to make the saucer fly back and forth across the screen.
   - **9.7.** Save the drawing as *MySaucer* in the C:\Steps3D\Lesson06 folder.

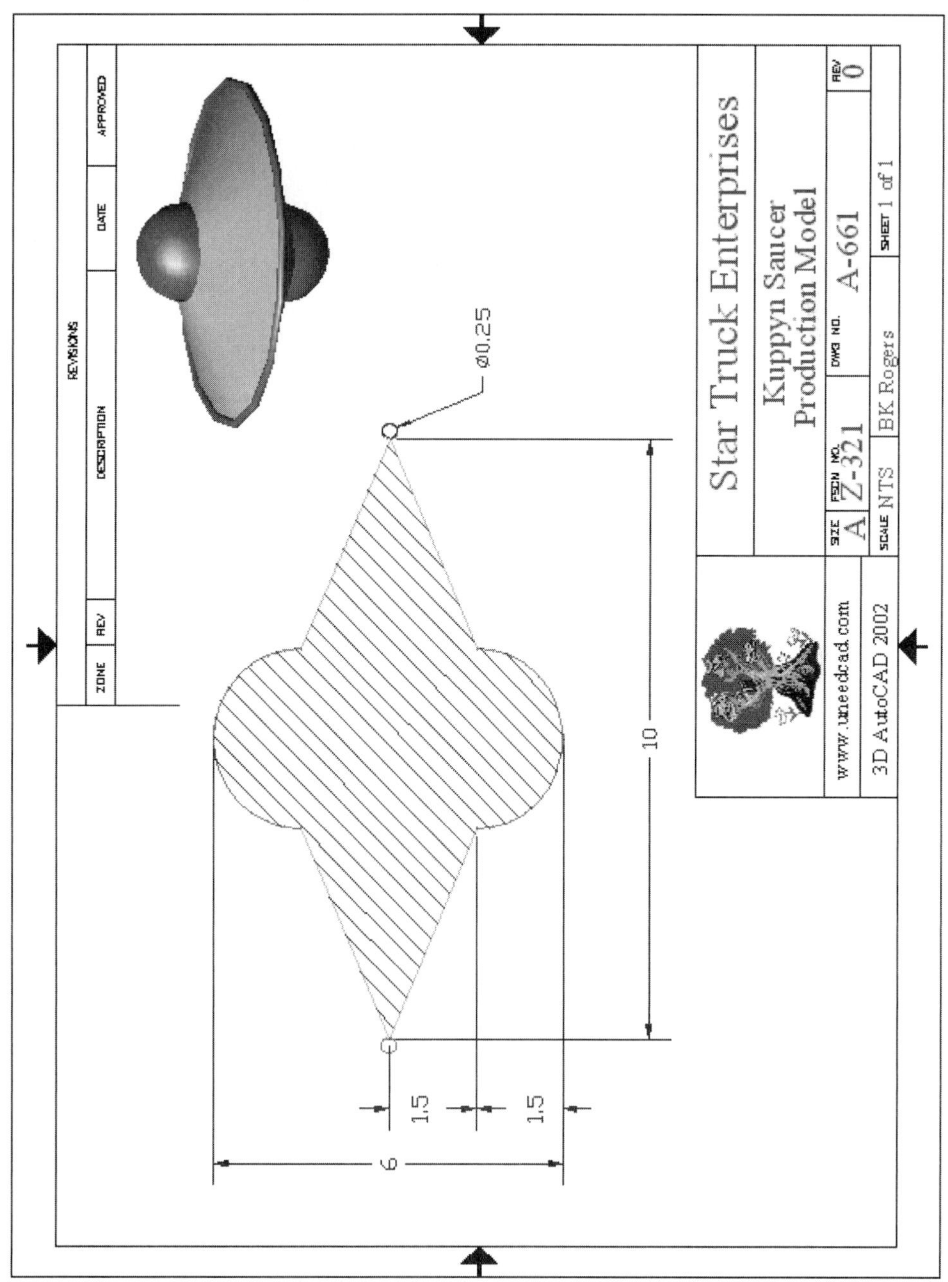

FIG. 6.6.9 Flying Saucer

10. Create the aquarium aerator drawing shown in Figure 6.6.10. The following hints will help.
  10.1. Use the *lesson 06 template* to begin.
  10.2. Change the layer colors as needed.
  10.3. Use these tools: box, donut, and dish.
  10.4. Viewport scales are a uniform 1:1.
  10.5. Text uses the Times New Roman font.
  10.6. Save the drawing as *MyAerator* in the C:\Steps3D\Lesson06 folder.

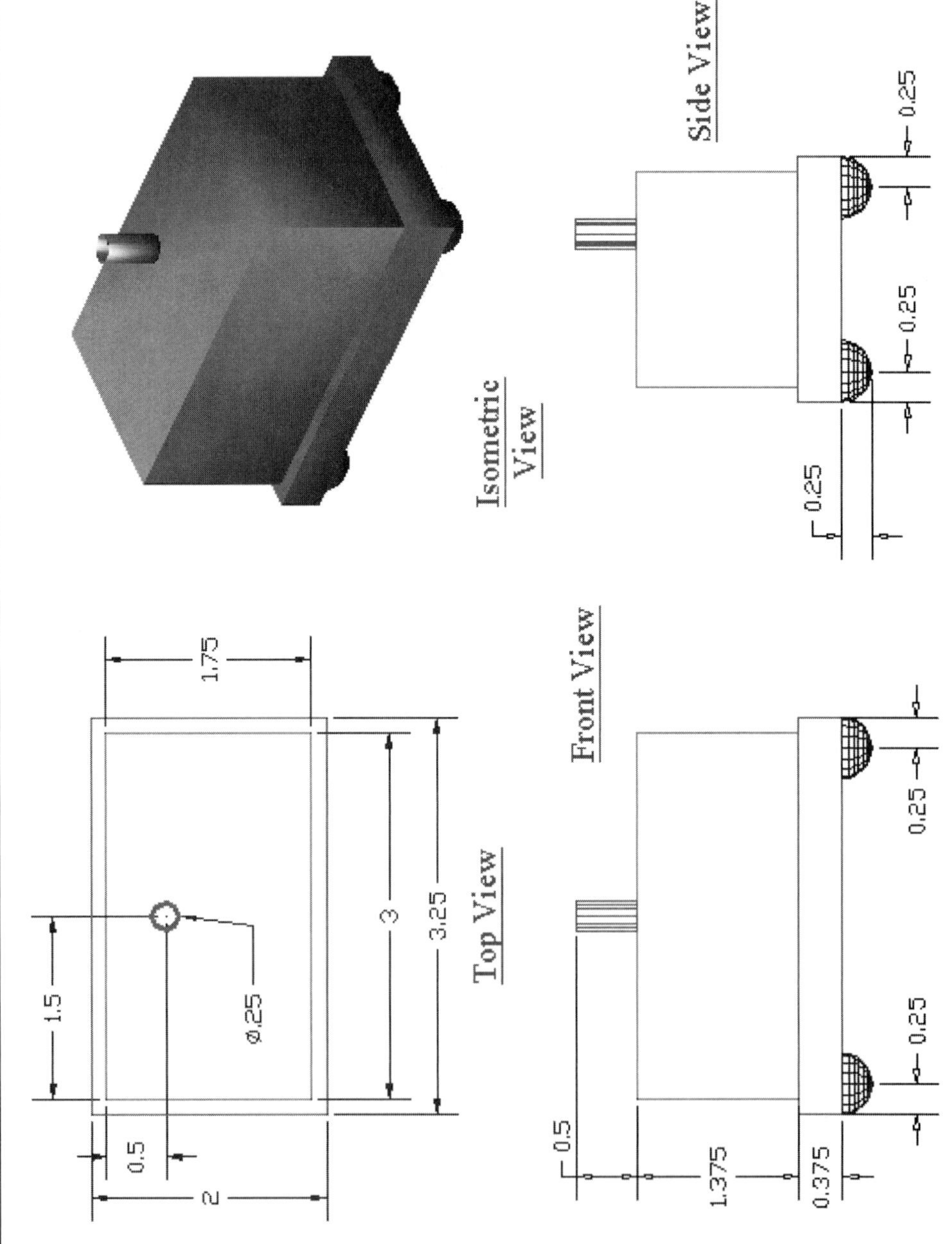

FIG. 6.6.10 Aerator

11. Create the trailer light drawing shown in Figure 6.6.11. The following hints will help.

11.1. Use the *lesson 06 template* to begin.

11.2. Change the layer colors as needed.

11.3. Use these tools: box, donut, pyramid, and cone.

11.4. Viewport scales are a uniform 1:2.

11.5. Text uses the Times New Roman font.

11.6. The sidelight requires the UCS be aligned with the side to be drawn properly.

11.7. Save the drawing as *MyLight* in the C:\Steps3D\Lesson06 folder.

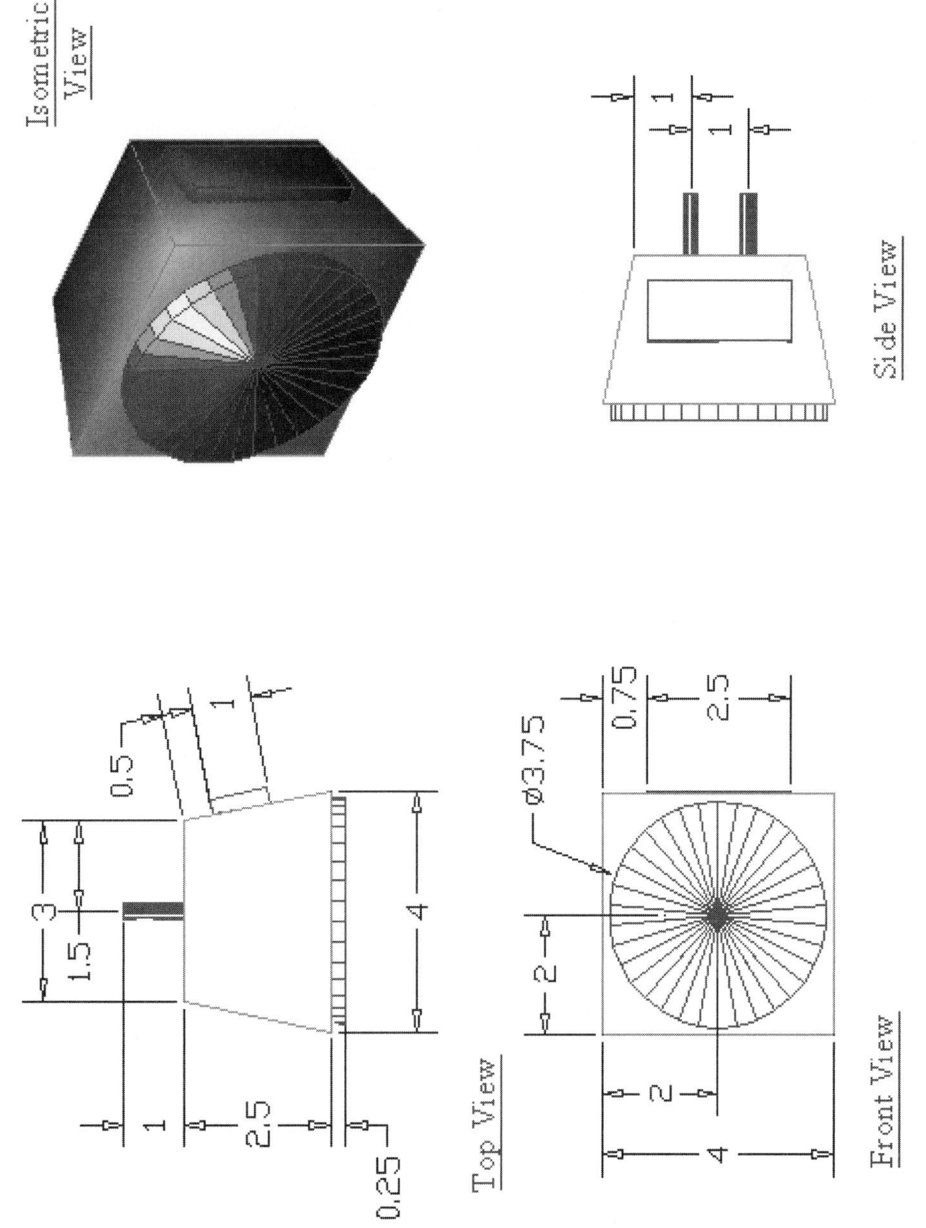

FIG. 6.6.11 Trailer Light

12. Create the microphone drawing shown in Figure 6.6.12. The following hints will help.
    12.1. Use the *lesson 06 template* to begin.
    12.2. Change the layer colors as needed.
    12.3. Use these tools: box, cone, sphere, and wedge.
    12.4. The UCS is tricky on this one. Align it with the cone to draw the button. Use the UCS to help you rotate the microphone so that it sits atop the wedge.
    12.5. The wedge is $\frac{1}{4}''$ wide.
    12.6. Save the drawing as *MyMicrophone* in the C:\Steps3D\Lesson06 folder.

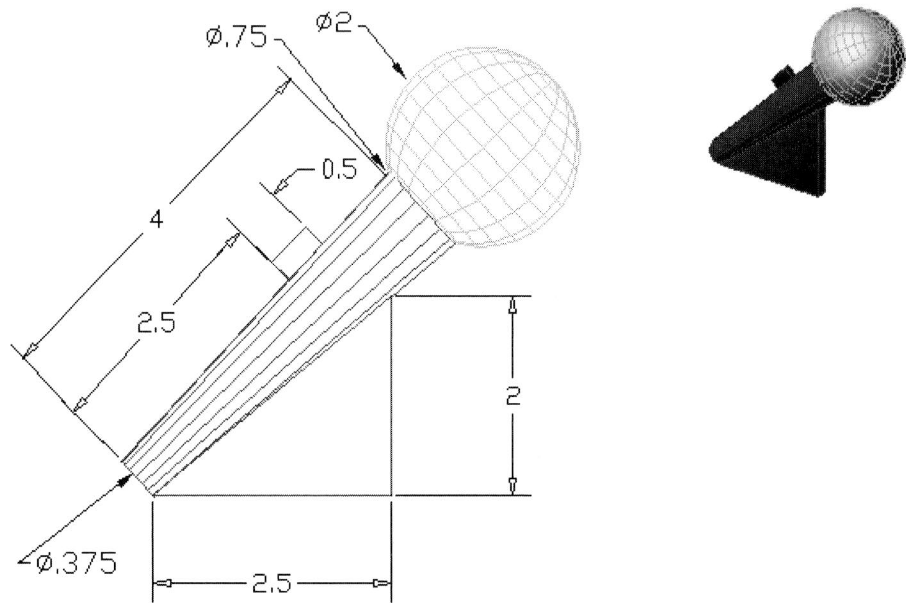

FIG. 6.6.12 Microphone

13. Create the coffee table drawing shown in Figure 6.6.13. The following hints will help.
    13.1. Use these tools: cone, torus, and region.
    13.2. The torus is 36″ diameter and the tube is 1″ diameter.
    13.3. The legs are 21″ long and extend 2″ below the bottom shelf.
    13.4. I use the Gouraud Shademode.
    13.5. Save the drawing as *MyCoffee Table* in the C:\Steps3D\Lesson06 folder.

FIG. 6.6.13 Coffee Table

14. Create the wagon drawing shown in Figure 6.6.14. The following hints will help.

14.1. Use these tools: cone, torus, box, and dome.

14.2. The wheel tori are 4″ diameter with 1″ diameter tubes.

14.3. The axles are 1″ diameter × 8″ long cones.

14.4. The axles are 12″ apart.

14.5. The wagon floor is 18″ × 6″ × $\frac{1}{2}$″.

14.6. The outer boards are 2$\frac{1}{2}$″ wide and spaced $\frac{1}{2}$″ apart.

14.7. The inner boards are 1$\frac{1}{2}$″ wide.

14.8. I use the Gouraud Shademode.

14.9. Save the drawing as *MyWagon* in the C:\Steps3D\Lesson06 folder.

FIG. 6.6.14 Wagon

15. Create the pyramid in sphere drawing shown in Figure 6.6.15. The following hints will help.

15.1. Use these tools: sphere, torus, and pyramid.

15.2. The sphere is 16″ diameter. (You will need to explode it and erase some of the 3D Faces.)

15.3. The pyramid is 5″ squared on the base × 5″ high.

15.4. The torus is 10″ diameter with a 1″ diameter tube.

15.5. The pyramid is hatched to create the brick pattern.

15.6. I use the **gOuraud+edges** Shademode to show both the surfaces and the hatching.

15.7. Save the drawing as *MyPyrSph* in the C:\Steps3D\Lesson06 folder.

FIG. 6.6.15 Pyramid in Sphere

16. Create the raised sphere drawing shown in Figure 6.6.16. The following hints will help.
    16.1. Use these tools: wedge, box, and pyramid.
    16.2. The sphere is the drawing we created in Exercise 15. I inserted it as a block at $\frac{1}{8}''$ scale. (Be sure the UCS in both drawings is equal to the WCS. We will discuss more on three-dimensional blocks in Lesson 12.)
    16.3. The ramps are 8″ × 2″ × 2″.
    16.4. The center box is 4″ × 4″ × 2″.
    16.5. The pyramid is 4″ × 4″ × 2″ (with a 2″ × 2″ top).
    16.6. The torus is 10″ diameter with a 1″ diameter tube.
    16.7. The pyramid is hatched to create the brick pattern.
    16.8. I use the **gOuraud+edges** Shademode to show both the surfaces and the hatching.
    16.9. Save the drawing as *MyTemple* in the C:\Steps3D\Lesson06 folder.

FIG. 6.6.16 Raised Sphere

17. Create the lamp drawing shown in Figure 6.6.17. The following hints will help.
    17.1. Use these tools: cone.
    17.2. The center pole is 6′ tall × 1″ diameter.
    17.3. The base is 12″ diameter on the bottom and 1″ diameter on the top. It is 2″ high.
    17.4. The top is 1″ diameter on the bottom and 12″ diameter on the top. It is 6″ high.
    17.5. The switch is $\frac{1}{2}''$ diameter 0× $\frac{1}{2}''$ high. It is located halfway up the center pole.
    17.6. Save the drawing as *MyLamp* in the C:\Steps3D\Lesson06 folder.

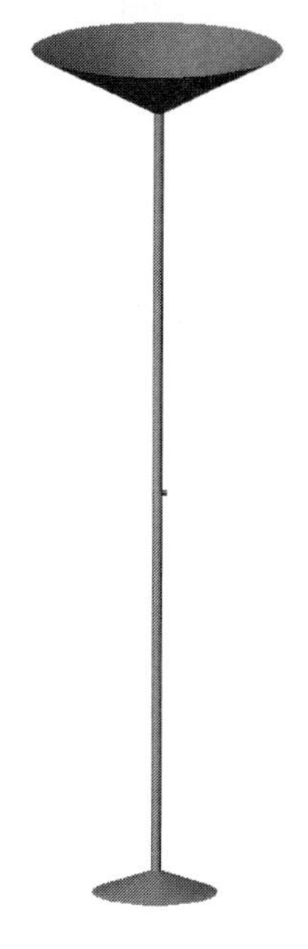

FIG. 6.6.17 Lamp

6.7 REVIEW QUESTIONS

1. through 8. List the eight predefined Surface Models.

9. Surface Models are created as __________.

10. When exploded, a Surface Model becomes a series of __________.

11. Commands used to create predefined Surface Models must be preceded with the characters __________.

12. Use the __________ command to draw any six-sided box whose sides, top, and bottom are parallel or perpendicular to the current UCS.

13. A __________ is a box whose sides, top, and bottom are all equal.

14. When drawing a wedge, you can change the __________ to help control the direction of the slope.

15. through 18. List the four types of pyramid you can draw in AutoCAD.

19. A __________ is a pyramid with only four triangles.

20. All pyramids are __________.

21. The top of a pointed pyramid is called the __________.

22. An AutoCAD pyramid with two triangles, two quadrilaterals, and a rectangular base is called a __________.

23. (T or F) It is possible to draw a pyramid with a larger top than base.

24. (T or F) A cone's top must be smaller than its base.

25. (T or F) To point a cone downward, simply make the height a negative number.

26. A __________ is the upper half of a sphere.

27. A __________ is the lower half of a sphere.

28. A __________ looks like the inner tube of a truck tire.

29. (T or F) You can use the fillet command to soften the edges of a box.

30. (T or F) You can create concentric spheres with the offset command.

31. (T or F) You can create multiple copies of a pyramid with the array command.

32. (T or F) You can remove part of a sphere by exploding it and erasing the 3D Faces.

LESSON 7

Complex Surface Models

Following this lesson, you will

- Know how to build more complex Surface Models
  - ***Rulesurf***
  - ***Revsurf***
  - ***Tabsurf***
  - ***Edgesurf***
  - ***3DMesh***
  - ***PFace***
- Know how to control the number of surfaces used to draw a Surface Model
  - ***Surftab1***
  - ***Surftab2***

In Lesson 6, you discovered some simple tools that you can use to create Surface Models. But what if you need a model that does not easily translate into one of the predefined Surface Models? For example, suppose you need to draw an I-Beam, a piping elbow, or an ornate lamp. Which predefined model would you use?

The answer, of course, is that none of the predefined tools would help. Well then, would you have to draw a Wireframe Model (a stick figure) and stretch the surfaces over it?

That might work for the I-Beam but not for the piping elbow or the ornate lamp.

The truth is that these tools (Wireframe Models and predefined Surface Models) were designed for simple objects, not for complex constructions. But take heart, AutoCAD provides other tools that will help you deal easily with more intricate designs.

In Lesson 7, we will examine tools for creating complex Surface Models. Here we will conclude our study of Surface Model creation techniques with a look at the procedures needed to put the razzle-dazzle in your three-dimensional drawing.

Let's get started!

7.1 Controlling the Number of Surfaces—*Surftab1* and *Surftab2*

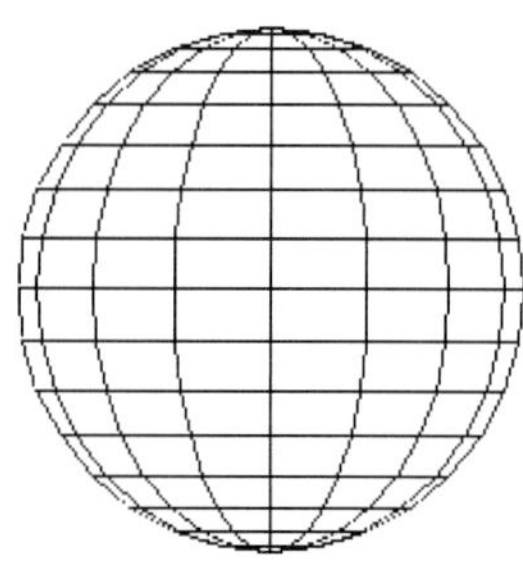

FIG. 7.1a Sphere

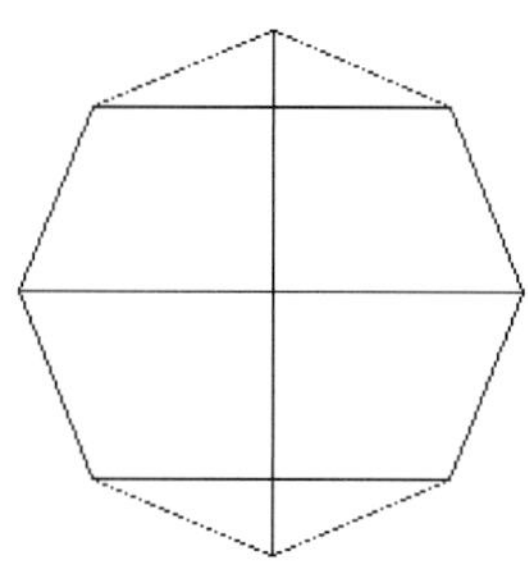

FIG. 7.1.b Revsurfed Arc

When you drew the sphere, dome, and dish in our last lesson, AutoCAD asked you for the number of segments (or faces) you wanted to use in defining the object. Remember that we defined longitudinal and latitudinal segments differently so that you could see the distinction.

That approach worked well for a predefined shape. But when you draw complex shapes, AutoCAD cannot know what you are doing. So it cannot ask you for the number of segments you will need to define the object. Still, that information will be required for your complex object to take the shape you want.

For this reason, AutoCAD established two system variables to define the number of faces it will use to create an object. The first—**Surftab1**—defines the number of surfaces AutoCAD will use to create a linear object, or the number of surfaces it will use to create the circumference (axial direction) of a round (or arced) object. The second—**Surftab2**—defines the number of surfaces AutoCAD will use to create latitudinal sections (along the path of rotation) of an object.

Compare the drawings in Figures 7.1a, 7.1b, and 7.1c. Each drawing represents a sphere.

- Figure 7.1a was drawn using default settings (16 longitudinal and latitudinal segments) and the ***AI_Sphere*** command.
- Figure 7.1b was drawn using the ***Revsurf*** command (Section 7.2.3) with **Surftab1** and **Surftab2** both set to 4.

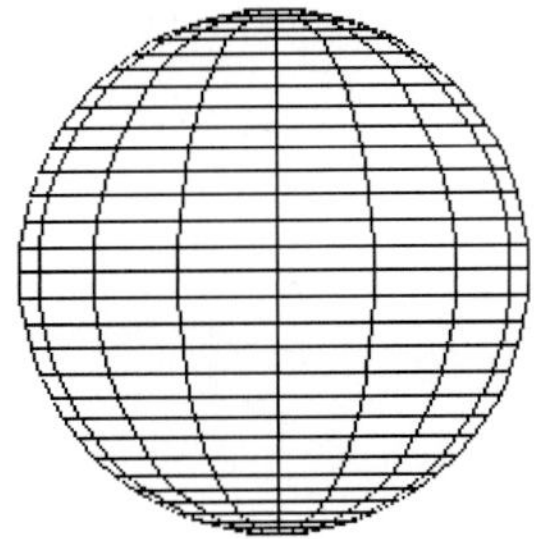

FIG. 7.1c Revsurfed Arc

- Figure 7.1c was drawn using the ***Revsurf*** command with **Surftab1** set to 16 and **Surftab2** set to 32.

Notice the difference between Figures 7.1b and 7.1c. Both were drawn using the same command with the same size arc and identical axes. The only difference was the **Surftab1** and **Surftab2** settings. In Figure 7.1b, AutoCAD used four faces to define the object along the circumference and along the path of revolution. In Figure 7.1c, AutoCAD used 16 faces to define the object along the circumference and 32 along the path of revolution. Here you see another important aspect of the **Surftab1** and **Surftab2** system variables—*their settings affect the shape of the object being drawn.*

Make a small copy of Figure 7.1c and write the **Surftab1** and **Surftab2** settings on it. Tape it to your monitor as a guide until you are comfortable with each.

We will set **Surftab1** and **Surftab2** as needed throughout the exercises in this lesson.

7.2 Different Approaches for Different Goals

AutoCAD provides four basic and two advanced commands to handle the drawing of complex shapes. You will probably enjoy the basic commands—they are lots of fun! The advanced commands, however, are more challenging and may take some time to master.

The basic commands all have one thing in common—they all use something two dimensional as a guide to create a three-dimensional object. But remember, a two-dimensional object can exist in Z-Space. That is, an object can have any two of the three properties required for a three-dimensional object (length, width, and height). The command you use to create the three-dimensional object will provide the third property. This will become clear once you have used the commands.

We will discuss the four basic commands in this section and save the advanced commands for the next one. Let's get started.

7.2.1 Follow the Path—The Tabsurf Command

The ***Tabsurf*** command is one of the easiest. You need a basic shape—circle, arc, polyline, and splines make great shapes—and something to indicate a path. AutoCAD will expand the shape into three dimensions along the path you identify.

The command sequence looks like this:

Command: *tabsurf*

Select object for path curve: *[select the object that will give shape to your three-dimensional object]*

Select object for direction vector: *[select an object that will tell AutoCAD the direction in which to expand the shape]*

This will become clearer with some practice.

You can access the ***Tabsurf*** command (and other complex surface commands discussed in this lesson) from the Surfaces toolbar or from the Draw pull-down menu. Follow this path for the pull-down menu commands:

Draw—Surfaces—Tabulated Surfaces (or other complex surface command)

WWW 7.2.1.1 Do This: Using Tabsurf to Create a Three-Dimensional Object

I. Open the *train.dwg* file in the C:\Steps3D\Lesson07 folder. The drawing looks like Figure 7.2.1.1a. (This will be a fun project. We will use the basic commands for drawing complex shapes to create a three-dimensional toy train.)

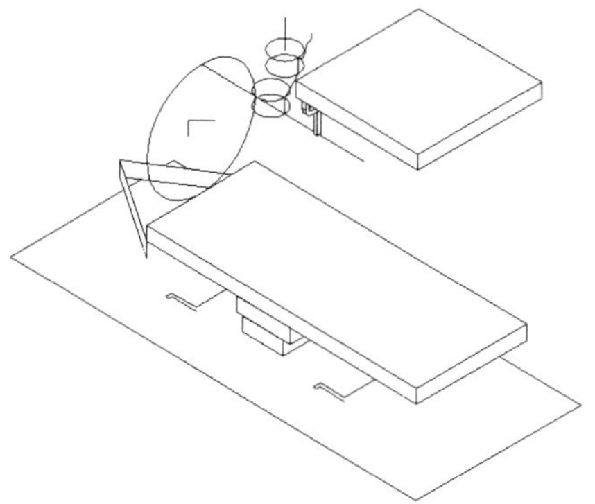

FIG. 7.2.1.1a *Train.dwg*

II. Set the current layer to **Tank**.

III. Follow these steps:

TOOLS	COMMAND SEQUENCE	STEPS
No Button Available	**Command:** *surftab1* **Enter new value for SURFTAB1 <6>:** *20*	**1.** Set the **Surftab1** system variable to 20 for a more defined shape.
Tabulated Surface Button	**Command:** *tabsurf*	**2.** Enter the ***Tabsurf*** command by typing ***tabsurf*** at the command prompt or selecting the **Tabulated Surface** button from the Surfaces toolbar.

continued

TOOLS	COMMAND SEQUENCE	STEPS
	Select object for path curve: ***[select the circle]***	**3.** (Refer to Figure 7.2.1.1.3 for Steps 3 and 4.) AutoCAD wants you to select the object for path curve—the *shape*. Select the circle indicated.

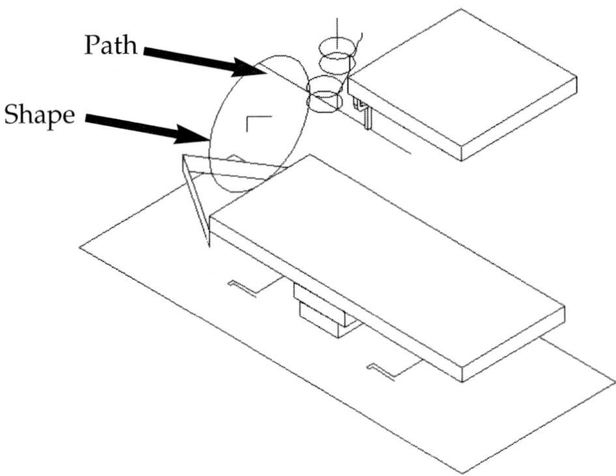

FIG. 7.2.1.1.3 Select These Objects

continued

TOOLS	COMMAND SEQUENCE	STEPS
	Select object for direction vector: *[select the line]*	**4.** AutoCAD wants to know in which direction to expand the shape—the *path*. Select the line indicated. (Select next to where the arrow points in Figure 7.2.1.1.3.) Your drawing looks like Figure 7.2.1.1.4. [*Note:* First AutoCAD determines the path by the selected object. But then it determines the direction for the three-dimensional object by *where* you select on the **object for direction vector**. Try repeating this step, but select the other end of the line (then undo until your drawing again looks like Figure 7.2.1.1.4).]

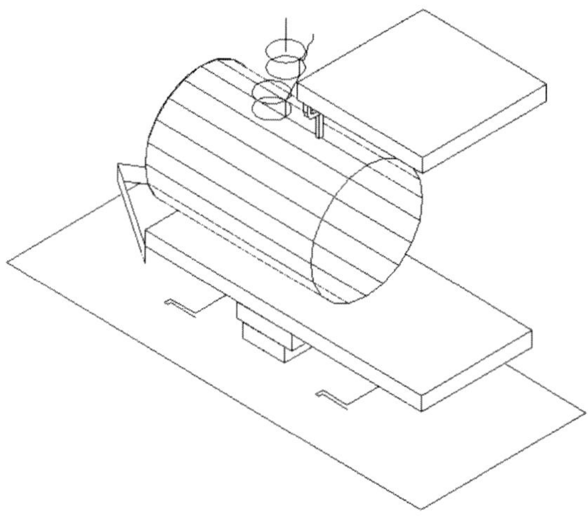

FIG. 7.2.1.1.4 Completed Tank

TOOLS	COMMAND SEQUENCE	STEPS
	**Command:** *z*	**5.** Zoom in around the smokestack (the stacked circles atop the tank).
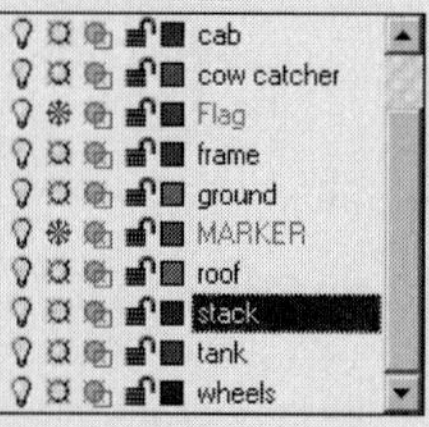	**Command:** *la*	**6.** Set the **stack** layer current.

continued

TOOLS	COMMAND SEQUENCE	STEPS
	**Command:** ***tabsurf***	**7.** Use the ***Tabsurf*** command to expand the circles along the lines. Notice that the path is independent of the UCS. Your drawing looks like Figure 7.2.1.1.7. 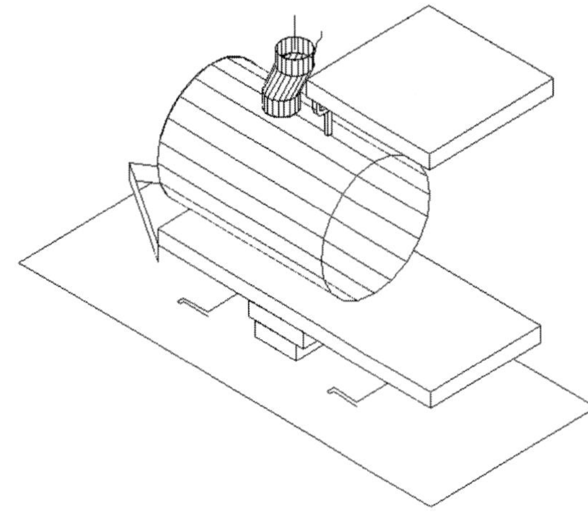 **FIG. 7.2.1.1.7** Tank with Smokestack (after zooming back out)
	**Command:** ***qsave***	**8.** Save the drawing, but do not exit.

Some things you may have noticed about the ***Tabsurf*** command and need to remember include:

- The layer of the new object is based on the current layer at the time it is drawn and not on the layer of the original shape or path.
- The part of the path AutoCAD uses to define the new object is the endpoint—a curved path will not produce a curved object.
- The original shape and path remain intact after the three-dimensional object is drawn—put them on a separate layer that can be frozen later.
- Where you pick on the path can affect the direction of the expansion.
- The UCS does not affect the expansion.

We used circles in our exercise, but ***Tabsurf*** will work on any predefined shape provided the shape is a single object. Polylines and Splines are particularly useful in creating shapes for ***Tabsurf*** expansion.

Let's take a look at another complex Surface Modeling command.

7.2.2 Add a Surface Between Objects—The Rulesurf Command

Use the ***Rulesurf*** command when you have two existing objects and want to place a surface between them. It is particularly useful when creating surfaces between uneven objects or objects of different size.

The command sequence is

Command: ***rulesurf***

Current wire frame density: SURFTAB1=20 ***[AutoCAD reminds you of the current Surftab1 setting; Surftab2 does not affect Rulesurf]***

Select first defining curve: ***[select the first edge of the surface to be created]***

Select second defining curve: ***[select the opposite edge of the surface to be created]***

Similarities between ***Rulesurf*** and ***Tabsurf*** include:

- The layer of the new object is based on the current layer at the time it is drawn and not on the layer of the original shape or path.
- The original edges remain intact after the three-dimensional object is drawn.
- Where you pick on the path can affect the expansion. You should pick in the same vicinity on both edges (toward the same endpoints).
- The UCS does not affect the expansion.

Let's try the ***Rulesurf*** command on our train's cow catcher.

WWW 7.2.2.1 Do This: Using Rulesurf to Create a Three-Dimensional Object

I. Be sure you are still in the *train.dwg* file. If not, open it now (it is in the C:\Steps3D\Lesson07 folder).

II. Restore the **−111** view.

III. Set the **tank** layer current.

IV. Follow these steps:

TOOLS	COMMAND SEQUENCE	STEPS
	**Command:** *reg* **Select objects:** *[select the circle]* **Select objects:** *[enter]* **1 loop extracted.** **1 Region created.**	**1.** Turn the circle in the front of the tank into a region. (This will improve viewing later.)
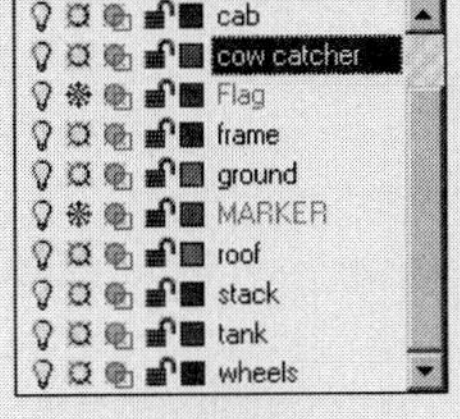	**Command:** *la*	**2.** Set the **cow catcher** layer current.
 Ruled Surface Button	**Command:** *rulesurf*	**3.** Enter the ***Rulesurf*** command by typing ***rulesurf*** at the command prompt or picking the **Ruled Surface** button on the Surfaces toolbar.

continued

TOOLS	COMMAND SEQUENCE	STEPS
	Current wire frame density: SURFTAB1=20 **Select first defining curve:** *[select the first edge]* **Select second defining curve:** *[select the second edge]*	**4.** (Refer to Figure 7.2.2.1.4.) AutoCAD needs to know where to draw the surface. Select the edges as indicated. If the surface appears crossed, erase it and try again. When you select the edges, pick in the same general location of each. (If you have trouble selecting the edges, hold down the control key and select until the edge is found.)

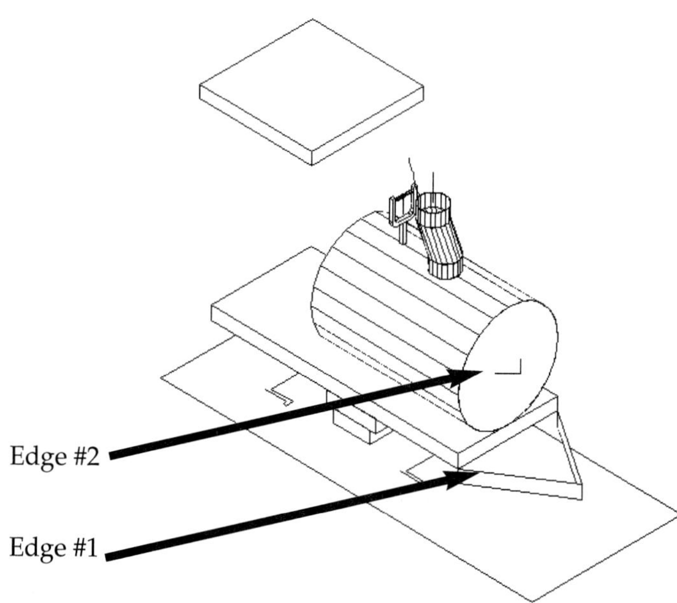

FIG. 7.2.2.1.4 Edges

continued

TOOLS	COMMAND SEQUENCE	STEPS
	**Command:** ***rulesurf***	**5.** Repeat Steps 3 and 4 for the other side of the cow catcher. Your drawing looks like Figure 7.2.2.1.5.

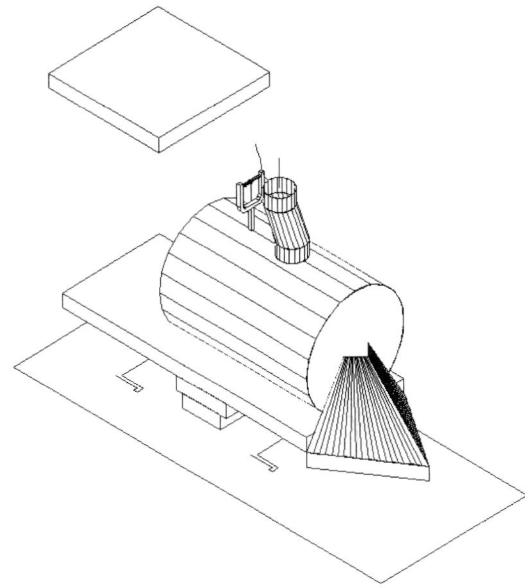

FIG. 7.2.2.1.5 Completed Cow Catcher

TOOLS	COMMAND SEQUENCE	STEPS
	**Command:** *qsave*	**6.** Save the drawing, but do not exit.

Like ***Tabsurf***, any type of object will do for an edge—the fancier the original object, the fancier the results!

Speaking of fancy, let's look at the ***Revsurf*** command!

7.2.3 Creating Circular Surfaces—The Revsurf Command

Revsurf is one of the more popular of AutoCAD's Surface Modeling commands. That could be because ***Revsurf*** is so simple to use. But it is more likely because of the nifty objects you can draw with it!

Like the ***Tabsurf*** command, ***Revsurf*** begins with an object that will define its basic shape and another object that will define its path (or, in the case of ***Revsurf***, its axis). Time and care should be devoted to creating the basic shape since a well-defined shape will be reflected in the final object. Although other objects may occasionally be required (like a circle as a basic shape to define a piping elbow), I would use polylines or splines almost exclusively. They tend to produce some truly professional results!

The ***Revsurf*** command sequence looks like this:

Command: ***revsurf***

Current wire frame density: SURFTAB1=20 SURFTAB2=6 ***[AutoCAD reports the current settings for both Surftab1 and Surftab2. Both will be needed for this procedure.]***

Select object to revolve: ***[select the object that defines the basic shape of the object you wish to create]***

Select object that defines the axis of revolution: ***[select an object that defines the axis around which you will revolve the shape]***

Specify start angle <0>: ***[specify a starting angle]***

Specify included angle (+ = ccw, − = cw) <360>: ***[tell AutoCAD if you want a fully or partially revolved shape. The default—360°—defines a full revolution. For less than a full revolution, enter the degrees that define the arc you wish to fill.]***

Like ***Tabsurf*** and ***Rulesurf***, the UCS does not affect ***Revsurf***. However, you might need to adjust it when creating the basic shape you intend to revolve.

Let's take a look at the ***Revsurf*** command.

7.2.3.1 Do This: Using Revsurf to Create a Three-Dimensional Object

I. Be sure you are still in the *train.dwg* file. If not, open it now (it is in the C:\Steps3D\Lesson07 folder).

II. Restore the **Bell** view.

III. Set the **Stack** layer current.

IV. Follow these steps:

TOOLS	COMMAND SEQUENCE	STEPS
 Revolved Surfaces Button	**Command:** ***revsurf***	**1.** Enter the ***Revsurf*** command by typing ***revsurf*** at the command prompt or picking the **Revolved Surface** button on the Surfaces toolbar.

continued

TOOLS	COMMAND SEQUENCE	STEPS
	Current wire frame density: SURFTAB1=20 SURFTAB2=6	**2.** AutoCAD reports the **Surftab1** and **Surftab2** settings. These suit our purpose, so we will continue.
	Select object to revolve:	Select the spline rising from the top of the smokestack as the object to revolve.
	Select object that defines the axis of revolution:	**3.** Select the line rising from the center of the smokestack as your **axis of revolution**.
	Specify start angle <0>: *[enter]*	**4.** Accept the **start angle** and **included angle** defaults.
	Specify included angle (+ = ccw, – = cw) <360>: *[enter]*	
	**Command:** *revsurf*	**5.** Repeat Steps 1 to 4 for the Bell assembly (be sure to use the **Bell** layer). Your drawing looks like Figure 7.2.3.1.5.

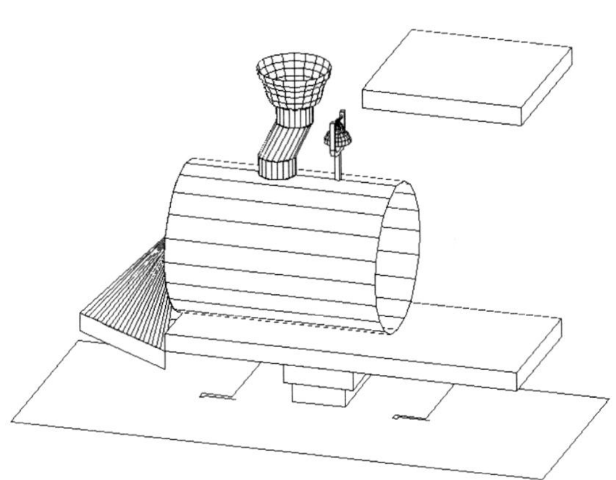

FIG. 7.2.3.1.5 Completed Smokestack and Bell

TOOLS	COMMAND SEQUENCE	STEPS
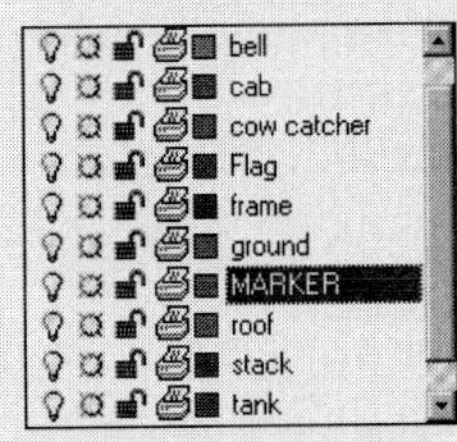	**Command:** *la*	**6.** Thaw the **MARKER** layer. Notice the nodes, but also notice the lines that appear as axes for the wheel shapes.

continued

TOOLS	COMMAND SEQUENCE	STEPS
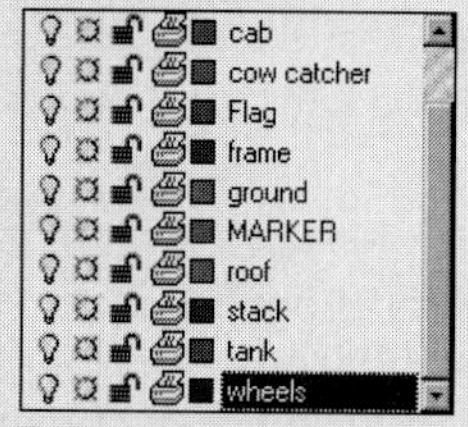 cab, cow catcher, Flag, frame, ground, MARKER, roof, stack, tank, wheels	**Command:** *la*	**7.** Set the **Wheels** layer current.
	**Command:** *revsurf*	**8.** Repeat Steps 1 to 4 for both wheels using the lines on the **MARKER** layer as the axes. (Refreeze the **MARKER** layer when you have finished.) Your drawing looks like Figure 7.2.3.1.8.
		FIG. 7.2.3.1.8 Wheels Added
	**Command:** *qsave*	**9.** Save the drawing, but do not exit.

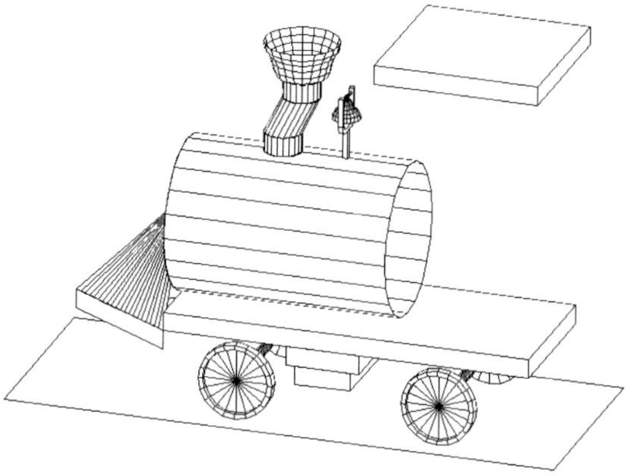

Was that fun?

But remember that I am providing the basic shapes for these exercises. It is a bit more involved (although not difficult) when you draw them yourself!

Our train is starting to take shape (as is our expertise with some cool new commands). Have you tried viewing the model with the Gouraud Shademode? It looks very nice (especially if you freeze layer **0**).

But we still have to draw the cab and the ground beneath the wheels. Let's not waste a moment—full steam ahead!

7.2.4 Using Edges to Define a Surface Plane—The Edgesurf Command

Edgesurf is actually one of the simplest of the complex surface commands. But I have placed it at the end of the basic commands because it makes a good transition to the more advanced commands.

Edgesurf creates a surface *plane*. That does not mean that it creates a surface along the X-, Y-, or Z-planes but rather a plane like an open field. It does not have to be flat, although it is not the best tool for very complex surfaces.

The ***Edgesurf*** command uses four edges to define a plane. The edges can be parallel to one another or skewed in any direction.

The command sequence simply asks for the four edges:

Command: ***edgesurf***

Current wire frame density: SURFTAB1=20 SURFTAB2=6 ***[AutoCAD reminds you of the Surftab1 and Surftab2 settings. Like Revsurf, both will be needed here.]***

Select object 1 for surface edge: ***{select the objects that will define the }***

Select object 2 for surface edge: ***{boundaries for the surface. You can }***

Select object 3 for surface edge: ***{select them in any order, but the order may affect the final appearance of the plane.}***

Select object 4 for surface edge:

Command:

We will use ***Edgesurf*** to create the ground beneath our train's wheels.

WWW 7.2.4.1 Do This: Using Edgesurf to Create a Three-Dimensional Object

I. Be sure you are still in the *train.dwg* file. If not, open it now (it is in the C:\Steps3D\Lesson07 folder).

II. Remain in the **Bell** view but zoom out so you can see the ground.

III. Set the **Ground** layer current.

IV. Follow these steps:

TOOLS	COMMAND SEQUENCE	STEPS
 Edge Surface Button	**Command:** ***edgesurf***	**1.** Enter the ***Edgesurf*** command by typing ***edgesurf*** at the command prompt or picking the **Edge Surface** button on the Surfaces toolbar.
	Current wire frame density: SURFTAB1=20 SURFTAB2=6 **Select object 1 for surface edge:**	**2.** AutoCAD reports the current **Surftab1** and **Surftab2** settings and then asks you to select the edges of your object.
	Select object 2 for surface edge: **Select object 3 for surface edge:** **Select object 4 for surface edge:**	Select the four lines that form the boundary of the ground (pick one of the shorter lines first). Your drawing looks like Figure 7.2.4.1.2.

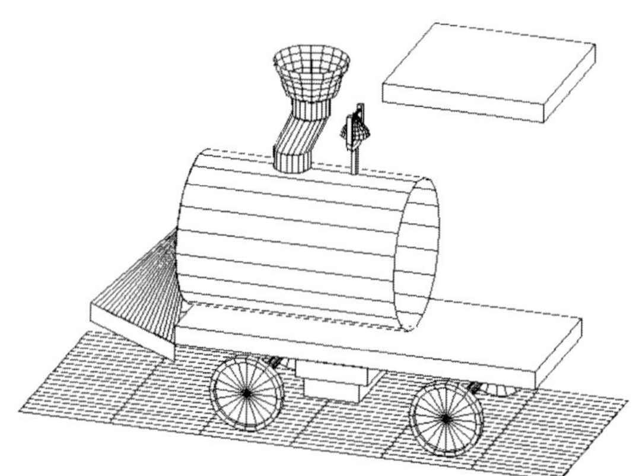

FIG. 7.2.4.1.2 *Ground Added*

TOOLS	COMMAND SEQUENCE	STEPS
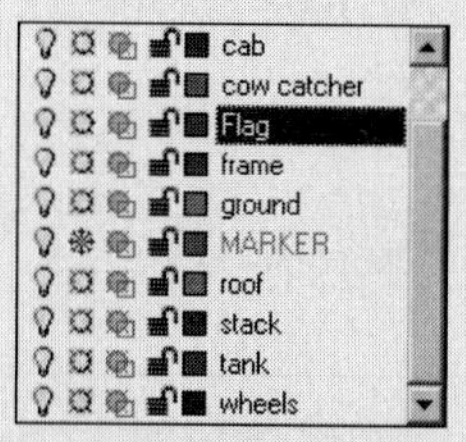	**Command:** ***la***	**3.** You have seen how ***Edgesurf*** works. But let me show you what it can do with a little imagination. Thaw the **Flag** layer and set it current. Notice the outline of the flag atop the roof (refer to Figure 7.2.4.1.5).
	Command: ***surftab2*** **Enter new value for SURFTAB2 <6>:** ***20***	**4.** Set **Surftab2** to ***20.*** This will enhance our resolution.

continued

TOOLS	COMMAND SEQUENCE	STEPS
	**Command:** ***edgesurf*** **Current wire frame density: SURFTAB1=20 SURFTAB2=20** **Select object 1 for surface edge:** **Select object 2 for surface edge:** **Select object 3 for surface edge:** **Select object 4 for surface edge:**	**5.** Now do an ***Edgesurf*** using the four sides (two lines and two splines) of the flag as your edges. Your drawing looks like Figure 7.2.4.1.5. 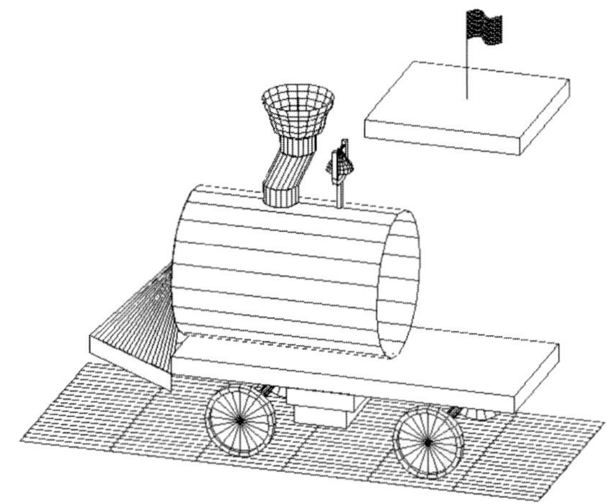 FIG. 7.2.4.1.5 Edged Surfaces
	**Command:** ***qsave***	**6.** Save the drawing, but do not exit.

How is that for a bit of razzle-dazzle?!

This concludes the basic Surface Model commands. But there is one part of our train we have yet to draw—the cab. We could create it using simple ***3DFace*** commands. However, that would give us several objects with which to deal later. There is a way to create the cab as a single object just as the sphere, box, torus, and other predefined Surface Models are single objects. That involves the advanced Surface Model commands, which we will look at next.

7.3 More Complex Surfaces

There are actually two advanced Surface Model commands—***3DMesh*** and ***PFace***. I do not recommend either for the faint of heart.

AutoCAD invented these commands for the user to create objects similar to the predefined Surface Models so the user can manipulate many surfaces as a single object (as in a single sphere rather than dozens of faces). But be forewarned: Creating an object with either the ***3DMesh*** or ***PFace*** command means manually specifying *every vertex on the object*! Besides that, you must identify the vertices *in a specific order*!

Does that sound like a lot of work? It is! (That's why I call this the *Advanced* text.) But in AutoCAD's defense, I must add that these commands are actually better suited for lisp routines or other third-party programs. You might say that you are on the border where CAD operation ends and CAD programming begins.

We will start with the ***3DMesh*** command.

> A third-party program is one that is designed to use AutoCAD as a base. In other words, AutoCAD becomes something like a CAD Operating System (as Windows is your computer's operating system). The third-party program builds on AutoCAD by providing shortcuts toward a specific end. Popular third-party programs include *Propipe, ProISO,* and others for the petrochemical industry, AutoCAD's own *Mechanical Desktop* and *Architectural Desktop* for related industries, and others.

7.3.1 Creating Meshes with the 3DMesh Command

The ***3DMesh*** command is similar to the ***Edgesurf*** command. (The similarity is akin to that between a sculptor and a whittler—both will give you a carving. But what the sculptor produces will embarrass the whittler.) Both work well in creating that open-field look. But where four edges define the ***Edgesurf*** object, you have no limit to the number of defined vertices with the ***3DMesh*** command. As I have mentioned, however, it requires tedious effort to identify each vertex involved.

The command sequence looks like this:

Command: *3dmesh*

Enter size of mesh in M direction: ***[tell AutoCAD how many lines are required to define the columns of faces you will need]***

Enter size of mesh in N direction: ***[tell AutoCAD how many lines are required to define the rows of faces you will need]***

Specify location for vertex (0, 0): ***[this prompt will repeat for each vertex (intersection) of lines defining the rows and columns]***

Command:

Notice that AutoCAD defines the rows and columns in terms of **M** and **N**. This helps avoid any confusion with the X-, Y-, and Z-axes. ***3DMesh*** works independently of the UCS.

There is an interesting point to remember when defining the size of the mesh in terms of rows and columns. Notice that AutoCAD does not ask for the number of rows and columns, but rather asks for the number of lines required to define the rows and columns. This is because you (and AutoCAD) will be working with the vertices that create the surface, not the spaces between the vertices. The easiest way to determine the number of lines required is simply to add one to the number of rows and columns you want.

This will become clearer in our next exercise. Let's draw a hill in front of our train.

WWW 7.3.1.1 Do This: Using 3DMesh to Create a Three-Dimensional Surface

I. Be sure you are still in the *train.dwg* file. If not, open it now (it is in the C:\Steps3D\Lesson07 folder).

II. Thaw the **Marker** layer.

III. Set the **ground** layer current.

IV. Begin in the **Bell** view, but pan and orbit so you can see the nodes at the front of the train.

V. Be sure your running OSNAP has been set to **Node** (clear all other settings).

VI. Follow these steps:

TOOLS	COMMAND SEQUENCE	STEPS
 3D Mesh Button	**Command:** ***3dmesh***	**1.** Enter the ***3DMesh*** command by typing ***3dmesh*** at the command prompt or picking the **3D Mesh** button on the Surfaces toolbar.
	Enter size of mesh in M direction: ***6*** **Enter size of mesh in N direction:** ***6***	**2.** Tell AutoCAD you want 5 rows and 5 columns. (Remember that you need 6 lines to define 5 rows or columns.) (Refer to Figure 7.3.1.2.)

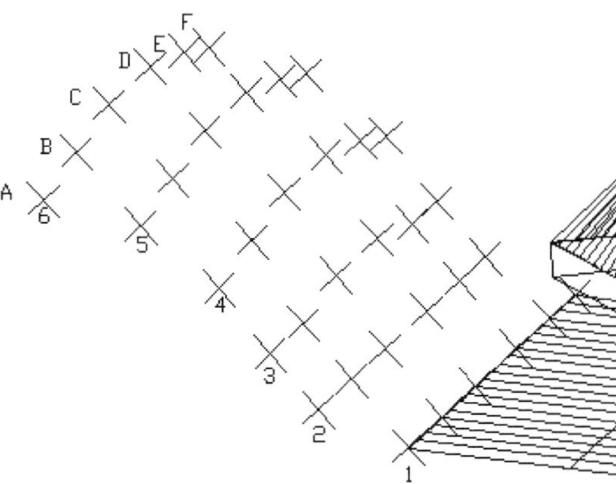

FIG. 7.3.1.2 Rows and Columns

continued

TOOLS	COMMAND SEQUENCE	STEPS
	Specify location for vertex (0, 0):	**3.** Now we will identify the vertices. Select nodes A-1 through A-6 sequentially. (*Hint:* Use running OSNAPs.)
	Specify location for vertex (0, 1):	
	Specify location for vertex (0, 2):	
	Specify location for vertex (0, 3):	
	Specify location for vertex (0, 4):	
	Specify location for vertex (0, 5):	
	Specify location for vertex (1, 0): *[prompt will repeat for each vertex]*	**4.** Follow Step 3 for rows B through F. (Be sure to select the nodes sequentially.)
cab, cow catcher, Flag, frame, ground, MARKER, roof, stack, tank, wheels	**Command:** *la*	**5.** Freeze the **Marker** layer. Your drawing looks like Figure 7.3.1.5.
		FIG. 7.3.1.5 Hill Has Been Drawn
	Command: *qsave*	**6.** Save the drawing, but do not exit.

Note that, once the basic shape of our hill has been defined by using the ***3DMesh*** command, you can add or remove faces using the ***Pedit*** command. We will look at that in more detail in Lesson 8.

Did you find it tedious having to select a node to define each of the 36 vertices? Imagine what it is like defining a large area! Bear in mind that I provided the nodes as a guide for this exercise. Normally, you will identify the location and place the nodes as well (or enter coordinates at the **Specify location** prompt). Do you see now why I described this command as the edge between CAD operating and CAD programming? You will often create a 3D Mesh using a lisp routine (or even a Visual Basic program) in conjunction with coordinates defined in a database or spreadsheet. This is really the only way to create large surfaces (like mountains and valleys).

But wait! The ***PFace*** command has even more options!

7.3.2 Creating Meshes with the PFace Command

We still have not created our cab. Why did we not use the ***3DMesh*** command? Simply because it does not lend itself easily to creating surfaces with holes (or, in the case of our cab, with windows).

In some instances, the ***PFace*** command actually appears easier to use than the ***3DMesh*** command. You do not have to enter coordinates sequentially—at least not as you did with the ***3DMesh*** command. In fact, you will identify all the vertices making up the object and then tell AutoCAD which vertex to use for which face. All you have to remember is which vertex is which. AutoCAD will do the rest. But with the ***PFace*** command, you will also have the opportunity to change the color and/or layer of each face. This might come in handy for construction walk-throughs.

The command sequence for the ***PFace*** command is

Command: *pface*

Specify location for vertex 1: *[this prompt repeats for each vertex; specify the location of all the vertices]*

Specify location for vertex X or <define faces>: *[when all the vertices have been identified, hit enter to define the faces]*

Face 1, vertex 1:

Enter a vertex number or [Color/Layer]: *[here you will tell AutoCAD which vertex to use for each face]*

Face 1, vertex 2:

Enter a vertex number or [Color/Layer] <next face>: *[hit enter to identify the vertices on the next face; the prompt will repeat until each face has been identified. Type C or L to change the color or layer of the face]*

Command:

This command sequence is a bit tricky, but it will be clearer when you complete the next exercise. Trickier still will be the identification of the vertex locations. This may involve some math and a comfortable understanding of the Cartesian Coordinate System. I will provide the vertex locations for our cab so that you can concentrate on the workings of the ***PFace*** command.

Let's begin. [The cab will have a front and two sides (drawn as three separate objects for simplicity). Each will consist of four faces framing an opening for a window.]

WWW 7.3.2.1 Do This: Using *PFace* to Create a Three-Dimensional Object

I. Be sure you are still in the *train.dwg* file. If not, open it now (it is in the C:\Steps3D\Lesson07 folder).

II. Set the **Cab** layer current.

III. Restore the **Bell** view.

IV. Clear all running OSNAPs.

V. Follow these steps:

TOOLS	COMMAND SEQUENCE	STEPS
No Button Available	**Command:** *pface*	**1.** Enter the ***PFace*** command by typing *pface* at the command prompt. There is no button, hotkey, or pull-down menu selection for this command.

continued

TOOLS	COMMAND SEQUENCE	STEPS
	Specify location for vertex 1: *7,1,1.5*	**2.** We will draw the front of the cab first. Enter the coordinates indicated at the prompts.
	Specify location for vertex 2 or <define faces>: *7,5,1.5*	
	Specify location for vertex 3 or <define faces>: *7,5,5.75*	
	Specify location for vertex 4 or <define faces>: *7,1,5.75*	
	Specify location for vertex 5 or <define faces>: *7,1.75,5.75*	
	Specify location for vertex 6 or <define faces>: *7,1.75,7.75*	
	Specify location for vertex 7 or <define faces>: *7,1,7.75*	
	Specify location for vertex 8 or <define faces>: *7,1,8.5*	
	Specify location for vertex 9 or <define faces>: *7,5,8.5*	
	Specify location for vertex 10 or <define faces>: *7,5,7.75*	
	Specify location for vertex 11 or <define faces>: *7,4.25,7.75*	
	Specify location for vertex 12 or <define faces>: *7,4.25,5.75*	
	Specify location for vertex 13 or <define faces>: *7,5,5.75*	
	Specify location for vertex 14 or <define faces>: *[enter]*	**3.** Hit *enter* to define the faces.

continued

TOOLS	COMMAND SEQUENCE	STEPS
	Face 1, vertex 1:	**4.** Identify the bottom face (Face 1) as indicated.
	Enter a vertex number or [Color/Layer]: *1*	
	Face 1, vertex 2:	
	Enter a vertex number or [Color/Layer] <next face>: 2	
	Face 1, vertex 3:	
	Enter a vertex number or [Color/Layer] <next face>: *3*	
	Face 1, vertex 4:	
	Enter a vertex number or [Color/Layer] <next face>: *4*	
	Face 1, vertex 5:	**5.** Hit ***enter*** to move to the next face (Face 2).
	Enter a vertex number or [Color/Layer] <next face>: *[enter]*	
	Face 2, vertex 1:	**6.** Identify the vertices for the second face as indicated.
	Enter a vertex number or [Color/Layer]: *4*	
	Face 2, vertex 2:	
	Enter a vertex number or [Color/Layer] <next face>: *5*	
	Face 2, vertex 3:	
	Enter a vertex number or [Color/Layer] <next face>: *6*	
	Face 2, vertex 4:	
	Enter a vertex number or [Color/Layer] <next face>: 7	

continued

TOOLS	COMMAND SEQUENCE	STEPS
	Face 2, vertex 5:	**7.** Hit ***enter*** to move to the next face (Face 3).
	Enter a vertex number or [Color/Layer] <next face>: *[enter]*	
	Face 3, vertex 1:	**8.** Identify the vertices for the third face as indicated.
	Enter a vertex number or [Color/Layer]: *7*	
	Face 3, vertex 2:	
	Enter a vertex number or [Color/Layer] <next face>: *8*	
	Face 3, vertex 3:	
	Enter a vertex number or [Color/Layer] <next face>: *9*	
	Face 3, vertex 4:	
	Enter a vertex number or [Color/Layer] <next face>: *10*	
	Face 3, vertex 5:	**9.** Hit ***enter*** to move to the next face (Face 4).
	Enter a vertex number or [Color/Layer] <next face>: *[enter]*	

continued

TOOLS	COMMAND SEQUENCE	STEPS
	Face 4, vertex 1: **Enter a vertex number or [Color/Layer]:** *10* **Face 4, vertex 2:** **Enter a vertex number or [Color/Layer] <next face>:** *11* **Face 4, vertex 3:** **Enter a vertex number or [Color/Layer] <next face>:** *12* **Face 4, vertex 4:** **Enter a vertex number or [Color/Layer] <next face>:** *13*	**10.** Identify the vertices for the fourth face as indicated.
	Face 4, vertex 5: **Enter a vertex number or [Color/Layer] <next face>:** *[enter]*	**11.** Hit *enter* to complete this face.
	Face 5, vertex 1: **Enter a vertex number or [Color/Layer]:** *[enter]*	**12.** Hit *enter* again to complete the command. Your drawing looks like Figure 7.3.2.1.12.

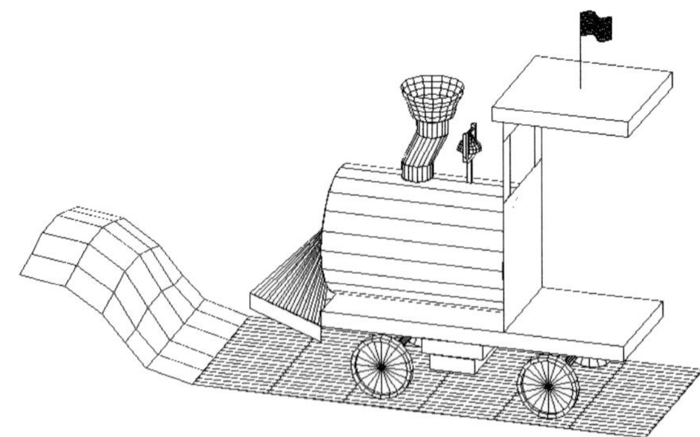

FIG. 7.3.2.1.12 Front of Cab

TOOLS	COMMAND SEQUENCE	STEPS
	**Command:** *qsave*	**13.** Save the drawing, but do not exit. (This exercise continues.)

Now you are saying to yourself, "I drew it . . . I see it . . . but I don't know how I did it." That is an understandable reaction to this exercise. Let me explain what you did.

- Look closely at the new mesh. You will see four faces (you may need to orbit slightly to see the top one). The 13 coordinates you entered in Step 2 are the coordinates of each corner of the faces (some coordinates are used twice). As you entered the coordinates, AutoCAD identified it with a number (**Specify location for vertex 6**, and so forth).
- In Steps 4, 6, 8, and 10, you told AutoCAD which coordinates to use to identify a specific corner of a specific face (**Face 1, vertex 2**, and so forth).

So you see, the complexity lies not in the command itself but in the amount of data required (and in calculating that data).

TOOLS	COMMAND SEQUENCE	STEPS
		14. Repeat Steps 1–13 using the following coordinates to draw the first side wall.

NUMBER	COORDINATE	NUMBER	COORDINATE	NUMBER	COORDINATE
1	11,1,1.5	6	10.25,1,7.75	11	7.75,1,7.75
2	7,1,1.5	7	11,1,7.75	12	7.75,1,5.75
3	7,1,5.75	8	11,1,8.5	13	7,1,5.75
4	11,1,5.75	9	7,1,8.5		
5	10.25,1,5.75	10	7,1,7.75		

TOOLS	COMMAND SEQUENCE	STEPS
	Command: *co*	**15.** Copy the new wall to the other side of the cab.

continued

TOOLS	COMMAND SEQUENCE	STEPS
	Command: *vpoint* **Current view direction: VIEWDIR= 7.0000,−22.0000,9.0000** **Specify a view point or [Rotate] <display compass and tripod>:** ***−30,21,6***	**16.** Change the viewpoint as indicated, set the **Shademode** to Gouraud, and freeze layer **0**. Your drawing looks like Figure 7.3.2.1.16. FIG. 7.3.2.1.16 Completed Train
	Command: *qsave*	**17.** Save the drawing.

Be proud of yourself! You have accomplished AutoCAD's 3D Surface commands!

7.4 Extra Steps

Try to incorporate all you have learned thus far into the train drawing.

- Adjust the views so you can see it from all sides.
- Freeze the **ground** layer and use the Continuous Orbiter to make the train revolve about the screen.
- Set up the train drawing for plotting:
  - Show it in three views and an isometric.
  - Dimension it.
  - Put it on a title block with your school's name.

7.5 What Have We Learned?

Items covered in this lesson include:

- *Controlling the number of surfaces on a Surface Model*
- *Basic and Advanced Surface Modeling Commands*
  - ***Surftab1***
  - ***Surftab2***
  - ***Rulesurf***
  - ***Tabsurf***
  - ***Revsurf***
  - ***Edgesurf***
  - ***3DMesh***
  - ***PFace***

Congratulations! You have finished AutoCAD's Wireframe and Surface Modeling commands. You have really come a long way in seven lessons!

The decisions you will now face concern which procedure or method you will need to create the objects that you want to create. The best help you can get for that is *practice*! So work through the problems at the end of this lesson until you are comfortable with your new abilities.

When you have finished with the exercises, go on to Lesson 8. There we will discuss the three-dimensional aspects of several editing tools you already know and some new ones that are specific to three-dimensional drawings. Then, at least where Wireframe and Surface Modeling is concerned, your training will be complete. After that we will start a whole new ballgame—we will learn how to create Solid Models!

So do the problems, pat yourself on the back for having come this far, and then move onward—ever onward!

7.6 EXERCISES

1. Create the Window Guide drawing in Figure 7.6.1. The following information will help.
   1.1. Use the *ANSI A Title Block* found in the \AutoCAD\Template folder.
   1.2. Use the Times New Roman font at $\frac{3}{16}''$ and $\frac{1}{8}''$ sizes.
   1.3. Adjust the dimstyle as needed (I used the **Small Dot** arrowhead).
   1.4. Create layers as needed.
   1.5. The object is a tabulated Surface Model created from a polyline shape.
   1.6. Use either a region or a 3D Face to close the ends.
   1.7. The Shademode used for the isometric figure is **Flat+Edges**.
   1.8. Save the drawing as *MyWinGuide* in the C:\Steps3D\Lesson07 folder.

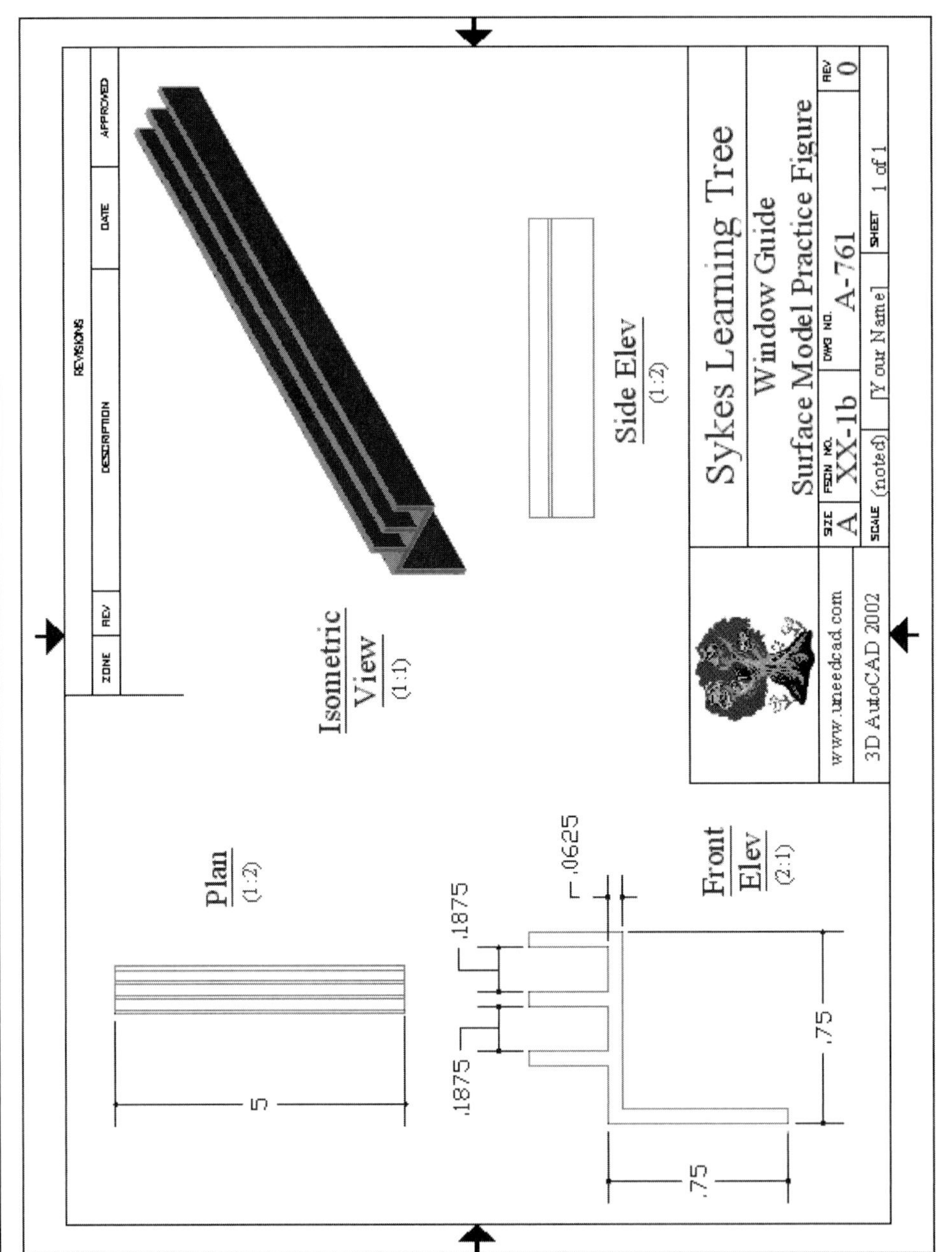

FIG. 7.6.1 Window Guide

2. Create the Light Fixture drawing in Figure 7.6.2. The following information will help.
   2.1. Use the *ANSI A Title Block* found in the \AutoCAD\Template folder.
   2.2. Use the Times New Roman font at $\frac{3}{16}$″ and $\frac{1}{8}$″ sizes.
   2.3. Adjust the dimstyle as needed.
   2.4. Create layers as needed.
   2.5. I used a **Surftab1** setting of 32 and a **Surftab2** setting of 6.

2.6. The object is a simple Revolved Surface Model. I created the shape on one layer and the Revolved Surface Model on another. I did the cross section by adjusting the viewport and freezing unnecessary layers.

2.7. Save the drawing as *MyFixture* in the C:\Steps3D\Lesson07 folder.

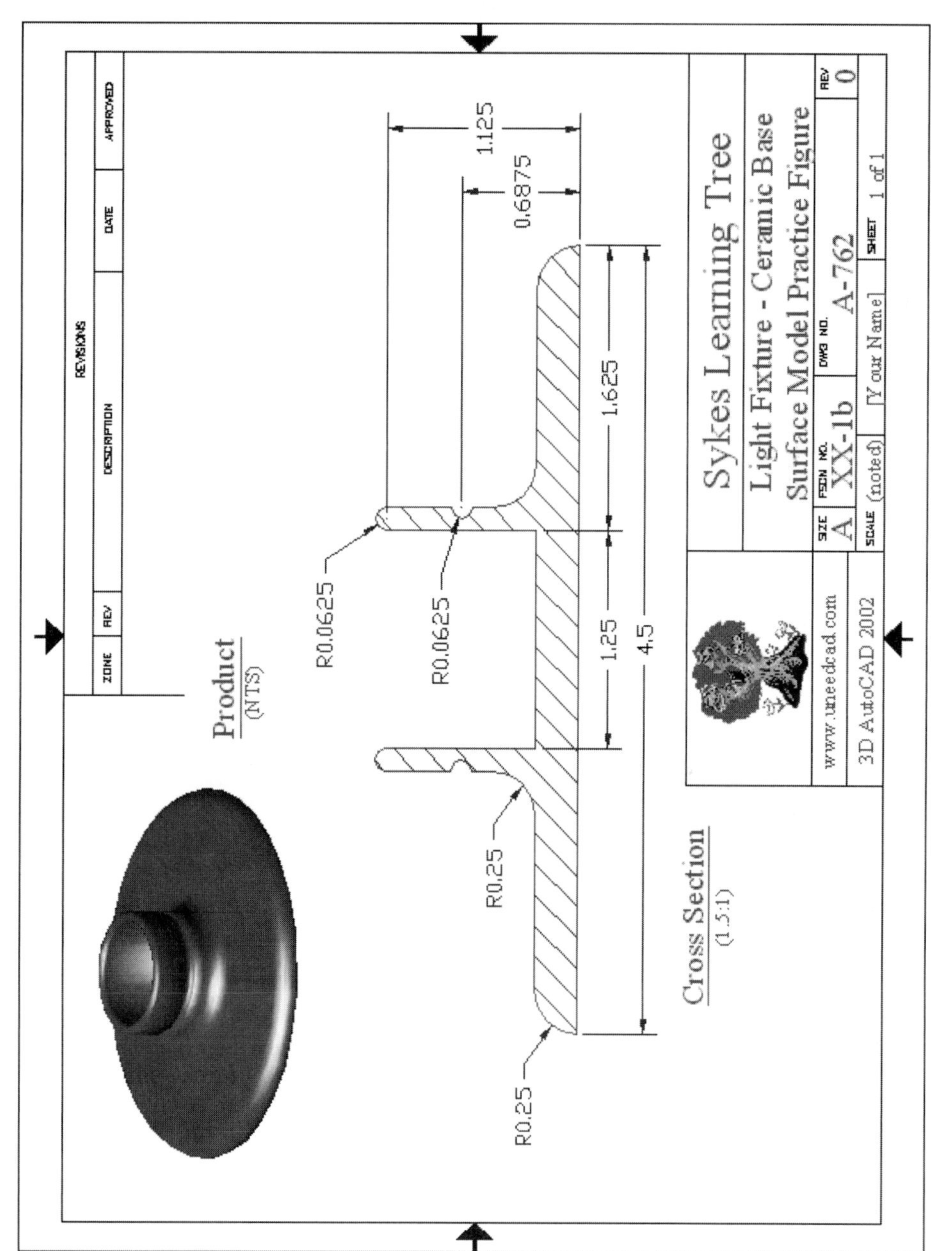

FIG. 7.6.2 Light Fixture

3. Create the Alan Wrench drawing in Figure 7.6.3. The following information will help.

   3.1. Use the *ANSI A Title Block* found in the \AutoCAD\Template folder.

   3.2. Use the Times New Roman font at $\frac{3}{16}''$ and $\frac{1}{8}''$ sizes.

3.3. Adjust the dimstyle as needed (I used the **Small Dot** arrowhead).

3.4. Create layers as needed.

3.5. I used the default settings for both surftabs.

3.6. This object is made up of two Tabulated Surfaces and a Revolved Surface. I used six-sided polygons as my basic shapes.

3.7. Save the drawing as *MyWrench* in the C:\Steps3D\Lesson07 folder.

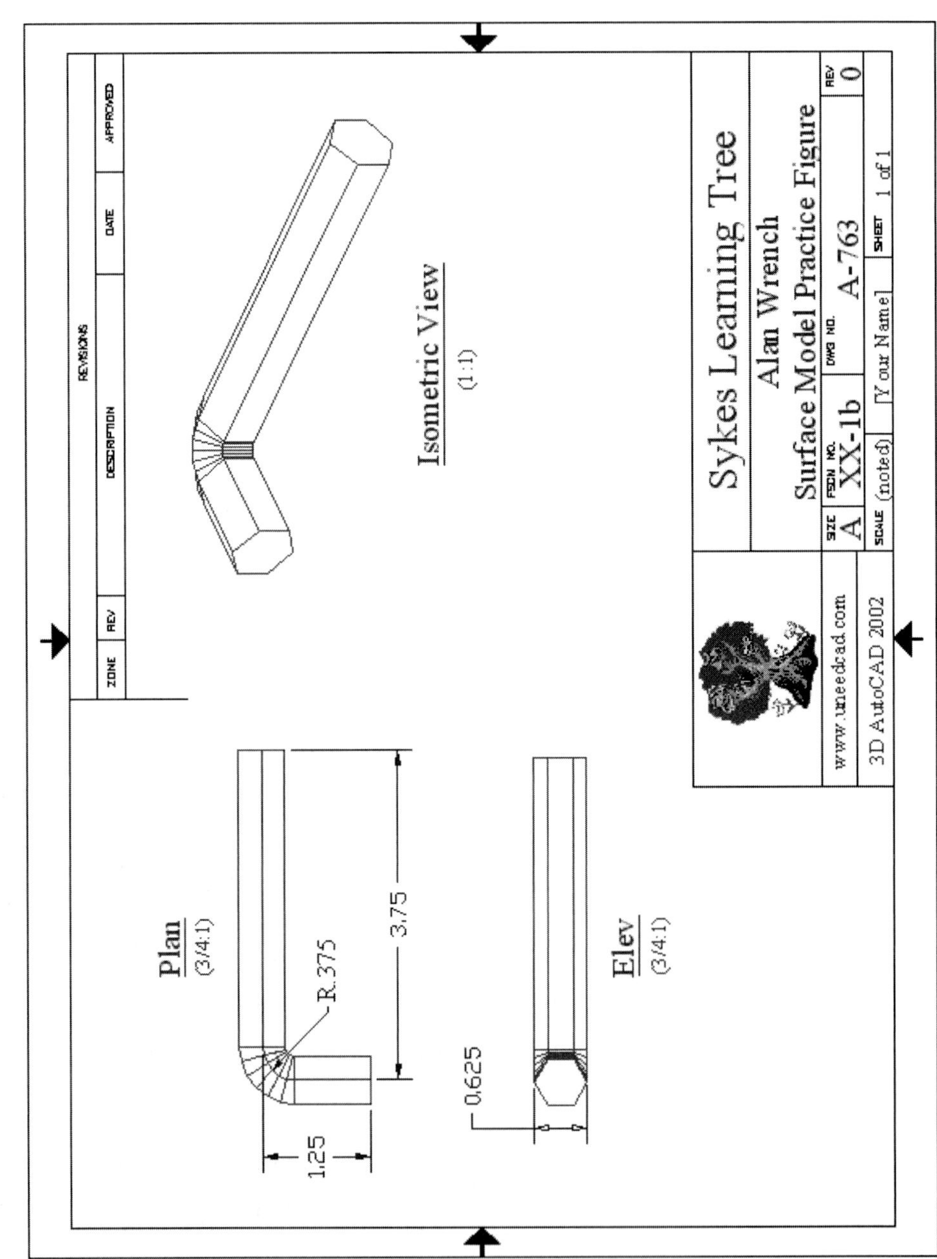

FIG. 7.6.3 Alan Wrench

4. Create the caster drawing in Figure 7.6.4. The following information will help.

4.1. Adjust the dimstyle as needed.

4.2. Create layers as needed (you will need more than you might think).

4.3. I used 16 as my setting for both surftabs.

4.4. The spindle is a Revolved Surface.

4.5. The upper plate is an Edged Surface.

4.6. The frame is a *single* polygon mesh (use the ***PFace*** command).

4.7. The axle is a Revolved Surface.

4.8. The wheel is a Revolved Surface with a hole in it for the axle.

4.9. The ball bearings are $\frac{1}{8}$" diameter spheres.

4.10. The Product view uses the Gouraud Shademode.

4.11. To create the sections, use the same technique you used in Exercise 2.

4.12. Save the drawing as *MyCaster* in the C:\Steps3D\Lesson07 folder.

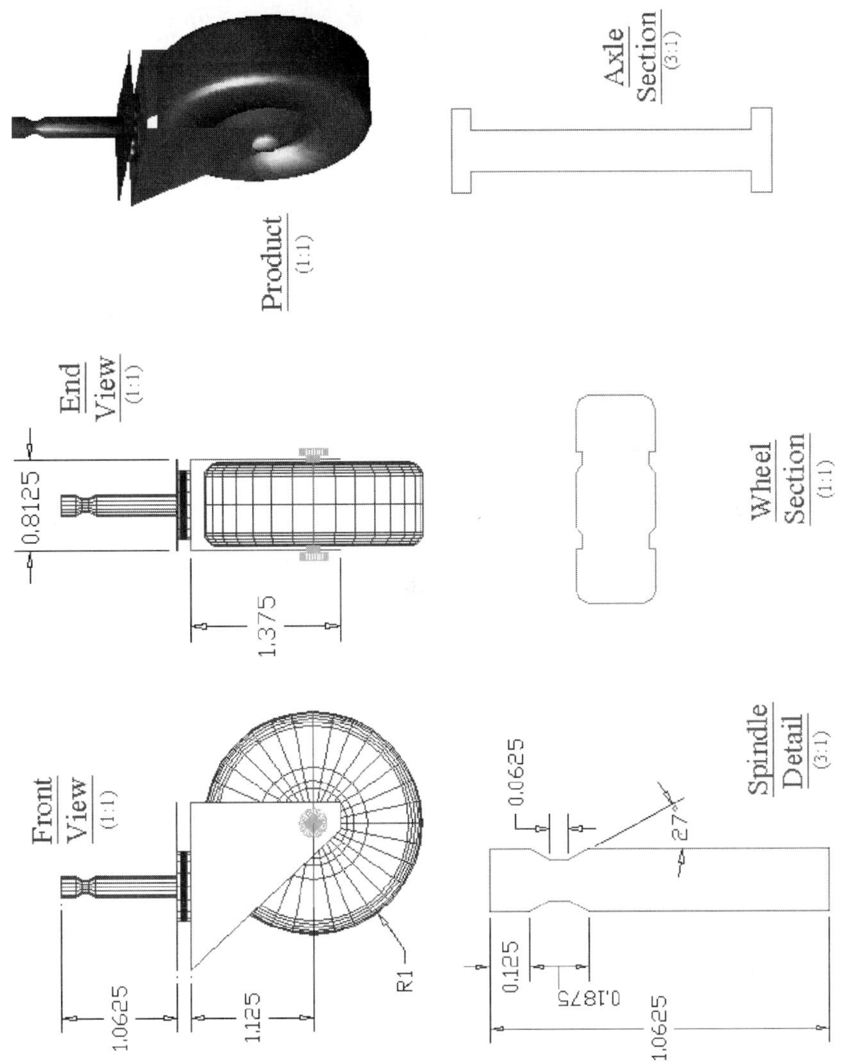

FIG. 7.6.4 Caster

5. Create the Toothpaste Tube drawing in Figure 7.6.5. The following information will help.
   5.1. The main tube is $7\frac{1}{4}''$ long $\times$ 2″ wide on the flat end. The round end has an additional $\frac{1}{4}''$ bubble.
   5.2. The round end is $1\frac{1}{4}''$ diameter.
   5.3. The cap is $\frac{1}{2}''$ long, $\frac{5}{8}''$ diameter, at the base, and $\frac{1}{2}''$ diameter at the top.
   5.4. Use ***Edgesurf*** to create the body of the tube.
   5.5. Use ***Revsurf*** to create the cap and the bubble-end of the tube.
   5.6. Save the drawing as *MyToothpaste* in the C:\Steps3D\Lesson07 folder.

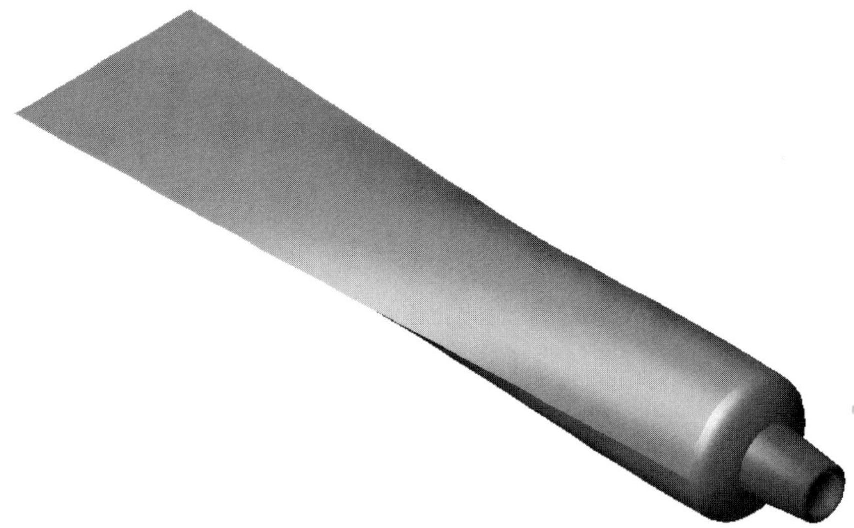

FIG. 7.6.5 Toothpaste

6. Create the Lighter drawing in Figure 7.6.6. The following information will help.
   6.1. The main bottle is $2\frac{1}{4}''$ tall and is based on an ellipse that is 1″ $\times$ $\frac{1}{2}''$.
   6.2. The top is based on half the bottle's ellipse and is $\frac{1}{2}''$ tall.
   6.3. The button is also based on half the bottle's ellipse, is $\frac{1}{16}''$ thick, and is at an angle of 15°.
   6.4. The striker wheel is $\frac{5}{16}''$ wide and $\frac{1}{4}''$diameter.
   6.5. Use ***Revsurf*** to create the striker wheel.
   6.6. Use ***Edgesurf*** to create the bottle and the top.
   6.7. Use regions where needed.
   6.8. Save the drawing as *MyLighter* in the C:\Steps3D\Lesson07 folder.

FIG. 7.6.6 Lighter

7. Create the Remote drawing in Figure 7.6.7. The following information will help.
   - **7.1.** The main face is $5\frac{3}{4}''$ long × 2″ wide.
   - **7.2.** There is an additional $\frac{1}{2}''$ molded arc on the sides and ends.
   - **7.3.** The thickness of the instrument is $\frac{1}{2}''$.
   - **7.4.** Round buttons are $\frac{3}{8}''$ diameter and $\frac{1}{4}''$ diameter domes.
   - **7.5.** Ellipse buttons are $\frac{1}{2}'' \times \frac{1}{4}''$.
   - **7.6.** Other buttons are either pyramids or tabsurfed polyline with regions closing the tops. These are $\frac{1}{8}''$ high.
   - **7.7.** Use Times New Roman font at a $\frac{1}{8}''$ text height.
   - **7.8.** Save the drawing as *MyRemote* in the C:\Steps3D\Lesson07 folder.

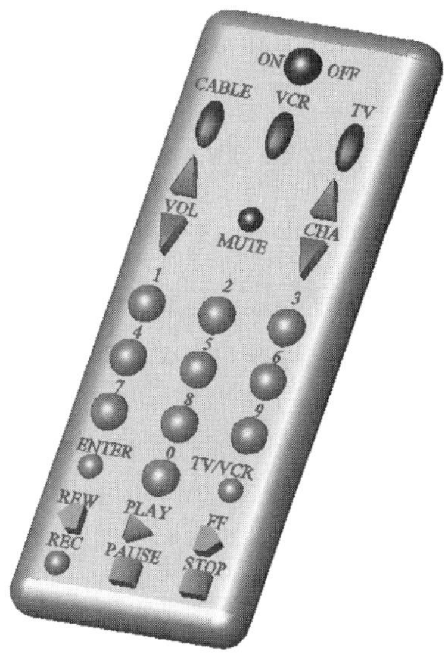

FIG. 7.6.7 Remote

8. Create the racer drawing in Figure 7.6.8b. The $\frac{1}{2}''$ grid in Figure 7.6.8a will help.
   8.1. Save the drawing as *MyRacer* in the C:\Steps3D\Lesson07 folder.

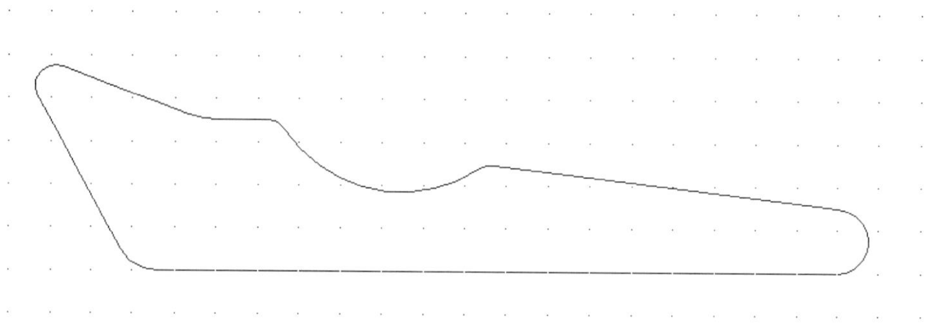

FIG. 7.6.8a Details

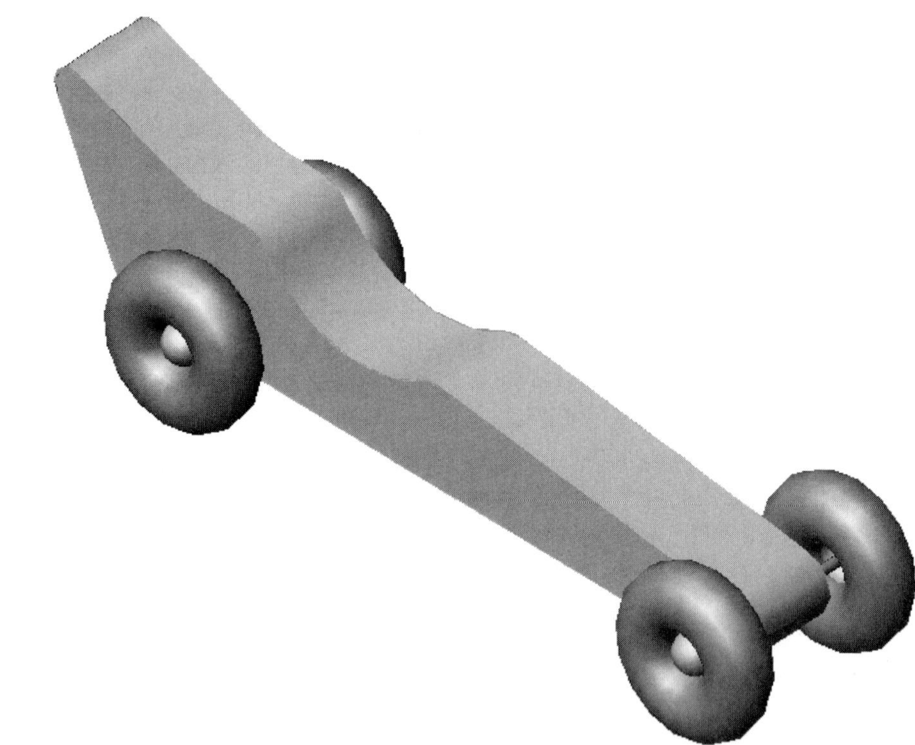

FIG. 7.6.8b Racer

7.7 REVIEW QUESTIONS

1. __________ defines the number of surfaces AutoCAD will use to create a linear object.

2. __________ defines the number of surfaces AutoCAD will use to create latitudinal sections.

3. (T or F) Surftab settings affect the shape of a Surface Model being drawn.

4. through 7. List AutoCAD's four basic commands for drawing complex Surface Models.

a.

b.

c.

d.

8. and 9. What are the two things needed to create a Surface Model using the Tabsurf command?

a.

b.

10. Which surftab setting will create a more defined shape—6 or 60?

11. (T or F) When using the Tabsurf command, the path indicated must exist on the X-Y plane of the current UCS.

12. When using any of the complex Surface Model commands, the layer of the created object depends on the (current layer, layer of the basic shape).

13. (T or F) When using the Tabsurf command, a curved path will *not* create a curved object.

14. (T or F) When using any of the complex Surface Model commands, the original shape remains intact.

15. ***Tabsurf*** will work on any predefined shape provided the shape is a __________.

16. and 17. Which two complex Surface Modeling commands use the Surftab2 setting?

a.

b.

18. Use the __________ command to create circular Surface Models.

19. (T or F) The Edgesurf command draws only flat planes.

20. and 21. What are the two advanced complex Surface Modeling commands?

a.

b.

22. (T or F) AutoCAD's advanced complex Surface Modeling commands are better suited for programmers than CAD operators.

23. (T or F) When using either the 3DMesh or the PFace command, the user must manually identify every vertex on the object he is creating.

24. and 25. When using the 3DMesh command, if you wanted five columns of faces, you would enter the size of mesh __________ as __________.

26. Use the __________ command to create the Surface Model if you need to change the layer of a specific face.

27. through 32. Identify these buttons.

27. 28.  29.  30.  31. 32. 

PART IV

Simple Model Editing

This part of our text contains this lesson:

LESSON 8

Z-Space Editing

Following this lesson, you will

- Know how to use AutoCAD's basic editing tools in Z-Space
  - ***Pedit***
  - ***Properties***
  - ***Grips***
  - ***Trim and Extend***
  - ***Align***
- Know how to use basic Z-Space-specific editing tools
  - ***Rotate3d***
  - ***Mirror3d***
  - ***3DArray***

It was just about here in our basic text that we began to look at editing tools. So it is appropriate that we stop now to look at how those editing tools work both on three-dimensional objects and on two-dimensional objects drawn in Z-Space.

You will find little difference in the way some tools and procedures work, but the differences in others may unsettle you. You will find still others to be brand new (although strangely familiar). Regardless of their differences or newness, however, you will find each tool we discuss in this lesson to be invaluable in your three-dimensional efforts. As they did in the two-dimensional world, editing tools will enhance your speed and drawing ability in Z-Space.

To keep it simple, I will divide the tools into two categories of study—Familiar (two-dimensional tools with which you are already familiar), and New (three-dimensional tools).

Let's start with Familiar.

8.1 Three-Dimensional Uses for Familiar (Two-Dimensional) Tools

As we studied editing tools in our basic text, we occasionally came across a prompt that I said would appear in the advanced text. AutoCAD designed these prompts to allow you to continue using some of the more common (and useful) tools when you made the transition into Z-Space. The tools—***Trim***, ***Extend***, and ***Align***—were not difficult to learn in the first book. And now that you are familiar with them, covering their three-dimensional functions will be a snap!

Once we have looked at those, we will look at the Object Properties Manager and some of the things it can do for a Surface Model.

Lastly, we will take a new look at the ***Pedit*** command. You might be surprised (if not thrilled) at what you find!

Let's start at the beginning.

8.1.1 Trimming and Extending in Z-Space

Trimming and extending in Z-Space begin very much like trimming and extending in two-dimensional space. In fact, the commands are the same, so all you must learn is the option required to control what gets trimmed/extended in a three-dimensional view.

Remember how the **Edgemode** system variable controlled the **Edge** option in both ***Trim*** and ***Extend*** commands (Section 8.1.2 of the basic text)? It still holds true in Z-Space, but there is an additional system variable to consider now—**Projmode**. Like **Edgemode**, **Projmode** affects both the ***Trim*** and ***Extend*** commands. But where **Edgemode** controls your ability to trim/extend to an imaginary extension of the selected cutting edge/boundary, **Projmode** controls how the ***Trim*** and ***Extend*** commands behave in three-dimensional space.

There are two ways to set the **Projmode** system variable—by accessing the **Project** option at the **[Project/Edge/Undo]** prompt of either command, or by entering ***Projmode*** at the command prompt. The command prompt requires that you enter a number code for the option you wish to use; the **Project** option of the ***Trim/Extend*** command presents the available settings. The number codes and their corresponding settings follow.

CODE	SETTING	FUNCTION
0	None	This is called the *True 3D* setting. It requires that both the cutting edge/boundary and the object to trim/extend be in the same plane. That is, they must actually intersect or, using the **Edgemode** system variable, intersect at an imaginary extension.
1	UCS	(AutoCAD's default setting) When active, this setting projects the cutting edge/boundary and object to trim/extend onto the XY plane of the current UCS and then performs the task as though the objects exist in two-dimensional space.
2	View	When active, this setting projects the cutting edge/boundary and object to trim/extend onto the current view as though your monitor's screen is the XY plane. It then performs the task as though the objects exist in two-dimensional space.

Let's see how these settings work in a couple of exercises (one for the ***Trim*** command and one for the ***Extend*** command).

For a two-dimensional study of the ***Trim*** command, go to Section 8.1.1 of the basic text.

WWW 8.1.1.1 Do This: Trimming in Z-Space

I. Open the *trim.dwg* in the C:\Steps3D\Lesson08 folder. The drawing looks like Figure 8.1.1.1a. (The boxes are wireframe lines with no faces.)

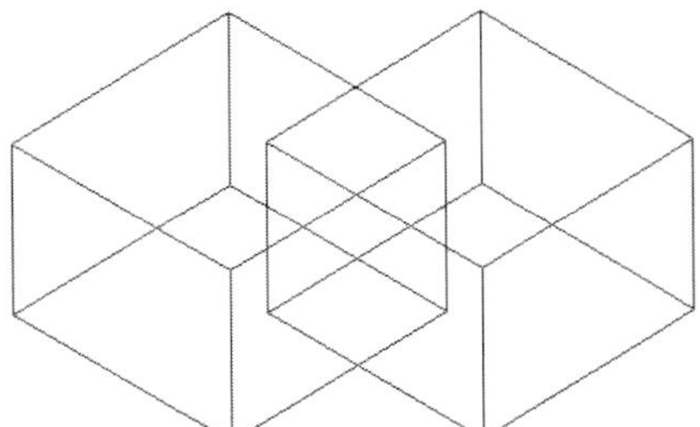

FIG. 8.1.1.1a *Trim.dwg*

II. Be sure the **Edgemode** system variable is set to ***1***.

III. Follow these steps:

TOOLS	COMMAND SEQUENCE	STEPS
No Button Available	**Command:** *projmode* **Enter new value for PROJMODE <1>:** ***0***	**1.** Let's begin by setting the **Projmode** system variable to zero (the True 3D setting).
	Command: ***tr*** **Current settings: Projection=None Edge=Extend** **Select cutting edges . . .** 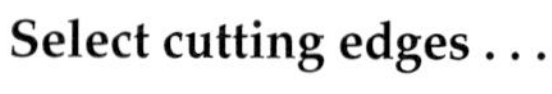 **Select objects:** **Select objects:** ***[enter]***	**2.** Now begin the ***Trim*** command and select the line indicated in Figure 8.1.1.1.2 as your cutting edge. 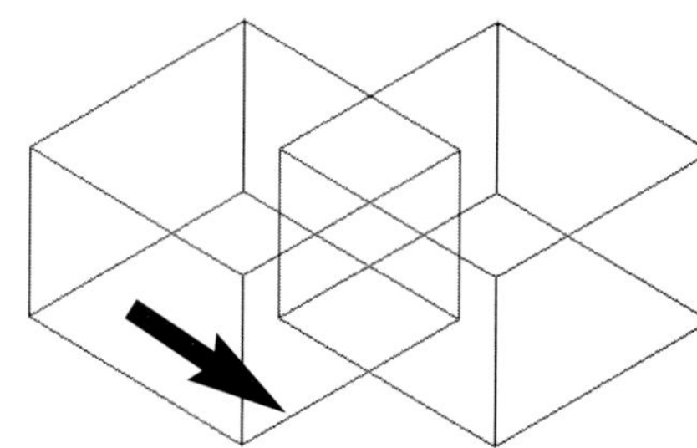 FIG. 8.1.1.1.2
	Select object to trim or shift-select to extend or [Project/Edge/Undo]:	**3.** Now select the lines indicated in Figure 8.1.1.1.3 to trim. Select the bottom line first. Notice that the lower line trims, but the upper line does not. With the **Projmode** system variable set to zero, the lines must be on the same plane (as I explained in the chart on p. 307). The upper line does not intersect the cutting edge so it did not trim. 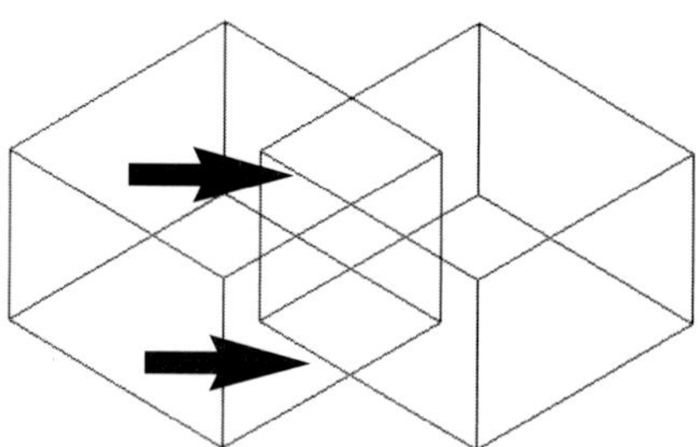 FIG. 8.1.1.1.3
	Select object to trim or shift-select to extend or [Project/Edge/Undo]: ***p*** **Enter a projection option [None/Ucs/View] <None>:** ***u***	**4.** Now, without leaving the command, change the **Projmode** to the **UCS** setting as shown.

continued

TOOLS	COMMAND SEQUENCE	STEPS
	Select object to trim or shift-select to extend or [Project/Edge/Undo]:	**5.** Now trim the line that would not trim previously. It trims now because AutoCAD projects the **cutting edge** and **object to trim** against the XY plane of the current UCS (as if both lines were drawn in 2D space).
	Select object to trim or shift-select to extend or [Project/Edge/Undo]: *[enter]*	**6.** Hit *enter* to complete the command. Your drawing looks like Figure 8.1.1.1.6. 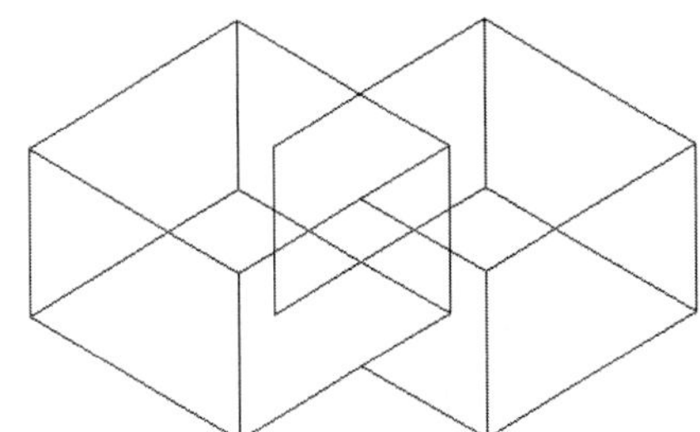 **FIG. 8.1.1.1.6** Trimmed Lines
	**Command:** *tr*	**7.** Repeat Step 2.
	Select object to trim or shift-select to extend or [Project/Edge/Undo]:	**8.** Now select the line indicated in Figure 8.1.1.1.8 to trim. Notice that the line will not trim. The **Projmode** system variable setting of ***1*** (UCS) means that the lines must intersect in a two-dimensional projection of the current UCS. The line does not intersect the cutting edge, so it did not trim. 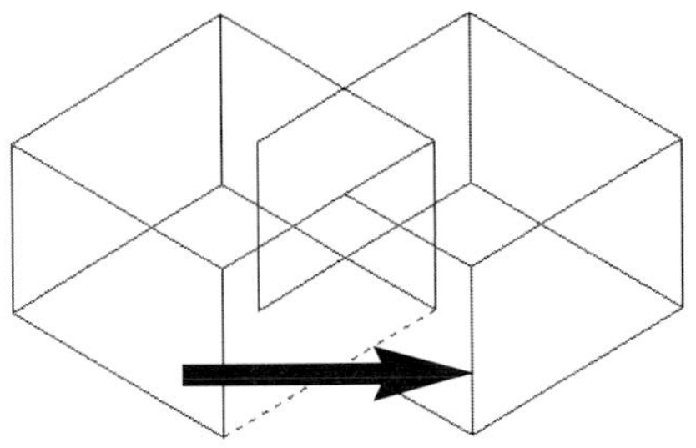 **FIG. 8.1.1.1.8** Select This Line to Trim

continued

TOOLS	COMMAND SEQUENCE	STEPS
	Select object to trim or shift-select to extend or [Project/Edge/Undo]: *p* **Enter a projection option [None/Ucs/View] <Ucs>:** *v*	**9.** Now, without leaving the command, change the **Projmode** to the **View** setting as indicated.
	Select object to trim or shift-select to extend or [Project/Edge/Undo]:	**10.** Now trim the line that would not trim previously. It trims now for two reasons: (1) AutoCAD has projected the **cutting edge** and **object to trim** against your screen (the current view) as if your screen defined the XY plane, and (2) AutoCAD has extended the cutting edge according to the **Edgemode** setting.
	Select object to trim or shift-select to extend or [Project/Edge/Undo]: *[enter]*	**11.** Hit *enter* to complete the command. Your drawing looks like Figure 8.1.1.1.11. 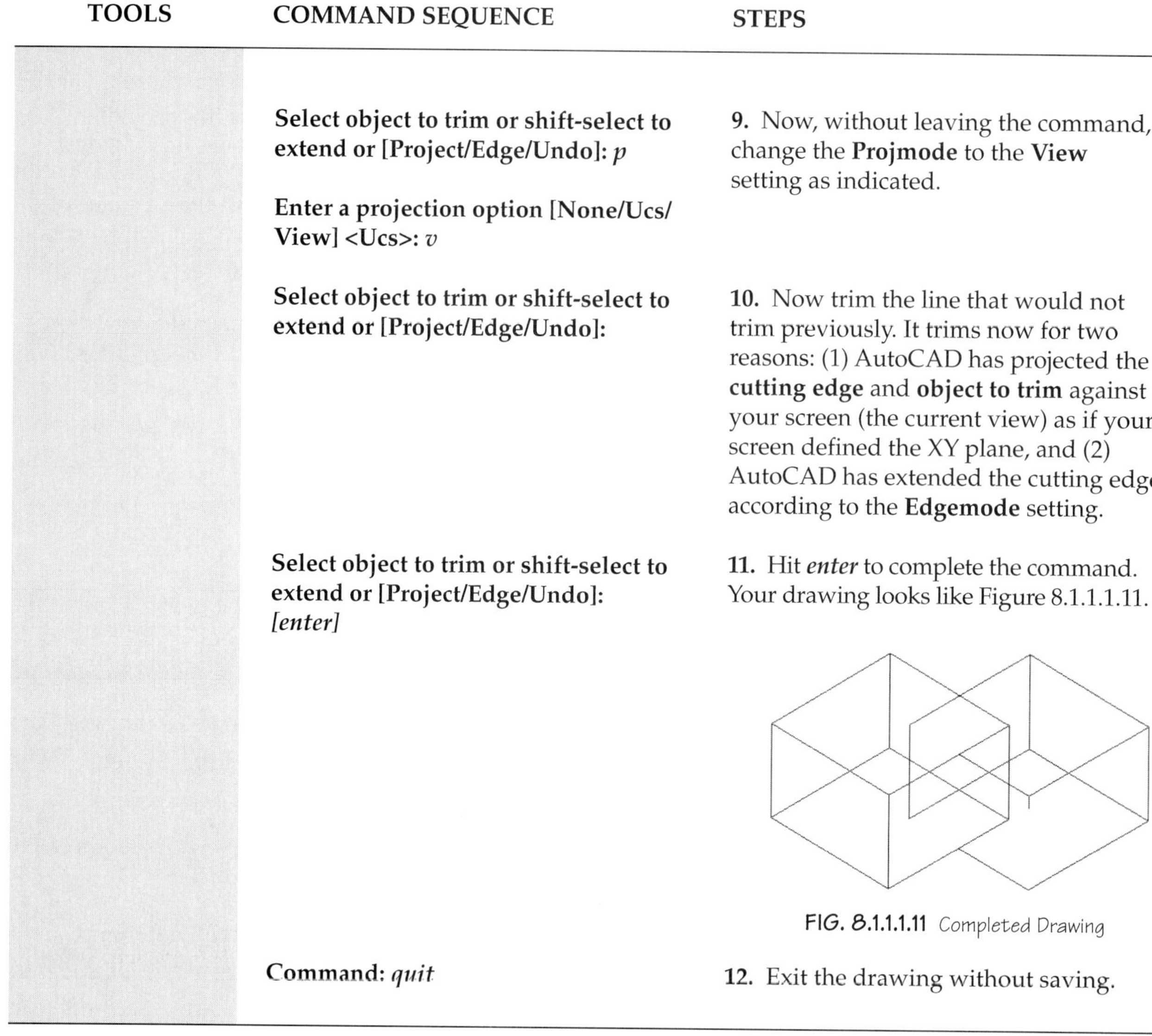 FIG. 8.1.1.1.11 Completed Drawing
	Command: *quit*	**12.** Exit the drawing without saving.

And now, let's look at the ***Extend*** command.

For a two-dimensional study of the ***Extend*** command, go to Section 8.1.2 of the basic text.

WWW 8.1.1.2 Do This: Extending in Z-Space

I. Open the *ext.dwg* in the C:\Steps3D\Lesson08 folder. The drawing looks like Figure 8.1.1.2a.

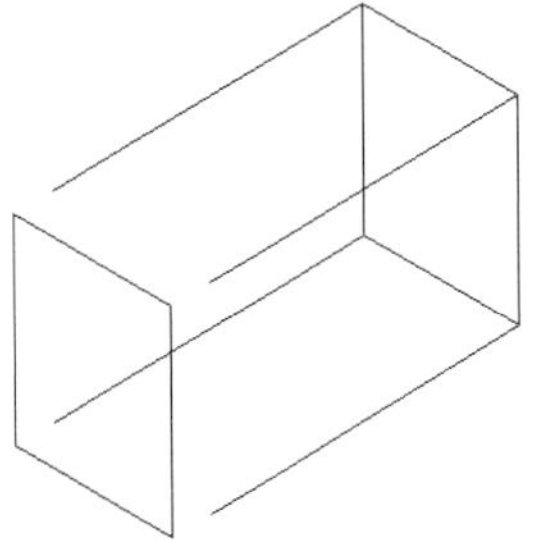

FIG. 8.1.1.2a *Ext.dwg*

II. Be sure the **Edgemode** system variable is set to ***1***.

III. Follow these steps:

TOOLS	COMMAND SEQUENCE	STEPS
No Button Available	**Command:** ***projmode*** **Enter new value for PROJMODE <1>:** ***0***	1. We will begin again by setting the **Projmode** system variable to zero.
	Command: ***ex*** **Current settings: Projection=None Edge=Extend** **Select boundary edges . . .** **Select objects:** **Select objects:** ***[enter]***	2. Begin the ***Extend*** command and select the line indicated in Figure 8.1.1.2.2 as your boundary edge. 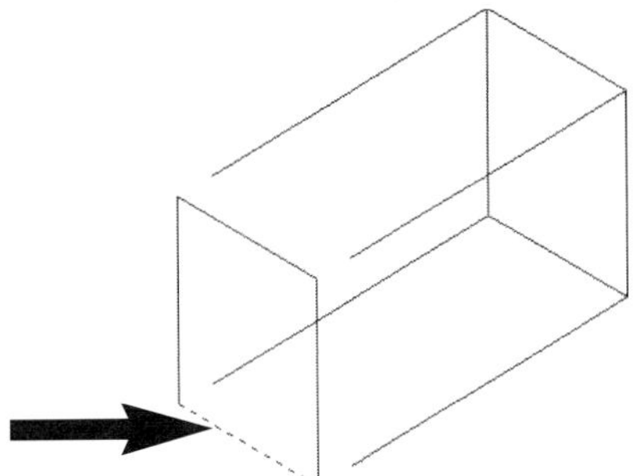 FIG. 8.1.1.2.2 Select the Boundary Edge

continued

TOOLS	COMMAND SEQUENCE	STEPS
	Select object to extend or shift-select to trim or [Project/Edge/Undo]:	**3.** Now select the lines indicated in Figure 8.1.1.2.3 to extend. Select the bottom lines first. Notice that the lower lines extend but not the upper lines. As in the ***Trim*** command, with **Projmode** set to ***0***, the lines must be in the same XY plane. The upper lines do not share the boundary edge's plane, so they did not extend.

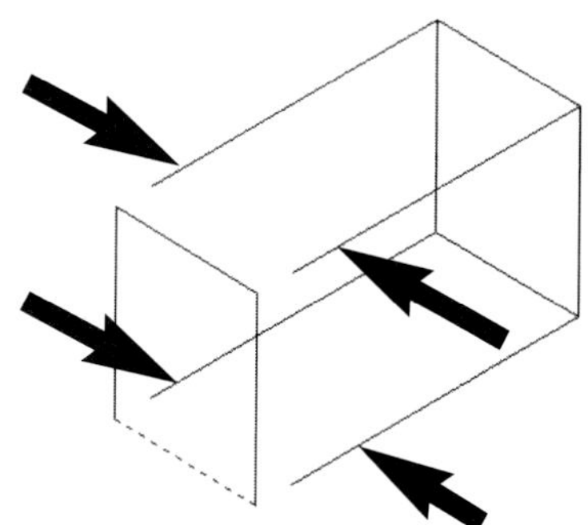

FIG. 8.1.1.2.3 Extend These Lines

TOOLS	COMMAND SEQUENCE	STEPS
	Select object to extend or shift-select to trim or [Project/Edge/Undo]: *p* **Enter a projection option [None/Ucs/View] <None>:** *u*	**4.** Without leaving the command, change **Projmode** to the **UCS** setting, as shown.
	Select object to extend or shift-select to trim or [Project/Edge/Undo]:	**5.** Now extend the lines that would not extend previously. They extend now because AutoCAD has projected them against the XY plane of the current UCS.

continued

TOOLS	COMMAND SEQUENCE	STEPS
	Select object to extend or [Project/ Edge/Undo]: ***[enter]***	**6.** Hit ***enter*** to complete the command. Your drawing looks like Figure 8.1.1.2.6. 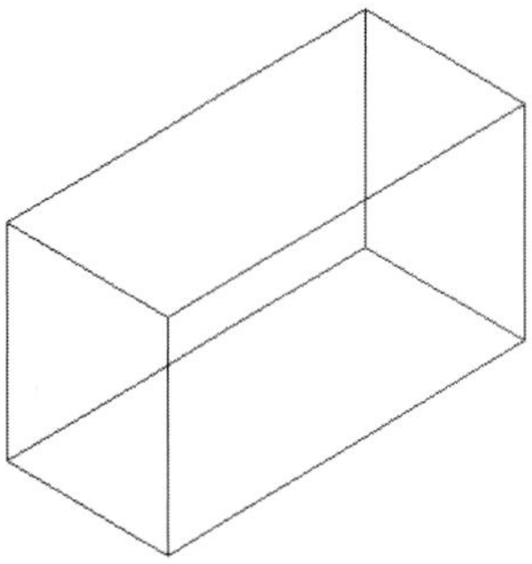 FIG. 8.1.1.2.6 Extended Lines
	**Command:**	**7.** Repeat Step 2, but select the boundary edge indicated in Figure 8.1.1.2.7. 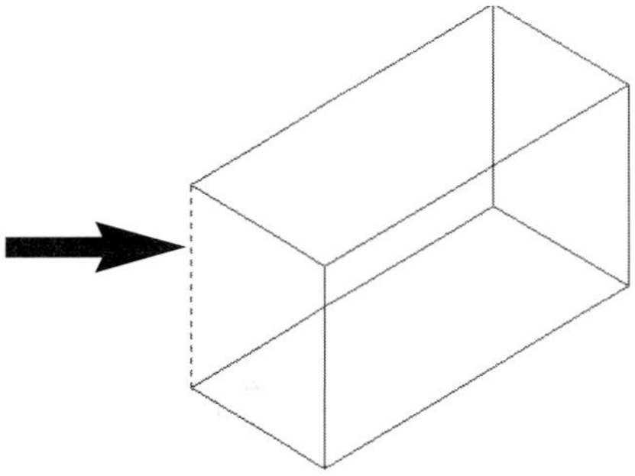 FIG. 8.1.1.2.7 Select This Boundary Edge

continued

TOOLS	COMMAND SEQUENCE	STEPS
	Select object to extend or shift-select to trim or [Project/Edge/Undo]:	**8.** Select the line indicated in Figure 8.1.1.2.8 to extend. Notice that the line will not extend. With **Projmode** set to ***1***, the lines must intersect in a two-dimensional projection of the current UCS. The lines do not, so the selected **object to extend** did not extend. FIG. 8.1.1.2.8 Select This Boundary Edge
	Select object to extend or shift-select to trim or [Project/Edge/Undo]: *p* **Enter a projection option [None/Ucs/View] <Ucs>:** *v*	**9.** Without leaving the command, change the **Projmode** to the **View** setting, as shown.
	Select object to extend or shift-select to trim or [Project/Edge/Undo]:	**10.** Now extend the line that would not extend previously. As with the ***Trim*** command, it extends now because AutoCAD is looking at the lines projected against your screen (the current view).

continued

TOOLS	COMMAND SEQUENCE	STEPS
	Select object to extend or shift-select to trim or [Project/Edge/Undo]: ***[enter]***	**11.** Hit ***enter*** to complete the command. Your drawing looks like Figure 8.1.1.2.11. 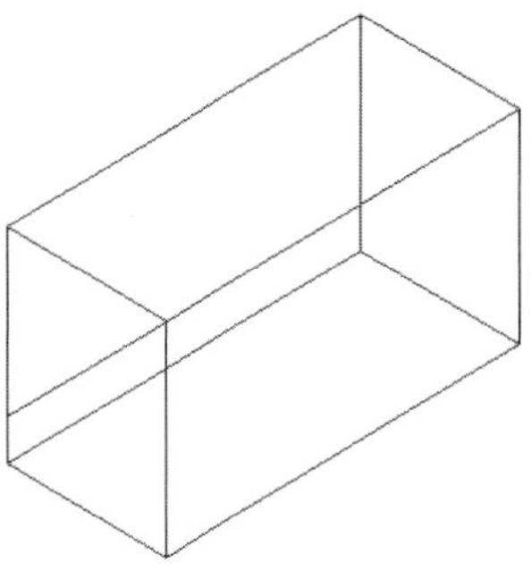 FIG. 8.1.1.2.11 Completed Drawing
	Command: ***quit***	**12.** Exit the drawing without saving.

You have seen that, although still fairly simple to use, the ***Trim*** and ***Extend*** commands have some different options with which you must become familiar if you are to use them to your full advantage in Z-Space.

But there are some additional things that I should highlight before continuing.

- These commands work on the same objects for which you used them in 2D space—you cannot trim/extend a 3D Face, 3D Mesh, Region, or Solid.
- You cannot use a 3D Face, 3D Mesh, or Solid as a cutting edge or boundary edge when trimming/extending.
- You *can*, however, use a Region as a cutting edge or boundary edge when trimming or extending.

Let's look at how another 2D command works with three-dimensional objects. Let's look at the ***Align*** command.

8.1.2 Aligning Three-Dimensional Objects

When you aligned objects in the basic text (Section 8.2.2), you used two source points and two destination points. The main difference between that two-dimensional exercise and aligning three-dimensional objects is that AutoCAD requires three points of alignment for the three-dimensional object.

But there is also another difference. When you aligned two-dimensional objects, AutoCAD asked if you wanted to scale the objects to the alignment points. You will not have that option with three-dimensional objects. But you can always use the ***Scale*** command once the objects are aligned.

For a two-dimensional study of the ***Align*** command, go to Section 8.2.2 of the basic text.

Let's perform a three-dimensional alignment using AutoCAD's ***Align*** command.

8.1.2.1 Do This: Aligning Three-Dimensional Objects

I. Open the *align.dwg* in the C:\Steps3D\Lesson08 folder. The drawing looks like Figure 8.1.2.1a. We will align the eastern face of the ridged pyramid with the top of the box.

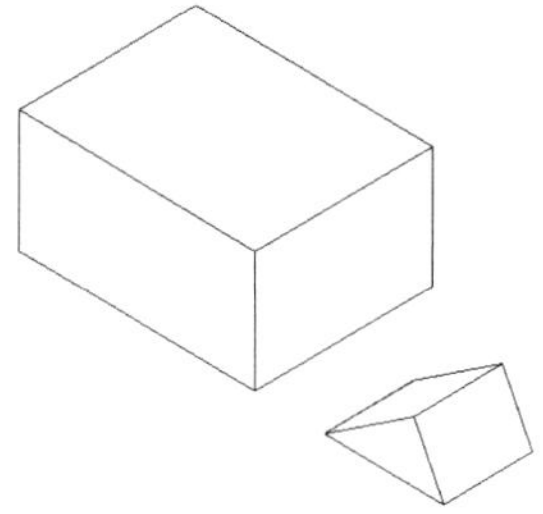

FIG. 8.1.2.1a *Align.dwg*

II. Follow these steps:

TOOLS	COMMAND SEQUENCE	STEPS
No Button Available	**Command:** ***al***	**1.** Enter the ***Align*** command.
	Select objects:	**2.** Select the wedge.
	Select objects: ***[enter]***	

continued

TOOLS	COMMAND SEQUENCE	STEPS
	Specify first source point: ***[Point 1a]*** **Specify first destination point:** ***[Point 1b]*** **Specify second source point:** ***[Point 2a]*** **Specify second destination point:** ***[Point 2b]*** **Specify third source point or <continue>:** ***[Point 3a]*** **Specify third destination point:** ***[Point 3b]***	**3.** (Refer to Figure 8.1.2.1.3a.) Select the alignment points as indicated. Your drawing looks like Figure 8.1.2.1.3b.

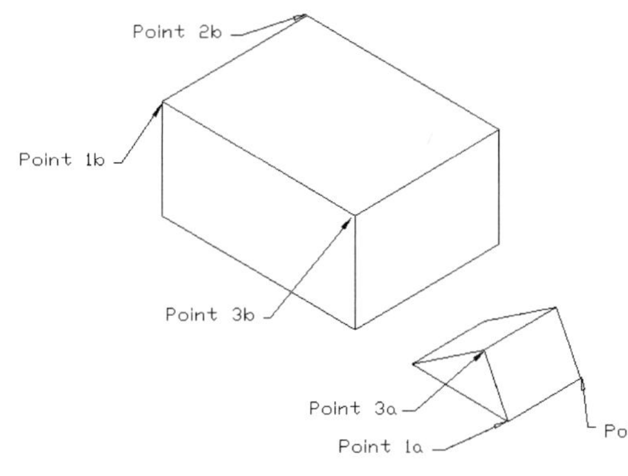

FIG. 8.1.2.1.3a Use These Alignment Points

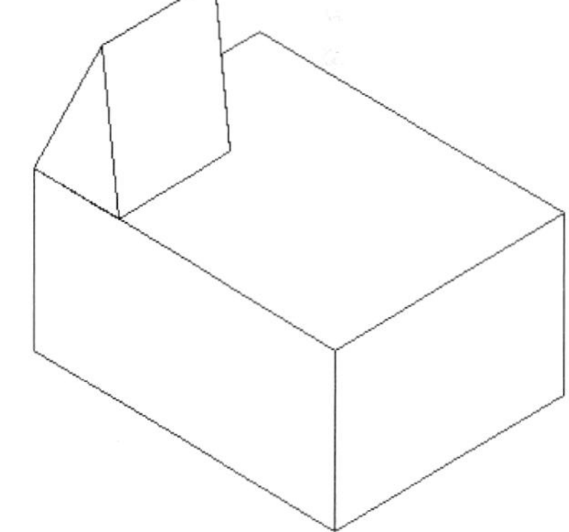

FIG. 8.1.2.1.3b Completed Alignment

TOOLS	COMMAND SEQUENCE	STEPS
	Command: ***quit***	**4.** Exit the drawing without saving it.

I wish they were all that easy!

The really bright side to the ***Align*** command is that is does not care what types of objects are being aligned. You can align the objects you aligned in 2D space or you can align 3D Faces, 3D Meshes, Regions, or Solids!

8.1.3 Three-Dimensional Object Properties

When you began creating Surface Models, you opened the door to a wide variety of new objects—3D Faces, 3D Meshes, Regions, and Solids—that you may need to modify at one time or another.

Your list is immediately halved, however, because Regions and Solids have no editable properties. Additionally, 3D Faces have very few (and very elementary) editable properties, so you can relax in your approach to three-dimensional object properties.

On the other hand, 3D Meshes can make you long for the simplicity of a two-dimensional world!

We will spend some time with the different approaches to editing 3D Meshes later, but for now, let's begin by examining the 3D Face properties AutoCAD makes available in the Object Properties Manager (OPM). Refer to Figure 8.1.3a as we consider the possibilities.

General	
Color	ByLayer
Layer	obj1
Linetype	——— ByLayer
Linetype scale	1.0000
Plot style	ByColor
Lineweight	——— ByLayer
Hyperlink	
Geometry	
Vertex	1
Vertex X	4.0000
Vertex Y	1.0000
Vertex Z	1.0000
Edge 1	Visible
Edge 2	Visible
Edge 3	Visible
Edge 4	Visible

FIG. 8.1.3a OPM Showing 3D Face Properties

- The General section contains property information with which you are already familiar. (For the basics on how to use the OPM, see Section 7.5.2 in the basic text.)
- The Geometry section contains editable information for the specific 3D Face that has been selected.
  - The **Vertex** row identifies a specific vertex on the 3D Face. AutoCAD identifies the vertex on the drawing with an "X"—similar to the way it identifies a vertex when editing with the ***Pedit*** command's **Edit Vertex** option. When the user picks in the Vertex row, a set of directional arrows appears in the value column. Use these to scroll through the vertices or type in the number of the vertex you wish to modify.
  - The **Vertex X, Vertex Y,** and **Vertex Z** rows present the corresponding coordinate value for that vertex. The coordinate values reflect the current UCS. When the user picks one of these rows, AutoCAD presents a **Pick Point** button. The user may use this button to pick a point on the screen, or he may enter a typed number in the value column to change the location of the vertex.
  - The **Edge** rows are toggles that can be used to change the visibility of specific 3D Face edges.

Let's take a look at the OPM in action.

WWW 8.1.3.1 Do This: Using the OPM on Three-Dimensional Objects

I. Open the *3Dfaces.dwg* in the C:\Steps3D\Lesson08 folder. The drawing looks like Figure 8.1.3.1a. (The open box is made up of 3D Faces; the rectangle is a Region, and the other box is a Solid.)

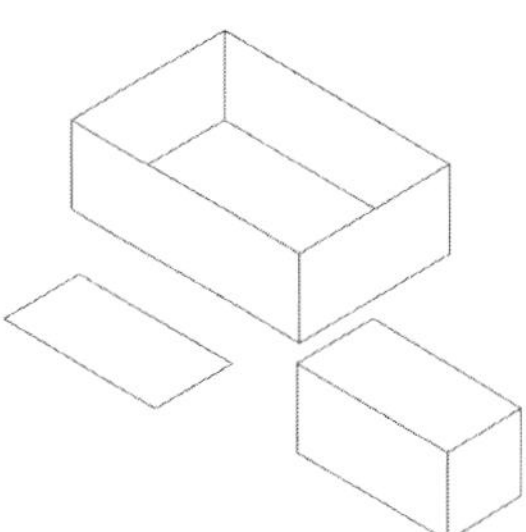

FIG. 8.1.3.1a *DFaces.dwg*

II. Follow these steps:

TOOLS	COMMAND SEQUENCE	STEPS
 Properties Button	**Command:** *props*	**1.** Open the Object Properties Manager. Dock it to the left side of the screen (if necessary) and center the display. **2.** Select the Region (the flat green rectangle). Notice the Geometry section of the OPM (Figure 8.1.3.1.2). Two properties are shown for reference, but neither is accessible for modification (both are gray).

Geometry	
Area	2.0000
Perimeter	6.0000

FIG. 8.1.3.1.2 Region Properties

continued

TOOLS	COMMAND SEQUENCE	STEPS

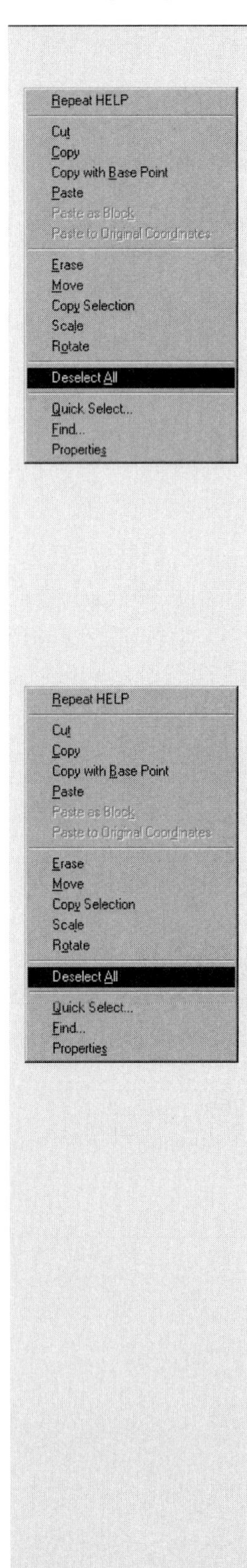

3. Deselect the Region either by hitting the **Esc** key or selecting **Deselect All** from the cursor menu.

4. Repeat Step 2, but this time select the Solid box.

Notice that no Geometry is available for reference or editing.

5. Repeat Step 3.

6. Select the front 3D Face on the open box.

Notice the Geometry section of the OPM (refer to Figure 8.1.3a, p. 318).

continued

TOOLS	COMMAND SEQUENCE	STEPS

Geometry	
Vertex	4
Vertex X	1.0000
Vertex Y	1.0000
Vertex Z	1.0000

7. Let's use the OPM to perform some modifications. Change the **Vertex** that you will edit to ***4***. (Pick in the **Vertex** row and use the directional arrow buttons to change the vertex.) Notice an "X" identifies the vertex on the 3D Face (Figure 8.1.3.1.7).

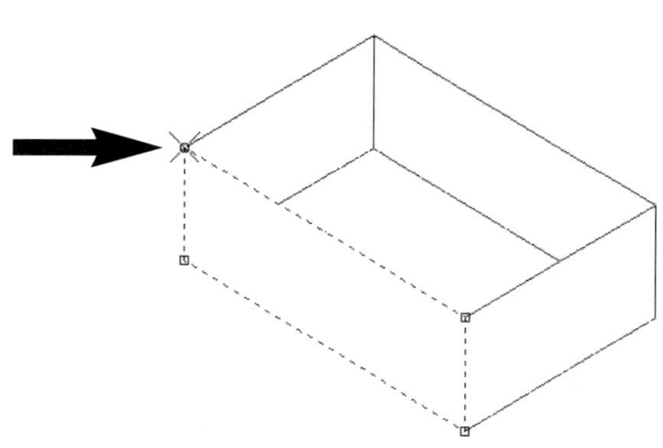

FIG. 8.1.3.1.7 Vertex 4

Geometry	
Vertex	4
Vertex X	2.5
Vertex Y	1.0000
Vertex Z	1.0000

8. Change the value of **Vertex X** to **2.5**. Notice the change on the 3D Face. (*Note:* You must hit ***enter*** after changing the value for AutoCAD to accept the change.)

Geometry	
Vertex	1
Vertex X	4.0000
Vertex Y	1.0000
Vertex Z	1.0000
Edge 1	Visible
Edge 2	Visible
Edge 3	Visible
Edge 4	Visible

Visible
Hidden

9. Now make **Edge 4** invisible, as shown. Notice the change in the 3D Face (Figure 8.1.3.1.9).

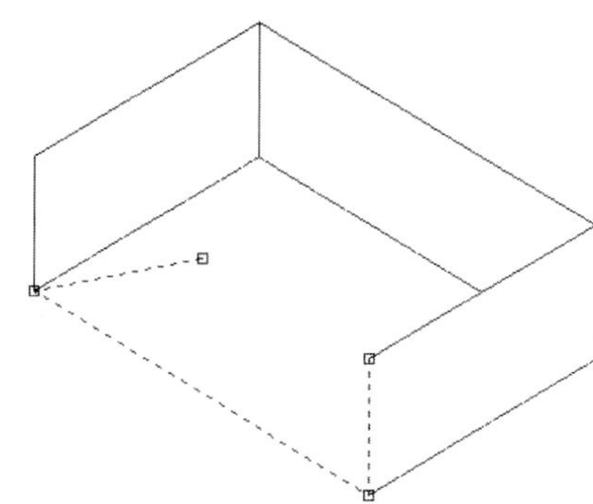

FIG. 8.1.3.1.9 Altered Vertex and 3D face

Command: *quit*

10. Exit the drawing without saving the changes.

As you can see, although you cannot modify a Region or Solid, modifying a 3D Face with the OPM is quite easy.

8.1.4 Modifying a 3D Mesh

3D Mesh modification is considerably more complicated than 3D Face modification primarily because it is a more complex object. When you modify a 3D Face, you have only the one object with which to work. That object has three or four vertices and edges. You have nothing else with which to work that might complicate matters.

A 3D Mesh, on the other hand, has any number of vertices, several Mesh values, and even a polyline Fit/Smooth value.

Luckily, AutoCAD has provided three methods for modifying 3D Meshes. These are the ***Pedit*** command, the OPM, and Grips. Each has its place, and knowing when to use each procedure will go a long way toward preserving your sanity when facing a 3D Mesh with dozens (or hundreds) of vertices.

Let's start with the ***Pedit*** command.

8.1.4.1 Using Pedit to Modify a 3D Mesh

Remember how much fun you had with the ***Pedit*** command in the basic text? I told you then that you would probably never need the **Edit vertex** tier of options—at least not in the two-dimensional world. Well, you are not in Kansas anymore. But this is where you get the payoff for struggling through that exercise that covered the **Edit vertex** options.

The ***Pedit*** command looks slightly different when you select a 3D Mesh instead of a polyline. This is the sequence:

Enter an option [Edit vertex/Smooth surface/Desmooth/Mclose/Nclose/Undo]:

- The **Edit vertex** options resemble the same options you received when you selected a two-dimensional polyline. But it has some additional tools. It looks like this:

Current vertex (0,0).

Enter an option [Next/Previous/Left/Right/Up/Down/Move/REgen/eXit] <N>:

- The first thing you will notice is that AutoCAD identifies the vertex both with an "X" (as it did on the polyline) and by M-column and N-row coordinate at the command line.
- The **Next/Previous** tools work just as they did for a polyline—to maneuver along the mesh from vertex to vertex.
- The **Left/Right/Up/Down** tools supplement the **Next/Previous** tools, making it easier to maneuver to a specific vertex without having to pass through countless vertices to get there.

- The **Move** option, of course, allows the user to move the currently selected vertex to a new point.
- **REgen** and **eXit** work the same on 2D and 3D objects. (**Regen** regenerates the mesh/polyline being edited, and **eXit** exits this tier of options.)

- **Mclose/Mopen** and **Nclose/Nopen** serve the same function as the **Open/Close** option of the 2D ***Pedit*** command. But on the 3D Mesh, AutoCAD draws a closing line between first and last points of the M-columns or N-rows.
- As always, **Undo** undoes the last modification. (Remember, do not confuse the **Undo** option with the ***Undo*** command, which undoes the last command.)
- **Smooth surface** creates a curved shape from the 3D Mesh. This handy tool is really quite useful for images that will be rendered (more on Rendering in Lesson 13).

  There are three types of smooth surface (Figure 8.1.4.1a)—Quadratic B-Spline, Cubic B-Spline, and Bezier. The type of surface created with the **Smooth surface** option depends on the current setting of the **Surftype** system variable (refer to Figure 8.1.4.1a). Two other system variables control the number of M-columns and N-rows on the smoothed 3D Mesh. These are **Surfu** (to control the number of M-columns) and **Surfv** (to control the number of N-rows).

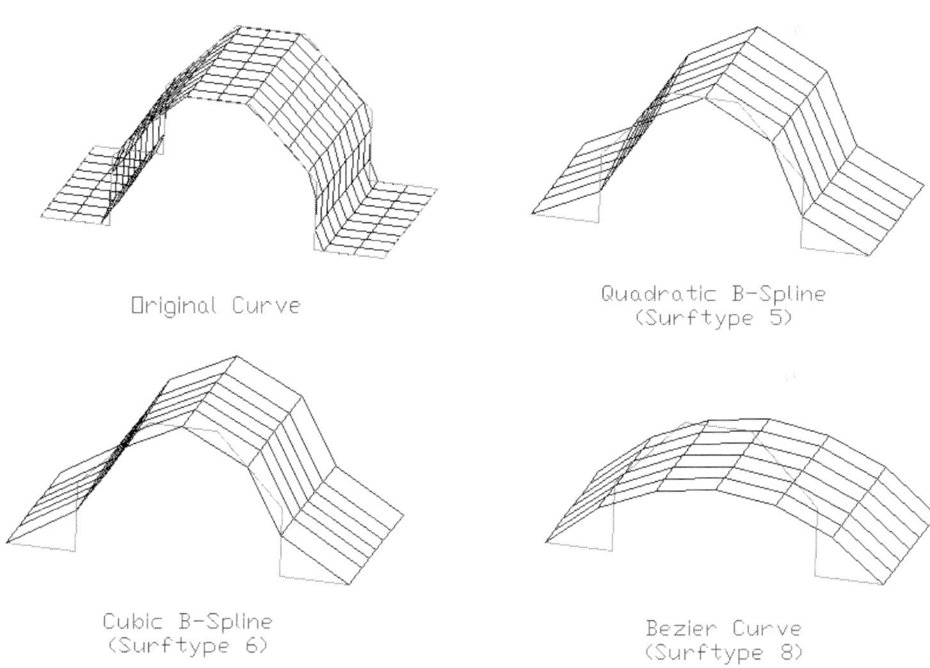

FIG. 8.1.4.1a Smooth Surfaces

- Of course, the **Desmooth** option removes any changes made with the **Smooth surface** option.

Let's experiment with the ***Pedit*** command and 3D Meshes.

WWW 8.1.4.1.1 Do This: Using *Pedit* on 3D Meshes

I. Open the *3DMesh.dwg* in the C:\Steps3D\Lesson08 folder. The drawing looks like Figure 8.1.4.1.1a.

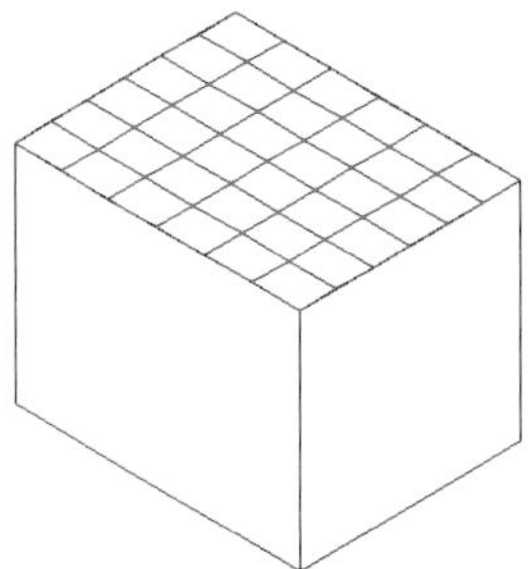

FIG. 8.1.4.1.1a *DMesh.dwg*

II. Close the OPM.

III. Follow these steps:

TOOLS	COMMAND SEQUENCE	STEPS
Edit Polyline Button (Modify II Toolbar)	**Command:** ***pe***	**1.** Enter the ***Pedit*** command.
	Select polyline or [Multiple]:	**2.** Select the 3D Mesh atop the figure.
Enter Cancel Edit vertex Smooth surface Desmooth Mclose Nclose Undo Pan Zoom	**Enter an option [Edit vertex/Smooth surface/Desmooth/Mclose/Nclose/Undo]:** ***e***	**3.** Tell AutoCAD to use the **Edit vertex** option.

continued

TOOLS	COMMAND SEQUENCE	STEPS
	Enter an option [Next/Previous/Left/ Right/Up/Down/Move/REgen/eXit] <N>:*[enter]*	**4.** Hit enter three times (accepting the **Next** option) to move the locator to the middle of the east end of the 3D Mesh (Figure 8.1.4.1.1.4). (The **Current vertex** will be 0,3.)

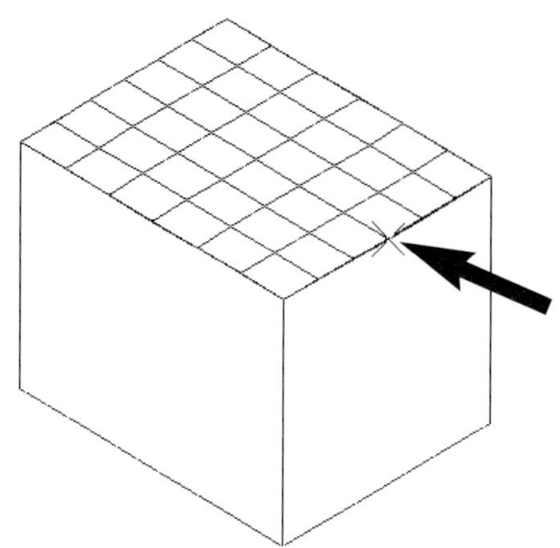

FIG. 8.1.4.1.1.4 Vertex 0,3

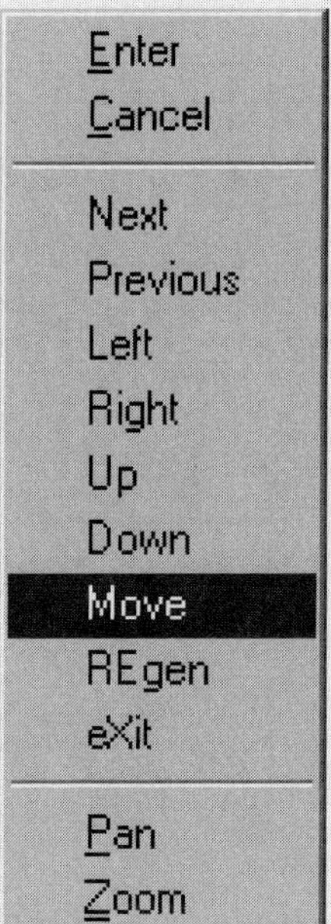

TOOLS	COMMAND SEQUENCE	STEPS
	Enter an option [Next/Previous/Left/ Right/Up/Down/Move/REgen/eXit] <N>: *m*	**5.** Use the **Move** option to move the vertex upward 1.5 units as shown. Your drawing looks like Figure 8.1.4.1.1.5.
	Specify new location for marked vertex: ***@0,0,1.5***	

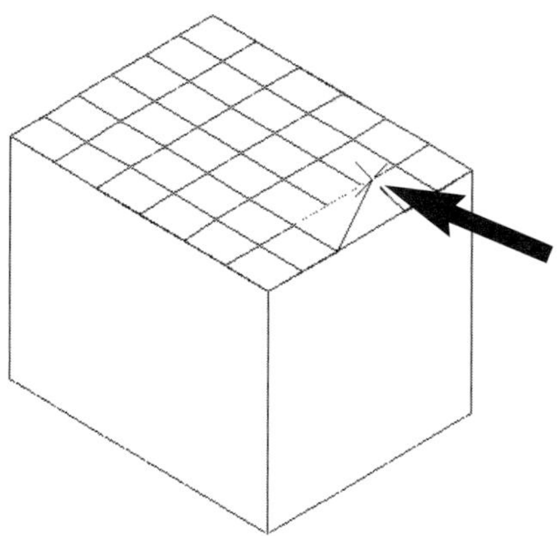

FIG. 8.1.4.1.1.5 Moved Vertex

continued

TOOLS	COMMAND SEQUENCE	STEPS

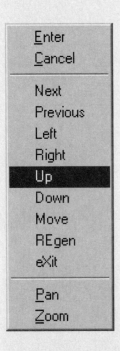

Enter
Cancel
Next
Previous
Left
Right
Up
Down
Move
REgen
eXit
Pan
Zoom

Enter an option [Next/Previous/Left/Right/Up/Down/Move/REgen/eXit] <N>: *u*

6. Use the **Up** option to move the locator to vertex 1,3 (Figure 8.1.4.1.1.6).

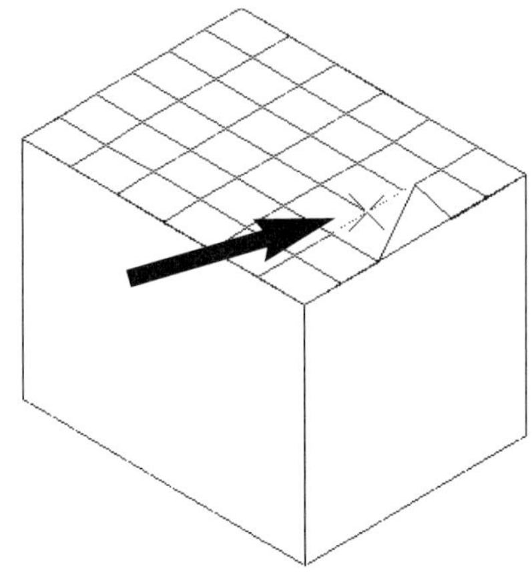

FIG. 8.1.4.1.1.6 Vertex 1,3

Enter an option [Next/Previous/Left/Right/Up/Down/Move/REgen/eXit] <U>: *m*

Specify new location for marked vertex: *@0,0,1.5*

7. Repeat Step 5.

8. Repeat Steps 6 and 7 until the entire column has been raised. Your drawing looks like Figure 8.1.4.1.1.8.

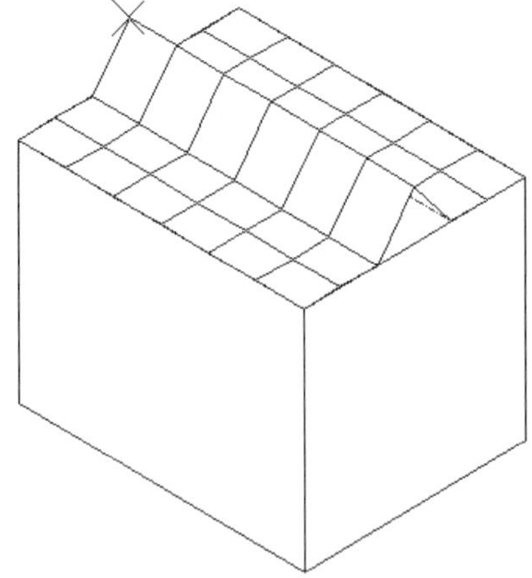

FIG. 8.1.4.1.1.8 Raised Column of Vertices

continued

TOOLS | **COMMAND SEQUENCE** | **STEPS**

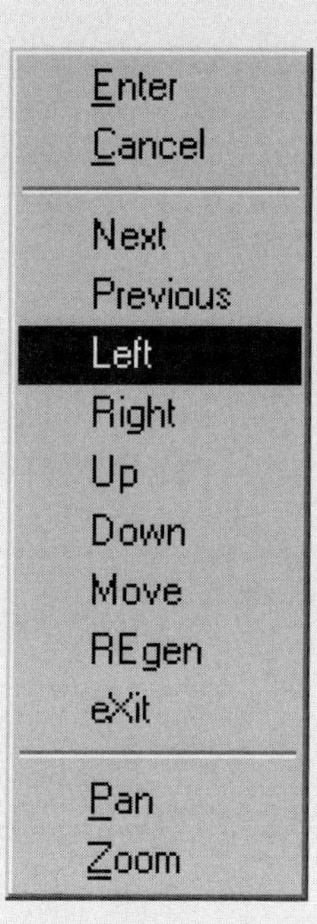

Enter an option [Next/Previous/Left/ Right/Up/Down/Move/REgen/eXit] <U>: *l*

9. Use the **Left** option to move the locator to vertex 6,2 (Figure 8.1.4.1.1.9).

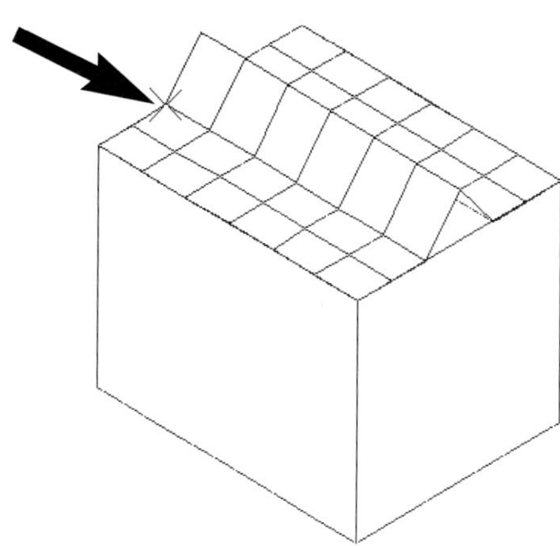

FIG. 8.1.4.1.1.9 Vertex 6,2

Enter an option [Next/Previous/Left/ Right/Up/Down/Move/REgen/eXit] <L>: *m*

Specify new location for marked vertex: *@0,0,.75*

10. Move the vertex upward three fourths of a unit as shown.

Enter
Cancel
Next
Previous
Left
Right
Up
Down
Move
REgen
eXit
Pan
Zoom

Enter an option [Next/Previous/Left/ Right/Up/Down/Move/REgen/eXit] <L>:

11. Move the locator **Down** to the next vertex and repeat Step 10. Repeat this procedure until the roof looks like Figure 8.1.4.1.1.11. (You will use the **Right** option to get to the other side of the ridge.)

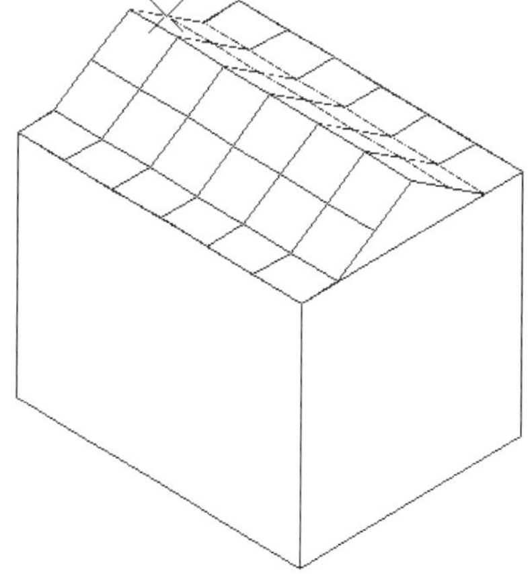

FIG. 8.1.4.1.1.11 Peaked Roof

continued

TOOLS	COMMAND SEQUENCE	STEPS
Enter Cancel Next Previous Left Right Up Down Move REgen eXit Pan Zoom	**Enter an option [Next/Previous/Left/ Right/Up/Down/Move/REgen/eXit] <U>:** *x*	**12.** Exit the command as shown.
	Enter an option [Edit vertex/Smooth surface/Desmooth/Mclose/Nclose/ Undo]: *[enter]*	
	Command: *surftype* **Enter new value for SURFTYPE <6>:** *5*	**13.** Now we will experiment with different roof shapes. Set the **Surftype** to 5 for a Quadratic B-Spline.
	Command: *surfu* **Enter new value for SURFU <6>:** *12* **Command:** *surfv* **Enter new value for SURFV <6>:** *18*	**14.** Set the **Surfu** and **Surfv** system variables as indicated for a more rounded roof.
	Command: *pe* **Select polyline or [Multiple]:**	**15.** Repeat the ***Pedit*** command and select the same 3D Mesh.
Enter Cancel Edit vertex Smooth surface Desmooth Mclose Nclose Undo Pan Zoom	**Enter an option [Edit vertex/Smooth surface/Desmooth/Mclose/Nclose/ Undo]:** *s*	**16. Smooth** the surface.
	Enter an option [Edit vertex/Smooth surface/Desmooth/Mclose/Nclose/ Undo]: *[enter]*	**17.** Exit the command. Your drawing looks like Figure 8.1.4.1.1.17. 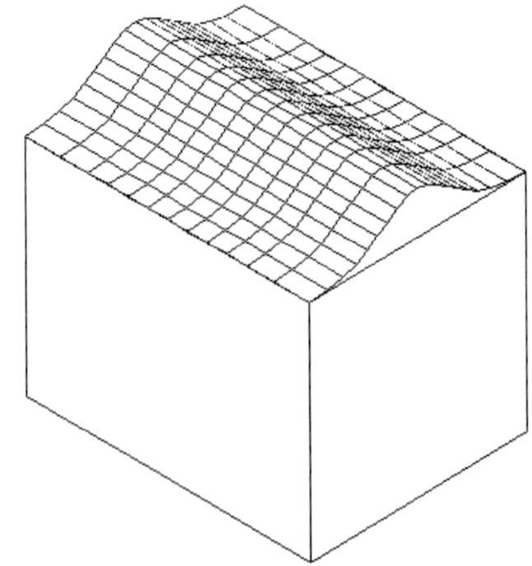 **FIG. 8.1.4.1.1.17** Quadratic B-Spline Curvature of the Roof

continued

TOOLS	COMMAND SEQUENCE	STEPS
		18. Repeat Steps 15 through 17 with the Surftype set to 6 (Cubic B-Spline). It will be difficult to see the difference, but if you look closely, you will notice that the Cubic B-Spline is slightly more curved (Figure 8.1.4.1.1.18).
		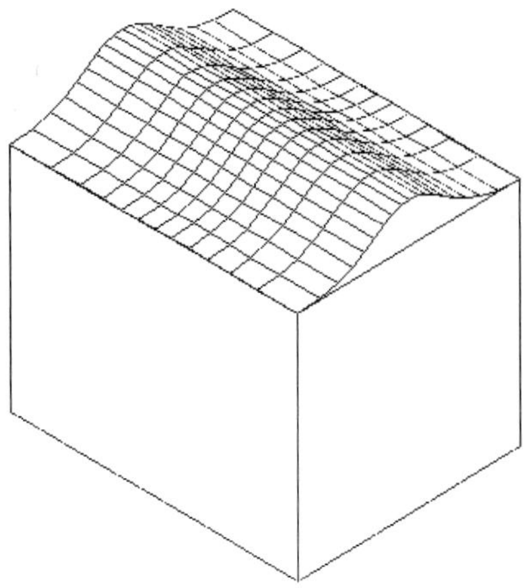 FIG. 8.1.4.1.1.18 Cubic B-Spline
	**Command:** *qsave*	**19.** Save the drawing, but do not exit.

Experiment with the Shademode for each of the different types of roofs. Which do you like best? (Return the Shademode to **Hidden**.)

Let's look next at using the OPM to edit the 3D Mesh.

8.1.4.2 Using the OPM to Modify a 3D Mesh

The OPM offers the same options as the ***Pedit*** command but makes it easier to select a specific vertex (if you know its M,N coordinate). [Refer to Figure 8.1.4.2a for the following discussion.]

Geometry	
Vertex	1
Vertex X	10.0000
Vertex Y	1.0000
Vertex Z	7.0000
Mesh	
M closed	No
N closed	No
M density	13
N density	19
M vertex count	7
N vertex count	7
Misc	
Fit/Smooth	Cubic

FIG. 8.1.4.2a OPM Showing 3D Mesh Properties

- Vertices work the same as they did when you modified the 3D Face in Exercise 8.1.3.1. The only difference is the possible number of vertices with which to work.
- Mesh properties include four that you can change and two for reference.
  - **M closed** and **N closed** are toggles. They work like the **Close** option of the ***Pedit*** command. Remember that the **M** value controls columns of faces and the **N** value controls rows. I generally rely on AutoCAD to set these values when I create a Surface Model—I have not found the situation where it fails to set them properly at design time.
  - **M** and **N density** control the density of columns and rows on the 3D Mesh. These are based on the values of the **Surfu** and **Surfv** system variables except that they reflect the number of lines defining the rows/columns (rather than the number of rows/columns).
  - The user cannot change the **M vertex count** and **N vertex count**. AutoCAD gives these numbers as a reference.
- The **Fit/Smooth** option works like the **Smooth vertex** option of the ***Pedit*** command.

Let's experiment with 3D Meshes and the OPM.

8.1.4.2.1 Do This: Using the OPM on 3D Meshes

I. Be sure you are still in the *3DMesh.dwg* file in the C:\Steps3D\Lesson08 folder. If not, open it now.

II. Open the OPM.

III. Follow these steps:

TOOLS	COMMAND SEQUENCE	STEPS

1. Select the roof. Notice that the OPM changes to reflect the properties of the 3D Mesh (Figure 8.1.4.2a).

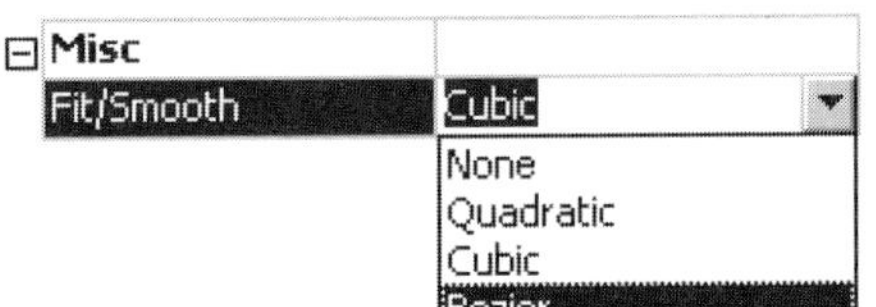

2. Change the type of surface to **Bezier** as indicated. Notice how much softer the curve is than the other two you have seen (Figure 8.1.4.2.1.2).

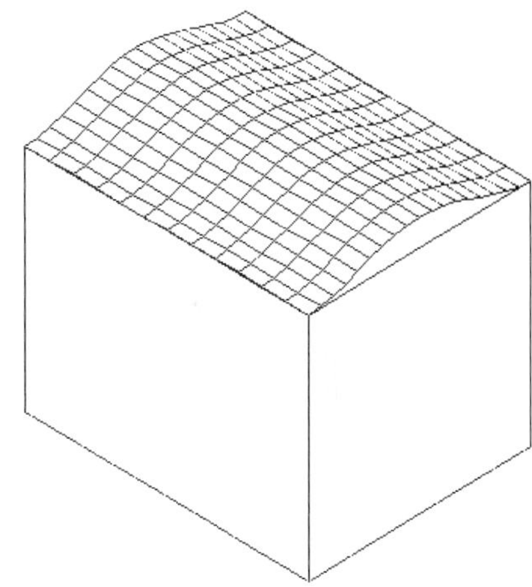

FIG. 8.1.4.2.1.2 Bezier Roof

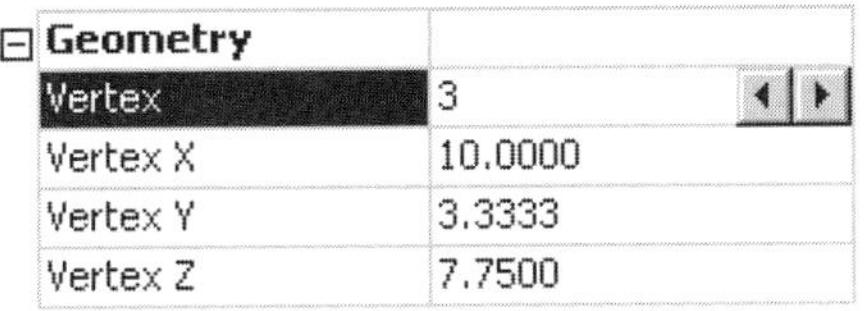

3. We will use the OPM to seal both ends of the roof against the wall. Make vertex **3** active. Do this by selecting the **Vertex** row and typing **3** in the value column or using the arrows to go to **3**.

continued

TOOLS	COMMAND SEQUENCE	STEPS

Geometry	
Vertex	3
Vertex X	10.0000
Vertex Y	3.3333
Vertex Z	7.0000

4. Change the value of **Vertex Z** to 7. Do this by typing **7** in the value column of **Vertex Z** (this is the easy approach) or by using the **Pick** button to enter a three-dimensional coordinate.

Notice the change on the drawing.

5. Repeat Steps 3 and 4 for vertices 4, 5, 45, 46, and 47. Your drawing looks like Figure 8.1.4.2.1.5.

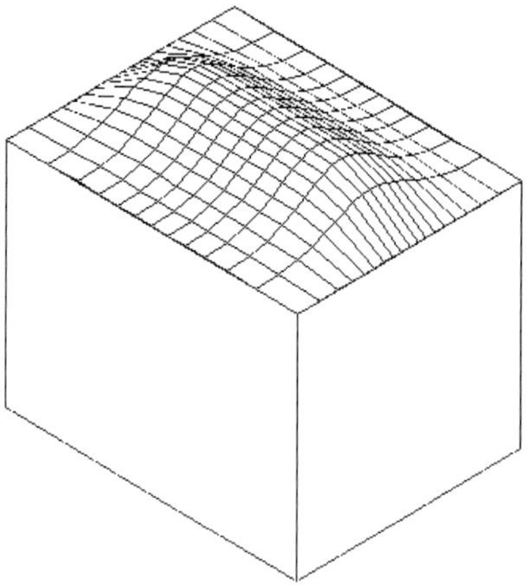

FIG. 8.1.4.2.1.5 New Roof

Command: *qsave*

6. Save the drawing, but do not exit.

Again, experiment with the Shademode settings. Orbit the view to see the building from all sides and then return it to this view.

Which procedure do you like best so far? Certainly the OPM is easiest, if you know which vertex you wish to edit.

We will look at grips next.

8.1.4.3 Using Grips to Modify a 3D Mesh

There is very little to add to what you have already learned about grips (Lesson 17 of the basic text). But I want to show you how easy it is to modify a 3D Mesh using grips.

Let's get right to it.

8.1.4.3.1 Do This: Using Grips to Modify 3D Meshes

I. Be sure you are still in the *3DMesh.dwg* file in the C:\Steps3D\Lesson08 folder. If not, open it now.

II. Close the OPM.

III. Set the running OSNAP to **Node** and clear all other settings.

IV. Follow these steps:

TOOLS	COMMAND SEQUENCE	STEPS
	**Command:** *la*	**1.** Thaw the **Marker** layer. Notice the nodes above the roof.
		2. Select the roof. Notice the grips.
		3. Pick the center grip at the top of the roof (use the coordinate display to the left on the status bar—the grip is at coordinate 5.5,4.5,8.5).
		4. Stretch the 3D Mesh to the center node above the roof.

continued

TOOLS	COMMAND SEQUENCE	STEPS
		5. Stretch the 3D Mesh using the grip at point 7,4.5,8.5 to the eastmost node and the grip at point 4,4.5,8.5 to the westmost node. Your drawing looks like Figure 8.1.4.3.1.5.

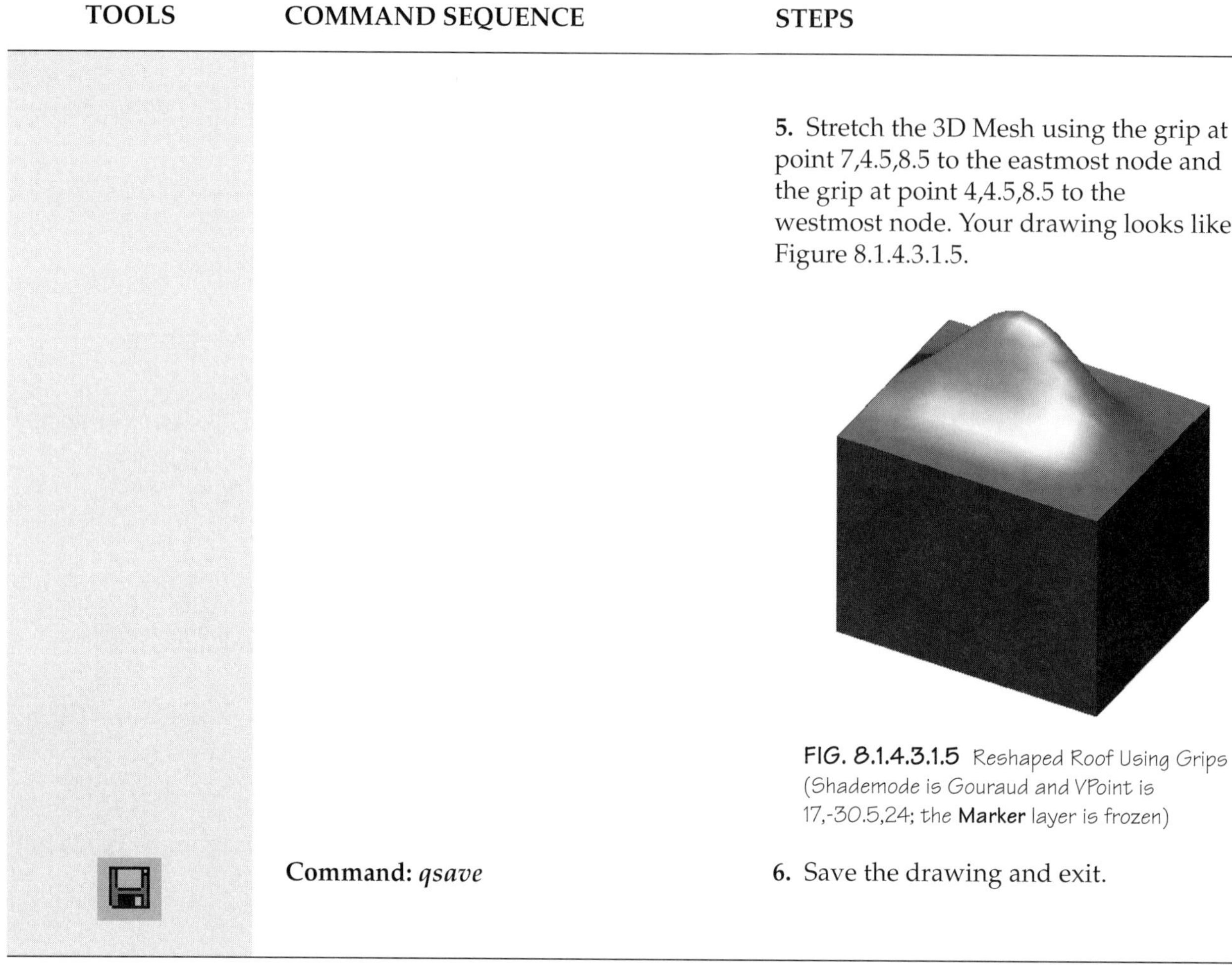

FIG. 8.1.4.3.1.5 Reshaped Roof Using Grips (Shademode is Gouraud and VPoint is 17,-30.5,24; the **Marker** layer is frozen)

TOOLS	COMMAND SEQUENCE	STEPS
	Command: *qsave*	6. Save the drawing and exit.

You can see how much easier it is to move a vertex using grips than any other method. The only requirement is that the destination point be known!

8.2 Editing Tools Designed for Z-Space

You have seen how several modification tools you already knew have been adapted to help you in Z-Space and with three-dimensional objects. It is good to maintain some familiarity between the 2D and 3D worlds.

In this section, we will look at some new tools designed specifically for working in Z-Space, but as their names imply (***Rotate3d***, ***Mirror3d***, and ***3DArray***), they serve familiar functions. The major difference between these and their two-dimensional counterparts involves the use of axes rather than base or rotation points.

Let's look at each.

8.2.1 Rotating About an Axis— The Rotate3d Command

Rotating about a base point was easy—you simply selected what to rotate and a base point. Then you told AutoCAD what angle you wanted.

Rotating about an axis is slightly more complex. But if you ever need to rotate an object in Z-Space, you will find the ***Rotate3d*** command irreplaceable. It works like this:

Command: *Rotate3d*

Current positive angle: ANGDIR=counterclockwise ANGBASE=0 *[AutoCAD reminds you how the drawing was set up]*

Select objects: *[select the object(s) you want to rotate]*

Select objects: *[hit enter when you have completed the selection set]*

Specify first point on axis or define axis by [Object/Last/View/Xaxis/Yaxis/Zaxis/2points]: *[select a point on the axis about which you wish to rotate the objects]*

Specify second point on axis: *[select a second point to identify the axis]*

Specify rotation angle or [Reference]: *[tell AutoCAD how much to rotate the object(s)]*

Command:

It might look frightening compared with the ***Rotate*** command, but once you have used it, you will find it fairly simple. Let's consider each of the axis-defining options.

- The default option is simply to specify **2points** on the axis. AutoCAD needs you to define the axis of rotation by picking any two points on the axis. Once you have done that, AutoCAD will prompt you to

  Specify rotation angle or [Reference]:

  Then tell AutoCAD how much to rotate the selected objects.

- The **Object** option is probably the easiest. If you have an object drawn that can serve as an axis, all you have to do is select it. When you choose the **Object** option, AutoCAD prompts

  Select a line, circle, arc, or 2D-polyline segment:

  - If you select a line, AutoCAD uses the line as your axis of rotation.
  - If you select a circle or arc, AutoCAD rotates the objects parallel to the plane of the circle or arc and about an imaginary axis drawn through the center of it.
  - AutoCAD treats a straight 2D-polyline segment as a line, and a 2D-polyline arc as an arc.

- The **Last** option refers to the last axis you used in the ***Rotate3d*** command.
- When you select the **View** option, AutoCAD rotates the objects about an imaginary axis drawn perpendicular to your monitor's screen.
- The **Xaxis/Yaxis/Zaxis** options align the axis of rotation with the X-, Y-, or Z-axis that runs through a selected point. AutoCAD prompts

  Specify a point on the Y [or X or Z] axis <0,0,0>:

  Enter the point's coordinates or pick it on the screen.

  Let's try it!

> The ***Rotate3d*** command (and the other 3D commands in this section) can also be found in the Modify pull-down menu. Follow this path:
>
> *Modify—3D Operation—Rotate 3D (or Mirror 3D or 3D Array)*

WWW 8.2.1.1 Do This: Rotating Objects in Z-Space

I. Open the *ro3d.dwg* file in the C:\Steps3D\Lesson08 folder. The drawing looks like Figure 8.2.1.1a.

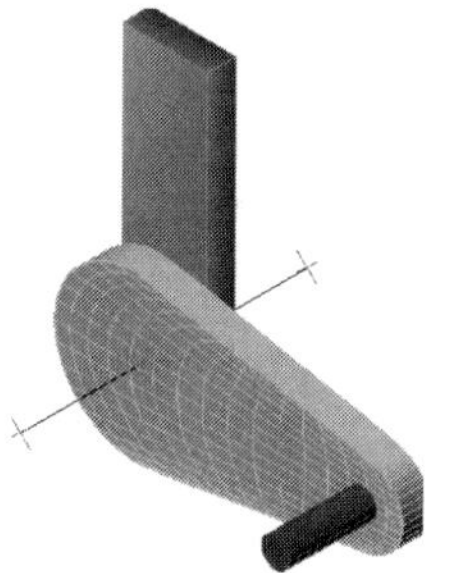

FIG. 8.2.1.1a *Ro3d.dwg*

II. Follow these steps:

TOOLS	COMMAND SEQUENCE	STEPS
No Button Available	**Command:** ***rotate3d***	**1.** Enter the ***Rotate3d*** command by typing it at the command prompt. (There is no hotkey or toolbar button.)

continued

TOOLS	COMMAND SEQUENCE	STEPS
	Select objects:	**2.** Select the handle and then confirm the selection.
	Select objects: *[enter]*	
	Specify first point on axis or define axis by [Object/Last/View/Xaxis/Yaxis/Zaxis/ 2points]:	**3.** We will begin by selecting two points to define the axis of rotation (the default). Select the node at the end of the line in front of the handle . . .
	Specify second point on axis:	**4.** . . . and then select the node at the other end of the line.
	Specify rotation angle or [Reference]: 45	**5.** Rotate the handle 45°. The drawing looks like Figure 8.2.1.1.5.

Notice that the handle rotated downward. When we selected points on the axis, AutoCAD assumed the direction we defined (from the first node to the second) to be the positive Z-direction of our rotation. It then rotated the object counterclockwise. (Use the right-hand rule to verify this for yourself.)

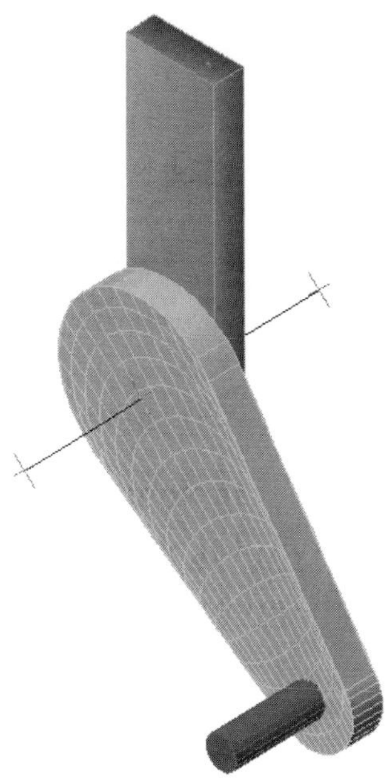

FIG. 8.2.1.1.5 First Rotation

continued

TOOLS	COMMAND SEQUENCE	STEPS
	Command: *[enter]*	**6.** We will use an object to define our axis of rotation this time. Repeat the command.
	Select objects:	**7.** Select the handle again.
	Select objects: *[enter]*	
Enter Cancel **Object** Last View Xaxis Yaxis Zaxis 2points Pan Zoom	**Specify first point on axis or define axis by [Object/Last/View/Xaxis/Yaxis/Zaxis/ 2points]:** *o*	**8.** Now choose the **Object** option.
	Select a line, circle, arc, or 2D-polyline segment:	**9.** Select the line between the two nodes. (*Note:* I drew the line from the front node to the rear node—thus defining the +Z-direction for the object).
	Specify rotation angle or [Reference]: −45	**10.** Rotate the handle −45°. It returns to its original position.
	Command: *−vp*	**11.** Next we will try the **View** option. Reset the Viewpoint to 0,−1,0 for a front view of the objects. (*Caution:* Do *not* use the *front view* button on the View toolbar as it will also change the UCS.)
	Current view direction: VIEWDIR=1.0000,−1.0000,1.0000	
	Specify a view point or [Rotate] <display compass and tripod>: *0,−1,0*	
	Command: *rotate3d*	**12.** Repeat Steps 1 and 2.
Enter Cancel Object Last **View** Xaxis Yaxis Zaxis 2points Pan Zoom	**Specify first point on axis or define axis by [Object/Last/View/Xaxis/Yaxis/Zaxis/ 2points]:** *v*	**13.** Select the **View** option.
	Specify a point on the view direction axis <0,0,0>:	**14.** Select the node in the center of the large end of the handle.
	Specify rotation angle or [Reference]: *135*	**15.** Rotate the handle 135°. This time, AutoCAD assumes the view represents a plan view of the drawing (with +Z rising outward from the monitor).

continued

TOOLS	COMMAND SEQUENCE	STEPS
	**Command:** *z*	 **16.** Restore the previous view. Your drawing looks like Figure 8.2.1.1.16. 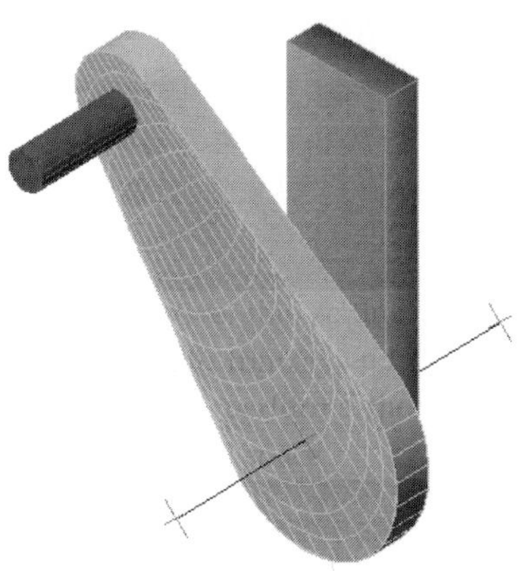 FIG. 8.2.1.1.16 Handle Rotated at 135 Degrees
	Command: *rotate3d*	**17.** Our last option will be to rotate the handle about the Y-axis (the axis along which the line is drawn). (Turn on the UCS icon to make this clear.) Repeat Steps 1 and 2.
Enter Cancel Object Last View Xaxis Yaxis Zaxis 2points Pan Zoom	**Specify first point on axis or define axis by [Object/Last/View/Xaxis/Yaxis/Zaxis/2points]:** *y*	**18.** Choose the **Yaxis** option.
	Specify a point on the Y axis <0,0,0>:	**19.** Select one of the nodes on the line . . .
	Specify rotation angle or [Reference]: *135*	**20.** . . . and tell AutoCAD to rotate the handle 135°. The handle returns to its original position.
	Command: *quit*	**21.** Exit the drawing without saving it.

As you can see, the only real difficulty in three-dimensional rotations is deciding which option to use (and remembering in which direction the positive Z-axis runs)!

8.2.2 Mirroring Three-Dimensional Objects—The Mirror3d Command

The differences between the ***Rotate3d*** and ***Rotate*** commands are really quite similar to the differences between the ***Mirror3d*** and ***Mirror*** commands. Rather than selecting a point around which to rotate an object in 2D space, you had to pick two points on an axis to satisfy the ***Rotate3d*** command. Rather than picking two points on a mirror *line* as you did in 2D space, you must pick three points to identify a mirror *plane* (the actual face of the mirror) when using the ***Mirror3d*** command.

The options offered by the ***Mirror3d*** command are also very similar to those presented by the ***Rotate3d*** command.

Command: *Mirror3d*

Select objects: *[select the object(s) you want to mirror]*

Select objects: *[hit enter when you have completed the selection set]*

Specify first point of mirror plane (3 points) or [Object/Last/Zaxis/View/XY/YZ/ZX/3points] <3points>: *{use these to}*

Specify second point on mirror plane: *{identify the mirror}*

Specify third point on mirror plane: *{plane}*

Delete source objects? [Yes/No] <N>: *[this option is the same as the 2D Mirror command—hit enter to keep the source objects or type Y to remove them]*

Command:

Let's get right to an exercise.

WWW 8.2.2.1 Do This: Mirroring Objects in Z-Space

I. Open the *Star.dwg* in the C:\Steps3D\Lesson08 folder. The drawing looks like Figure 8.2.2.1a.

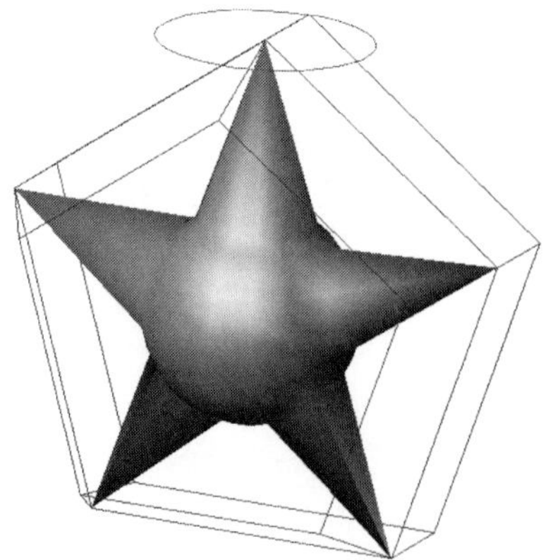

FIG. 8.2.2.1a *Star.dwg*

II. Follow these steps:

TOOLS	COMMAND SEQUENCE	STEPS
No Button Available	**Command:** ***mirror3d***	**1.** Enter the ***Mirror3d*** command. There is no hotkey or toolbar button.
	Select objects:	**2.** Select the star and then confirm the selection.
	Select objects: ***[enter]***	
	Specify first point of mirror plane (3 points) or [Object/Last/Zaxis/View/XY/YZ/ZX/3points] <3points>: ***[select Point 1]***	**3.** We will use the default **3points** approach first. Pick the points indicated in Figure 8.2.2.1.3.
	Specify second point on mirror plane: ***[select Point 2]***	
	Specify third point on mirror plane: ***[select Point 3]***	

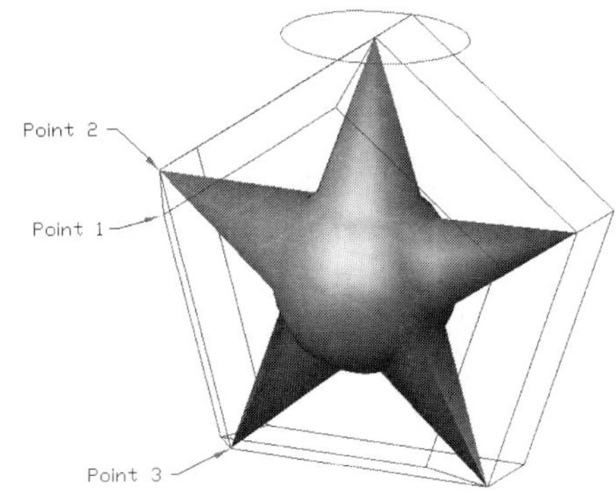

FIG. 8.2.2.1.3 Select These Points

TOOLS	COMMAND SEQUENCE	STEPS
	Delete source objects? [Yes/No] <N>: ***[enter]***	**4.** Do not delete the source objects. Your drawing looks like Figure 8.2.2.1.4a. The star has been mirrored along the plane you identified (look at it in plan view—Figure 8.2.2.1.4b—for a better understanding of the angles).

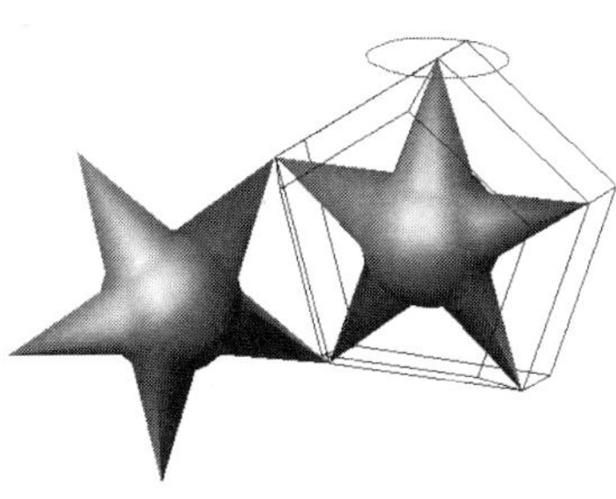

FIG. 8.2.2.1.4a Mirrored Star—3-Point Approach

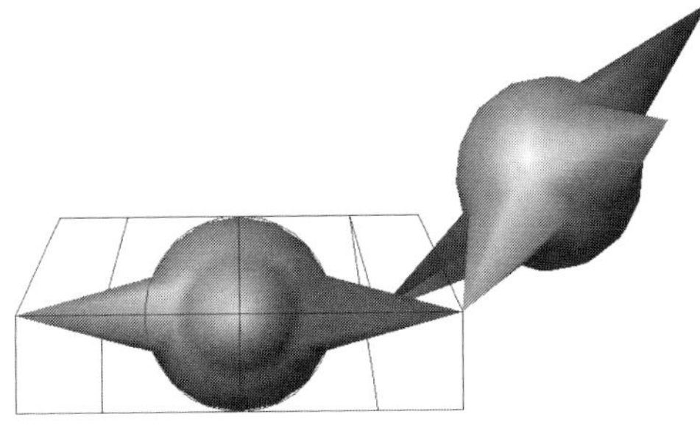

FIG. 8.2.2.1.4b Plan View of the Same Image

TOOLS	COMMAND SEQUENCE	STEPS
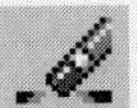	**Command:** ***e***	**5.** Erase the new star.
	Command: ***mirror3d***	**6.** Let's use the **Object** option to stand the star on its head. Repeat Steps 1 and 2.

continued

TOOLS	COMMAND SEQUENCE	STEPS
Enter Cancel Object Last Zaxis View XY YZ ZX 3points Pan Zoom	**Specify first point of mirror plane (3 points) or [Object/Last/Zaxis/View/XY/YZ/ZX/3points] <3points>:** *o*	**7.** Choose the **Object** option.
	Select a circle, arc, or 2D-polyline segment:	**8.** Select the star's halo (the circle).
	Delete source objects? [Yes/No] <N>: *y*	**9.** This time, delete the source objects. The star has been mirrored using the plane in which the circle was drawn. Your drawing looks like Figure 8.2.2.1.9.

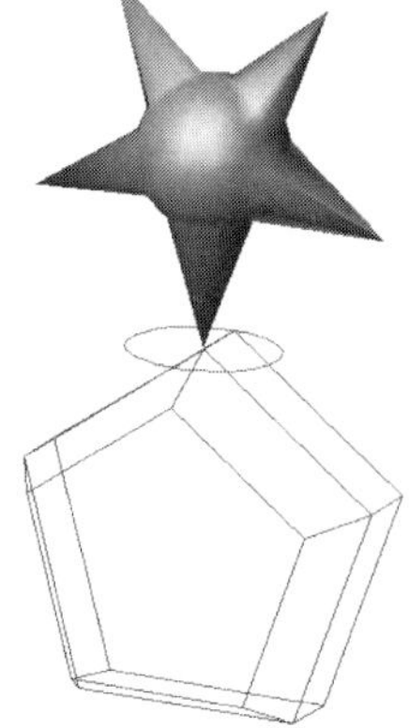

FIG. 8.2.2.1.9
Mirrored Star—Object Approach

TOOLS	COMMAND SEQUENCE	STEPS
	Command: *mirror3d*	**10.** Now we will mirror the star using the YZ plane. Repeat Steps 1 and 2. (Turn on the UCS icon to identify the YZ plane.)
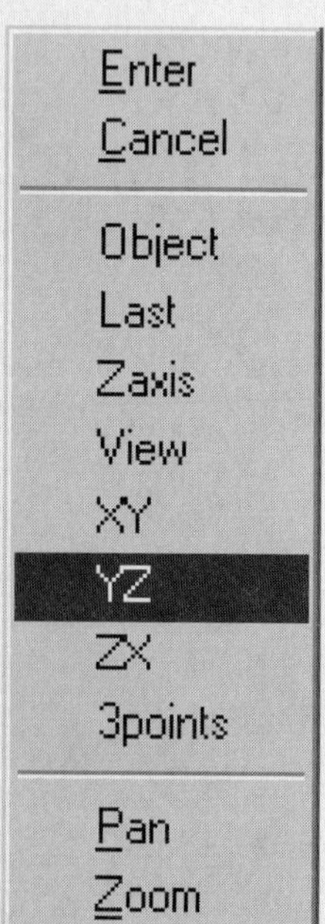	**Specify first point of mirror plane (3 points) or [Object/Last/Zaxis/View/XY/YZ/ZX/3points] <3points>:** *yz*	**11.** Choose the **YZ** option and select the leftmost point of the star.
	Specify point on YZ plane <0,0,0>:	

continued

TOOLS	COMMAND SEQUENCE	STEPS
	Delete source objects? [Yes/No] <N>: *[enter]*	**12.** Do not delete the source objects. Your drawing looks like Figure 8.2.2.1.12.
	Command: *quit*	**13.** Exit the drawing without saving your changes.

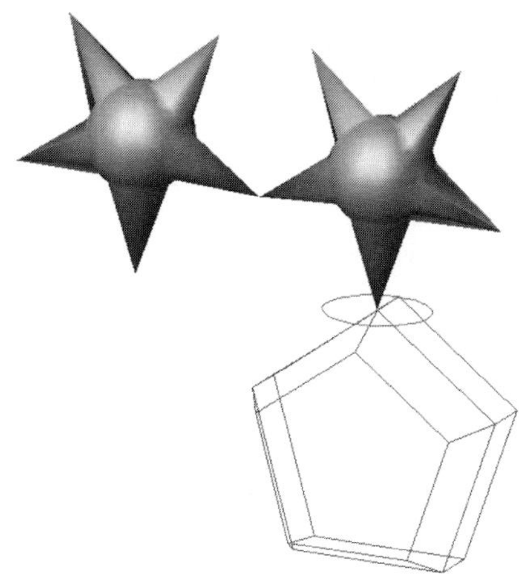

FIG. 8.2.2.1.12 Mirrored Star in the YZ Plane

If there were only one suggestion I could make about both the ***Rotate3d*** and ***Mirror3d*** commands, it would be to always check your image from more than one (preferably three or four) viewpoints. Remember that, in Z-Space, object positions seen from one angle are not necessarily true three-dimensional positions.

8.2.3 Arrayed Copies in Three Dimensions—The 3DArray Command

Of the three modification commands in this section, the ***3DArray*** command most closely resembles its two-dimensional counterpart. In fact, the only difference between the two-dimensional Rectangular Array and the three-dimensional Rectangular Array is the addition of prompts for number and spacing of levels. The only difference between the two-dimensional Polar Array and the three-dimensional Polar Array is that, rather than selecting a center point of the array, the user must identify two points on an axis.

Let's array some objects in Z-Space.

8.2.3.1 Do This: Arraying Objects in Z-Space—Rectangular Arrays

I. We will begin this exercise by creating a three-dimensional piperack. Open the *3darray-rec.dwg* in the C:\Steps3D\Lesson08 folder. The drawing looks like Figure 8.2.3.1a.

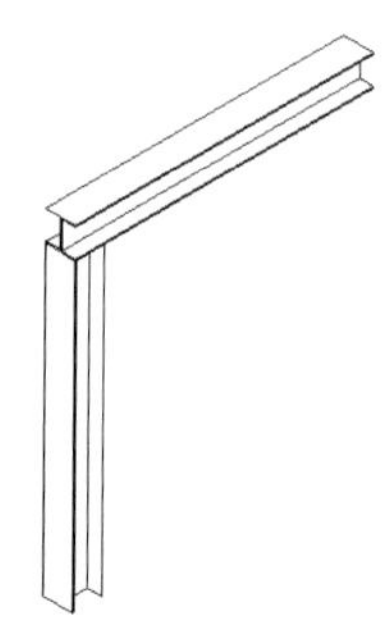

FIG. 8.2.3.1a *3DArray-Rec.dwg*

II. Follow these steps:

TOOLS	COMMAND SEQUENCE	STEPS
No Button Available	**Command:** *3a*	**1.** Enter the ***3DArray*** command by typing ***3darray*** or ***3a*** at the command line. There is no toolbar button.
	Select objects: **Select objects:** *[enter]*	**2.** Select the vertical 10′ I-Beam, and then confirm the selection.
	Enter the type of array [Rectangular/ Polar] <R>: *[enter]*	**3.** Accept the default **Rectangular** type of array.
	Enter the number of rows (---) <1>: *2* **Enter the number of columns (| | |) <1>:** *3* **Enter the number of levels (. . .) <1>:** *2*	**4.** Tell AutoCAD you want two rows, three columns, and two levels.

continued

TOOLS	COMMAND SEQUENCE	STEPS
	Specify the distance between rows (---): *9′* **Specify the distance between columns (| | |):** *15′* **Specify the distance between levels (. . .):** *11′*	**5.** Specify the distances as shown. Your drawing looks like Figure 8.2.3.1.5. (Zoom out as required to see the entire drawing.) 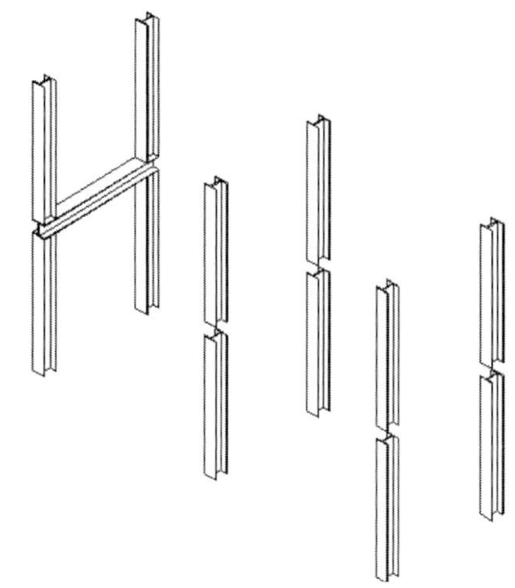 FIG. 8.2.3.1.5 Arrayed Column (hidden lines removed for clarity)
	Command: *3a*	**6.** Now array the horizontal support. Repeat the ***3DArray*** command.
	Select objects: **Select objects:** *[enter]*	**7.** Select the horizontal support and confirm the selection.
	Enter the type of array [Rectangular/ Polar] <R>: *[enter]*	**8.** Accept the default **Rectangular** type of array.
	Enter the number of rows (---) <1>: *[enter]* **Enter the number of columns (| | |) <1>:** *3* **Enter the number of levels (. . .) <1>: 2**	**9.** You will want to create one row, three columns, and two levels . . .

continued

TOOLS	COMMAND SEQUENCE	STEPS
	Specify the distance between columns (| | |): *15′* **Specify the distance between levels (...):** *11′*	**10.** . . . at the spacing indicated. Your drawing looks like Figure 8.2.3.1.10. FIG. 8.2.3.1.10 Completed Drawing (hidden lines removed for clarity)
	Command: *saveas*	**11.** Save the drawing as *MyPiperack.dwg* in the C:\Steps3D\Lesson08 folder, and then exit.

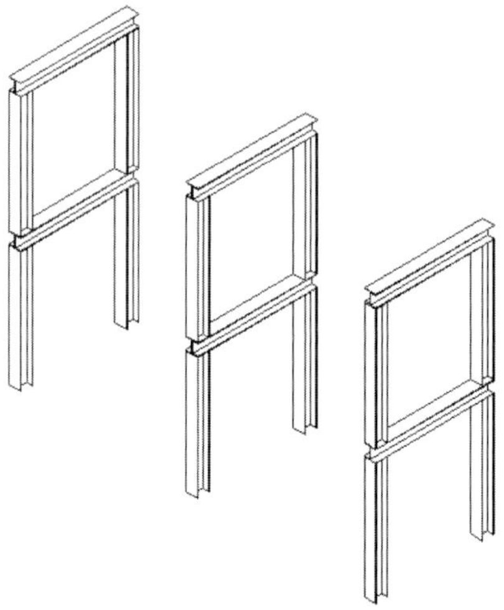

WWW 8.2.3.2 Do This: Arraying Objects in Z-Space—Polar Arrays

I. Now we will use the Polar option of the ***3DArray*** command. Open the *3darray-polar.dwg* file in the C:\Steps3D\Lesson08 folder. The drawing looks like Figure 8.2.3.2a.

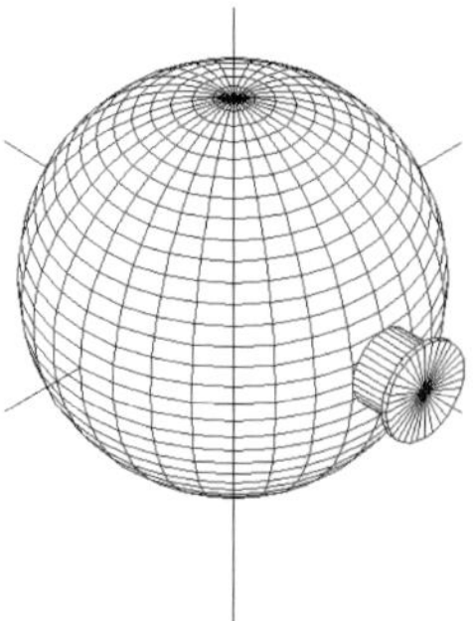

FIG. 8.2.3.2a *3DArray-Polar.dwg* (hidden lines removed for clarity)

II. Set the **Intersection** and **Endpoint** Running OSNAPs. Clear all other settings.

III. Follow these steps:

TOOLS	COMMAND SEQUENCE	STEPS
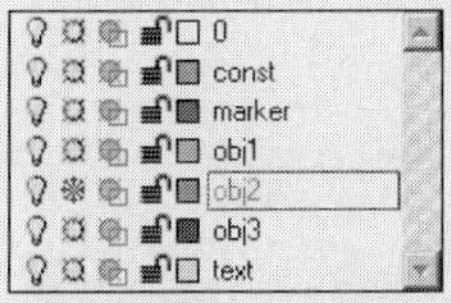	**Command:** *la*	**1.** This procedure is much easier if we remove the sphere—otherwise it will be impossible to pick the center of the array properly. So begin by freezing the **Obj2** layer.
No Button Available	**Command:** *3a*	**2.** Enter the **3DArray** command by typing **3darray** or **3a** at the command line.
	Select objects:	**3.** Select the nozzle and then confirm the selection.
	Select objects: *[enter]*	
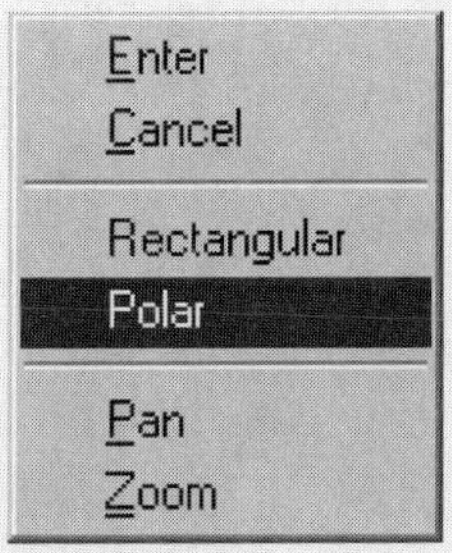	**Enter the type of array [Rectangular/Polar] <R>:** *p*	**4.** Tell AutoCAD you want to create a **Polar** array.
	Enter the number of items in the array: *4*	**5.** We will create four copies of the nozzle and fill a full circle. (You might notice that the order of the prompts differs slightly from that of the ***Array*** command. But you can relax; all the prompts are still there.)
	Specify the angle to fill (+ = ccw, − = cw) <360>: *[enter]*	
	Rotate arrayed objects? [Yes/No] <Y>: *[enter]*	**6.** We do want to rotate the nozzles as they are copied.
	Specify center point of array: *int*	**7.** Select the intersection of the guidelines as the **center point of array**.

continued

TOOLS	COMMAND SEQUENCE	STEPS
	Specify second point on axis of rotation:	**8.** The only prompt the ***3DArray*** command has that the ***Array*** command does not is that the ***3DArray*** command requires you to identify an **axis of rotation** rather than just a center point. Pick either endpoint of the north–south horizontal line. Your drawing looks like Figure 8.2.3.2.8.

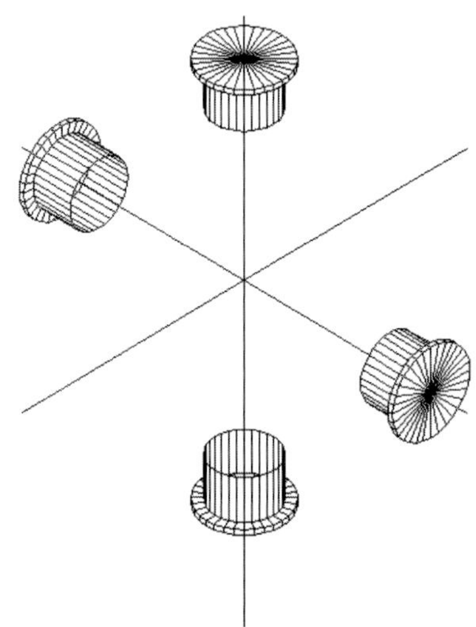

FIG. 8.2.3.2.8 Polar Arrayed Nozzles (hidden lines removed for clarity)

continued

TOOLS	COMMAND SEQUENCE	STEPS
	Command: *3a*	**9.** Repeat Steps 2 through 8, but this time select an endpoint on the vertical line in Step 8. Your drawing looks like Figure 8.2.3.2.9.

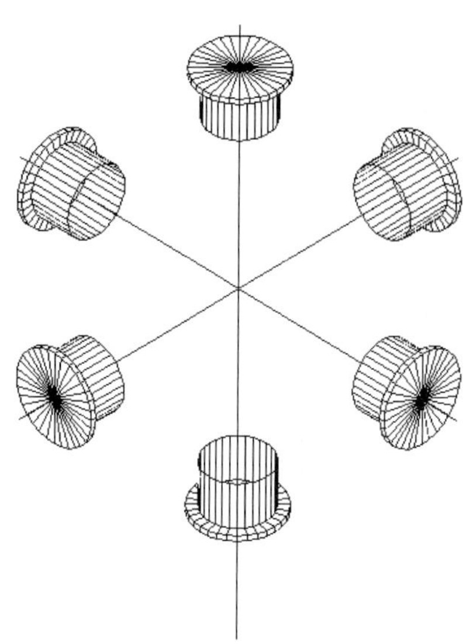

FIG. 8.2.3.2.9 Both Polar Arrays

10. Thaw the **Obj2** layer, freeze the **Marker** layer, and set the Shademode to **Gouraud**. Your drawing looks like Figure 8.2.3.2.10.

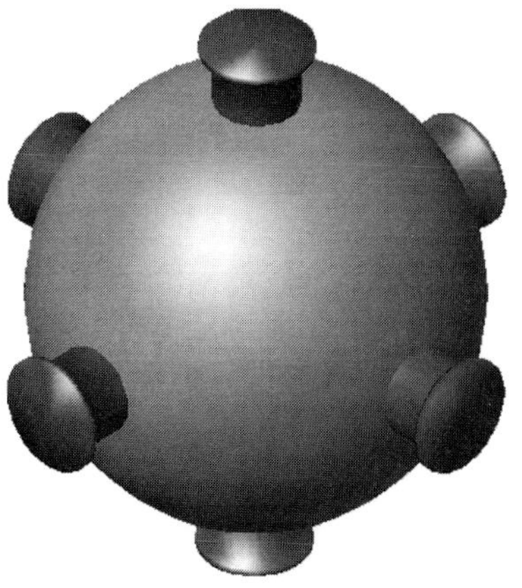

FIG. 8.2.3.2.10 Completed Drawing

continued

TOOLS	COMMAND SEQUENCE	STEPS
	Command: ***saveas***	**11.** Save the drawing as *Weird Vessel.dwg* in the C:\Steps3D\Lesson08 folder and then exit.

8.3 Extra Steps

Create several 3D Meshes—similar to those shown in Figure 8.1.4.1a (p. 323). Use different shapes to begin—hat or stair shapes are good as starters, but do not limit yourself. Use the ***Edgesurf*** command to help you.

Once you have four or five meshes, experiment with the different **Smooth surface** options of the ***Pedit*** command.

It is an important step in your training to combine the different tools you have learned.

- Try editing each mesh before and after the mesh has been smoothed and note the difference in outcome.
- Try doing the same editing chores using different Shademode settings. Which setting is easier? Which editing tool (Pedit, OPM, or Grips) is easiest for each Shademode setting?

8.4 What Have We Learned?

Items covered in this lesson include

- *Two-dimensional modifying tools used on three-dimensional objects*
  - ***Pedit***
  - ***Trim***
  - ***Extend***
  - ***Align***
  - ***Grips***
  - ***The Object Properties Manager***
- *Tools designed specifically for Z-Space*
  - ***Surftype***
  - ***Surfv*** *and* ***Surfu***
  - ***Rotate3d***
  - ***Mirror3d***
  - ***3DArray***

This has been a busy lesson, but you have learned so much!

When combined with your knowledge of Wireframe and Surface Modeling (and some practice), these tools will enable you to create almost any structure you wish to draw. With some creative use of the Shademode system variable, you can produce professional-quality, colorful drawings of almost anything for any industry!

But what must you have that I cannot provide?

Practice . . . Practice . . . Practice!

Remember: Only through practice does training become experience. And it is experience that creates successful, efficient, economical, and sound designs; and it is experience that earns top dollar!

So repeat any lesson as needed for the proper training, and then work through the exercises at the end of the lesson for experience.

Our next lesson begins the wonderful world of Solid Modeling. There you will see things that are guaranteed to amaze and confound, bemuse and befuddle. But, above all, you will see why Solid Modeling is the future of CAD.

8.5 EXERCISES

1. Using the *Star-Root.dwg* file in the C:\Steps3D\Lesson08 folder, create the star drawing we used in Exercise 8.2.2.1. (*Hint:* Grips make this exercise much easier.)

2. Create the conveyor belt drawing shown in Figure 8.5.2. Follow these guidelines.

- **2.1.** Draw only one shaft and one roller (use the ***Revsurf*** command for best results).
- **2.2.** Use the ***3DArray***, ***Rotate3d***, and ***Mirror3d*** commands to arrange the guides and the rollers on the guides.
- **2.3.** Use splines and the ***Rulesurf*** command to create the belt.
- **2.4.** I used a **Surftab1** setting of 18 for the shaft and roller, and **Surftab1** setting of 100 and **Surftab2** setting of 36 when I created the belt.
- **2.5.** Save the drawing as *MyBelt.dwg* in the C:\Steps3D\Lesson08 folder.

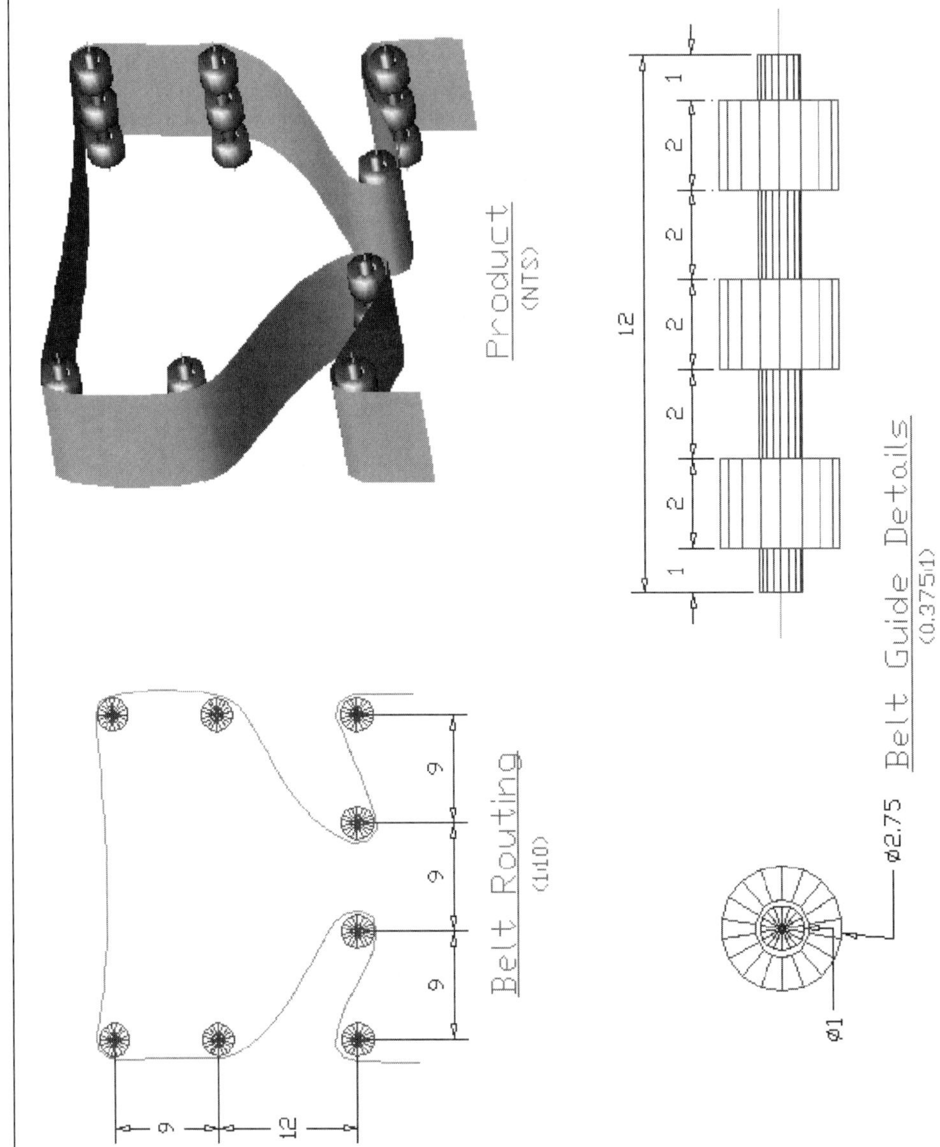

FIG. 8.5.2 Conveyor Belt

3. Starting with the *MyPiperack.dwg* file you created in Exercise 8.2.3.1 (or the *Piperack.dwg* file if that one is not available), create the piping drawing shown in Figure 8.5.3. Follow these guidelines.
   3.1. The tank has a 15′ diameter and a 10′ height. The top is a 3′-high pointed cone.
   3.2. Pipe is 12″ diameter (12.75″ OD,or outer diameter).
   3.3. Elbows are 18″ from open face to centerline of bend.
   3.4. There is a $\frac{1}{8}$″ gasket between the flange and the nozzle at the tank.
   3.5. **Surftab1** and **Surftab2** values are 16.

3.6. The dike wall around the tank is 2′ high. The top of the wall is one mesh grid wide.

3.7. I used ***Revsurf*** to create the elbows and ***Rulesurf*** to create the pipe.

3.8. Save the drawing as *MyPipingPlan.dwg* in the C:\Steps3D\Lesson08 folder.

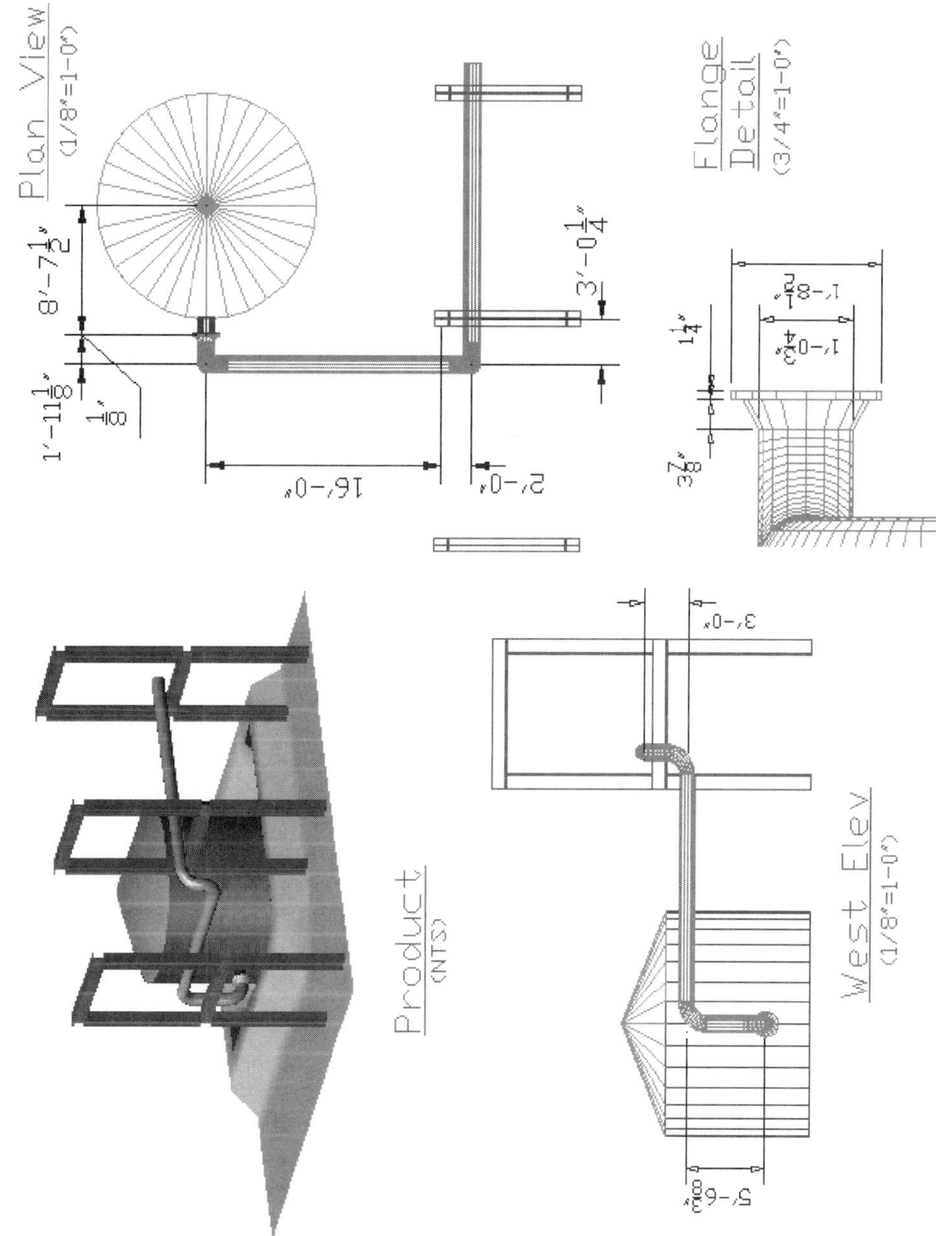

FIG. 8.5.3 Piping

4. Create the propeller drawing shown in Figure 8.5.4. Follow these guidelines.

4.1. The blade is a three-dimensional curve—use a spline as the arc and rise to the end of the upper line as shown in the *top blade detail*. Use as many vertices as you need—but I would not use less than five.

4.2. I used a **Surftab1** setting of 8 to create the hub, and a **Surftab1** setting of 16 and **Surftab2** setting of 18 to create the blade.

4.3. Once the blade is drawn, turn it into a block. Insert the block into its proper place on the hub but then explode it.

4.4. Use the ***Rotate3d*** command to rotate the blade 105° on the hub.

4.5. Use the 3D Mesh editing tools you learned in this lesson to attach the ends of the blade to the hub.

4.6. (*Hint:* The ***Stretch*** command works as well in Z-Space as it did in 2D space.)

4.7. Save the drawing as *MyProp.dwg* in the C:\Steps3D\Lesson08 folder.

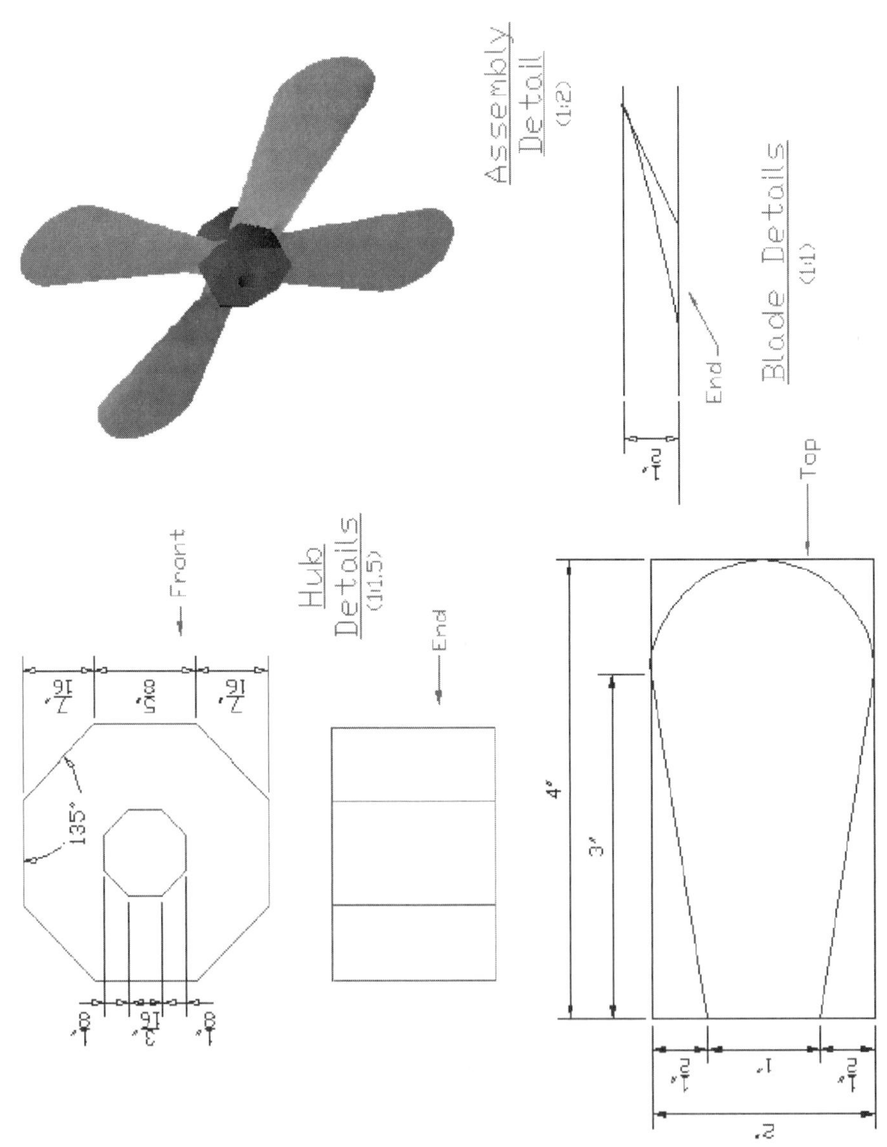

FIG. 8.5.4 Propeller

5. Create the three-dimensional chess drawing shown in Figure 8.5.5. Follow these guidelines.
   5.1. Each square is $1\frac{1}{2}''$.
   5.2. The boards are rotated at 15° increments.
   5.3. The post is 1″ diameter.
   5.4. The frames are $\frac{1}{2}''$ wide × $\frac{3}{4}''$ deep.
   5.5. The boards are 8″ apart.
   5.6. Save the drawing as *My3DChess.dwg* in the C:\Steps3D\Lesson08 folder.

FIG. 8.5.5 Three-Dimensional Chess

6. This is another challenge! Create the curl drawing shown in Figure 8.5.6. Follow these guidelines.
   6.1. I started with a 1″ line.
   6.2. There are 30 faces in all.
   6.3. The ring is ~$4\frac{1}{4}''$ diameter (I started with a line at 1,1 and arrayed it about point 4,4).
   6.4. I used three layers and two colors.
   6.5. The faces rotate 180°.
   6.6. Save the drawing as *MyCurl.dwg* in the C:\Steps3D\Lesson08 folder.

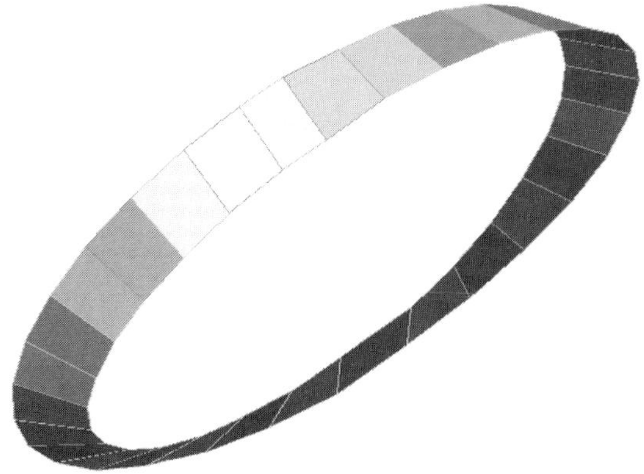

FIG. 8.5.6 Curl

7. Create the sailboat drawing shown in Figure 8.5.7. Follow these guidelines.
   7.1. This is a toy sailboat. The boat itself is 6″ × 2″ × $\frac{3}{4}$″.
   7.2. The keel is 3″ below the bottom of the boat.
   7.3. The mast is 7″ long × $\frac{1}{8}$″ diameter.
   7.4. The boom is 5″ long × $\frac{1}{8}$″ diameter.
   7.5. Save the drawing as *MySBoat.dwg* in the C:\Steps3D\Lesson08 folder.

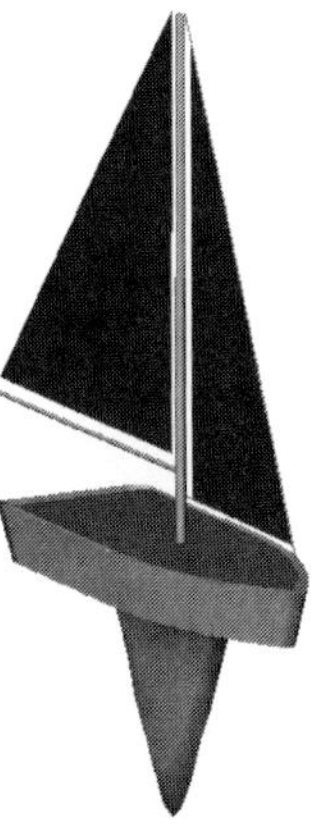

FIG. 8.5.7 Sailboat

8.6 REVIEW QUESTIONS

Answer the following questions on a separate sheet of paper.

1. __________ controls how the Trim and Extend commands behave in Z-Space.

2. You can set the above system variable by selecting the __________ option at either the Trim or Extend command's prompt.

3. What is the true 3D setting for the Projmode system variable?

4. Setting the Projmode system variable to __________ means that AutoCAD will look at cutting edges and objects to trim in a two-dimensional projection of the current UCS.

5. (T or F) You cannot trim or extend part of a 3D Mesh.

6. (T or F) You cannot use a 3D Face as a cutting edge.

7. (T or F) You cannot use a Region as a boundary when extending.

8. (T or F) You cannot scale three-dimensional objects as part of the Align command.

9. (T or F) Regions and 3D Faces have no editable properties.

10. Which would you use to edit a 3D Face? (Pedit, OPM, neither)

11. and 12. Name the two methods for hiding an edge of a 3D Face.

a.

b.

13. through 15. List the three methods for modifying a 3D Mesh.

a.

b.

c.

16. When using the Pedit command on a 3D Mesh, the __________ option creates a curved shape from the 3D Mesh.

17. through 19. List the three types of smooth surfaces.

a.

b.

c.

20. The __________ system variable controls the type of smooth surface that is created with the Pedit command.

21. (T or F) You can change the number of M or N vertices of a 3D Mesh using the OPM.

22. The major difference between the new tools discussed in this lesson and their two-dimensional counterparts involves using an __________ rather than base or rotation points.

23. When using the View option of the Rotate3d command, AutoCAD rotates the objects about __________.

PART V

Advanced Modeling

This part of our text contains these lessons:

9. Solid Modeling Building Blocks
10. Composite Solids
11. Editing 3D Solids
12. Three-Dimensional Blocks and Three-Dimensional Plotting Tools

LESSON 9

Solid Modeling Building Blocks

Following this lesson, you will

- Know how to create AutoCAD's Solid Modeling Building Blocks
  - ***Box***
  - ***Wedge***
  - ***Cone***
  - ***Sphere***
  - ***Cylinder***
  - ***Torus***
  - ***Extrude***
  - ***Revolve***
- Know how and why to use AutoCAD's Isolines system variable

Understanding some of the history of three-dimensional AutoCAD might help you prepare for this lesson.

AutoCAD began its trek into Z-Space by creating the Z-axis. The Z-axis gave users the ability to create three-dimensional lines and circles for the first time. AutoCAD called this development Wireframe Modeling.

But although the creation of a Z-axis was no small feat for programmers, Wireframe Modeling came up short in its usefulness to draftsmen. After all, a skeleton without skin is a fairly transparent accomplishment.

AutoCAD "covered" the need by developing Surface Modeling. Here, the user gained the *3DFace* (and related) commands that could be used to "stretch a blanket" over the wireframe. This appeared to solidify AutoCAD's three-dimensional experiment. But the success, like its models, was hollow.

AutoCAD programmers still dreamed of a model that would be "just like the real thing." That is, they wanted the computer to be able to reflect mass properties, solids where the object was solid, and spaces where the solid was empty. They wanted a solid object to *be* a solid object—not a loose conglomeration of circles and lines. So AutoCAD developed Solid Modeling.

Obviously, I could not give you the full history in these few paragraphs. The reason for these paragraphs, then, is to let you know that developers of Solid Modeling had Wireframe and Surface Modeling on which to build.

What does that mean to you now? Simply, that having studied the intricacies of the more primitive modeling techniques, you are well prepared (better, perhaps, than you might think) for tackling this newest—and most remarkable—of AutoCAD's modeling tools.

9.1 What Are Solid Modeling Building Blocks?

Most people refer to Solid Modeling building blocks as primitive solids. But, frankly, that term is not as descriptive as it might be. Building blocks are toys with which we all played as children. You are already familiar with their basic shapes—box, wedge, cone, cylinder, sphere, and torus. You studied all of these, except cylinder, as part of your predefined Surface Models. (A cylinder is simply a cone with equal radii at both ends.)

Additionally, we will include homemade shapes as part of our building blocks (didn't you wish you could do that when you were a child?). To create these, we will use the solids equivalent of the ***Revsurf*** command—***Revolve***—and a command that turns 2D objects into 3DSolids—***Extrude***.

Therefore, to answer the question, "What are Solid Modeling building blocks?" (for the test), let me give you a quick definition. Solid Modeling building blocks are predefined and user-defined solid shapes with which you build your model.

Let's look at each of them.

9.2 Extruding 2D Regions and Solids

One of the easiest ways to create a three-dimensional solid is simply to *extrude* a two-dimensional object. This means that AutoCAD will take the two-dimensional object and "stretch" it or "pull" it into Z-Space. The objects on which AutoCAD can perform this engineering marvel are 3D Faces, closed polylines, circles, ellipses, closed splines, donuts, regions, and 2D solids. The results may surprise you!

The command sequence looks like this:

Command: ***extrude*** **(or** ***ext*****)**

Current wire frame density: ISOLINES=4

Select objects: ***[select the objects you want to extrude]***

Select objects: ***[hit enter to confirm the selection]***

Specify height of extrusion or [Path]: ***[tell AutoCAD how far into Z-Space you want to "stretch" the object]***

Specify angle of taper for extrusion <0>: ***[specify a taper angle, if desired]***

Command:

There are not many options to confuse you, but what they can do will astound you. Let's look at each line.

- AutoCAD first lets you know how many *Isolines* it will use to display the object. Let me explain isolines.

Remember when you drew Surface Models? You had to identify the number of faces to use by answering some prompts or adjusting the values of the **Surftab1** and **Surftab2** system variables.

When drawing a solid object, the shape is unaffected by the Surftab settings. A round solid object is round regardless of the number of lines AutoCAD uses to show that it is round. But using a large number of lines to show something is round takes a bit more memory and regeneration time, so AutoCAD allows you to control the number. You control the number of lines used to draw a rounded solid object with the **Isolines** system variable.

This will become clearer in our next exercise.

- The first option occurs right after the **Select objects:** prompts. Here you can tell AutoCAD how "tall" to make the object (how far to stretch it into Z-Space), or you can select an object that will define the extrusion **Path**. The path object can be a line, arc, or 3DPoly. The results can be quite elaborate.
- Another option that can produce elaborate results is the **taper for extrusion** option. The default (**0**) produces a nice straight extrusion. An angle entry, however, can turn a box into a pyramid!

> You can also access the ***Extrude*** command using the Draw pull-down menu. Follow this path:
>
> *Draw—Solids—Extrude*

Let's extrude some objects.

WWW 9.2.1 Do This: Extruding into Z-Space

I. Open the *regions & solids.dwg* in the C:\Steps3D\Lesson09 folder. The drawing looks like Figure 9.2.1a. (The top two IBeams are regions, the third IBeam is a polyline, the square is a solid, and the circle is a circle.)

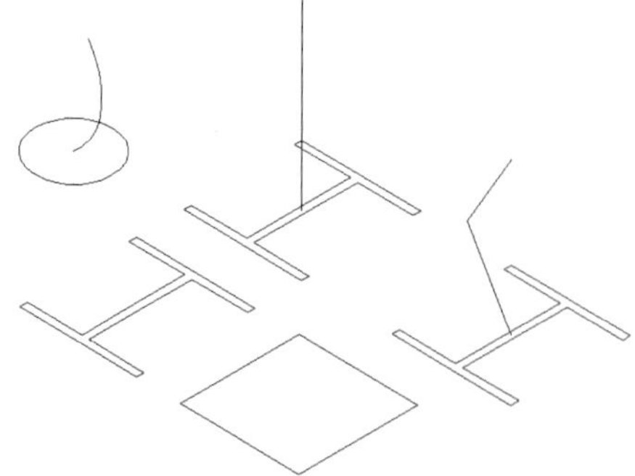

FIG. 9.2.1a regions & solids.dwg

II. Set the **Obj1** layer current.

III. Follow these steps:

TOOLS	COMMAND SEQUENCE	STEPS
 Extrude Button	**Command:** ***ext***	**1.** Enter the ***Extrude*** command by typing ***extrude*** or ***ext*** at the command prompt. Or you can pick the **Extrude** button on the Solids toolbar.
	Current wireframe density: ISOLINES=4	**2.** Select the lower-left IBeam and confirm the selection.
	Select objects:	
	Select objects: ***[enter]***	
	Specify height of extrusion or [Path]: ***5***	**3.** Enter a **height of extrusion** of 5 and accept the default **angle of taper for extrusion**. The IBeam looks like Figure 9.2.1.3. Notice that the original object disappears and that the new 3D Solid object is created on the current layer.
	Specify angle of taper for extrusion <0>: ***[enter]***	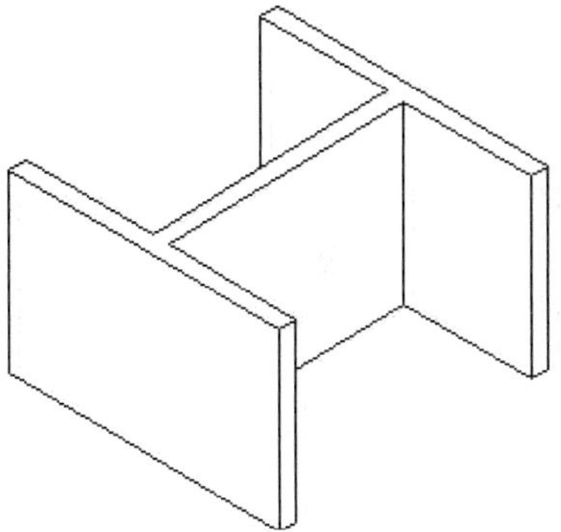 FIG. 9.2.1.3 Extruded IBeam (hidden lines removed)
	**Command:** ***[enter]***	**4.** Repeat the ***Extrude*** command.
	Current wireframe density: ***ISOLINES=4***	**5.** Select the IBeam directly behind the first (the one with the straight line rising from it).
	Select objects:	
	Select objects: ***[enter]***	

continued

TOOLS	COMMAND SEQUENCE	STEPS
	**Specify height of extrusion or [Path]:** *p*	**6.** Tell AutoCAD to use a **Path** to guide the extrusion . . .
	Select extrusion path:	**7.** . . . and select the line in the center of the IBeam. Your drawing looks like Figure 9.2.1.7.

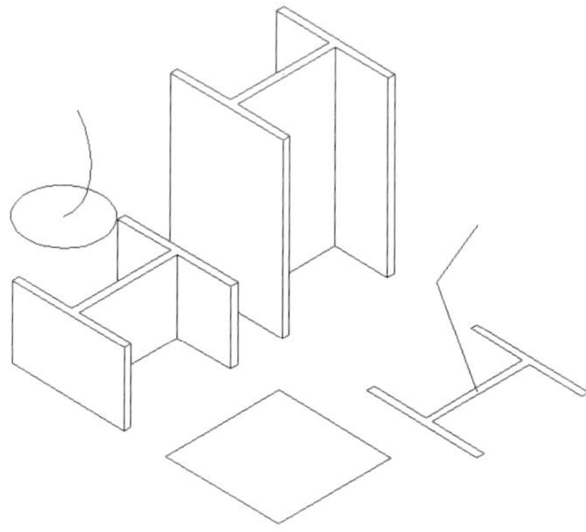

FIG. 9.2.1.7 IBeam Extruded Along a Straight Path (hidden lines removed)

TOOLS	COMMAND SEQUENCE	STEPS
	**Command:** *[enter]*	**8.** Repeat Steps 4 through 7 for the other IBeam using the 3D polyline as the path. Your drawing looks like Figure 9.2.1.8. Notice the difference when the path is not straight.

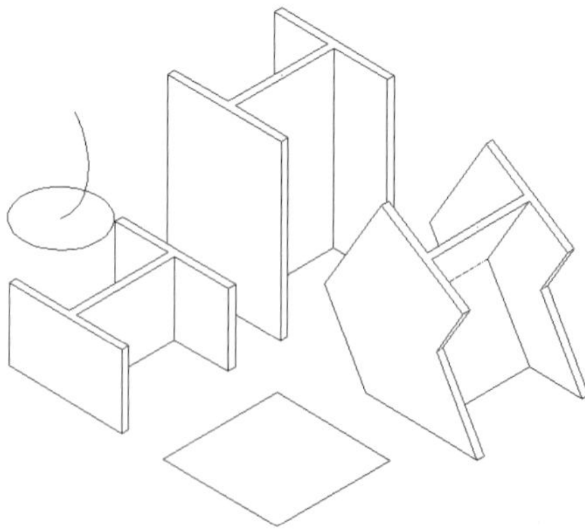

FIG. 9.2.1.8 Nonlinear Path Extrusion (hidden lines removed)

continued

TOOLS	COMMAND SEQUENCE	STEPS
	**Command:** *[enter]*	**9.** Repeat Step 8 on the circle. Notice how difficult it is to tell what you have drawn (Figure 9.2.1.9).

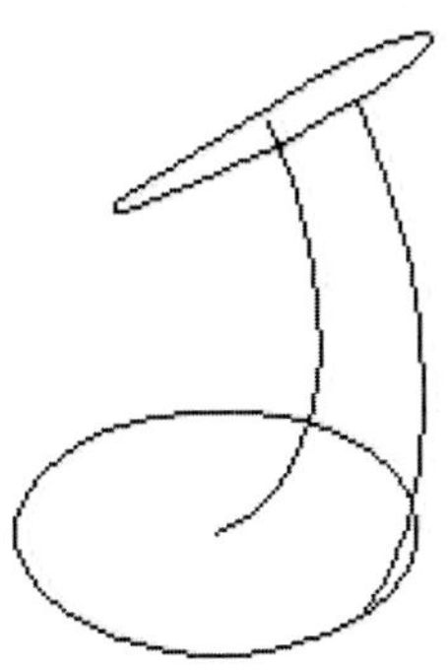

FIG. 9.2.1.9 Circle Extruded Along a Nonlinear Path (hidden lines shown for clarity)

TOOLS	COMMAND SEQUENCE	STEPS
No Button Available	**Command:** *isolines*	**10.** Set the **Isolines** system variable to *24*.
	Enter new value for ISOLINES <4>: *24*	
	Command: *re*	**11.** Regenerate the drawing. Your drawing looks like Figure 9.2.1.11.

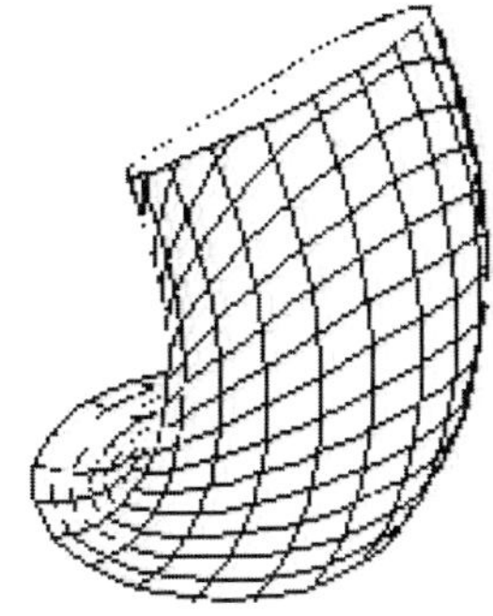

FIG. 9.2.1.11 Isolines Set to 24 (hidden lines removed)

TOOLS	COMMAND SEQUENCE	STEPS
 Extrude Button	**Command:** *ext*	**12.** Now let's look at the last prompt. Repeat the ***Extrude*** command and select the solid (the square).
	Current wire frame density: ISOLINES=24	
	Select objects:	
	Select objects: *[enter]*	
	Specify height of extrusion or [Path]: *5*	**13.** Use *5* as the **height of extrusion** . . .

continued

TOOLS	COMMAND SEQUENCE	STEPS
	Specify angle of taper for extrusion <0>: *30*	**14.** . . . but give it an **angle of taper** of *30*°. Your drawing looks like Figure 9.2.1.15.
		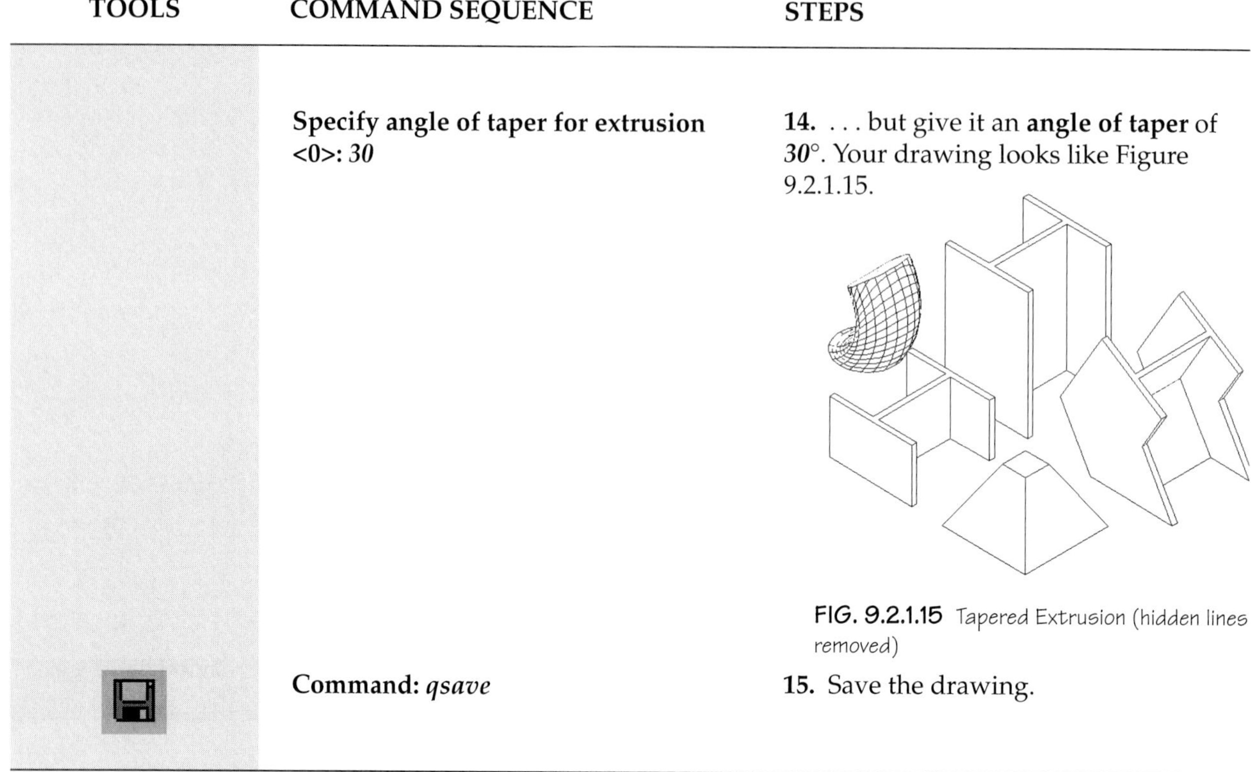 FIG. 9.2.1.15 Tapered Extrusion (hidden lines removed)
	Command: *qsave*	**15.** Save the drawing.

Are you beginning to see why solids are the tool of choice for most three-dimensional work? But wait! We have much, much more to cover!

9.3 Drawing the Blocks

Extruding two-dimensional objects into Z-Space is handy. But solids offer many of the same predefined shapes that you used in Surface Modeling plus one additional shape. We will look at these now, and then we will look at the ***Revolve*** command. But the real marvels of Solid Modeling—the nifty tricks that make it so very valuable—will have to wait for Lessons 10 and 11.

Let's look at the predefined Solid Modeling shapes and their similarities to (and differences from) their Surface Modeling counterparts.

9.3.1 Box

You will use the ***Box*** command to draw any size box whose sides are parallel or perpendicular to the current UCS. This is the command sequence:

Command: *box*
Specify corner of box or [CEnter] <0,0,0>: *[identify the first corner of the box]*
Specify corner or [Cube/Length]: *[identify the opposite corner of the box]*
Specify height: *[tell AutoCAD how tall to make the box]*
Command:

The first thing you probably noticed is that the command sequence is shorter than the ***AI_Box*** command's sequence. Indeed, the ***Box*** command has only three prompts to ***AI_Box***'s five. But the ***Box*** command's prompts offer more options. Let's see.

- The first prompt asks for a **corner** of the box. Satisfy this prompt by picking a point on the screen or entering a coordinate.

  The alternative to specifying the first corner is to specify the **CEnter** of the box. Access this option by typing *C* or *CE*. AutoCAD will respond with a prompt to specify the center of the box:

  Specify center of box <0,0,0>:

  Once you locate the center of the box, AutoCAD will then continue with the remaining prompts.
- Next, AutoCAD asks you to specify the opposite **corner** of the box. You may notice a programming flaw when it does—normally, a corner prompt uses a rubber band box on the screen to help you select corners (as it does with the ***Rectangle*** command). Here you will use the rubber band line normally used when drawing lines or polylines. AutoCAD will use the point you select to determine the length and width of the box. It will then prompt you for the height.

  The **Cube** option will prompt you to **Specify length:** and use the value you enter as length, width, and height for the cube.

  The **Length** option will prompt you to **Specify length:** as the **Cube** option did but will follow that prompt with prompts for **width** and **height**, as well.

> You can also access the ***Box*** command (as well as the other commands in this section) using the Draw pull-down menu. Follow this path:
>
> *Draw—Solids—[commands]*

We will draw some boxes to see these options.

9.3.1.1 Do This: Drawing Solid Boxes

I. Start a new drawing from scratch.

II. Adjust the viewpoint to see the drawing from a SE Isometric View (1,−1,1).

III. Follow these steps:

TOOLS	COMMAND SEQUENCE	STEPS
Box Button	**Command:** ***box***	**1.** Enter the ***Box*** command by typing ***box*** at the command prompt. Or you can pick the **Box** button on the Solids toolbar.
	Specify corner of box or [CEnter] <0,0,0>: ***4,4***	**2.** Specify the corners of the box as shown.
	Specify corner or [Cube/Length]: ***@4,2***	
	Specify height: ***1.5***	**3.** Give it a **height** of ***1.5*** units. That was simple, was it not? Your drawing looks like Figure 9.3.1.1.3.
		FIG. 9.3.1.1.3 Box
	Command: ***[enter]***	**4.** This time let's draw a cube. Repeat the command.
Enter Cancel CEnter Pan Zoom	**Specify corner of box or [CEnter] <0,0,0>:** ***c***	**5.** We will use the **CEnter** option.
	Specify center of box <0,0,0>: ***5,5,2.5***	**6.** And place the center as shown.
	Specify corner or [Cube/Length]: ***c***	**7.** Tell AutoCAD to draw a **Cube**.

continued

TOOLS	COMMAND SEQUENCE	STEPS

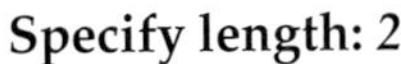

Specify length: *2*

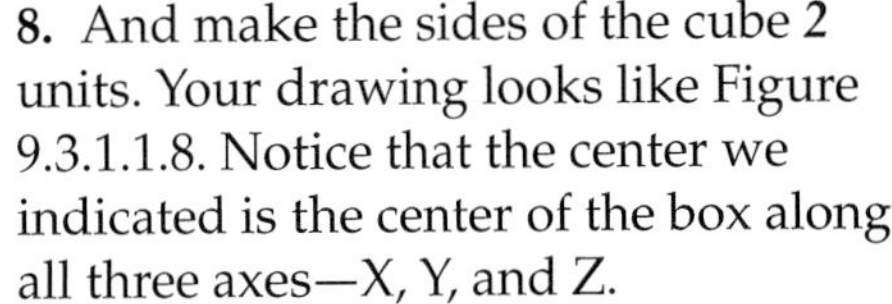

8. And make the sides of the cube **2** units. Your drawing looks like Figure 9.3.1.1.8. Notice that the center we indicated is the center of the box along all three axes—X, Y, and Z.

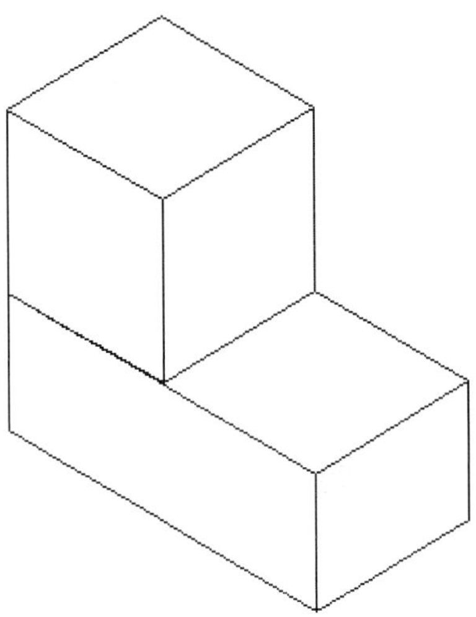

FIG. 9.3.1.1.8 Cube Drawn on Center (hidden lines removed)

Command: *[enter]*

9. We will draw one more to see the **Length** option. Repeat the command.

Specify corner of box or [CEnter] <0,0,0>:

10. Pick the corner of the existing box at coordinates 6,4,1.5 as the first **corner**.

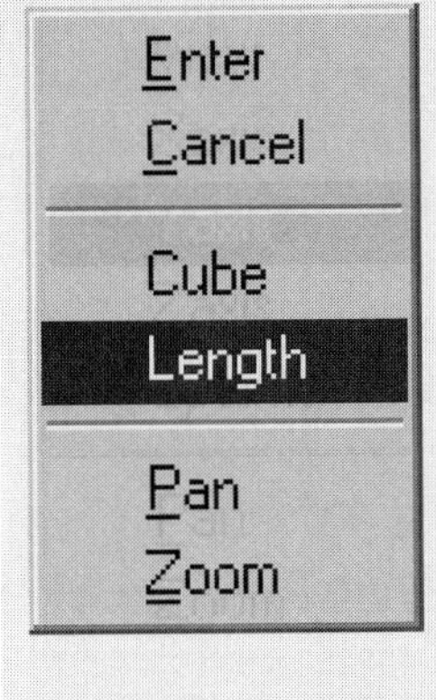

Specify corner or [Cube/Length]: *l*

11. Use the **Length** option.

continued

TOOLS	COMMAND SEQUENCE	STEPS
	Specify length: *2* **Specify width:** *2* **Specify height:** *2*	**12.** And specify the **length**, **width**, and **height** as shown. Your drawing looks like Figure 9.3.1.1.12. FIG. 9.3.1.1.12 Completed Drawing
	Command: *save*	**13.** Save the drawing as *MyBlocks—Boxes.dwg* in the C:\Steps3D\Lesson09 folder.

Does it remind you of playing with blocks when you were a child? Well, now you can make a living playing with those blocks!

■ 9.3.2 Wedge

The similarities between the ***AI_Box*** command and the ***AI_Wedge*** command hold true for the ***Box*** and ***Wedge*** commands as well. The command sequence for the ***Wedge*** command looks like this:

Command: *wedge* **(or** *we***)**

Specify first corner of wedge or [CEnter] <0,0,0>: *[identify the first corner of the wedge (this will be the right-angled corner)]*

Specify corner or [Cube/Length]: *[identify the opposite corner of the wedge]*

Specify height: *[tell AutoCAD how tall to make the wedge]*
Command:

Look familiar? The prompts and the options are identical to those of the ***Box*** command. The only additional information you need is to know that the first corner of the wedge identifies the right angle.

We will draw a couple of wedges for practice.

9.3.2.1 Do This: Drawing Solid Wedges

I. Start a new drawing from scratch.

II. Adjust the viewpoint to see the drawing from a SE Isometric View (1,−1,1).

III. Follow these steps:

TOOLS	COMMAND SEQUENCE	STEPS
Wedge Button	**Command:** *we*	**1.** Enter the ***Wedge*** command by typing ***wedge*** or ***we*** at the command prompt. Or you can pick the **Wedge** button on the Solids toolbar.
	Specify first corner of wedge or [CEnter] <0,0,0>: *1,1*	**2.** Start the wedge as shown.
	Specify corner or [Cube/Length]: *@−4,2* **Specify height:** *1.5*	**3.** Point the wedge away from the screen by using a negative **X** value, as shown, and give it a height of ***1.5*** units. Your wedge looks like Figure 9.3.2.1.3. FIG. 9.3.2.1.3 *Wedge*
	Command: *[enter]*	**4.** Now we will use the **Cube** option. Repeat the command.

continued

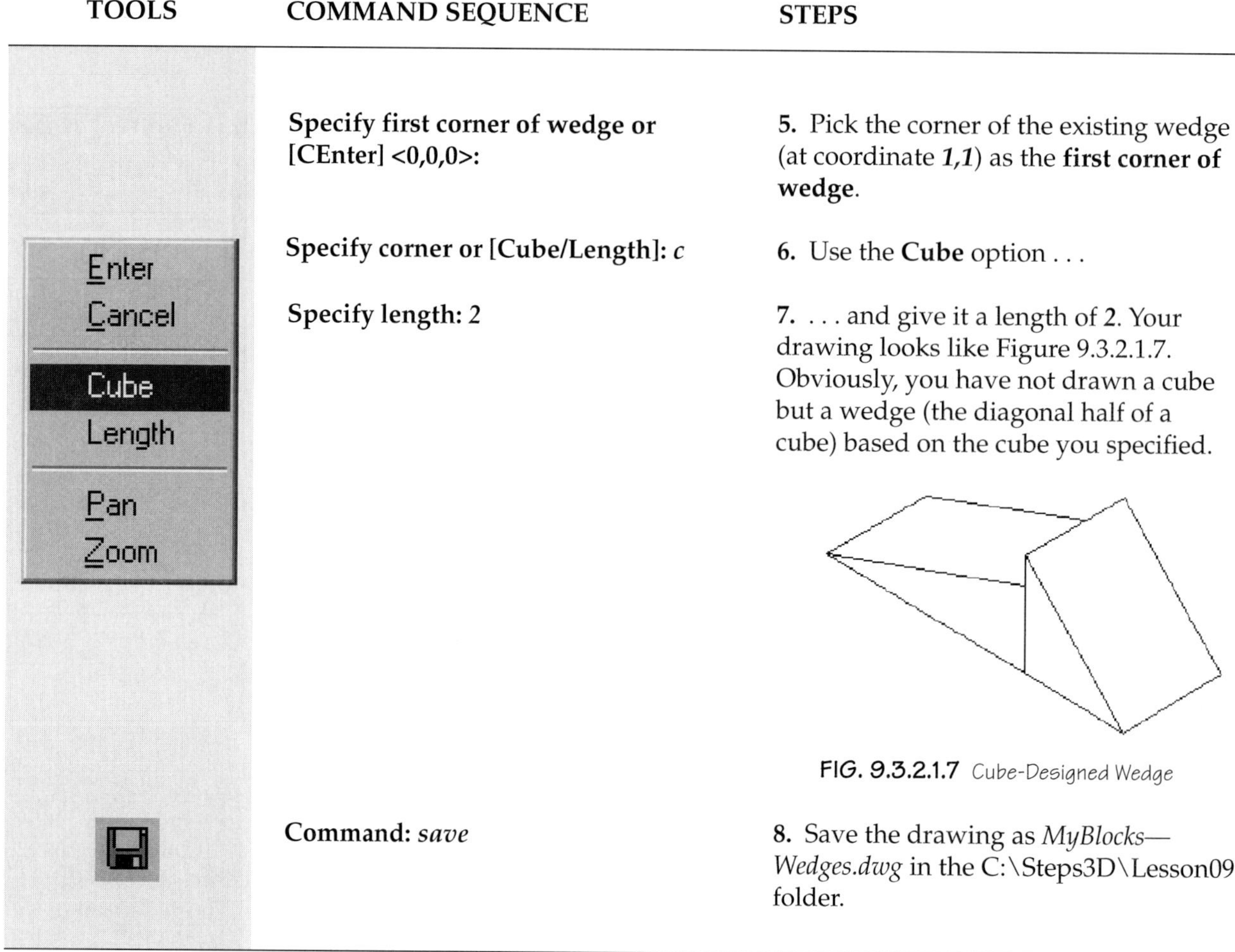

TOOLS	COMMAND SEQUENCE	STEPS
	Specify first corner of wedge or [CEnter] <0,0,0>:	**5.** Pick the corner of the existing wedge (at coordinate ***1,1***) as the **first corner of wedge**.
Enter Cancel Cube Length Pan Zoom	**Specify corner or [Cube/Length]:** *c*	**6.** Use the **Cube** option . . .
	Specify length: 2	**7.** . . . and give it a length of **2**. Your drawing looks like Figure 9.3.2.1.7. Obviously, you have not drawn a cube but a wedge (the diagonal half of a cube) based on the cube you specified. **FIG. 9.3.2.1.7** Cube-Designed Wedge
	Command: *save*	**8.** Save the drawing as *MyBlocks—Wedges.dwg* in the C:\Steps3D\Lesson09 folder.

You probably noticed that the ***Wedge*** command does not have a rotation angle prompt like the ***AI_Wedge*** command did. You can orient the solid wedge as you draw it (using positive or negative numbers), or you can use the ***Rotate*** or ***Rotate3D*** command to point it in the desired direction.

9.3.3 Cones and Cylinders

Although the command sequence for solid cones is shorter (and easier) than its Surface Model counterpart, it was not shortened without sacrifice. But the sacrifices are offset by some new opportunities.

The differences between the two mean that

- you cannot draw a solid cylinder with the ***Cone*** command (you will use the ***Cylinder*** command instead);
- all solid cones come to a point at one end, so creating a megaphone shape becomes more difficult;

- it is possible to draw an *elliptical* solid cone but not an elliptical Surface Model cone;
- drawing solid cones and cylinders is often faster and produces more rounded shapes.

The ***Cone*** and ***Cylinder*** command sequences are almost identical. The ***Cone*** command looks like this:

Command: *cone*

Current wire frame density: ISOLINES=4

Specify center point for base of cone or [Elliptical] <0,0,0>: *[identify the center point for the base of the cone]*

Specify radius for base of cone or [Diameter]: *[identify the radius for the base of the cone]*

Specify height of cone or [Apex]: *[tell AutoCAD how tall to make the cone]*

Command:

And the ***Cylinder*** command sequence looks like this:

Command: *cylinder*

Current wire frame density: ISOLINES=4

Specify center point for base of cylinder or [Elliptical] <0,0,0>: *[identify the center point for the base of the cylinder]*

Specify radius for base of cylinder or [Diameter]: *[identify the radius for the base of the cylinder]*

Specify height of cylinder or [Center of other end]: *[tell AutoCAD how tall to make the cylinder]*

Command:

The options are fairly straightforward. Let's take a look.

- Before starting, of course, AutoCAD reminds you of the **Isolines** setting.
- The first option of both commands is an opportunity to draw elliptical cones or cylinders. Simply type ***E*** to access this option. AutoCAD's prompts will change slightly to resemble the standard ***Ellipse*** command prompts:

Specify axis endpoint of ellipse for base of cone or [Center]:

Specify second axis endpoint of ellipse for base of cone:

Specify length of other axis for base of cone:

- The next option allows the user to specify a base radius or diameter (type ***D*** for the diameter option).
- The last lines of each prompt ask for the same thing, although they are worded a bit differently. An **Apex** or **Center of other end** allows the user to draw cones or cylinders that are not straight up and down. Use one of these options and pick an off-center point to change the direction to which the cone or cylinder points.

Try your hand at the solid approach to cones and cylinders in an exercise.

9.3.3.1 Do This: Drawing Solid Cones and Cylinders

I. Start a new drawing from scratch.

II. Adjust the viewpoint to see the drawing from a SE Isometric View (1,−1,1).

III. Set the **Isolines** system variable to 24 for clarity.

IV. Follow these steps:

TOOLS	COMMAND SEQUENCE	STEPS
Cone Button	**Command:** ***cone***	**1.** Enter the ***Cone*** command by typing ***cone*** at the command prompt. Or you can pick the **Cone** button on the Solids toolbar. (We will complete the sequence with the ***Cone*** command. Then we will repeat it using the ***Cylinder*** command.)
	Current wire frame density: ISOLINES=24 **Specify center point for base of cone or [Elliptical] <0,0,0>:** *2,8*	**2.** We will use default options on the first cone/cylinder. Place the first cone at coordinate *2,8* (the first cylinder at coordinate *8,8*).
	Specify radius for base of cone or [Diameter]: 2 **Specify height of cone or [Apex]:** *4*	**3.** Give the cone/cylinder a base radius of 2 and a height of **4**.

continued

TOOLS	COMMAND SEQUENCE	STEPS
Cylinder Button	**Command:** ***cylinder***	**4.** Repeat Steps 1 through 3 using the ***Cylinder*** command. Your drawing looks like Figure 9.3.3.1.4.
	Command: ***cone***	**5.** Let's use our new commands to draw an elliptical cone and then an elliptical cylinder. Repeat the ***Cone*** command.
	Current wire frame density: ISOLINES=24	**6.** Choose the **Elliptical** option.
	Specify center point for base of cone or [Elliptical] <0,0,0>: ***e***	
	Specify axis endpoint of ellipse for base of cone or [Center]: ***0,4***	**7.** Place the **axis endpoint of ellipse for base of cone** at coordinate ***0,4***. (Place the **axis endpoint of ellipse for base of cylinder** at ***6,4***.)
	Specify second axis endpoint of ellipse for base of cone: ***4,4***	**8.** Place the **second axis endpoint of ellipse for base of cone** at coordinate ***4,4***. (Place the **second axis endpoint of ellipse for base of cylinder** at ***10,4***.)
	Specify length of other axis for base of cone: ***1***	**9.** The **length of other axis** should be ***1*** . . .
	Specify height of cone or [Apex]: ***4***	**10.** . . . and the height should be ***4***.
	Command: ***cylinder***	**11.** Repeat Steps 5 through 10 for the ***Cylinder*** command as indicated. Your drawing looks like Figure 9.3.3.1.11.

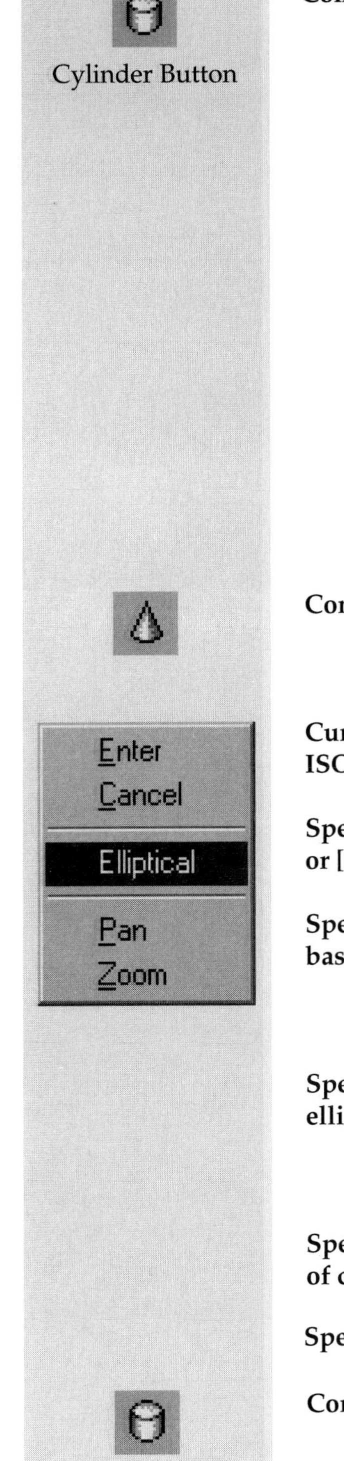

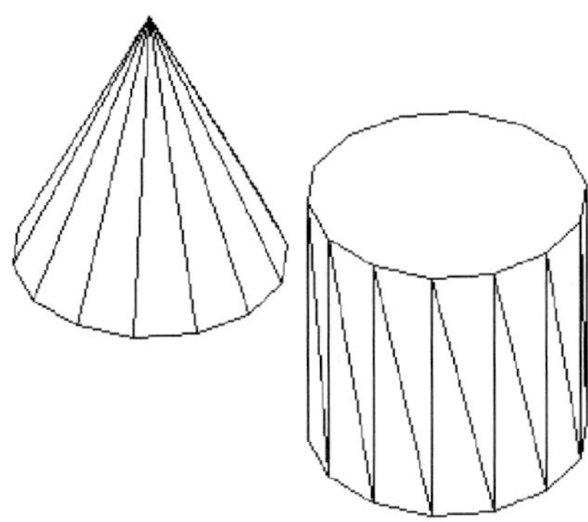

FIG. 9.3.3.1.4 Cone and Cylinder (hidden lines removed)

continued

TOOLS	COMMAND SEQUENCE	STEPS

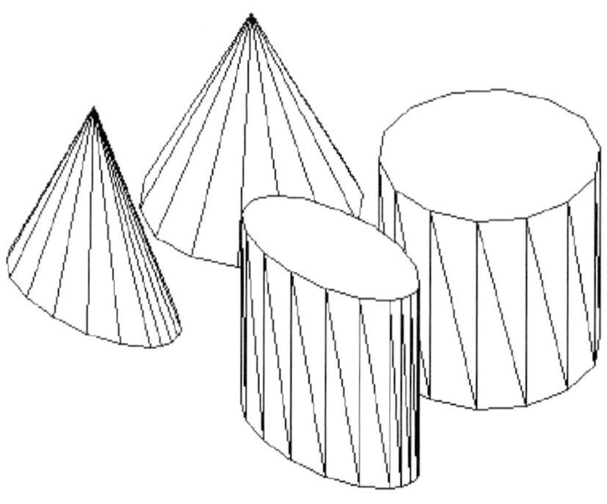

FIG. 9.3.3.1.11 Elliptical Cone and Cylinder (hidden lines removed)

TOOLS	COMMAND SEQUENCE	STEPS
	Command: ***cone***	**12.** Now use the **Apex/Center of other end** option to change the direction of the cone/cylinder. Repeat the ***Cone*** command.
	Current wire frame density: ISOLINES=24	**13.** Place the base point of the cone at ***2,0,2***. (Place the base point of the cylinder at ***8,0,2***.)
	Specify center point for base of cone or [Elliptical] <0,0,0>: ***2,0,2***	
Enter Cancel Diameter Pan Zoom	**Specify radius for base of cone or [Diameter]:** ***d***	**14.** Set the **diameter** of the base at ***4***.
	Specify diameter for base of cone: ***4***	
	**Specify height of cone or [Apex]:** ***a***	**15.** This time, use the **Apex** (or **Center of other end**) option. Place the **Apex** of the cone at ***2,−4,2***. (Place the **Center of other end** of the cylinder at ***8,−4,2***.)
	Specify apex point: ***2,−4,2***	

continued

TOOLS	COMMAND SEQUENCE	STEPS
	Command: *cylinder*	**16.** Repeat Steps 12 through 15 using the ***Cylinder*** command as indicated. Your drawing looks like Figure 9.3.3.1.16.
	Command: *save*	**17.** Save the drawing as *MyBlocks—Cones.dwg* in the C:\Steps3D\Lesson09 folder.

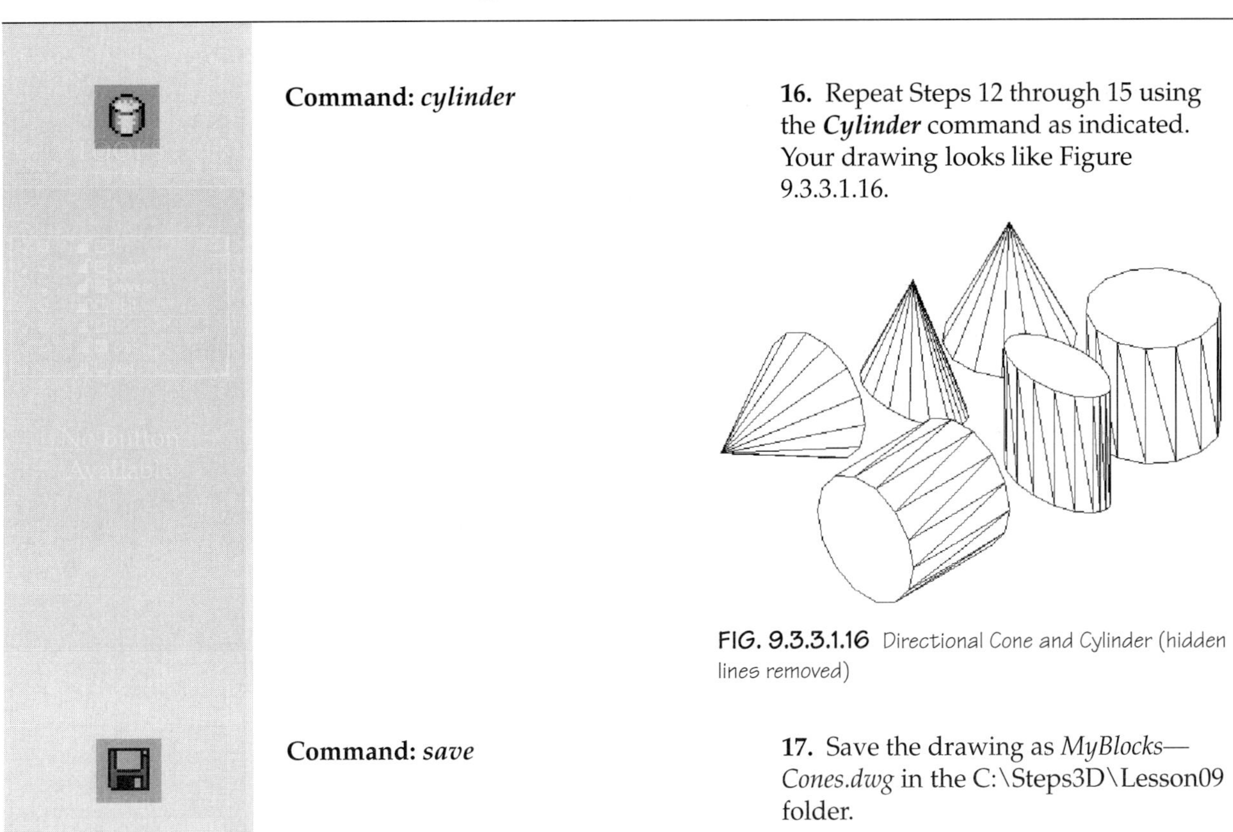

FIG. 9.3.3.1.16 Directional Cone and Cylinder (hidden lines removed)

It is interesting that these commands use the same procedures to produce such similar objects. Perhaps, in the future, AutoCAD will reduce them to one command with a **Cone/Cylinder** option.

9.3.4 Sphere

The sphere is another object whose production was greatly simplified between creation of the ***AI_Sphere*** command and the solid ***Sphere*** command. Indeed, we have gone from five prompts and three options to two prompts and one option! And the option is the common radius/diameter choice available in so many commands.

Here is the solid ***Sphere*** command sequence:

Command: *sphere*

Current wire frame density: ISOLINES=4

Specify center of sphere <0,0,0>: *[identify the center of the sphere]*

Specify radius of sphere or [Diameter]: *[how big do you want it?]*

Command:

Although AutoCAD does not prompt for the number of longitudinal or latitudinal segments, it is a good idea to set the **Isolines** system variable to a large enough number for proper viewing. But that is something you should do early in the drawing session. It does not have to be repeated for each command.

Draw a sphere.

9.3.4.1 Do This: Drawing a Solid Sphere

I. Start a new drawing from scratch.

II. Adjust the viewpoint to see the drawing from a SE Isometric View (1,−1,1).

III. Set the **Isolines** system variable to 64 for clarity.

IV. Follow these steps:

TOOLS	COMMAND SEQUENCE	STEPS
Sphere Button	**Command:** ***sphere***	**1.** Enter the ***Sphere*** command by typing ***sphere*** at the command line. Or you can pick the **Sphere** button on the Solids toolbar.
	Current wire frame density: ISOLINES=64	**2.** Locate the **center of sphere** as indicated . . .
	Specify center of sphere <0,0,0>: ***4,4,4***	
	Specify radius of sphere or [Diameter]: ***2***	**3.** . . . and give it a radius of **2**. Your drawing looks like Figure 9.3.4.1.3. FIG. 9.3.4.1.3 Sphere (hidden lines removed)
	Command: ***save***	**4.** Save the drawing as *MyBlocks—Sphere.dwg* in the C:\Steps3D\Lesson09 folder.

There is nothing else to show you about spheres. AutoCAD simplicity—what a marvel!

You will notice the lack of a ***Dome*** or ***Dish*** command on the Solids toolbar. That is because these objects are not normally solid. If, however, you need a solid dome or dish, you can use the ***Subtract*** command covered in the next lesson to create it.

9.3.5 Torus

There is a subtle difference in the way you drew the Surface Model torus and how you will draw a solid torus. But the difference will drive you crazy if you are not aware of it.

The difference lies in the way you size the torus itself (as opposed to sizing the tube of the torus). When you gave a radius or diameter for the Surface Model torus, you were indicating how large it would be from the center to the outer edge of the torus. When you give a radius or diameter for a solid torus, you are indicating the distance from the center of the torus to the center of the tube that forms the torus.

Consider the tori shown in Figure 9.3.5a. The torus on the left is a Surface Model; the torus on the right is a Solid Model. Both have a torus diameter of 4 and a tube diameter of 1. But the torus diameter of the Surface Model measures the distance to the *outer edge* of the tube, whereas the diameter of the Solid Model measures the distance to the *center* of the tube. Bear this in mind when drawing surface or solid tori.

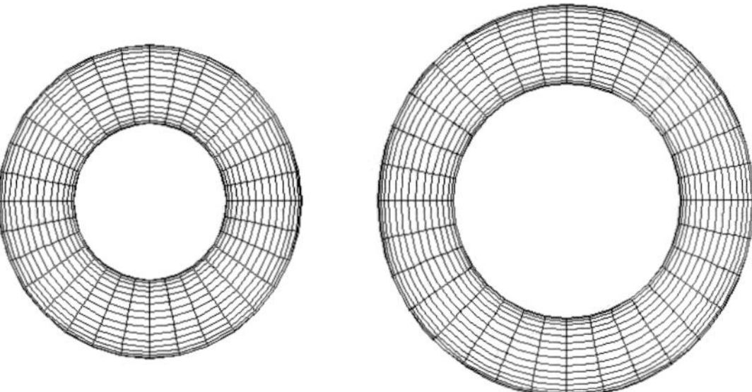

FIG. 9.3.5a Tori

The command sequence for a solid torus (like the other solid sequences) is shorter than its Surface Model counterpart. It looks like this:

Command: ***torus*** **(or** ***tor*****)**

Current wire frame density: ISOLINES=4

Specify center of torus <0,0,0>: *[locate the center of the torus]*

Specify radius of torus or [Diameter]: *[indicate the size of the torus]*

Specify radius of tube or [Diameter]: *[indicate the size of the tube that will make up the torus]*

Command:

As with the *Sphere* command, it is a good idea to set the **Isolines** system variable to a large enough number for proper viewing.

Draw a torus.

9.3.5.1 Do This: Drawing a Solid Torus

I. Start a new drawing from scratch.

II. Adjust the viewpoint to see the drawing from a SE Isometric View (1,−1,1).

III. Set the **Isolines** system variable to 64 for clarity.

IV. Follow these steps:

TOOLS	COMMAND SEQUENCE	STEPS
Torus Button	**Command:** *tor*	**1.** Enter the *Torus* command by typing *torus* or *tor* at the command line. Or you can pick the **Torus** button on the Solids toolbar.
	Current wire frame density: ISOLINES=64	**2.** Locate the torus as indicated.
	Specify center of torus <0,0,0>: *4,4,1*	
	Specify radius of torus or [Diameter]: *3* **Specify radius of tube or [Diameter]:** *.5*	**3.** Size the torus and the tube as indicated. Your drawing looks like Figure 9.3.5.1.3. **FIG. 9.3.5.1.3** Torus (hidden lines removed)
	Command: *[enter]*	**4.** The *Torus* command cries for experimentation. Let's play a little. What happens when the tube diameter is larger than the torus diameter? Repeat the *Torus* command.

continued

TOOLS	COMMAND SEQUENCE	STEPS
	Current wire frame density: ISOLINES=64	**5.** Let's put this torus in the center of the first one.
	Specify center of torus <0,0,0>: *4,4,2*	
	Specify radius of torus or [Diameter]: *−3*	**6.** Just for fun, let's give the radius of the torus a negative number . . .
	Specify radius of tube or [Diameter]: *6*	**7.** . . . and the tube a larger number. Your drawing looks like Figure 9.3.5.1.7 (okay, I used the Shademode to enhance the image, but you can, too). (Whoa, cool! See what you can discover with a bit of experimentation!) FIG. 9.3.5.1.7 Football-Shaped Torus
	Command: *save*	**8.** Save the drawing as *MyBlocks—Torus.dwg* in the C:\Steps3D\Lesson09 folder.

Oh, the fun you can have with a computer, AutoCAD, time, and a little imagination!

9.4 Creating More Complex Solids Using the *Revolve* Command

After we studied the predefined Surface Model objects in Lesson 6, we spent another lesson studying more complex Surface Models. We covered six commands: ***Rulesurf***, ***Revsurf***, ***Tabsurf***, ***Edgesurf***, ***3DMesh***, and ***PFace***.

Tabsurf is easily replaced by the ***Extrude*** command we saw at the beginning of this lesson. But it may please you to know that, with one exception, the rest of the surface-specific commands have no solid equivalents.

The exception involves your favorite command (and mine)—***Revsurf***. Remember the nifty shapes we created on our train back in Lesson 7 (the top of the smokestack, the wheels, the bell)? It would be a shame not to be able to create such objects as solids.

For that reason, AutoCAD has provided the ***Revolve*** command. But unlike the other solid commands and their Surface Modeling counterparts, ***Revolve*** is just a bit more difficult to use than ***Revsurf***. But this is mostly because of the additional options involved. Here is the command sequence:

Command: ***revolve*** **(or** ***rev*****)**

Current wire frame density: ISOLINES=4

Select objects: ***[select the object that defines the basic shape of the object you wish to create—you may select multiple objects, but each object must be closed]***

Select objects: ***[hit enter to confirm the selection]***

Specify start point for axis of revolution or

define axis by [Object/X (axis)/Y (axis)]: ***[select a point on the axis of revolution]***

Specify endpoint of axis: ***[select another point to define the axis]***

Specify angle of revolution <360>: ***[tell AutoCAD how much of a revolution you want]***

Command:

The first options do not occur until AutoCAD prompts you for an **axis of revolution**. Then you have four.

- The default option requires that you specify a point on the axis. AutoCAD will then ask you to specify another point.
- You may also define the axis by **Object**. When you choose this option, AutoCAD asks you to **Select an object.** Select an object that exists in the current XY plane and AutoCAD will do the rest.

One of the main differences between ***Revsurf*** and ***Revolve*** is that ***Revsurf*** will create an object through revolution *without regard to the UCS*. ***Revolve*** requires that the axis of rotation exist in the current UCS.

Another important difference is that the shape being revolved with the ***Revolve*** command must be a *closed* shape. Ideal objects to revolve include polylines, polygons, rectangles, circles, ellipses, and regions.

- The **X (axis)** or **Y (axis)** option will revolve the object about the selected axis using coordinate 0,0 as the center of the revolution.

- AutoCAD presents the last option after you have made the axis of revolution decision. This option allows you to control the **angle of revolution** (how much of a revolution do you want?). Simply enter an angle in degrees.

You can also access the ***Revolve*** command using the Draw pull-down menu. Follow this path:

Draw—Solids—Revolve

Let's see the ***Revolve*** command in action.

WWW

9.4.1 Do This: Drawing a 3DSolid with the *Revolve* Command

I. Open the *finial.dwg* file in the C:\Steps3D\Lesson09 folder. The drawing looks like Figure 9.4.1a.

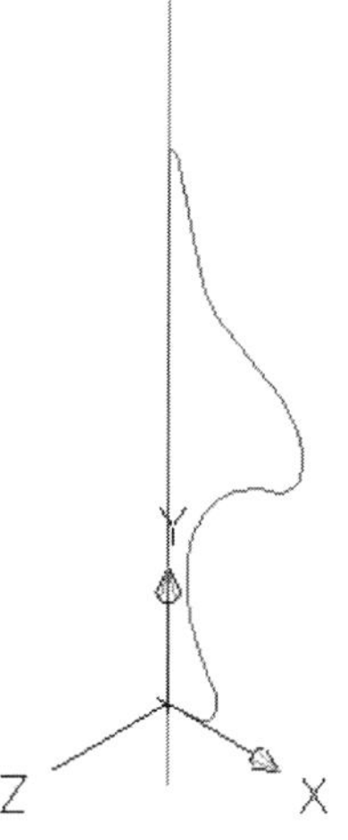

FIG. 9.4.1a Finial.dwg

II. Notice the orientation of the UCS and where it is centered; then turn ***off*** the UCS icon.

III. Be sure the **obj1** layer and the Gouraud Shademode are current.

IV. Follow these steps:

TOOLS	COMMAND SEQUENCE	STEPS
 Revolve Button	**Command:** *rev*	**1.** Enter the ***Revolve*** command by typing ***revolve*** or ***rev*** at the command prompt. Or you can pick the **Revolve** button on the Solids toolbar.
	Select objects:	**2.** Select the shape and confirm the selection.
	Select objects: *[enter]*	
	Specify start point for axis of revolution or define axis by [Object/X (axis)/ Y (axis)]: *_endpt*	**3.** Using OSNAPs, pick the endpoints of the vertical line to define your **axis of revolution**. (Pick the bottom endpoint first.)
	Specify endpoint of axis: *_endpt*	
	Specify angle of revolution <360>: *270*	**4.** Revolve the object ***270°***. Your drawing looks like Figure 9.4.1.4. Notice that the solid is created on the current layer.

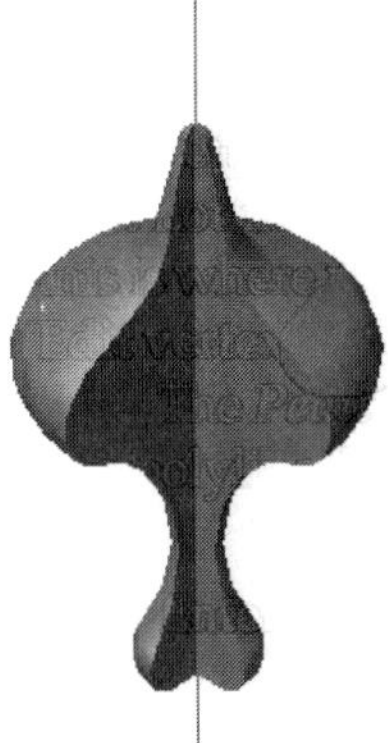

FIG. 9.4.1.4 Revolved Shape (three-quarter finial)

TOOLS	COMMAND SEQUENCE	STEPS
	Command: *u*	**5.** Undo the change.
	Command: *rev*	**6.** Let's use an object to define our axis. Repeat Steps 1 and 2.
Enter Cancel Object X (axis) Y (axis) Pan Zoom	**Specify start point for axis of revolution or define axis by [Object/X (axis)/Y (axis)]:** *o*	**7.** Tell AutoCAD you will use an **Object** to define the **axis of revolution**.
	Select an object:	**8.** Then select the vertical line.

continued

TOOLS	COMMAND SEQUENCE	STEPS
	Specify angle of revolution <360>: *[enter]*	**9.** Accept the default ***360°*** this time. Your drawing looks like Figure 9.4.1.9. FIG. 9.4.1.9 Full Finial
	Command: *u*	**10.** Undo the change.
	Command: *rev*	**11.** Let's use the Y-axis to define our axis of revolution. Repeat Steps 1 and 2.
	Specify start point for axis of revolution or define axis by [Object/X (axis)/Y (axis)]: *y*	**12.** Tell AutoCAD to revolve the objects about the Y-axis.
	Specify angle of revolution <360>:	**13.** Accept the **360°** default rotation. Your drawing again looks like Figure 9.4.1.9 (see Step 9).
	Command: *u*	**14.** Undo the change.
	Command: *[enter]*	**15.** Let's see what happens when we use the X-axis to define our axis of revolution. Repeat Steps 1 and 2.

continued

TOOLS	COMMAND SEQUENCE	STEPS
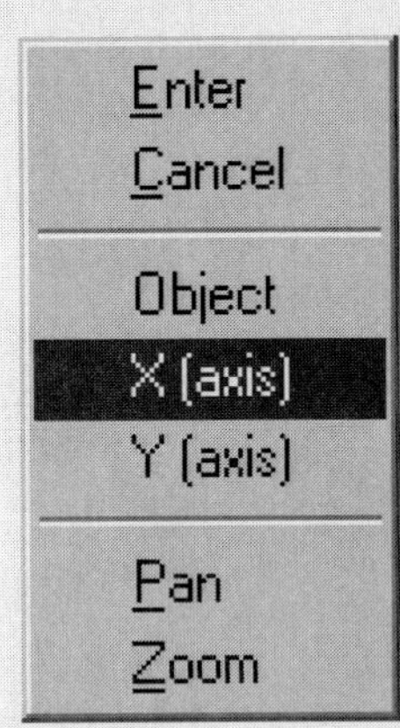 	**Specify start point for axis of revolution or define axis by [Object/X (axis)/Y (axis)]:** *x*	**16.** This time, tell AutoCAD to revolve the objects about the X-axis . . .
	Specify angle of revolution <360>:	**17.** . . . and accept the **360°** default rotation. Your drawing now looks like Figure 9.4.1.17 (Your finial has become an ashtray—does that deserve another "Whoa, cool?").  **FIG. 9.4.1.17** Ashtray (rotated to hold the ashes)
	Command: *saveas*	**18.** Save the drawing as *MyAshtray.dwg* in the C:\Steps3D\Lesson09 folder.

9.5 Extra Steps

- You will notice a second CD in the box in which AutoCAD was shipped. This is the AutoCAD Learning Assistant (ALA). Follow the instructions included in the box to install the ALA (if you have not already done so). Access the ALA from within AutoCAD by selecting **Learning Assistant** under the Help pull-down menu. Take some time to get acquainted with it.

  A good place to begin will be the section on Creating Basic 3D Solids. Follow this path on the Contents page:

  Tutorials—Working in Three Dimensions—Creating Basic 3D Solids

  (You might also look at Creating 3D Surfaces.)

  View the demo(s) and then pick the **Try It** jump at the top of the section. This will place an instructional window atop AutoCAD's window, which will lead you through an exercise.

- Familiarize yourself with the various other categories in the ALA and return to it for help and reinforcement as often as necessary.

9.6 What Have We Learned?

Items covered in this lesson include

- *AutoCAD's Solid Modeling Building Blocks*
  - ***Extrude***
  - ***Box***
  - ***Wedge***
  - ***Cone***
  - ***Sphere***
  - ***Cylinder***
  - ***Torus***
  - ***Revolve***
- *Support for the building blocks*
  - ***Isolines***

This has been another fun lesson! (We need these occasionally.) The commands have been simple and straightforward.

In Lesson 9, you saw how to draw familiar shapes as solids rather than simple Surface Models. You also had the opportunity to use AutoCAD's ***Extrude*** command—this one is the basis for most 2D-to-3D conversion packages. Did you feel like a kid again—opening a new box of blocks for the first time and exploring each wooden shape? Did your mind slip ever so slightly into that thin mist that inevitably precedes any great discovery? Did you start to create vague mental objects using the shapes as building blocks? How many times did you begin a thought with the words, "I can use this for . . . " or "This is a lot easier than . . . "?

The Solid Modeling bug has bitten you!

Actually, you may not be quite bitten . . . yet. But wait until you finish Lessons 10 and 11! There you will get to play with your new building blocks in ways you never dreamed possible back in your nursery. You will see ways to combine blocks that were simply not possible until the advent of the computer. Wait until you see . . . .

But first we must finish this lesson. Do the exercises. Get some practice. Answer the Review Questions. And then proceed!

9.7 EXERCISES

To get the opportunity to compare Solid Modeling to Surface Modeling, repeat the exercises you did in those lessons. Use solids whenever possible.

1. **through 6.** Create the drawings in Exercises 6.6.9 through 6.6.14 (in Lesson 6) using solids instead of Surface Models. Save the drawings to the C:\Steps3D\Lesson09 folder.
7. **through 12.** Create the drawings in Exercises 7.6.1 through 7.6.3, and Exercises 7.6.6 through 7.6.8 (in Lesson 7) using solids instead of Surface Models. Save the drawings to the C:\Steps3D\Lesson09 folder.

13. Create the paper clip drawing shown in Figure 9.7.13.
    - **13.1.** The drawing is set up and dimensioned using metrics.
    - **13.2.** The paper clip is a single solid object.
    - **13.3.** Save the drawing as *MyClip.dwg* in the C:\Steps3D\Lesson09 folder.

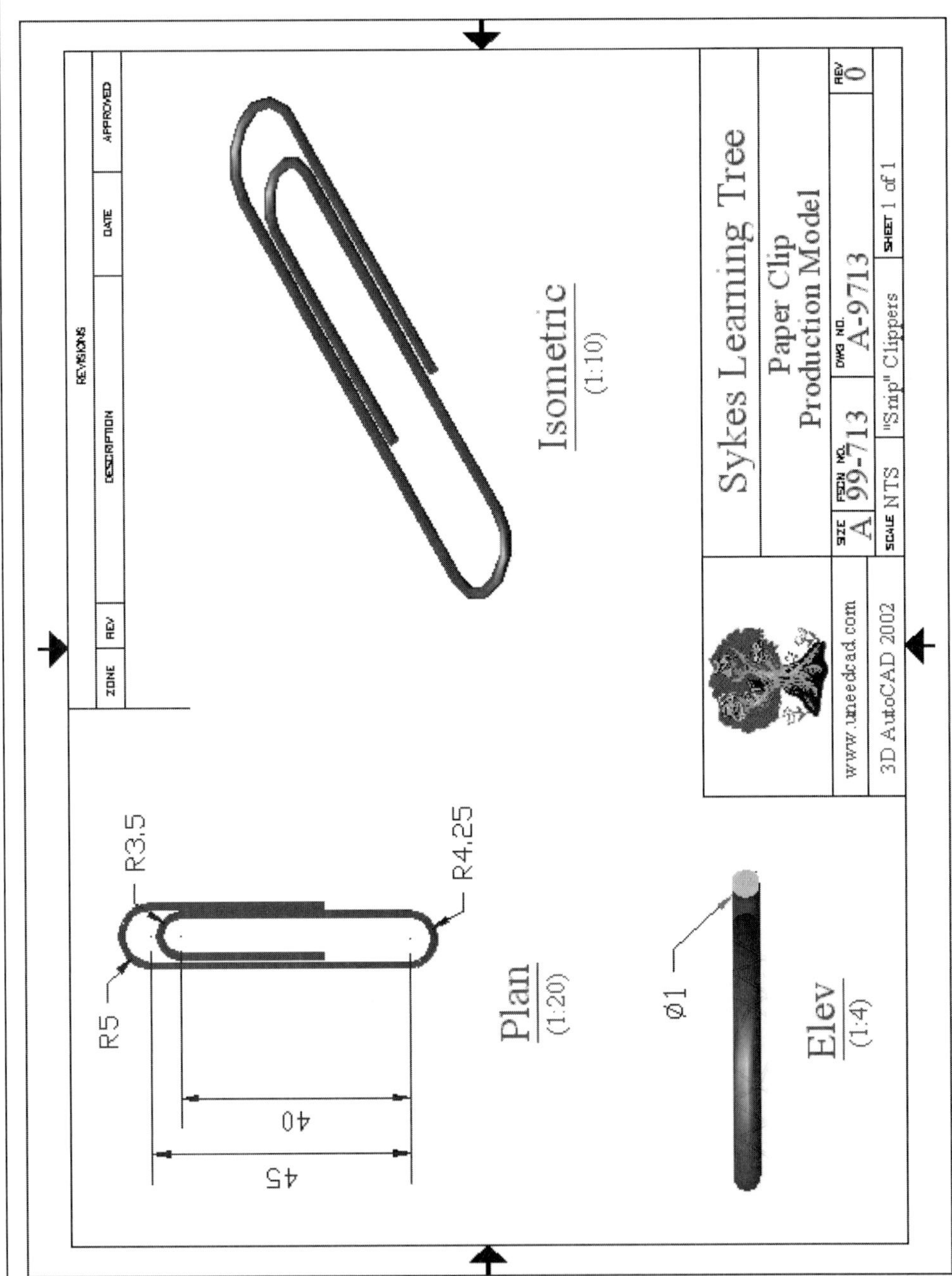

FIG. 9.7.13 Paper Clip

14. Create the fan cover drawing in Figure 9.7.14.
    - **14.1.** Each of the wires is $\frac{1}{16}''$ in diameter (including the torus around the frame).
    - **14.2.** The center plate is $\frac{1}{8}''$ thick.
    - **14.3.** Save the drawing as *MyFanCover.dwg* in the C:\Steps3D\Lesson09 folder.

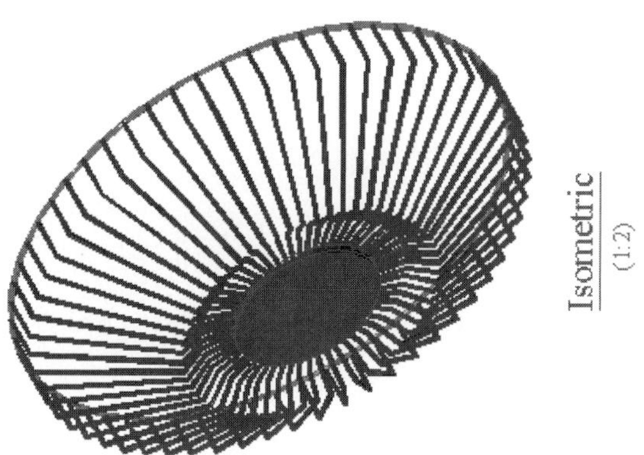

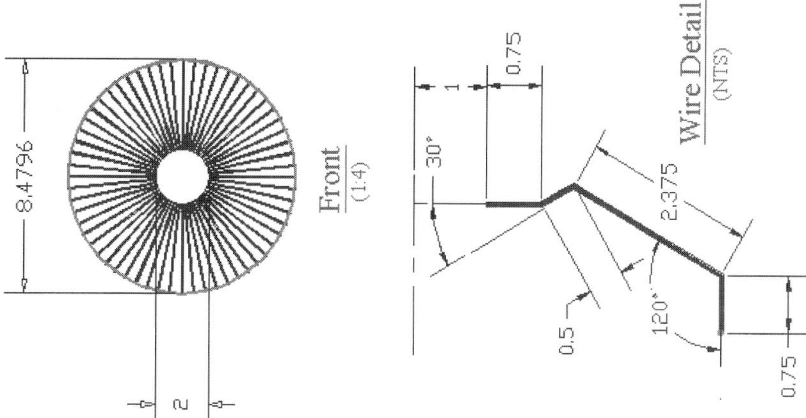

FIG. 9.7.14 Fan Cover

15. Create the round planter drawing shown in Figure 9.7.15. Follow these guidelines.

15.1. Use the *ANSI A Title Block* found in the \Acad2002\Template folder.

15.2. Text size is $\frac{3}{16}''$ and $\frac{1}{8}''$.

15.3. Save the drawing as *MyPlanter.dwg* in the C:\Steps3D\Lesson09 folder.

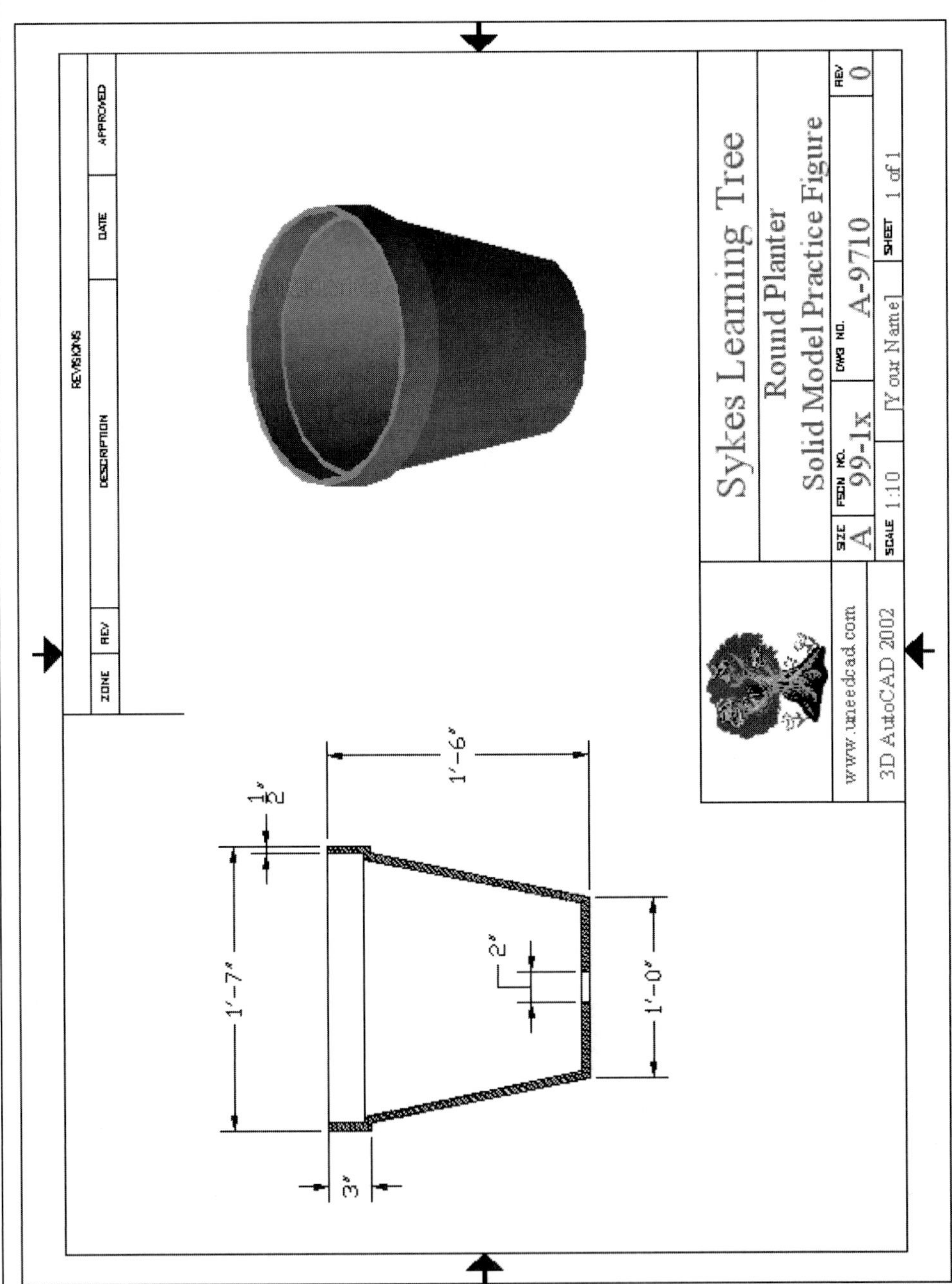

FIG. 9.7.15 Round Planter

16. Create the double helix drawing shown in Figure 9.7.16. Follow these guidelines.
    16.1. The balls are 1″ diameter.
    16.2. The rods are $\frac{1}{8}$″ diameter × 1″ long.
    16.3. Each pairing rotates 15°.
    16.4. Save the drawing as *MyGenes.dwg* in the C:\Steps3D\Lesson09 folder.

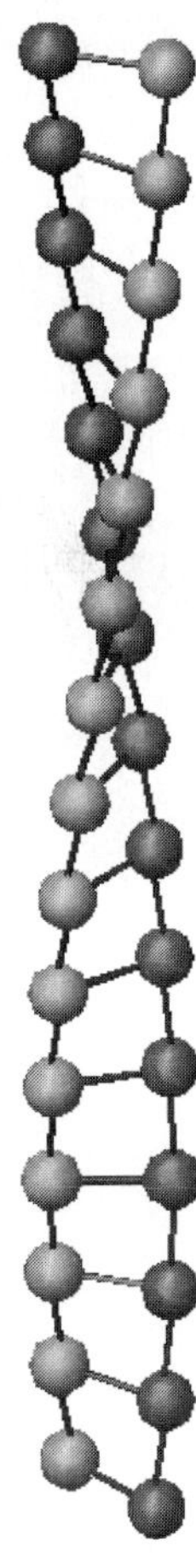

FIG. 9.7.16 Double Helix

17. Create the fence drawing shown in Figure 9.7.17. Follow these guidelines.

- **17.1.** The posts are 4 × 4s ($3\frac{1}{2}''$ × $3\frac{1}{2}''$).
- **17.2.** The slats are 1 × 4s ($\frac{3}{4}''$ × $3\frac{1}{2}''$). (I started with splines and turned them into regions.)
- **17.3.** The fence is 6″ above the ground.
- **17.4.** The center rail is a 1 × 2 ($\frac{3}{4}''$ × $1\frac{1}{2}''$).
- **17.5.** Save the drawing as *MyFence.dwg* in the C:\Steps3D\Lesson09 folder.

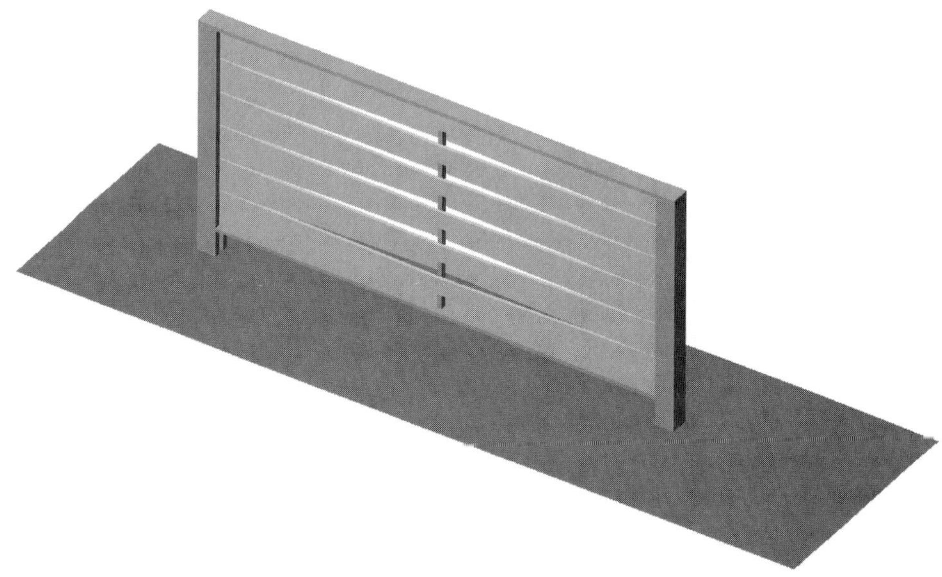

FIG. 9.7.17 *Fence*

18. Create the patio planter box drawing shown in Figure 9.7.18. Follow these guidelines.

18.1. Use the *ANSI A Title Block* found in the \Acad2002\Template folder.

18.2. Text size is $\frac{3}{16}''$ and $\frac{1}{8}''$.

18.3. Save the drawing as *MyPlanterBox.dwg* in the C:\Steps3D\Lesson09 folder.

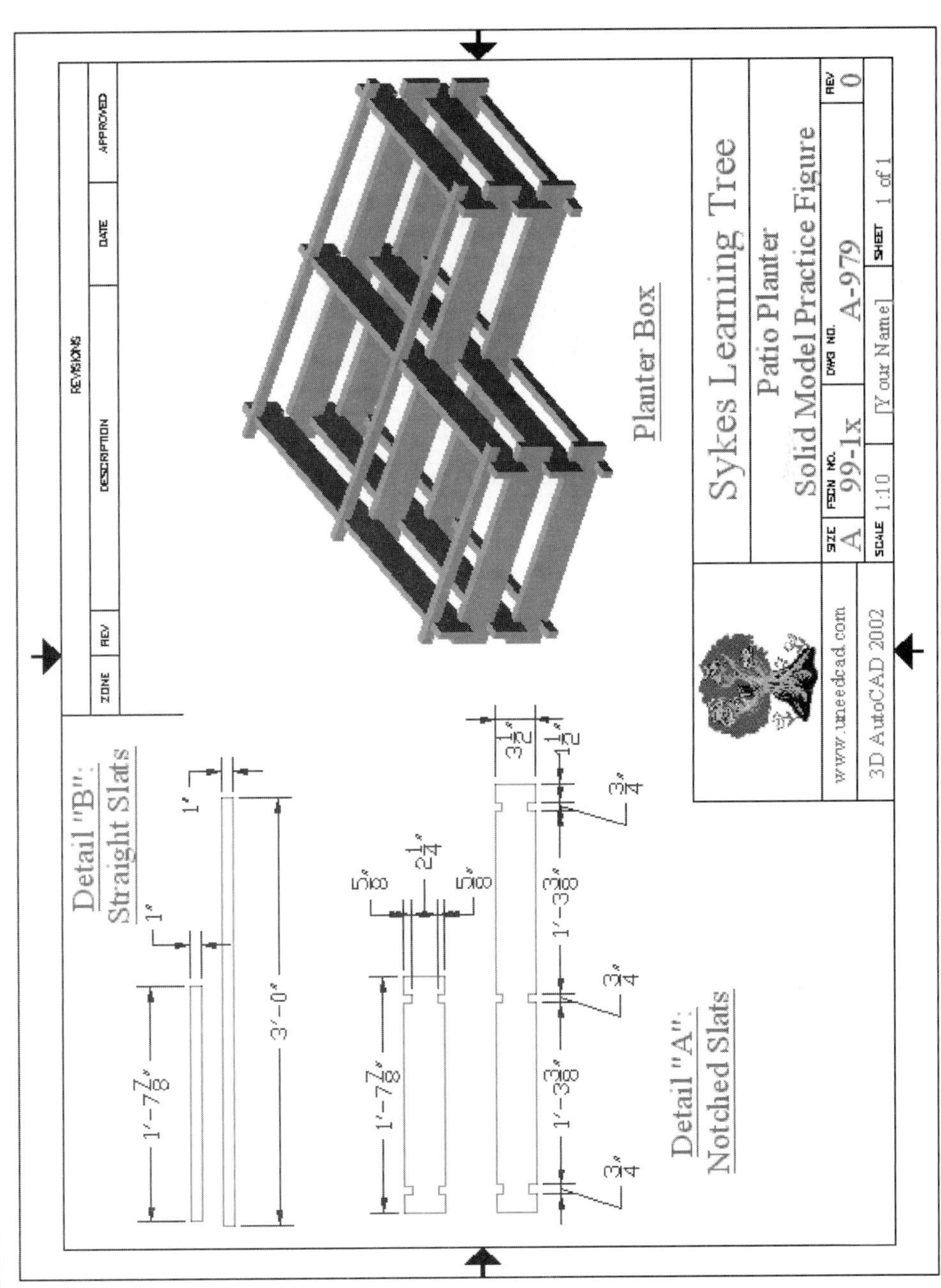

FIG. 9.7.18 Patio Planter Box

9.8 REVIEW QUESTIONS

Answer these questions on a separate sheet of paper.

1. A __________ is a cone with equal radii at both ends.
2. The __________ command creates 3D solids from two-dimensional regions and solids.
3. __________ are solid shapes—predefined and user defined—with which you build your model.
4. Control the number of lines used to draw a rounded object with the __________ system variable.
5. To draw a solid pyramid, use the __________ option of the Extrude command.
6. (T or F) It is necessary to redraw an object to view changes in the Isolines display.
7. (T or F) It is necessary to regenerate an object to view changes in the Isolines display.
8. (T or F) The Cube option of the Box command prompts only for the length of the box.
9. The Center option of the Box command identifies the center of the box along (the X- and Y-axes, the X-, Y-, and Z-axes).
10. Which prompt of the Wedge command identifies the location of the right angle?
11. Orient the solid wedge using the Rotate (command, option).
12. Use the __________ command to draw a solid cylinder.
13. (T or F) Unlike the AI_Cone command, you can draw an elliptical cone using the Cone command.
14. (T or F) There is no command to create a solid Dome or Dish.
15. Using the AI_Torus command, the size of the torus refers to the (distance from the center to the outer edge, distance from the center to the center of the tube).
16. Using the Torus command, the size of the torus refers to the (distance from the center to the outer edge, distance from the center to the center of the tube).
17. The Surface Modeling command that most closely resembles the solid Revolve command is __________.
18. When using the Object option to define the axis of revolution of the Revolve command, the object selected (must, does not have to) exist in the current XY plane.
19. Unlike the shape selected during the Revsurf command, the shape selected during the Revolve command must be __________.
20. (T or F) Unlike the Revsurf command, the Revolve command does not allow the user to control the angle of revolution.
21. The __________ command forms the basis for most 2D-to-3D conversion packages.

LESSON 10

Composite Solids

Following this lesson, you will

- Know how to create composite solids from AutoCAD's solid building blocks using these commands:
  - ***Union***
  - ***Subtract***
  - ***Intersect***
  - ***Slice***
  - ***Interfere***
- Know how to calculate mass properties of a solid
- Know how to create a cross section using the ***Section*** command
- Know how to shape solids using these commands:
  - ***Fillet***
  - ***Chamfer***

I think I can . . . I think I can . . . I think I can . . .

Watty Piper's *The Little Engine That Could*

You have made it through the beginnings of Solid Modeling. You have experienced successes and near misses throughout your study, but the semester is half over. You may be tired and thinking more about Christmas or Easter or Labor Day than AutoCAD. You may be wondering, "Why AutoCAD . . . why school . . . why spend all this time and money to educate (or reeducate) myself?"

Let's pause for a paragraph or two for some words of encouragement. Let me tell you where you are in the overall scheme of (AutoCAD) things.

In all professions there is a turning point—the point where the draftsman becomes the engineer, where the painter becomes the artist, the idea becomes the design. In every life there is (hopefully) a time where adolescence gives way to adulthood. In the world of computer drafting, you are at that turning point. You are about to leave the CAD Draftsman designation behind and become a true CAD Operator.

In the next two lessons, you will discover how to take the building blocks—3D Solids and all of the basic and advanced modifying tools you have learned (and some you will learn now)—and create *objects*. (Notice I did not say "create *drawings*.") You will show the objects you create *in* drawings, but be assured that you will be creating objects.

Once you have accomplished that very doable goal, I will show you how to apply materials to those objects—how to show the wood grain on a table or make glass transparent. We will cover this in the lesson on rendering.

But for now, let me offer these words of encouragement: Approach these lessons with the confidence of a graduate moving into graduate school. You have many successes under your belt, but the best is yet to come!

You may have noticed that AutoCAD has two Solids toolbars—the first is simply *Solids* and the second is *Solids Editing*. Between them, there are 32 opportunities for creating or modifying three-dimensional solid objects. We have already discussed eight of these—the Object Creation commands (*Box, Wedge, Cone, Cylinder, Sphere, Torus, Extrude,* and *Revolve*). I will group the remaining 24 into loose categories to help your understanding. These categories include Construction/Shaping Tools (*Slice, Section, Interfere, Union, Subtract, Intersect, Fillet,* and *Chamfer*), Solid Editing Tools (*Solidedit*), and Print Setup commands (*Solprof, Soldraw,* and *Solview*).

Obviously, that list does not add up to 24. The Solid Editing Tools consist of a single command; but like *Pedit*, it is a multifaceted command.

We will consider the Construction/Shaping Tools in Lesson 10, and then the *Solidedit* commands in Lesson 11. We will save the Print Setup commands for Lesson 12.

Let's begin.

10.1 Many Become One—Solid Construction Tools

When you were a child, did you ever wish you could fuse your playing blocks together in order to preserve a particularly clever building effort? You wanted to keep that castle or tower forever to demonstrate your prowess with the tools of your trade. You wanted your family and friends to be able to see—years from now—how you built the perfect model!

And then your sister rode through on her tricycle and your dreams were shattered.

Well, the programmers at AutoCAD had sisters, too. So they created a way to permanently fuse their computer blocks so that no one could ever disassemble them. Then they followed their childhood fantasies and created ways to remove parts of their blocks by using different shapes to define the carving. And they invented ways to find interferences between their blocks and to create cross sections . . .

. . . and their childhood dreams became reality in *Solid Modeling Construction Tools*.

Let's see how they work.

10.1.1 Union

The ***Union*** command behaves very much like a computer-controlled welding rod. It combines two solid objects into one. But unlike the welding rod, it leaves no seams that can break!

It is one of the simplest tools you will ever hope to find. The command sequence is

Command: ***union*** **(or** ***uni*****)**
Select objects: *[select the solids you wish to weld]*
Select objects: *[hit enter to confirm the selection]*
Command:

They just do not come any easier. But the value of the ***Union*** command cannot be overstated. It turns simple objects like cylinders and boxes into production models like flanges, tools, doorstops, doorknobs, and much, much more.

> You can also access the ***Union*** command (as well as the ***Subtract*** and ***Intersect*** commands) using the Modify pull-down menu. Follow this path:
>
> *Modify—Solids Editing—Union*

We have to try this one. We will create a flange over the next few exercises by using two construction tools and several cylinders.

WWW 10.1.1.1 Do This: Welding Solid Objects with the *Union* Command

I. Open the *Flange.dwg* file in the C:\Steps3D\Lesson10 folder. The drawing looks like Figure 10.1.1.1a.

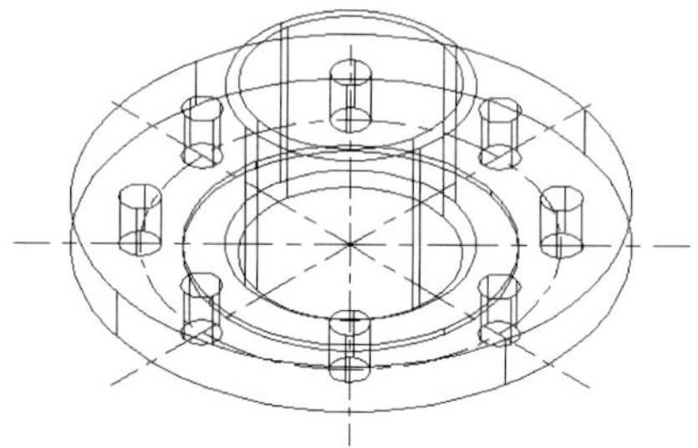

FIG. 10.1.1.1a *Flange.dwg*

II. Follow these steps:

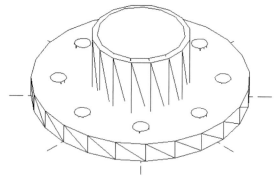

TOOLS	COMMAND SEQUENCE	STEPS
	Command: ***hide***	**1.** Remove hidden lines. Your drawing looks like Figure 10.1.1.1.1. Notice that the center cylinder disappears into the bottom cylinder with no visible connection. FIG. 10.1.1.1.1 Hidden Lines Removed
	Command: ***re***	**2.** Regenerate the drawing.

continued

TOOLS	COMMAND SEQUENCE	STEPS
 Union Button	**Command:** *uni*	**3.** Enter the ***Union*** command by typing ***union*** or ***uni*** at the command prompt. Or you can pick the **Union** button on the Solids Editing toolbar.
	Select objects:	**4.** Select the three cylinders indicated in Figure 10.1.1.1.4. 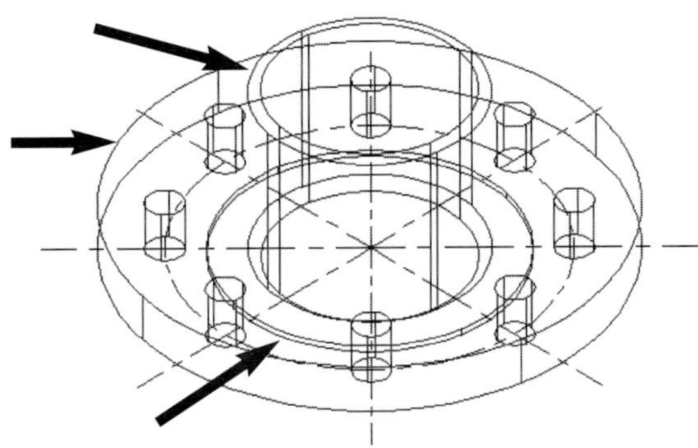 FIG. 10.1.1.1.4 Select These Cylinders
	Select objects: *[enter]*	**5.** Confirm the selection. Your drawing looks like Figure 10.1.1.1.5. The selected cylinders have become a single unit (try erasing one of them to verify this). 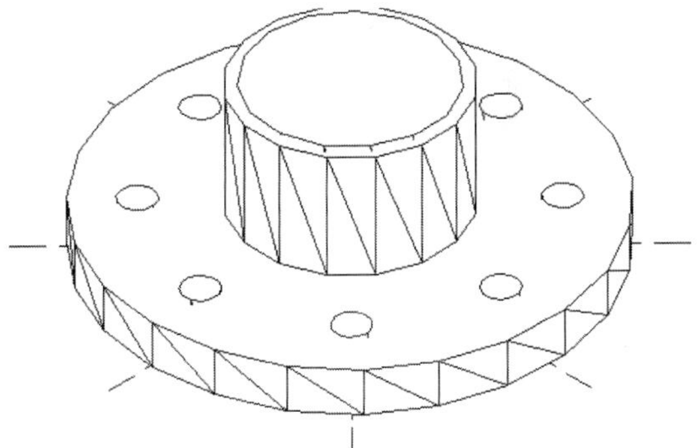 FIG. 10.1.1.1.5 Welded Cylinders (hidden lines removed for clarity)
	 **Command:** *qsave*	**6.** Save the drawing, but do not exit.

Of course, the ***Union*** command is only one side of the coin. If you can add objects to each other, you should be able to remove one object from another as well.

Look at the ***Subtract*** command.

10.1.2 Subtract

We created a solid flange in our last exercise, but a flange has little use if nothing can flow through it. Enter the ***Subtract*** command.

You are already familiar with the ***Subtract*** command from Lesson 5. We used it in Section 5.3.3 to put windows in our walls. ***Subtract*** works the same on 3D Solids as it did on regions.

We will use it to remove the bolt holes and the core of our flange.

WWW 10.1.2.1 Do This: Removing One Solid from Another

I. Be sure you are still in the *Flange.dwg* file in the C:\Steps3D\Lesson10 folder. If not, open it now.

II. Follow these steps:

TOOLS	COMMAND SEQUENCE	STEPS
 Subtract Button	**Command:** *su*	**1.** Enter the ***Subtract*** command by typing ***subtract*** or ***su*** at the command prompt. Or you can pick the **Subtract** button on the Solids Editing toolbar.
	SUBTRACT Select solids and regions to subtract from . . . **Select objects:** **Select objects:** *[enter]*	**2.** AutoCAD asks you to select the object from which you wish to remove something. Select the solid you created in our last exercise (select the outermost cylinder). Then confirm the selection.

continued

TOOLS	COMMAND SEQUENCE	STEPS
	Select solids and regions to subtract . . . **Select objects:** **Select objects:** *[enter]*	**3.** AutoCAD now wants to know what to remove. Select the innermost cylinder and each of the smaller cylinders arrayed about the flange (the bolt holes). Then confirm the selection. Your drawing looks like Figure 10.1.2.1.3. 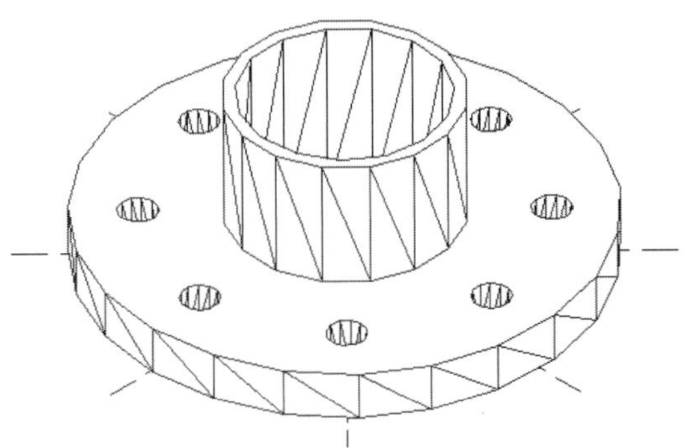 FIG. 10.1.2.1.3 Bolt Holes and Core Removed (hidden lines removed for clarity)
	**Command:** *qsave*	**4.** Save and close the drawing.

These first two exercises have been fairly easy and straightforward. But take a moment and fill in the blanks in the following sentences with as many answers as you can (time yourself and see how many answers you can find in 60 seconds):

I can use the ***Union*** command to create __________ out of __________.
I can use the ***Subtract*** command to create __________ out of __________.

Here are some hints:

- Look about the room and consider objects on the desk, floor, walls, and shelves.
- Imagine that you have the blocks with which you played as a child, but now you have a bottle of glue, a drill, and a chisel, as well.

Are you beginning to see the possibilities?

10.1.3 Intersect

The ***Intersect*** command comes in handy when creating intricate multisided figures. It works by removing everything that does not intersect something else. This will become clearer with an exercise, but first look at the command sequence:

Command: *intersect* **(or** *in***)**
Select objects: *[select objects that intersect each other]*
Select objects: *[hit enter to confirm the selection]*
Command:

(If only all commands accomplished as much—as easily!)
Let's see what we can do with the ***Intersect*** command.

10.1.3.1 Do This: Creating Objects at Intersections

I. Open the *Emerald.dwg* file in the C:\Steps3D\Lesson10 folder. The drawing looks like Figure 10.1.3.1a. (It is two octagons extruded at 30° to become two 3D Solid objects.)

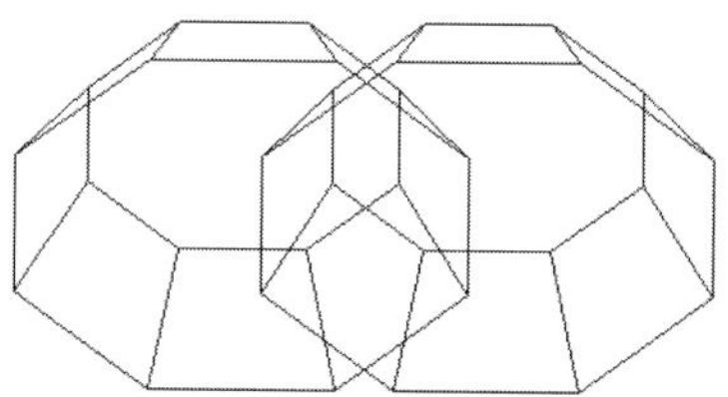

FIG. 10.1.3.1a *Emerald.dwg*

II. Follow these steps:

TOOLS	COMMAND SEQUENCE	STEPS
No Button Available	**Command:** *mirror3d* **Select objects:** *[select both octagons]* **Select objects:** *[enter]* **Specify first point of mirror plane (3 points) or [Object/Last/Zaxis/View/XY/YZ/ZX/3points] <3points>:** *[select the three points indicated in Figure 10.1.3.1.1 to define the mirror plane atop the existing solids]* **Delete source objects? [Yes/No] <N>:** *[enter]*	**1.** Let's make this really interesting. Create two more octagon solids using the ***Mirror3d*** command as shown. (Refer to Figure 10.1.3.1.1.) 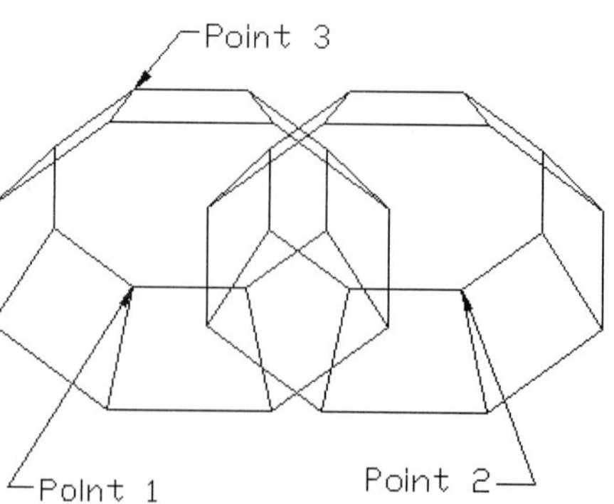 **FIG. 10.1.3.1.1** Select These Points

continued

TOOLS	COMMAND SEQUENCE	STEPS
	**Command:** ***m*** **Select objects:** ***[select the two new solids]*** **Select objects:** ***[enter]*** **Specify base point or displacement:** ***0,0,−.5*** **Specify second point of displacement or <use first point as displacement>:** ***[enter]***	**2.** Now move the new solids down one-half unit in Z-Space. (I will use the displacement method.) Your drawing looks like Figure 10.1.3.1.2 (four overlapping octagon 3D solids). 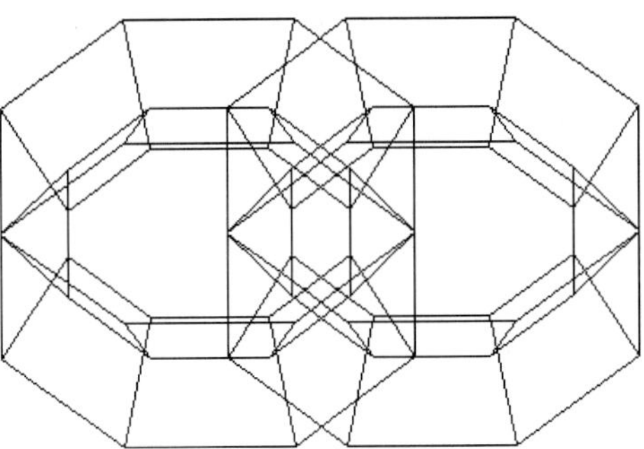 **FIG. 10.1.3.1.2** Four Solid Octagons
 Intersect Button	**Command:** ***in***	**3.** And now for the nifty part: Enter the ***Intersect*** command by typing ***intersect*** or ***in*** at the command prompt. Or you can pick the **Intersect** button on the Solids Editing toolbar.
	Select objects: **Select objects:** ***[enter]***	**4.** Select the four octagon solids and then confirm the selection.

continued

TOOLS	COMMAND SEQUENCE	STEPS
	Command: *−vp* **Current view direction: VIEWDIR=0.0000,−1.0000,1.0000** **Specify a view point or [Rotate] <display compass and tripod>:** *1,−1,1*	**5.** Adjust the viewpoint for clarity. Your drawing looks like Figure 10.1.3.1.5.
	**Command:** *qsave*	**6.** Save the drawing, but do not exit.

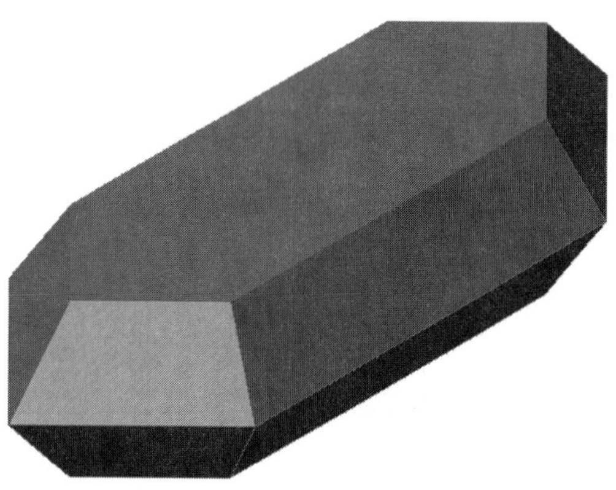

FIG. 10.1.3.1.5 Emerald (shown in Gouraud+Edges Shademode)

Wow! What else can we do?!

■ 10.1.4 Slice

Did you know that the value of precious stones often increases when they are cut just right? Let's cut our emerald.

The command we will use is called ***Slice***. Use the ***Slice*** command to make a straight cut or remove a piece of an object as if cutting it away with a knife. The sequence offers more options than the others we have seen in this lesson, but that means more opportunities to cut it the way you want it cut. It looks like this:

Command: *slice* **(or** *sl***)**

Select objects: *[select the solid object to cut]*

Select objects: *[hit enter to confirm the selection]*

Specify first point on slicing plane by [Object/Zaxis/View/XY/YZ/ZX/3points] <3points>: *[pick three points on the object to define the slicing plane]*

Specify second point on plane:

Specify third point on plane:

Specify a point on desired side of the plane or [keep Both sides]: *[pick a point on the side of the object you wish to keep]*
Command:

The options do not appear until after the object you wish to slice has been selected. They should be familiar from your mastery of the ***Rotate3d*** and ***Mirror3d*** commands, but let's go over them again to be sure.

- The default option requires that you select **3points** to define a slicing plane. This is like drawing the knife blade that will be slicing through the object.
- The **Object** option is still the easiest. If you have an object (circle, ellipse, arc, spline, or polyline) drawn through the object you want to slice, you can select it as your slicing plane.
- The **Zaxis** option is difficult to follow. It prompts like this:

  Specify a point on the section plane:
  Specify a point on the Z-axis (normal) of the plane:

  - The first prompt is asking for a point on the slicing plane.
  - The next prompt is asking for a point on the Z-axis of the slicing plane. You use this point to orient the slicing plane—essentially by picking a point to define which way is "up" if you are standing on the slicing plane.
- The **XY/YZ/ZX** options allow you to define the slicing plane by identifying a single point on the chosen plane (the **XY** plane, the **YZ** plane, or the **ZX** plane). AutoCAD defines these planes according to the current UCS.
- The last option occurs at the final prompt. It allows you to keep either a selected piece (the default) or both pieces of the object after it has been sliced.

You can also access the ***Slice*** command (as well as the ***Interfere*** and ***Section*** commands) using the Draw pull-down menu. Follow this path:

Draw—Solids—Slice

Let's cut our gemstone.

10.1.4.1 Do This: Slicing 3D Solid Objects

I. Be sure you are still in the *Emerald.dwg* file in the C:\Steps3D\Lesson10 folder. If not, open it now.

II. Follow these steps:

TOOLS	COMMAND SEQUENCE	STEPS
 Slice Button	**Command:** ***sl***	**1.** Enter the ***Slice*** command by typing ***slice*** or ***sl*** at the command prompt. Or you can pick the **Slice** button on the Solids toolbar.
	Select objects: **Select objects:** *[enter]*	**2.** Select the emerald and confirm the selection.
	Specify first point on slicing plane by [Object/Zaxis/View/XY/YZ/ZX/3points] <3points>: *[select point 1]* **Specify second point on plane:** *[select point 2]* **Specify third point on plane:** *[select point 3]*	**3.** (Refer to Figure 10.1.4.1.3.) Select the points indicated.

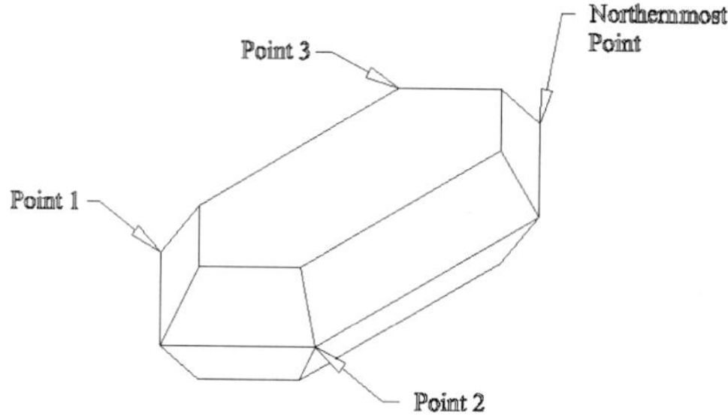

FIG. 10.1.4.1.3 Select These Points

TOOLS	COMMAND SEQUENCE	STEPS
	Specify a point on desired side of the plane or [keep Both sides]:	**4.** Pick the northernmost endpoint (see Figure 10.1.4.1.3) on the emerald (indicating that you wish to keep that section of the gemstone). Your drawing looks like Figure 10.1.4.1.4.

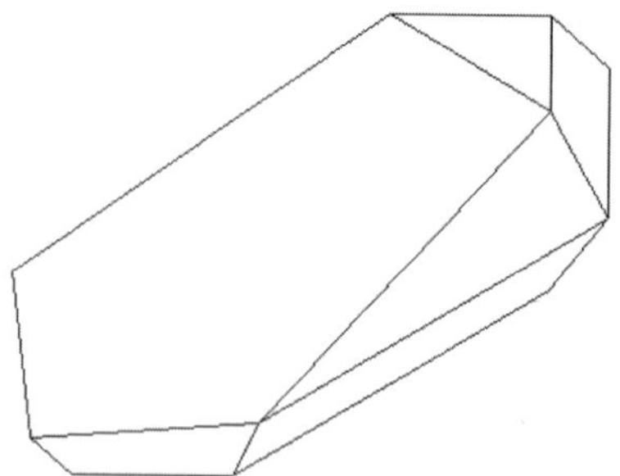

FIG. 10.1.4.1.4 Sliced Stone

continued

TOOLS	COMMAND SEQUENCE	STEPS

Command: *u*

5. Undo the change.

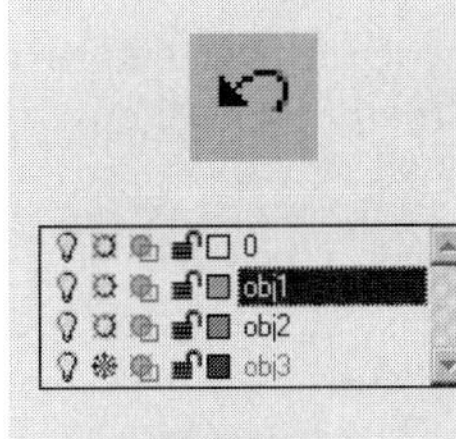

Command: *la*

6. Let's try the **Object** option. First, thaw the **obj1** layer. Notice the circle that intersects the emerald (Figure 10.1.4.1.6).

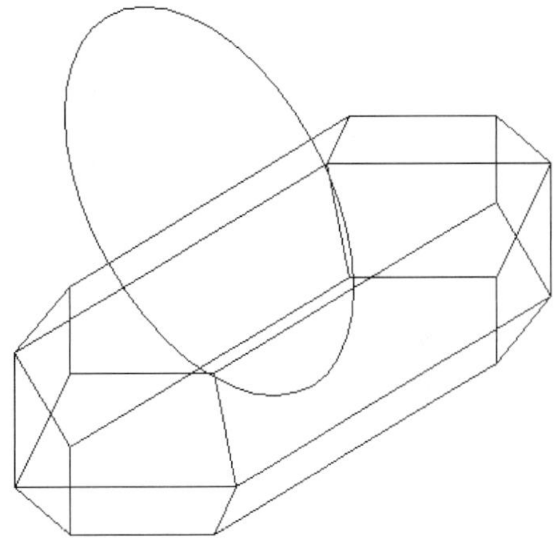

FIG. 10.1.4.1.6 Use the Object Option

Command: *sl*

7. Repeat Steps 1 and 2.

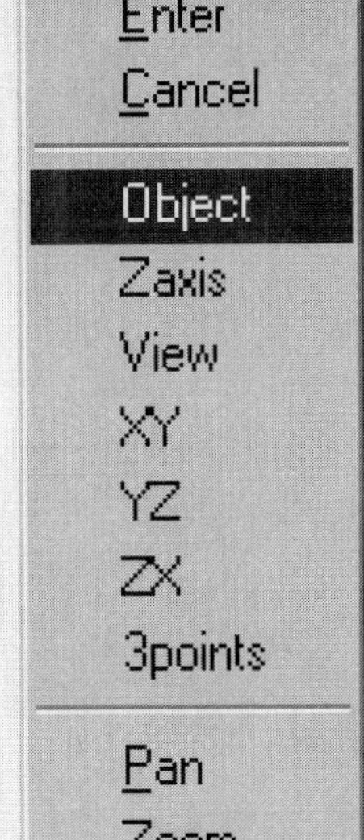

Specify first point on slicing plane by [Object/Zaxis/View/XY/YZ/ZX/3points] <3points>: *o*

8. Choose the **Object** option.

Select a circle, ellipse, arc, 2D-spline, or 2D-polyline:

9. Select the circle . . .

continued

TOOLS	COMMAND SEQUENCE	STEPS
	Specify a point on desired side of the plane or [keep Both sides]:	**10.** . . . and pick the northernmost point on the emerald. Your drawing looks like Figure 10.1.4.1.10.
		FIG. 10.1.4.1.10 Sliced Using the Circle as a Slicing Plane (Shademode=Hidden)
	Command: *u*	**11.** Undo the change.
	Command: *la*	**12.** Now we will try the **Zaxis** option. First, freeze the **obj1** layer and thaw the **obj3** layer. Notice the line that retreats from the center of the object.
		FIG. 10.1.4.1.12 Thawed OBJ3 Layer
	Command: *sl*	**13.** Repeat Steps 1 and 2.

continued

TOOLS	COMMAND SEQUENCE	STEPS
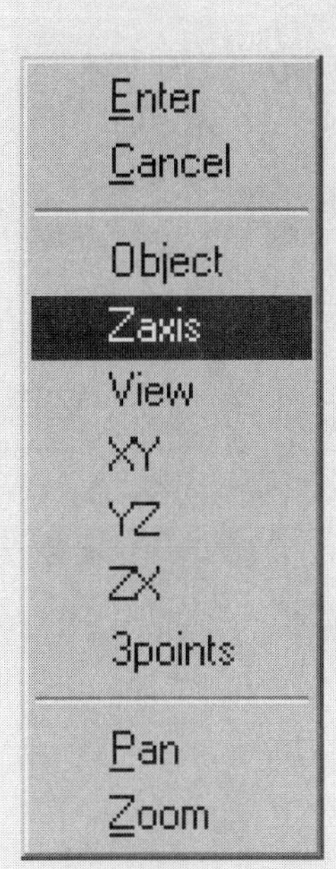	**Specify first point on slicing plane by [Object/Zaxis/View/XY/YZ/ZX/3points] <3points>:** *z*	**14.** Choose the **Zaxis** option.
	Specify a point on the section plane:	**15.** Pick the endpoint of the line where it meets the emerald. The slicing plane will pass through this point.
	Specify a point on the Z-axis (normal) of the plane:	**16.** Pick the other endpoint of the line. The slicing plane will be *perpendicular* to the line you identified with the last pick.
	Specify a point on desired side of the plane or [keep Both sides]: *b*	**17.** This time, let's **keep Both sides**. A line appears through the emerald.
	**Command:** *m* **Select objects:** *[select the southern piece of the emerald]* **Select objects:** *[enter]* **Specify base point or displacement:** *0,−.5* **Specify second point of displacement or <use first point as displacement>:**	**18.** Use the displacement method of the *Move* command to separate the two pieces of the emerald. Your drawing looks like Figure 10.1.4.1.18. 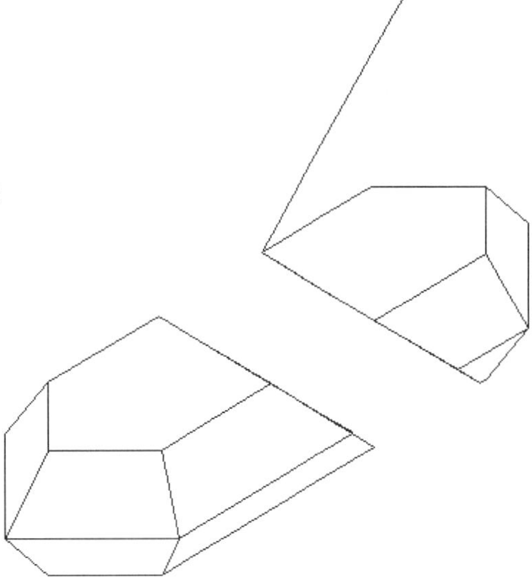 FIG. 10.1.4.1.18 Sliced Along the Z-Axis
	**Command:** *u*	**19.** Undo the changes until the emerald is one piece again.
	Command: *sl*	**20.** Repeat Steps 1 and 2.

continued

TOOLS	COMMAND SEQUENCE	STEPS
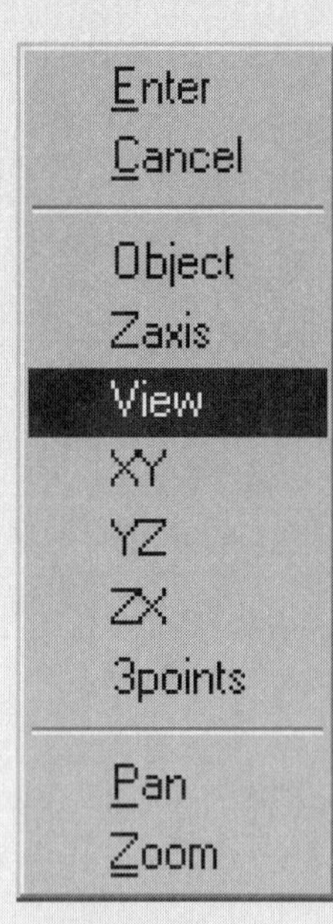	**Specify first point on slicing plane by [Object/Zaxis/View/XY/YZ/ZX/3points] <3points>:** *v*	**21.** Use the **View** option.
	Specify a point on the current view plane <0,0,0>:	**22.** Pick the endpoint of the line where it meets the emerald . . .
	Specify a point on desired side of the plane or [keep Both sides]:	**23.** . . . and keep the back part of the gemstone. Your drawing looks like Figure 10.1.4.1.23. AutoCAD has created a slicing plane parallel to your view and through the point you specified in Step 22.

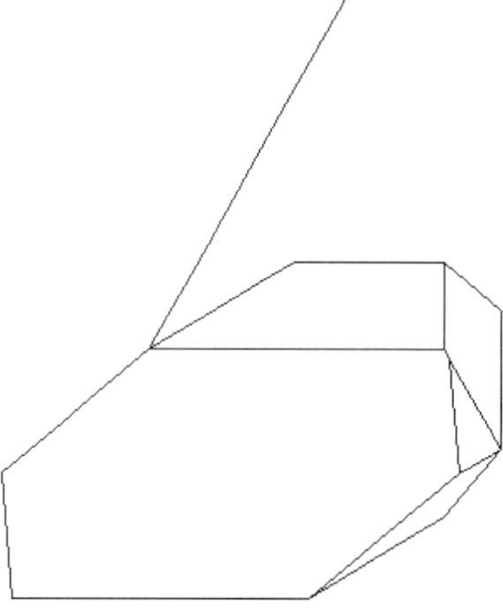

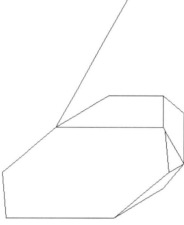

FIG. 10.1.4.1.23 Results of a View Specified Slicing Plane

TOOLS	COMMAND SEQUENCE	STEPS
	**Command:** *u*	**24.** Undo the changes.
	**Command:** *sl*	**25.** Repeat Steps 1 and 2.
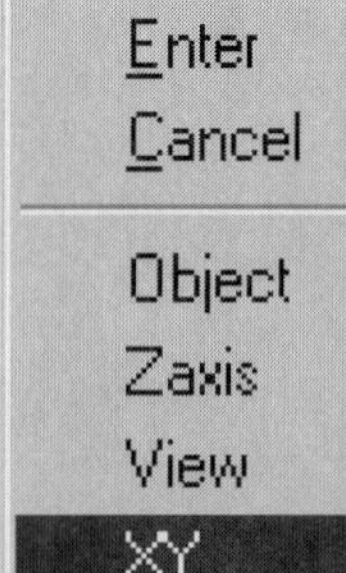	**Specify first point on slicing plane by [Object/Zaxis/View/XY/YZ/ZX/3points] <3points>:** *xy*	**26.** Now we will slice along a UCS plane. Use the **XY** plane.
	Specify a point on the XY-plane <0,0,0>:	**27.** Select the front point (southernmost) on the emerald. AutoCAD will cut through this point.

continued

TOOLS	COMMAND SEQUENCE	STEPS
	Specify a point on desired side of the plane or [keep Both sides]:	**28.** Keep the bottom of the emerald. Your drawing looks like Figure 10.1.4.1.28.
		FIG. 10.1.4.1.28 Sliced Along a UCS Plane
	Command: ***qsave***	**29.** Save the drawing and exit.

As I said, the ***Slice*** command is slightly more involved than the commands we learned earlier, but you can see why.

Most people find one method of doing things easier than other methods. With the ***Slice*** command, AutoCAD gives you plenty of methods from which to choose. Knowing all the ways to accomplish the intended goal, however, may save you some time and hassle later when the preferred method refuses to work.

Suppose you had to determine the volume of the object we created in our last exercise (the cut emerald). Can you think of an easy way? I cannot.

AutoCAD provides a tool to make the calculation easier (okay, it does it for you)—***Massprop***. The ***Massprop*** command will compute not only the volume of the selected object but also the mass, bounding box, centroid, moments and products of inertia, radii of gyration, and principle moments and directions about the centroid. All you have to do is enter the command and select the object! (And your boss spent all those years in engineering school learning how to do this on a slide rule!)

10.1.5 Interfere

Using the ***Interfere*** command, the designer can identify problems cheaply and easily *before* construction finds them.

This is a designer's delight. ***Interfere*** identifies places in a drawing where one solid interferes with another. You will use it more as a checking tool once the drawing has been completed than as a drawing tool itself—although you can use it to draw an interference.

The command sequence looks like this:

Command: *interfere* **(or** *inf***)**

Select first set of solids:

Select objects: *[identify the solids you want to check]*

Select second set of solids:

Select objects: *[identify a second set of solids if you wish to check one against the other]*

Comparing X solids against Y solids.

Interfering solids: *[AutoCAD tells you how many objects interfere with other objects]*

Interfering pairs: *[AutoCAD tells you how many occurrences of interference it has discovered]*

Create interference solids? [Yes/No] <N>: *[if you want, AutoCAD will create a solid from the interference—much as it does with the* **Intersect** *command except that nothing will be removed]*

Highlight pairs of interfering solids? [Yes/No] <N>: *[if you want, AutoCAD will show you each interference, one at a time]*

Command:

AutoCAD presents no options that might confuse you, but there is a quirk that can be useful. If you select all the objects to check at the first selection prompt (**Select first set of solids:**) and simply hit enter at the second prompt (**Select second set of solids:**), AutoCAD will check all of the solids in the selection set against each other. Otherwise, AutoCAD checks objects in the first selection set against objects in the second selection set only.

Let's see how it works.

10.1.5.1 Do This: Interference Detection

I. Open the *pipe10.dwg* file in the C:\Steps3D\Lesson10 folder. The drawing looks like Figure 10.1.5.1a. (It is a simple piping plan with a two-level piperack. Can you see any obvious interferences?)

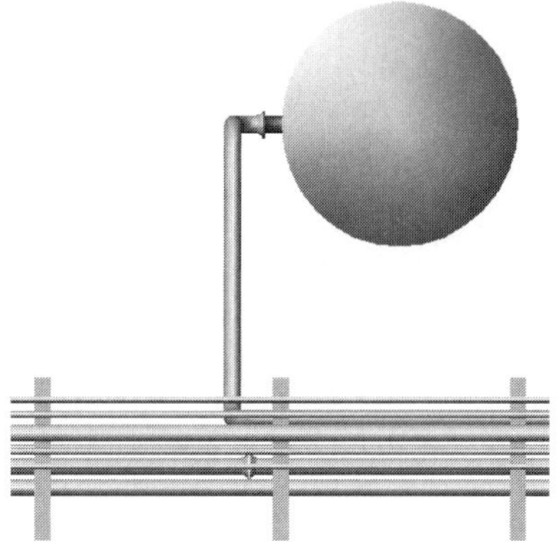

FIG. 10.1.5.1a *Pip10.dwg*

II. Follow these steps:

TOOLS	COMMAND SEQUENCE	STEPS
 Interfere Button	**Command: *inf***	**1.** Enter the ***Interfere*** command by typing ***interfere*** or ***inf*** at the command prompt. Or you can pick the **Interfere** button on the Solids toolbar.
	Select first set of solids: **Select objects: *all*** **Select objects: *[enter]***	**2.** We will check the entire drawing for interferences. At the first **Select objects** prompt, type ***all***, and then confirm the selection set.
	Select second set of solids: **Select objects: *[enter]*** **No solids selected.** **Comparing 38 solids with each other.**	**3.** We will check all of the solids against each other, so hit ***enter*** at the second **Select objects** prompt. AutoCAD tells you that it is comparing the solids with each other (this may take a few moments).

continued

TOOLS	COMMAND SEQUENCE	STEPS
	Interfering solids: 3 **Interfering pairs: 2**	**4.** AutoCAD found three solids hitting each other in two instances of interference. Notice that it highlights the interfering solids (Figure 10.1.5.1.4).

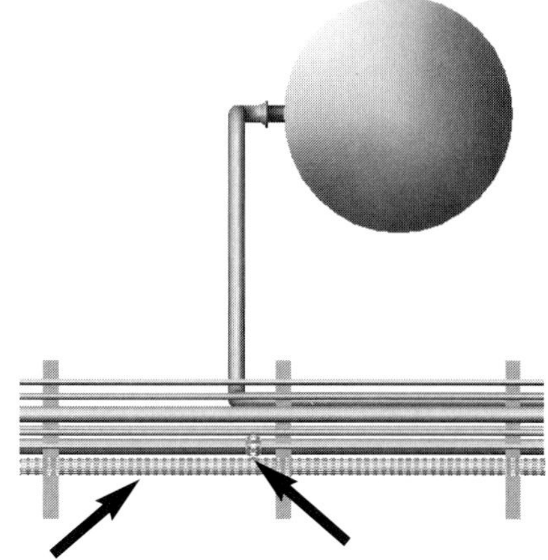

FIG. 10.1.5.1.4 Interferences Shown

TOOLS	COMMAND SEQUENCE	STEPS
	Create interference solids? [Yes/No] <N>: *[enter]*	**5.** We do not need AutoCAD to create a solid at the interference . . .
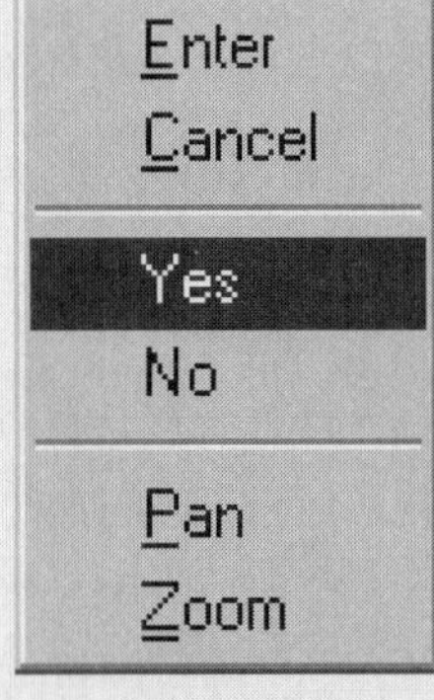	**Highlight pairs of interfering solids? [Yes/No] <N>:** *y*	**6.** . . . but we are not sure which objects interfere (flange against flange or two instances of flange against pipe). So we will ask AutoCAD to highlight the interfering pairs. AutoCAD highlights a flange and the pipe.
Enter Cancel Next pair eXit Pan Zoom	**Enter an option [Next pair/eXit] <Next>:** **Enter an option [Next pair/eXit] <Next>:** *x*	**7.** Hit ***enter*** to see the other interference. AutoCAD highlights the other flange and the pipe. Enter ***X*** or select **exit** from the cursor menu to end the command.
	Command: *quit*	**8.** Exit the drawing without saving it.

In a few simple steps, you have located a problem that might have cost tons of money in redesign and construction costs.

We have another timesaver to see, but first let's visit some old friends.

10.2 Using Some Old Friends on Solids—*Fillet* and *Chamfer*

Remember how much fun you had drawing the outhouse door back in Lesson 8 of the basic text? You used the ***Fillet*** and ***Chamfer*** commands to make the corners (twice). Where would you be if you could not use those convenient tools on 3D Solids?

Luckily, AutoCAD saw the need to round and mitre corners on solid objects and made the tools available—with a few necessary adjustments. Look at the command sequences when these two are used on solids (we will begin with the ***Fillet*** command):

Command: ***Fillet*** **(or *f*)**

Current settings: Mode=TRIM, Radius=0.5000

Select first object or [Polyline/Radius/Trim]: *[select a solid]*

Enter fillet radius <0.5000>: *[accept or change the radius]*

Select an edge or [Chain/Radius]: *[select the edge to fillet]*

Command:

The command begins just as it did when you studied it in the basic text. But when you select a solid object at the **Select first object** prompt, AutoCAD recognizes the solid and asks for some different information.

- It immediately prompts for a radius—something it did not do for a two-dimensional object (although the default radius has not changed).
- You can hit enter at the **Select an edge** prompt and AutoCAD will assume that you intend to fillet the edge you selected at the **Select first object** prompt. It will then proceed to fillet that edge. Or you can choose one of the other options:
  - When you pick a single edge on the surface of a solid while using the **Chain** option, AutoCAD should automatically pick the other lines on that surface that are sequential and tangential to the one you selected. [Frankly, I have never been impressed by the way this works (or does not work).]
  - The **Edge** option simply allows you to select the edges to fillet one at a time.
  - The **Radius** option allows you to change the radius of each edge you select.

The command sequence for the ***Chamfer*** command is

Command: ***chamfer*** **(or *cha*)**

(TRIM mode) Current chamfer Dist1=0.5000, Dist2=0.5000

Select first line or [Polyline/Distance/Angle/Trim/Method]: *[select a solid]*

Base surface selection . . .

Enter surface selection option [Next/OK (current)] <OK>: *[each edge naturally has two surfaces that are next to it; hit enter if the correct surface is highlighted or type N to toggle between the surfaces until the appropriate one highlights]*

Specify base surface chamfer distance <0.5000>: *[enter the chamfer distances]*
Specify other surface chamfer distance <0.5000>:
Select an edge or [Loop]: *[select the edge to chamfer]*
Command:

- The first option, as explained, allows you to select the correct surface to chamfer.
- The next two options—**Specify base surface chamfer distance** and **specify other surface chamfer distance**—allow you to accept or change the chamfer distances (notice that there is no **Angle** option here as there is for two-dimensional objects).
- The last option—**Select an edge or [Loop]**—allows you to pick the edges to chamfer individually or, when you use the **Loop** option, collectively around the entire surface.

Let's try the ***Fillet*** and ***Chamfer*** commands on a solid.

WWW 10.2.1 Do This: Solid Fillets and Chamfers

I. Open the *Flange.dwg* file in the C:\Steps3D\Lesson10 folder. If you have not completed it yet, open the *Flange-done.dwg* file instead. We will countersink the bolt holes, mitre the weld neck (the upper cylinder), and fillet the edge.

II. Follow these steps:

TOOLS	COMMAND SEQUENCE	STEPS
	Command: *f*	**1.** Let's begin with a simple fillet. Enter the ***Fillet*** command by typing ***fillet*** or ***f*** at the command prompt. Or you can pick the **Fillet** button on the Modify toolbar.
	Select first object or [Polyline/ Radius/Trim]:	**2.** Select the top surface of the base of the flange.
	Enter fillet radius <0.5000>: *.25*	**3.** Set the radius to one-quarter unit.

continued

TOOLS	COMMAND SEQUENCE	STEPS

Select an edge or [Chain/Radius]: *[enter]*

4. Hit ***enter*** to complete the command. Your drawing looks like Figure 10.2.1.4.

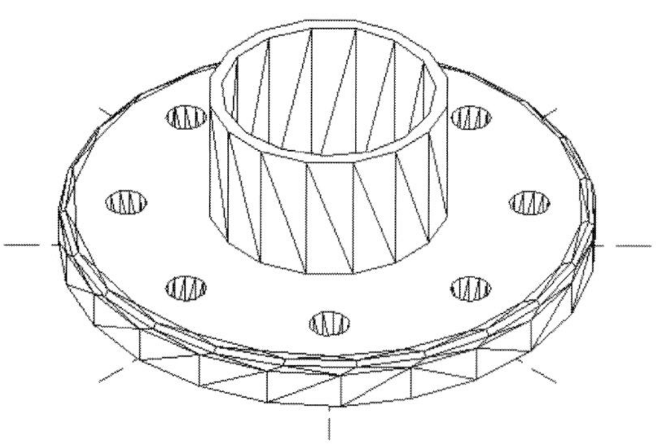

FIG. 10.2.1.4 Filleted Base (hidden lines removed)

Command: ***cha***

5. Now we will mitre the weld neck. Enter the ***Chamfer*** command by typing ***chamfer*** or ***cha*** at the command prompt. Or you can pick the **Chamfer** button on the Modify toolbar.

Select first line or [Polyline/ Distance/Angle/Trim/Method]:

6. Select the upper cylinder . . .

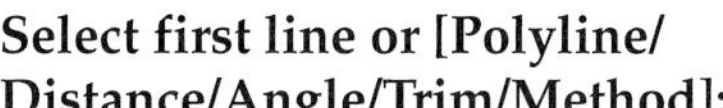
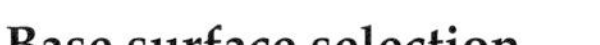
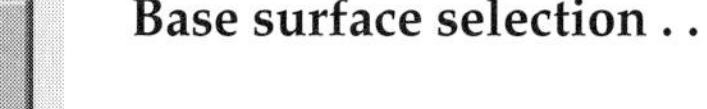

Base surface selection . . .

Enter surface selection option [Next/OK (current)] <OK>: *n*

Enter surface selection option [Next/OK (current)] <OK>: *[enter]*

7. . . . and adjust the surface selected until just the outer circle of the cylinder is highlighted.

Specify base surface chamfer distance <0.5000>: *.125*

Specify other surface chamfer distance <0.5000>: *.125*

8. Set the chamfer distances to one-eighth unit.

continued

TOOLS	COMMAND SEQUENCE	STEPS
	Select an edge or [Loop]: **Select an edge or [Loop]:** *[enter]*	**9.** Select the outer edge of the upper cylinder and then confirm the selection. Your drawing looks like Figure 10.2.1.9.

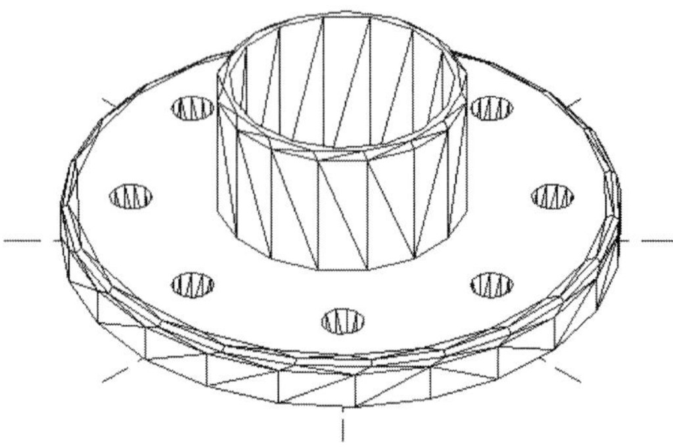

FIG. 10.2.1.9 Chamfered Weld Neck (hidden lines removed)

TOOLS	COMMAND SEQUENCE	STEPS
	Command: *[enter]*	**10.** Now countersink the bolt holes. Repeat the ***Chamfer*** command.
	Select first line or [Polyline/ Distance/Angle/Trim/Method]:	**11.** Select the upper surface of the base of the flange.
	Base surface selection . . .	
	Enter surface selection option [Next/OK (current)] <OK>: *[enter]*	
	Specify base surface chamfer distance <0.1250>: *.25*	**12.** Set the chamfer distances to one-quarter unit.
	Specify other surface chamfer distance <0.1250>: *.25*	

continued

TOOLS	COMMAND SEQUENCE	STEPS
	Select an edge or [Loop]: **Select an edge or [Loop]:** *[enter]*	**13.** Select the upper circle around each of the bolt holes. Then hit ***enter*** to complete the command. Your drawing looks like Figure 10.2.1.13.
		FIG. 10.2.1.13 Completed Flange (shown in Gouraud Shademode)
	Command: *qsave*	**14.** Save the drawing, but do not exit. Save the drawing again as *MyFlange12.dwg* in the C:\Steps3D\Lesson12 folder (we will do more with it later). Close the drawing.

Now let's look at that other timesaver—the ***Section*** command.

10.3 Creating Cross Sections the Easy Way—The *Section* Command

Have you ever completed the tedious cross section of an object only to discover that you missed something (perhaps a line or an arc that was difficult to see)? Well, AutoCAD has just the tool for you!

The ***Section*** command creates cross sections of solid objects. And it is one of AutoCAD's easier commands to master!

The command sequence is

Command: *section* **(or** *sec***)**

Select objects: *[select one or more solids to section]*

Select objects: *[hit enter to confirm the selection]*

Specify first point on Section plane by [Object/Zaxis/View/XY/YZ/ZX/3points] <3points>: *[identify three points on the Section plane (to define it)]*

Specify second point on plane:

Specify third point on plane:

Command:

It is really just that simple. AutoCAD does the rest and places the section inside the objects being sectioned. Move it to a suitable place on the drawing, add section (hatch) lines, and you are finished.

Some things to note about the ***Section*** command:

- The options for defining the Section plane are identical to those used to define a Slice plane.
- The section that AutoCAD creates is a region. You can hatch a region, or you can explode it into lines and arcs.
- The section created is aligned with the Section plane—rotate it as necessary to align it to the UCS.
- AutoCAD creates the Section on the current layer.

We will create a cross section of our flange.

10.3.1 Do This: Creating Cross Sections

I. Reopen the *Flange.dwg* file (or the *Flange-done.dwg* file) in the C:\Steps3D\Lesson10 folder.

II. Remove the hidden lines.

III. Follow these steps:

TOOLS	COMMAND SEQUENCE	STEPS
Section Button	**Command:** *sec*	**1.** Enter the ***Section*** command by typing ***section*** or ***sec*** at the command prompt. Or you can pick the **Section** button on the Solids toolbar.
	Select objects:	**2.** Select the flange and confirm the selection.
	Select objects: *[enter]*	

continued

TOOLS	COMMAND SEQUENCE	STEPS
	Specify first point on Section plane by [Object/Zaxis/View/XY/YZ/ZX/3points]<3points>:	**3.** Pick the westernmost endpoint of the east–west centerline.
	Specify second point on plane:	**4.** Pick the other endpoint of the same line.
	Specify third point on plane:	**5.** Pick the center of the top of the flange. Notice that AutoCAD creates a section inside the flange (Figure 10.3.1.5).

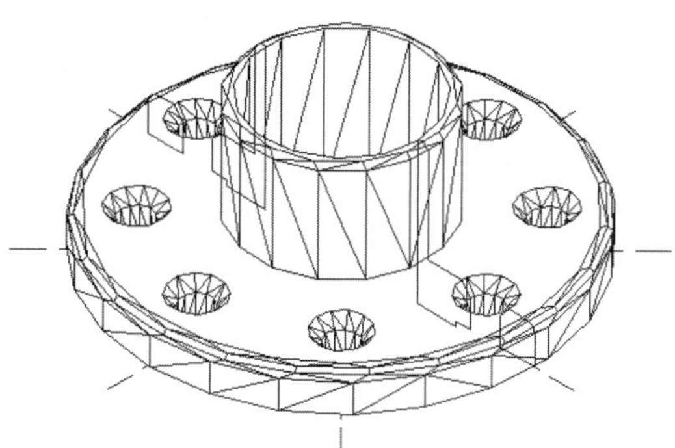

FIG. 10.3.1.5 Section Created

TOOLS	COMMAND SEQUENCE	STEPS
	Command: *m*	**6.** Move the section, as indicated, to see it better. (I selected the *last* item created and moved it using the displacement method.)
	Select objects: *l*	
	Select objects: *[enter]*	
	Specify base point or displacement: *12,0*	
	Specify second point of displacement or <use first point as displacement>: *[enter]*	

continued

TOOLS	COMMAND SEQUENCE	STEPS
	**Command:** *−vp* **Current view direction: VIEWDIR=1.0000,−1.0000,1.0000** **Specify a view point or [Rotate] <display compass and tripod>:** *0,−1,0*	**7.** Adjust the view to see the objects from the front. Your drawing looks like Figure 10.3.1.7.

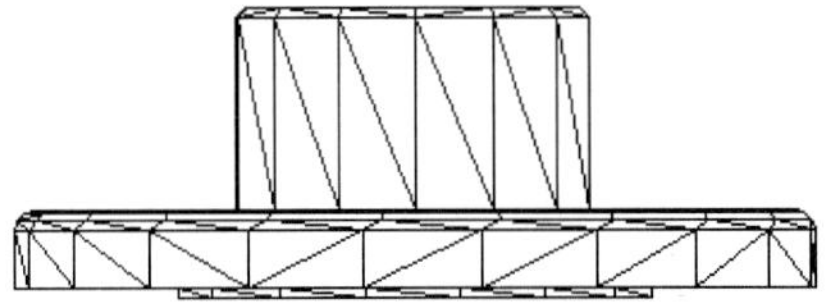
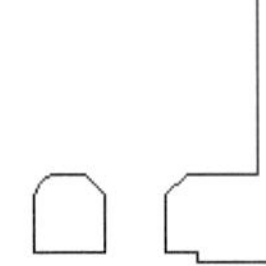
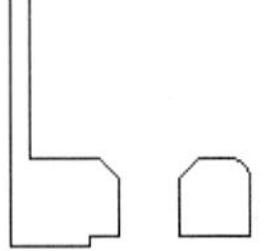

FIG. 10.3.1.7 Sectional View (Layer C1 frozen and hidden lines removed for clarity)

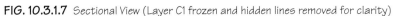

8. You may now add hatching and centerlines to your cross section.

How does that compare to drawing a cross section from scratch?

10.4 Extra Steps

Go back to the list of items you created at the end of Section 10.1.2 (p. 403). Take a few hours (or an afternoon) and see how many of them you can draw using the tools you learned in this lesson. I cannot think of a better way to gain experience (or identify questions).

Some hints for this exercise:

- Do not attempt anything that will not fit in a shoebox.
- One of those flexible, 6″ rulers with inches on one side and millimeters on the other will serve you well (now and in the future).
- Try (at first) to limit yourself to objects that will require no more than three of the basic shapes you have learned.
- You will find other terrific objects to draw in garages and kitchens.

10.5 What Have We Learned?

Items covered in this lesson include:

- *Tools used to create Composite Solids*
  - ***Union***
  - ***Subtract***
  - ***Intersect***
  - ***Slice***
  - ***Interfere***
- *Tools used to shape solids*
  - ***Fillet***
  - ***Chamfer***
- *Other Solid Modeling Tools*
  - ***Section***
  - ***Massprop***

Well, what do you think? Wouldn't it have been fun to have these tools when you were playing with blocks as a child?

As I promised, you have stopped drawing pictures of things and have actually begun creating objects using the tools in AutoCAD's "shop." I hope you can sense the potential of these tools from what you have seen here.

When I was in junior high school, I read a book by Jack London called *Call of the Wild*. It was about a dog that was taken from an easy life in the Northwest and forced to pull a sled in the Klondike during the Gold Rush. Buck (the dog) had many adventures (learning experiences) as he adapted to the wild frontier life of the arctic. But all the while—with increasing intensity—he felt a call from the wild to move out on his own. He experimented with the urging—often leaving camp for days at a time to explore the wilderness. In the end, after learning all that he could in the safety and comfort of the camps, he answered the call and moved out to live with the other wild creatures.

At this point in your AutoCAD training, you should be experimenting on your own, just as Buck did. You will find thrills—and chills—as you discover things about the software that even the masters do not know. You will make some mistakes, but the adventure lies in overcoming the mistakes (that is what makes learning fun).

In a few short chapters, you will be on your own (with the other wild creatures in the design world). Learn all that you can now!

10.6 EXERCISES

1. **through 8.** Create the "su" drawings in Appendix B using solids. Use solid primitives and the composite solid creation tools you learned in this lesson to make each drawing a single object. Save the drawings in the C:\Steps3D\Lesson10 folder.
9. Create the hinge shown in Figure 10.6.9. Refer to the following guidelines.
   9.1. The hinge is a single solid object.
   9.2. Fully dimension the hinge as shown.
   9.3. Place it with the title block of your choice on an 11″ × $8\frac{1}{2}$″ sheet of paper.
   9.4. Save the drawing as *MyHinge.dwg* in the C:\Steps3D\Lesson10 folder.

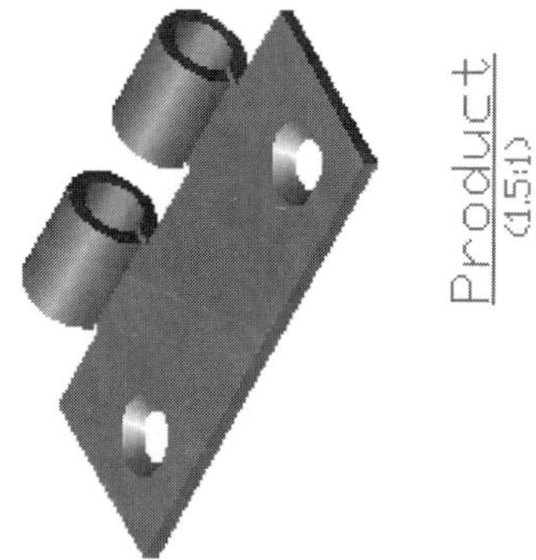

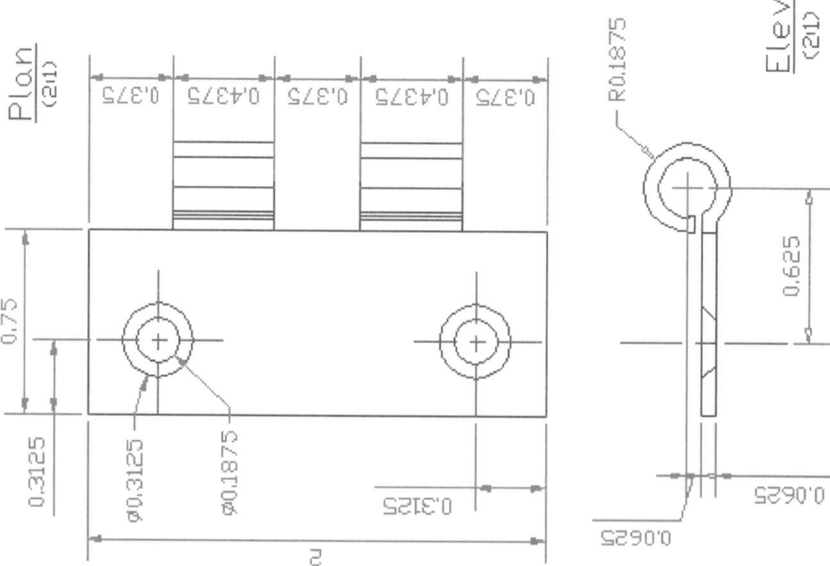

FIG. 10.6.9 Hinge

10. Create the flange shown in Figure 10.6.10. Refer to the following guidelines.

10.1. The flange is a single solid object.

10.2. Create the sections and fully dimension the flange as shown.

10.3. Place it with the title block of your choice on an 11″ × $8\frac{1}{2}$″ sheet of paper.

10.4. Bolt holes are $\frac{3}{8}$″ diameter.

10.5. The center hole is 2.25″ diameter.

10.6. Save the drawing as *MyFlange.dwg* in the C:\Steps3D\Lesson10 folder.

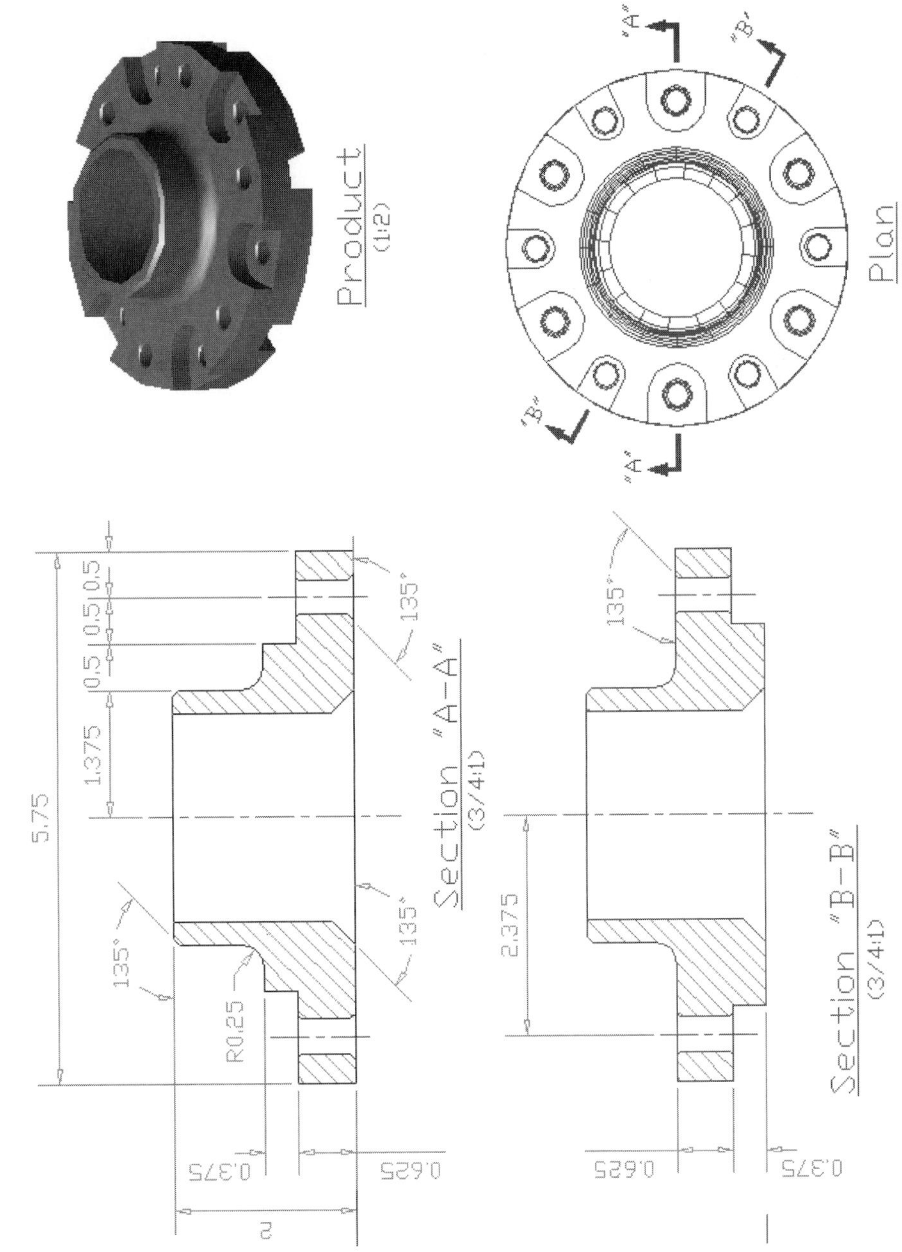

FIG. 10.6.10 Flange

11. Create the flange gear shown in Figure 10.6.11. Refer to the following guidelines.
    11.1. The flange gear is a single solid object.
    11.2. Fully dimension the object as shown.
    11.3. Place it with the title block of your choice on an 11″ × $8\frac{1}{2}$″ sheet of paper.
    11.4. Save the drawing as *MyFlangeGear.dwg* in the C:\Steps3D\Lesson10 folder.

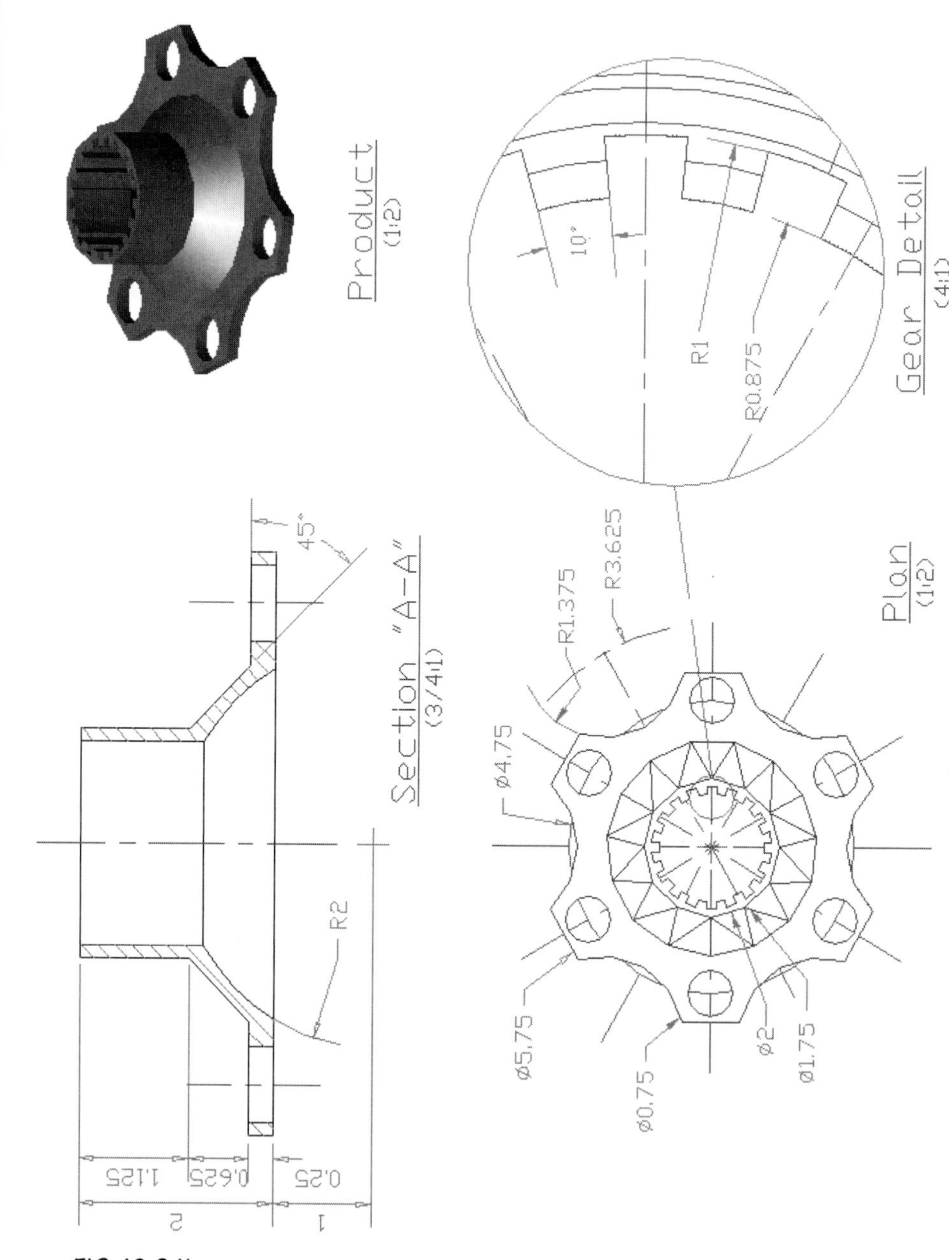

FIG. 10.6.11 Flange Gear

12. Create the floating support and anchor shown in Figure 10.6.12. Refer to the following guidelines.
    - **12.1.** Each piece is a single solid object. (*Hint:* The top of the brace was created with wedges whose length and height were 4″.)
    - **12.2.** Fully dimension the objects as shown.
    - **12.3.** Place the drawing with the title block of your choice on an 11″ × $8\frac{1}{2}$″ sheet of paper.
    - **12.4.** Save the drawing as *MyAnchor.dwg* in the C:\Steps3D\Lesson10 folder.

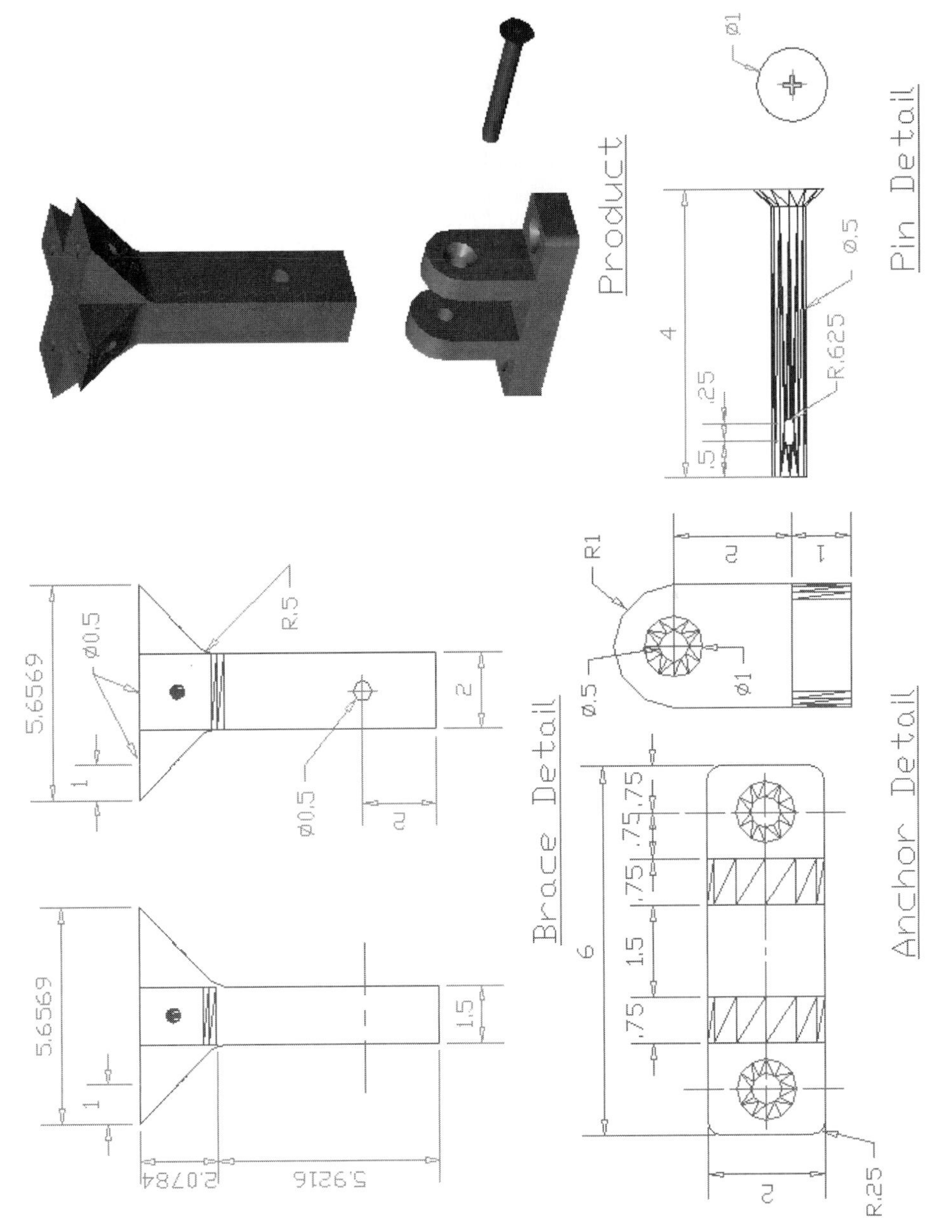

FIG. 10.6.12 Floating Support and Anchor

13. Create the dining chair shown in Figure 10.6.13. Refer to the following guidelines.

13.1. Each leg begins at 1″ diameter, but balloons to $1\frac{1}{2}$″ in the middle.

13.2. The leg bracing is $\frac{3}{4}$″ diameter; the back dowels are $\frac{1}{2}$″diameter.

13.3. The back support is 1″ squared.

13.4. Fully dimension the objects as shown.

13.5. Place the drawing with the title block of your choice on a 17″ × 11″ sheet of paper.

13.6. Save the drawing as *MyDiningChair.dwg* in the C:\Steps3D\Lesson10 folder.

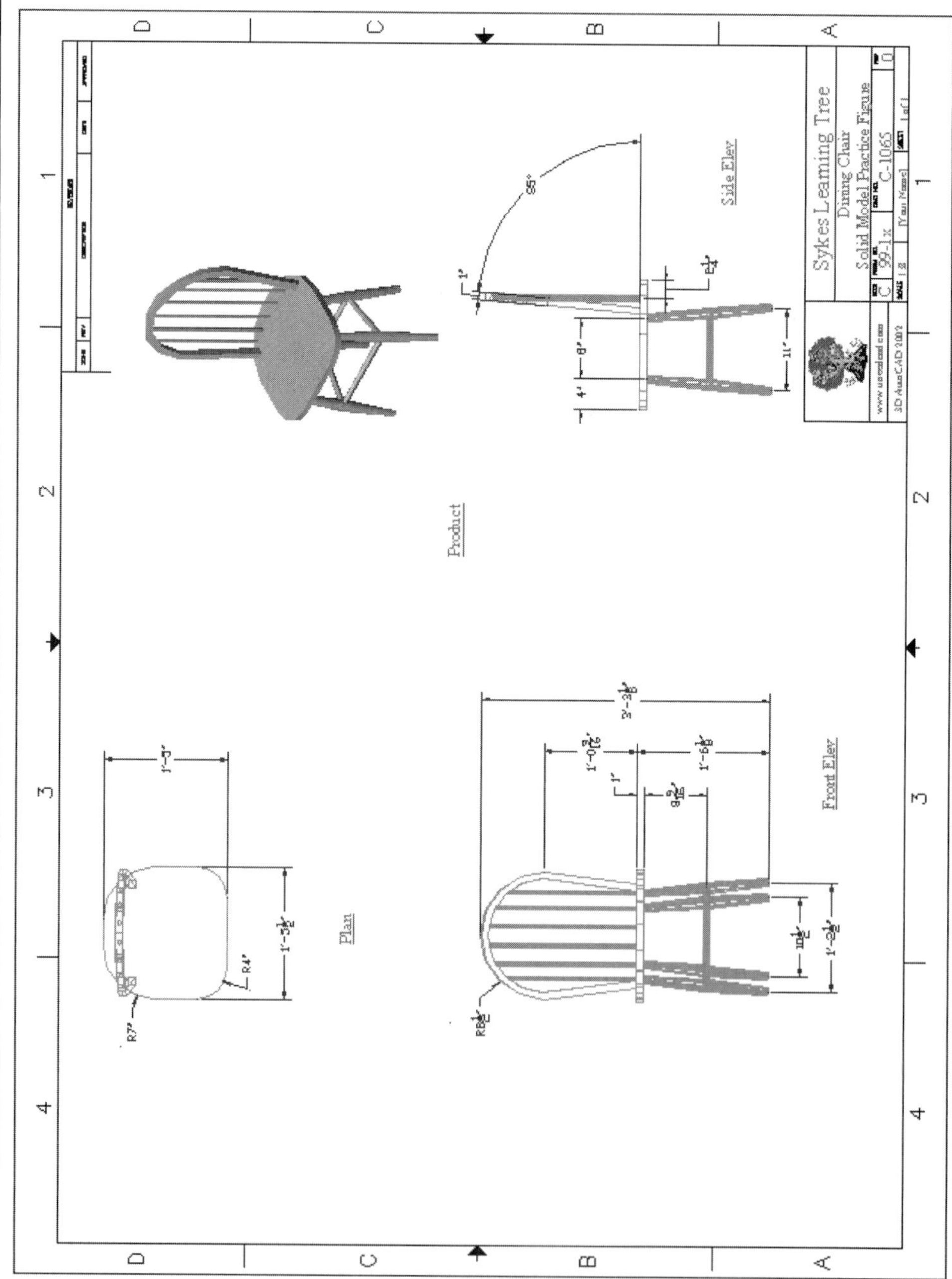

FIG. 10.6.13 Dining Chair

14. Create the table lamp shown in Figure 10.6.14. Refer to the following guidelines.

14.1. The base is a solid object.

14.2. The top is a $\frac{1}{8}''$ thick hollow glass ball.

14.3. Fully dimension the objects as shown.

14.4. Place the drawing with the title block of your choice on an $11'' \times 8\frac{1}{2}''$ sheet of paper.

14.5. Save the drawing as *MyTableLamp.dwg* in the C:\Steps3D\Lesson10 folder.

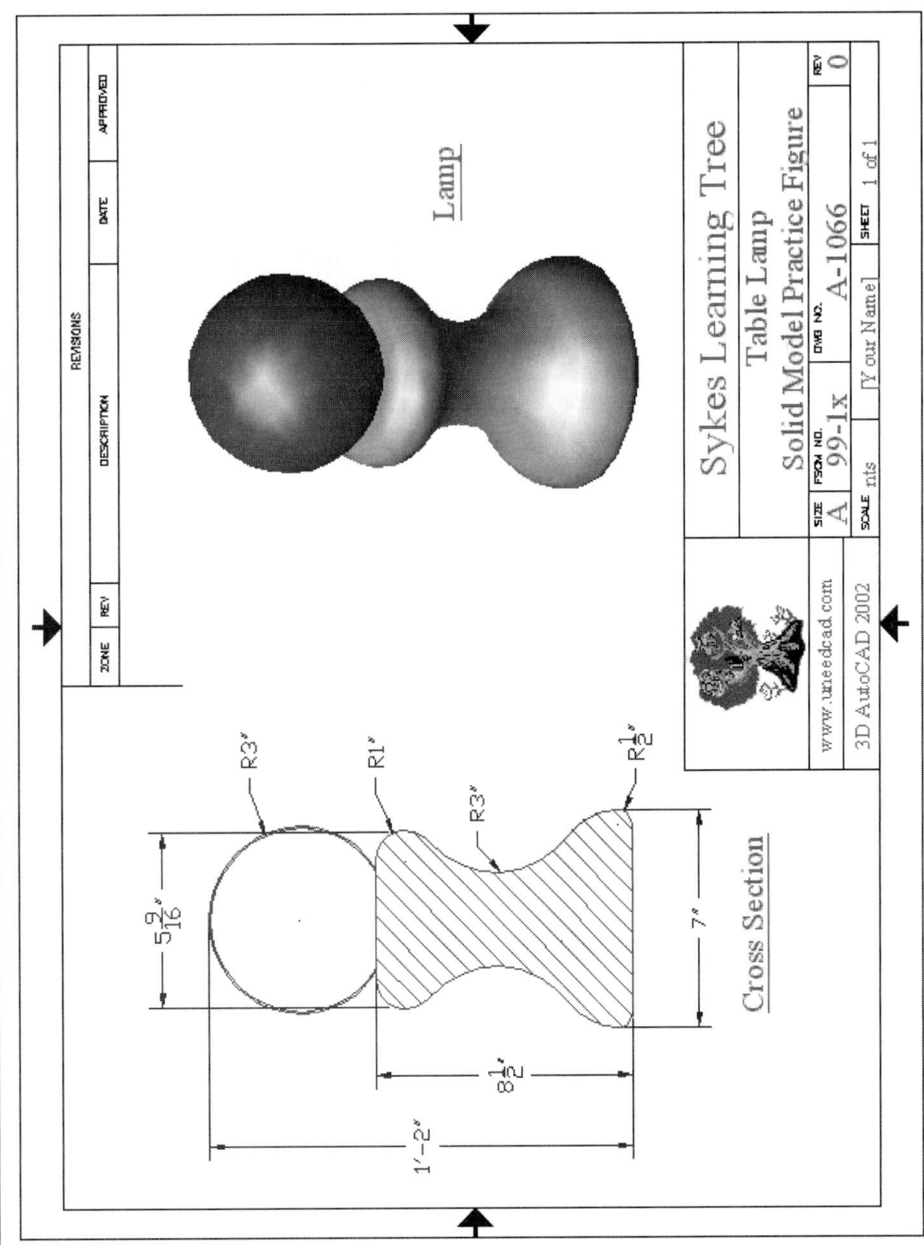

FIG. 10.6.14 Table Lamp

15. Create the cross in pool shown in Figure 10.6.15. Refer to the following guidelines.

15.1. Each piece (including the water) is a separate solid object.

15.2. Fully dimension the objects as shown.

15.3. Save the drawing as *MyCross.dwg* in the C:\Steps3D\Lesson10 folder.

Thanks to Casey Peel for permission to use this drawing. For more of Mr. Peel's drawings, visit his Web site at *http://www.peelinc.com/cpeel/creations/index.html.*

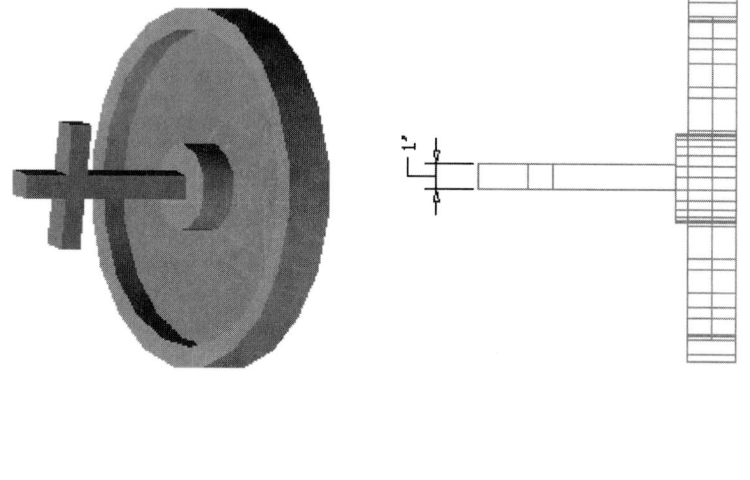

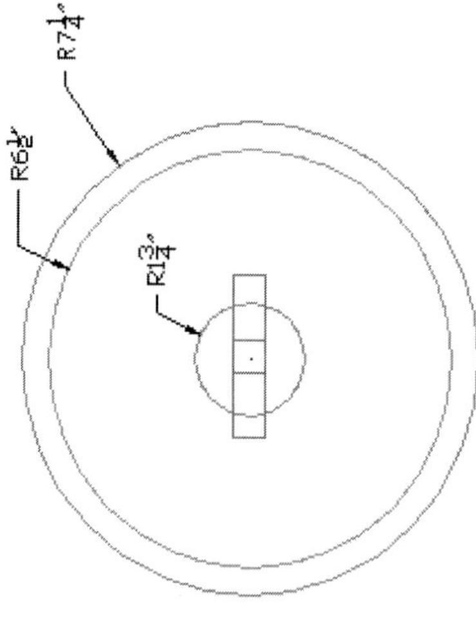

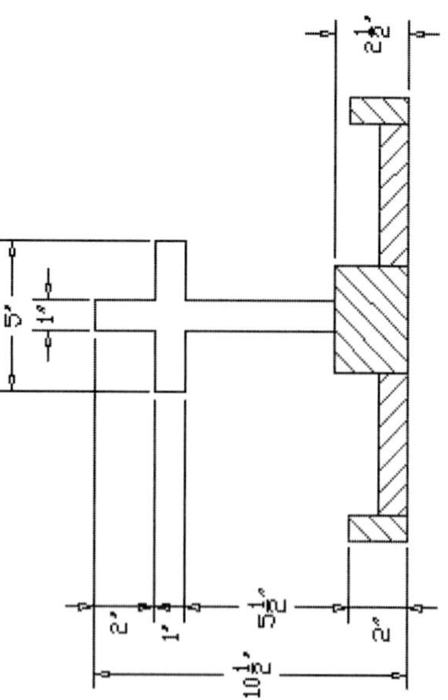

FIG. 10.6.15 Cross in Pool

10.7 REVIEW QUESTIONS

Write the correct answer on a separate sheet of paper.

1. The __________ command behaves like a computer-controlled welding rod.

2. Use the __________ command to remove one solid shape from another.

3. The Intersect command (a) removes everything that intersects between solids, (b) removes everything that does not intersect between solids.

4. Use the __________ command to cut through a solid object as though you are using a knife.

5. When using the Zaxis option of the Slice command, where will the point on the Z-axis (normal) of the plane be?

6. The __________ command will compute the volume of a selected solid object.

7. Which command helps the draftsman find design interferences *before* construction?

8. (T or F) There is no difference between filleting solids and filleting two-dimensional objects.

9. (T or F) You can change the fillet radius on the fly when filleting solids.

10. (T or F) There is no difference between chamfering solids and chamfering two-dimensional objects.

11. (T or F) There is no Angle option when chamfering a solid.

12. The __________ command will automatically create cross sections of solid objects.

13. The section that AutoCAD creates is a (solid, region, polyline).

LESSON 11

Editing 3D Solids

Following this lesson, you will

- Know how to use AutoCAD's ***SolidEdit*** command and its subcommands:
  - Face
    - Extrude
    - Move
    - Rotate
    - Offset
    - Taper
    - Delete
    - Copy
    - coLor
  - Edge
    - Copy
    - coLor
  - Body
    - Imprint
    - seParate solids
    - Clean

- **Shell**
- **Check**
- Know how to use the **SolidCheck** system variable

Over the course of your studies, I have pointed out many of AutoCAD's redundant features. (Indeed, by now you know me to be a great advocate of AutoCAD redundancy.) With the advent of AutoCAD 2000, a new feature appeared that duplicated some other features of 3D Solid editing you have already learned. But this command—*SolidEdit*—had some new routines and some new twists that made it a favorite to solid modelers everywhere.

Unfortunately, *SolidEdit* is not a simple command. In fact, it is a command in the tradition of *Pedit* or *Splinedit.* In other words, expect a multitiered command with multiple options per tier. But the wonders of those options will make Solid Modeling easier (and more fun) than you ever thought possible.

Let's take a look.

11.1 A Single Command, But It Does So Much—*SolidEdit*

Actually, as a command by itself, ***SolidEdit*** does not accomplish a thing. The ***SolidEdit*** command should be considered a ticket into a realm where 15 new commands dwell (17 if you consider **Undo** and **eXit**)—each capable of something beneficial to the solid modeler.

> Most of you will not remember that AutoCAD's original dimensioning tool is called a **Dim** prompt. From there, the user issued one of the many dimension commands (linear, angular, etc.). Think of what dimensioning looks like today, and then imagine what the future might hold for the ***SolidEdit*** command.

If we tried to study ***SolidEdit*** as a single command, we might find it somewhat overwhelming. But luckily, AutoCAD divided the command options into three categories—**Face**, **Edge**, and **Body**. In fact, AutoCAD's ***SolidEdit*** command prompt looks like this:

Enter a solids editing option [Face/Edge/Body/Undo/eXit] <eXit>:

Each of the options (categories) presents a separate tier of choices designed to help modify a solid object. (The other two options—**Undo** and **eXit**—are the standard options for most commands. **Undo** undoes the last procedure in the command; **eXit** completes the command and returns you to the command prompt.) We will use these natural divisions to study each option as a category, or grouping, of several routines.

AutoCAD also provides a Solids Editing toolbar with buttons that quickly access each of the commands in the categories. We will use these buttons throughout our lesson.

11.2 Changing Faces—The Face Category

The **Face Category** contains the bulk of ***SolidEdit***'s commands. This category includes commands (or options) designed to alter the faces of a solid.

To get to the **Face Category**'s options, follow this sequence:

Command: ***solidedit***

Enter a solids editing option [Face/Edge/Body/Undo/eXit] <eXit>: ***f***

[Extrude/Move/Rotate/Offset/Taper/Delete/Copy/coLor/Undo/eXit] <eXit>:

You can then select the routine you wish to use.

> Although faces occupy essentially the same place on 3D Solids as they did on Surface Models, remember that they are not 3D Faces. They are simply sides of a 3D Solid.

Of course, an easier way to access a specific **SolidEdit** routine would be simply to pick the desired choice on the Solids Editing toolbar.

Let's look at each of the routines as though they were individual commands.

11.2.1 Changing the Thickness of a 3D Solid Face—The Extrude Option

Have you tried to stretch a 3D Solid? If so, you have noticed that, once created, you cannot change the shape or dimensions of individual sides (faces) of the 3D Solid. And, if you have tried to extrude a 3D Solid, you have seen that you cannot.

So how do you change the individual faces of a 3D Solid? Well, prior to AutoCAD 2000, you could not—unless you added a 3D Solid using the ***Union*** command. But that was tedious, at best, and quite inefficient.

One of the ways AutoCAD responded to the need to change 3D Solids was by providing the **Extrude** option of the **Face Category**. The option works identically to the ***Extrude*** command—but only on selected faces. Here is the sequence:

Command: *solidedit*

Enter a solids editing option [Face/Edge/Body/Undo/eXit] <eXit>: *f*

[Extrude/Move/Rotate/Offset/Taper/Delete/Copy/coLor/Undo/eXit] <eXit>: *e*

Select faces or [Undo/Remove]: *[pick an edge(s) of the face you wish to extrude—AutoCAD will highlight the two faces that form that edge]*

Select faces or [Undo/Remove/ALL]: *[if you wish to extrude only one of the highlight faces, tell AutoCAD you wish to Remove a face]*

Remove faces or [Undo/Add/ALL]: *[select an edge of the face you wish to remove—select a face that is not shared with the face you do wish to extrude]*

Remove faces or [Undo/Add/ALL]: *[hit enter to complete the selection]*

Specify height of extrusion or [Path]: *[these two options are identical to the Extrude command's sequence]*

Specify angle of taper for extrusion <0>:

AutoCAD will then extrude the selected face and return to the **Face Category** of the ***SolidEdit*** command.

> The **Extrude** option of the ***SolidEdit*** command (as well as the other options discussed in this lesson) can also be reached via the Modify pull-down menu. Follow this path:
>
> *Modify—Solids Editing—Extrude Faces (or the desired option)*

Let's give it a try.

WWW 11.2.1.1 Do This: Extruding a 3D Solid Face

I. Open the *SE-Box.dwg* file in the C:\Steps3D\Lesson11 folder. The drawing looks like Figure 11.2.1.1a. (The current viewpoint is 1,−2,1.)

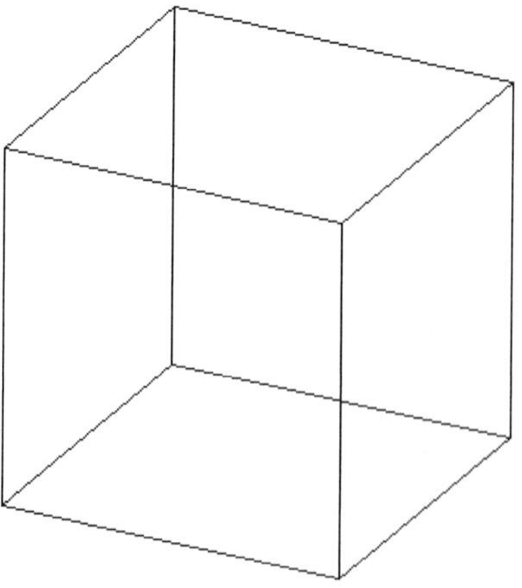

FIG. 11.2.1.1a *SE-Box.dwg*

II. Follow these steps:

TOOLS	COMMAND SEQUENCE	STEPS
 Extrude Faces Button	**Command:** ***solidedit*** **Solids editing automatic checking: SOLIDCHECK=1** **Enter a solids editing option [Face/Edge/Body/Undo/eXit] <eXit>:** ***f*** **Enter a face editing option [Extrude/Move/Rotate/Offset/Taper/Delete/Copy/coLor/Undo/eXit] <eXit>:** ***e***	**1.** Enter the command sequence shown to access the **Extrude** option of the **Face Category**. Or you may pick the **Extrude Faces** button on the Solids Editing toolbar. (*Note:* Picking the **Extrude faces** button replaces the entire command sequence shown in this step. Proceed to Step 2.)
	Select faces or [Undo/Remove]:	**2.** Select the upper-east edge (Figure 11.2.1.1.2). 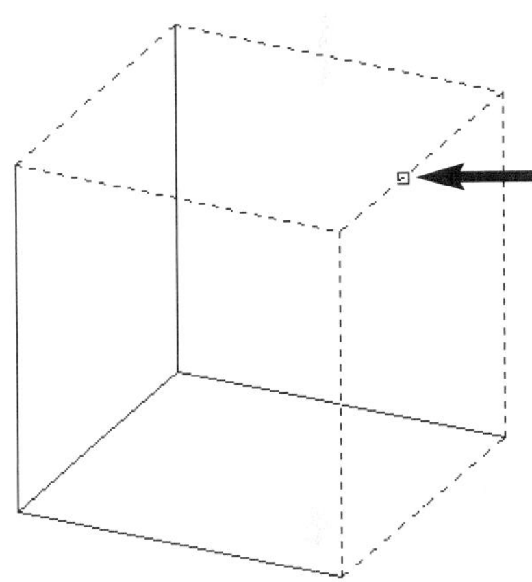 FIG. 11.2.1.1.2 Select This Edge
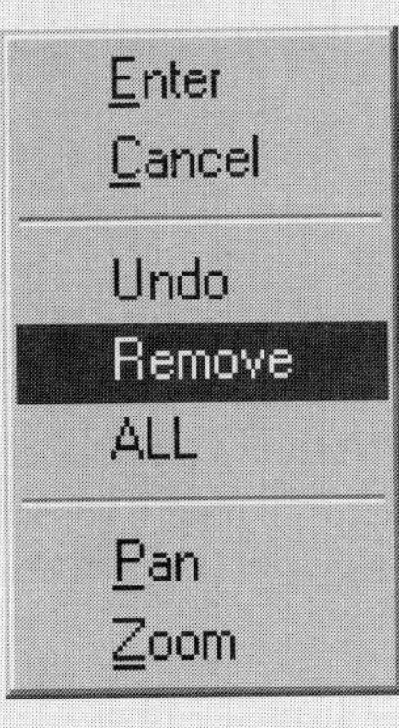	**Select faces or [Undo/Remove/ALL]:** ***r***	**3.** Tell AutoCAD you wish to remove a face from the selection set.
	Remove faces or [Undo/Add/ALL]: **Remove faces or [Undo/Add/ALL]:** ***[enter]***	**4.** Select an edge on the eastern face, and then hit ***enter*** to continue.
	Specify height of extrusion or [Path]: ***1*** **Specify angle of taper for extrusion <0>:** ***30***	**5.** Tell AutoCAD to use an extrusion **height** of ***1*** and a **taper angle** of ***30°***.

continued

TOOLS	COMMAND SEQUENCE	STEPS
	Solid validation started. **Solid validation completed.** **Enter a face editing option [Extrude/Move/Rotate/Offset/Taper/ Delete/Copy/coLor/Undo/eXit] <eXit>:** *[enter]*	**6.** By default, AutoCAD validates that the task you have outlined is possible and then extrudes the object.
	Solids editing automatic checking: SOLIDCHECK=1 **Enter a solids editing option [Face/ Edge/Body/Undo/eXit] <eXit>:** *[enter]*	**7.** Hit *enter* twice to exit the command. Your drawing looks like Figure 11.2.1.1.7. 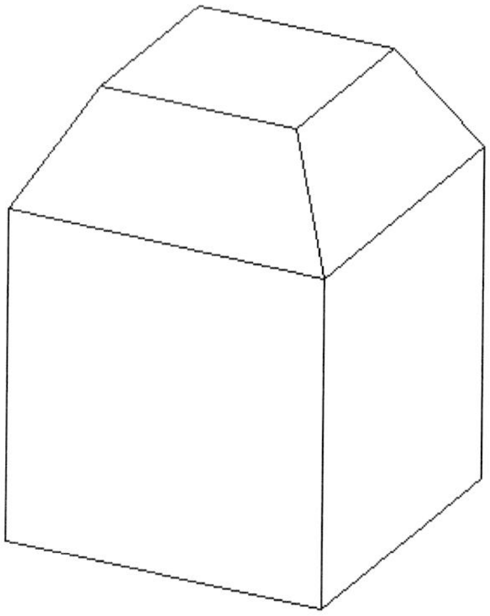 **FIG. 11.2.1.1.7** Extruded Face of a 3D Solid (hidden lines removed)
	**Command:** *qsave*	**8.** Save the drawing, but do not exit.

Next, we will look at a similar option.

11.2.2 Moving a Face on a 3D Solid

The **Move** routine of the **Face Category** proves to be quite handy when it becomes necessary to relocate part of a 3D Solid—such as a bolt hole—that was improperly placed. This handy tool was sorely missed in previous releases and will, no doubt, prove as valuable to the solid editor as the ***Move*** command does to two-dimensional CAD draftsmen.

The command sequence looks like this:

Command: *solidedit*

Enter a solids editing option [Face/Edge/Body/Undo/eXit] <eXit>: *f*

[Extrude/Move/Rotate/Offset/Taper/Delete/Copy/coLor/Undo/eXit] eXit>: *m*

Select faces or [Undo/Remove]: *[pick an edge of the face you wish to move; as with the Extrude option, AutoCAD will highlight the two faces that form that edge]*

Select faces or [Undo/Remove/ALL]: *[if you wish to move only one of the highlight faces, tell AutoCAD you wish to Remove a face]*

Remove faces or [Undo/Add/ALL]: *[select an edge of the face you wish to remove—select a face that is not shared with the face you do wish to move]*

Remove faces or [Undo/Add/ALL]: *[hit enter to complete the selection]*

Specify a base point or displacement: *[the next options are identical to the basic two-dimensional Move command's options]*

Specify a second point of displacement:

AutoCAD will then move the selected face and return to the **Face Category** of the ***SolidEdit*** command.

Let's give it a try.

11.2.2.1 Do This: Moving a 3D Solid Face

I. Be sure you are still in the *SE-Box.dwg* file in the C:\Steps3D\Lesson11 folder. If not, open it now.

II. Follow these steps:

TOOLS	COMMAND SEQUENCE	STEPS
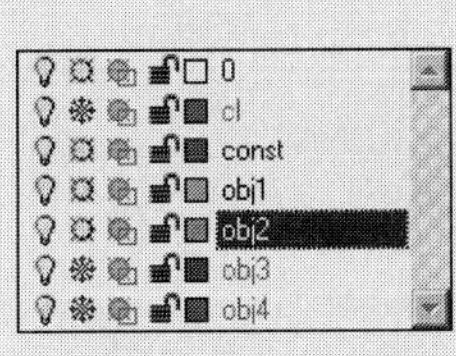	**Command:** *la*	**1.** Thaw the **obj2** layer. Notice the cylinder that appears inside the box (Figure 11.2.2.1.1). 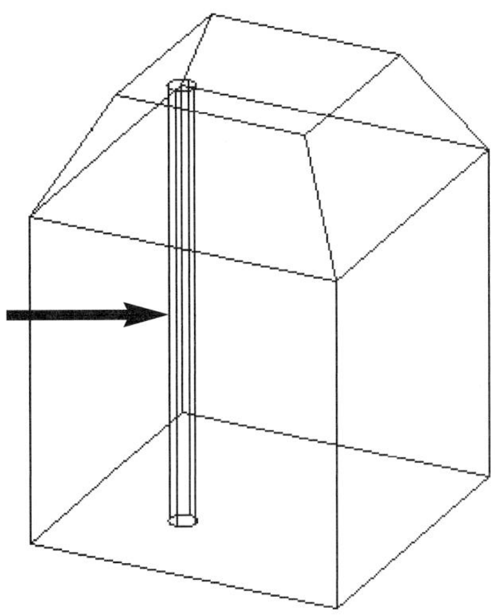 FIG. 11.2.2.1.1 Cylinder

continued

TOOLS	COMMAND SEQUENCE	STEPS
	**Command:** ***su***	**2.** Use the ***Subtract*** command to subtract the cylinder from the box. Your drawing looks like Figure 11.2.2.1.2. 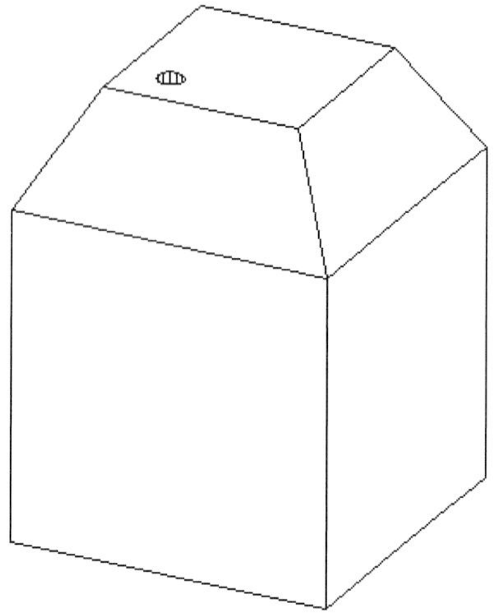 **FIG. 11.2.2.1.2** 3D Solid with Hole (hidden lines removed)
 Move Faces Button	**Command:** ***solidedit*** **Solids editing automatic checking: SOLIDCHECK=1** **Enter a solids editing option [Face/ Edge/Body/Undo/eXit] <eXit>:** ***f*** **Enter a face editing option [Extrude/Move/Rotate/Offset/Taper/ Delete/Copy/coLor/Undo/eXit] <eXit>:** ***m***	**3.** Enter the command sequence shown to access the **Move** option of the **Face Category**. Or you can pick the **Move Faces** button on the Solids Editing toolbar.
	Select faces or [Undo/Remove]:	**4.** Select the top of the hole. AutoCAD highlights the top of the hole and the topmost face of the 3D Solid.
Enter Cancel Undo Remove ALL Pan Zoom	**Select faces or [Undo/Remove/ALL]:** ***r*** **Remove faces or [Undo/Add/ALL]:** **Remove faces or [Undo/Add/ALL]:** ***[enter]***	**5.** Tell AutoCAD you want to remove a face from the selection set, and then select the topmost face of the 3D Solid. Hit ***enter*** to continue.

continued

TOOLS	COMMAND SEQUENCE	STEPS
	Specify a base point or displacement: ***1,1***	**6.** I will use the displacement method to move the hole 1 unit east and 1 unit north on the 3D Solid.
	Specify a second point of displacement: ***[enter]***	
	Solid validation started. **Solid validation completed.**	**7.** As with the **Extrude** routine, AutoCAD validates the procedure before actually moving the hole.
	Enter a face editing option [Extrude/Move/Rotate/Offset/Taper/Delete/Copy/coLor/Undo/eXit] <eXit>: ***[enter]***	**8.** Hit ***enter*** twice to exit the command. Your drawing looks like Figure 11.2.2.1.8.
	Solids editing automatic checking: SOLIDCHECK=1 **Enter a solids editing option [Face/Edge/Body/Undo/eXit] <eXit>:** ***[enter]***	FIG. 11.2.2.1.8 Moved Hole (hidden lines removed)
	Command: ***qsave***	**9.** Save the drawing, but do not exit.

Consider for a moment the old way of "moving" a hole.

- First, you would have to create a solid over the existing hole.
- Next, you would use the ***Union*** command to fill in the hole.
- Then you would create a cylinder with the appropriate size and height in the new location.
- You would conclude by subtracting the new cylinder from the solid.

Try doing it this way. It will really make you appreciate the ***SolidEdit*** command! Next we will rotate a face on the 3D Solid.

11.2.3 Rotating Faces on a 3D Solid

Like the other **Face Category** options, **Rotate** emulates another command. But in the case of the **Rotate** routine, it does not emulate the ***Rotate*** command but rather the ***Rotate3d*** command. In other words, you will have the opportunity to rotate a 3D Solid face about an axis (as opposed to a point).

The command sequence looks like this:

Command: *solidedit*

Enter a solids editing option [Face/Edge/Body/Undo/eXit] <eXit>: *f*

[Extrude/Move/Rotate/Offset/Taper/Delete/Copy/coLor/Undo/eXit] <eXit>: *r*

Select faces or [Undo/Remove]:]: *[pick an edge of the face you wish to rotate; AutoCAD will highlight the two faces that form that edge]*

Select faces or [Undo/Remove/ALL]: *[if you wish to rotate only one of the highlight faces, tell AutoCAD you wish to Remove a face]*

Remove faces or [Undo/Add/ALL]: *[select an edge of the face you wish to remove—select a face that is not shared with the face you do wish to rotate]*

Remove faces or [Undo/Add/ALL]: *[hit enter to complete the selection]*

Specify an axis point or [Axis by object/View/Xaxis/Yaxis/Zaxis] <2points>: *[the rest of the options are identical to the Rotate3d command's options]*

Specify the second point on the rotation axis:

Specify a rotation angle or [Reference]:

Are you ready to try it?

11.2.3.1 Do This: Rotating a 3D Solid Face

I. Be sure you are still in the *SE-Box.dwg* file in the C:\Steps3D\Lesson11 folder. If not, open it now.

II. Follow these steps:

TOOLS	COMMAND SEQUENCE	STEPS
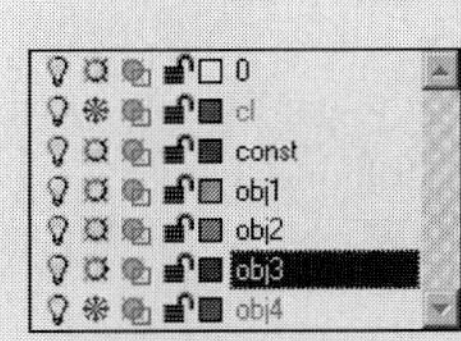	**Command:** *la*	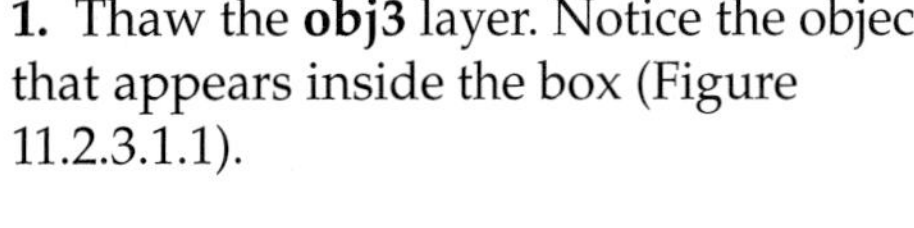 **1.** Thaw the **obj3** layer. Notice the object that appears inside the box (Figure 11.2.3.1.1). 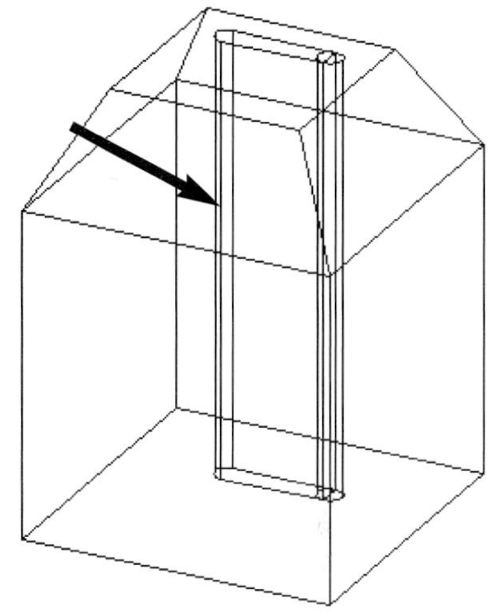 **FIG. 11.2.3.1.1** New Object
	**Command:** *su*	**2.** Use the ***Subtract*** command to subtract the object from the box. Your drawing looks like Figure 11.2.3.1.2. 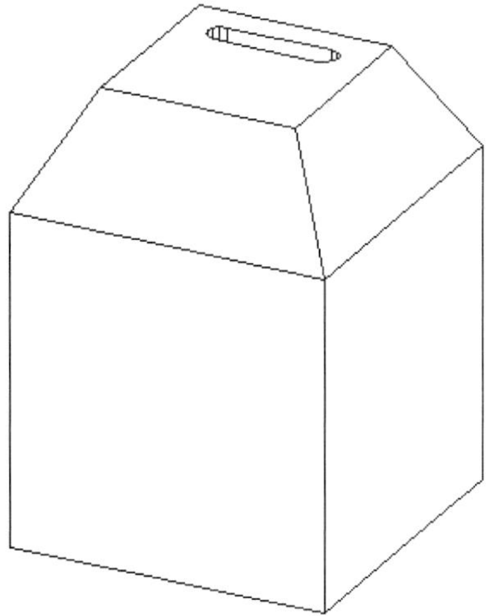 **FIG. 11.2.3.1.2** Slotted Solid (hidden lines removed)

continued

TOOLS	COMMAND SEQUENCE	STEPS
 Rotate Faces Button	**Command:** *solidedit*	**3.** Enter the command sequence shown to access the **Rotate** option of the **Face Category**. Or you can pick the **Rotate Faces** button on the Solids Editing toolbar.
	Solids editing automatic checking: SOLIDCHECK=1 **Enter a solids editing option [Face/Edge/Body/Undo/eXit] <eXit>:** *f*	
	Enter a face editing option [Extrude/Move/Rotate/Offset/Taper/Delete/Copy/coLor/Undo/eXit] <eXit>: *r*	
	Select faces or [Undo/Remove/ALL]:	**4.** Select the four faces forming the slot, and then hit ***enter*** to continue.
	Select faces or [Undo/Remove/ALL]: *[enter]*	
	Specify an axis point or [Axis by object/View/Xaxis/Yaxis/Zaxis] <2points>: *[select the upper-center point]*	**5.** Select the upper- and lower-center points indicated in Figure 11.2.3.1.5. (You must pick the upper-center point first to properly set the Z-axis.)
	Specify the second point on the rotation axis: *[select the lower-center point]*	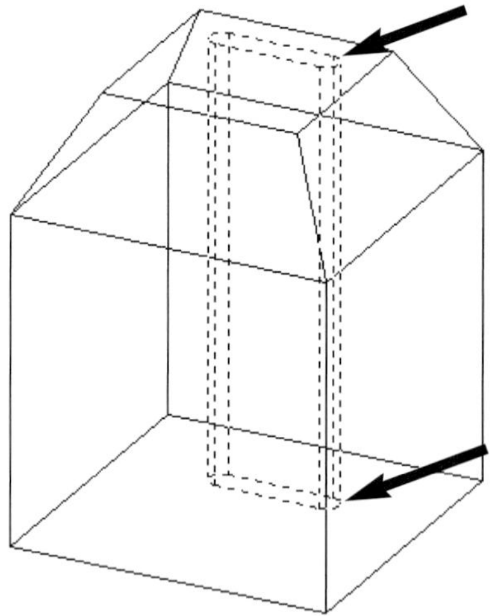 **FIG. 11.2.3.1.5** Select These Center Points to ID the Rotation Axis
	Specify a rotation angle or [Reference]:−*45*	**6.** Rotate the slot −45°. (If you selected the lower-center point first in Step 6, you must rotate +45°.)

continued

TOOLS	COMMAND SEQUENCE	STEPS
	Enter a face editing option [Extrude/Move/Rotate/Offset/Taper/ Delete/Copy/coLor/Undo/eXit] <eXit>: *[enter]* **Solids editing automatic checking: SOLIDCHECK=1** **Enter a solids editing option [Face/ Edge/Body/Undo/eXit] <eXit>:** *[enter]*	**7.** Hit ***enter*** twice to complete the command. Your drawing looks like Figure 11.2.3.1.7. 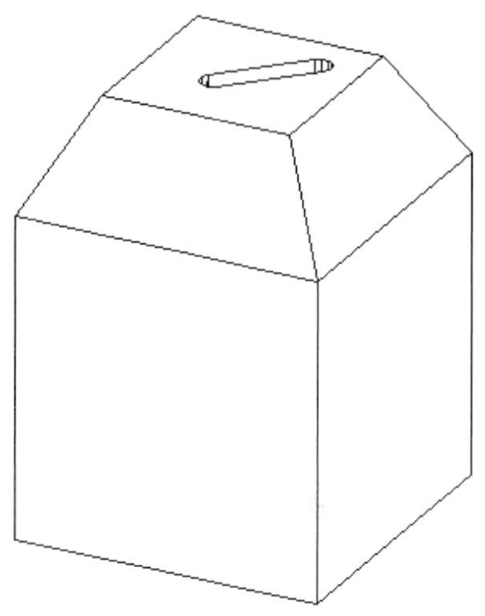 **FIG. 11.2.3.1.7** Rotated Slot (hidden lines removed)
	**Command:** *qsave*	**8.** Save the drawing, but do not exit.

Imagine the trouble you would have had accomplishing this task without the ***SolidEdit*** command!

11.2.4 Offsetting Faces on a 3D Solid

The **Offset** routine of the **Face Category** works very much like the two-dimensional command. There are, however, some quirks about it that the user must know to avoid frustration.

The first of these quirks lies in the direction of the offset. When using the two-dimensional command, the user picks the direction of the offset on the screen or by coordinate input. In Z-Space, this might present problems (since picking a point on the screen does not work well in Z-Space). Instead, the user controls the direction of the offset by using a positive or negative number to identify the distance of the offset. But here is the quirk: The positive number does not increase the size of the face being offset (it will not increase the size of the slot, as you will see). Rather, it increases the *volume of the solid* (thus *decreasing* the size of the slot). A negative number, of course, has the opposite effect.

The second quirk is actually an omission on AutoCAD's part. Whereas the user can offset an object through a point in two-dimensional space (using the ***Offset*** command), no such option is presented when using the ***SolidEdit*** command. The CAD operator will miss this convenience. (Hopefully, AutoCAD will remedy this oversight in the future.)

The command sequence for the **Offset** option is

Command: *solidedit*

Enter a solids editing option [Face/Edge/Body/Undo/eXit] <eXit>: *f*

[Extrude/Move/Rotate/Offset/Taper/Delete/Copy/coLor/Undo/eXit] <eXit>: *o*

Select faces or [Undo/Remove]:]: *[pick an edge of the face you wish to offset; AutoCAD will highlight the two faces that form that edge]*

Select faces or [Undo/Remove/ALL]: *[if you wish to offset only one of the highlight faces, tell AutoCAD you wish to Remove a face]*

Remove faces or [Undo/Add/ALL]: *[select an edge of the face you wish to remove—select a face that is not shared with the face you do wish to offset]*

Remove faces or [Undo/Add/ALL]: *[hit enter to complete the selection]*

Specify the offset distance: *[enter the distance you wish to offset the selected face(s)]*

Try enlarging the slot a bit.

11.2.4.1 Do This: Offsetting a 3D Solid Face

I. Be sure you are still in the *SE-Box.dwg* file in the C:\Steps3D\Lesson11 folder. If not, open it now.

II. Follow these steps:

TOOLS	COMMAND SEQUENCE	STEPS
 Offset Faces Button	**Command:** *solidedit* **Solids editing automatic checking: SOLIDCHECK=1** **Enter a solids editing option [Face/Edge/Body/Undo/eXit] <eXit>:** *f* **Enter a face editing option [Extrude/Move/Rotate/Offset/Taper/Delete/Copy/coLor/Undo/eXit] <eXit>:** *o*	**1.** Enter the command sequence shown to access the **Offset** option of the **Face Category**. Or you may pick the **Offset Faces** button on the Solids Editing toolbar.

continued

TOOLS	COMMAND SEQUENCE	STEPS
	Select faces or [Undo/Remove/ALL]: **Select faces or [Undo/Remove/ALL]:** *[enter]*	**2.** Select the four faces forming the slot, and then hit ***enter*** to continue.
	Specify the offset distance: −.*125*	**3.** We want to increase the size of the slot (*decreasing* the volume of the solid), so we will enter a negative number. Offset the slot by $\frac{1}{8}''$ as indicated.
	Enter a face editing option [Extrude/Move/Rotate/Offset/Taper/Delete/Copy/coLor/Undo/eXit] <eXit>: *[enter]* **Solids editing automatic checking: SOLIDCHECK=1** **Enter a solids editing option [Face/Edge/Body/Undo/eXit] <eXit>:** *[enter]*	**4.** Hit ***enter*** twice to complete the command. Your drawing looks like Figure 11.2.4.1.4. 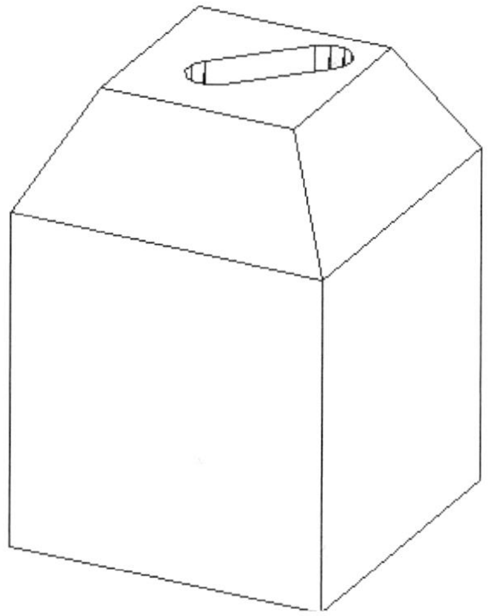 **FIG. 11.2.4.1.4** Enlarged Slot (hidden lines removed)
	Command: *qsave*	**5.** Save the drawing, but do not exit.

11.2.5 Tapering Faces on a 3D Solid

Tapering a face on a 3D Solid is not difficult, but you will need to watch the positive and negative numbers just as you did when you offset a face. The command sequence is

Command: *solidedit*

Enter a solids editing option [Face/Edge/Body/Undo/eXit] <eXit>: *f*

[Extrude/Move/Rotate/Offset/Taper/Delete/Copy/coLor/Undo/eXit] <eXit>: *t*

Select faces or [Undo/Remove]:]: *[pick an edge of the face you wish to taper; AutoCAD will highlight the two faces that form that edge]*

Select faces or [Undo/Remove/ALL]: *[if you wish to taper only one of the highlight faces, tell AutoCAD you wish to Remove a face]*

Remove faces or [Undo/Add/ALL]: *[select an edge of the face you wish to remove—select a face that is not shared with the face you do wish to taper]*

Remove faces or [Undo/Add/ALL]: *[hit enter to complete the selection]*

Have you noticed the similarities in the prompts and instructions for all of the routines that we have seen so far?

Specify the base point: *[the base point does not have to be on the face itself; essentially, you are using the base point and second point to identify a direction, or axis, for the taper]*

Specify another point along the axis of tapering: *[identify a second point along the axis]*

Specify the taper angle: *[tell AutoCAD how much of an angle you wish to create—remember, a positive number will enlarge a hole in the direction of the axis you indicated; a negative number, of course, will reduce the hole]*

Let's taper a hole in our solid.

11.2.5.1 Do This: Tapering a 3D Solid Face

I. Be sure you are still in the *SE-Box.dwg* file in the C:\Steps3D\Lesson11 folder. If not, open it now.

II. Follow these steps:

TOOLS	COMMAND SEQUENCE	STEPS
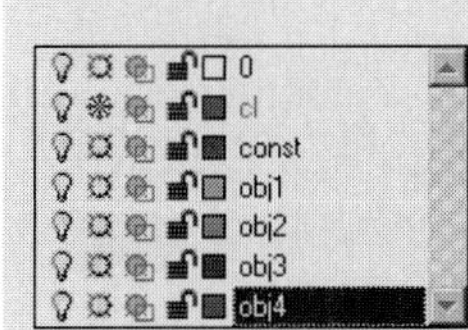	**Command:** *la*	**1.** Thaw the **obj4** layer. Notice the cylinder that appears inside the box (Figure 11.2.5.1.1).
	**Command:** *su*	**2.** Use the ***Subtract*** command to subtract the cylinder from the box. Your drawing looks like Figure 11.2.5.1.2.

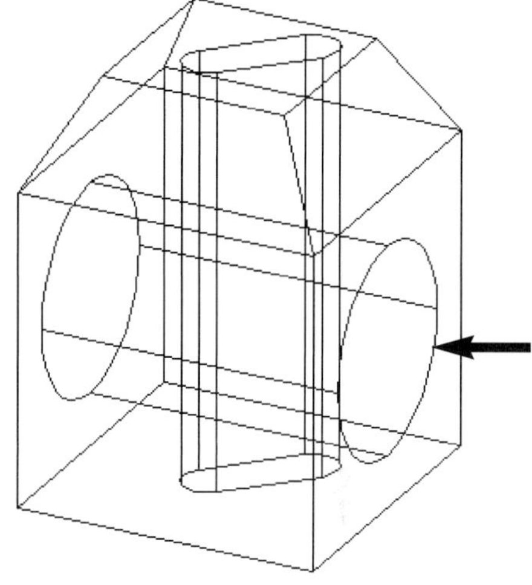

FIG. 11.2.5.1.1 New Cylinder

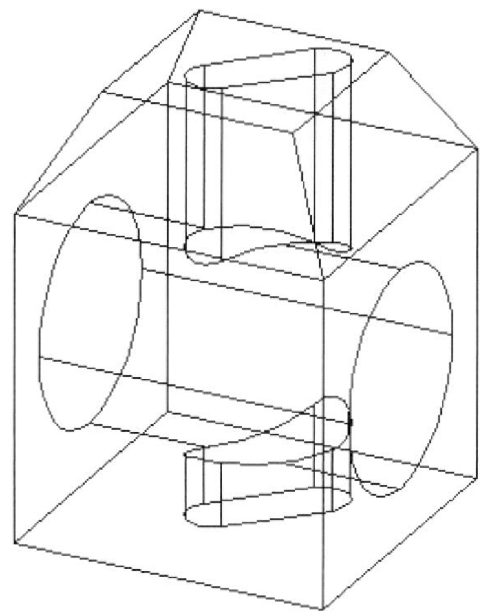

FIG. 11.2.5.1.2 Hole in Solid

continued

TOOLS	COMMAND SEQUENCE	STEPS
 Taper Faces Button	**Command:** *solidedit* **Solids editing automatic checking: SOLIDCHECK=1** **Enter a solids editing option [Face/ Edge/Body/Undo/eXit] <eXit>:** *f* **Enter a face editing option [Extrude/Move/Rotate/Offset/Taper/ Delete/Copy/coLor/Undo/eXit] <eXit>:** *t*	**3.** Enter the command sequence shown to access the **Taper** routine of the **Face Category**. Or you may pick the **Taper Faces** button on the Solids Editing toolbar.
	Select faces or [Undo/Remove/ALL]: **Select faces or [Undo/Remove/ALL]:** *[enter]*	**4.** Select one of the isolines defining the large hole, and then hit ***enter*** to continue.
	Specify the base point: **Specify another point along the axis of tapering:**	**5.** Use the eastern (right) center of the large hole as the base point and the center of the other end as the other **point along the axis of tapering**.
	Specify the taper angle: −5	**6.** We will reduce the size of the hole as it moves westward. Enter a negative **taper angle** of 5° as indicated.
	Enter a face editing option [Extrude/Move/Rotate/Offset/Taper/ Delete/Copy/coLor/Undo/eXit] <eXit>: *[enter]* **Solids editing automatic checking: SOLIDCHECK=1** **Enter a solids editing option [Face/ Edge/Body/Undo/eXit] <eXit>:** *[enter]*	**7.** Hit ***enter*** twice to complete the command. Your drawing looks like Figure 11.2.5.1.7. 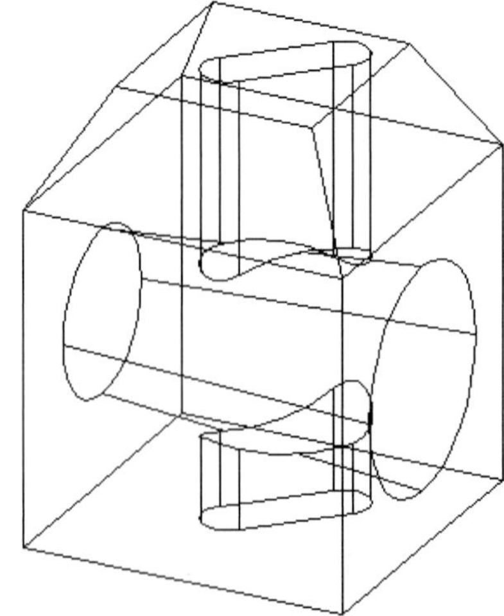 **FIG. 11.2.5.1.7** Tapered Hole

continued

TOOLS	COMMAND SEQUENCE	STEPS
	**Command:** *qsave*	**8.** Save the drawing, but do not exit.

11.2.6 Deleting 3D Solid Faces

Our next routine provides a method for removing some faces (like fillets, chamfers, holes, etc.) from a 3D Solid. The command sequence is one of the easiest (no points or axes to identify).

Command: *solidedit*

Enter a solids editing option [Face/Edge/Body/Undo/eXit] <eXit>: *f*

[Extrude/Move/Rotate/Offset/Taper/Delete/Copy/coLor/Undo/eXit] <eXit>: *d*

Select faces or [Undo/Remove]:]: *[pick an edge of the face you wish to delete; AutoCAD will highlight the faces that form that edge]*

Select faces or [Undo/Remove/ALL]: *[hit enter to complete the selection]*

Suppose we want to get rid of the large hole altogether. We will use the **Delete** routine.

11.2.6.1 Do This: Deleting a 3D Solid Face

I. Be sure you are still in the *SE-Box.dwg* file in the C:\Steps3D\Lesson11 folder. If not, open it now.

II. Follow these steps:

TOOLS	COMMAND SEQUENCE	STEPS
 Delete Faces Button	**Command:** *solidedit* **Solids editing automatic checking: SOLIDCHECK=1** **Enter a solids editing option [Face/ Edge/Body/Undo/eXit] <eXit>:** *f* **Enter a face editing option [Extrude/Move/Rotate/Offset/Taper/ Delete/Copy/coLor/Undo/eXit] <eXit>:** *d*	**1.** Enter the command sequence shown to access the **Delete** routine of the **Face Category**. Or you may pick the **Delete Faces** button on the Solids Editing toolbar.
	Select faces or [Undo/Remove/ALL]: **Select faces or [Undo/Remove/ALL]:** *[enter]* **Enter a face editing option [Extrude/Move/Rotate/Offset/Taper/ Delete/Copy/coLor/Undo/eXit] <eXit>:** *[enter]* **Solids editing automatic checking: SOLIDCHECK=1** **Enter a solids editing option [Face/ Edge/Body/Undo/eXit] <eXit>:** *[enter]*	**2.** Select the large, tapered hole (you will find it easier to select one of the internal isolines defining the face). Then hit ***enter*** three times to complete the command. Your drawing looks like Figure 11.2.6.1.2. 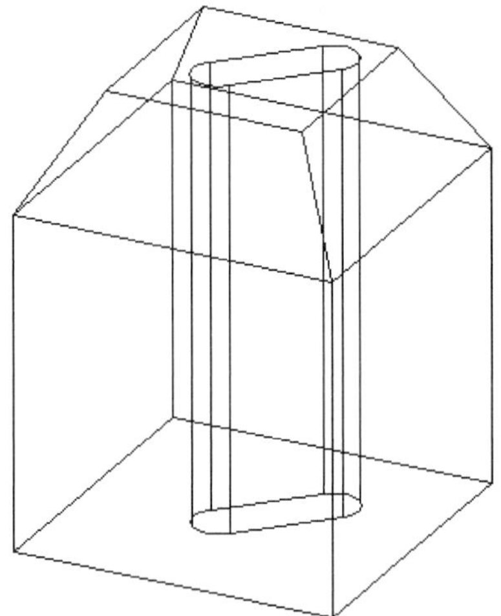 **FIG. 11.2.6.1.2** 3D Solid After Deleting the Tapered Hole
	**Command:** *qsave*	**3.** Save the drawing, but do not exit.

11.2.7 Copying 3D Solid Faces as Regions or Bodies

Use the **Copy** routine of the **Face Category** to create copies of one or more faces of a 3D Solid. AutoCAD creates the copies as regions or bodies, which you can explode into individual lines, arcs, circles, and so forth, or extrude into new 3D Solid objects. Unlike the results of the ***Copy*** command, however, *the new objects exist on the layer that was current when the copies were created.*

A *body* is any structure that represents a solid or a Non-Uniform Rational B-Spline (NURBS) surface.

It is as simple to use as the ***Copy*** command. The command sequence is

Command: *solidedit*

Enter a solids editing option [Face/Edge/Body/Undo/eXit] <eXit>: *f*

[Extrude/Move/Rotate/Offset/Taper/Delete/Copy/coLor/Undo/eXit] <eXit>: *c*

Select faces or [Undo/Remove]:]: *[pick an edge of the face you wish to copy; AutoCAD will highlight the two faces that form that edge]*

Select faces or [Undo/Remove/ALL]: *[remove unwanted faces or hit enter to complete the selection]*

Specify a base point or displacement: *[the last prompts are the same as the Copy command's prompts]*

Specify a second point of displacement:

We will copy the top faces of our solid.

11.2.7.1 Do This: Copying a 3D Solid Face

I. Be sure you are still in the *SE-Box.dwg* file in the C:\Steps3D\Lesson11 folder. If not, open it now.

II. Follow these steps:

TOOLS	COMMAND SEQUENCE	STEPS
 Copy Faces Button	**Command:** *solidedit* **Solids editing automatic checking: SOLIDCHECK=1 Enter a solids editing option [Face/Edge/Body/Undo/eXit] <eXit>:** *f* **Enter a face editing option [Extrude/Move/Rotate/Offset/Taper/ Delete/Copy/coLor/Undo/eXit] <eXit>:** *c*	**1.** Enter the command sequence shown to access the **Copy** routine of the **Face Category**. Or you may pick the **Copy Faces** button on the Solids Editing toolbar.
	Select faces or [Undo/Remove/ALL]: **Select faces or [Undo/Remove/ALL]:** *[enter]*	**2.** Select the top face and the four angled faces around it. Hit *enter* to continue.
	Specify a base point or displacement: *5,0* **Specify a second point of displacement:** *[enter]*	**3.** Use the displacement method to copy the faces five units to the right as indicated.
	Enter a face editing option **[Extrude/Move/Rotate/Offset/Taper/ Delete/Copy/coLor/Undo/eXit] <eXit>:** *[enter]* **Solids editing automatic checking: SOLIDCHECK=1** **Enter a solids editing option [Face/ Edge/Body/Undo/eXit] <eXit>:** *[enter]*	**4.** Hit *enter* twice to complete the command. Your drawing looks like Figure 11.2.7.1.4.

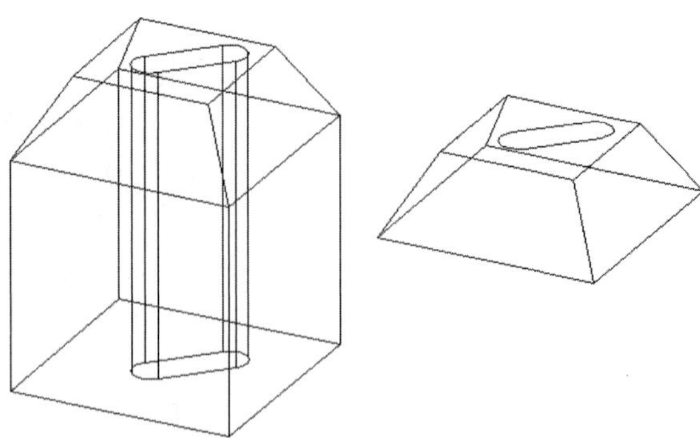

FIG. 11.2.7.1.4 *Copied Faces*

continued

TOOLS	COMMAND SEQUENCE	STEPS
	Command: *li*	**5.** Perform a ***List*** on one of the faces to verify that it is a region.
	Command: *e*	**6.** Erase the new objects.

11.2.8 Changing the Color of a Single Face

The **coLor** routine of the **Face Category** is useful if you intend to shade or remove hidden lines from your drawing. It helps to distinguish between the different faces.

The command sequence is

Command: *solidedit*

Enter a solids editing option [Face/Edge/Body/Undo/eXit] <eXit>: *f*

[Extrude/Move/Rotate/Offset/Taper/Delete/Copy/coLor/Undo/eXit] <eXit>: *l*

Select faces or [Undo/Remove]:]: *[pick an edge of the face whose color you wish to change—AutoCAD will highlight the two faces that form that edge]*

Select faces or [Undo/Remove/ALL]: *[remove unwanted faces or hit enter to complete the selection]*

[AutoCAD presents the Color Selection dialog box; select the color you wish the face(s) to be]

Let's make the slot a different color and view our 3D Solid using the Gouraud Shademode.

11.2.8.1 Do This: Changing the Color of a 3D Solid Face

I. Be sure you are still in the *SE-Box.dwg* file in the C:\Steps3D\Lesson11 folder. If not, open it now.

II. Follow these steps:

TOOLS	COMMAND SEQUENCE	STEPS
 Color Faces Button	**Command:** *solidedit* **Solids editing automatic checking: SOLIDCHECK=1** **Enter a solids editing option [Face/Edge/Body/Undo/eXit] <eXit>:** *f* **Enter a face editing option [Extrude/Move/Rotate/Offset/Taper/ Delete/Copy/coLor/Undo/eXit] <eXit>:** *l*	**1.** Enter the command sequence shown to access the **coLor** routine of the **Face Category**. Or you can pick the **Color Faces** button on the Solids Editing toolbar.
	Select faces or [Undo/Remove/ALL]: **Select faces or [Undo/Remove/ALL]:** *[enter]*	**2.** Select the faces that form the slot, and then hit *enter* to continue.
	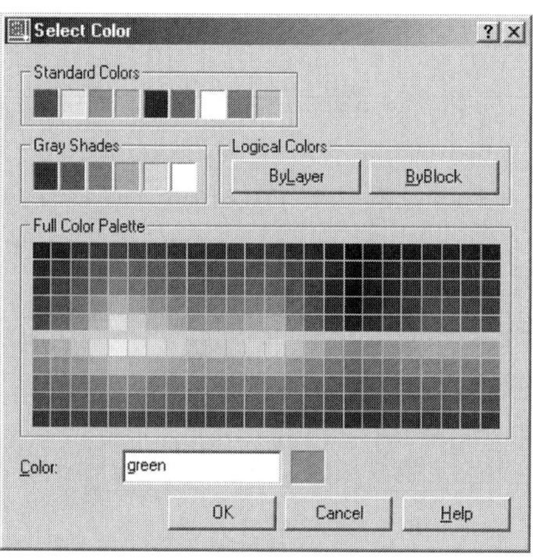	**3.** AutoCAD presents the Select Color dialog box. Select **Green**.
	Enter a face editing option [Extrude/Move/Rotate/Offset/Taper/ Delete/Copy/coLor/Undo/eXit] <eXit>: *[enter]* **Solids editing automatic checking: SOLIDCHECK=1** **Enter a solids editing option [Face/ Edge/Body/Undo/eXit] <eXit>:** *[enter]*	**4.** Hit *enter* twice to complete the command.

continued

TOOLS	COMMAND SEQUENCE	STEPS
	**Command:** *shademode* **Current mode: 2D wireframe** **Enter option [2D wireframe/3D wireframe/Hidden/Flat/Gouraud/ fLat+edges/gOuraud+edges] <2D wireframe>:** *g*	**5.** Set the Shademode system variable to **Gouraud**. Your drawing looks like Figure 11.2.8.1.5. 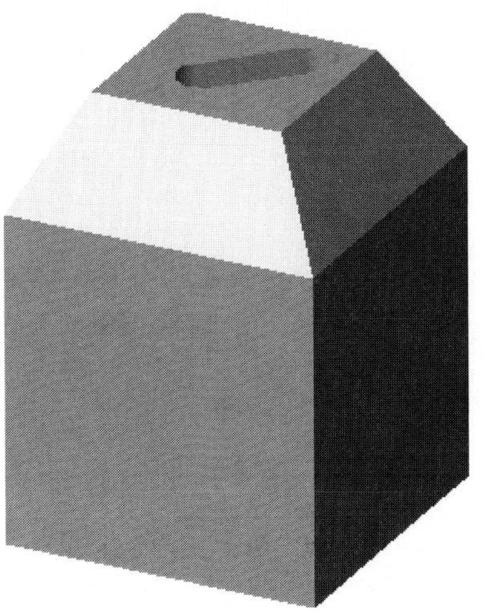 FIG. 11.2.8.1.5 Colored and Shaded 3D Solid
	**Command:** *qsave*	**6.** Save the drawing, but do not exit.

11.3 Modifying Edges—The Edge Category

The **Edge Category** contains only two real options (besides the **Undo/eXit** options). Both of these—**Copy** and **coLor**—repeat options found in the **Face Category**. But here they are for use on single edges rather than entire faces.

The command sequence to access the **Edge** options of the ***SolidEdit*** command is

Command: *solidedit*

Enter a solids editing option [Face/Edge/Body/Undo/eXit] <eXit>: *e*

Enter an edge editing option [Copy/coLor/Undo/eXit] <eXit>:

Prompts for both the **Copy** option and the **CoLor** option are identical to their counterparts in the **Face Category**.

Let's look at each in an exercise.

WWW 11.3.1 Do This: Changing Edges on a 3D Solid

I. Be sure you are still in the *SE-Box.dwg* file in the C:\Steps3D\Lesson11 folder. If not, open it now.

II. Change the **Shademode** setting back to **2D**.

III. Set **Const** as the current layer.

IV. Follow these steps:

TOOLS	COMMAND SEQUENCE	STEPS
 Color Edges Button	**Command:** *solidedit* **Solids editing automatic checking: SOLIDCHECK=1** **Enter a solids editing option [Face/ Edge/Body/Undo/eXit] <eXit>:** *e* **Enter an edge editing option [Copy/coLor/Undo/eXit] <eXit>:** *l*	**1.** Enter the command sequence shown to access the **coLor** routine of the **Edge Category**. Or you can pick the **Color Edges** button on the Solids Editing toolbar.
	Select edges or [Undo/Remove]: **Select edges or [Undo/Remove]:** *[enter]*	**2.** Select the lowermost and easternmost edge of the 3D Solid (Figure 11.3.1.2), and then hit *enter* to continue. 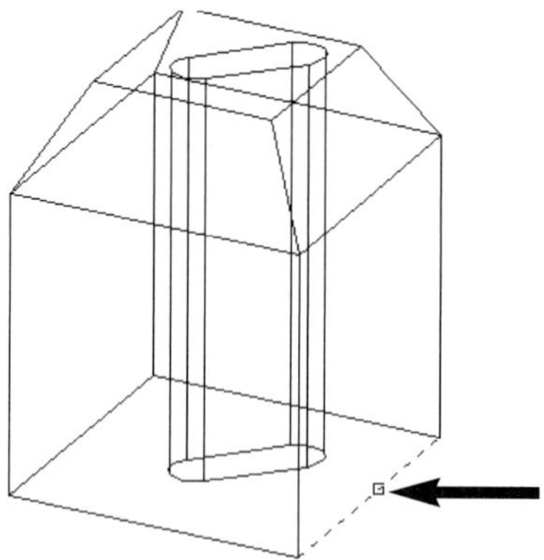 **FIG. 11.3.1.2** Select This Edge

continued

TOOLS	COMMAND SEQUENCE	STEPS
	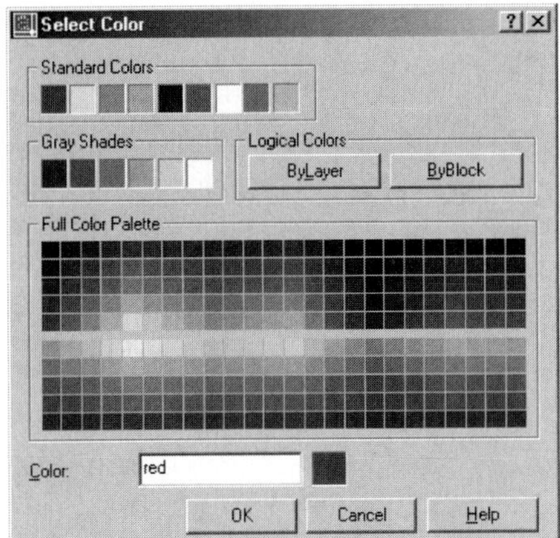	**3.** AutoCAD presents the Select Color dialog box. Select **Red**.
 Copy Edges Button	**Enter an edge editing option [Copy/coLor/Undo/eXit] <eXit>:** *c*	**4.** AutoCAD changes the color of the selected line and then returns to the **edge editing option** prompt. Tell it you want to copy an edge as shown (or you can pick the **Copy Edges** button on the Solids Editing toolbar).
	Select edges or [Undo/Remove]: **Select edges or [Undo/Remove]:** *[enter]*	**5.** Select the same edge as in Step 2 and one of the adjoining edges (Figure 11.3.1.5). Hit *enter* to continue. 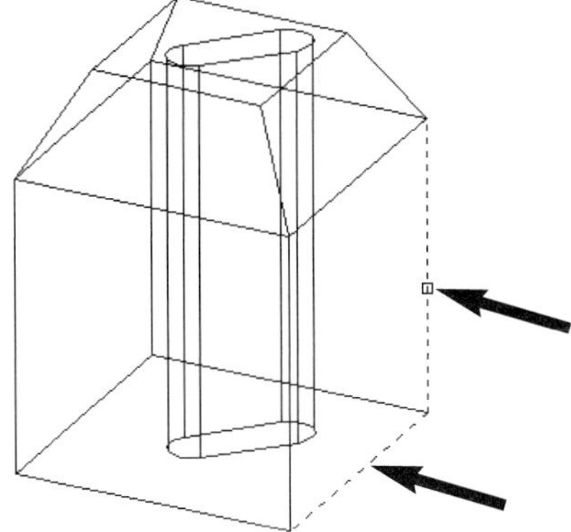 FIG. 11.3.1.5 Select These Edges
	Specify a base point or displacement: *2,0* **Specify a second point of displacement:**	**6.** Use the displacement method to copy the edges two units to the east, as indicated.

continued

TOOLS	COMMAND SEQUENCE	STEPS
	Enter an edge editing option [Copy/coLor/Undo/eXit] <eXit>: *[enter]*	**7.** Exit the command. Your drawing looks like Figure 11.3.1.7.
	Solids editing automatic checking: SOLIDCHECK=1 **Enter a solids editing option [Face/Edge/Body/Undo/eXit] <eXit>:** *[enter]*	Notice that both copies have been placed on the current (**Const**) layer and that both have assumed the characteristic color of that layer regardless of their layer and color on the 3D Solid. **FIG. 11.3.1.7** *Copied Lines*
	Command: *u*	**8.** Undo the previous changes.

So you see that not much difference occurs between these procedures and their counterparts in the **Face Category**—except for the obvious effect on edges rather than faces.

Our next category, however, will be quite different!

11.4 Changing the Whole 3D Solid—The Body Category

The **Body Category** includes routines to modify a 3D Solid as a whole. All of its five options (except the **Undo/eXit** options) are new and have no counterparts in the 2D or 3D modification worlds. We will look at each.

To access the **Body Category**'s options, follow this sequence:

Command: *solidedit*

Enter a solids editing option [Face/Edge/Body/Undo/eXit] <eXit>: *b*

[Imprint/seParate solids/Shell/cLean/Check/Undo/eXit] <eXit>:

11.4.1 Imprinting an Image onto a 3D Solid

The **Imprint** routine of the **Body Category** "imprints" (or draws) an image of a selected object—arc, circle, line, 2D or 3D polyline, ellipse, spline, region, or body—onto a 3D solid. Essentially, the imprint is a two-dimensional representation of the object on one of the faces of the 3D Solid.

Once the impression has been made, *the line (or arc, spline, etc.) actually becomes a defining edge for a new face on the 3D Solid.* So you can use this to help create new faces where they are needed.

This will become clearer with an exercise.

The command sequence to use the **Imprint** option is

Command: *solidedit*

Enter a solids editing option [Face/Edge/Body/Undo/eXit] <eXit>: *b*

[Imprint/seParate solids/Shell/cLean/Check/Undo/eXit] <eXit>: *i*

Select a 3D solid: *[select the 3D Solid on which you wish to make the impression]*

Select an object to imprint: *[select the object you wish to imprint]*

Delete the source object <N>: *[AutoCAD allows you the opportunity to keep or delete the object you are using to create your impression]*

Select an object to imprint: *[you may continue to imprint objects or hit enter to complete the option]*

Let's see what we can do with **Imprint**.

WWW 11.4.1.1 Do This: Imprinting Edges on a 3D Solid

I. Be sure you are still in the *SE-Box.dwg* file in the C:\Steps3D\Lesson11 folder. If not, open it now.

II. Follow these steps:

TOOLS	COMMAND SEQUENCE	STEPS
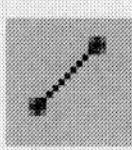	**Command:** *l*	**1.** Draw a line between the midpoints of the vertical edges defining the western face of the 3D Solid. (We will use this line to imprint a new edge.) Your drawing will look like Figure 11.4.1.1.1.
		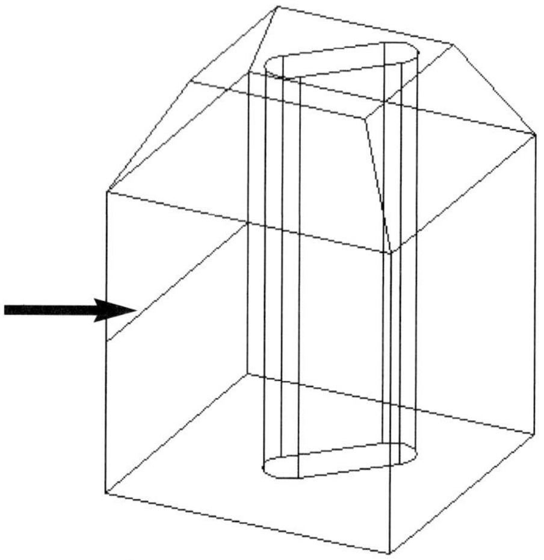 FIG. 11.4.1.1.1 New Line
 Imprint Button	**Command:** *solidedit* **Solids editing automatic checking: SOLIDCHECK=1** **Enter a solids editing option [Face/Edge/Body/Undo/eXit] <eXit>:** *b* **Enter a body editing option [Imprint/seParate solids/Shell/cLean/Check/Undo/eXit] <eXit>:** *i*	**2.** Enter the command sequence shown to access the **Imprint** routine of the **Body Category**. Or you can pick the **Imprint** button on the Solids Editing toolbar.
	Select a 3D solid:	**3.** Select the 3D Solid.
	Select an object to imprint:	**4.** Select the line you created in Step 1.
	Delete the source object <N>: *y*	**5.** We will not need the line after the impression is made, so allow AutoCAD to delete it.

continued

TOOLS	COMMAND SEQUENCE	STEPS
	Select an object to imprint: *[enter]* **Enter a body editing option [Imprint/seParate solids/Shell/cLean/ Check/Undo/eXit] <eXit>:** *[enter]* **Solids editing automatic checking: SOLIDCHECK=1** **Enter a solids editing option [Face/ Edge/Body/Undo/eXit] <eXit>:** *[enter]*	**6.** We can continue to imprint objects, but we will not need to do so now. So hit *enter* three times to complete the command.
	Command: *solidedit*	**7.** Follow the procedure outlined in Exercise 11.2.3.1 to rotate the new face 30°. The completed drawing will look like Figure 11.4.1.1.7. **FIG. 11.4.1.1.7** New Rotated Face
	Command: *qsave*	**8.** Save the drawing.

You can probably see that **Imprint** will be one of the more useful of the ***SolidEdit*** command's options. You may find it easier to imprint and modify than to create a new 3D Solid and join it (via the ***Union*** command) to an existing 3D Solid.

11.4.2 Separating 3D Solids with the seParate Solids Routines

At first glance, the **seParate solids** option looked very promising—after all, it separates 3D Solids into their constituencies. Simply put, this means that, if a 3D Solid were created from a box and a cylinder, it would separate the 3D Solid into the box and cylinder again. The way it works, however, *you can only separate the constituent objects when they do not actually touch.*

Still, there will be times when you find the **seParate solids** option quite handy. You will see this in our exercise.

The command sequence is one of the simplest:

Command: *solidedit*

Enter a solids editing option [Face/Edge/Body/Undo/eXit] <eXit>: *b*

[Imprint/seParate solids/Shell/cLean/Check/Undo/eXit] <eXit>: *p*

Select a 3D solid: *[select the solid you wish to separate]*

Let's take a look.

11.4.2.1 Do This: Separating Parts of a 3D Solid

I. Open the *SE-Box-2.dwg* file in the C:\Steps3D\Lesson11 folder. The drawing looks like Figure 11.4.2.1a.

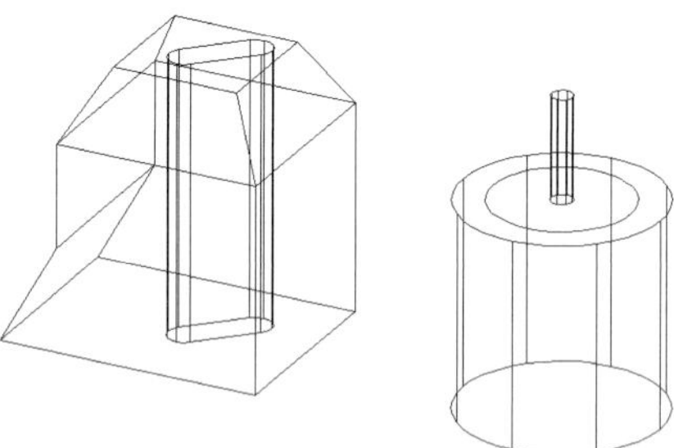

FIG. 11.4.2.1a *SE-Box-2.dwg*

II. Use the ***List*** command to verify that all objects shown are part of a single 3D Solid.

III. Follow these steps:

TOOLS	COMMAND SEQUENCE	STEPS
 Separate Button	**Command:** *solidedit*	1. Enter the command sequence shown to access the **seParate solids** routine of the **Body Category**. Or you may pick the **Separate** button on the Solids Editing toolbar.
	Solids editing automatic checking: SOLIDCHECK=1 **Enter a solids editing option [Face/ Edge/Body/Undo/eXit] <eXit>:** *b*	
	Enter a body editing option [Imprint/seParate solids/Shell/cLean/ Check/Undo/eXit] <eXit>: *p*	
	Select a 3D solid:	2. Select either of the objects on the screen (as you have seen, they are both part of a single 3D Solid).
	Enter a body editing option [Imprint/seParate solids/Shell/cLean/ Check/Undo/eXit] <eXit>: *[enter]*	3. Hit *enter* twice to complete the command.
	Solids editing automatic checking: SOLIDCHECK=1 **Enter a solids editing option [Face/ Edge/Body/Undo/eXit] <eXit>:** *[enter]*	
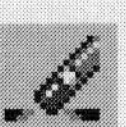	**Command:** *e*	4. Erase the object on the right to verify that the 3D Solids have separated.
	**Command:** *u*	5. Undo the erasure.
	**Command:** *qsave*	6. Save the drawing, but do not exit.

11.4.3 Clean

The **Clean** option of the **Body Category** removes extra (redundant) edges and vertices—including imprinted and unused edges—from a 3D Solid. Use it as a final cleanup tool once you have completed your 3D Solid.

The command sequence is identical to that of the **seParate solids** option—and is, therefore, one of AutoCAD's simplest.

Did you notice the extra circular edge at the top of the new 3D Solid? We do not need this one, so we will use the **Clean** option to remove it.

Let's take a look.

11.4.3.1 Do This: Cleaning Up a 3D Solid

I. Be sure you are still in the *SE-Box-2.dwg* file in the C:\Steps3D\Lesson11 folder. If not, open it now.

II. Follow these steps:

TOOLS	COMMAND SEQUENCE	STEPS
 Clean Button	**Command:** *solidedit* **Solids editing automatic checking: SOLIDCHECK=1** **Enter a solids editing option [Face/Edge/Body/Undo/eXit] <eXit>:** ***b*** **Enter a body editing option [Imprint/seParate solids/Shell/cLean/Check/Undo/eXit] <eXit>:** ***l***	**1.** Enter the command sequence shown to access the **Clean** routine of the **Body Category**. Or you may pick the **Clean** button on the Solids Editing toolbar.
	Select a 3D solid:	**2.** Select the round 3D Solid (on the right).
	Enter a body editing option [Imprint/seParate solids/Shell/cLean/Check/Undo/eXit] <eXit>: ***[enter]*** **Solids editing automatic checking: SOLIDCHECK=1** **Enter a solids editing option [Face/Edge/Body/Undo/eXit] <eXit>:** ***[enter]***	**3.** Hit ***enter*** twice to complete the command. The object looks like Figure 11.4.3.1.3 (notice that the extra circular edge on the top has been removed). 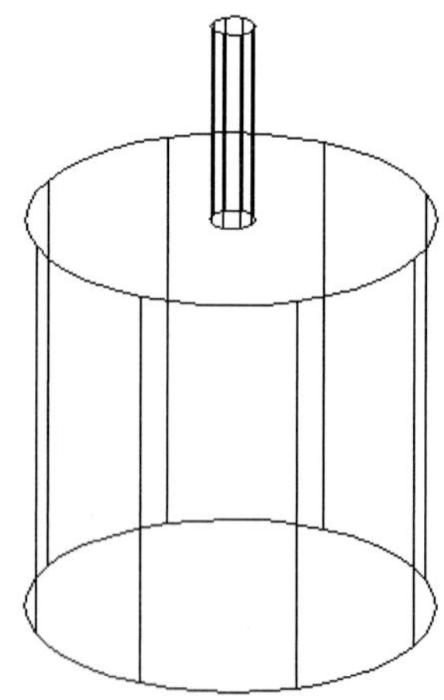 **FIG. 11.4.3.1.3** Removed Edge
	**Command:** *qsave*	**4.** Save the drawing, but do not exit.

■ 11.4.4 Shell

The **Shell** routine is one of the niftiest in the ***SolidEdit*** stable. With it, the user can convert a 3D Solid into a solid object similar to a Surface Model. In other words, the user can convert a 3D Solid into a hollow "shell" made up of a single 3D Solid object.

To better understand this, consider your computer's monitor. Imagine the monitor with all the "guts" taken out—leaving just the plastic shell. The shell is a single solid object. The **Shell** routine was designed to create such objects!

The command sequence resembles those in the **Face Category**:

Command: *solidedit*

Enter a solids editing option [Face/Edge/Body/Undo/eXit] <eXit>: *b*

[Imprint/seParate solids/Shell/cLean/Check/Undo/eXit] <eXit>: *s*

Select a 3D solid: *[select the 3D Solid you wish to shell]*

Remove faces or [Undo/Add/ALL]: *[select an edge of the face(s) you wish to remove]*

Remove faces or [Undo/Add/ALL]: *[hit enter to complete the selection]*

Enter the shell offset distance: *[this figure defines the thickness of your shell]*

Let's create a shell from our original object.

WWW 11.4.4.1 Do This: Shelling a 3D Solid

I. Be sure you are still in the *SE-Box-2.dwg* file in the C:\Steps3D\Lesson11 folder. If not, open it now.

II. Follow these steps:

TOOLS	COMMAND SEQUENCE	STEPS
 Shell Button	**Command:** *solidedit* **Solids editing automatic checking: SOLIDCHECK=1** **Enter a solids editing option [Face/Edge/Body/Undo/eXit] <eXit>:** *b* **Enter a body editing option [Imprint/seParate solids/Shell/cLean/Check/Undo/eXit] <eXit>:** *s*	**1.** Enter the command sequence shown to access the **Shell** routine of the **Body Category**. Or you may pick the **Shell** button on the Solids Editing toolbar.
	Select a 3D solid:	**2.** Select the original 3D Solid (the one on the left).

continued

TOOLS	COMMAND SEQUENCE	STEPS
	Remove faces or [Undo/Add/ALL]: **Remove faces or [Undo/Add/ALL]:** *[enter]*	**3.** Remove the bottommost and southernmost edge (Figure 11.4.4.1.3). Hit ***enter*** to continue.

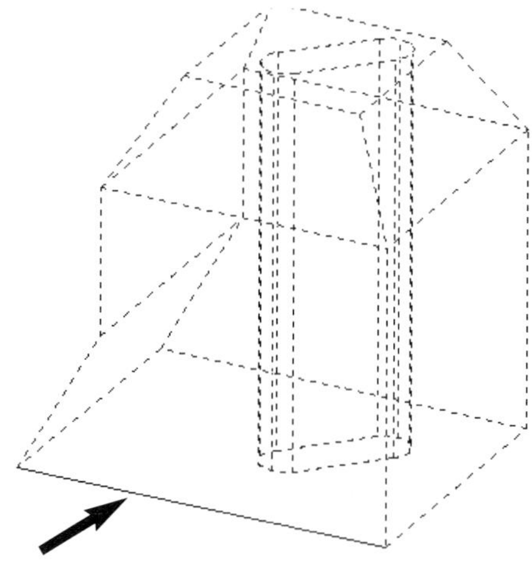

FIG. 11.4.4.1.3 Remove This Edge

TOOLS	COMMAND SEQUENCE	STEPS
	Enter the shell offset distance: ***1/16***	**4.** Make the shell thickness $\frac{1}{16}''$.
	Enter a body editing option **[Imprint/seParate solids/Shell/cLean/Check/Undo/eXit] <eXit>:** *[enter]* **Solids editing automatic checking: SOLIDCHECK=1** **Enter a solids editing option [Face/Edge/Body/Undo/eXit] <eXit>:** *[enter]*	**5.** Hit ***enter*** twice to complete the command. Your drawing looks like Figure 11.4.4.1.5.

FIG. 11.4.4.1.5 Shelled Object (Shademode=Gouraud)

TOOLS	COMMAND SEQUENCE	STEPS
	**Command:** *qsave*	**6.** Save the drawing.

11.4.5 Checking to Be Certain You Have an ACIS Solid

Have you noticed this note at the beginning of each of the options you have used in the *SolidEdit* command?

Solids editing automatic checking: SOLIDCHECK=1

This is telling you that the **SolidCheck** system variable has been set to **1** (that is, it has been activated or turned **On**). This means that AutoCAD will automatically check any 3D Solid objects selected for editing to verify that they are valid ACIS solids.

All this means is that 3D Solids created in AutoCAD can be used by other software that uses ACIS.

ACIS is a solid modeling format created by Spatial Technology, Inc.

The command sequence is identical to that of the **seParate solids** and **Clean** routines and will return the message

This object is a valid ACIS solid

if the object is a valid ACIS solid.

Frankly, this is another of AutoCAD's redundancies. Leaving the **SolidCheck** system variable set to **1** (the default) will guarantee that AutoCAD automatically checks any 3D Solid you try to edit. Using the **SolidCheck** system variable's default, you will never have to worry about ACIS (unless the object fails the verification).

If the object fails the verification, it is a good idea to redraw it.

11.5 Extra Steps

Demonstrations for many of the items covered in this lesson can be viewed through the AutoCAD Learning Assistant. Play the Editing Faces of 3D Solids video to supplement your reading. Follow this path in the Learning Assistant:

AutoCAD 2002—Tutorials—Working in 3 Dimensions—Editing Faces of 3D Solids

11.6 What Have We Learned?

Items covered in this lesson include

- *Tools used to edit 3D Solid Faces, including*
  - *Extrude*
  - *Move*
  - *Rotate*
  - *Offset*
  - *Taper*
  - *Delete*
  - *Copy*
  - *coLor*
- *Tools used to edit 3D Solid Edges, including*
  - *Copy*
  - *coLor*
- *Tools used to edit 3D Solid Bodies, including*
  - *Imprint*
  - *seParate solids*
  - *Clean*
  - *Shell*
  - *Check*
- *The* ***SolidCheck*** *system variable*

Wow! What a lesson! Did you ever imagine a single command could have so many different options?

You have learned many ways to create and modify 3D Solids. As I promised, you are no longer simply a CAD draftsman. By experience and training, you have become a CAD operator. You no longer draw. Now you create actual objects in the computer. There is very little left in the three-dimensional world for you to learn!

In our next lesson, I will show you how to handle blocks in Z-Space. I will also show you some tools to help you plot the objects you have learned to create. It will be an easier and less involved lesson than this one, so you can relax a bit. After that, we will look at Rendering the objects you create (making them look "real" by assigning materials to them). Then we will leave Z-Space and cover some other advanced tools you need to know before completing your training.

But first, as always, let's practice what we have learned.

11.7 EXERCISES

1. Open the *Slotted Guide #1.dwg* file in the C:\Steps3D\Lesson11 folder. Using only the procedures discussed in this lesson, create the drawing in Figure 11.7.1.
   - **1.1.** Remember that a negative number entered as an extrusion height will extrude *into* the object.
   - **1.2.** Remember that a negative number entered as a tapering angle will angle outward.
   - **1.3.** Save the drawing as *MySG#1.dwg* in the C:\Steps3D\Lesson11 folder.

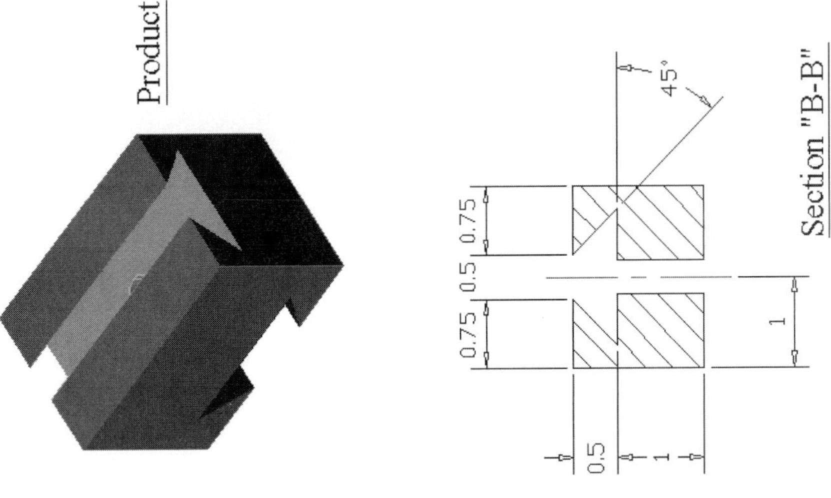

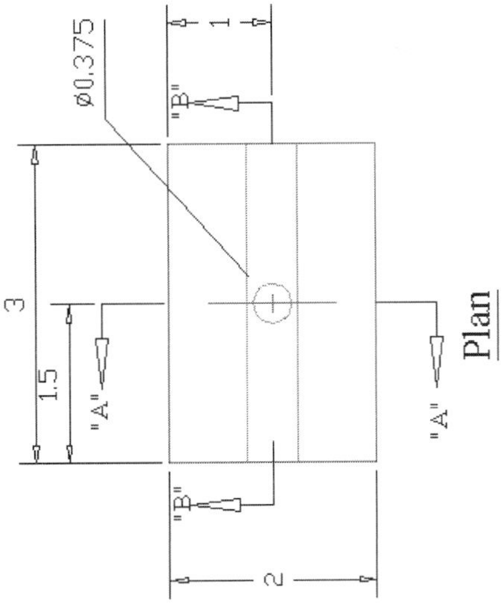

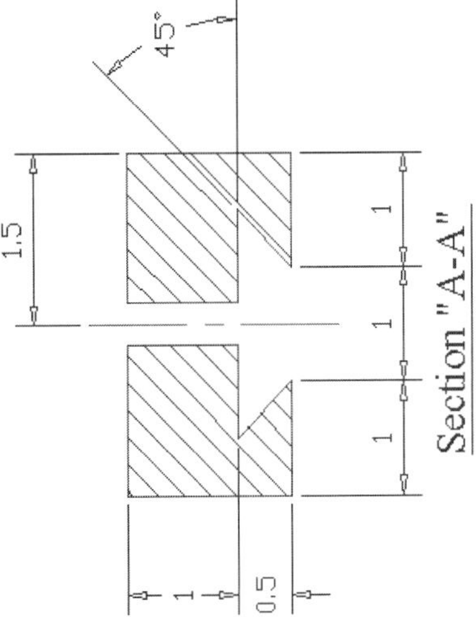

FIG. 11.7.1 *Slotted Guide #1.dwg*

2. Open the *Slotted Guide #2.dwg* file in the C:\Steps3D\Lesson11 folder. Using only the procedures discussed in this lesson, create the drawing in Figure 11.7.2.
   2.1. Save the drawing as *MySG#2.dwg* in the C:\Steps3D\Lesson11 folder.

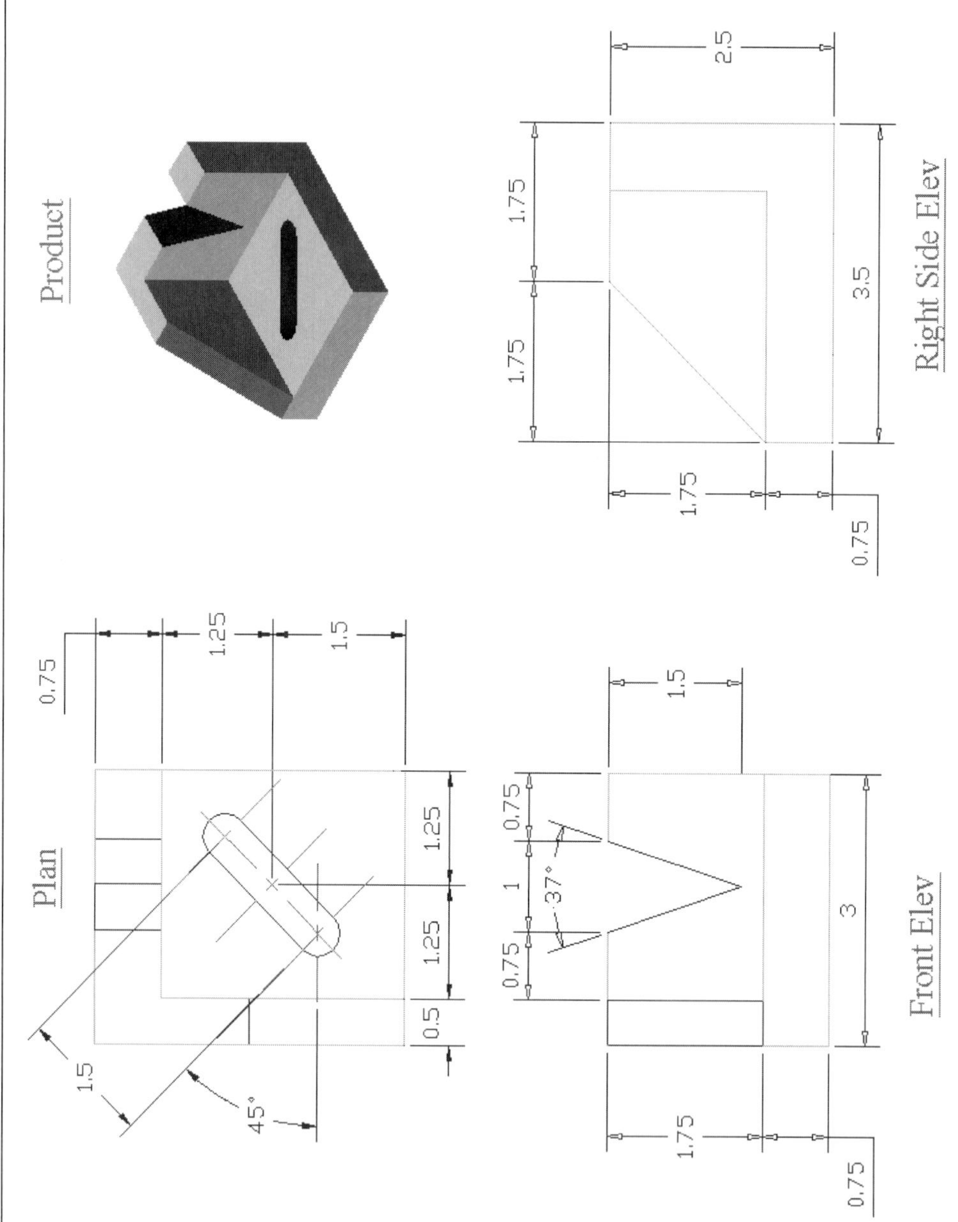

FIG. 11.7.2 *Slotted Guide #2.dwg*

3. Create the corner bracket drawing in Figure 11.7.3.
   - **3.1.** Use a $\frac{1}{16}''$ fillet along the edges.
   - **3.2.** The rounded indentations are visible front and back.
   - **3.3.** Save the drawing as *MyCB.dwg* in the C:\Steps3D\Lesson11 folder.

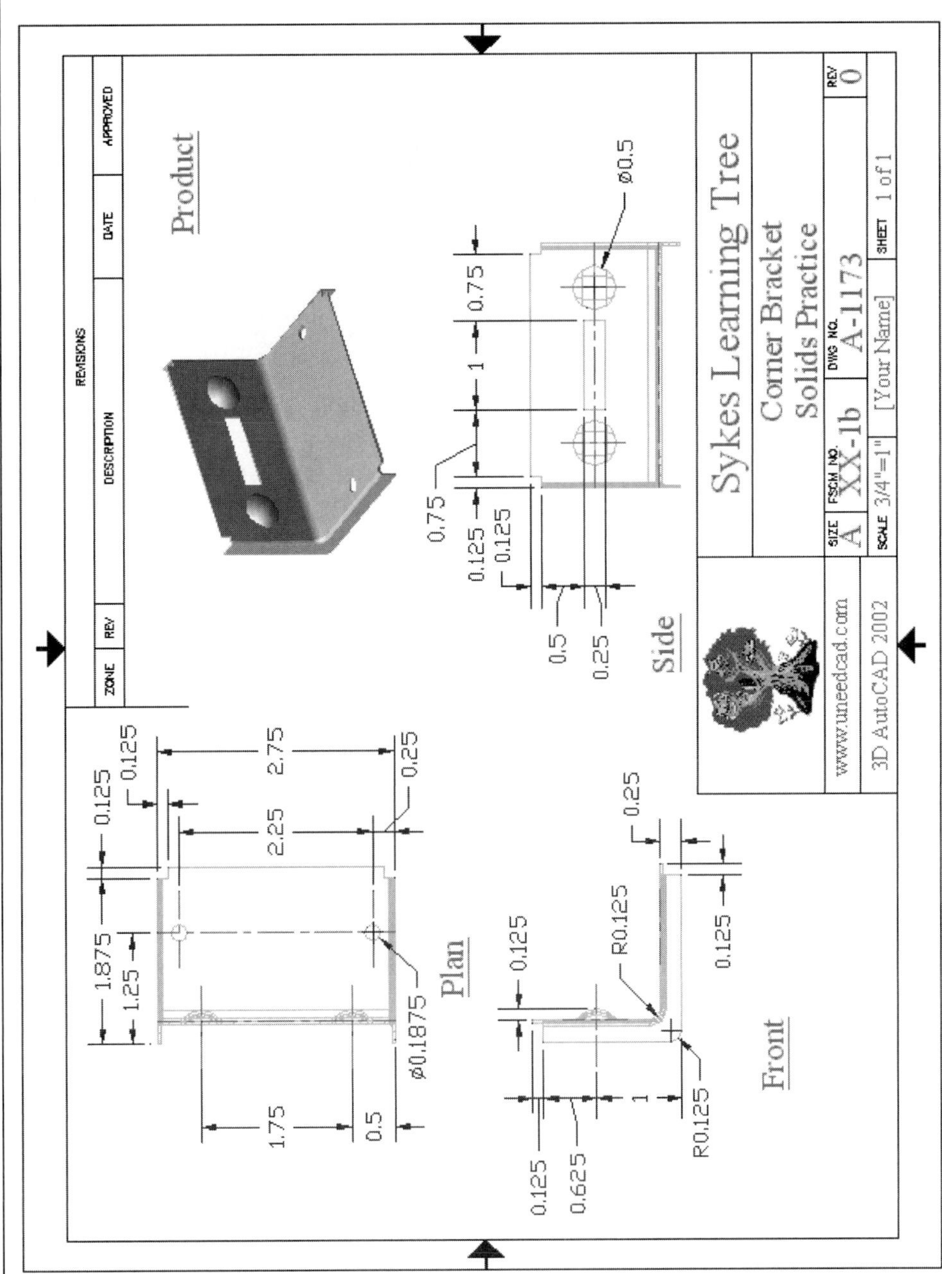

FIG. 11.7.3 *Corner Bracket. dwg*

4. Create the lid drawing in Figure 11.7.4.

   4.1. Save the drawing as *MyLid.dwg* in the C:\Steps3D\Lesson11 folder.

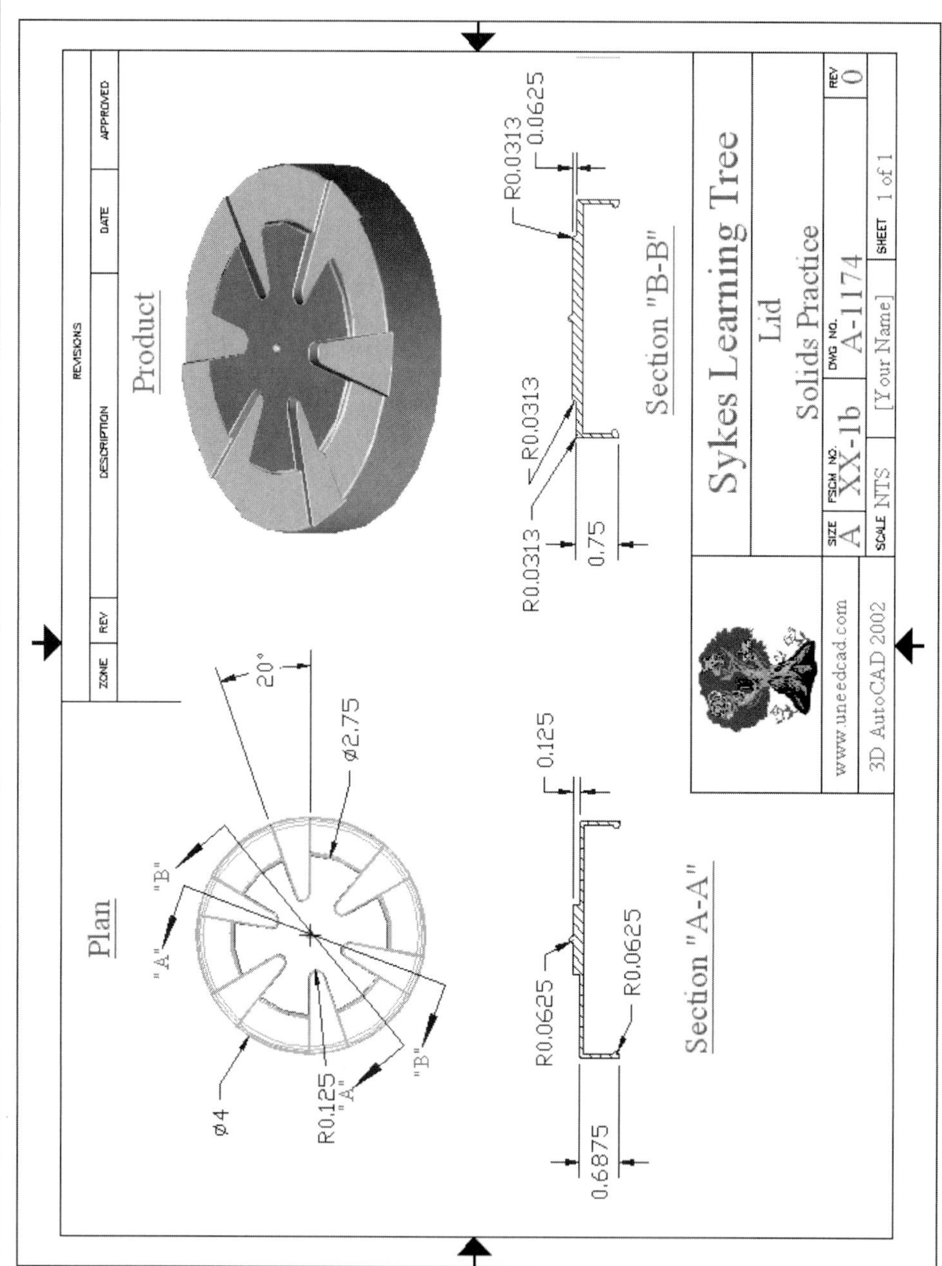

FIG. 11.7.4 *Lid.dwg*

5. Create the plug drawing in Figure 11.7.5.

   5.1. Save the drawing as *MyPlug.dwg* in the C:\Steps3D\Lesson11 folder.

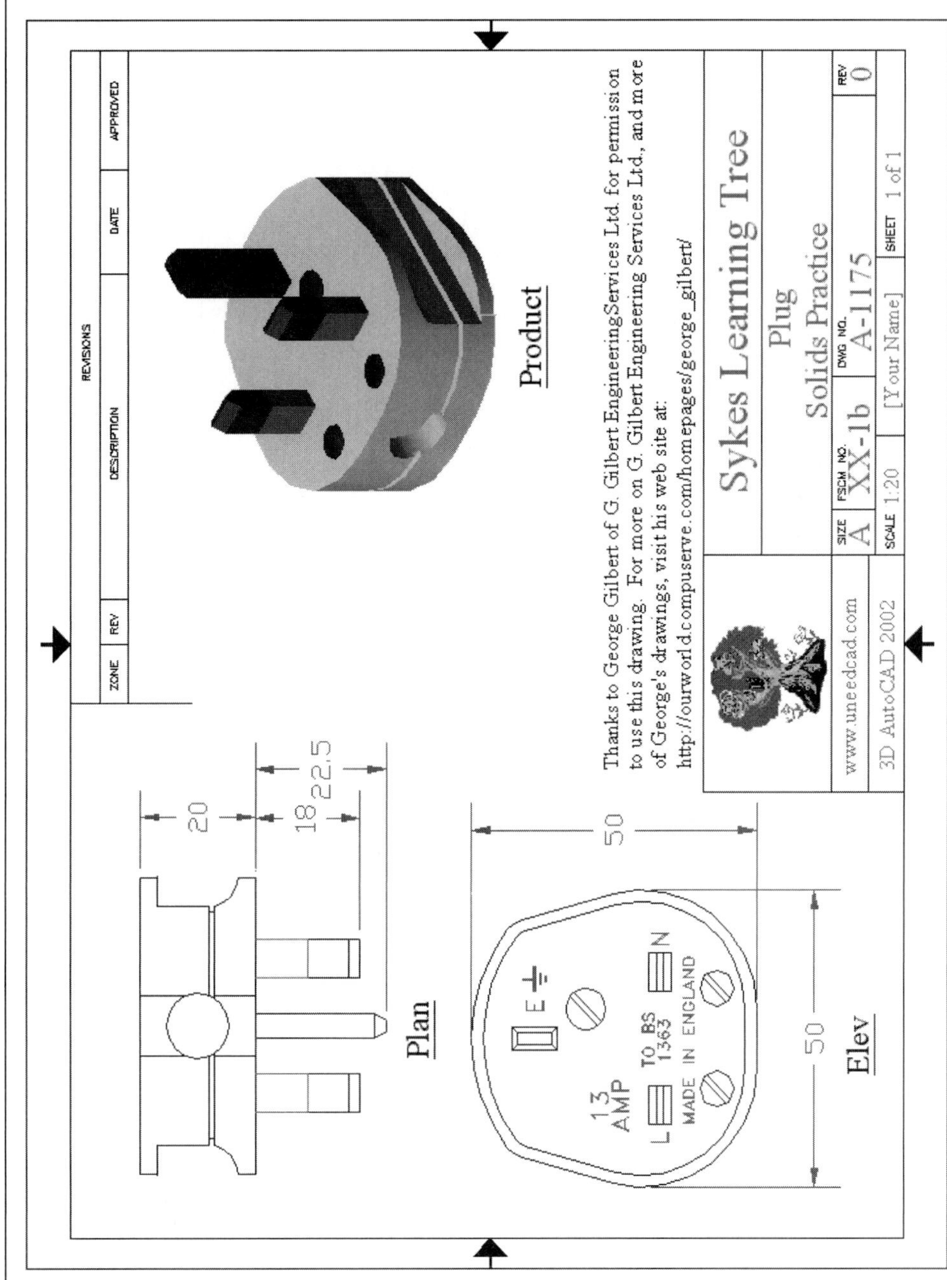

FIG. 11.7.5 *Plug.dwg*

6. Create the switch drawing in Figure 11.7.6.
   6.1. Save the drawing as *Switch.dwg* in the C:\Steps3D\Lesson11 folder.

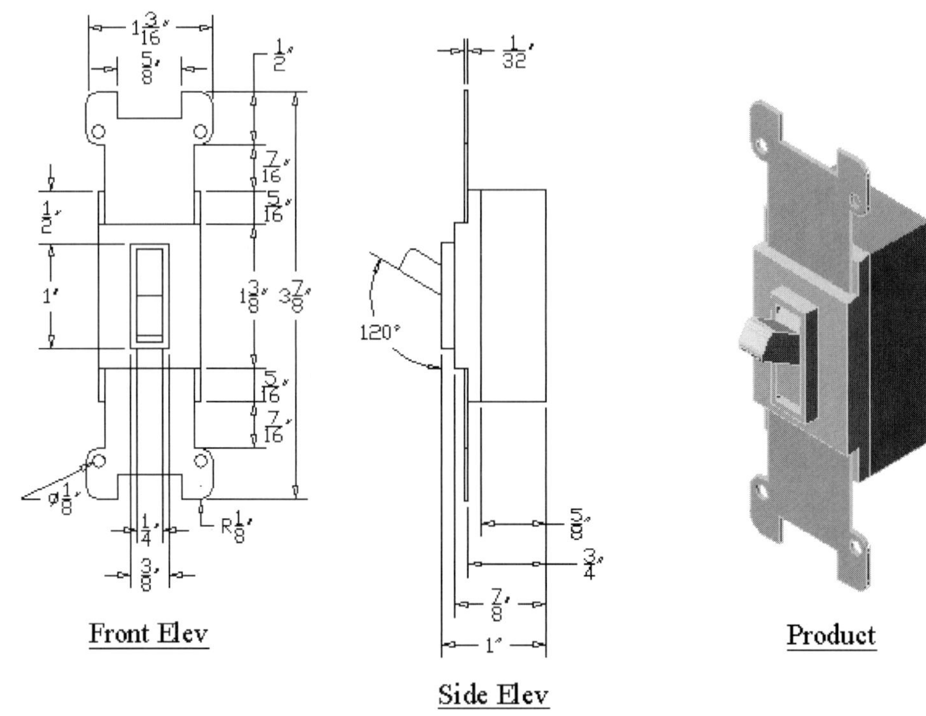

FIG. 11.7.6 *Switch.dwg*

7. Create the wheel drawing in Figure 11.7.7.
   7.1. Place this drawing on a C-size (22″ × 17″) sheet of paper.
   7.2. Fillet the rim and hub with a $\frac{1}{4}$″ fillet.
   7.3. Save the drawing as *MyWheel.dwg* in the C:\Steps3D\Lesson11 folder.

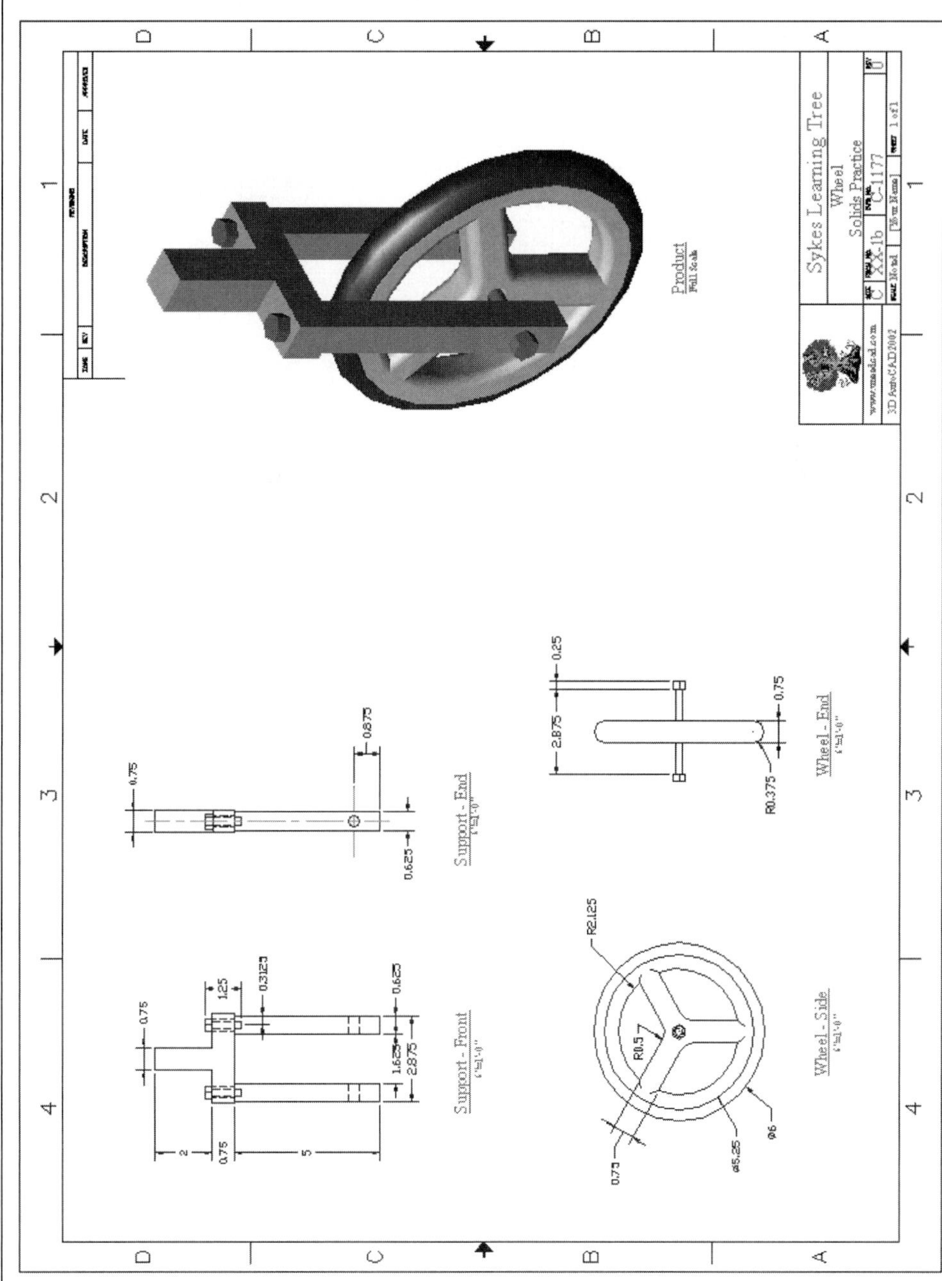

FIG. 11.7.7 *MyWheel.dwg*

8. Create the level drawing in Figure 11.7.8.
   8.1. Do not join the glass pieces to the body of the level.
   8.2. Save the drawing as *MyLevel.dwg* in the C:\Steps3D\Lesson11 folder.

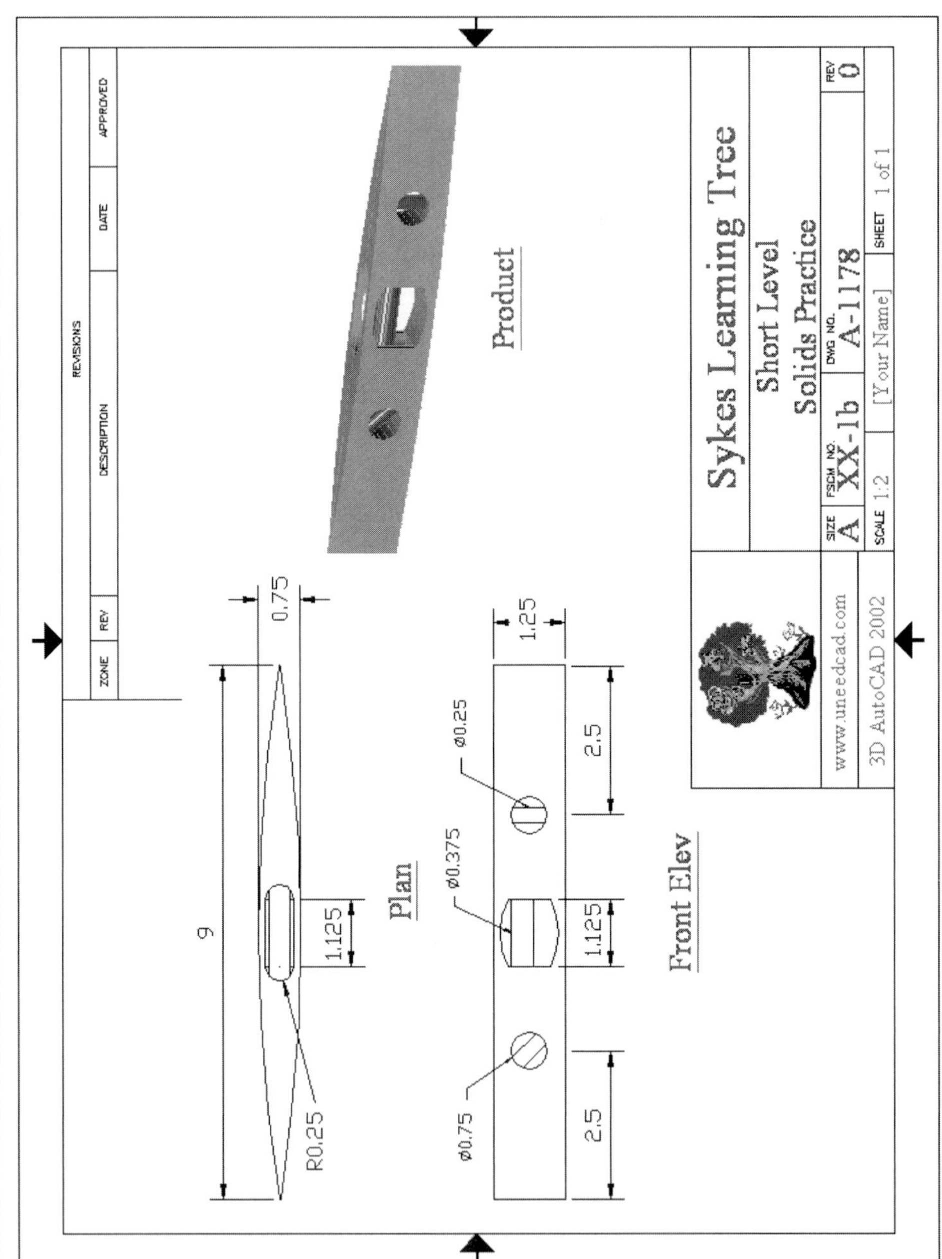

FIG. 11.7.8 *MyLevel.dwg*

11.8 REVIEW QUESTIONS

Please write your answers on a separate sheet of paper.

1. through 3. List the three categories of SolidEdit commands.

a.

b.

c.

4. The __________ category contains the bulk of SolidEdit's commands.

5. Use the __________ routine of the Face Category to change the location and taper angle of a face.

6. Use the __________ routine of the Face Category to relocate part of a solid that was improperly placed.

7. The Rotate routine of the Face Category emulates the (Rotate, Rotate3D) command.

8. The user controls the direction of the Face Category's Offset by using __________.

9. Using a positive number in response to the offset distance prompt of the Offset routine will cause the (size of a slot, volume of the 3D Solid) to increase.

10. Use the __________ routine of the Face Category to change a straight hole to a cone-shaped hole.

11. Use the __________ routine of the Face Category to remove a hole from a 3D Solid.

12. When using the Copy routine of the Face Category to create copies of a face, the copies are __________.

13. To change the color of a single edge of a 3D Solid, use the Color routine of the __________ Category.

14. and 15. Use the __________ routine of the __________ Category to create a new edge on a 3D Solid.

16. Consider the 3D Solids in Figures 11.8.16a and 11.8.16b. On which would the Separate Solids routine of the Body Category work?

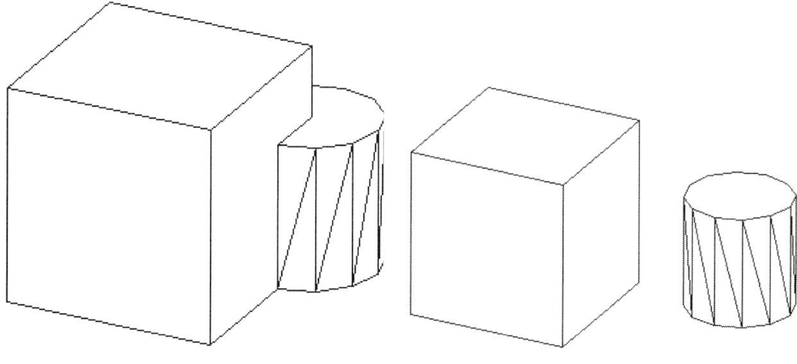

FIG. 11.8.16a FIG. 11.8.16b

17. Use the __________ option of the Body Category to remove unwanted or unused edges on a 3D Solid.

18. through 31. Identify the following buttons by function and category.

18. 19. 20. 21. 22. 23. 24.

25. 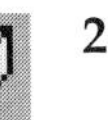 26. 27. 28. 29. 30. 31. 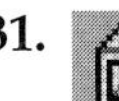

LESSON 12

Three-Dimensional Blocks and Three-Dimensional Plotting Tools

Following this lesson, you will

- Know how to use blocks in Z-Space
  - Creating three-dimensional blocks
  - Inserting three-dimensional blocks
- Know how to use the Solid Plotting Tools
  - ***Solview***
  - ***Soldraw***
  - ***Solprof***

As I mentioned when concluding the last lesson, there is very little left for you to learn with respect to creating three-dimensional objects in AutoCAD. This lesson, then, will serve as a wrap-up of Z-Space methods and techniques before we move on to Rendering.

In Lesson 12, we will first consider the behavior of blocks in a three-dimensional world. While the differences between two-dimensional blocks and three-dimensional blocks can be dramatic, they do not necessarily have to be difficult. We will consider the effects of Z-Space and working planes on creation and insertion of blocks as well as the use of attributes on a three-dimensional block.

Then we will discuss three special tools designed to help you set up and plot 3D Solids with considerably less difficulty than you might have had previously.

Let's begin.

12.1 Using Blocks in Z-Space

As with two-dimensional blocks, three-dimensional blocks can save the CAD operator a tremendous amount of time and effort. But there are a few things the three-dimensional operator must consider.

12.1.1 Three-Dimensional Blocks and the UCS

First among these considerations is the working plane (the current UCS). *AutoCAD creates blocks against the plane of the current UCS* (Figure 12.1.1a)—*not* the WCS. In other words, the XYZ values of the current UCS (the X-axis, Y-axis, and Z-axis values of the object) become part of the block definition.

Likewise, AutoCAD inserts blocks by matching the axis values of the block to the current UCS (Figure 12.1.1b).

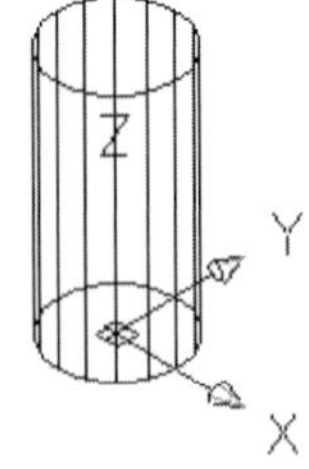

FIG. 12.1.1a Creating Block

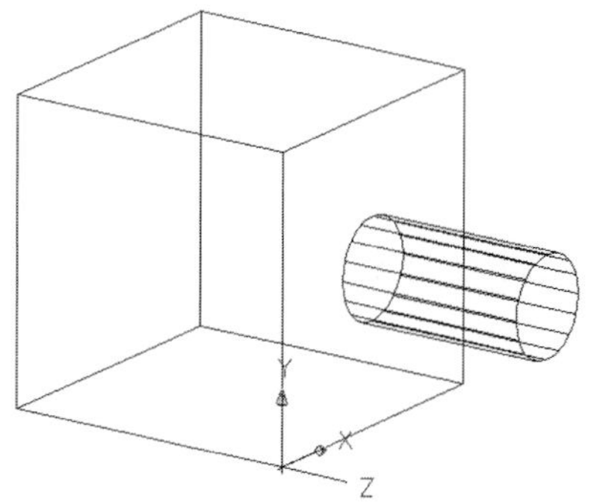

FIG. 12.1.1b Inserting Block

We will see this in a series of three exercises. First, we will create two blocks—an elbow and some pipe. Our blocks will have two simple attributes defining what they are and their size. Second, we will utilize our UCS and insertion scale factors to insert the blocks in a simple piping configuration. Third, we will extract attribute data that will give us a running total of the amount of pipe we have used.

Let's begin.

WWW 12.1.1.1 Do This: Creating 3D Blocks

I. Open the *Blocks.dwg* file in the C:\Steps3D\Lesson12 folder. The drawing looks like Figure 12.1.1.1a.

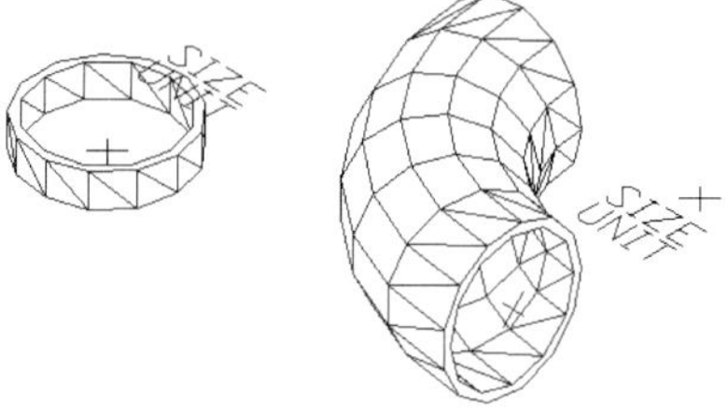

FIG. 12.1.1.1a *Blocks.dwg*

II. Notice that the elbow is open in the +X and +Y directions. Note also that the elbow and the pipe are drawn to scale as 4″ fittings, and that the height of the pipe is 1″.

III. Follow these steps:

TOOLS	COMMAND SEQUENCE	STEPS
	Command: *b*	**1.** Make a note of the current UCS, and then make blocks from the two objects you see. The block on the left should be called *Pipe*—use the node as the insertion point (include the node and the two attributes in the block). The block on the right should be called *Ell*—use the node inside the eastern opening of the elbow as the insertion point (include all three nodes and the two attributes in the block).
		2. Use the ***WBlock*** command to write both of the blocks to the C:\Steps3D\Lesson12 folder.
	Command: *qsave* **Command:** *close*	**3.** Save and close the drawing.

Now we will look at some new variations of the ***Insert*** command.

12.1.2 Inserting Three-Dimensional Blocks

The second three-dimensional block consideration involves the insertion scale of the block. In two-dimensional drafting, you could scale a block along the X- or Y-axis. Now you have an additional axis along which you can scale the block. You should give special attention to the use of a three-dimensional block because of the effect scale might have. Consider the images in Figures 12.1.2a, b, c, and d.

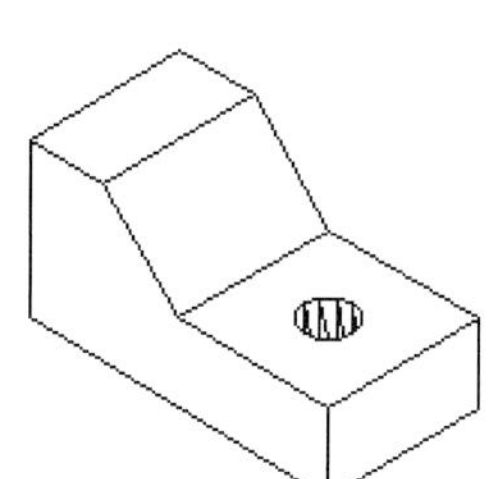

FIG. 12.1.2a Block Inserted with XYZ Axes = 1

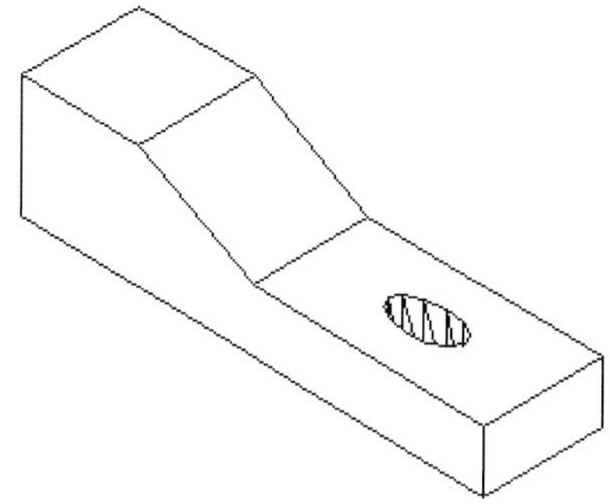

FIG. 12.1.2b Block Inserted with X-Axis = 2 (YZ Axes = 1)

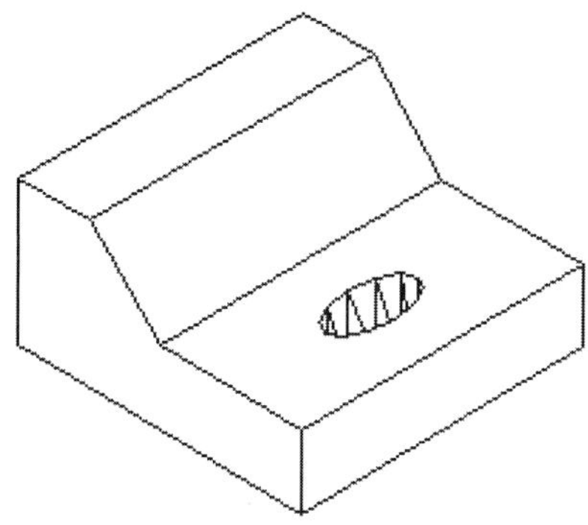

FIG. 12.1.2c Block Inserted with Y-Axis = 2 (XZ Axes = 1)

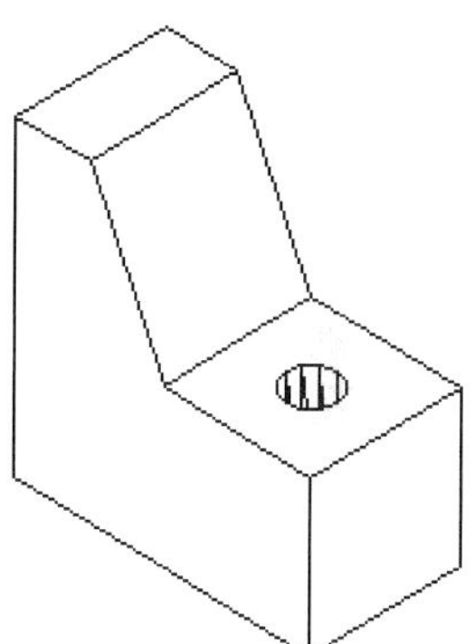

FIG. 12.1.2d Block Inserted with Z-Axis = 2 (XY Axes n = 1)

We will have an opportunity to use the scale options and see how the UCS affects the insertion when we insert our new blocks into a drawing. Let's get started!

WWW 12.1.2.1 Do This: Inserting 3D Blocks

I. Open the *Piping Configuration.dwg* file in the C:\Steps3D\Lesson12 folder. The drawing looks like Figure 12.1.2.1a. (The nodes have been set to help guide you through the block insertions. The **UCSIcon** system variable has been set to **ORigin**.)

II. Follow these steps:

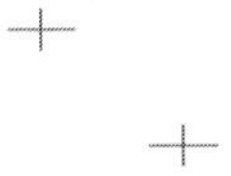

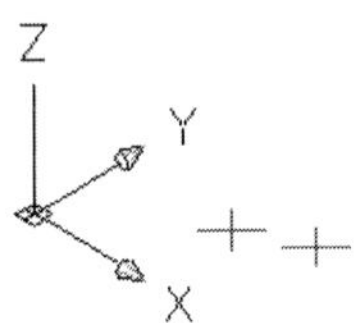

FIG. 12.1.2.1a *Piping Configuration.dwg*

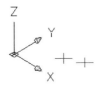

TOOLS	COMMAND SEQUENCE	STEPS
	Command: ***ucs***	**1.** Change the UCS as indicated in Figure 12.1.2.1.1. (*Hint:* Rotate the UCS 90° on the X-axis and then 270° on the Z-axis.)

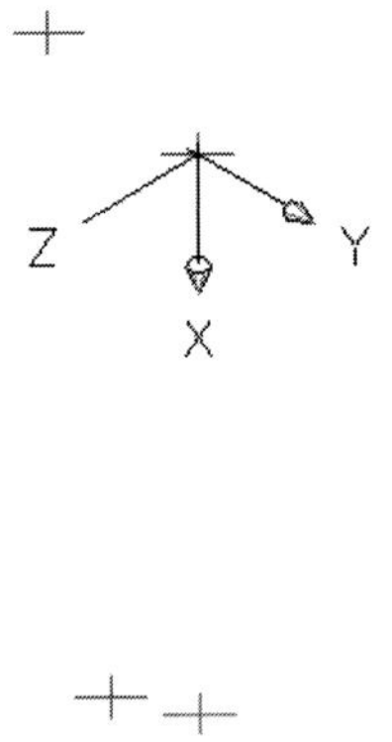

Z Y X

FIG. 12.1.2.1.1 Change the UCS

continued

TOOLS	COMMAND SEQUENCE	STEPS
	**Command:** ***i***	**2.** On the **Pipe** layer, insert the *ell* block at the 0,0,0 coordinate of the current UCS. (You created this block and placed it in the C:\Steps3D\Lesson12 folder in our last exercise.) Use a scale of 1 for each axis. Accept the default 4″ size. Your drawing looks like Figure 12.1.2.1.2.
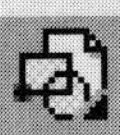	**Command:** ***i***	**3.** Add the rest of the elbows. (Place the UCS at each node and insert the elbows at 0,0.) Your drawing looks like Figure 12.1.2.3. (Your UCS icon may be in a different location.)

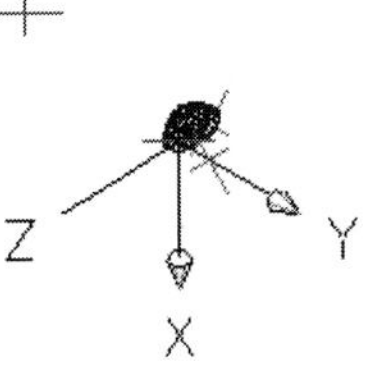

FIG. 12.1.2.1.2 Inserted Ell (hidden lines removed)

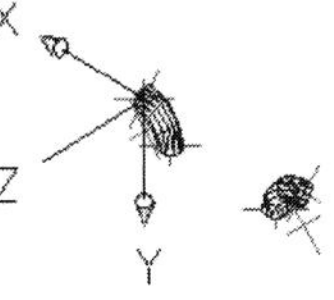

FIG. 12.1.2.3 Inserted Ell (hidden lines removed)

continued

TOOLS	COMMAND SEQUENCE	STEPS

Command: *ucs*

4. Reset the UCS to the WCS.

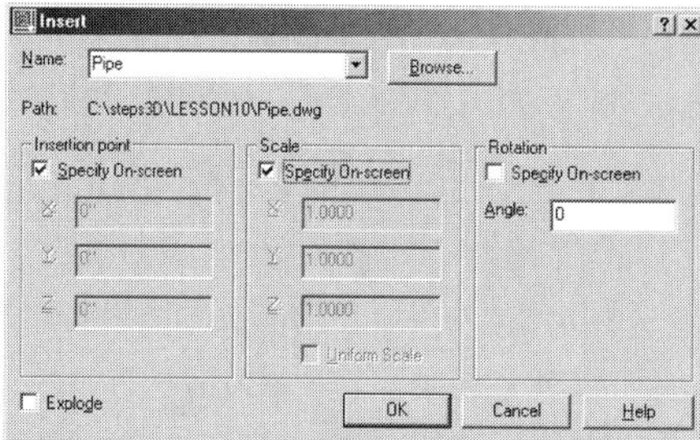

5. Now we will insert the pipe. We will use a scale factor to make it fit between the elbows. Tell AutoCAD you wish to insert the *pipe* block. Use the settings shown.

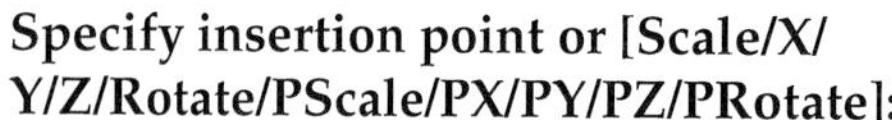

Specify insertion point or [Scale/X/Y/Z/Rotate/PScale/PX/PY/PZ/PRotate]:

6. Place the *Pipe* block at the upper node of the lower-right elbow.

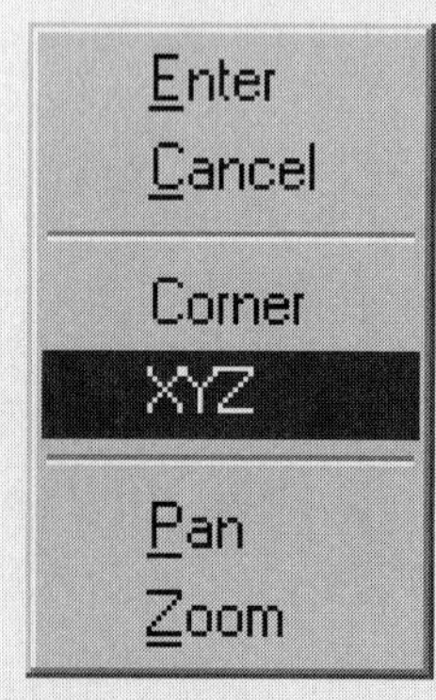

Enter X scale factor, specify opposite corner, or [Corner/XYZ] <1>: *xyz*

7. Now tell AutoCAD you wish to define the scale on each of the **XYZ** axes.

Specify X scale factor or [Corner] <1>: *[enter]*

Enter Y scale factor <use X scale factor>: *[enter]*

Specify Z scale factor or <use X scale factor>: *8′*

8. Accept the default scale for the X- and Y-axes but give the Z-axis a scale of 8′ (the distance between the two elbows). Since the height of the pipe was 1″, a scale of 8′ means that the pipe will be 8′ long.

What size is the unit?<4″>: *[enter]*

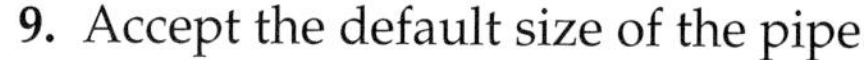

9. Accept the default size of the pipe.

continued

TOOLS	COMMAND SEQUENCE	STEPS
	**Command:** *i*	**10.** Repeat Steps 5 through 9 for the other vertical run of pipe. (Use the center of the upper end of the elbow as your insertion point.) Your drawing looks like Figure 12.1.2.1.10.

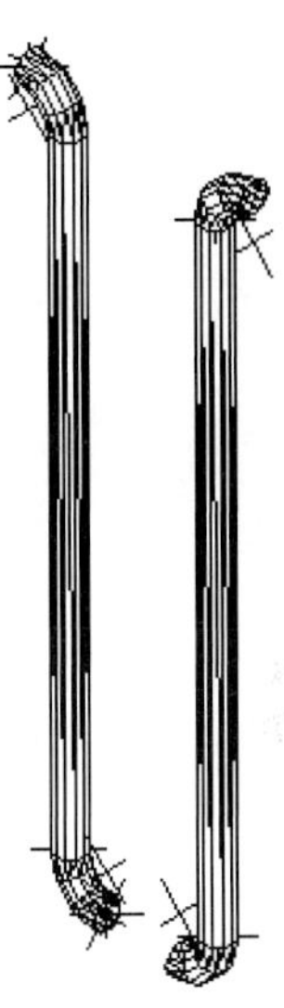

FIG. 12.1.2.1.10 Inserted Vertical Runs of Pipe

continued

TOOLS	COMMAND SEQUENCE	STEPS
		11. Adjust the UCS as needed to add the final run of pipe. The distance between the two elbows is 12″ . Your drawing looks like Figure 12.1.2.1.11.

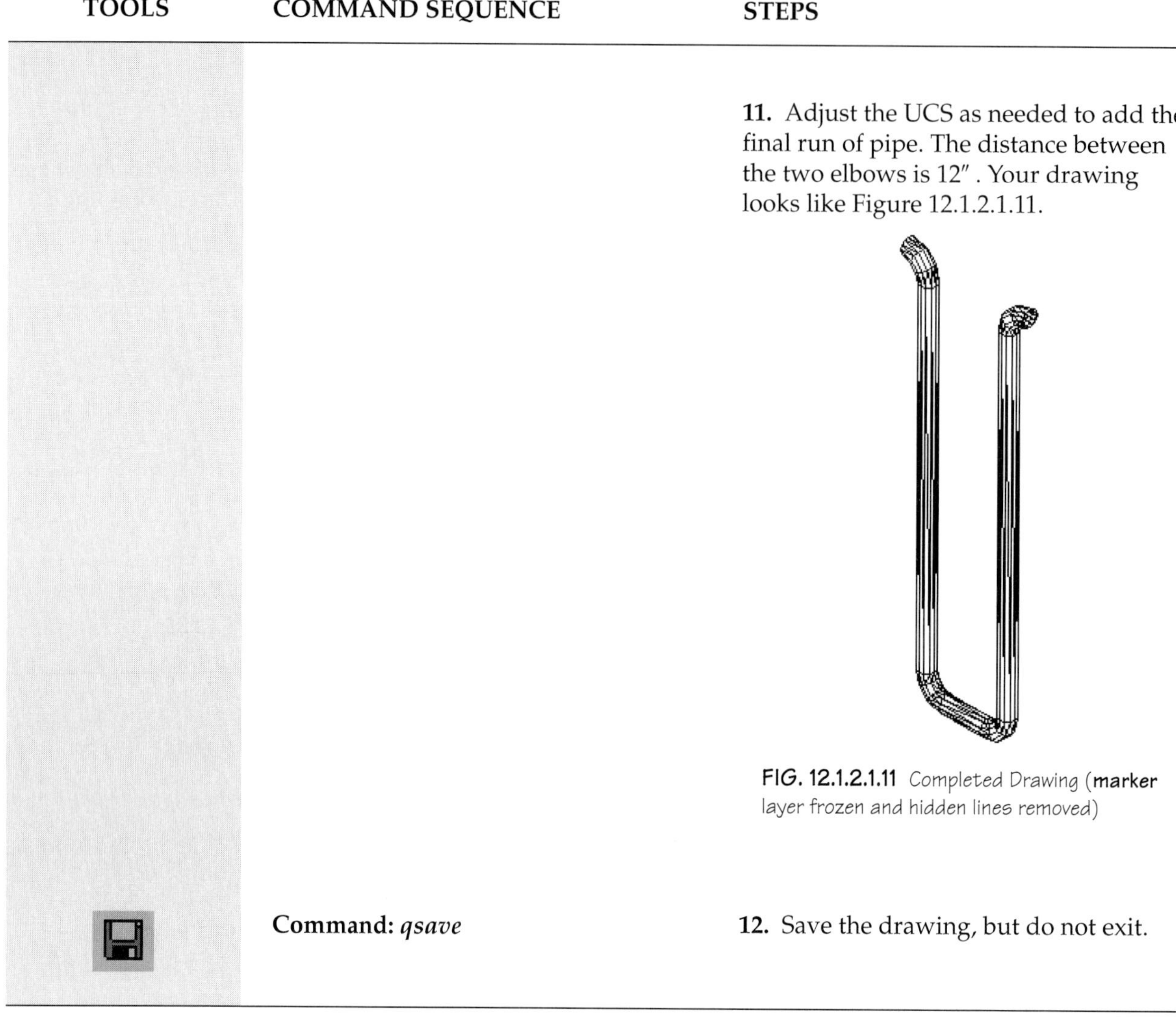

FIG. 12.1.2.1.11 Completed Drawing (**marker** layer frozen and hidden lines removed)

TOOLS	COMMAND SEQUENCE	STEPS
	Command: *qsave*	**12.** Save the drawing, but do not exit.

12.1.3 Making Good Use of Attributes

The last (and possibly most rewarding) thing we should consider when using three-dimensional blocks is the possible use of attributes. When combining the abilities you have already seen (in Sections 12.1.1 and 12.1.2) with a clever use of attributes, you will discover a remarkably useful way to create a bill of materials for most projects.

We will extract the attribute data attached to our blocks to see that the *pipe* blocks contain data about the length of each piece of pipe. This data is accurate enough to be used on a cutting list!

Sound nifty? Let's try it!

12.1.3.1 Do This: Extracting the Attributes

I. Be sure you are still in the *Piping Configuration.dwg* file in the C:\Steps3D\Lesson12 folder. If not, open it now.

II. Follow these steps:

TOOLS	COMMAND SEQUENCE	STEPS
	Command: ***attext*** 	**1.** Tell AutoCAD you wish to extract attribute data.
	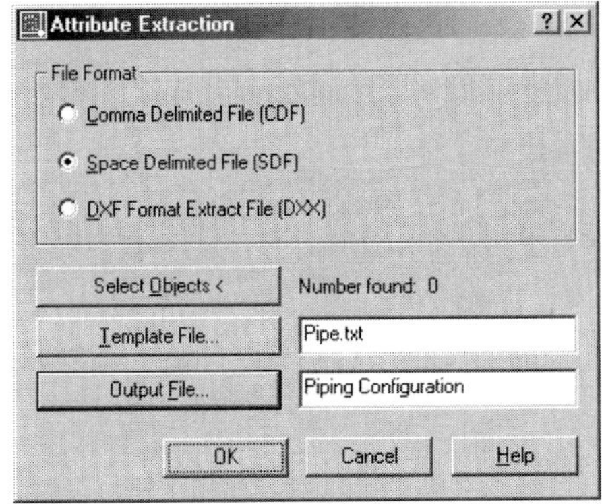	**2.** Create a **Space Delimited File** using the *Pipe.txt* template provided for you in the C:\Steps3D\Lesson12 folder. Accept the default output file, but be sure it is located in the C:\Steps3D\Lesson12 folder. Pick the **OK** button to continue.
	7 records in extract file. 	**3.** AutoCAD tells you how many records it created.
	**Command:** ***qsave***	**4.** Save the drawing.
	Command: ***notepad*** **File to edit: c:\Steps3D\lesson12\piping configuration.txt**	**5.** Open the *Piping Configuration.txt* file in the C:\Steps3D\Lesson12 folder. It looks like Figure 12.1.3.1.5.

```
90-degree elbow    4"          1.00000
90-degree elbow    4"          1.00000
90-degree elbow    4"          1.00000
90-degree elbow    4"          1.00000
pipe               4"         96.00000
pipe               4"         96.00000
pipe               4"         12.00000
```

FIG. 12.1.3.1.5 *Piping Configuration.txt*

Notice that each of the blocks used in the drawing has a listing for unit and size. Ignore the numerical column for the elbows, but notice the numbers in the numerical column beside the pipe units. This is the Z-Scale of each piece of pipe. We know that the Z-axis dimension of the block was 1, but we used the insertion scale to make the pipe long enough to fill the gaps between the elbows. So the Z-Scale you are seeing is actually the true length of the pipe! You can import this data into your database or spreadsheet (as you did in Lesson 20 of the basic text) and keep a running total of the amount of pipe used for the project!

Although we used pipe in our exercise, this method works as well when tracking board feet or lengths of steel. How might you use it in your profession?

12.2 Plotting a 3D Solid

We will conclude our study of 3D Solids with a group of special commands that AutoCAD designed to make plotting Solid Models easier. The "Sol Group" consists of three commands: ***Solview***, ***Soldraw***, and ***Solprof***. You will not find a finer example of teamwork in the CAD world. You will use the first command—***Solview***—to set up the layout (the Paper Space viewports). Then you will use the other two commands—***Soldraw*** and ***Solprof***—to create the actual drawings that go into the viewports.

Let's look at each.

12.2.1 Setting Up the Plot—The Solview Command

Of the three, ***Solview*** is the most complex command. It creates viewports according to user input. The viewports can be defined by the XY-plane of a user-defined UCS, or by calculating orthographic projections, auxiliary projections, and cross sections from a UCS viewport. ***Solview*** places the viewports on the **VPorts** layer (which it creates if necessary). It also creates viewport-specific layers for visible lines (*Viewname-vis*), hidden lines (*Viewname-hid*), dimensions (*Viewname-dim*), and hatching (*Viewname-hat*).

You must enter the ***Solview*** command while a Layout tab is active. AutoCAD responds with the initial ***Solview*** prompt:

Command: ***solview***

Enter an option [Ucs/Ortho/Auxiliary/Section]:

Let's consider each option.

- The **UCS** option creates a two-dimensional profile view of the object. It uses the XY-plane of a user-specified UCS to define the profile. AutoCAD responds to selection of the **UCS** option with the prompt:

Enter an option [Named/World/?/Current] <Current>: *[enter]*

Enter view scale <1.0000>: *[enter the scale for the view (if incorrect, you can rescale the view later using Zoom XP or the Scale control box on the Viewports toolbar)]*

Specify view center: *[pick a point where you would like the center point of the view]*

Specify view center <specify viewport>: *[reposition the view, if necessary, or hit enter to continue]*

Specify first corner of viewport: *[define the viewport by specifying opposite corners]*

Specify opposite corner of viewport:

Enter view name: *[give the viewport a unique name]*

The same sequence applies to the **Named** and **World** options, except that AutoCAD will precede the **Named** option sequence with a request for the name of the UCS to use. Use the **?** option to list the named UCSs available for use. Use the **UCS** option to create the first viewport—usually a front view or plan view of the 3D Solid.

- Use the **Ortho** option to create orthographic projections from an existing view. The command sequence is the same as with the **UCS** option.
- Creating an auxiliary view—a view perpendicular to an inclined face—is as easy as drawing an orthographic projection for AutoCAD. It responds to selection of the **Auxiliary** option with

Specify first point of inclined plane: *[specify two points that define the inclined plane]*

Specify second point of inclined plane:

Specify side to view from: *[pick a point from where you wish to see the inclined plane]*

AutoCAD continues with the options to size and locate the viewport.

- The **Section** option creates a cross section complete with section lines. (It takes the *Soldraw* command to actually create the section.) The sequence is

Specify first point of cutting plane:

Specify second point of cutting plane:

Specify side to view from:

Again, AutoCAD continues with the options to size and locate the viewport.

You will notice in our next exercise that, in fact, none of these options creates a drawing. What they do is *set up* a viewport for the orthographic, auxiliary, or

> cross-sectional drawings that you will create later with the ***Soldraw*** command. You will see the actual 3D Solid in each viewport until you use the ***Soldraw*** command.

All of these options will become much clearer with an exercise. Let's begin.

12.2.1.1 Do This: Using *Solview* to Set Up a Layout

I. Open the *Sol1.dwg* file in the C:\Steps3D\Lesson12 folder. It looks like Figure 12.2.1.1a.

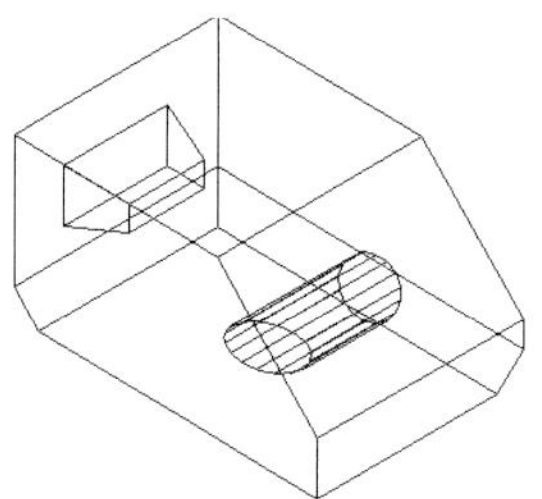

FIG. 12.2.1.1a *Sol1.dwg*

II. Activate the **Layout1** tab and set it up for a landscaped orientation on an $8\frac{1}{2}'' \times 11''$ sheet of paper. Erase any viewports that appear.

III. Follow these steps:

TOOLS	COMMAND SEQUENCE	STEPS
Setup View Button	**Command:** ***solview***	**1.** Enter the ***Solview*** command by typing ***solview*** at the command prompt (there is no hotkey). Or you can pick the **Setup View** button on the Solids toolbar.
Enter Cancel Ucs Ortho Auxiliary Section Pan Zoom	**Enter an option [Ucs/Ortho/ Auxiliary/Section]:** ***u***	**2.** Select the **UCS** option.

continued

TOOLS	COMMAND SEQUENCE	STEPS
	**Enter an option [Named/World/?/ Current] <Current>:** *n*	**3.** Tell AutoCAD you wish to use a **Named** UCS, and use the UCS called *Front*.
	Enter name of UCS to restore: *front*	
	Enter view scale <1.0000>: *.75*	**4.** We will use a three-quarter scale for our viewport.
	Specify view center: *3,3.5*	**5.** Center the viewport on Paper Space coordinates **3,3.5**. Confirm the location.
	Specify view center <specify viewport>: *[enter]*	
	Specify first corner of viewport: *1,4.5*	**6.** Size the viewport as indicated (you may pick approximate coordinates).
	Specify opposite corner of viewport: *5,2.5*	
	Enter view name: ***Front***	**7.** Call the view ***Front***. Your drawing looks like Figure 12.2.1.1.7.

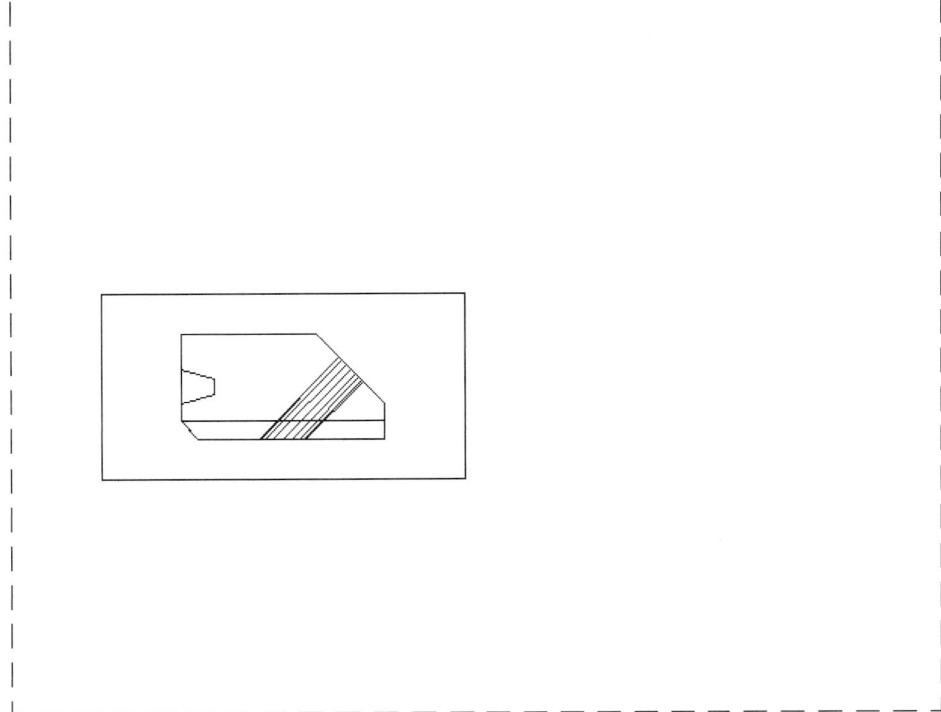

FIG. 12.2.1.1.7 UCS Viewport—Front

continued

TOOLS	COMMAND SEQUENCE	STEPS
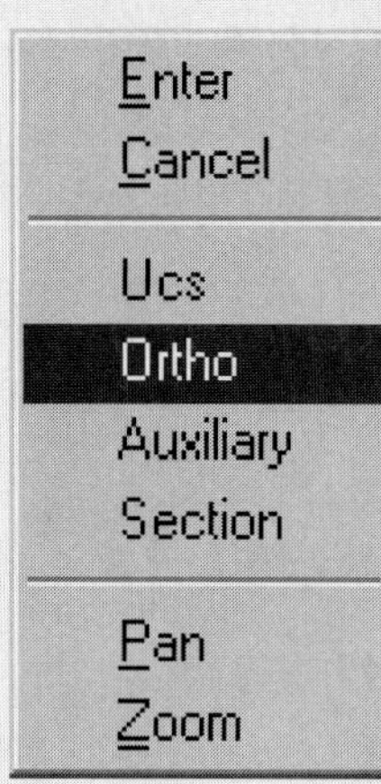	**Enter an option [Ucs/Ortho/ Auxiliary/Section]:** *o*	**8.** Now tell AutoCAD to create an orthographic projection.
	Specify side of viewport to project:	**9.** Pick a point on the right side of the existing viewport (notice that AutoCAD automatically uses the midpoint OSNAP) . . .
	Specify view center: *8,3.5* **Specify view center <specify viewport>:** *[enter]*	**10.** . . . and center the viewport at about the coordinates indicated. Confirm the location.
	Specify first corner of viewport: *6.5,4.5* **Specify opposite corner of viewport:** *9.5,2.5*	**11.** Locate the viewport at about the coordinates indicated.
	Enter view name: *Right*	**12.** Call the viewport ***Right***.
	Enter an option [Ucs/Ortho/ Auxiliary/Section]: *o*	**13.** Repeat Steps 8 through 12 to create a *Top* viewport as shown in Figure 12.2.1.1.13.

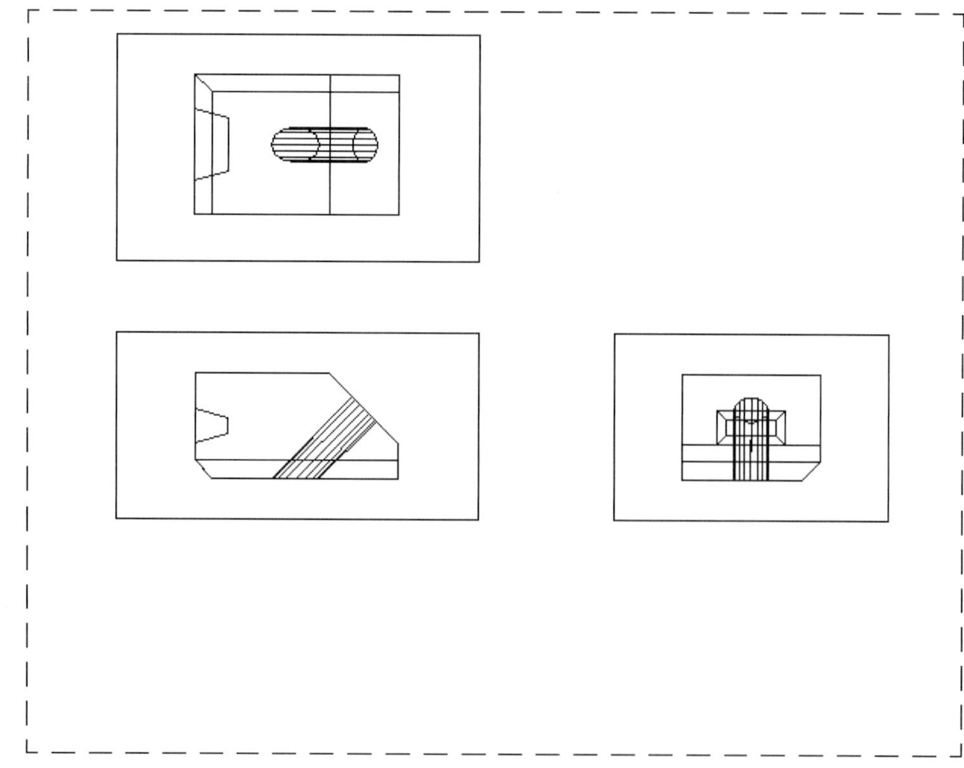

FIG. 12.2.1.1.13 *Orthographic Projections*

continued

TOOLS	COMMAND SEQUENCE	STEPS
Enter Cancel Ucs Ortho Auxiliary Section Pan Zoom	**Enter an option [Ucs/Ortho/ Auxiliary/Section]:** *a*	**14.** Now we will create an **Auxiliary** view of the inclined surface.
	Specify first point of inclined plane: _endp of **Specify second point of inclined plane: _endp of**	**15.** In the original viewport (*Front*), pick the endpoints of the inclined surface (pick anywhere in the *Front* viewport to activate it) . . .
	Specify side to view from: *[pick anywhere in the upper right quadrant of the viewport]*	**16.** . . . and tell AutoCAD you wish to view the surface from the upper-right corner of the viewport.
	Specify view center: **Specify view center <specify viewport>:** *[enter]*	**17.** Pick a point about even with the center of the upper viewport (*Top*). Confirm the location.
	Specify first corner of viewport: **Specify opposite corner of viewport:** **Enter view name:** *Aux*	**18.** Place the viewport around the auxiliary image (do not worry that the viewports overlap), and name the view *Aux*.

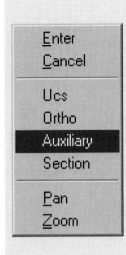

continued

TOOLS	COMMAND SEQUENCE	STEPS
	Enter an option [Ucs/Ortho/ Auxiliary/Section]: *[enter]*	**19.** Hit ***enter*** to complete the command. Then move the new viewpoint to the position shown in Figure 12.2.1.1.19.

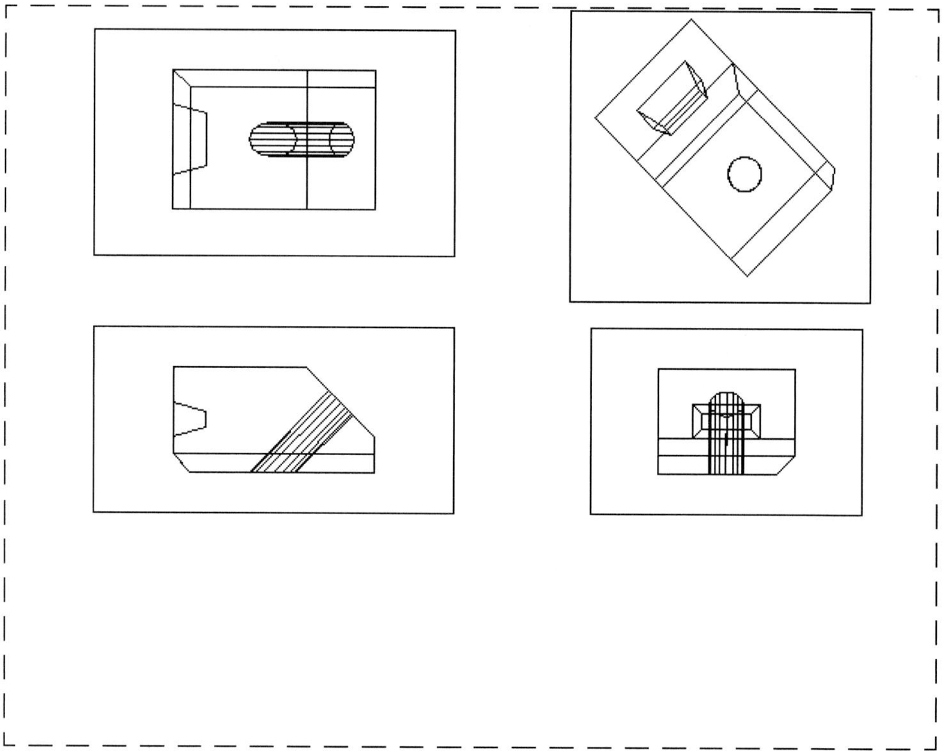

FIG. 12.2.1.1.19 Auxiliary View

TOOLS	COMMAND SEQUENCE	STEPS
	Command: ***qsave***	**20.** Save the drawing.
	**Command:** ***solview***	**21.** Repeat the ***Solview*** command.
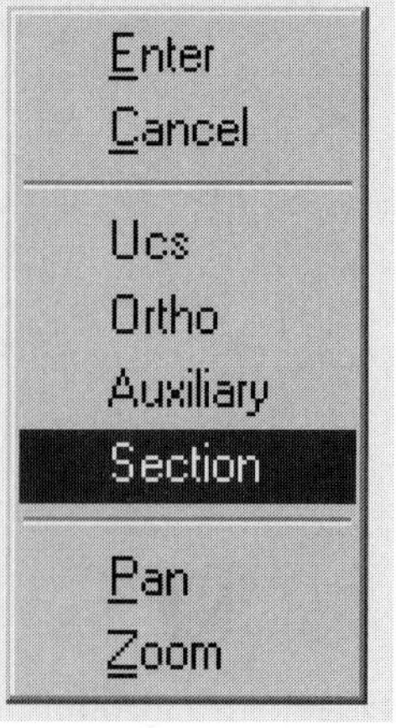 Enter Cancel Ucs Ortho Auxiliary Section Pan Zoom	**Enter an option [Ucs/Ortho/ Auxiliary/Section]:** ***s***	**22.** Select the **Section** option.

continued

TOOLS	COMMAND SEQUENCE	STEPS
	Specify first point of cutting plane: **Specify second point of cutting plane:**	**23.** In the upper-left viewport (*Top*), specify the cutting plane as shown in Figure 12.2.1.1.23 (use ortho).
	Specify side to view from: **Enter view scale <0.7500>:** *[enter]*	**24.** View the object from the lower quadrant of the viewport, and accept the default view scale.
	Specify view center: **Specify view center <specify viewport>:** *[enter]*	**25.** Center the sectional viewport below the original (*Front*) viewport. Confirm the location.

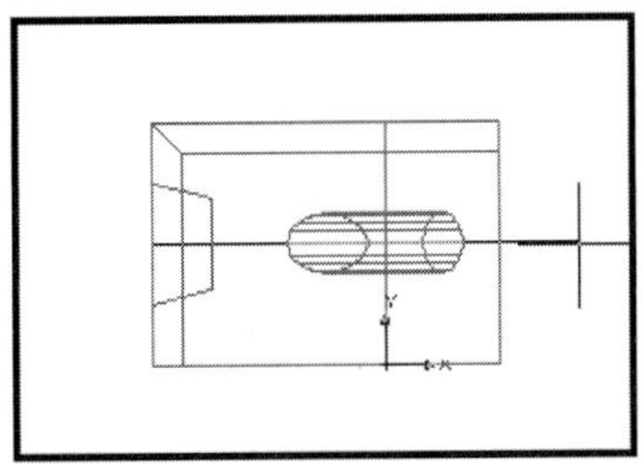

FIG. 12.2.1.1.23 Cutting Plane

continued

TOOLS	COMMAND SEQUENCE	STEPS
	Specify first corner of viewport: **Specify opposite corner of viewport:** **Enter view name:** ***Sect***	**26.** Place the viewport around the image, and call the view ***Sect***. Your drawing looks like Figure 12.2.1.1.26.

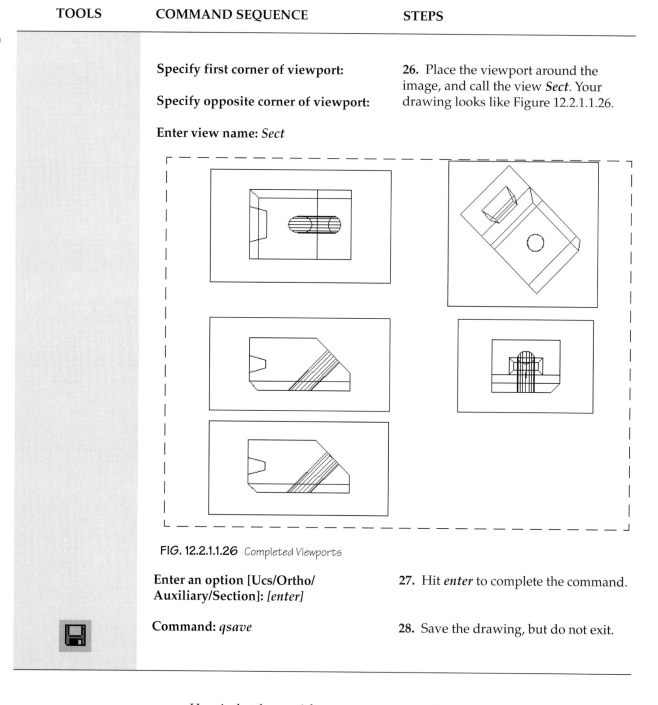

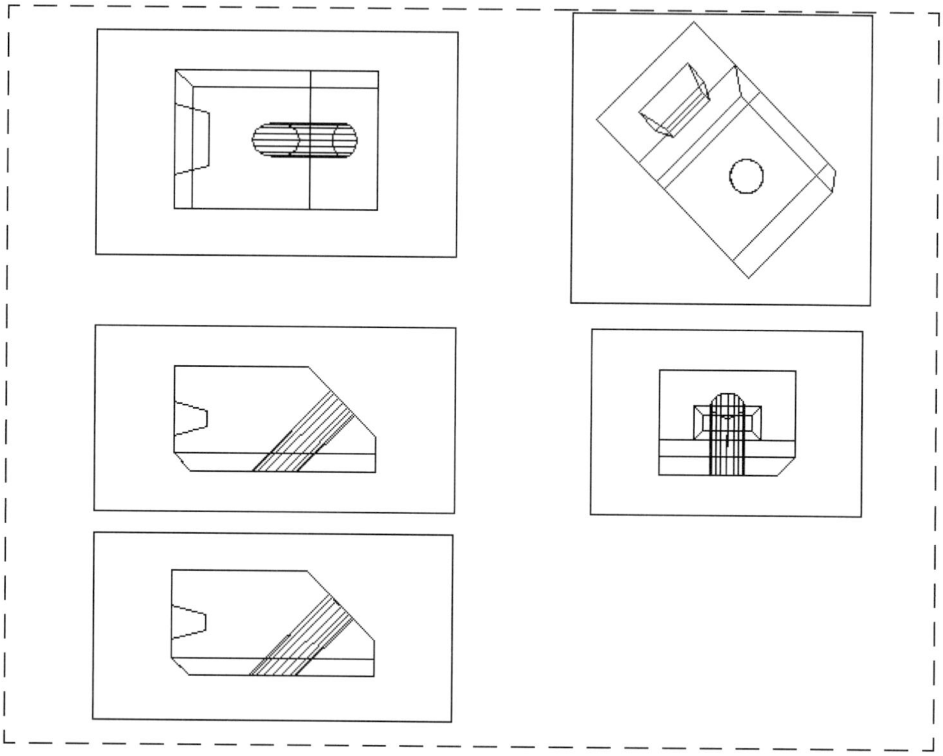

FIG. 12.2.1.1.26 Completed Viewports

TOOLS	COMMAND SEQUENCE	STEPS
	Enter an option [Ucs/Ortho/ Auxiliary/Section]: ***[enter]***	**27.** Hit ***enter*** to complete the command.
	**Command:** ***qsave***	**28.** Save the drawing, but do not exit.

How is that for a quick way to set up several viewports? If you look a little further than your immediate screen, you will find that AutoCAD has also set up layers specific to each viewport (it will use the ***VPLayer*** command to freeze each layer in all but the appropriate viewport).

Obviously, however, the drawing is not yet ready to plot—each viewport still shows the full 3D Solid. To complete the drawing, we need to show profiles in each viewport. Let's look at the ***Soldraw*** and ***Solprof*** commands next.

12.2.2 Creating the Plot Images—The Soldraw and Solprof Commands

Both ***Soldraw*** and ***Solprof*** create profiles in a viewport. The biggest difference is that ***Soldraw*** was designed to work specifically with viewports created by the ***Solview*** command. ***Solprof*** will create a profile in a viewport created by the ***MView*** or ***MVSetup*** commands. Additionally, ***Soldraw*** will create cross sections where they were set up with the ***Solview*** command.

A profile shows only those edges and/or silhouettes of a 3D Solid that are visible in the specific viewport when hidden lines are removed.

An important thing to remember about the ***Sol . . .*** commands is that they were designed to work only with solids. They will *not* work with surfaces or blocks.

The command sequence for ***Soldraw*** is one of AutoCAD's simplest:

Command: *soldraw*
Select viewports to draw . . . .
Select objects:

AutoCAD does the rest automatically. Try it.

All of the ***Sol . . .*** commands can be accessed through the Draw pull-down menu. Follow this path:

Draw—Solids—Setup—(Drawing, View, Profile)

WWW 12.2.2.1 Do This: Creating Profiles and Sections with Soldraw

I. Be sure you are still in the *Sol1.dwg* file in the C:\Steps3D\Lesson12 folder. If not, open it now.

II. Follow these steps:

TOOLS	COMMAND SEQUENCE	STEPS
 Setup Drawing Button	**Command:** ***soldraw***	**1.** Enter the ***Soldraw*** command by typing ***soldraw*** at the command prompt (there is no hotkey). Or you can pick the **Setup Drawing** button on the Solids toolbar.
	Select objects: **Select objects:** ***[enter]***	**2.** Select each of the viewports. Hit ***enter*** to complete the command. AutoCAD creates the profiles and sections. Your drawing looks like Figure 12.2.2.1.2.

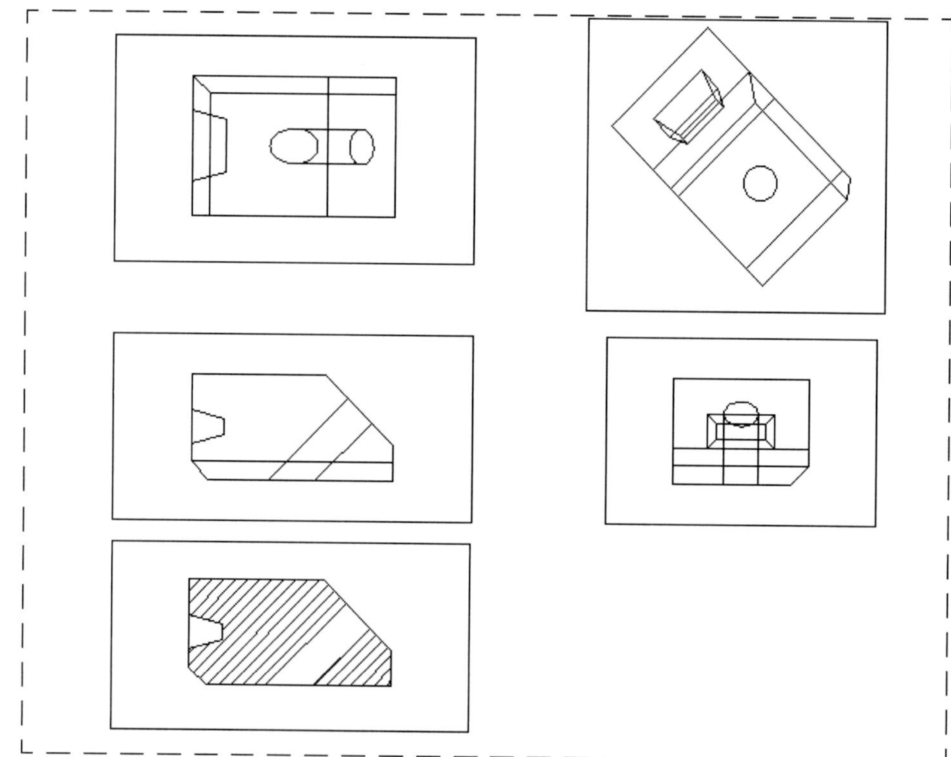

FIG. 12.2.2.1.2 Profiles Created with ***Soldraw***

TOOLS	COMMAND SEQUENCE	STEPS
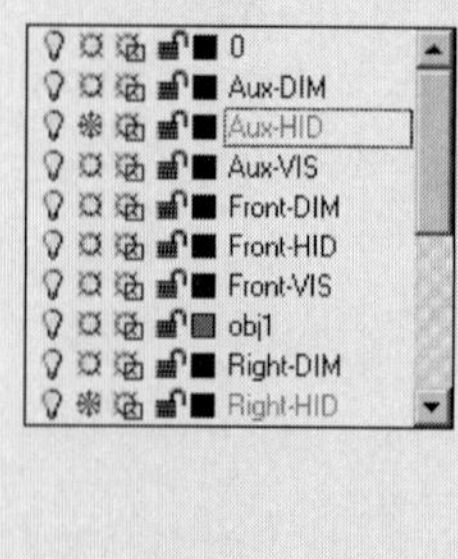	**Command:** ***la***	**3.** Not quite satisfied? Freeze all of the **[Name]-hid** layers except **Front-hid**.

continued

TOOLS	COMMAND SEQUENCE	STEPS
	Command: ***la***	**4.** Load the *Hidden* linetype and assign it to the **Front-hid** layer. Your drawing looks like Figure 12.2.2.1.4. (Happier now?)

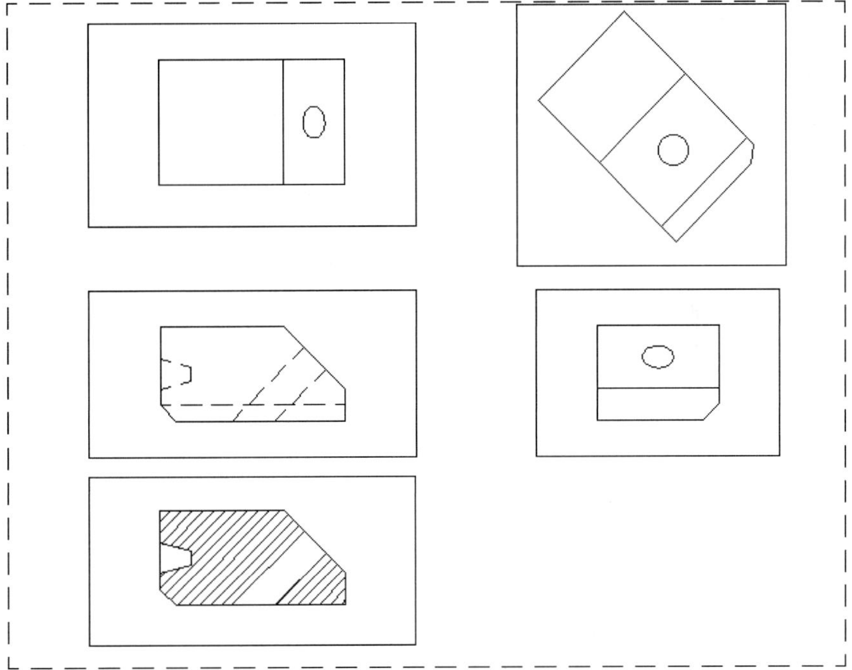

FIG. 12.2.2.1.4 Hid Layers Modified

TOOLS	COMMAND SEQUENCE	STEPS
	**Command:** ***qsave***	**5.** Save the drawing, but do not exit.

Solprof works almost as easily, but the profiles it creates are actually blocks. Here is the command sequence:

Command: ***solprof***
Select objects:
Select objects: ***[enter]***
Display hidden profile lines on separate layer? [Yes/No] <Y>:
Project profile lines onto a plane? [Yes/No] <Y>:
Delete tangential edges? [Yes/No] <Y>:

Let's look at the options.

- The first option—**Display hidden profile lines on separate layer? [Yes/No] <Y>:**—asks if you would like to place all profile lines on one layer or place the hidden lines on a separate layer. The default is to place hidden lines on a separate layer.

  When you accept the default (generally a good idea), AutoCAD places visible lines on layer *PV-[viewport handle]* and hidden lines on layer *PH-[viewport handle]*. By using the AutoCAD-assigned viewport handle as part of the layer, AutoCAD assures you of a unique layer name. This way you can freeze the layer or change the linetype of the hidden lines.
- The next option—**Project profile lines onto a plane? [Yes/No] <Y>:**—allows the user to create a two-dimensional profile by projecting the lines onto the view plane (the default), or to create three-dimensional lines.
- The last option—**Delete tangential edges? [Yes/No] <Y>:**—allows the user to remove tangential lines. These are objects (lines) that show the transition between arcs or circles. They are essentially the same things as isolines, except that they are actual objects.

Let's use the ***Solprof*** command to create an isometric view of our object.

12.2.2.2 Do This: *Creating Profiles with Solprof*

I. Be sure you are still in the *Sol1.dwg* file in the C:\Steps3D\Lesson12 folder. If not, open it now.

II. Create a new viewport in the lower-right corner of the layout (use the ***MView*** command).

III. Activate the new viewport and set up an isometric viewpoint (1,−1,1).

IV. Follow these steps:

TOOLS	COMMAND SEQUENCE	STEPS
Setup Profile Button	**Command:** *solprof*	**1.** Enter the ***Solprof*** command by typing ***solprof*** at the command prompt (there is no hotkey). Or you can pick the **Setup Profile** button on the Solids toolbar. (Be sure the new viewport is still active.)
	Select objects:	**2.** Select the 3D Solid.
	Select objects: *[enter]*	

continued

TOOLS	COMMAND SEQUENCE	STEPS
	Display hidden profile lines on separate layer? [Yes/No] <Y>: *[enter]* **Project profile lines onto a plane? [Yes/No] <Y>:** *[enter]* **Delete tangential edges? [Yes/No] <Y>:** *[enter]*	**3.** Accept the defaults for the next three prompts.
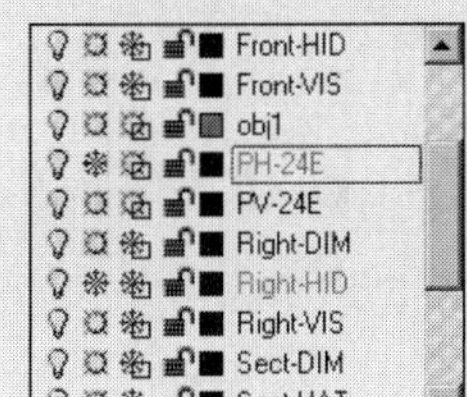	**Command:** *la*	**4.** Freeze the **PH-[viewport handle]** layer. (The viewport handle will vary. Use the list command to identify the layer of the hidden lines, if necessary.)

continued

TOOLS	COMMAND SEQUENCE	STEPS
	Command: *vplayer* **Enter an option [?/Freeze/Thaw/ Reset/Newfrz/Vpvisdflt]:** *f* **Enter layer name(s) to freeze:** *obj1* **Enter an option [All/Select/Current] <Current>:** *[enter]* **Enter an option [?/Freeze/Thaw/ Reset/Newfrz/Vpvisdflt]:** *[enter]*	**5.** Use the ***VPLayer*** command to freeze the **obj1** layer in the active viewport. Your drawing looks like Figure 12.2.2.2.5.

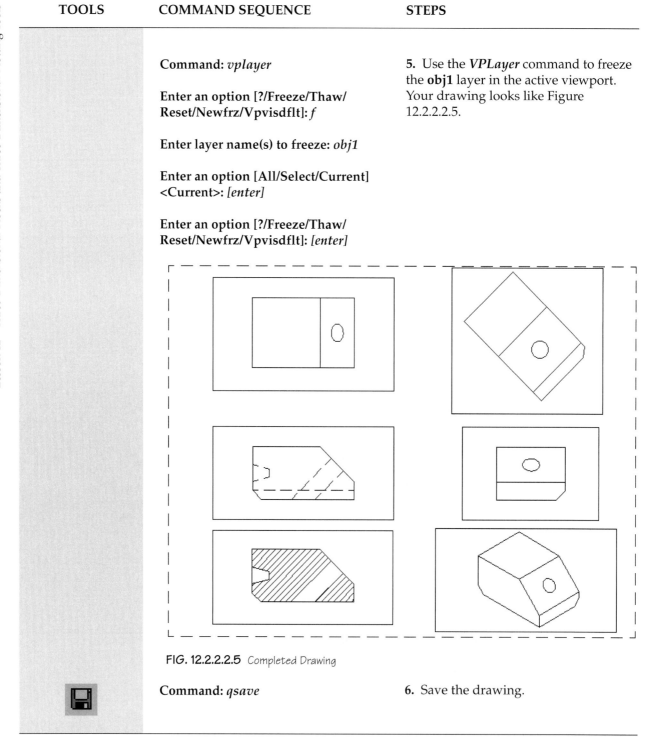

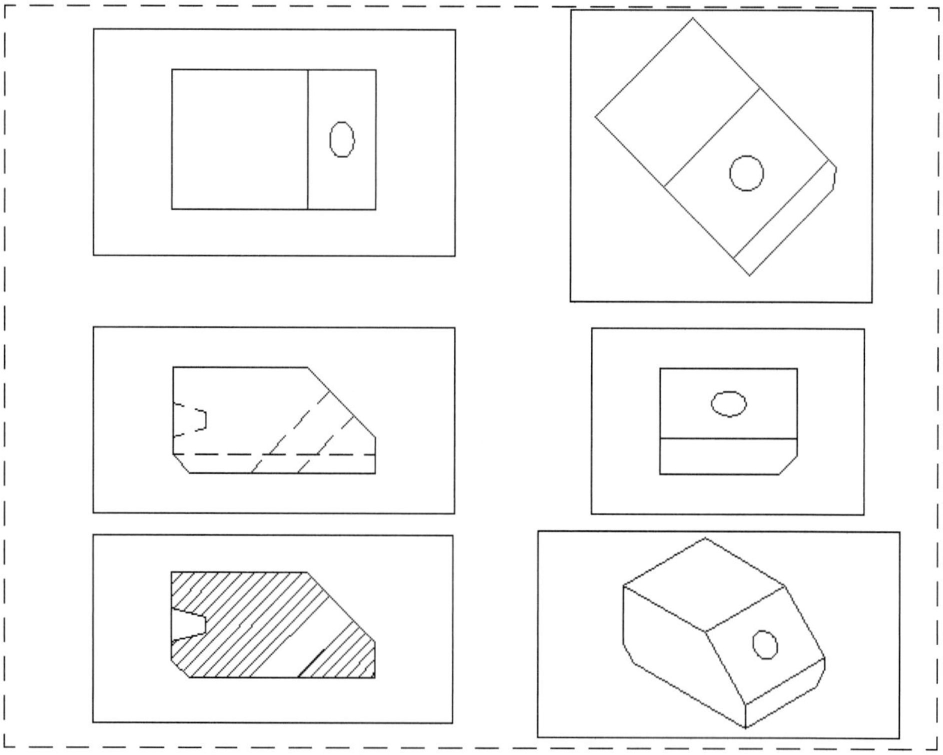

FIG. 12.2.2.2.5 Completed Drawing

TOOLS	COMMAND SEQUENCE	STEPS
	**Command:** *qsave*	**6.** Save the drawing.

You can now use other techniques you have learned to dimension each view, add appropriate text, and otherwise complete the drawing.

12.3 Extra Steps

Return to any of the drawings you created in the exercises at the end of Lessons 10 and 11. Create the plotting layouts shown in the exercises (if you created layouts, open Layout2 and recreate them). This will work best if you use drawings for which you have already created layouts—it will help you compare the method you used previously with the ***Sol . . .*** commands.

12.4 What Have We Learned?

Items covered in this lesson include

- *Three-dimensional uses and techniques for blocks*
- *The **Sol . . .** tools used to set up plots for 3D Solids*
  - ***Solview***
  - ***Soldraw***
  - ***Solprof***

In this lesson, you discovered some easier ways to set up a Paper Space plot and some new (and useful) techniques for working with blocks. And you wrapped up your study of three-dimensional drafting and modeling techniques. You can relax for two minutes and pat yourself on the back for having accomplished quite a lot of often difficult material. Then tackle the exercises at the end of the lesson.

In Lesson 13, you will see how to render a drawing. While not always useful as a drafting tool, rendering takes the CAD operator one step further—to adding material qualities to your objects. This means having a table that shows wood grain or a glass lamp that appears transparent. You will see how to show your drawing in perspective rather than isometric mode. You will create photographic-quality images suitable for brochures or posters, and much more!

So, complete the exercises and hurry into that place where AutoCAD meets computer graphics!

12.5 EXERCISES

1. Open the *Slotted Guide.dwg* file in the C:\Steps3D\Lesson12 folder. Create the layout shown in Figure 12.5.1.
   - **1.1.** *Hint:* The ***Sol . . .*** commands work best when the object is viewed through a 2D Shademode.
   - **1.2.** Save the drawing as *MySG.dwg* in the C:\Steps3D\Lesson12 folder.

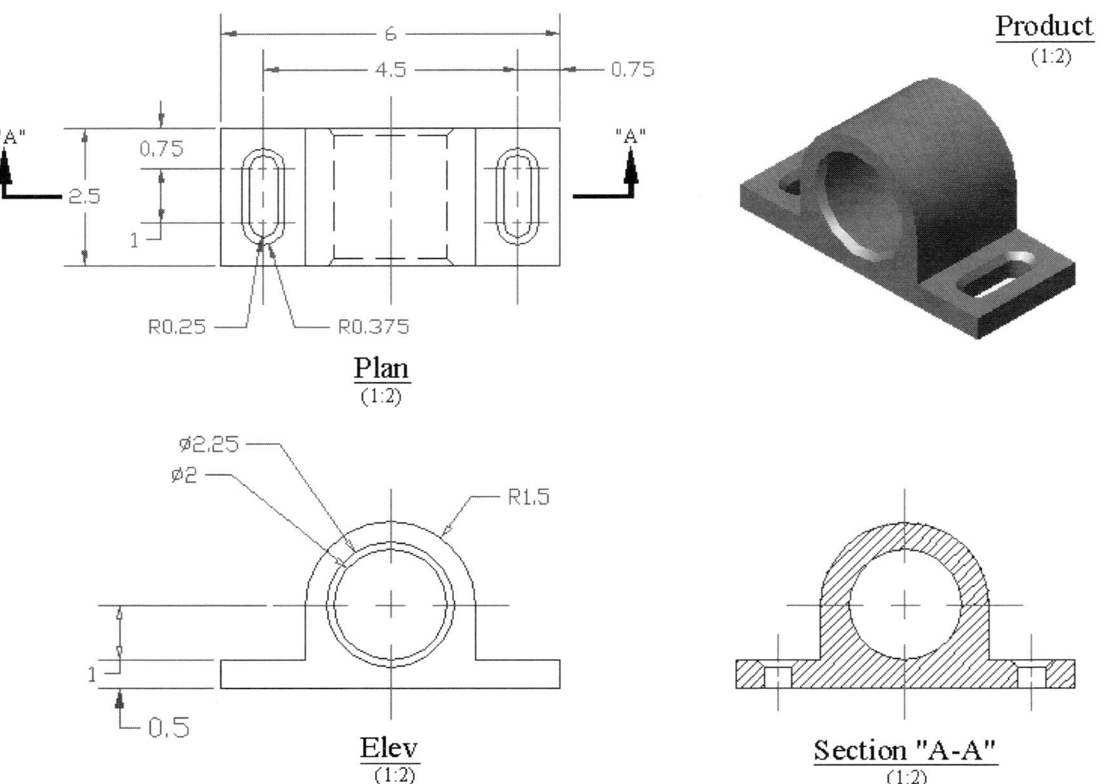

FIG. 12.5.1 *Slotted Guide.dwg*

2. Open the *My Flange 12.dwg* file you created in Lesson 10 (it should be in the C:\Steps3D\Lesson12 folder). If that one is not available, open the *Flange12.dwg* file instead. Create the layout shown in Figure 12.5.2.
   2.1. Most of the centerlines already exist on layer **Cl**.
   2.2. Save the drawing as *MyFlg.dwg* in the C:\Steps3D\Lesson12 folder.

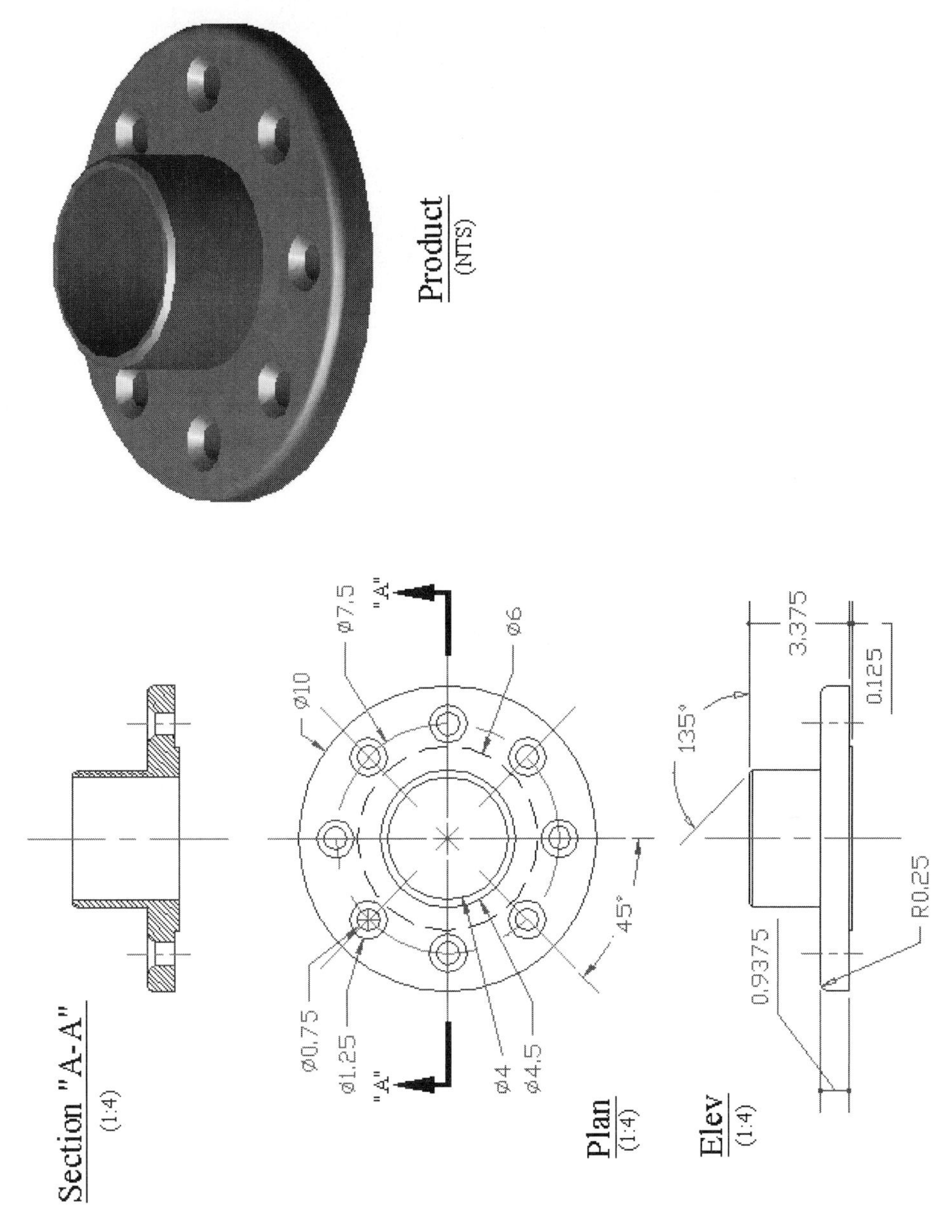

FIG. 12.5.2 *Flange12.dwg*

3. Open the *Jig1.dwg* in the C:\Steps3D\Lesson12 folder. Create the layout shown in Figure 12.5.3.
   3.1. Set up the drawing on a 17″ × 11″ sheet of paper.
   3.2. Save the drawing as *MyJig1.dwg* in the C:\Steps3D\Lesson12 folder.

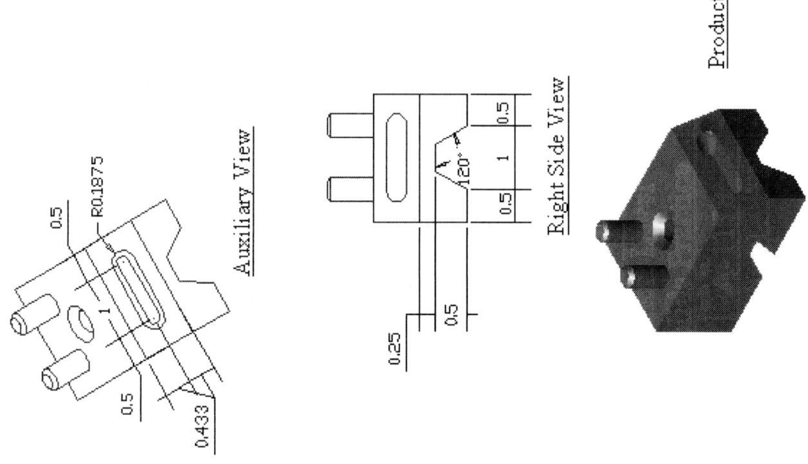

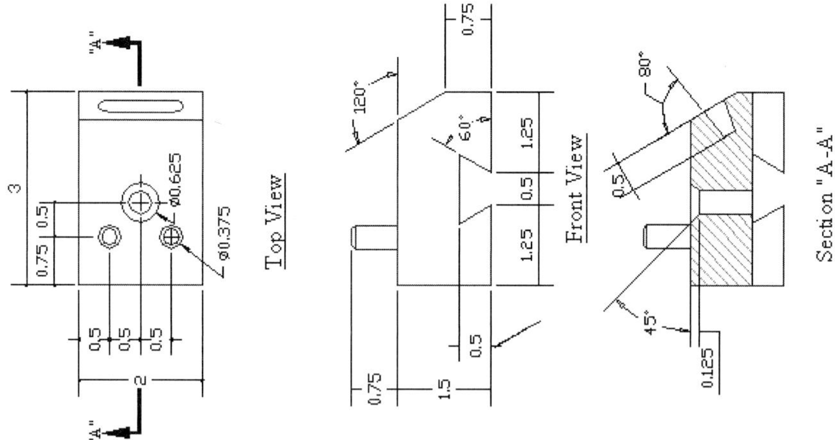

FIG. 12.5.3 *Jig1.dwg*

4. Open the *Thermometer.dwg* in the C:\Steps3D\Lesson12 folder. Create the layout shown in Figure 12.5.4.
   - **4.1.** Set up the drawing on an 11″ × 17″ sheet of paper.
   - **4.2.** Save the drawing as *MyThermometer.dwg* in the C:\Steps3D\Lesson12 folder.

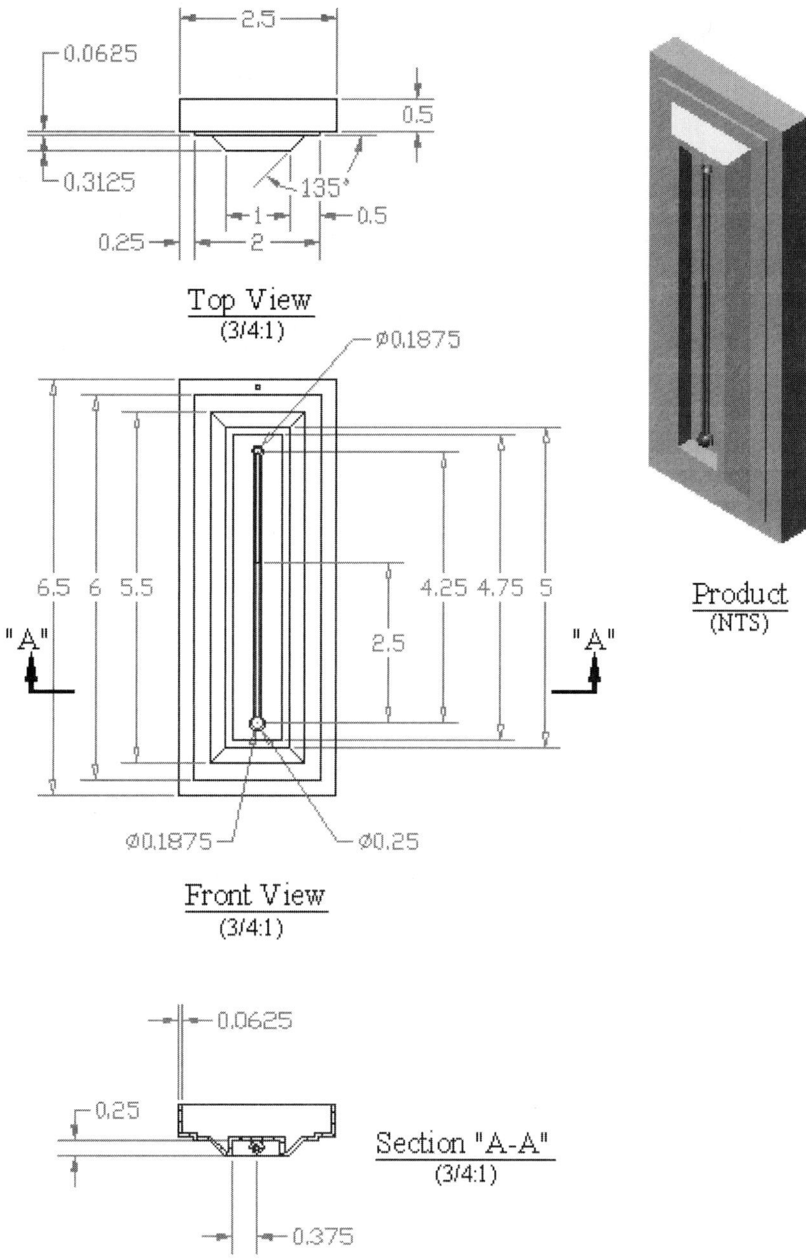

FIG. 12.5.4 *Thermometer.dwg*

5. Create the Service Cart drawing shown in Figure 12.5.5.
   5.1. Create the layout on an 11″ × 17″ sheet of paper.
   5.2. Adjust the Z-Scale and UCS as needed to use a single 2 × 2 block to build the frame.
   5.3. Use the caster you created in Lesson 6 (or the *Caster.dwg* file in the C:\Steps3D\Lesson12 folder) for the caster block.
   5.4. Use attributes and the ***Attext*** command to create the cutting list.
   5.5. You will notice that the ***Sol...*** commands will not work properly on blocks, so you will have to use the ***MView*** or ***MVSetup*** command to create your viewports.
   5.6. Save the drawing as *MyCart.dwg* in the C:\Steps3D\Lesson12 folder.

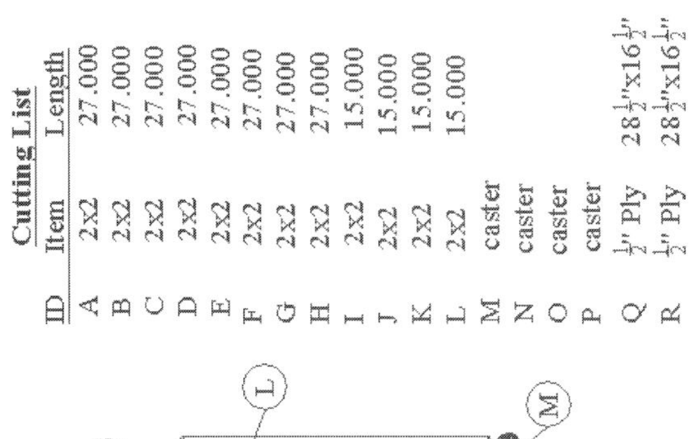

Cutting List

ID	Item	Length
A	2x2	27.000
B	2x2	27.000
C	2x2	27.000
D	2x2	27.000
E	2x2	27.000
F	2x2	27.000
G	2x2	27.000
H	2x2	27.000
I	2x2	15.000
J	2x2	15.000
K	2x2	15.000
L	2x2	15.000
M	caster	
N	caster	
O	caster	
P	caster	
Q	½" Ply	28½"x16½"
R	½" Ply	28½"x16½"

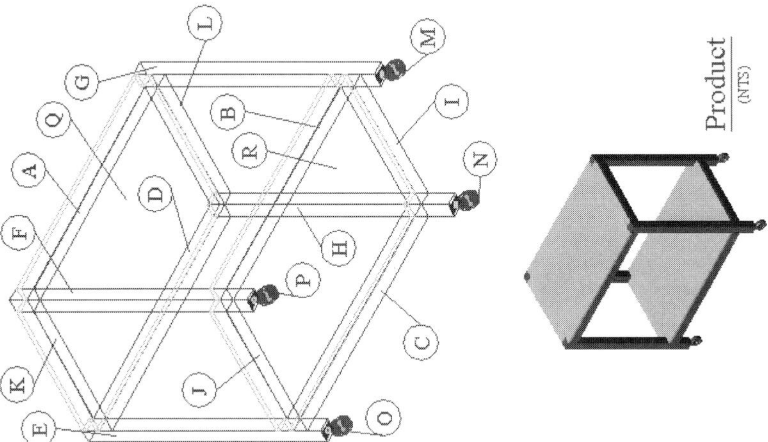

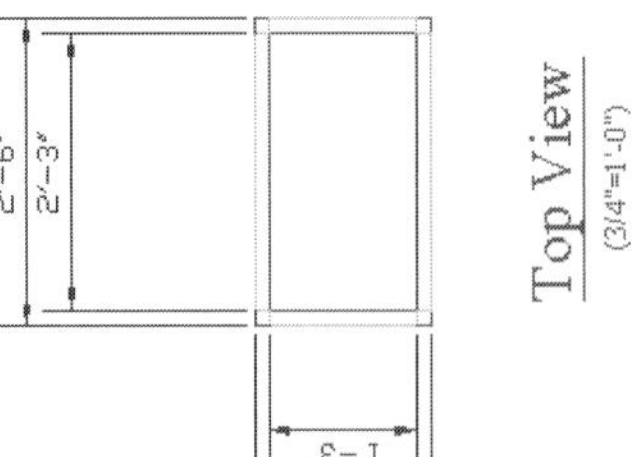

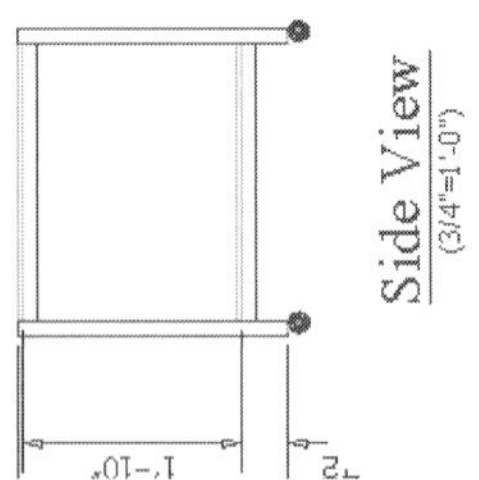

FIG. 12.5.5 Service Cart

6. Create the *1_2Ell* drawing shown in Figure 12.5.6.
   - **6.1.** Make sure the base point of the elbow is as indicated. (Use the ***Base*** command to move it, if necessary.)
   - **6.2.** Be sure the UCS = WCS when you finish.
   - **6.3.** Save the drawing as *My1_2Ell.dwg* in the C:\Steps3D\Lesson12 folder.

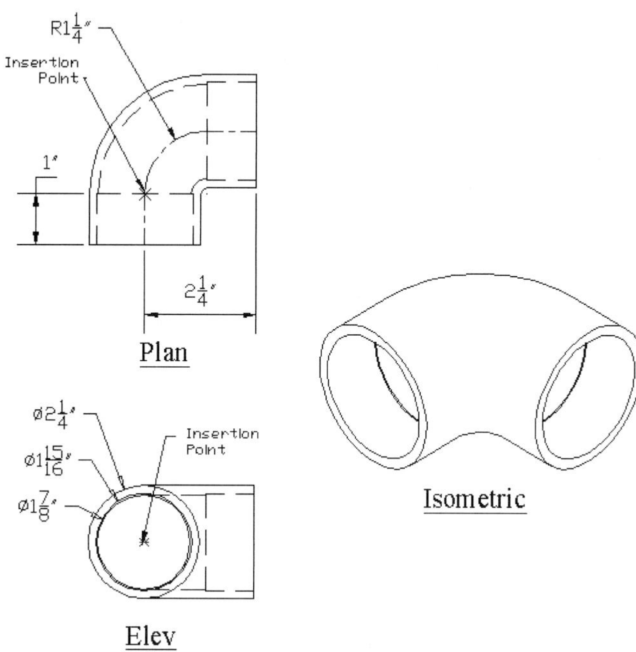

FIG. 12.5.6 *1_2Ell.dwg*

7. Create the *1_2Tee* drawing shown in Figure 12.5.7.
   - **7.1.** Make sure the base point of the tee is as indicated. (Use the ***Base*** command to move it, if necessary.)
   - **7.2.** Be sure the UCS = WCS when you finish.
   - **7.3.** Save the drawing as *My1_2Tee.dwg* in the C:\Steps3D\Lesson12 folder.

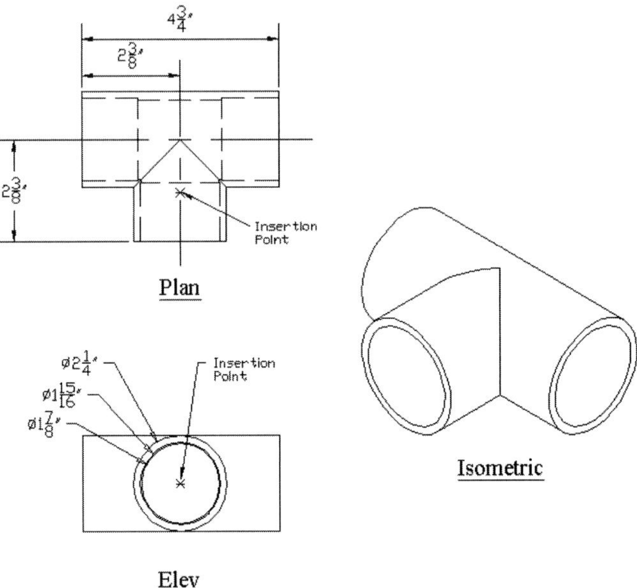

FIG. 12.5.7 *1_2Tee.dwg*

8. Create the Bike Rack drawing shown in Figure 12.5.8.
   - **8.1.** Use the elbow you created in Exercise 12.5.6. (If this is not available, use the *1_2Ell* drawing found in the C:\Steps3D\Lesson12 folder.)
   - **8.2.** Use the *1_2Pipe* drawing to provide the pipe between the elbows (just as you did in Exercise 12.1.2.1).
   - **8.3.** Be sure the UCS = WCS when you finish.
   - **8.4.** Save the drawing as *MyBikeRack.dwg* in the C:\Steps3D\Lesson12 folder.

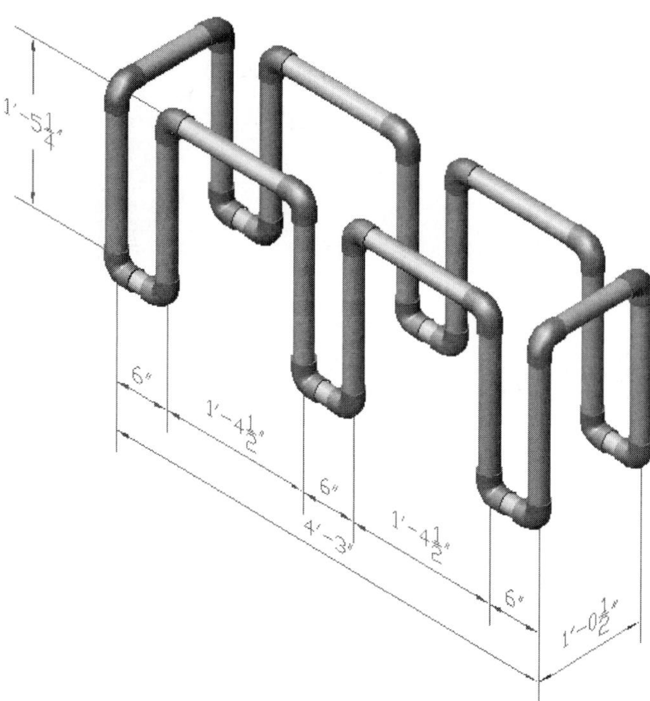

FIG. 12.5.8 *Bike Rack.dwg*

9. Create the Lawn Chair drawing shown in Figure 12.5.9.

9.1. Use the elbow you created in Exercise 12.5.6. (If this is not available, use the *1_2Ell* drawing found in the C:\Steps3D\Lesson12 folder.)

9.2. Use the tee you created in Exercise 12.5.7. (If this is not available, use the *1_2Tee* drawing found in the C:\Steps3D\Lesson12 folder.)

9.3. Use the *1_2Pipe* drawing to provide the pipe between the elbows (just as you did in Exercise 12.1.2.1).

9.4. Be sure the UCS = WCS when you finish.

9.5. Save the drawing as *MyLawnChair.dwg* in the C:\Steps3D\Lesson12 folder.

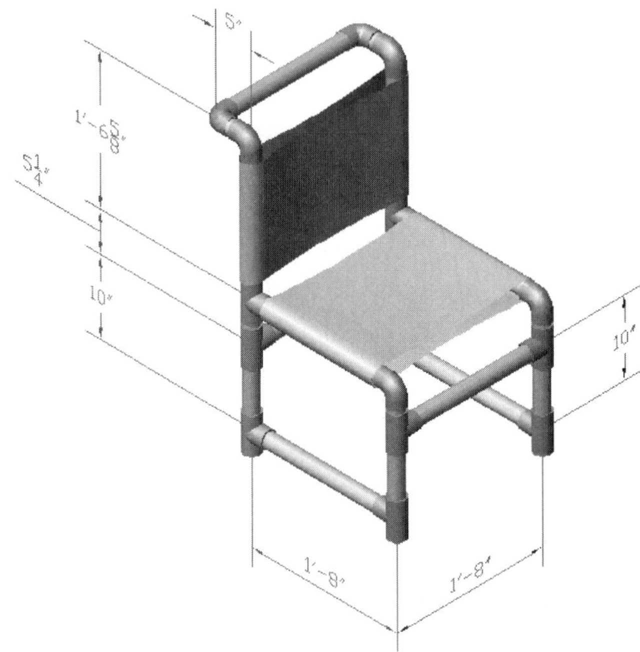

FIG. 12.5.9 *LawnChair.dwg*

10. Create the Patio Scene drawing shown in Figure 12.5.10.

10.1. Use the equipment you created in Exercises 12.5.8 and 12.5.9. (If these are not available, use the corresponding drawings found in the C:\Steps3D\Lesson12 folder.)

10.2. You created the garden fence in Lesson 9 and the fountain in Lesson 10. (Both are provided in the C:\Steps3D\Lesson12 folder if you did not save your drawings.)

10.3. Save the drawing as *MyPatioScene.dwg* in the C:\Steps3D\Lesson12 folder.

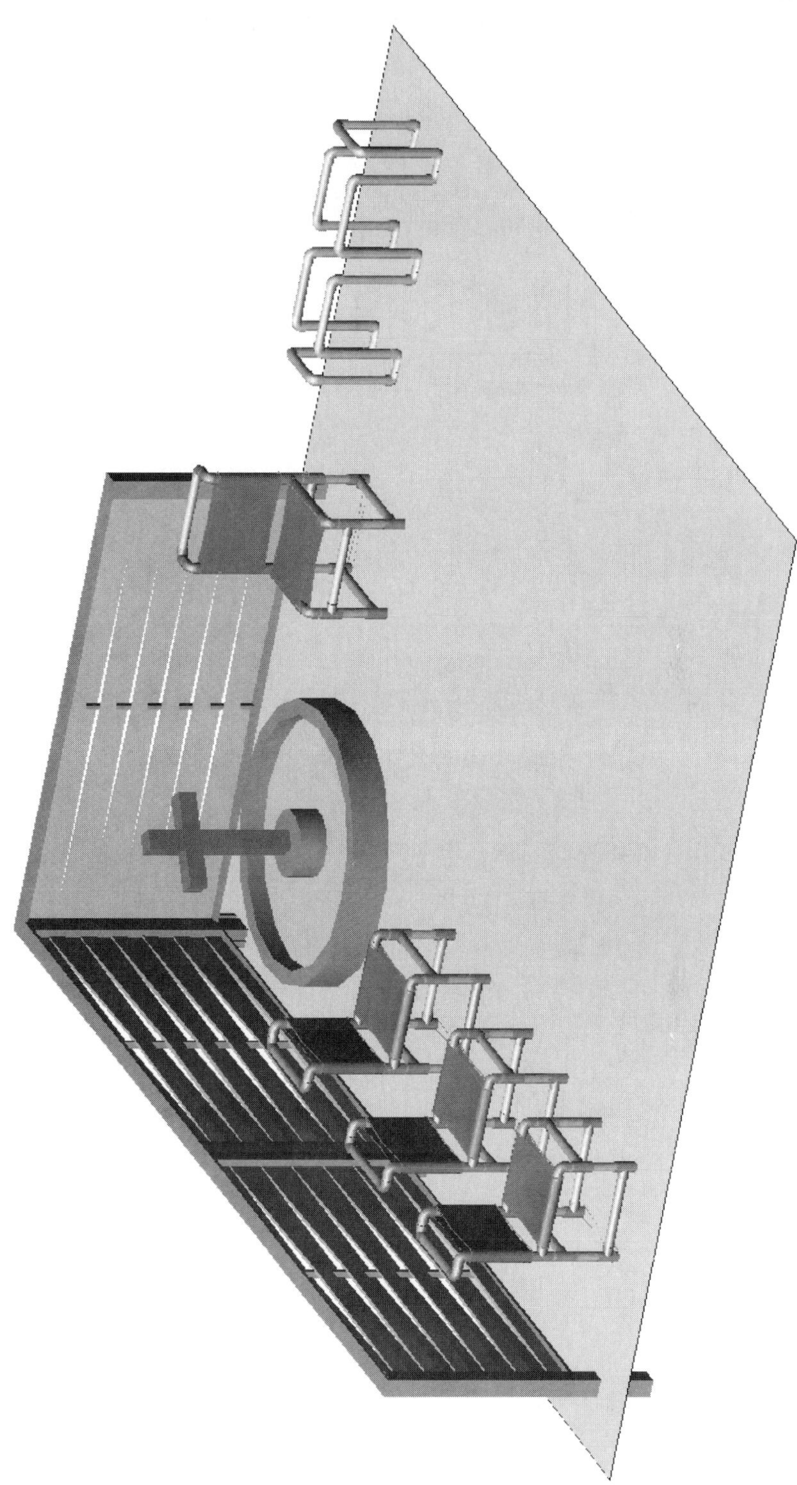

FIG. 12.5.10 *PatioScene.dwg*

12.6 REVIEW QUESTIONS

Please answer these questions on a separate sheet of paper.

1. (T or F) AutoCAD creates blocks against the plane of the current UCS.

2. AutoCAD inserts three-dimensional blocks by matching the __________ values of the block to the current UCS.

3. To be able to properly insert a three-dimensional block using a scale factor to size the block, the dimension of the object along the axis that will be scaled should be __________.

4. through 6. List the three commands that make up the Sol Group.

a.

b.

c.

7. Use the __________ command to set up the layout for plotting a 3D Solid.

8. Use the __________ command to create the actual drawings set up by the Solview command.

9. Use the __________ command to create profiles of a 3D Solid in a viewport.

10. through 13. List the four types of view Solview can create.

a.

b.

c.

d.

14. through 17. List the four things for which the Solview command creates layers.

a.

b.

c.

d.

18. Which of the initial four options of the Solview command should you use first?

19. Cross sections, orthographic projections, and auxiliary views are actually *drawn* by the (Solview, Soldraw, Solprof) command.

20. (T or F) Both Soldraw and Solprof create profiles in a viewport.

21. A __________ shows only those edges and/or silhouettes of a 3D Solid that are visible in the specific viewport when hidden lines are removed.

22. The (Soldraw, Solprof) command creates profiles that are actually blocks.

23. By default, Solprof will place hidden lines on (the same, a different) layer as/from the visible lines.

PART VI

Rendering and Xrefs

This part of our text contains these lessons:

LESSON

13

Is It Real or Is It Rendered?

Following this lesson, you will

- Know how to render an AutoCAD drawing
  - Rendering
  - Assigning materials
  - Adding graphics
  - Adding lights
  - Creating scenes

From childhood's hour I have not been
As others were—I have not seen
As others saw.

Alone—Edgar Allan Poe

Far better it is to dare mighty things, to win glorious triumphs, even though checkered by failure, than to take rank with those poor spirits who neither enjoy much nor suffer much, because they live in the gray twilight that knows not victory nor defeat.

Theodore Roosevelt

The measure of one's soul is calculated
not in successes or failures, but in the number of
attempts one is willing to make.

Anonymous

As you might guess from the three preceding quotes, you now face the most challenging of the lessons you will undertake in our *One Step at a Time* series. So before you start, think back to what you knew when you began Lesson 1 of *AutoCAD 2002: One Step at a Time*. You began each lesson with anticipation and a touch of anxiety, but you finished each knowing more than you did when you started. It has not always been easy, but you have persevered (or else you would not be here). Consider your accomplishments. And then take Teddy's advice and "dare mighty things" in Lesson 13.

13.1 What Is Rendering and Why Is It So Challenging?

Rendering is a procedure that takes the objects you have created and gives them properties to make them appear "real." The degree to which they appear real depends on a host of user-defined settings including assigned materials, types and positions of lights, and light intensity.

Why is rendering so challenging? Consider what Edgar Allan Poe said in the quote that began this lesson. Every individual will "see" a scene in a different way. Translating what your mind sees to what appears on the screen involves often subtle manipulation of several variables.

Remember Lesson 7—I told you that we had reached the edge between CAD operating and CAD programming. Well, in Lesson 13, you have reached the edge between CAD operating and art. Just as not every whittler is a sculptor, not every draftsman is an artist. This is where you face the challenge.

13.2 Beyond *Shademode*—The *Render* Command

It may fortify you to know that you have been using a rudimentary form of rendering all along when you used the ***Shademode*** command. But here again, consider the whittler and the sculptor. Whereas the ***Shademode*** command has a few options from which to choose, the ***Render*** command presents (quite literally) infinite possibilities. Fortunately, we will navigate the possibilities using dialog boxes.

Let's begin with the basic Render dialog box (Figure 13.2a). Access the dialog box by entering the ***Render*** command at the command prompt or picking the **Render** button on the Render toolbar. The first thing you will notice is that the dialog box has been sectioned into four frames and several spaces between the frames. Let's look.

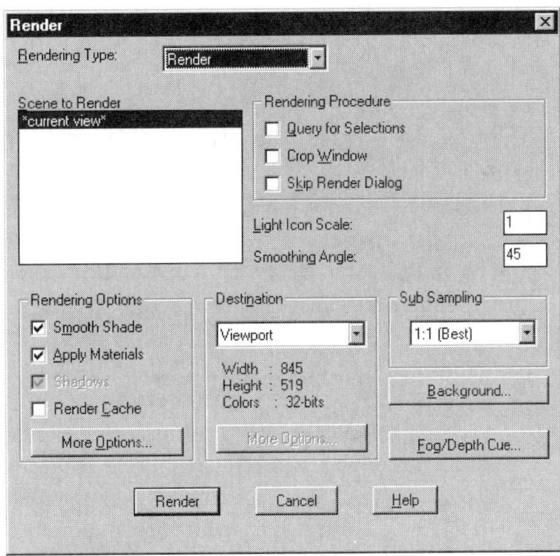

FIG. 13.2a Render Dialog Box

- There are three types of rendering available in the **Rendering Type** control box. These are (in order of quality from lowest to highest) **Render**, **Photo Real**, and **Photo Raytrace**. Each has its own options (more on these in a few moments) and each has its uses. To make it simple, remember that the lowest-quality renderer (**Render**) is fastest and that the highest quality (**Photo Raytrace**) is slowest. Even on a fast computer, rendering speeds remain an issue.

- The **Scene to Render** list box presents a selection list of available scenes to render. By default, AutoCAD will render the **current view**. But you will see how to create additional scenes in Section 13.6.
- The three check box options in the **Rendering Procedure** frame can help save time when rendering.
  - **Query for Selections** allows the user to render just those items selected.
  - **Crop Window** prompts the user to **Pick crop window to render**. Place a window around the area you wish to render. AutoCAD renders that area and hides the rest of the view.
  - Use the **Skip Render Dialog** to use the same settings for subsequent renderings. AutoCAD will not display the Render dialog box. To again display the dialog box, remove the check in the appropriate box in the Render Preferences dialog box (identical to the Render dialog box without the **Render** button). Access this dialog box with the ***RPref*** command.
- There are two unrelated (frameless) options below the **Rendering Procedure** frame.
  - When you add lights to your drawing, AutoCAD places an icon to mark the location of each. Use the **Light Icon Scale** text box to change the size of the icon if necessary for clarity. To determine the proper size, start with the drawing scale factor and adjust until you are satisfied.
  - The **Smoothing Angle** is the angle at which AutoCAD determines an edge when rendering. AutoCAD considers objects that form any angle greater than that shown in the **Smoothing Angle** text box to have an edge between them. If the objects form less of an angle, AutoCAD will render as though they are a single object.
- Pay particular attention to the options listed in the **Rendering Options** frame in the lower-left corner of the Render dialog box. Changes in these settings can dramatically affect the appearance of the rendered objects.
  - **Smooth Shade** smoothes edges on multifaceted surfaces (like spheres).
  - A check in the **Apply Materials** box tells AutoCAD to apply (when rendering) any materials that have been assigned to specific objects.
  - **Shadows** are only available for the **Photo Real** and **Photo Raytrace** types of rendering. When selected, AutoCAD will calculate shadows cast by objects as a result of any lights you have defined. The use of shadows in a rendered scene goes a long way toward creating a "real" appearance.
  - **Render Cache** can be a tremendous timesaver. When checked, AutoCAD writes rendering information to a file on the computer's hard disk. It then uses this information in subsequent renderings.
  - The **Rendering Type** determines which dialog box the **More Options . . .** button presents.
    - When the rendering type is **Render**, AutoCAD presents the Render Options dialog box (Figure 13.2b).

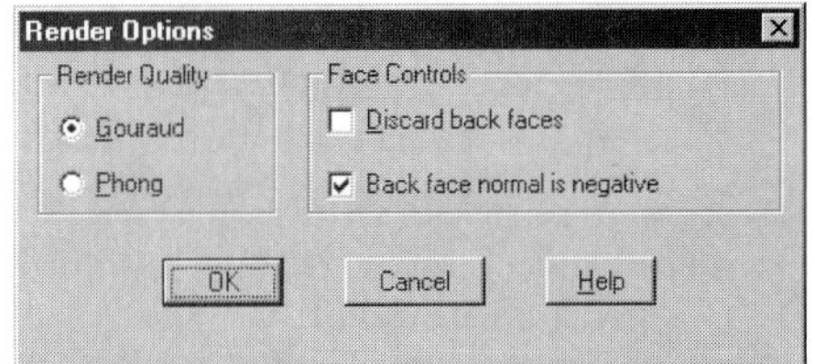

FIG. 13.2b Render Options Dialog Box

- The **Render Quality** frame allows the user to select between **Gouraud** rendering (this is what you are accustomed to seeing with the **Gouraud** option of the ***Shademode*** command) and **Phong** rendering (this is more sophisticated than Gouraud—it produces a more realistic image).
- The **Discard back faces** option of the **Face Controls** frame allows the user another opportunity to increase rendering speed. A check here tells AutoCAD not to consider back faces (those hidden with the ***Hide*** command) when rendering.

  The **Back face normal is negative** option sounds more complicated than it is. A check here tells AutoCAD that back is back and front is front. Remove the check and AutoCAD will consider the back faces to be the front (and vice versa). Then, if the **Discard back faces** option is checked, AutoCAD will render the back faces and hide the front ones!

➠ When the rendering type is **Photo Real**, AutoCAD presents the Photo Real Render Options dialog box (Figure 13.2c). Here you have four frames of options.

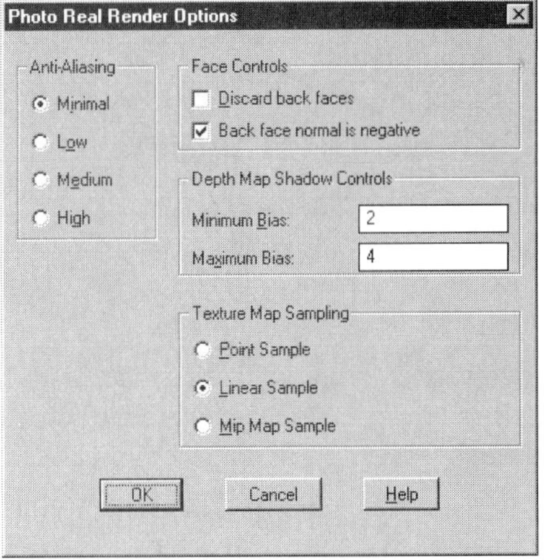

FIG. 13.2c Photo Real Rendering Options Dialog Box

- The **Anti-Aliasing** frame allows the user to control how jagged edges will appear in a rendered scene. **Minimal** anti-aliasing is faster but produces more jagged edges; **High** anti-aliasing has just the opposite effect.
- The **Face Controls** frame is identical to the same frame on the Render Options dialog box previously discussed.

- **Depth Map Shadow Controls** allow the user to adjust how a shadow is created. These settings are best left to AutoCAD, but if you notice problems with shadowing (i.e., shadows casting shadows), try adjusting these numbers. The **Minimum Bias** is generally between 2 and 20. The **Maximum Bias** value should be less than 10 above the **Minimum Bias** value.
- **Texture Map Sampling** allows the user three choices of what to do when a texture map is larger than the object to which it has been attached.

A **Texture Map** is an image (a bitmap or other graphic) projected onto an object (like a table or wall).

Point Sample produces a sharp image, but the lines may appear jagged.

Linear Sample's image is less focused, but the lines are not as jagged.

Mip Map Sample produces very soft edges, but lines may appear quite blurred.

➠ When the rendering type is **Photo Raytrace**, AutoCAD presents the Photo Raytrace Render Options dialog box (Figure 13.2d). Here you have five frames of options. Fortunately, only two of the frames are new.

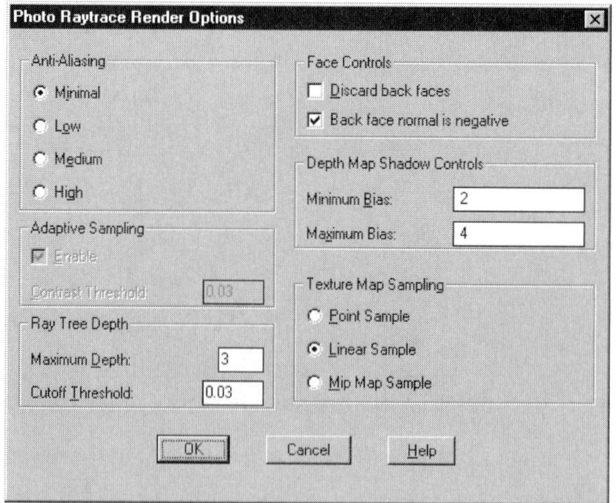

FIG. 13.2d Photo Raytrace Render Options

- **Adaptive Sampling** is only available for the bottom three **Anti-Aliasing** options. It provides a tool to speed up anti-aliasing. Enter a value between 0 and 1 in the **Contrast Threshold** box—the higher the number, the faster the rendering but the lower the quality.

- The **Ray Tree Depth (Maximum Depth)** setting allows the user to control the amount of reflected or refracted light rays in a rendering. Higher numbers yield better results but take longer. AutoCAD recommends a maximum value of 10.

  The **Cutoff Threshold** controls how far a ray of light will travel. Again, higher numbers produce better-quality renderings but take longer.

■ Use the **Destination** frame of the Render dialog box (Figure 13.2a, p. 525) to tell AutoCAD where to place the rendering. Choices include

- Place the rendering in the current **Viewport**.
- Open a separate **Render Window** in which to place the rendering.
- Create a separate graphics **File** for the rendering. When you select the **File** option, AutoCAD makes the **More Options . . .** button available. This button presents the File Output Configuration dialog box (Figure 13.2e). Options available in the different frames depend on the type of file selected in the **File Type** frame.

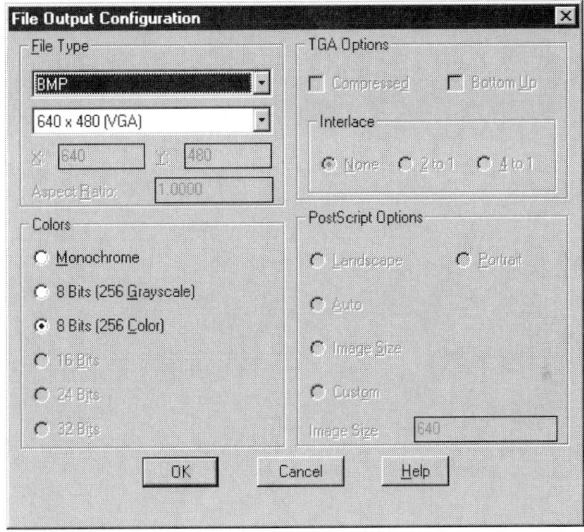

FIG. 13.2e File Output Configuration Dialog Box

  ➠ File types available in the control box include .BMP, .PCX, PostScript, .TGA, and .TIF.

  ➠ Below that is a resolution control box. Here the user controls the resolution of the output file (the higher the resolution, the finer the quality of the rendered file).

  ➠ The **Aspect Ratio** (width to height) is available when the user selects **User Defined** in the resolution control box.

- TGA options are available when you select the TGA file type.

  ➠ **Compressed** makes the final file size smaller. I always select this for efficiency.

- **Bottom Up** causes the file to be read from the lower-left corner rather than the upper-left corner.
- **Interlace** controls how the file will be read by a graphics program. I normally set this to 2 to 1 for more speed.

- The **Colors** frame allows the user to determine the number of colors used to create the file. The larger the number, the finer the quality. I usually set this to the highest quality available even though that tends to increase the size of the file.
- All of the options in the PostScript frame deal with size and orientation of the image.
  - **Portrait** stands the page up (i.e., 11″ × $8\frac{1}{2}$″) whereas **Landscape** lays it on its side (i.e., $8\frac{1}{2}$″ × 11″).
  - **Auto** automatically scales the image for you.
  - **Image Size** makes the image the actual size.
  - **Custom** uses the value in the **Image Size** box to set the size of the image in pixels.

- **Sub Sampling** (on the Render dialog box) speeds the rendering process by rendering only a ratio of the pixels. Highest quality but slowest rendering is 1:1 (render all pixels); lowest quality but fastest rendering is 8:1 (render every eighth pixel).
- The **Background** button calls the Background dialog box (Figure 13.2f). Here the user controls the background for the rendering. AutoCAD provides four options—these control what other options are available.

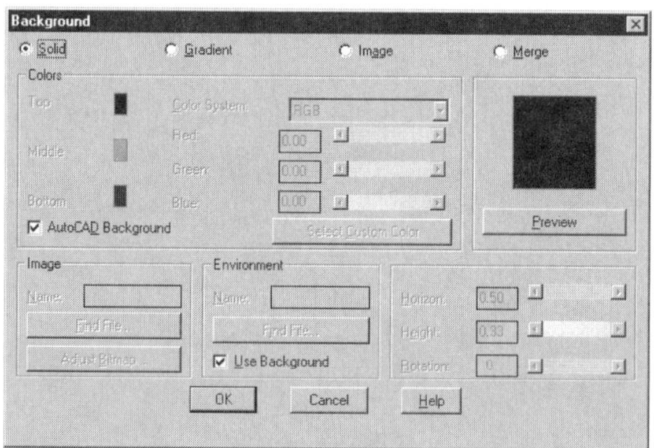

FIG. 13.2f Background Dialog Box

- **Solid** allows you to use a single-color background. You can use the current color (leave a check in the **AutoCAD Background** check box) or select/define a color in the **Colors** frame. (Preview your settings using the **Preview** button in the upper-right frame.)
- **Gradiant** creates a two- or three-color graduated background. When selected, AutoCAD makes the **Colors** frame available as well as the lower right frame. Use the lower-right frame to define the size of the graduations. (Set the **Height** value to ***0*** for a two-color background.)

- The **Image** option, of course, allows the user to use an image in the background. Possible file types you can use include .BMP, .PNG, .JPG, .TGA, .TIF, .GIF, and .PCX. Once you have selected an image, the **Adjust Bitmap** button will present a dialog box that will allow you to adjust the location and tiling of the image.
- The **Merge** option uses the current background image as the background.
- The **Environment** option (frame), when used with a **Photo Real** type of rendering, causes a mirroring effect. When used with a **Photo Raytrace** type, AutoCAD uses the image to effect changes to light reflection and refraction in the rendering.

■ The **Fog/Depth Cue . . .** button on the Render dialog box calls the Fog/Depth Cue dialog box (Figure 13.2g). Here you can fog (tint) the objects being rendered as well as the background of the rendering.

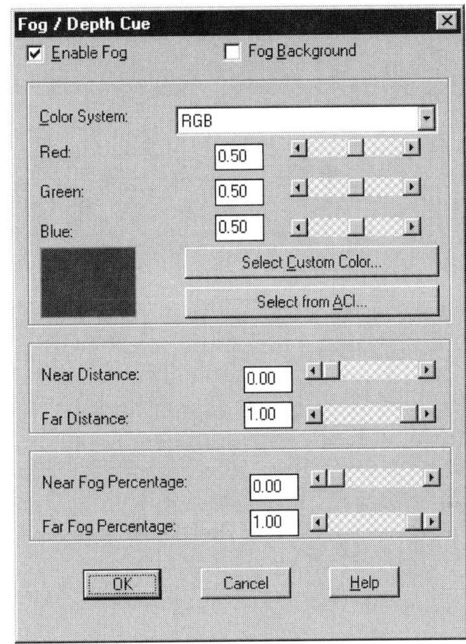

FIG. 13.2g Fog/Depth Cue Dialog Box

- **Enable Fog**, when selected alone, causes the objects in the drawing to be tinted according to the color defined in the uppermost frame. When **Fog Background** is selected, the entire image will be tinted.
- Use the uppermost frame of the Fog/Depth Cue dialog box to define the color for the fogging.
  The **Color System** control box provides two methods for selecting colors—**RGB** (Red, Green, Blue) and **HLS** (Hue, Lightness, Saturation). When **RGB** is current, adjust color intensity using the **Red:**, **Green:**, and **Blue:** slider bars. When **HLS** is current, adjust color intensity using the **Hue:**, **Lightness:**, and **Saturation:** slider bars. (*Note:* These slider bars replace the **Red:**, **Green:**, and **Blue:** slider bars.)

The **Select Custom Color . . .** button calls a standard Windows custom color dialog box whereas the **Select from ACI . . .** button presents AutoCAD's Color dialog box.

The box in the lower-left corner of the frame will present the color that you have defined.

- The next frame provides values AutoCAD uses to determine where to begin and end the fog. Values are percentages (from 0 to 1) of the distance from the camera to the back working plane.
- The last frame provides values AutoCAD uses to determine how much fog to place at the **Near** and **Far Distance** points.

Well, what do you think? I counted at least seven primary dialog boxes. I would not dare count the number of variables. Do you begin to see why there are infinite possibilities to render a drawing? Do you begin to see why this is the most challenging lesson in our course? (Remember, we have just covered the Render dialog box. We have not looked at materials or lighting . . . yet!)

To remove the rendering from a drawing (to return it to its previous state), simply regenerate the drawing (with the ***Regen*** command).

But let's pause to acquire some hands-on experience before we look at adding materials to our rendering.

You can also access all of the commands in this lesson via the View pull-down menu. Follow this path:

View—Render—[command]

WWW 13.2.1 Do This: Discovering Rendering

I. Open the *Rendering Project.dwg* file in the C:\Steps3D\Lesson13 folder. The drawing looks like Figure 13.2.1a.

FIG. 13.2.1a *Rendering Project.dwg*

II. Follow these steps:

TOOLS	COMMAND SEQUENCE	STEPS
 Gouraud Shaded Button	**Command:** ***shademode***	**1.** First, we will compare basic types of rendering. Use the ***Shademode*** command to Gouraud-shade the drawing. Note the time required to complete the command. Your drawing looks like Figure 13.2.1.1.

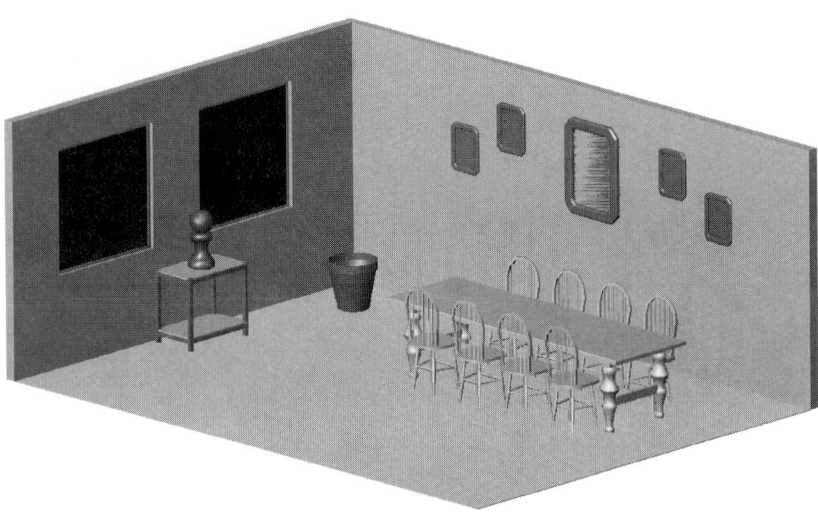

FIG. 13.2.1.1 *Gouraud-Shaded Drawing*

TOOLS	COMMAND SEQUENCE	STEPS
 Render Button	 **Command:** ***rr***	**2.** Enter the ***Render*** command by typing ***render*** or ***rr*** at the command prompt. Or you can pick the **Render** button on the Render toolbar.
	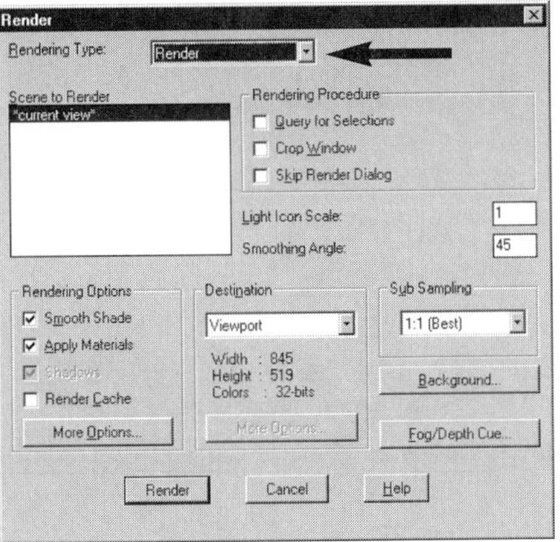	**3.** Using the **Render** type, as indicated, pick the **Render** button to render the drawing. (Use defaults for all other settings.) Compare the differences between the basic **Render** type and the Gouraud Shademode. ***Render*** took just a little more time but produced a finer-quality image than ***Shademode***. Unfortunately, however, *you cannot work on a rendered drawing as you can on a shaded drawing.*

continued

TOOLS	COMMAND SEQUENCE	STEPS

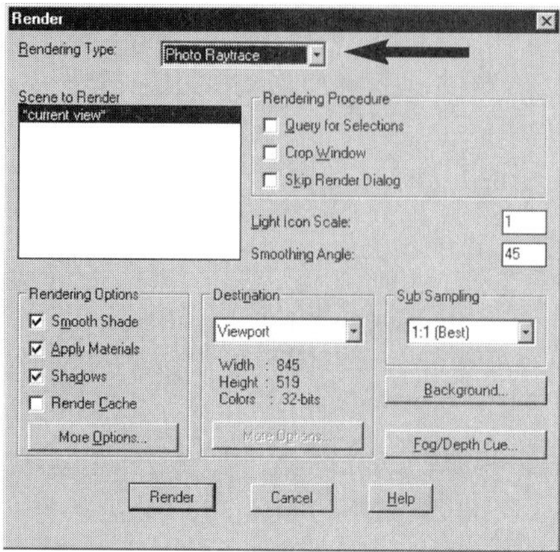

4. Compare the **Render** type rendering to a **Photo Raytrace** type rendering. Repeat Steps 2 and 3 using the **Photo Raytrace Rendering Type**. Your drawing looks like Figure 13.2.1.4.

Notice the differences. The **Photo Raytrace** type took longer but produced a slightly better quality in the rendering.

Let's try some of the options.

FIG. 13.2.1.4 Photo Raytrace Type of Rendering

Command: *rr*

5. Repeat the *Render* command.

continued

TOOLS	COMMAND SEQUENCE	STEPS

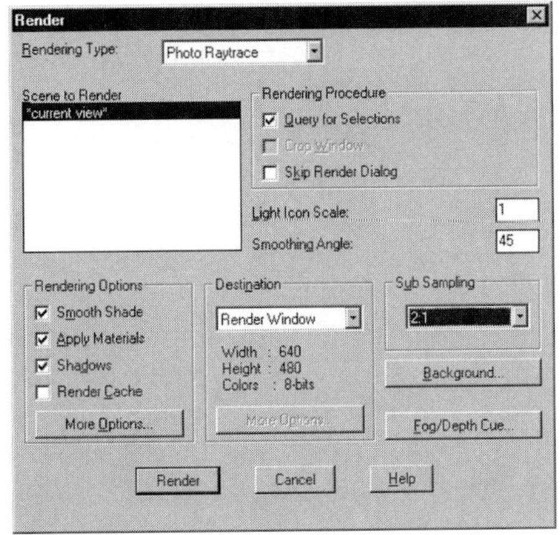

6. (We will continue with the **Photo Raytrace** type of rendering throughout the rest of the lesson.)

We will render only part of the drawing (to save time). Tell AutoCAD to **Query for Selections** (for specific objects to render).

Send the rendering to the **Render Window . . .**
. . . and speed the rendering by setting the **Sub Sampling** to 2:1.

Pick the **Render** button to continue.

Select objects:

Select objects: *[enter]*

7. AutoCAD prompts you to select the objects to render. Place a selection window around the table and chairs.

Your drawing looks like Figure 13.2.1.7. Consider the results.

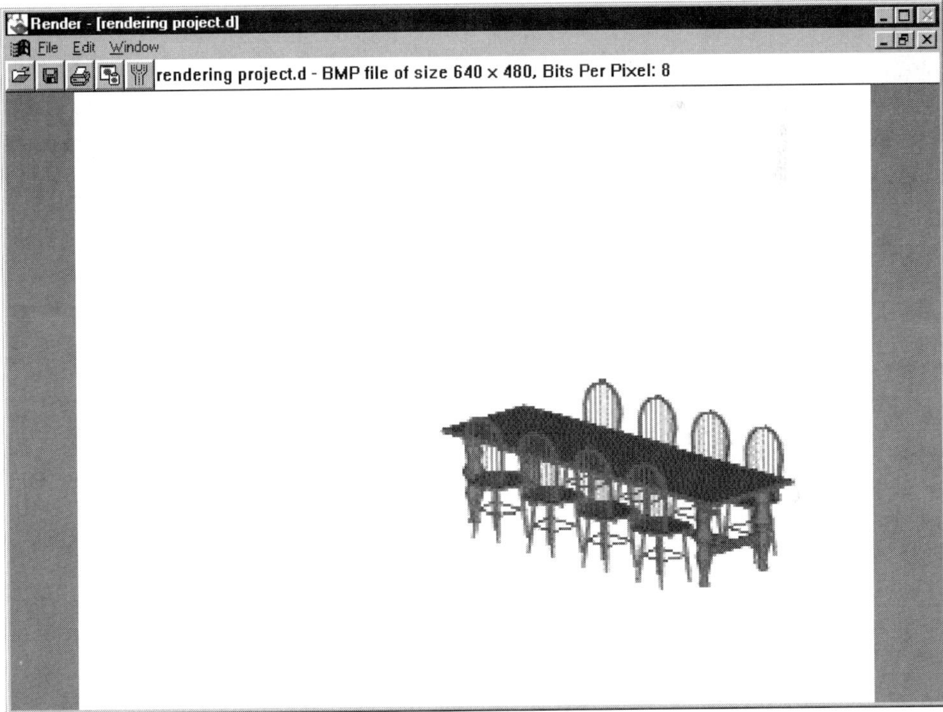

FIG. 13.2.1.7 Render Window

continued

TOOLS	COMMAND SEQUENCE	STEPS

- The rendering moved fairly quickly because you only rendered part of the drawing and your **Sub Sampling** was halved.
- The rendering was placed into a separate window. Take a moment to examine the buttons and pull-down menus for the Render window. Pay particular attention to the **Options** selection under the **File** pull-down menu. There you can adjust the quality of future images.
- Notice the poor quality of the rendering. This is a result of the **Sub Sampling** changes you made. You can do this to render quickly—to make adjustments in the settings — but you will want the final rendering to use the ***1:1*** **Sub Sampling** setting.
- You can minimize the Render window when you wish to return to AutoCAD. To close it, go to the Load/Unload Applications dialog box (use the ***Appload*** command or the **Load Application** option under the Tools pull-down menu) and unload **ACRender.arx**.

Command: *rr*

8. Repeat the ***Render*** command and set the **Rendering Procedure, Sub Sampling,** and **Destination** frames to their defaults.

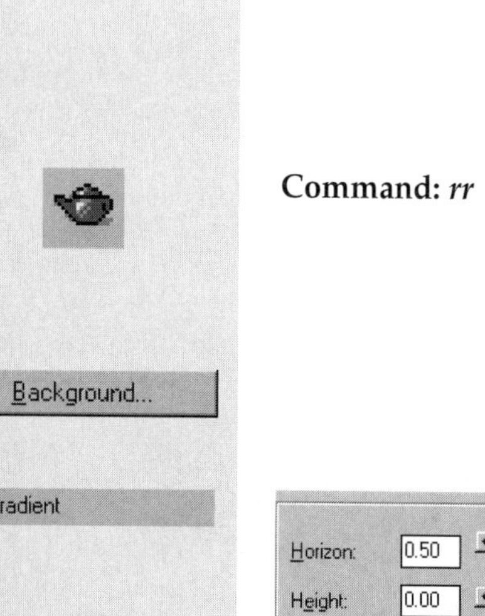

9. Let's play with the background. Pick the **Background** button.

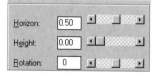

10. We will use a two-color gradient background. Put a bullet next to **Gradient**, and set the **Height** to ***0.***

continued

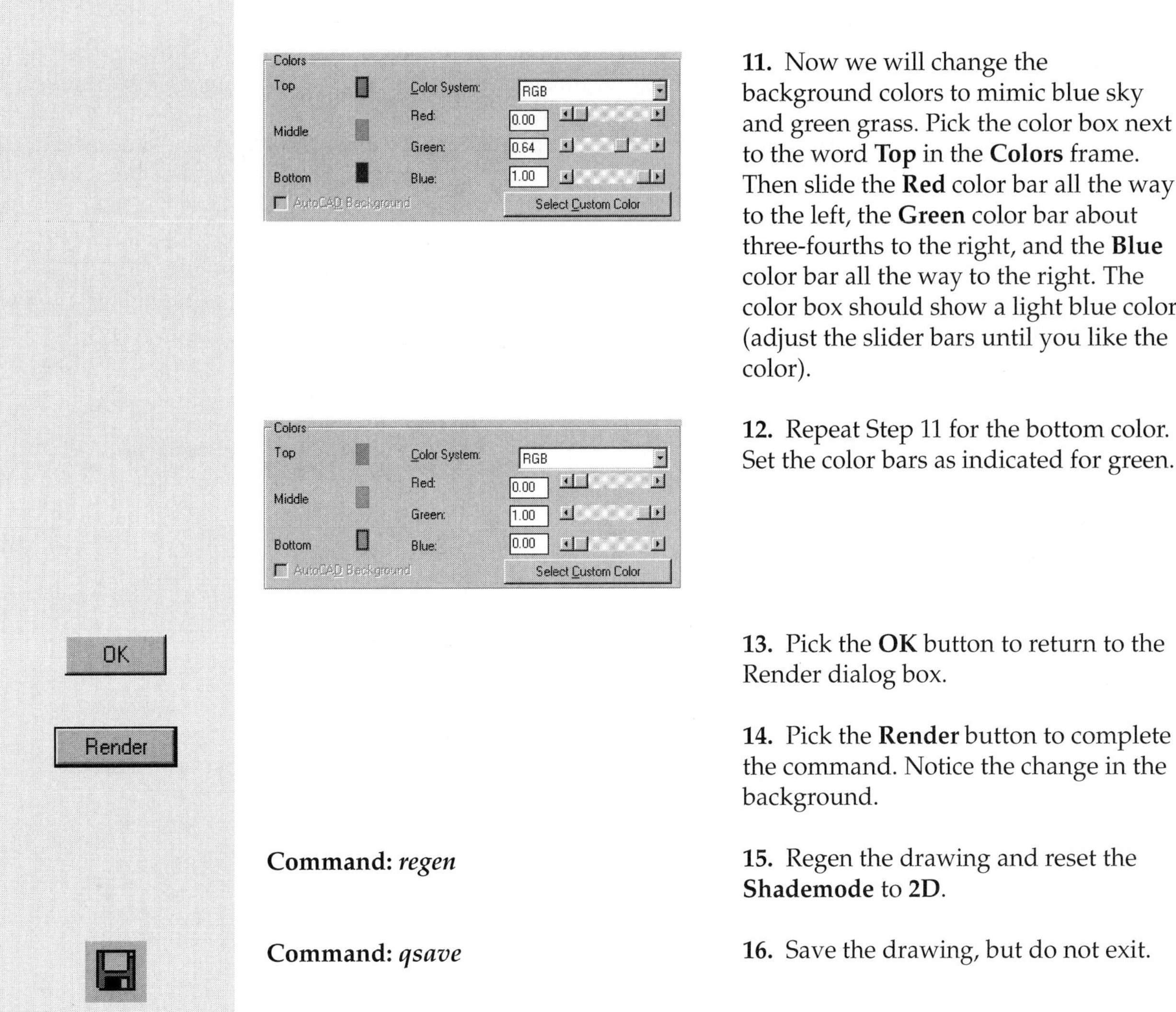

TOOLS	COMMAND SEQUENCE	STEPS
	Colors: Top, Middle, Bottom; Color System: RGB; Red: 0.00; Green: 0.64; Blue: 1.00; AutoCAD Background; Select Custom Color	**11.** Now we will change the background colors to mimic blue sky and green grass. Pick the color box next to the word **Top** in the **Colors** frame. Then slide the **Red** color bar all the way to the left, the **Green** color bar about three-fourths to the right, and the **Blue** color bar all the way to the right. The color box should show a light blue color (adjust the slider bars until you like the color).
	Colors: Top, Middle, Bottom; Color System: RGB; Red: 0.00; Green: 1.00; Blue: 0.00; AutoCAD Background; Select Custom Color	**12.** Repeat Step 11 for the bottom color. Set the color bars as indicated for green.
OK		**13.** Pick the **OK** button to return to the Render dialog box.
Render		**14.** Pick the **Render** button to complete the command. Notice the change in the background.
	Command: ***regen***	**15.** Regen the drawing and reset the **Shademode** to **2D**.
	Command: ***qsave***	**16.** Save the drawing, but do not exit.

We could easily spend a hundred pages exploring the rest of the possibilities, but you should have the general idea. Take some time (once you complete the lesson) to continue exploring on your own.

You have seen the basics of the ***Render*** command, but so far, the rendered drawing is fairly unimpressive. It still looks like a cartoon—bright and colorful but not real. Next we will begin to add reality to our image by assigning material values to the various objects.

Let's proceed.

13.3 Adding Materials to Make Your Solids Look Real

As you will soon see, adding materials to an object can mean the difference between colorful cartoon images and images that come close to photographic realism. And luckily, you can accomplish it fairly easily.

To understand materials, think of them as paint (or wallpaper). The object does not actually become wood (or granite, etc.). Rather, it has the image of wood painted onto it. AutoCAD achieves this by attaching an image file (usually a bitmap) to the surfaces of the objects. The only trick involved for the user, then, is to know which image file to use. AutoCAD provides a library full of possible images from which to choose. If these do not satisfy the user's needs, however, AutoCAD helps to create new images (or modify old ones)!

AutoCAD makes four categories of materials available: **Standard** (plain with no markings), **Granite, Marble,** or **Wood**. The last three contain markings that reflect properties of that type of material.

Begin the process of attaching materials in your drawing with the ***RMat*** command (or you can pick the **Materials** button on the Render toolbar). AutoCAD presents the Materials dialog box (Figure 13.3a). Let's take a look.

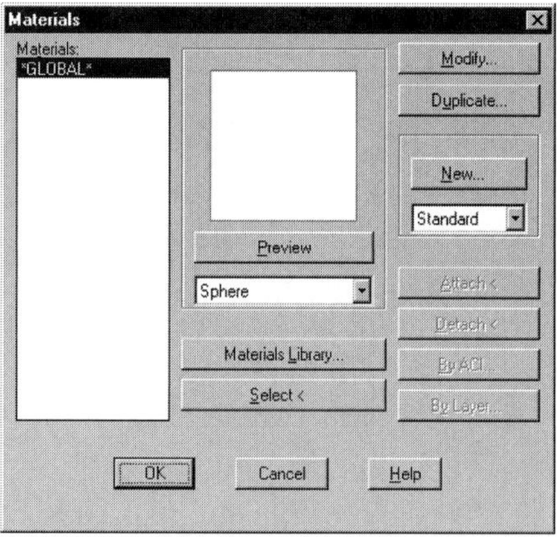

FIG. 13.3a Materials Dialog Box

- The first thing you will probably notice is the **Materials** list box on the left side of the dialog box. Here AutoCAD will list all the materials currently loaded and available for use. By default, AutoCAD has no materials loaded.
- The frame to the right of the **Materials** list box allows the user to preview the material currently highlighted in the list box. Use the control box at the bottom of the frame to tell AutoCAD that you wish to preview the material against a **Sphere** or a **Cube**. Use the **Preview** button to create the preview in the window above the button.

- The **Select** button (below the **Preview** frame) returns you to the graphics screen where you can select an object. AutoCAD then returns you to the Materials dialog box and highlights the material currently attached to the object. Use this to identify materials already assigned to specific objects.
- The **Materials Library . . .** button presents the Materials Library dialog box (Figure 13.3b). This is where you will load materials to use in your drawing. Let's take a look at our options.

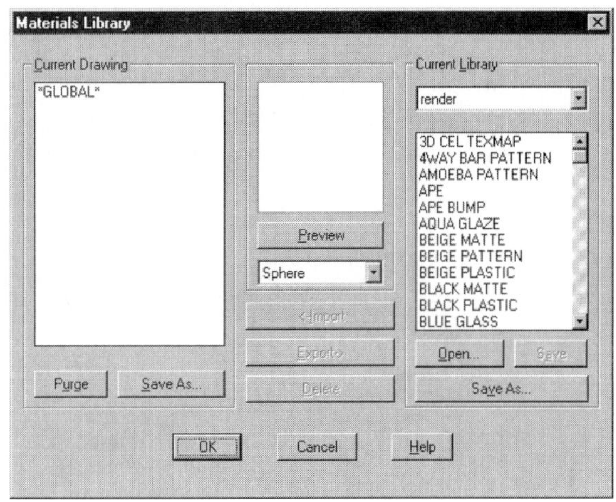

FIG. 13.3b Materials Library Dialog Box

- The **Current Drawing** frame presents a list box that shows all the materials loaded and available in the current drawing. Use the **Purge** button to remove unused materials and the **Save As . . .** button to save the list (as an .MLI file). You can use a saved list in another drawing.
- Use the **Preview** frame just as you did in the Materials dialog box.
- The **Current Library** frame presents all the materials available in the library shown in the upper control box. Use the **Open** button to open a different *.MLI* file (Materials LIbrary). Use the **Save** or **Save As . . .** buttons to save the library.
- Use the **<-Import** and **Export->** buttons to load or unload materials currently highlighted in the list box or the **Current Library** frame's selection box.
- The **Delete** button will remove selected materials from the current drawing or the material library. (It is not a good idea to remove materials from the library as they then become unavailable for future use.)
- The **OK** button will return you to the Materials dialog box.

You can also access the Materials Library using the ***MatLib*** command or selecting the **Materials Library** button on the Render toolbar. If you access the Materials dialog box in one of these ways, the **OK** button will return you to the command prompt.

- Use the **New** button on the Materials dialog box to create user-defined materials. When you pick the **New** button, AutoCAD presents one of four New . . . Material dialog boxes. The specific dialog box presented depends on the materials category displayed in the selection box below the button.

  - The New Standard Material dialog box (Figure 13.3c) allows the user to create a solid-color material. This type of material is most useful for plastic or metal surfaces.

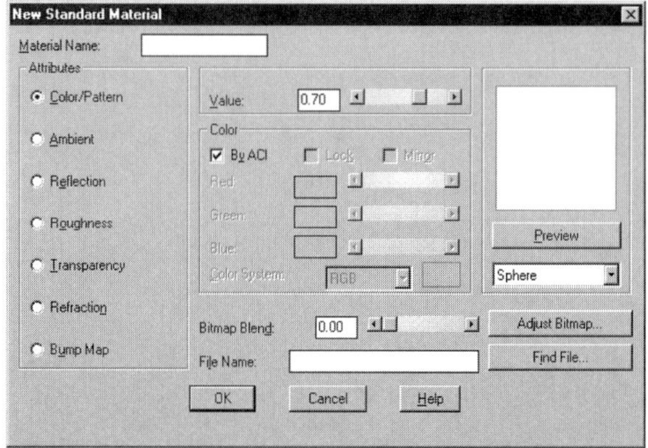

FIG. 13.3c New Standard Material Dialog Box

  - Begin by entering a unique name for your new material in the **Material Name:** text box.
  - The **Attributes** frame presents several ways to adjust the appearance of the new material. Adjust the value of the attributes using the **Value** and **Color** frames.
    - **Color/Pattern:** This option allows you to adjust the main color of the material.
    - **Ambient:** Use this option to adjust the shadow color of the material.
    - **Reflection:** This option allows you to change the reflective (highlighted) color of the new material.
    - **Roughness:** Roughness refers to the size of the reflective area (the shininess of the object). A higher value means a larger reflective area.
    - **Transparency:** Controls the transparency of the material. A value of 1 is opaque. Use the **File Name:** text box to assign an opacity map (a bitmap) to this material. When using a Photo Raytrace or Photo Real render type, transparency tends to diminish toward the edges of the object.
    - **Refraction:** (Applies only to the Photo Raytrace render type.) Allows you to adjust how much the light will "bend" around the material. Use this in conjunction with transparency to control what happens to light passing through an object.
    - **Bump Map:** (According to AutoCAD's glossary, a bump map is "a map in which brightness values are translated into apparent changes in the height of the surface of an object.") A bullet in the Bump Map attribute allows the user to specify a bump map in the Bitmap Blend **File Name:** text box.

- The **Preview** frame works just as the other preview frames we have discussed.
- To assign a bitmap to your new material, use the **Find File . . .** button in the lower-right corner of the dialog box. This is how you would create a new material using a scanned image.
- Access the Adjust Material Bitmap Placement dialog box (Figure 13.3d) with the **Adjust Bitmap . . .** button. Adjust the size and location of the bitmap here.

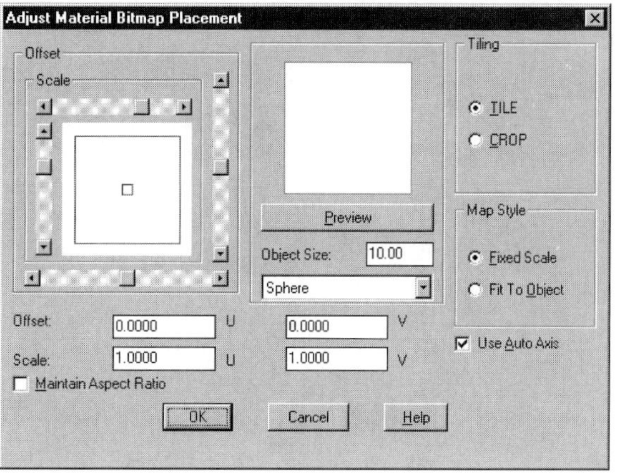

FIG. 13.3d Adjust Material Bitmap Placement Dialog Box

With attribute variations for the specific category of material, the other New . . . Material dialog boxes are identical to the New Standard Material dialog box. Additionally, you may use the **Modify . . .** and **Duplicate . . .** buttons to adjust material attributes using the same dialog boxes as the New . . . Material dialog boxes.

AutoCAD makes the four buttons in the lower-right corner of the Materials dialog box available only when there are materials listed in the Materials list box.

- Use the **Attach <** button to attach the material highlighted in the list box to an object in the drawing. AutoCAD returns you to the graphics screen to make your selection(s). The **Attach <** button will also highlight the objects to which the selected material is currently attached.
- Use the **Detach <** button to remove a material from an object. AutoCAD returns you to the graphics screen to select the object(s).
- Use the **By ACI . . .** button to attach materials to objects according to the color of the objects.
- Use the **By Layer . . .** button to attach materials to objects according to the layer on which the objects reside.

You can assign materials to any object or block in a drawing, but 3D Faces and 3D Solids produce the best results.

This section has produced a lot of "material" to absorb, but it will be easier to understand after you have completed an exercise. Let's begin.

WWW 13.3.1 Do This: Adding Materials for Rendering

I. Be sure you are still in the *rendering project.dwg* file in the C:\Steps3D\Lesson13 folder. If not, open it now.

II. Follow these steps:

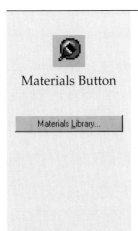

TOOLS	COMMAND SEQUENCE	STEPS
	**Command:** *rmat*	**1.** Open the Materials dialog box by entering ***RMat*** at the command prompt or by picking the **Materials** button on the Render toolbar. **2.** Access the Materials Library dialog box by picking the **Materials Library . . .** button. (*Note:* We could have accessed the library directly from the command line by typing ***MatLib*** at the prompt or by picking the **Materials Library** button on the Render toolbar. But this way we can load and assign materials in one procedure.) **3.** In the **Current Library** frame's list box, select **Amoeba Pattern**. [*Note:* If the **Amoeba Pattern** (or any of the materials used in this exercise) is not available, pick the down arrow next to **render** and select the **Rendering Project** library. If you do not see that library, use the **Open** button to access it in the C:\Steps3D\Lesson13 folder.]

continued

TOOLS	COMMAND SEQUENCE	STEPS

4. Pick the **<-Import** button to copy this material to the current drawing.

5. Repeat Steps 2 and 3 to import the materials shown.

6. Pick the **OK** button to continue. AutoCAD returns you to the Materials dialog box.

7. Let's create an additional material. Select Marble in the **New** frame control box, and then pick the **New . . .** button. AutoCAD presents the New Marble Material dialog box.

Material Name: MYMARBLE

8. Call the material *MyMarble*.

Color
By ACI
Mirror
Red: 0.69
Green: 0.00
Blue: 0.41
Color System: RGB

9. Put a bullet next to **Vein Color** in the **Attributes** frame and set the colors as indicated.

10. Put a bullet next to Scale in the **Attributes** frame and set the value to *6.25*.

continued

TOOLS	COMMAND SEQUENCE	STEPS
 OK		**11.** Pick the **OK** button to continue. Notice that *MYMARBLE* has been added to the list of available materials (Figure 13.3.1.11).

GLOBAL
AMOEBA PATTERN
BLUE GLASS
BLUE METALIC
BROWN MATTE
MYMARBLE
TILE GOLDGRANITE
WHITE GLASS
WOOD - DARK ASH
WOOD - WHITE ASH

FIG. 13.3.1.11 New Material

TOOLS	COMMAND SEQUENCE	STEPS
Attach <		**12.** Now let's attach materials to objects in our drawing. Select the **Amoeba Pattern** material from the **Materials** list and then pick the **Attach <** button.
	Select objects to attach "AMOEBA PATTERN" to: **Select objects:** *[enter]*	**13.** AutoCAD returns to the graphics screen and asks you to select the objects to which you want to attach the material. Pick the floor. Hit ***enter*** to continue.
 OK		**14.** Pick the **OK** button to complete the command.
	**Command:** *rr*	**15.** We will use the **Amoeba Pattern** to simulate carpet. Render just the floor (use the **Query for Selections** procedure and select the floor).

continued

TOOLS	COMMAND SEQUENCE	STEPS
		16. Repeat the ***RMat*** command and Steps 12 to 14 to assign the materials indicated in Figure 13.3.1.16.

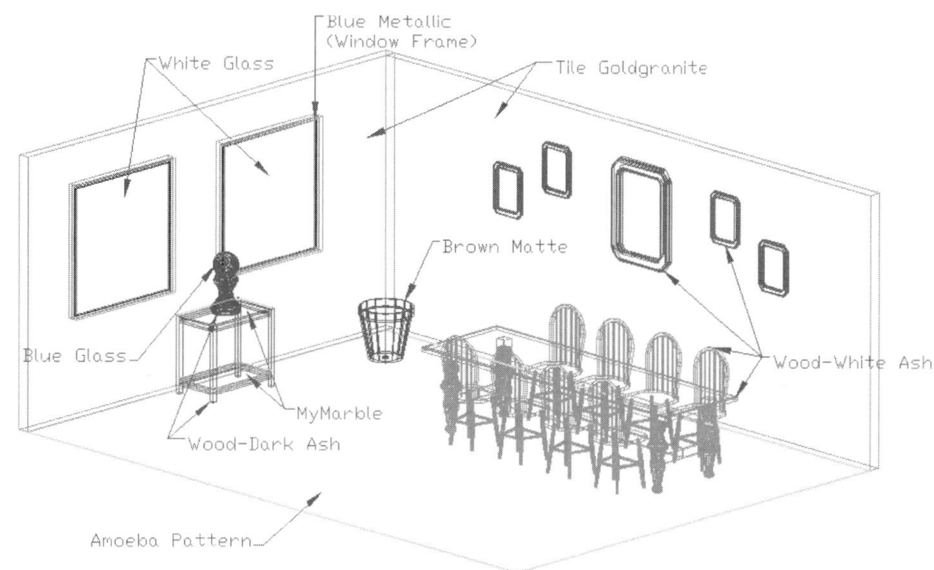

FIG. 13.3.1.16 Assign These Materials

TOOLS	COMMAND SEQUENCE	STEPS
	**Command:** *rr*	**17.** Using the **Photo Raytrace** render type, render the entire drawing. Notice the time it takes to render. Your drawing looks like Figure 13.3.1.17. (Compare it with Figure 13.2.1.4 in our last exercise.)

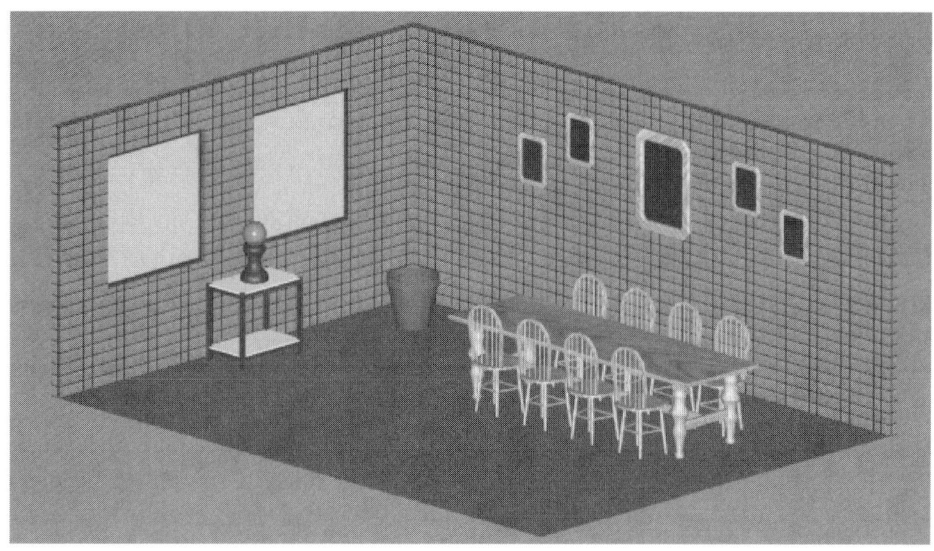

FIG. 13.3.1.17 Rendered with Materials

continued

TOOLS	COMMAND SEQUENCE	STEPS
	Command: *qsave*	**18.** Save the drawing, but do not exit.

You can say, "Wow!" if you want, but we are not quite there yet. We need to add some more touches to make our image look as real as possible.

Our next step will be to add some graphics—pictures in the frames, a plant in the pot, and a tree outside. Then we will add some lighting as a final touch.

13.4 Special Effects—Adding Other Graphic Images to Your Drawing

When I was in my late twenties—some centuries back—I had had my own apartment for many years. I was comfortable. Then one day my mother asked if I could give my baby sister a place to live for a while. She was still young and recently out on her own. My first reaction, as you might imagine, was to be aghast at the idea (I mean who wants their baby sister living with them?). Still, I could not say no to Mama.

When she moved in, my sister completely redecorated my bachelor pad. This really did not bother me much (it needed a good cleaning anyway). But when she brought in a truckload of plants . . . I was amazed by how much life they brought into my apartment.

We need a plant (and some photographs) to make our dining room as homey as Sue made my apartment. (She left some time later, taking her plants, and I felt completely abandoned! Gosh, I missed those plants!)

Adding additional graphics—the AutoCAD term is Landscaping—to your drawing is very much like adding materials. You will find a Landscaping Library—*Render.lli*—in the Support folder. This library holds a few graphics you can use, but AutoCAD also allows you to import graphics into this file. You can even create your own library.

There are a few differences between attaching materials and landscaping.

- You do not have to attach landscaping to an object. It can be freestanding in the drawing.
- You cannot access the Landscape Library from the Landscape New dialog box. There are separate commands—***LSNew*** to access the Landscape New dialog box, and ***LSLib*** to access the Landscape Library dialog box.
- There is a separate command for modifying the size and position of landscaping—***LSEdit***. But luckily it uses the same dialog box as the ***LSNew*** command.

Let's begin with the Landscape New dialog box (Figure 13.4a).

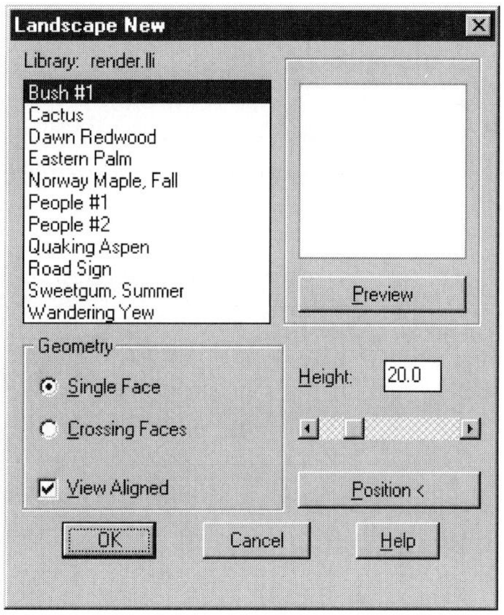

FIG. 13.4a Landscape New Dialog Box

- Select the image you wish to use from the list box in the upper-left corner of the dialog box.
- Preview the image by picking the **Preview** button in the frame next to the list box.
- The **Geometry** frame has two options.
  - **Single Face** (a single occurrence of the image) or **Crossing Faces** (two images crossing at 90° through the center—like a cardboard Christmas tree). I recommend the **Single Face—Crossing Faces** does not look real enough for me.
  - A check in the **View Aligned** box will ensure that the image appears to be three dimensional (flat against the screen) from any viewing angle. Remove the check to view the image from one direction only (you will see these in the exercises).
- Use the **Height** text box to control the size of the image.
- Pick the **Position <** button to place the image in the drawing. AutoCAD will prompt

  Choose the location of the base of the landscape object.

Let's add a plant inside our dining room and a tree outside.

WWW 13.4.1 Do This: Adding Landscaping for Rendering

I. Be sure you are still in the *rendering project.dwg* file in the C:\Steps3D\Lesson13 folder. If not, open it now.

II. Follow these steps:

TOOLS	COMMAND SEQUENCE	STEPS
 Landscape New Button	**Command:** *lsnew*	**1.** Enter the ***LSNew*** command at the command prompt or pick the **Landscape New** button on the Render toolbar. AutoCAD presents the Landscape New dialog box.
	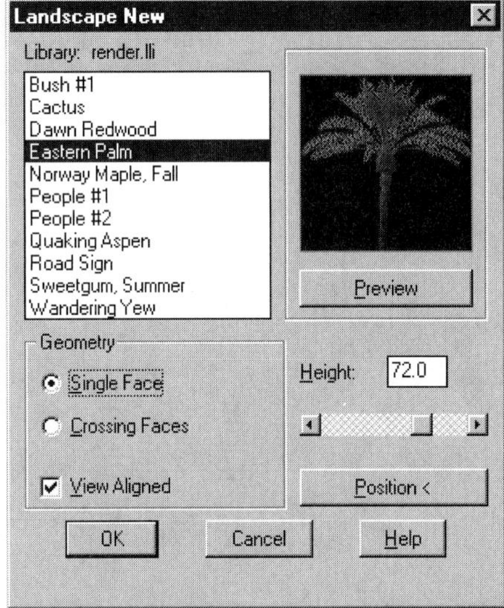	**2.** Select the **Eastern Palm** image and set the parameters indicated. Pick the **Position <** button to continue.
	Choose the location of the base of the landscape object *12′1,14′7,1′3*	**3.** AutoCAD asks where to place the image. We will put it in the planter; enter the coordinates shown. AutoCAD returns to the Landscape New dialog box.
OK		**4.** Pick the **OK** button to complete the command.

continued

TOOLS	COMMAND SEQUENCE	STEPS
		5. Repeat Steps 1 to 4 to add the **Dawn Redwood** outside the windows. Make the image 7′ high, single faced, and view aligned. Position it at coordinates ***6′,14′,0.*** Your drawing looks like Figure 13.4.1.5. (Notice that markers appear to locate the images. Like materials, the actual image will not appear until the scene is rendered.)

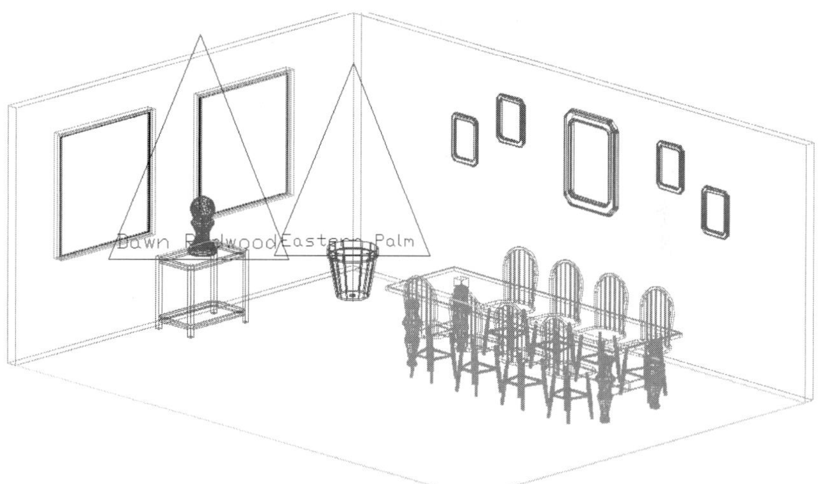

FIG. 13.4.1.5 Landscaping Markers

TOOLS	COMMAND SEQUENCE	STEPS
	**Command:** *qsave*	**6.** Save the drawing, but do not exit.

We will render the scene after our next exercise. First, however, let's take a look at the Landscape Library.

Call the Landscape Library dialog box (Figure 13.4b) with the ***LSLib*** command. For such a tiny box, this one provides some very useful opportunities. Let's look at these.

FIG. 13.4b Landscape Library Dialog Box

- The list box, of course, shows the images available in the library file shown above the box.
- The **Modify . . .** and **New . . .** buttons call the same dialog box (Figure 13.4c), although it has two different names. Use this box to add (or modify) an image to the library.

FIG. 13.4c Landscape Library New Dialog Box

- The **Default Geometry** frame looks like the **Geometry** frame of the Landscape New dialog box. Here you can set the defaults for your new image that will appear in the Landscape New dialog box.
- Enter a unique name for your new image in the **Name:** text box.
- Enter the image file you wish to use in the **Image File:** text box, or use the **Find File . . .** button to locate it.

- Enter the **Opacity Map File:** name in the appropriate text box, or use the **Find File . . .** button to locate it. (AutoCAD's glossary defines an opacity map as the "[p]rojection of opaque and transparent areas onto objects, creating the effect of a solid surface with holes or gaps.") As AutoCAD requires the entry of both an image file and an opacity map file, I generally specify the same file in both text boxes. This does not, however, allow for shadows. I would use a .gif or .taa file with a transparent background as an opacity map file to provide shadows.

- Use the **Delete** button (back in the Landscape New dialog box) to remove an image from the library.
- Use the **Save . . .** button to save changes to the current library or to create a new library.
- Use the **Open . . .** button to open another library file.

We will add some graphics to our Landscape Library and place them in the picture frames on our wall.

WWW 13.4.2 Do This: Adding Images to the Landscaping Library

I. Be sure you are still in the *rendering project.dwg* file in the C:\Steps3D\Lesson13 folder. If not, open it now.

II. Thaw the **Marker** layer.

III. Restore the **frames** view. (Note that the UCS remains = WCS.)

IV. Follow these steps:

TOOLS	COMMAND SEQUENCE	STEPS
 Landscape Library Button	**Command:** *lslib*	**1.** Enter the ***LSLib*** command or pick the **Landscape Library** button on the Render toolbar. AutoCAD presents the Landscape Library dialog box (Figure 13.4b).
New...		**2.** Pick the **New . . .** button to access the Landscape Library New dialog box (Figure 13.4c).

continued

TOOLS	COMMAND SEQUENCE	STEPS

3. We will want to view the images within the frames regardless of our viewing angle, so remove the check from the **View Aligned** box in the **Default Geometry** frame.

Name: Aloysius
Image File: C:\steps3D\LESS Find File...
Opacity Map File: C:\steps3D\LESS Find File...

4. Call the new image *Aloysius*, and use the **Find File . . .** button to locate the *Aloysius.gif* file in the C:\Steps3D\Lesson13 folder. (Be sure to look for a .gif file.) Do this for both the **Image File** and the **Opacity Map File**.

5. Pick the **OK** button to continue. AutoCAD returns to the Landscape Library dialog box. Notice that **Aloysius** has become an available image.

6. Repeat Steps 2 through 4 for the following images: *Barbara*, *Kevin*, *Starbuck*, and *Boys*. (These are all .gif files located in the C:\Steps3D\Lesson13 folder.)

7. Pick the **OK** button to continue.

8. AutoCAD presents the Landscape Library Modification message box (Figure 13.4.2.8), giving you the opportunity to discard your changes. Pick the **Save Changes . . .** button.

FIG. 13.4.2.8 Landscape Library Modification Message Box

9. AutoCAD asks for the location of the library file to save. It defaults to the Render.lli file. Pick the **Open** button to complete the command.

continued

TOOLS	COMMAND SEQUENCE	STEPS
	**Command:** *lsnew*	**10.** Now we will insert the new images. Enter the ***LSNew*** command or pick the **Landscape New** button on the Render toolbar.
		11. Notice that the new images are available in the list box. Select **Kevin**. Give the image a height of 14″ and position it at the node of the lower-left frame.
OK		**12.** Pick the **OK** button to complete the command.
		13. Repeat Steps 11 and 12 for the remaining images. From left to right, they are Kevin, Starbuck, Barbara (large frame—28″), Aloysius, and Boys. Your drawing looks like Figure 13.4.2.13.

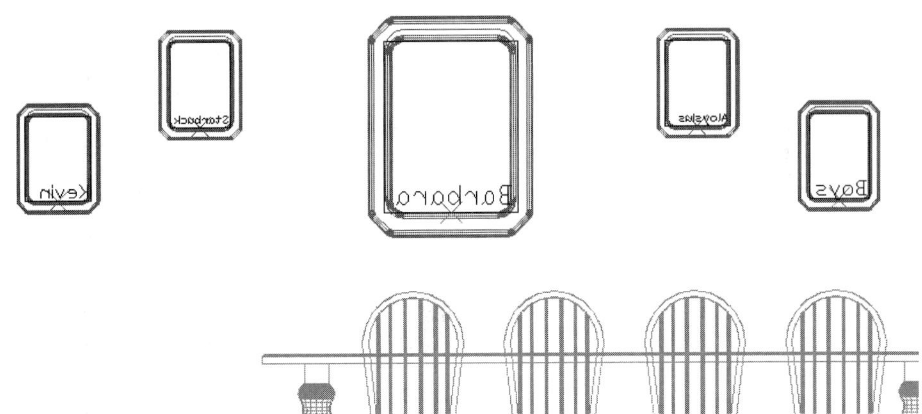

FIG. 13.4.2.13 Location of Images

TOOLS	COMMAND SEQUENCE	STEPS
	**Command:** *v*	**14.** Restore the **Base** view.

continued

TOOLS	COMMAND SEQUENCE	STEPS
	**Command:** *rr*	**15.** Render the drawing. It looks like Figure 13.4.2.15.

FIG. 13.4.2.15 Rendered Scene

TOOLS	COMMAND SEQUENCE	STEPS
	**Command:** *qsave*	**16.** Save the drawing, but do not exit.

Compare our latest rendering with previous ones. Our dining room looks better and better! But it still does not quite look real. We have one more thing to add.

13.5 Lights and Angles

Then God said, "Let there be light," and there was light. God saw how good the light was. . . . —the first day.

Genesis 1:3

Perhaps we can better understand the importance of light when we consider that it was the first thing He created.

AutoCAD provides four types of lighting. These include one that AutoCAD defines and the user controls—**Ambient Light**, and three that the user defines and controls—**Point Light**, **Spotlight**, and **Distant Light**.

- **Ambient Light** lights all surfaces with equal intensity. It has no actual source, but the user can control its intensity.
- A **Point Light** works like a lightbulb. It spreads rays in all directions from a single source. It dissipates as it moves away from the source, and it casts shadows.
- A **Spotlight** works like a **Point Light**, except that it can be pointed in a single direction.
- A **Distant Light** mimics the sun. In fact, the user can define the location of a **Distant Light** in terms of planetary location and time of day.

You can use any combination of one, two, three, or all types of light in your rendering.

Call the Lights dialog box (Figure 13.5a) with the ***Light*** command.

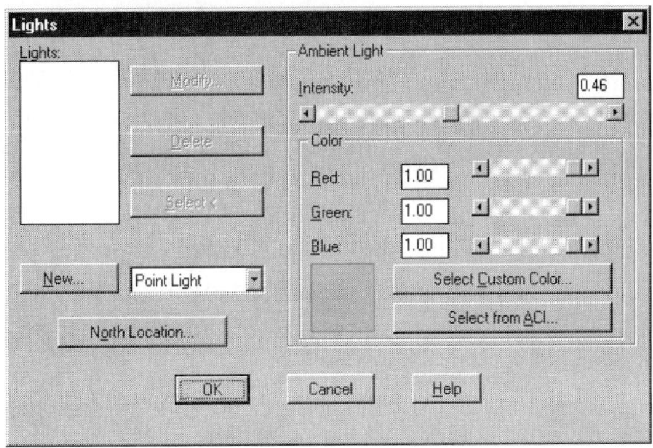

FIG. 13.5a Lights Dialog Box

- Let's begin with the **Ambient Light** frame.
  - The **Color** subframe allows the user to determine the color of the ambient light. Full **Red**, **Green**, and **Blue** make white light. The user can change the color by degrees using the slider bars or select a color using the **Select Custom Color . . .** or **Select from ACI . . .** buttons.
  - Control the intensity (brightness) of the **Ambient Light** using the **Intensity:** slider bar. Or you may enter a number from 0 (no light) to 1 (brightest setting) in the text box.

FIG. 13.5b Point Light Icon

FIG. 13.5c Spotlight Icon

FIG. 13.5d Distant Light Icon

- The **Lights:** list box shows all of the lights currently available in the drawing.
- The **Modify** button calls a specific dialog box for **Point Light**, **Spotlight**, or **Distant Light**, depending on which has been selected in the list box. These dialog boxes are identical to their New __ Light dialog box counterparts discussed later.
- The **Delete** button, of course, removes a light from the drawing's database. A deleted light is no longer available for use.
- The **Select <** button returns you to the graphics screen where you can select a light icon (see Figures 13.5b to 13.5d). AutoCAD then returns you to the Lights dialog box and identifies the light you have selected by highlighting it in the list box.
- The **North Location . . .** button presents the North Location dialog box (Figure 13.5e). Here the user can set north according to a specific UCS, the WCS, or by angle in the XY-plane.

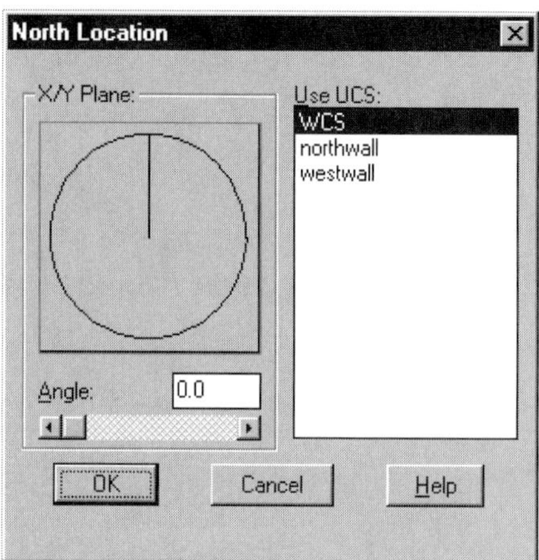

FIG. 13.5e North Location Dialog Box

- To add a new light to the drawing, select the type of light you want from the New control box (next to the **New** button), and then pick the **New . . .** button. The dialog box presented depends on the type of light you want to add. Let's look at each.
  - AutoCAD has divided the New Point Light dialog box (Figure 13.5f) into four frames and one open area.

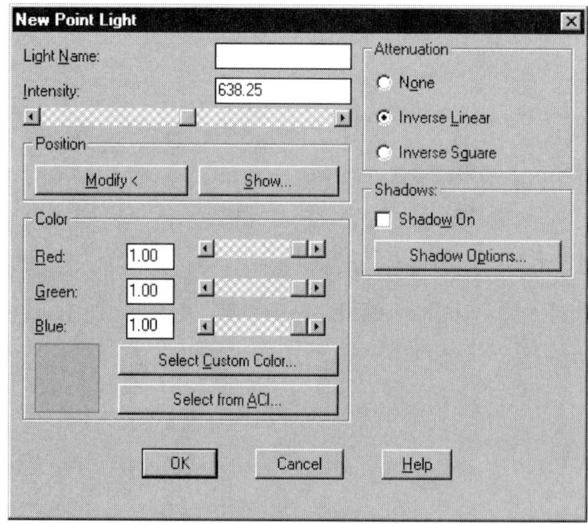

FIG. 13.5f New Point Light Dialog Box

- Put a unique name for your new point light in the **Light Name:** text box in the upper-left corner of the dialog box. Limit the name to eight characters or less.
- Use either the slider bar or the text box to enter the **Intensity:** of the light. It might be easier for you to think in terms of wattage—how powerful a lightbulb would you use?
- The **Modify <** button in the **Position** frame returns you to the graphics screen and prompts you to

Enter light location <current>:

You may pick a point on the screen or enter coordinates for your point light. (Remember that if you pick an arbitrary point, AutoCAD assumes a Z-axis value of 0.)

The **Show . . .** button presents the Show Point Light Position dialog box (Figure 13.5g). This box identifies the X, Y, and Z coordinates of the light.

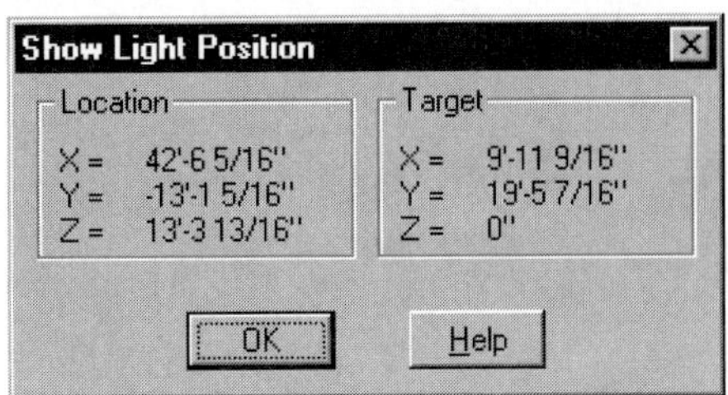

FIG. 13.5g Show Point Light Position Dialog Box

- The **Color** frame works as it has in other Rendering dialog boxes. Use this one to set the color of the Point Light.
- **Attenuation** refers to how light dissipates over distance.
  - **None** means that distant objects will reflect as much light from this Point Light as closer objects reflect.
  - **Inverse Linear** is normal reflectivity. In other words, an object twice as far away as another object will reflect half the light the closer one does. This is the default setting and appropriate for most situations.
  - **Inverse Square** is similar to **Inverse Linear** but works with squared numbers. Or, in our previous example, the distant object will reflect one-quarter the light that the closer one reflected.
- For a more real rendering, place a check in the **Shadow On** box in the **Shadow** frame. You can control the type of shadow with settings in the Shadow Options dialog box (Figure 13.5h) accessed by picking the **Shadow Options . . .** button.

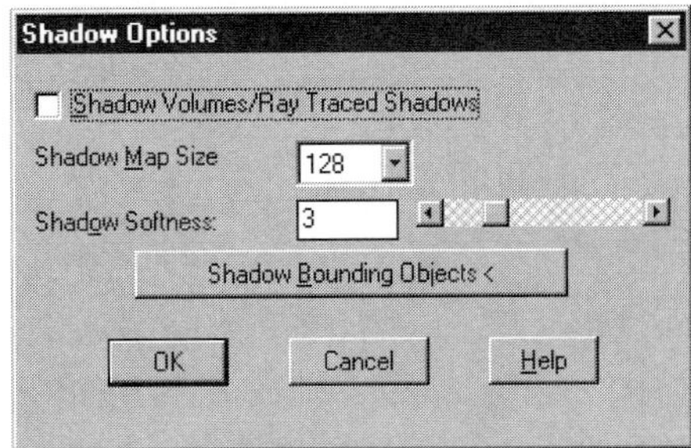

FIG. 13.5h Shadow Options Dialog Box

- The default option (a check in the **Shadow Volumes/Ray Traced Shadows** box) is the "normal" shadow display.
- Control the accuracy of the shadow with the value in the **Shadow Map Size** control box. The larger the number (from 64 to 4096), the more accurate the shadow. However, larger numbers mean more rendering time. I have never found the need to increase the number beyond the default 128.
- **Shadow Softness** refers to sharpness of the shadow. Again, I have never found the need to alter the default.
- The **Shadow Bounding Objects** < button allows the user to modify a selected set of objects whose shadows are clipped by the bounding box.

- The New Spotlight dialog box (Figure 13.5i) contains the same prompts as the New Point Light dialog box with two additions.

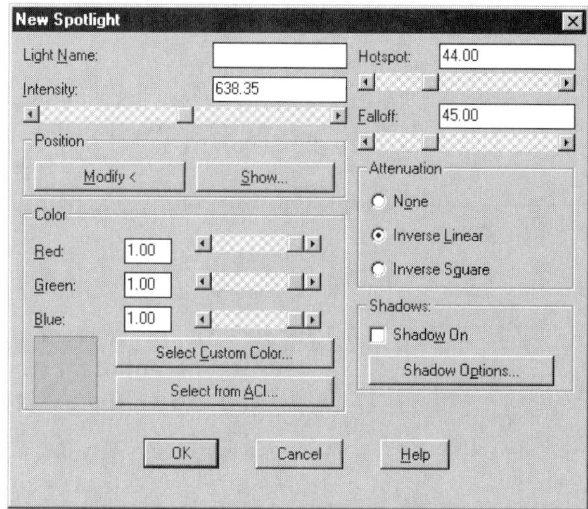

FIG. 13.5i New Spotlight Dialog Box

- ➠ The **Hotspot** value determines the angle (from 0° to 160°) of the main beam of light (the center of the light). Use this to assign a direction for your spotlight to point.
- ➠ The **Falloff** value determines the size of the full cone of light (the field angle). Use this to focus or widen the spotlight.

- The New Distant Light dialog box (Figure 13.5j) contains the same **Name**, **Intensity**, **Color**, and **Shadow** options as the first two. But here we have some useful tools for locating the light source (the sun).

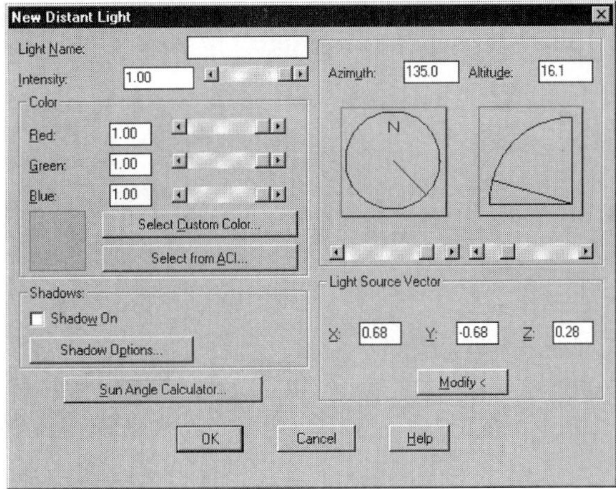

FIG. 13.5j New Distant Light Dialog Box

- Use the upper-right frame to locate the sun by **Azimuth** (N-S-E-W direction) and **Altitude** (how high in the sky).
- Use the **Light Source Vector** frame to locate the sun by coordinates. The **Modify** < button allows you to locate the light by location and direction.
- The **Sun Angle Calculator . . .** button presents the preferred method for locating the sun—the Sun Angle Calculator dialog box (Figure 13.5k). Here you can allow AutoCAD to determine the location of the sun by entering a date, time, and location (latitude and longitude).

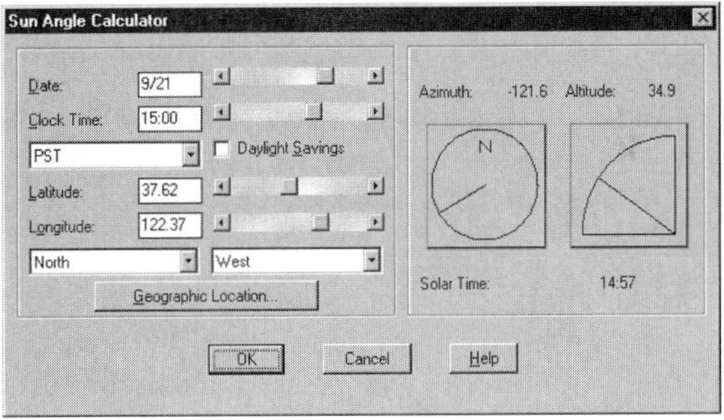

FIG. 13.5k Sun Angle Calculator Dialog Box

Sound difficult? Pick the **Geographic Location . . .** button. AutoCAD presents the Geographic Location dialog box (Figure 13.5l). Here you can select a city anywhere in the world using the City control box. Or you can simply pick a point on the map! (Use the Continental control box above the map to change the map shown.)

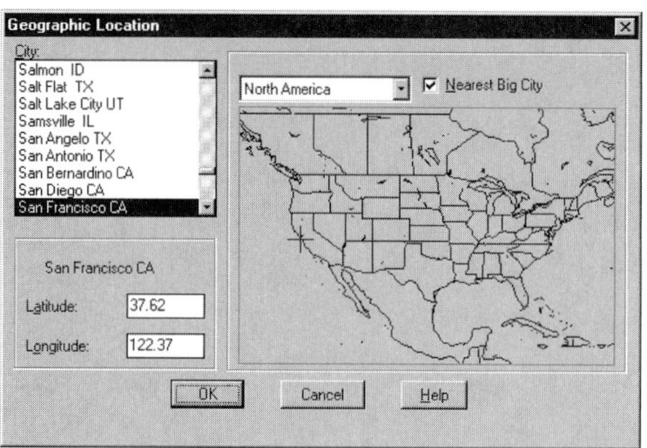

FIG. 13.51 *Geographic Location Dialog Box*

It really cannot get any easier than that!

With so much information to manage, does your appreciation for dialog boxes continue to grow?

We will add three lights to our dining room—two Point Lights and a Distant Light.

13.5.1 Do This: Let There Be Light!

I. Be sure you are still in the *rendering project.dwg* file in the C:\Steps3D\Lesson13 folder. If not, open it now.

II. Regenerate the drawing.

III. Follow these steps:

TOOLS	COMMAND SEQUENCE	STEPS
Lights Button	**Command:** ***light***	**1.** We will begin by placing a lightbulb in our lamp. Enter the ***Light*** command or pick the **Lights** button on the Render toolbar.
	New... Point Light	**2.** Set the type of light to Point Light and pick the **New . . .** button. AutoCAD presents the New Point Light dialog box (Figure 13.5f).

continued

TOOLS	COMMAND SEQUENCE	STEPS
	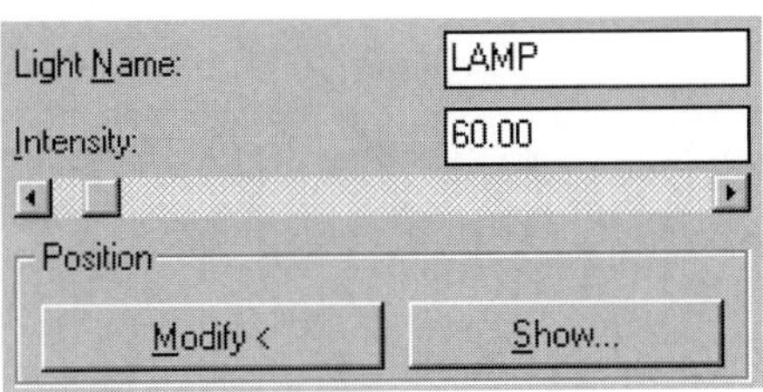	**3.** Call the new light *Lamp*, set the intensity to that of a 60-watt bulb, and then pick the **Modify <** button in the **Position** frame.
	Enter light location <current>:	**4.** Use OSNAPs to locate the light in the center of the lamp (between the windows). (A node marks the spot.)
		**5.** Place a check in the **Shadow On** check box to be sure our lamp casts shadows.
OK		**6.** Pick the **OK** button to return to the Lights dialog box and again to complete the command. AutoCAD places an icon showing you where the light will be located (Figure 13.5.1.6). (If you cannot see the icon, use the ***RPref*** command and set the **LightIconScale** to **24**.)

FIG. 13.5.1.6 Point Light Icon (Light Icon Scale—Render dialog box—is 24; hidden lines removed)

continued

TOOLS	COMMAND SEQUENCE	STEPS
	Command: *light*	**7.** Repeat Steps 1 through 6 to add a ceiling light (call it *Ceiling*). The light should have the intensity of a 90-watt bulb and be located at coordinates ***27′−6″, 4′, 8′***. Remember to turn on the shadows.
	Command: *[enter]*	**8.** Now let's locate the sun. Repeat the ***Light*** command.
	New... Distant Light	**9.** Set the type of light to Distant Light and pick the **New . . .** button. AutoCAD presents the New Distant Light dialog box (Figure 13.5j).
	Light Name: SUN	**10.** Call the new light *Sun*.
Sun Angle Calculator...		**11.** Pick the **Sun Angle Calculator . . .** button to call the Sun Angle Calculator dialog box.
	Date: 3/12 Clock Time: 15:00 CST Daylight Savings Latitude: 37.62 Longitude: 122.37 North West Geographic Location...	**12.** Set the date/time to March 12 at 3:00 P.M. CST. Then pick the **Geographic Location . . .** button to continue. AutoCAD presents the Geographic Location dialog box (Figure 13.5l).
	Geographic Location City Hood OR Hopkinsville KY Hoquiam WA Hot Springs AR Houghton MI Houghton Lake MI Houston TX Hudspeth TX Humble TX North America Nearest Big City Houston TX Latitude: 29.76 Longitude: 95.36 OK Cancel Help	**13.** Pick a point near **Houston, Texas,** as indicated.
OK		**14.** Pick the **OK** button twice to return to the New Distant Light dialog box.

continued

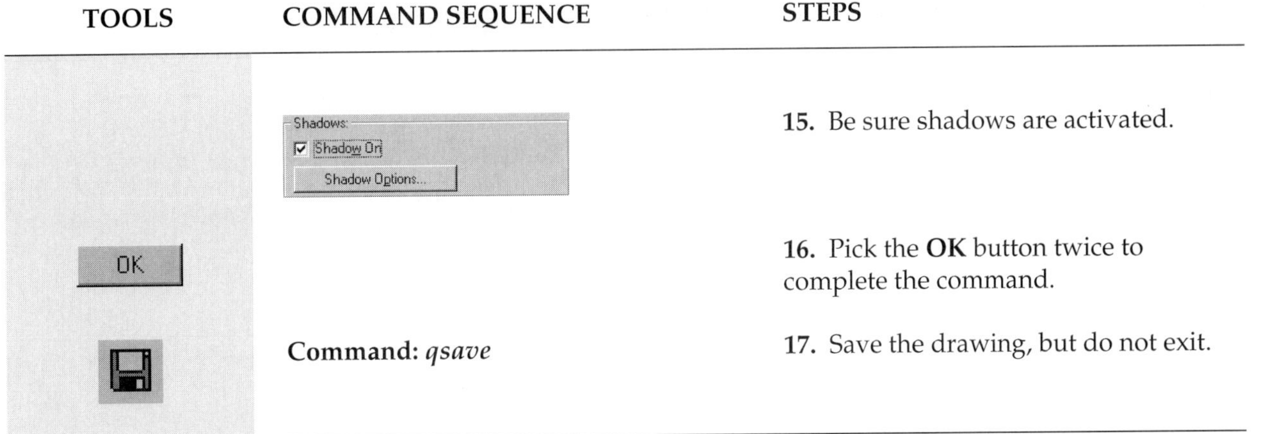

TOOLS	COMMAND SEQUENCE	STEPS
		15. Be sure shadows are activated.
		16. Pick the **OK** button twice to complete the command.
	Command: *qsave*	**17.** Save the drawing, but do not exit.

We have added the lights, but we need to create a scene to use the lights. We will do that next and then render our drawing.

13.6 Creating a Scene

Perhaps the easiest part of rendering—creating a scene—involves nothing more than telling AutoCAD which lights to use and which view to render.

The *Scene* command calls the Scenes dialog box (Figure 13.6a). AutoCAD lists available scenes in the list box and offers three choices (buttons) of things you can do.

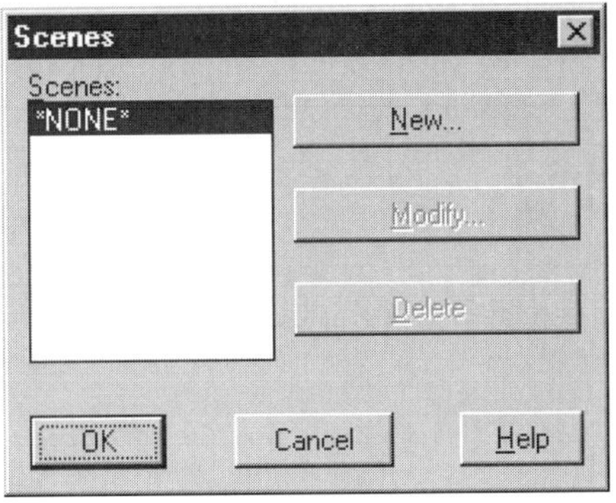

FIG. 13.6a Scenes Dialog Box

- The **New . . .** and **Modify . . .** buttons call the dialog box shown in Figure 13.6b. Here the user designates which (existing) view to use in this scene along with which light(s) to use.

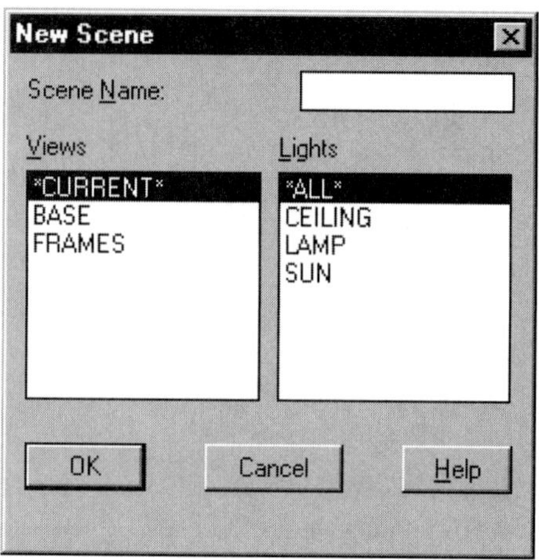

FIG. 13.6b New Scene Dialog Box

The only real difference between the New Scene and Modify Scene dialog boxes is that the New Scene dialog box requires that you give your new scene a unique name. The Modify Scene dialog box allows you to change the name, view, or lights but does not require anything.

- The **Delete . . .** button, of course, allows you to remove a scene from the drawing's database.

Let's make a scene!

13.6.1 Do This: Make a Scene!

I. Be sure you are still in the *rendering project.dwg* file in the C:\Steps3D\Lesson13 folder. If not, open it now.

II. Follow these steps:

TOOLS	COMMAND SEQUENCE	STEPS
Scenes Button	**Command:** *scene*	**1.** Enter the *Scene* command or pick the **Scenes** button on the Render toolbar.
New...		**2.** Pick the **New . . .** button on the Scene dialog box.

continued

TOOLS	COMMAND SEQUENCE	STEPS

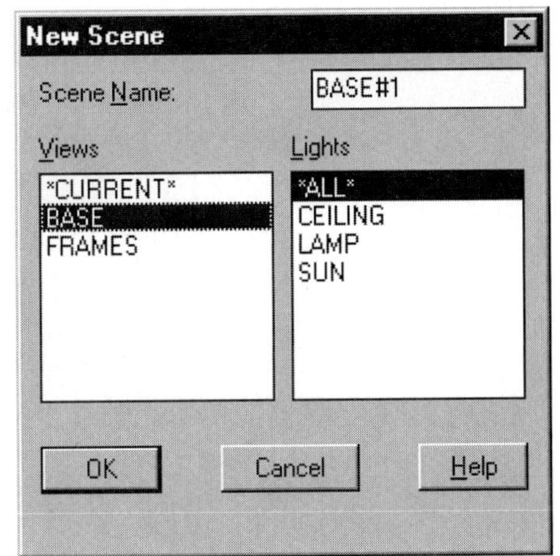

3. Call the scene *Base#1*. Select the **Base** view and use **All** the lights in the drawing.

Pick the **OK** button to continue.

4. Notice that **BASE#1** is listed in the available **Scenes** list box (Figure 13.6.1.4).

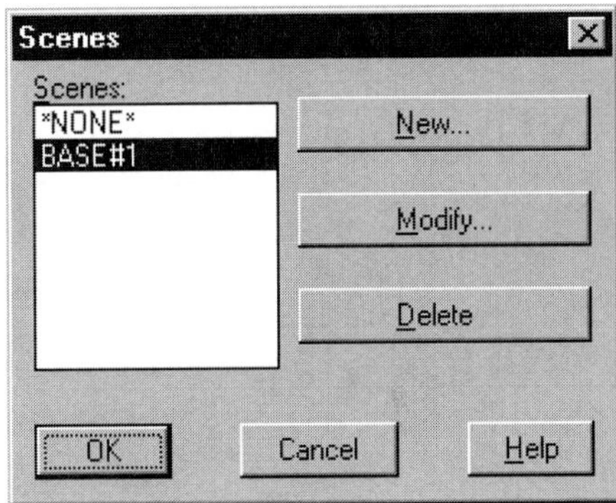

FIG. 13.6.1.4 Scenes List Box

5. Repeat Steps 1 to 3 to create the scenes shown in the following chart.

SCENE	VIEW	LIGHT(S)
BASE#2	Base	Ceiling
BASE#3	Base	Ceiling and Sun
BASE#4	Base	Ceiling and Lamp
FRAME#1	Frames	Ceiling

continued

TOOLS	COMMAND SEQUENCE	STEPS
		6. The Scenes dialog box looks like Figure 13.6.1.6. Pick the **OK** button to complete the command.

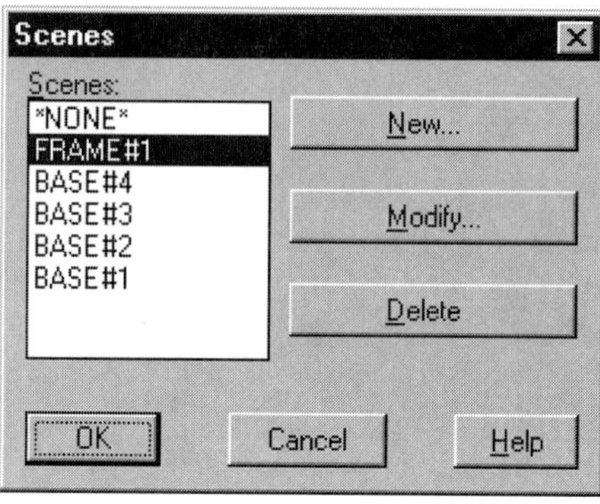

FIG. 13.6.1.6 Scenes Dialog Box

Command: *scene*

7. Now let's modify our scenes. Repeat the ***Scene*** command.

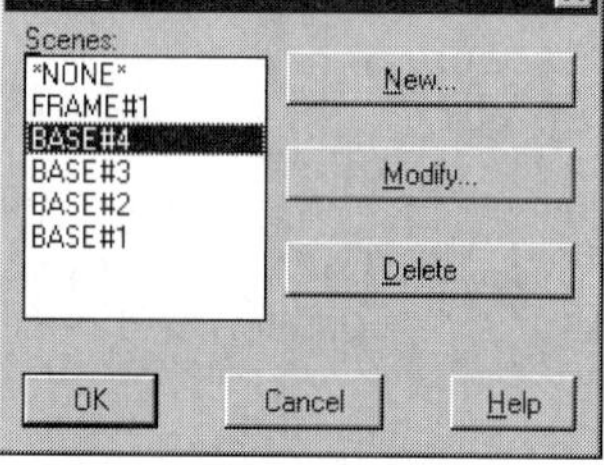

8. Select the **Base#4** scene in the **Scenes:** list box and pick the **Modify . . .** button.

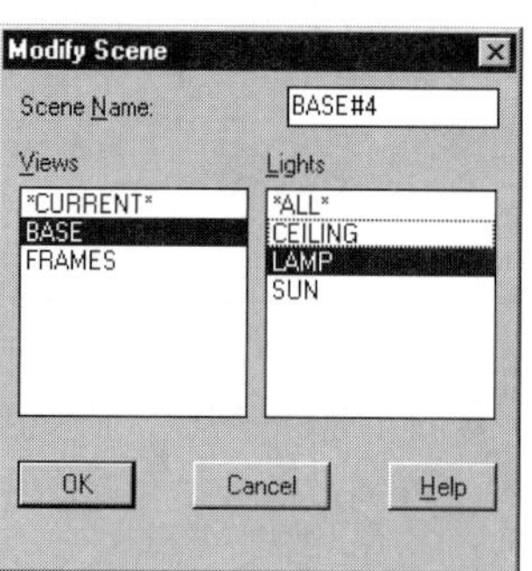

9. Remove the **Ceiling** light. (Hold down the control key while selecting **CEILING**.)

Pick the **OK** button to continue.

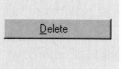

10. Remove the **Base#3** scene by selecting it in the list box and then picking the **Delete . . .** button. AutoCAD prompts with an "Are you sure" dialog box.

continued

TOOLS	COMMAND SEQUENCE	STEPS
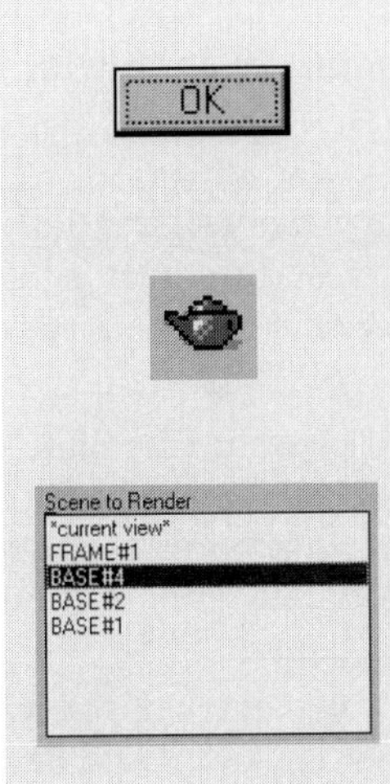		**11.** Pick the **OK** button to confirm the deletion, and again to complete the command.
	Command: *rr*	**12.** Enter the ***Render*** command or pick the **Render** button on the Render toolbar.
		13. Notice the scenes you just created are now shown in the **Scene to Render** list box. Render each for comparison. (The **Base#1** rendering is shown in Figure 13.6.1.13.)

FIG. 13.6.1.13 Base #1 Rendered

TOOLS	COMMAND SEQUENCE	STEPS
	**Command:** *qsave*	**14.** Save the drawing.

Did you notice the lights and shadows? This image is truly photographic quality.

AutoCAD is not designed to plot a rendered drawing. You can, however, render the drawing to a file and print the rendered file through a graphics program (such as MS Paint).

13.7 Extra Steps

There are two additional—although less frequently used—commands with which you should experiment in rendering.

- The first is ***RPref*** (for Render Preferences). This command presents essentially the same dialog box the ***Render*** command presents. The biggest difference is the replacement of the **Render** button with an **OK** button. Use this box to set rendering defaults.
- The second is ***Stats*** (for Render Statistics). This command presents the Statistics dialog box, which provides detailed information about the last rendering. Details include type of rendering, scene rendered, time to completion, the size of the rendering, and much, much more.

Redo the renderings on each of the scenes you created in the last exercise and compare the statistics on each. Then set up the rendering preferences you would like to use for defaults in the future.

13.8 What Have We Learned?

Items covered in this lesson include:

- *Rendering commands and techniques*
  - *Assigning materials*
  - *Adding graphics*
  - *Adding lights*
  - *Creating scenes*
- *Commands*
  - ***Render***
  - ***RMat***
  - ***MatLib***
  - ***LSNew***
  - ***LSLib***
  - ***LSEdit***
  - ***Light***
  - ***Scene***
  - ***RPref***
  - ***Stats***

You have accomplished a great deal with the completion of Lesson 13. In this lesson you have conquered the bridge between CAD operation and art. This is as far as AutoCAD goes toward the creation of design imagery. (Beyond this, you will have to get some tools and build the objects!)

Let's tackle some final exercises and answer some questions!

13.9 EXERCISES

1. Open the *emerald13.dwg* file in the C:\Steps3D\Lesson13 folder. My rendering appears in Figure 13.9.1.
   - **1.1.** Assign materials to the emerald and tabletop. (I used **Green Glass** and **Mottled Marble**. I changed the transparency of the glass to a value of ***0.45***.)
   - **1.2.** Assign a background. (I used a three-color gradient.)
   - **1.3.** Place a light(s). (I used a single-point light with an intensity of 10.7 located at coordinates 18,4,9.)
   - **1.4.** Render the drawing.
   - **1.5.** Repeat Steps 1.1 to 1.4 using a different set of assignments.

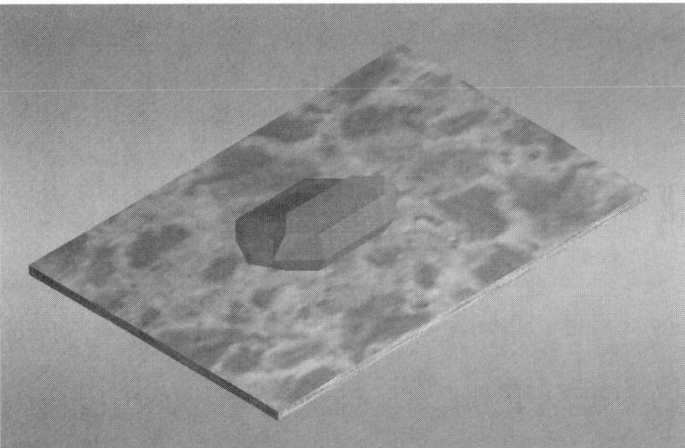

FIG. 13.9.1 *Emerald.dwg*

2. Open the *caster13.dwg* file in the C:\Steps3D\Lesson13 folder. My rendering appears in Figure 13.9.2.
   - **2.1.** Assign materials to the objects. I used
     - **2.1.1.** Bright Olive (bearings)
     - **2.1.2.** Bumpy Metal (flooring)
     - **2.1.3.** Chrome Gifmap (wheel)
     - **2.1.4.** Dark Olive Matte (axle, spindle, bearing case)
     - **2.1.5.** Sand Texture (frame)
   - **2.2.** Place a light(s). (I used a single-point light with an intensity of 27.45 located at coordinates 0,−10,4.)
   - **2.3.** Render the drawing.
   - **2.4.** Repeat Steps 2.1 to 2.3 using a different set of assignments.

FIG. 13.9.2 *Caster13.dwg*

3. Open the *pipe13.dwg* file in the C:\Steps3D\Lesson13 folder. My rendering appears in Figure 13.9.3.
   3.1. Assign materials to the objects. I used:
      3.1.1. Beige Plastic (tank and nozzle)
      3.1.2. Blue Matte (large pipe and fittings)
      3.1.3. Brown Matte (model platform)
      3.1.4. Olive Metal (pipe rack)
      3.1.5. Red Matte (small pipe)
   3.2. Assign a background. (I used the HLS Color System for a two-color gradient. I made both colors a light blue/cyan color.)
   3.3. Place a light(s). (I used a distant light with an ambient light intensity of 0.45. The unit is located in a plant in New Orleans. The graphic was created at 3:00 P.M. in late September.)
   3.4. Render the drawing.
   3.5. Repeat Steps 3.1 to 3.4 using a different set of assignments.

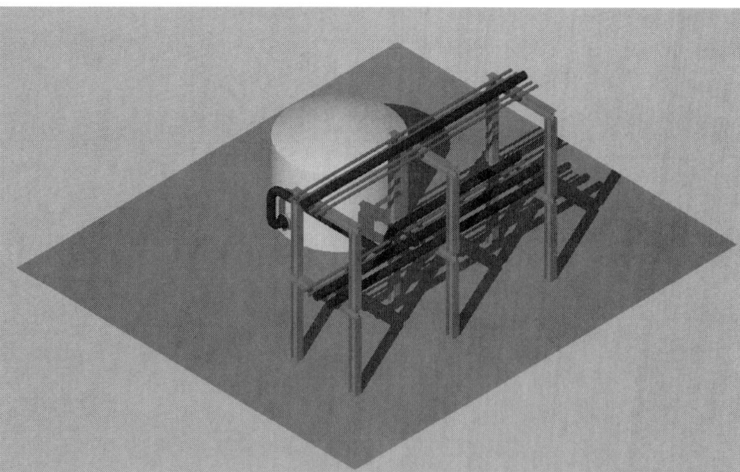

FIG. 13.9.3 *Pipe13.dwg*

4. Open the *train13.dwg* file in the C:\Steps3D\Lesson13 folder. My rendering appears in Figure 13.9.4.
   - **4.1.** Assign materials to objects. I used:
     - **4.1.1.** Ape (front of train)
     - **4.1.2.** Blue Plastic (cab, base, top of cattleguard)
     - **4.1.3.** Chrome Gifmap (wheels, smokestack, bell)
     - **4.1.4.** Cream Plastic (backdrop)
     - **4.1.5.** Red Plastic (water tank, undercarriage, base of cattleguard, flag)
     - **4.1.6.** Wood White Ash (bell frame, box, flagpole)
   - **4.2.** Attach a landscape person in the cab. (I used People #2.)
   - **4.3.** Assign a background. (I used a solid green background.)
   - **4.4.** Place a light(s). (I used a single spotlight with location of 0,−60,0 and a target location of 4,1,4.5. Ambient light intensity is 0.5.)
   - **4.5.** Render the drawing.
   - **4.6.** Repeat Steps 4.1 to 4.5 using a different set of assignments.

FIG. 13.9.4 *Train13.dwg*

You have quite a variety of exercises from which to choose in this lesson. Your next assignment is to return to any of the exercises you have completed in the text, assign materials, graphics, and lights as you deem necessary and then render the drawings. Following are several exercises you can do. (If you have not completed these drawings, they are available in the C:\Steps3D\Lesson13 folder.)

FIG. 13.9.5 C:\Steps3D\Lesson06\MyWagon (Save as *MyRWagon* in the C:\Steps3D\Lesson13 folder)

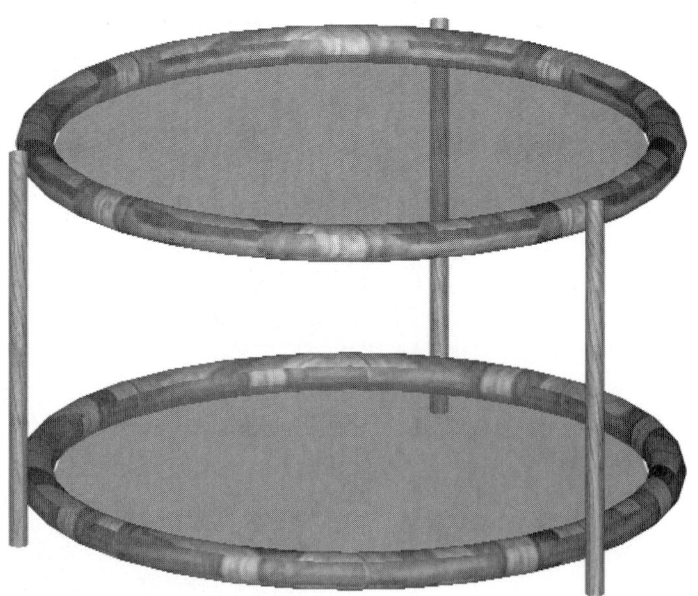

FIG. 13.9.6 C:\Steps3D\Lesson06\MyCoffeeTable (Save as *MyRCoffeeTable* in the C:\Steps3D\Lesson13 folder)

FIG. 13.9.7 C:\Steps3D\Lesson06\MyPyrSph (Save as *MyRPyrSph* in the C:\Steps3D\Lesson13 folder)

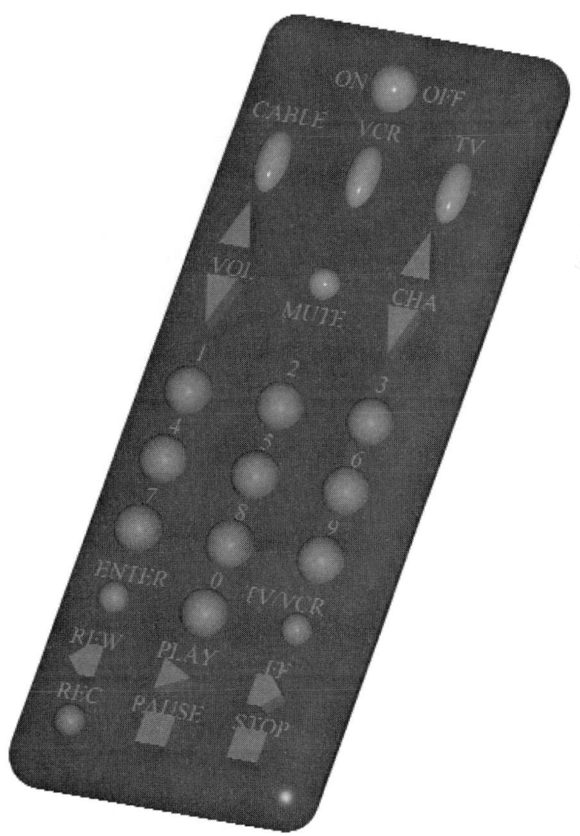

FIG. 13.9.8 C:\Steps3D\Lesson07\MyRemote (Save as *MyRRemote* in the C:\Steps3D\Lesson 13 folder)

FIG. 13.9.9 C:\Steps3D\Lesson08\My3Dchess (Save as MR3Dchess in the C:\Steps3D\Lesson13 folder)

FIG. 13.9.10 C:\Steps3D\Lesson08\MyBelt (Save as MyRBelt in the C:\Steps3D\Lesson13 folder)

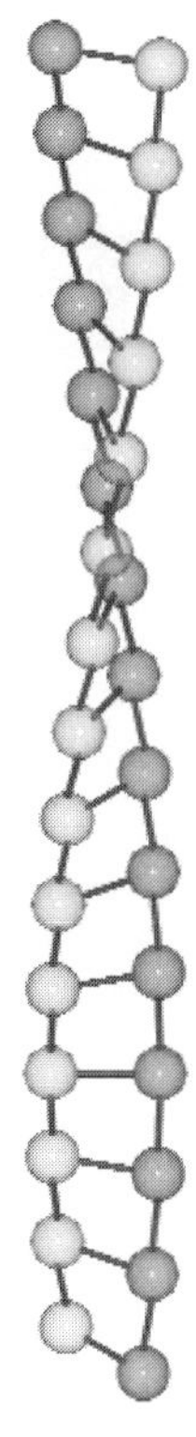

FIG. 13.9.11 C:\Steps3D\Lesson09\MyGenes (Save as *MyRGenes* in the C:\Steps3D\Lesson13 folder)

FIG. 13.9.12 C:\Steps3D\Lesson09\MyPlanter Box (Save as *MyRPlanterBox* in the C:\Steps3D\Lesson13 folder)

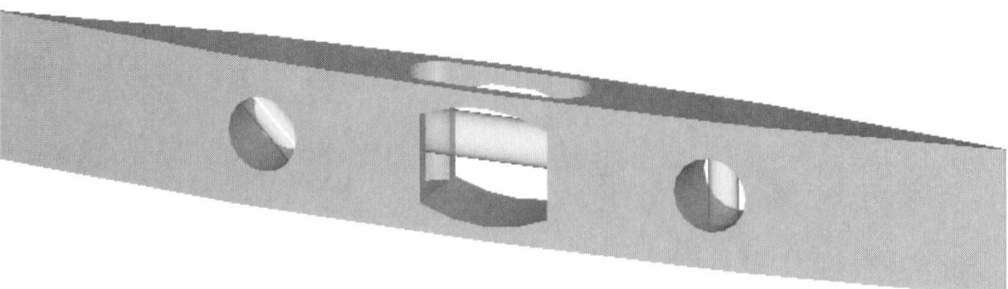

FIG. 13.9.13 C:\Steps3D\Lesson11\MyLevel (Save as *MyRLevel* in the C:\Steps3D\Lesson13 folder)

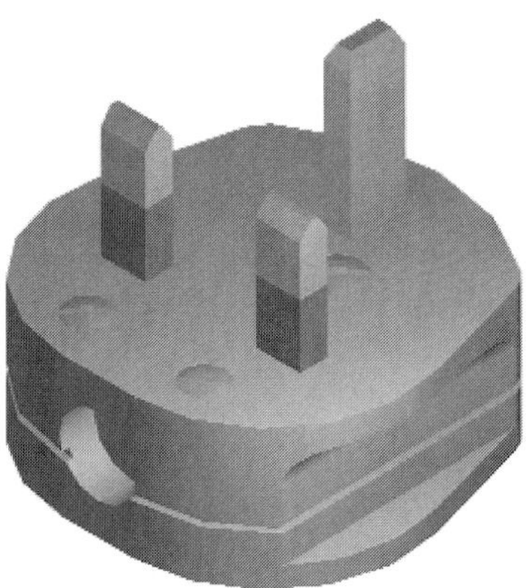

FIG. 13.9.14 C:\Steps3D\Lesson11\MyPlug (Save as *MyRPlug* in the C:\Steps3D\Lesson13 folder)

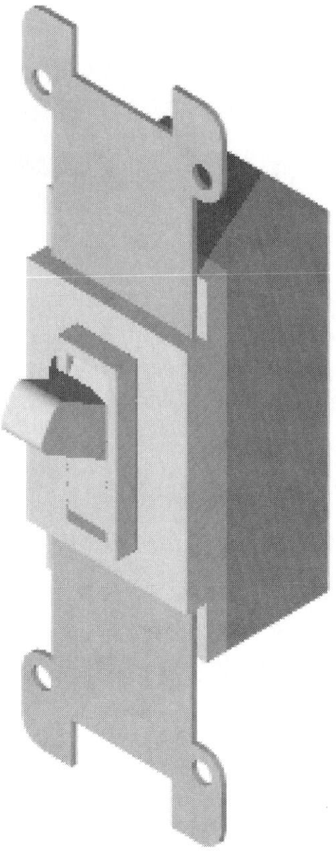

FIG. 13.9.15
C:\Steps3D\Lesson11\MySwtich (Save as *MyRSwitch* in the C:\Steps3D\Lesson13 folder)

FIG. 13.9.16 C:\Steps3D\Lesson11\MyWheel (Save as *MyRWheel* in the C:\Steps3D\Lesson13 folder)

FIG. 13.9.17 C:\Steps3D\Lesson12\MyPatioScene (Save as *MyRPatioScene* in the C:\Steps3D\Lesson13 folder)

5. Using other objects you have created in Lessons 6 through 13, redesign the patio scene. Some suggestions follow.
   5.1. Replace the fountain with the planter box.
   5.2. Place planters (Lesson 9) in the planter box and add plants.
   5.3. Add a sidewalk or some decking.
   5.4. Save the drawing as *MyOtherPatio.dwg* in the C:\Steps3D\Lesson13 folder.
6. Using other objects you have created in Lessons 6 through 13, redesign the room we created in our rendering project. Some suggestions follow.
   6.1. Replace the plant with the standing lamp (Lesson 6).
   6.2. Put the 3D Chess set on the table.
   6.3. Change the pictures on the wall.
   6.4. Save the drawing as *MyDen.dwg* in the C:\Steps3D\Lesson13 folder.

13.10 REVIEW QUESTIONS

Please write your answers on a separate sheet of paper.

1. __________ is a procedure that takes the objects you have created and gives them properties to make them appear "real."

2. The Render, Lights, and Scenes buttons are located on the __________ toolbar.

3. through 5. Place these three rendering types in order from lowest quality to highest: Photo Real, Render, Photo Raytrace.

a.

b.

c.

6. (T or F) AutoCAD allows the user to render just one or two objects without having to render the entire drawing.

7. What is the command to access the Render Preferences dialog box?

8. (T or F) It is not possible to change the size or location of the light icon.

9. When you do not want objects that are oriented at 40° to each other to be rendered as though they are a single object, change the __________ setting on the Render dialog box.

10. If your rendering does not show assigned materials, check the __________ box on the Render dialog box.

11. (T or F) Shadows are not available for all types of rendering.

12. (Gouraud, Phong) rendering produces a more realistic rendering.

13. and 14. When using the Photo Real type of rendering, minimize the jagged edges by setting the __________ frame to __________.

15. When controlling Depth Map Shadows, the difference between minimum and maximum bias should be no more than __________.

16. A texture map is __________.

17. through 19. List the three places AutoCAD can place a rendering.

a.

b.

c.

20. through 24. List the five types of files to which you can save a rendering.

a.

b.

c.

d.

e.

25. If your rendering includes only one out of every four pixels, your Sub Sampling is set to __________.

26. To use a two-color graduated background in your rendering, set the background type to __________.

27. Access the __________ dialog box to tint a drawing.

28. Which command will "un-render" a drawing?

29. and 30. To close the Render dialog box, use the __________ command to unload the __________.arx.

31. through 34. List the four categories of materials available for rendering.

a.

b.

c.

d.

35. The __________ command calls the Materials dialog box.

36. and 37. What are the two shapes against which you may preview a material?

38. To determine which material is currently attached to an object, use the __________ button on the Materials dialog box.

39. To determine to which objects the highlighted material is currently attached, use the __________ button.

40. (T or F) You can attach materials to objects according to the layer on which the object resides.

41. You do not have to attach (materials, landscaping) to an object.

42. through 45. List the four types of light available in a rendering.

a.

b.

c.

d.

46. __________ light lights all surfaces with equal intensity. It casts no shadows.

47. Use a __________ light works to simulate a lightbulb.

48. __________ refers to how light dissipates over distance.

49. Use the __________ to locate the sun according to city and time of day.

50. You must create a __________ to use the lights you have created when you render your drawing.

LESSON 14

Externally Referenced Drawings

Following this lesson, you will:

- Know how to reference one drawing from another
  - Know how to use the Xref Manager
  - Know how to attach, detach, and overlay a reference drawing
  - Know how to clip a reference to see just what you want to see
  - Understand reference drawings' dependent symbols
  - Know how to load, unload, and reload a reference
  - Know how to edit a referenced drawing from within the primary drawing
- Know how to permanently bind a referenced drawing to the primary drawing

Think way back to our discussion of layers in Lesson 7 of the basic text. I explained layers by referring to the presentation method *Encyclopedia Britannica* used to detail the human body. Let me repeat that story here.

> When I was a child (back when drafting was done on shovel blades with charcoal from the fire), one of the most coveted possessions of our household was a set of *Encyclopedia Britannica*. I spent hours exploring the world through those books, but my favorite site was the picture of the human body. I was not all that interested in anatomy—but I was fascinated by the way the body was shown. There was one page with an outline of the body. Then there were successive pages made of clear plastic overlays with the skeletal, reproductive, digestive, and circulatory systems. As these folded down atop each other, the body took shape. If one system was in the way, all I did was fold that sheet back. This is the idea behind **Layers** in AutoCAD.

This is also the idea behind externally referenced drawings—Xrefs.

There is, however, quite a difference between layers and Xrefs. We use layers, as you know, to control the display of and differentiate between objects in a drawing (much as we used linetypes and widths on the drawing board). On the other hand, we use Xrefs to save drawing time and computer memory by *sharing information.*

When working with Xrefs, file location is a critical consideration. For the exercises in this lesson to work properly with the files provided, the files must be located in one of two places.

1. The best location is the C:\Steps\Lesson14 folder. This site has been thoroughly tested to be sure the files work properly.
2. The files may be placed on a network or other *location provided the path is defined in the Project File Search Path* (**Files** tab of the Options dialog box). If you are not comfortable with the Options dialog box, however, and do not have a CAD guru who can help, *please do not attempt to make changes in the Options dialog box.* Use the first choice instead.

14.1 Working with Externally Referenced Drawings—Xrefs

Exactly what are Xrefs?

Xrefs—externally referenced drawings—are drawings called into another drawing as a referenced background or object. They are, in fact, quite similar to blocks with some notable exceptions:

- Unlike blocks, Xrefs do not occupy space within a drawing. That is, the drawing will not increase in size with the inclusion of an Xref.
- Whereas a block may contain attributed information, an Xref cannot. However, the referenced file may contain blocks with attributes, and the values of these attributes may be extracted from the primary drawing (the one doing the referencing).
- The primary drawing automatically reloads the referenced drawing whenever the primary drawing is accessed. Therefore, the reference is as current as the last time the primary drawing was opened.

What are the benefits of using Xrefs?

- An important benefit of using Xrefs is that another operator may edit the referenced drawing without tying up your primary drawing. The changes he makes become available to you as soon as you reload the reference.
- Like blocks, any number of primary drawings may use a single referenced drawing. But unlike blocks, updating the references is automatic. Consider a unit of a refinery. Each unit requires civil, structural, piping, and electrical plans. Generally, the structural designer will copy the civil drawing for a "foundation" for his work. Likewise, the piper and electrical designer will use the structural plan. Changes to the structural plan may go unnoticed for days or weeks by others (unless some extraordinary communication occurs). However, if the pipers and electrical designers Xref the structural plan,
  - they will not have to draw the background themselves.
  - any changes made by the structural designer will automatically show on the other's drawings with the next loading or reloading.

Let's take a look at how to use Xrefs.

14.1.1 Attaching and Detaching Xrefs to Your Drawing

Although you can use individual commands for each manipulation of a referenced drawing, AutoCAD provides a manager-type dialog box—the Xref Manager (Figure 14.1.1a)—to help with Xrefs.

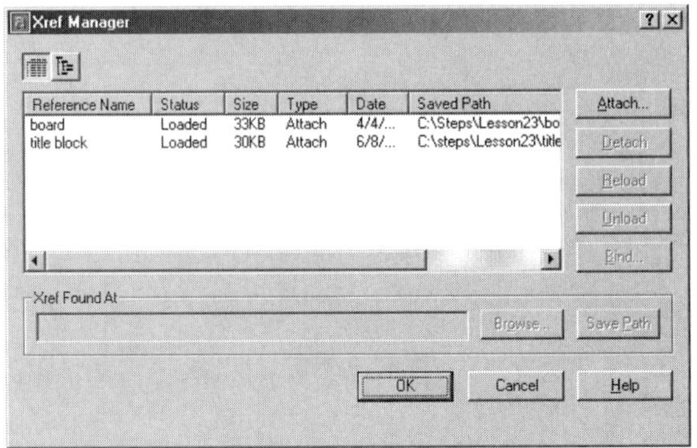

FIG. 14.1.1a Xref Manager

Let's take a look.

- AutoCAD allows you to view the items in the list box using either a **List View** (the default) or a **Tree View**. Toggle between types of views using the buttons in the upper left corner of the manager. (We will use the default **List View** in this lesson.)
- In the list box, AutoCAD provides several columns of information:
  - The **Reference Name** is the file name of the referenced drawing.
  - The drawing's **Status** will fall into one of several categories:
    - **Loaded** simply means that the drawing is currently attached.
    - An **Unloaded** reference will be removed from the primary drawing once the Xref Manager is closed. This is not a permanent condition. The reference remains intact and may be reloaded as desired.
    - A **Reloaded** designation means that AutoCAD will reload that reference when the Xref Manager closes.
    - An **Unreferenced** drawing is attached to the primary drawing but has been erased.
    - A drawing that no longer resides in the folder from which it was originally referenced (or in the search path defined in the Options dialog box) is marked in the **Status** column as **Not Found**.
    - If AutoCAD cannot read the referenced drawing, it marks it as **Unresolved**.
    - Xrefs can be nested. An **Orphaned** drawing was nested into a reference that is either unreferenced, unloaded, or not found.

- The **Size** column indicates the size of the referenced drawing.
- The user may either **Attach** or **Overlay** a reference (see the **Type** column). An attached drawing will go with the primary drawing if it is referenced by another drawing; an overlaid drawing will not (more on this in Section 14.1.4).
- The **Date** column indicates when the referenced drawing was last modified.
- The **Saved Path** column is a bit misleading. The path refers to the location of the drawing when it was originally referenced but *not necessarily where the reference is found*. Let me explain.

  When AutoCAD begins a drawing, it searches for referenced drawings in the *Saved Path* location. If it does not find it there, it searches the *Project File Search* Path defined in the Options dialog box. Then it searches the folder in which the current drawing resides. It will use the first file it finds with the appropriate name regardless of its location. But it will not change the information in the **Saved Path** column.

The **Project File Search Path** is defined on the **Files** tab of the Options dialog box (Figure 14.1.1b). Pick the "+" beside the **Project File Search Path** listing to see the folders AutoCAD will search. To add a folder, select the **Project File Search Path** listing and pick the **Add ...** button. AutoCAD will add a listing, and you must type in the desired name.

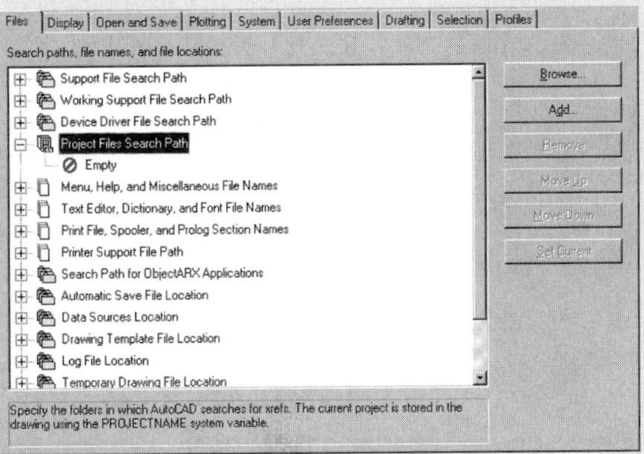

FIG. 14.1.1b: Files Tab of the Options Dialog Box

Then pick the plus beside the new project name, double-click on the **Empty** slot, and select the folder you wish to add to the search path.

Warning: Do not make changes in the Options dialog box without first consulting the CAD guru on your project.

For a video demonstration on setting up the Project Search Path, see the AutoCAD Learning Assistant's "Managing Shared Drawing Environments and Drawing Files" tutorial.

- Down the right side of the XRef Manager (Figure 14.1.1a), you will find five buttons.
  - The **Attach ...** button begins the ***XAttach*** command.
    The ***XAttach*** command begins with a Windows standard Select (Reference) File dialog box. There you will follow the path to the file you wish to reference. Once you have selected a file (and picked the **Open** button), AutoCAD presents the External Reference dialog box (Figure 14.1.1c).

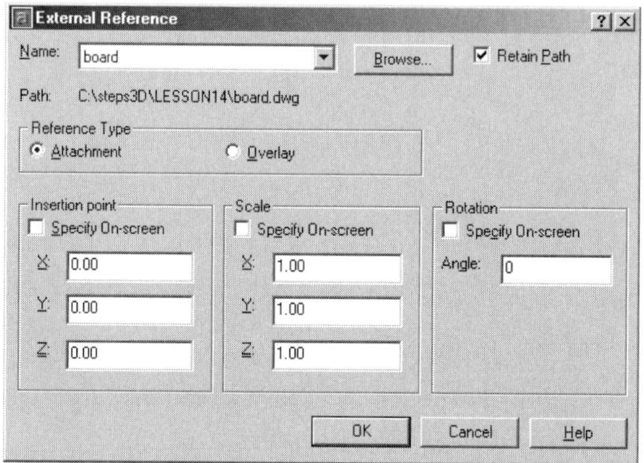

FIG. 14.1.1c External Reference Dialog Box

    - The **Name**: control box indicates the file you are attaching. You may pick the **Browse ...** button to select another file.
    - Leave a check in the **Retain Path** box to keep the path associated with the file. If you remove the check, AutoCAD will look for the file in the Project File Search Path or the current drawing's folder.
    - In the **Reference Type** frame, tell AutoCAD if you want your reference to be **Attached** or **Overlay**ed.
    - The **Insertion**, **Scale**, and **Rotation** frames are identical to their counterparts on the Insert dialog box (called by the ***Insert*** command).
  - Use the **Detach** button to remove references to the selected drawing. AutoCAD will detach the drawing when the Xref Manager closes. (*Note:* You cannot detach a nested reference. You must detach its primary drawing.)
  - **Unload** a drawing to remove a reference that you may want to use later. Unloading does not permanently remove the reference from the drawing, but it does remove it from display.
  - The **Reload** button marks the selected file for reloading when the Xref Manager closes. Use this button to update a reference without having to reopen your primary drawing, or to display an unloaded drawing.
  - Use the **Bind** button to permanently attach a reference to a primary drawing. (This is not the same as the ***XBind*** command, which we will discuss in Section 14.1.3.) AutoCAD presents the Bind Xrefs dialog box (Figure 14.1.1d) with two options.

FIG. 14.1.1d Xref Bind Dialog Box

As referenced information, dependent symbols are identified by the name of the referenced drawing followed by a bar and the symbol's name (i.e., **board | slots** is the **slots** layer on the referenced *board* drawing). The two options in the Bind Xrefs dialog box determine how Xref dependent symbols will be treated.

Dependent symbols are the layers, blocks, text styles, dimension styles, and linetypes that are part of a referenced drawing. To be available in the primary drawing, these symbols require that the referenced drawing be attached.

- **Binding** a referenced drawing causes AutoCAD to rename the dependent symbol but retain the referenced drawing's name in the new name. Thus, the **board | slots** layer will become **board0slots**. This approach means that you will always be able to trace where the symbol originated. [If the **board0slots** already exists, the number between the dollar signs increases (**board1slots**, **board2slots**, etc.).]
- Inserting a referenced drawing changes the referenced drawing into a block with the name of the referenced drawing becoming the name of the block. Dependent symbols become a part of the drawing but drop the name of the referenced drawing (i.e., **board | slots** becomes **slots**).

- The **Xref Found At** frame indicates where the selected drawing was found when AutoCAD loaded it. This is where AutoCAD actually found the drawing and may not be the same as the path.
  - Use the **Browse ...** button to select a different copy of the selected drawing to reference.
  - Use the **Save Path** button to redefine the saved path of the selected drawing to that shown in the **Xref Found At** box.

That was a lot of material to cover! Let's try our hands at Xrefing.
Here is the scenario for this lesson:

Your employer is developing a new product—a kit designed to help children learn about electricity. The kit will contain a circuit board where the student can attach a battery pack, switches, lights, resistors, and a galvanometer. The kit must be capable of creating any of several different wiring layouts.

Your job is to lay out some wiring diagrams of things the student can build using the objects listed. You have the initial board and component designs from the engineer, but some of these objects may change as the project develops. You do not have time to wait for engineering, so you will begin your layouts now using Xrefs so you can easily modify the component designs as they develop.

You can also access the XRef Manager by selecting **Xref Manager ...** or the ***XAttach*** command by selecting **External Reference ...** on the Insert pull-down menu.

WWW 14.1.1.1 Do This: Working with Xrefs

I. Start a new drawing using the *Start* template found in the C:\Steps3D\Lesson14 folder.

II. Save the drawing as *MyBoard* in the C:\Steps3D\Lesson14 folder.

III. Follow these steps:

TOOLS	COMMAND SEQUENCE	STEPS
 External Reference Button	**Command:** *xr*	**1.** We will begin by referencing our title block. Enter the ***Xref*** command by typing ***xref*** or ***xr*** at the command prompt. Or you can pick the **External Reference** button on the Reference toolbar.
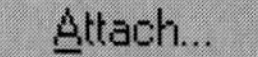		**2.** AutoCAD presents the Xref Manager. Pick the **Attach ...** button.
		3. AutoCAD presents the Select Reference File dialog box. Select *the title block.dwg* file in the C:\Steps3D\Lesson14 folder. (Double-click on the file name or pick the **Open** button to continue.)

continued

TOOLS | **COMMAND SEQUENCE** | **STEPS**

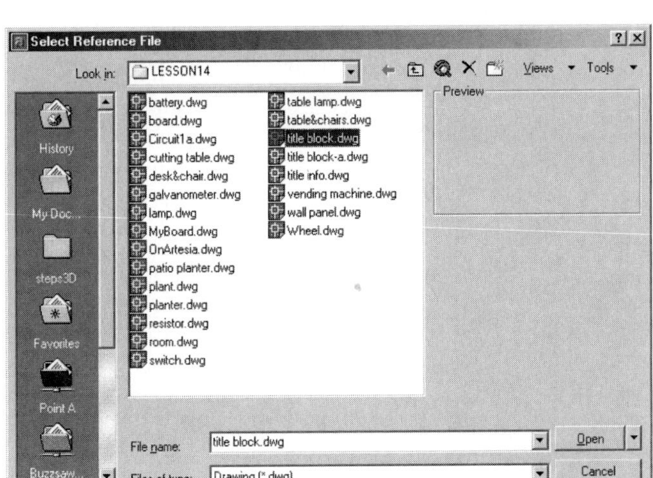

4. AutoCAD presents the External Reference dialog box. Be sure the selections match those shown.

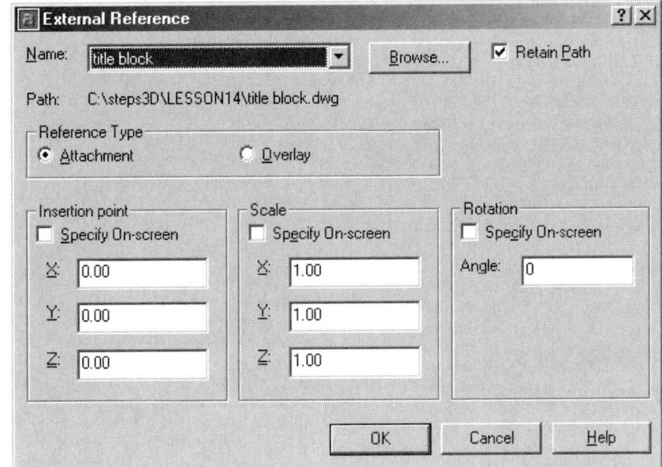

- Use the **Attachment Reference Type.**
- Remove the checks from the boxes in the three lower frames.
- Be sure there is a check in the **Retain Path** box.

Pick the **OK** button to continue.

continued

TOOLS	COMMAND SEQUENCE	STEPS

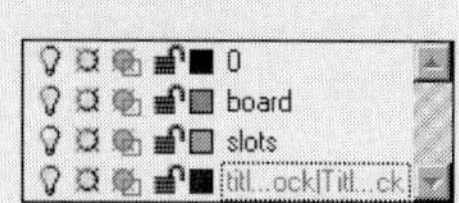

5. Check the **Layer** control box. Notice that AutoCAD has added the layer **title block | Title Block**. (The other layers were part of the template.) This is the layer on which the title block was created and has been referenced with the drawing. Notice that the layer is gray—it can be frozen, turned off, locked, or plotted, but it cannot be made current. You cannot draw on this layer because it is not actually part of the primary drawing.

6. Draw the board shown in Figure 14.1.1.1.6.

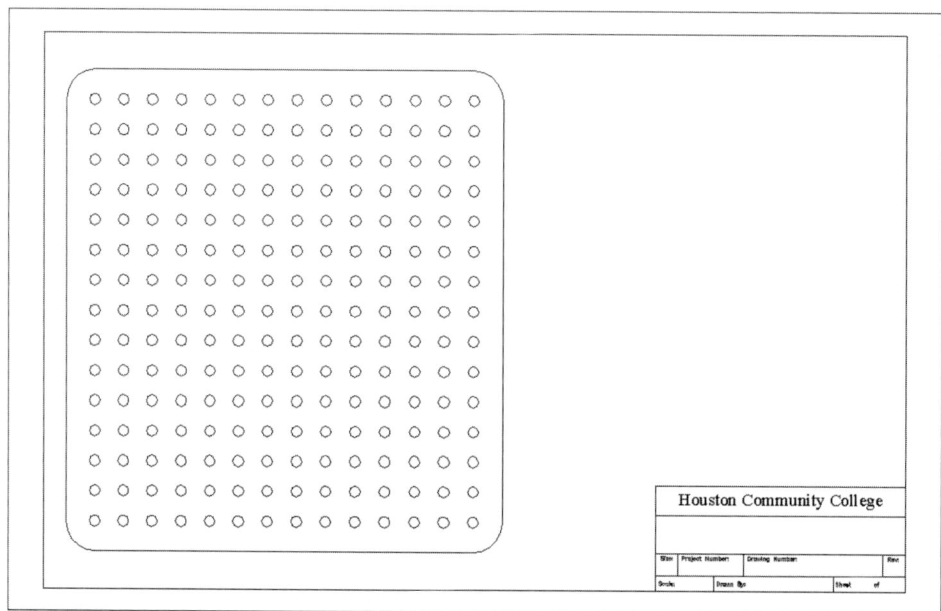

FIG. 14.1.1.1.6 *MyBoard.dwg*

- The rectangle's corners are at coordinates ***1,1*** and ***8.5,9***.
- The fillets are $\frac{1}{2}$".
- There are 15 rows and 14 columns of slots.
- The board is on the **board** layer.
- The slots are on the **slots** layer.
- The slots are $\frac{3}{16}$" diameter, $\frac{1}{2}$" apart, and begin at coordinate ***1.5,1.5***.

continued

TOOLS | **COMMAND SEQUENCE** | **STEPS**

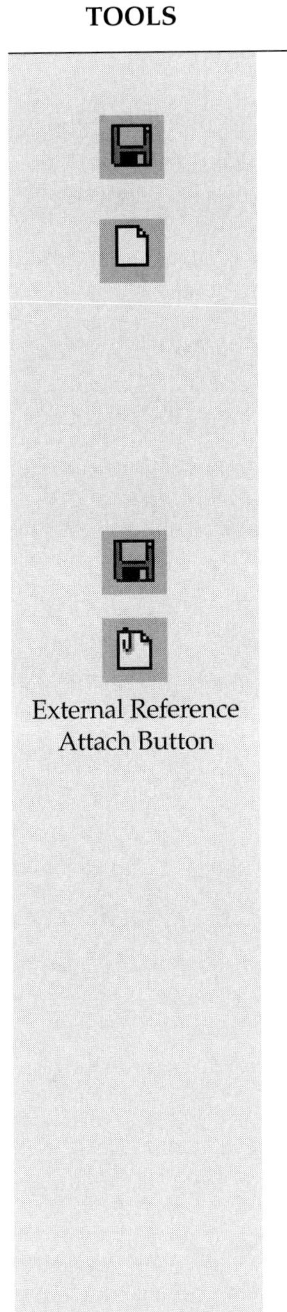

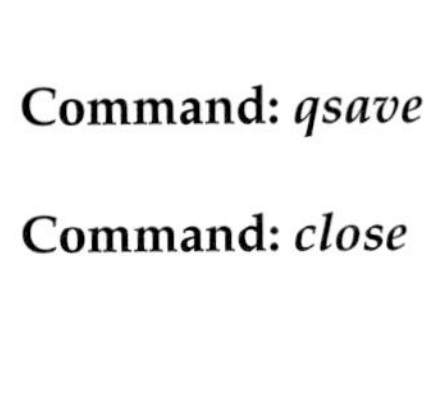

Command: ***qsave***

Command: ***close***

7. Save the drawing and close it.

8. Start a new drawing using the *Start* template found in the C:\Steps3D\Lesson14 folder. Save the drawing as *MyCircuit1* in the C:\Steps3D\Lesson14 folder.

9. Repeat Steps 1 to 4, but this time reference the *MyBoard.dwg* you created earlier in this exercise.

Command: ***qsave***

10. Save the drawing.

Command: ***xa***

11. Using the ***XAttach*** command, we will attach the battery and the switch.

Begin by entering ***xattach*** or ***xa*** at the command prompt. Or you can pick the **External Reference Attach** button on the Reference toolbar. (You will notice that this procedure is identical to the one we used to attach the *MyBoard.dwg* file except that we skip the Xref Manager.)

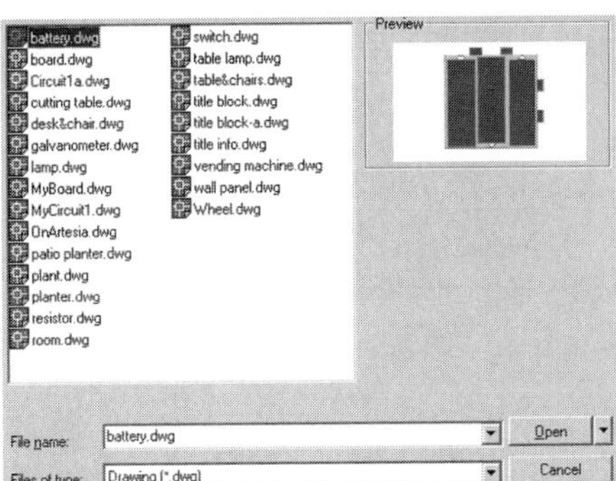

12. Repeat Step 3, but this time select the *battery.dwg* file.

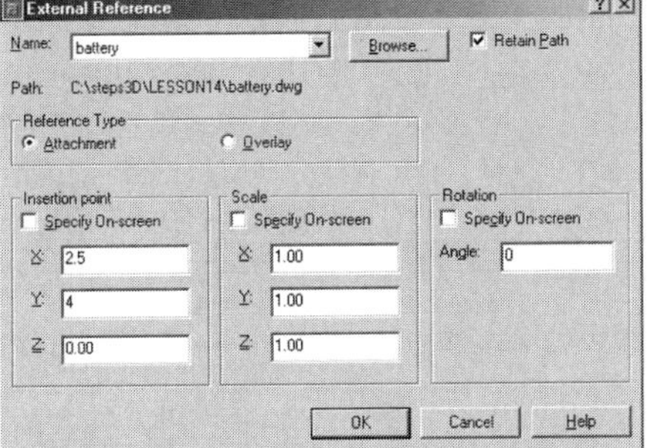

13. Insert the file at coordinates **2.5,4**.

continued

TOOLS	COMMAND SEQUENCE	STEPS
	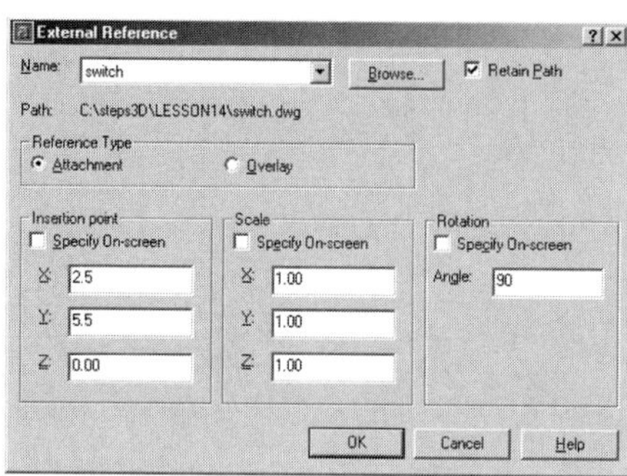	**14.** Repeat Steps 11 to 13 to insert the *switch.dwg* file at coordinates **2.5,5.5**. Be sure to insert this file at ***90°***. Your board looks like Figure 14.1.1.1.14.
		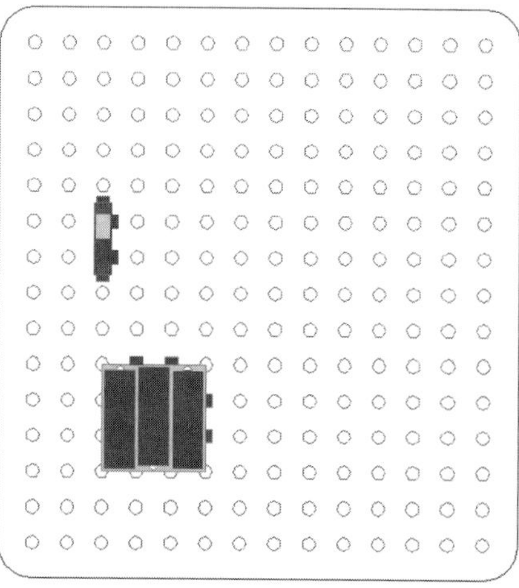 FIG. 14.1.1.1.14 Board with Battery and Switch
	Command: *qsave*	**15.** Save the drawing, but do not exit.

Notice the two pairs of wire connections on both the switch and the battery. Our engineers have not decided where to put the single required pair, so they have created two for now. We have a fair idea of which ones they will eventually use, but we do not want to change the actual component drawings yet. We can, however, alter the reference to show only those connections we want to show.

14.1.2 Removing Part of a Reference—The *XClip* Command

The tool needed to remove part of a referenced drawing is called ***XClip***. This is the command sequence:

Command: *xclip* **(or** *xc***)**

Select objects: *[select the reference(s) to clip]*

Select objects: *[hit enter to confirm the selection]*

Enter clipping option

[ON/OFF/Clipdepth/Delete/generate Polyline/New boundary] <New>: *[tell AutoCAD what you want to do]*

Specify clipping boundary:

[Select polyline/Polygonal/Rectangular] <Rectangular>: *[tell AutoCAD what type of clipping boundary you wish to use]*

The first option line presents several opportunities.

- **ON/OFF** are toggles for the clipping window. They determine whether AutoCAD will present only those portions of the referenced drawing visible through the clipping window (**ON**) or all of the referenced drawing (**OFF**).
- **Clipdepth** allows the user to set the front/back clipping planes of three-dimensional objects. It prompts

  Specify front clip point or [Distance/Remove]:

  Specify back clip point or [Distance/Remove]:

  A two-dimensional boundary must exist before you can define front or back clip points. Identify the clip points by coordinate or distance from the two-dimensional clipping boundary.
- Use **Delete** to remove a boundary.
- **Generate Polyline** will automatically draw a polyline along the clipping boundary. Again, a boundary must exist before AutoCAD can generate the polyline.
- **New boundary** (the default) permits you to identify a new clipping boundary.

The next line of options offers some choices for how to create the new boundary.

- Use the **Select polyline** option to use an existing polyline to define the boundary. The polyline does not have to be closed, but it must consist of only straight-line segments (no arcs) and must not intersect itself. (To create a "round" clipping boundary, use a polygon with a large number of sides.)
- Use the **Polygonal** option to create a multisided or nonlinear shape for a boundary (much like using a poly-window to create a selection set).
- Use the **Rectangular** option (the default) to use a window to define the clipping boundary.

AutoCAD provides a system variable to allow you to see the boundary even when it is not a polyline. The system variable is **XClipFrame**. A setting of ***0*** (the default) means the boundaries will be hidden. A setting of ***1*** will show the boudaries. AutoCAD provides a button—**External Reference Clip Frame**—on the Reference toolbar to help you toggle the system variable on and off.

You can also access the ***XClip*** command on the Modify pull-down menu. Follow this path:

Modify—Clip—Xref

We will remove the extra wire connectors from our battery and switch.

14.1.2.1 Do This: Clipping Xrefs

I. Be sure you are still in the *MyCircuit1.dwg* file. If not, open it now.

II. Follow these steps:

TOOLS	COMMAND SEQUENCE	STEPS
External Reference Clip	**Command:** *xc*	**1.** Enter the ***XClip*** command by typing ***xclip*** or ***xc*** at the command prompt. Or you may pick the **External Reference Clip** button on the Reference toolbar.
	Select objects: **Select objects:** *[enter]*	**2.** Select the battery and confirm the selection.
	Enter clipping option [ON/OFF/Clipdepth/Delete/generate Polyline/New boundary] <New>: *[enter]*	**3.** Accept the default **New boundary** option.
	Specify clipping boundary: **[Select polyline/Polygonal/ Rectangular] <Rectangular>:** *[enter]*	**4.** Tell AutoCAD you will create a **Rectangular** clipping boundary (the default).
	Specify first corner:	**5.** Place the **first corner** at the lower right corner of the battery (use OSNAPs) …

continued

TOOLS	COMMAND SEQUENCE	STEPS
	Specify opposite corner *2.5,4.25*	6. … and the **opposite corner** at the coordinates indicated. AutoCAD clips the reference and the battery now looks like Figure 14.1.2.1.6.

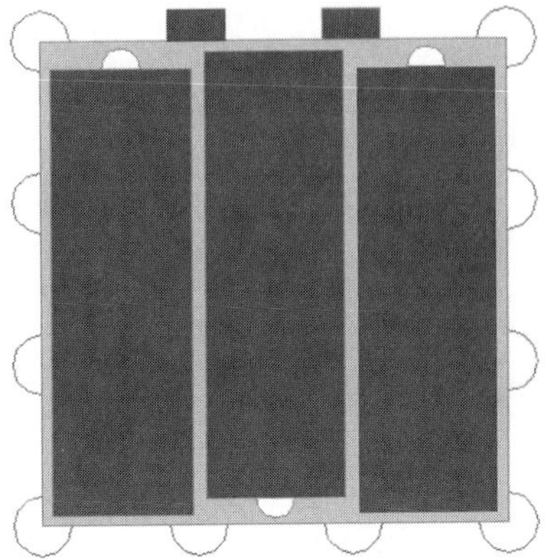

FIG. 14.1.2.1.6 Clipped Battery Reference

TOOLS	COMMAND SEQUENCE	STEPS
	**Command:** *xc*	7. Repeat Steps 1 to 6 to clip the side connections from the switch. Your board looks like Figure 14.1.2.1.7.

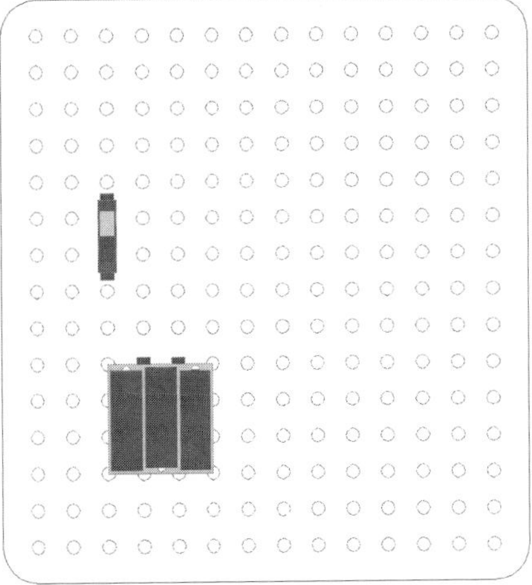

FIG. 14.1.2.1.7 Completed Board

TOOLS	COMMAND SEQUENCE	STEPS
	**Command:** *xr*	8. Have you noticed that the title block affects your ability to zoom in and out on the board with ease? Let's remove it temporarily while we work on our board. Open the Xref Manager.

continued

TOOLS	COMMAND SEQUENCE	STEPS

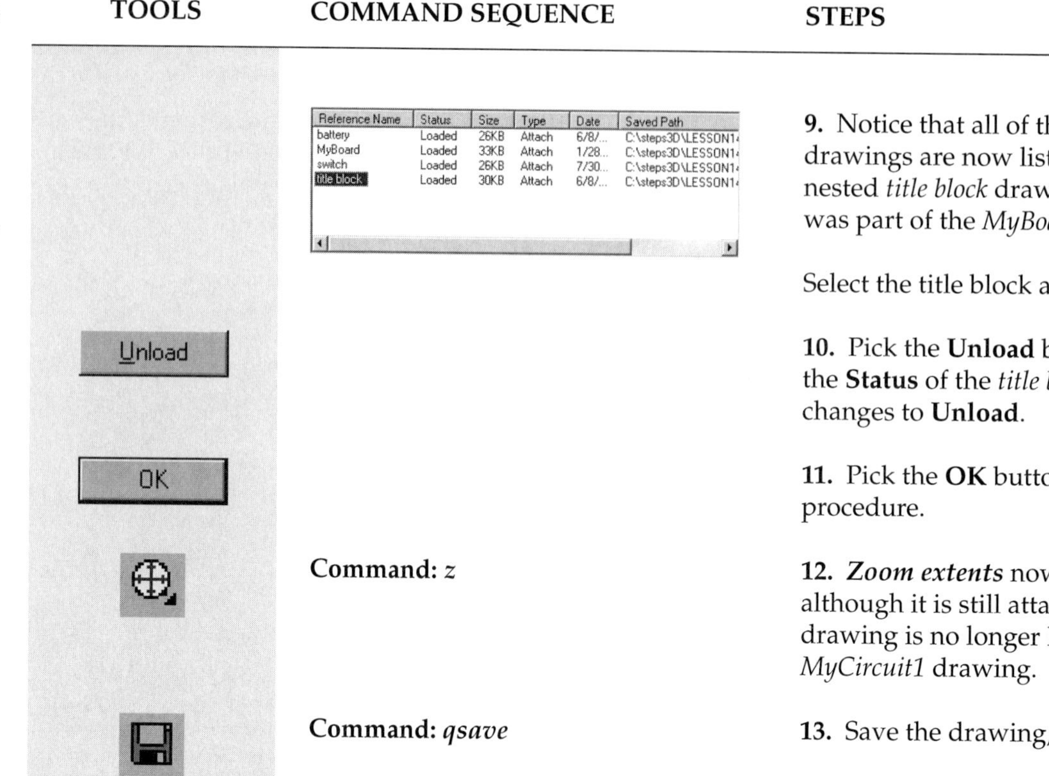

9. Notice that all of the referenced drawings are now listed—even the nested *title block* drawing (remember, it was part of the *MyBoard* drawing).

Select the title block as indicated.

10. Pick the **Unload** button. Notice that the **Status** of the *title block* reference changes to **Unload**.

11. Pick the **OK** button to complete the procedure.

Command: *z*

12. ***Zoom extents*** now to see that, although it is still attached, the *title block* drawing is no longer loaded into our *MyCircuit1* drawing.

Command: *qsave*

13. Save the drawing, but do not exit.

14.1.3 Xrefs and Dependent Symbols

AutoCAD allows two methods of permanently attaching referenced drawing data to the primary file—Binding and Xbinding. You will use the **Bind** button on the Xref Manager to permanently attach, or bind, an entire referenced drawing to the primary drawing. We discussed this in Section 14.1.1 and will demonstrate it in Section 14.4. But you can also attach parts (specific dependent symbols) of the referenced drawing individually to the primary drawing. The command for this is ***Xbind***, and it presents the Xbind dialog box (Figure 14.1.3a).

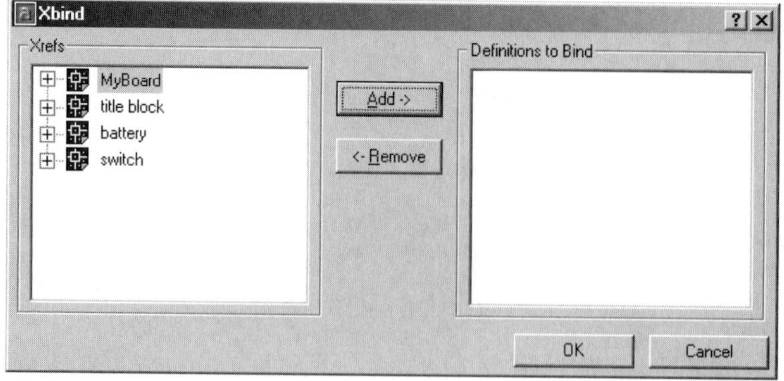

FIG. 14.1.3a Xbind Dialog Box

The Xbind dialog box is one of AutoCAD's easiest. Simply select the Dependent Symbol you wish to bind in the Xrefs frame, pick the **Add->** button, and **OK** your changes.

> You can also access the ***Xbind*** command on the Modify pull-down menu. Follow this path:
>
> *Modify—Object—External Reference—Bind ...*

Let's try one. The battery drawing has a **wire** layer and a **times** text style; we will add these to our primary file.

14.1.3.1 Do This: Xbinding Dependent Symbols

I. Be sure you are still in the *MyCircuit1.dwg* file. If not, open it now.

II. Follow these steps:

TOOLS	COMMAND SEQUENCE	STEPS
 External Reference Bind Button	**Command:** *xb*	**1.** Enter the ***Xbind*** command by typing ***Xbind*** or ***xb*** at the command prompt. Or you can pick the **External Reference Bind** button on the Reference toolbar.
	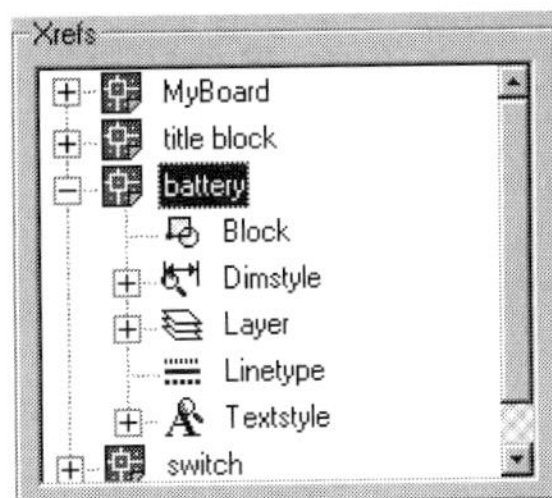	**2.** AutoCAD presents the Xbind dialog box (Figure 14.1.3a). Pick the "+" beside the battery reference. AutoCAD presents a list of Dependent Symbol Categories. Categories with symbols available for binding have a "+" beside them.
	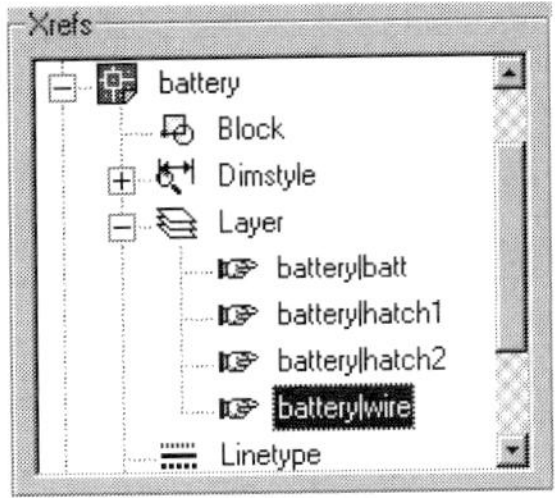	**3.** Pick the "+" beside the **Layer** category, and then select the **battery | wire** layer.

continued

TOOLS	COMMAND SEQUENCE	STEPS

4. Pick the **Add->** button. Notice that the **battery | wire** layer disappears from the **Xrefs** frame and appears in the **Definitions to Bind** frame.

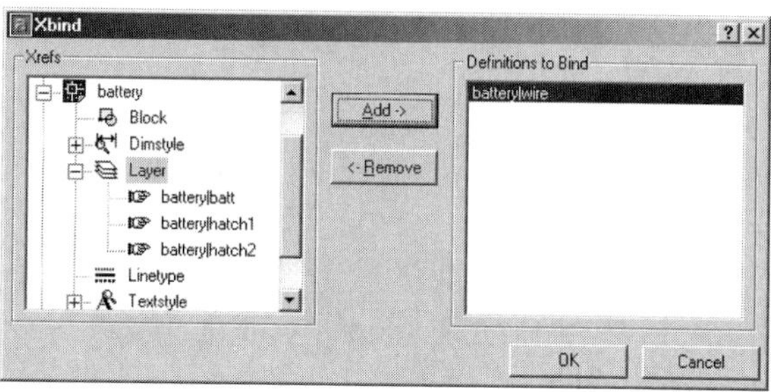

5. Pick the **OK** button to complete the command.

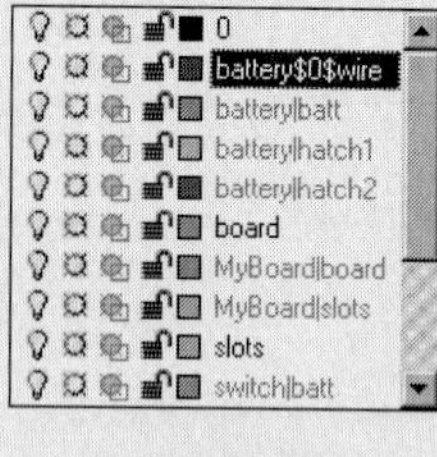

6. Check the **Layer** control box. Notice that the **battery | wire** layer has been replaced with **battery0wire**. You can now use this layer as you would any other layer in the primary drawing.

Command: *xb*

7. Repeat Steps 1 to 5 to bind the **battery | times** text style to the primary drawing. [Check your success by looking in the **Style Name** control box in the Text Style dialog box to be sure you have the **battery0times** style (Figure 14.1.3.1.7).]

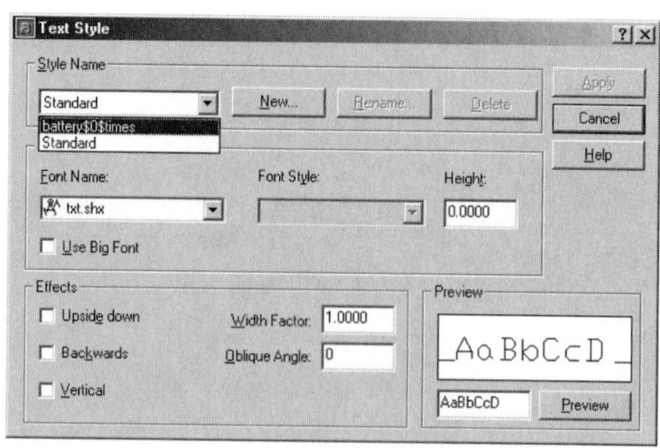

FIG. 14.1.3.1.7 Check to Find the **battery0times** Text Style

continued

TOOLS	COMMAND SEQUENCE	STEPS
	**Command:** *qsave*	**8.** Save the drawing, but do not exit.

14.1.4 Unloading, Reloading, and Overlaying Xrefs

In Exercise 14.1.2.1, we unloaded the *title block* reference to make our work easier. All we had to do to accomplish this was to select the drawing to unload (*title block*) and then pick the **Unload** button in the Xref Manager. Unloading a reference can speed work by reducing regeneration time. And as we saw, unloading a reference can remove unnecessary, distracting, and even obstructing objects from the display. But, eventually, the unloaded reference will probably need to be reloaded.

Reloading an unloaded reference is as easy as unloading it. Simply select the drawing to reload and pick the **Reload** button in the XRef Manager. We will reload the title block in our next exercise. First, let's consider the **Attach** versus **Overlay** type of reference.

Consider the diagram in Figure 14.1.4a.

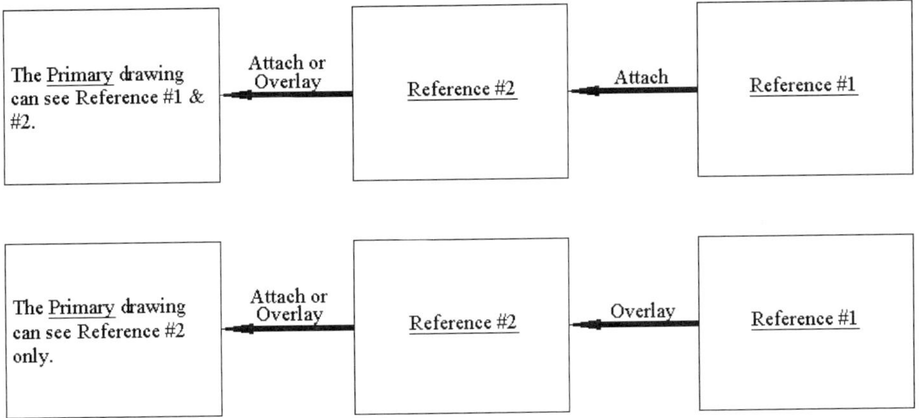

FIG. 14.1.4a Attach vs. Overlay

As you can see, the **Overlay** type of reference is effective only when used on a nested reference. In other words, overlaying a reference into the primary drawing will not affect the nested reference's visibility. To hide the nested reference, it must be overlaid into the drawing being referenced by the primary drawing.

We will see this in our next exercise. We will reload our *title block* (which is nested into the *MyBoard* drawing reference). [*MyBoard* (Reference #2 in the diagram) references *title block* (Reference #1) using the **Attach** type of reference; therefore, we can see it from the primary drawing (*MyCircuit1*).] In our exercise, we will change the reference type between *MyBoard* and *title block* and see how that affects *MyCircuit1*.

Let's begin.

14.1.4.1 Do This: Reloading and Overlaying References

I. Be sure you are still in the *MyCircuit1.dwg* file. If not, open it now.

II. Follow these steps:

TOOLS	COMMAND SEQUENCE	STEPS
	Command: *xr*	**1.** Call the XRef Manager.
Reload		**2.** Select the title block reference and then pick the **Reload** button.
OK		**3.** Pick the **OK** button to complete the procedure. Notice that the title block is again visible. (If necessary, ***zoom all*** to see it.)
	Command: *qsave* **Command:** *close*	**4.** Save and close the drawing.
		5. Open the *MyBoard* drawing.
	Command: *xr*	**6.** Call the XRef Manager.
	Reference Name | Status | Size | Type | Date | Saved Path title block | Loaded | 30KB | Overlay | 6/8/... | C:\steps3D\LESSON1	**7.** Double-click on the word **Attach** in the **Type** column. Notice that it changes to **Overlay**. (It is just that easy to change the reference type.)
OK		**8.** Pick the **OK** button to complete the procedure.
	Command: *qsave* **Command:** *close*	**9.** Save and close the drawing.
		10. Open the *MyCircuit1* drawing. Notice that the title block is no longer visible.

continued

TOOLS	COMMAND SEQUENCE	STEPS
	Command: *xr*	**11.** Call the XRef Manager. Notice that the *title block* drawing is no longer referenced.
		12. Repeat Steps 4 to 10, but this time set the type of reference to **Attach**.

14.2 Editing Xrefs

One of the nicest tools in the AutoCAD command family is our ability to edit a referenced drawing without having to leave the primary drawing. Even better is the fact that it is so easy to do!

> Although AutoCAD has made it quite simple to edit a referenced drawing, you should do so with caution. Remember that others may have referenced the same drawing and any changes made to it will reflect in their drawings as well.

Three commands make up the reference editing tools.

- *Refedit* begins the editing session. It prompts you to select the referenced objects to edit, like this:

  Command: *refedit*

  Select reference: *[select the referenced drawing]*

  [Here AutoCAD presents the Reference Edit dialog box (Figure 14.2a). Complete the options and pick the **OK** *button to continue.]*

  Select nested objects: *[select the objects that you wish to modify within the referenced drawing]*

  Select nested objects: *[enter to confirm the selection]*

  Use REFCLOSE or the Refedit toolbar to end reference editing session. *[AutoCAD lets you know how to end the editing session. It also displays the Refedit toolbar for your convenience.]*

The Reference Edit dialog box (Figure 14.2a) provides a list box showing the name of the selected reference and a **Preview** frame where you can see the referenced drawing. It also provides two options:

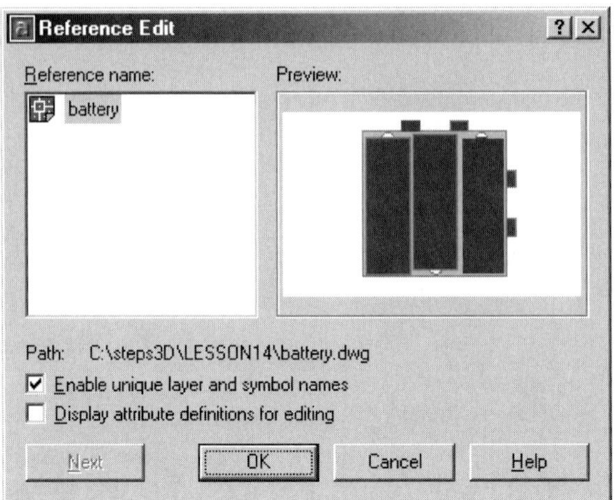

FIG. 14.2a Reference Edit Dialog Box

- **Enable unique layer and symbol names** controls how the layers of the referenced drawing will be made available to you during the edit. When this box is checked (the default) layers appear as **$[#]$[name]** (as in **0hatch1**). This makes it easy to find the layers immediately available during the editing session. (AutoCAD will group the layers together in the **Layer** control box.) When the box is cleared, layers appear by name only (as in **hatch1**) in alphabetical order—mixed in among the unavailable layers.
- **Display attribute definitions for editing** controls how attributes can be edited during the session.

  When a drawing with an attributed block appears in the **Reference name**: list box, the block appears as **[reference name] | [block name].**

  - A check in this box when the **reference name** is highlighted means that you will be able to edit the attribute *value*. The new value will be saved to the original (referenced) drawing.
  - A check in this box when the **block name** is highlighted means that you will be able to modify the attribute *definition*. Changes are saved to the original drawing, but the original value will remain intact. Subsequent insertions of the block, however, will contain the new attribute definition.
  - Leaving this box clear means that neither the value nor the definition of the attribute will be available for modification.

- Use ***Refset*** to add or remove referenced objects from the editing session. It prompts

  Transfer objects between the Refedit working set and host drawing …

  Enter an option [Add/Remove] <Add>: *[enter to add or type* **R** *to remove objects from the set]*

  Select objects: *[select the object(s) to add or remove]*

- ***Refclose*** ends the editing session. It prompts

  Enter option [Save/Discard reference changes] <Save>: *[enter to save the changes or type* **D** *to discard the changes]*

  [AutoCAD presents a warning box (Figure 14.2b) telling you what you are about to do]

  Regenerating model.

  1 xref instance updated

  battery redefined and reloaded.

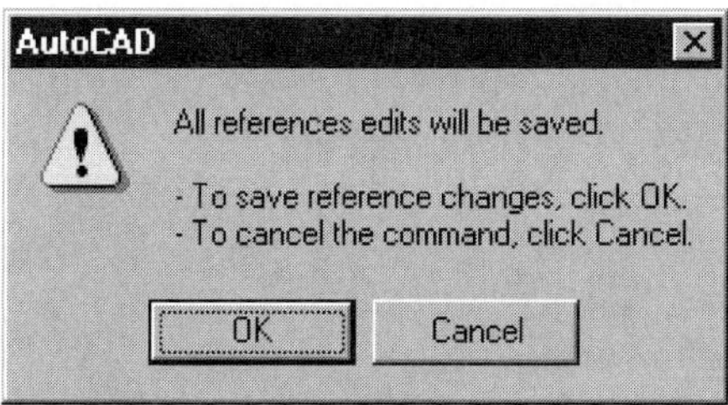

FIG. 14.2b Warning Box

AutoCAD also provides buttons on the Refedit toolbar to add or remove objects from the editing session (***Refset***) and to close the session saving or discarding your changes (***Refclose***).

In addition to the command line and toolbar approach, you may access the various ***Refedit*** commands via the Modify pull-down menu. Follow this path:

Modify—In-place Xref and Block Edit—[Edit command]

Let's try ***Refedit***.

Our engineer has determined where the wire connections should be on our battery and switch. We could open those drawings for the changes, but we are in the *MyCircuit1.dwg* file now and can make the changes here using ***Refedit***.

WWW 14.2.1 Do This: Editing Referenced Drawings

I. Be sure you are still in the *MyCircuit1.dwg* file. If not, open it now.

II. Follow these steps:

TOOLS	COMMAND SEQUENCE	STEPS
	Command: *xc*	**1.** First, let's remove the clipping planes. Enter the ***XClip*** command.
	Select objects:	**2.** Select the battery and the switch.
	Select objects: *[enter]*	
Enter Cancel ON OFF Clipdepth Delete generate Polyline New boundary Pan Zoom	**Enter clipping option [ON/OFF/Clipdepth/Delete/generate Polyline/New boundary] <New>:** *d*	**3.** Tell AutoCAD you want to **Delete** the clipping plane. AutoCAD presents both references in their entirety.
Edit Block or Xref Button	**Command:** *refedit*	**4.** Now we begin the editing session. Enter the ***Refedit*** command at the command prompt. There is no hotkey for this command, but you can pick the **Edit block or Xref** button on the Refedit toolbar.
	Select reference:	**5.** Select the battery.
OK		**6.** AutoCAD presents the Reference Edit dialog box (Figure 14.2a). We will use the default settings, so pick the **OK** button.

continued

TOOLS	COMMAND SEQUENCE	STEPS
	Select nested objects: **Select nested objects:** *[enter]* **Use REFCLOSE or the Refedit toolbar to end reference editing session.**	**7.** Select the wiring connections on the right side of the battery. (There are actually three objects—one hatching and two rectangles.)
	Command: *e*	**8.** AutoCAD makes only the wiring connections available for modification. Erase them.
Save Back Changes to Reference Button	**Command:** *refclose* **Enter option [Save/Discard reference changes] <Save>:** *[enter]*	**9.** Complete the ***Refedit*** command with the ***Refclose*** command. Hit ***enter*** to accept the **Save** option. Or you can pick the **Save back changes to reference** button on the Refedit toolbar.
OK		**10.** AutoCAD presents a warning box (Figure 14.2b). Pick the **OK** button to complete the command.
		11. Repeat Steps 4 to 9 to remove the right set of wiring connections on the switch.
	Command: *qsave* **Command:** *close*	**12.** Save and close the drawing.

14.3 Using Our Drawing as a Reference

Now that we have created a drawing with circuit board, battery, and switch, we can begin to create our wiring diagrams. We will plan on three layouts using the battery and switch in these locations, so we will use the *MyCircuit1.dwg* file as a reference over which we will create our layouts.

Let's begin.

14.3.1 Do This: Using Xrefs to Create Three Wiring Diagrams

I. Start a new drawing using the *Start* template in the C:\Steps3D\Lesson14 folder.

II. Follow these steps:

TOOLS	COMMAND SEQUENCE	STEPS
	Command: *xr*	**1.** Begin by referencing the *MyCircuit1* drawing. (Follow Steps 1 to 4 of Exercise 14.1.1.1.)
	Command: *xb*	**2.** Xbind the **battery | wire** layer and **title block | times** text style to your new drawing. (Use the procedure detailed in Exercise 14.1.3.1.)
		3. Rename the new layer to **Wire** and the new text style to **Times**.
	Command: *saveas*	**4.** Save the drawing as *MyCircuit1a.dwg* in the C:\Steps3D\Lesson14 folder.
	Command: *xa*	**5.** Reference the *lamp.dwg* file in the C:\Steps3D\Lesson14 folder and place it at coordinates ***6.5,6***.

continued

TOOLS	COMMAND SEQUENCE	STEPS
	Command: *spl*	**6.** Use splines to draw the wire shown in Figure 14.3.1.6. (Be sure to use the **Wire** layer.) Add the text on an appropriate layer. (Text size is $\frac{1}{8}$" and uses the **times** style.)

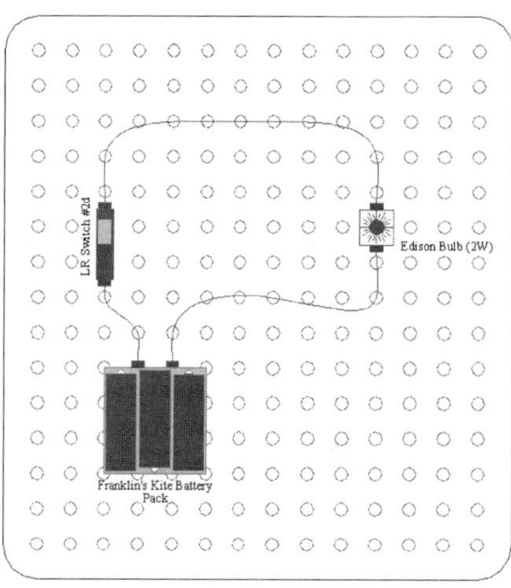

FIG. 14.3.1.6 *MyCircuit1a.dwg*

TOOLS	COMMAND SEQUENCE	STEPS
	Command: *i*	**7.** Insert the block file *title info* at the lower left corner of the title block (Figure 14.3.1.7). (Place it on its own layer, and fill in the data as appropriate for your situation.)

Houston Community College			
Wiring Project #1 Simple Light & Switch Diagram			
Size: B	Project Number: 10372	Drawing Number: B-14317	Rev: 0
Scale: NTS	Drawn By: T. Sykes	Sheet 1 of 1	

FIG. 14.3.1.7 Title Block Data

TOOLS	COMMAND SEQUENCE	STEPS
	Command: *qsave*	**8.** Save and close the drawing.
	Command: *close*	

continued

TOOLS	COMMAND SEQUENCE	STEPS
		9. Repeat Steps 1 to 8 (as needed) to create the drawings shown in Figures 14.3.1.9a and 14.3.1.9b. Adjust the title blocks to read Wiring Project #2, Galvanometer Diagram (drawing number) B-14319a, and Wiring Project #3, Resistor Diagram (drawing number) B-14319b. (Appropriate reference drawings have been provided in the C:\Steps3D\Lesson14 folder.)

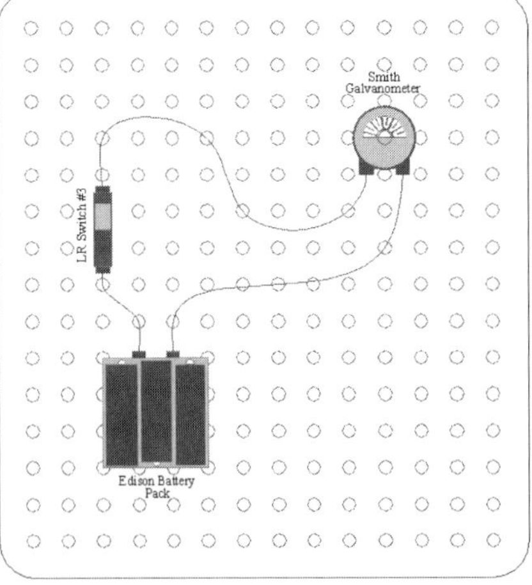

FIG. 14.3.1.9a Use the *Galvanometer.dwg* (save as *MyCircuit1b*)

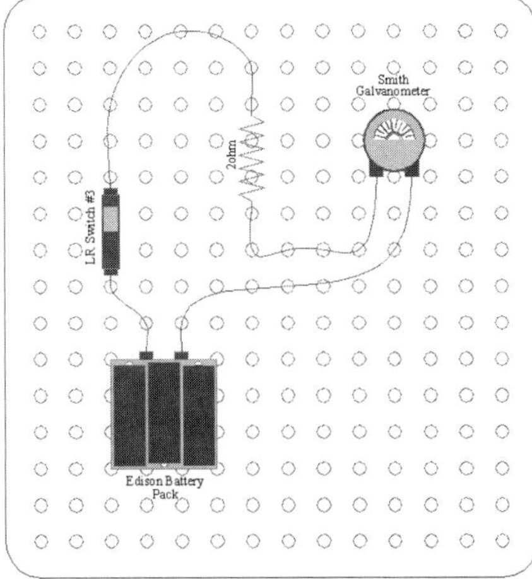

FIG. 14.3.1.9b Add the *Resistor.dwg* (save as *MyCircuit1c*)

10. Save the drawings as noted in the C:\Steps3D\Lesson14 folder.

Congratulations! You have completed three diagrams according to your original job requirements!

You will have an opportunity to create other diagrams at the end of this lesson. First, however, let's take a look at some special requirements for sending your referenced drawings to the client.

14.4 Binding an Xref to Your Drawing

The biggest problem that arises from the use of Xrefs lies in the location of the referenced file and how AutoCAD keeps track of that location.

By default, AutoCAD will look for referenced files in the **Saved Path** first, and then in folders listed in the **Project Files Search Path**. Again by default, the **Project Files Search Path** is empty. Therefore, you will need to add the location (path) of your references to the **Project Files Search Path** or rely on the **Saved Path**.

The problem develops when you decide to send your drawing to the client (or somewhere else). First, you must remember to send all the reference files along with the primary file. But even when you do this, the client may not (indeed, probably will not) place the files in a folder with the same name you were using. The result will be that the primary drawing will not be able to locate the references (your client gets frustrated and you look for a new job).

You could solve the problem by fully documenting necessary project/folder/path information and sending the documents along with the files. But this means that the client must read instructions about how to view your work—probably not a strong selling point for giving you more business.

You might use the eTransmit tool we discussed in Lesson 3 of our basic text, but there is another way. AutoCAD allows you to bind all the references to the primary drawing as blocks. Then you simply send the one file, and the client reads it with any AutoCAD program or viewer.

Binding references, however, dramatically increases the size of the drawing. So you need to wait until the project is complete before doing it. It might even be a good idea to save the bound drawing under a different name in case you need to do additional work on the original(s).

As we saw in our study of the XRef Manager (Section 14.1.1), binding is not difficult. Simply select the references to bind and pick the **Bind** button in the XRef Manager. AutoCAD will ask if you wish to **Bind** or **Insert** (via the Bind Xrefs dialog box—Figure 14.1.1d). (See the discussion of these options in Section 14.1.1.)

Let's see what happens when we bind our references.

WWW

14.4.1 Do This: Binding References

I. Open the *MyCircuit1a.dwg* file in the C:\Steps3D\Lesson14 folder. If this drawing is not available, open the *Circuit1a.dwg* file instead.

II. Follow these steps:

TOOLS	COMMAND SEQUENCE	STEPS
No Button Available	**Command:** *dwgprops*	**1.** Before we bind our references, let's see how large our drawing file is. Enter the command *dwgprops*.

continued

TOOLS	COMMAND SEQUENCE	STEPS
	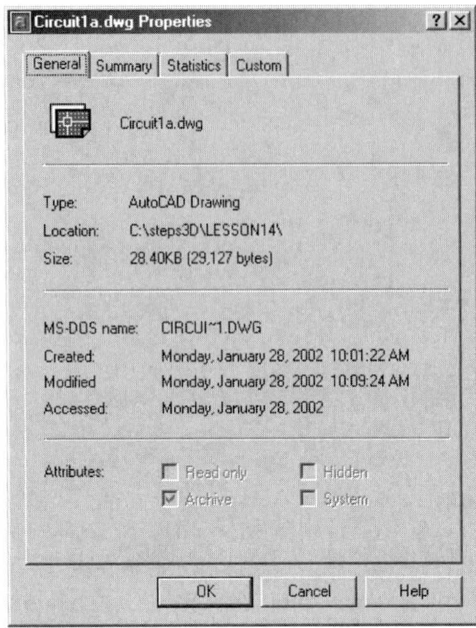	**2.** AutoCAD presents the (Drawing Name) Properties dialog box with information about the current drawing (*MyCircuit1a.dwg*). Note the size of the drawing, and then exit the dialog box (pick the **OK** button).
	**Command:** *xr*	**3.** Open the XRef Manager.
		4. Select the *Battery* reference. Notice that the **Bind** button is not available. The *Battery.dwg* file is nested into our primary drawing (it is there because it was referenced by the *Circuit1* drawing that, in turn, was referenced by our primary drawing). To bind a nested reference, bind its primary drawing.
		5. Select the *MyCircuit1* drawing and then pick the **Bind** button.
	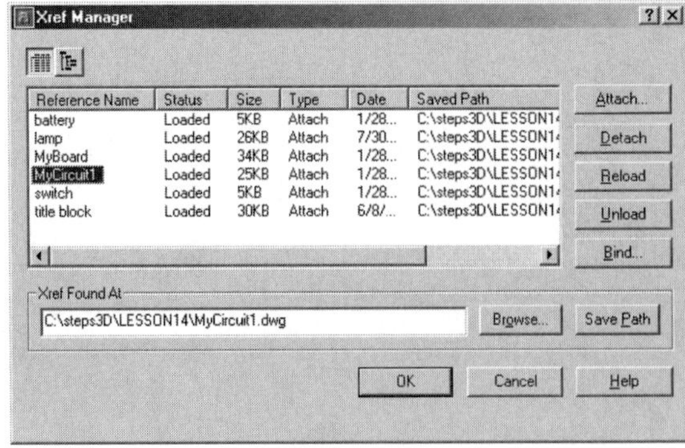	

continued

TOOLS | COMMAND SEQUENCE | STEPS

6. AutoCAD presents the Bind Xrefs dialog box. Remember, if you use the **Bind Bind Type**, dependent symbols adopt this format: **[ref name]$[#]$[layer]** (as in **battery0hatch1**). If you use the Insert Bind Type, dependent symbols drop the reference drawing name and **$[#]$** from their name.

Put a bullet next to **Insert** and pick the **OK** button.

7. AutoCAD returns you to the XRef Manager. Notice that all the references except *lamp* have been removed. Except for *lamp*, all the references were nested into our primary drawing via the *MyCircuit1.dwg* file. When it was bound, its references were also bound into the primary drawing.

8. Repeat Steps 4 to 6, this time binding the *lamp* reference.

9. Pick the **OK** button to complete the procedure.

10. AutoCAD has attached the references to the drawing as blocks. Look at the **Layer** control box to see the changes in how layers are identified. Notice that the reference drawing has been dropped from the name.

Command: *qsave*

11. Save the drawing, but do not exit.

continued

TOOLS | **COMMAND SEQUENCE** | **STEPS**

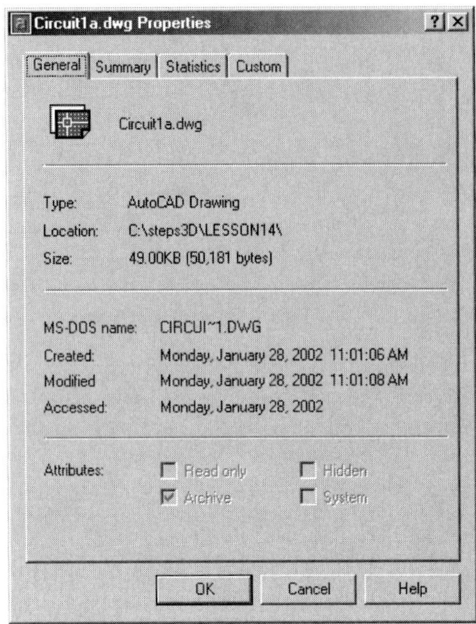

12. Repeat Steps 1 and 2 and compare the drawing size now with the size before binding the Xrefs. Notice that the size has almost doubled; this is how much drawing space you saved by using Xrefs! (Imagine how much help they will be in a 2- or 3-Mb drawing file!)

Command: *x*

13. Now explode all the blocks (except the title block information) and save the drawing. We do this for a comparison of drawing sizes (how large the drawing would have been had we simply drawn each object).

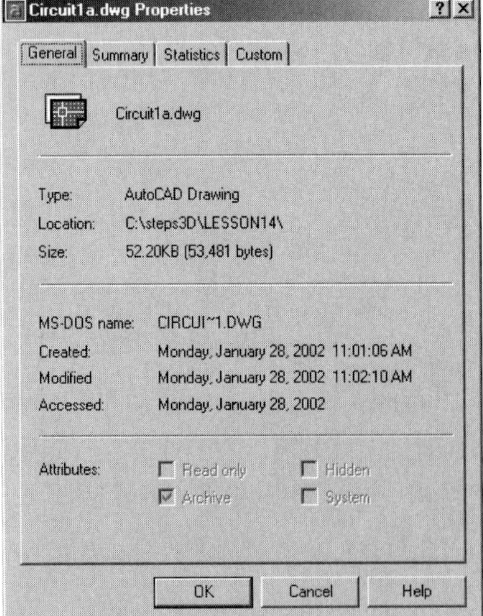

14. Repeat Steps 11 and 12. Notice how large the drawing file is now.

Command: *close*

15. Close the drawing. (Save the changes.)

You can now send the drawing to your client without fear of losing something in the transmittal!

14.5 Extra Steps

So what do you think of Xrefs? When used properly, they can be a tremendous time-saver. But something else is required. Let me tell you a story.

When I was working for one of the big petrochemical companies in Houston a few years ago, a friend of mine (another guru) was assigned to a new project. He was to set up the CAD system for the project.

For some wild reason (wild reasoning is not uncommon in petrochem), he decided to buck the norm and set up the project the way AutoCAD was designed to work—using things like attributes to track materials and Xrefs to save time. Jim worked diligently for weeks setting up and starting the project.

Then he was fired. It seemed the project's lead knew nothing about Xrefs and very little about attributes. All he saw was weeks gone with only a few drawings created (remember that proper setup of an AutoCAD project takes time in the beginning but saves time in the end).

The project lead hired a beginning CAD operator, had him teach himself about Xrefs and attributes and then spent more weeks disassembling, binding, exploding, and so forth all of the drawings and setups that Jim had created.

What is the moral of this story? Jim forgot one crucial fact of CAD operations. That fact involves communication. The majority of supervisors are simply not aware of AutoCAD's potential or proper use (yet). Jim did not explain to the boss what he was doing, nor did the boss bother to learn Jim's new system. He replaced it with something he understood (more expensive and time consuming but also more comfortable for him).

Your Extra Steps exercise is this: Go to your supervisor (or contact a supervisor in the industry in which you hope to work) and set up an interview. Ask if the company uses Xrefs and/or attributes to track materials. Then ask why or why not. If they are using Xrefs, try to convince them to stop (explain that this is an assignment and do not get too combative) and listen closely to their arguments. If they are not using Xrefs, try to convince them to do so. Again listen closely to their arguments.

> *Asking is only half the battle. Listening to the answer reveals the path to success.*
>
> Anonymous

14.6 What Have We Learned?

Items covered in this lesson include:

- *The XRef Manager*
- *Dependent Symbols*
- *Manipulating Xrefs—unloading, reloading, overlaying, and binding*
- *Editing Xrefs*
- *Commands*
  - ***Xref***
  - ***XAttach***
  - ***Xbind***
  - ***XClip***
  - ***Refedit***
  - ***Refclose***
  - ***Refset***
  - ***Dwgprops***

While only a fraction of the people to whom I have spoken about Xrefs actually use them, the number seems to be growing. Xrefs rank well behind blocks in popularity, but they can be almost as useful in their own way. Take some time to get comfortable with them in the exercises at the end of the lesson. Then talk it over with your employer and make an educated decision about how you will proceed.

Let's try a few more Xrefs.

14.7 EXERCISES

1. Using Xrefs whenever possible, create the drawing in Figure 14.7.1.

1.1. Use the following references (included in the C:\Steps3D\Lesson14 folder):

1.1.1. *Title block*

1.1.2. *Battery*

1.1.3. *Lamp*

1.1.4. *Galvanometer*

1.1.5. *MyBoard* (You created this in Exercise 14.1.1.1.)

1.1.6. *title info* (Insert this as a block to use the attributes.)

1.2. Create layers as needed. (You will need a wire and a text layer.)

1.3. Save the drawing as *MyCircuit1d.dwg* in the C:\Steps3D\Lesson14 folder.

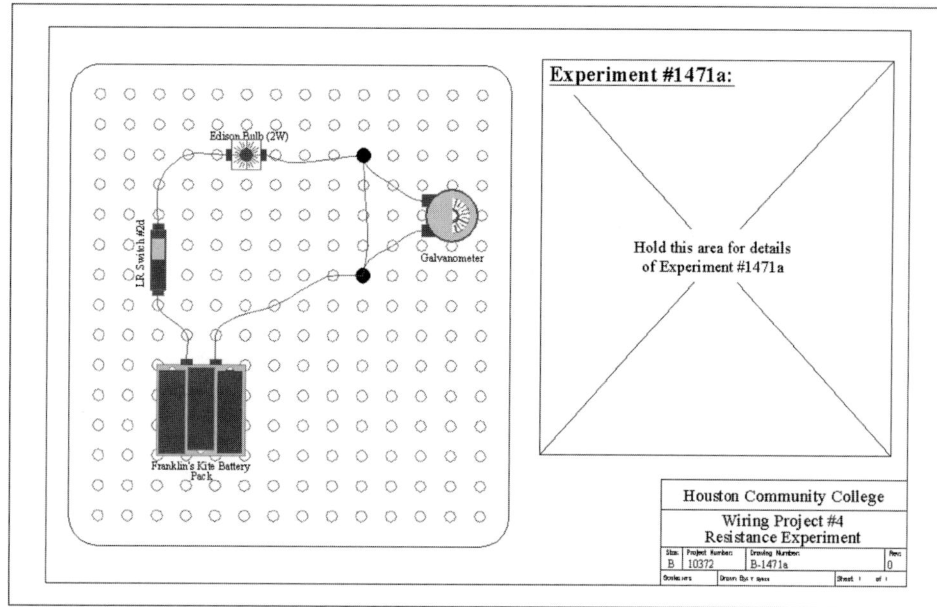

FIG. 14.7.1 *MyCircuit1d.dwg*

2. Create the drawings in Figures 14.7.2a and 14.7.2b, using Xrefs whenever possible.
   - **2.1.** Use the following references (included in the C:\Steps3D\Lesson14 folder):
     - **2.1.1.** *Title block-a*
     - **2.1.2.** Other drawings you might wish to create
     - **2.1.3.** *title info* (Insert this as a block to use the attributes.)
   - **2.2.** Create layers as needed. (You will need a pipe and a text layer.)
   - **2.3.** Save the drawings as *Pump Config 1.dwg* and *Pump Config 2.dwg* in the C:\Steps3D\Lesson14 folder.

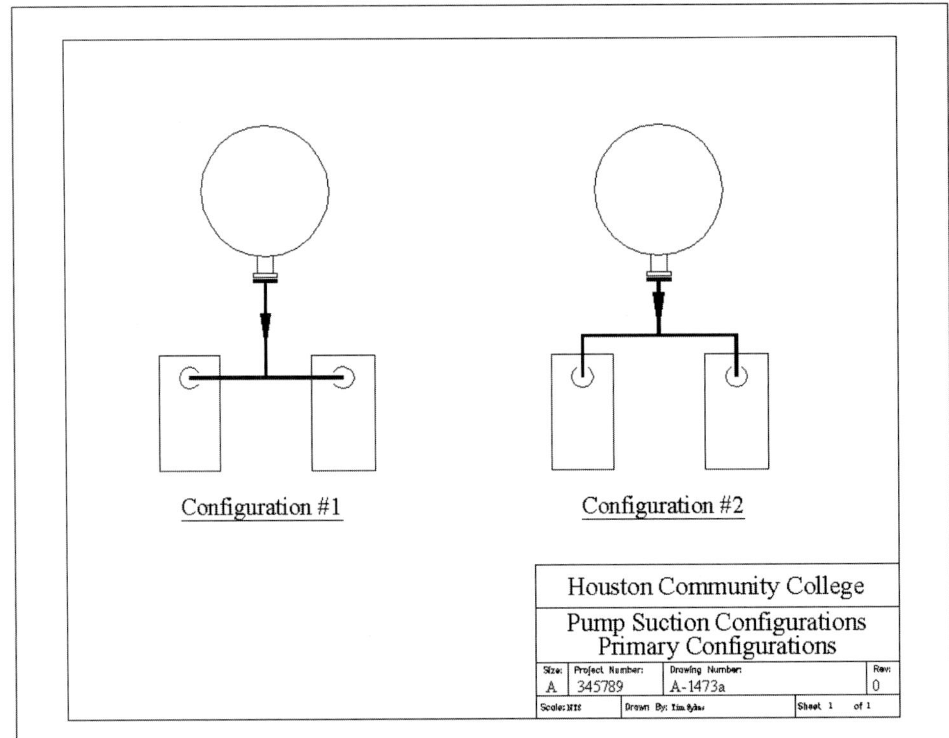

FIG. 14.7.2a *Pump Config 1.dwg*

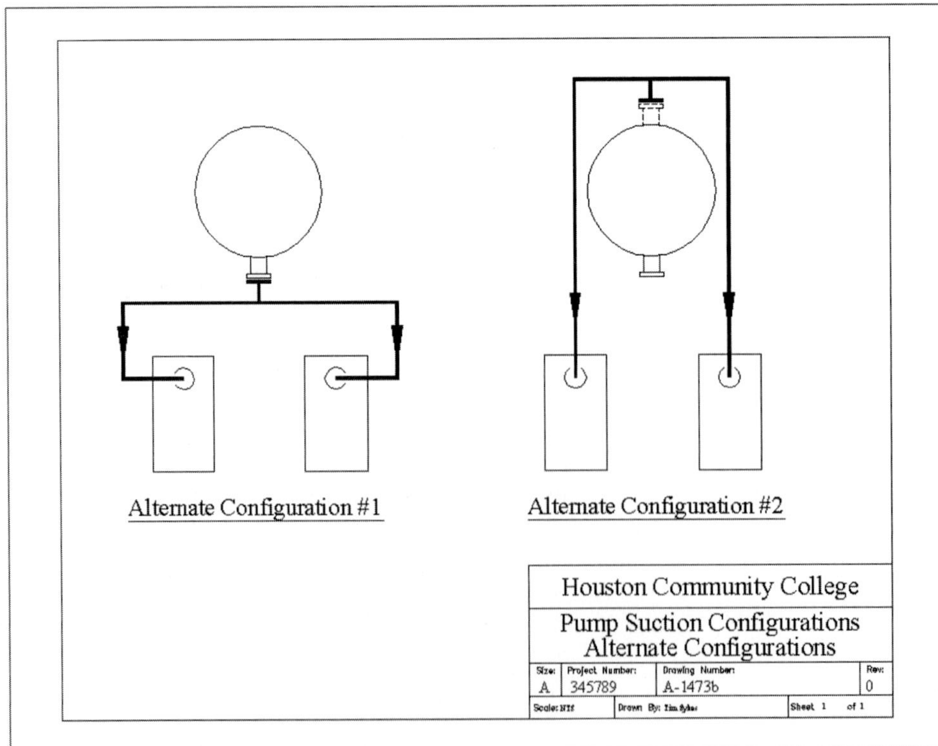

FIG. 14.7.2b *Pump Config 2.dwg*

3. Create the drawings in Figures 14.7.3a and 14.7.3b, using Xrefs whenever possible.
   - **3.1.** Use the following references (included in the C:\Steps3D\Lesson14 folder):
     - **3.1.1.** *Title block-a* (You will need to scale it for $\frac{1}{4}$"=1'-0" drawing on an 11" × $8\frac{1}{2}$" sheet of paper.)
     - **3.1.2.** *desk&chair*
     - **3.1.3.** *plant*
     - **3.1.4.** *room*
     - **3.1.5.** *table&chairs*
     - **3.1.6.** *vending machine*
     - **3.1.7.** *wall panel*
     - **3.1.8.** *title info* (Insert this as a block to use the attributes. You will need to scale it as well.)
   - **3.2.** Create layers as needed.
   - **3.3.** Save the drawings as *floor plan layout1.dwg* and *floor plan layout2.dwg* in the C:\Steps3D\Lesson14 folder.

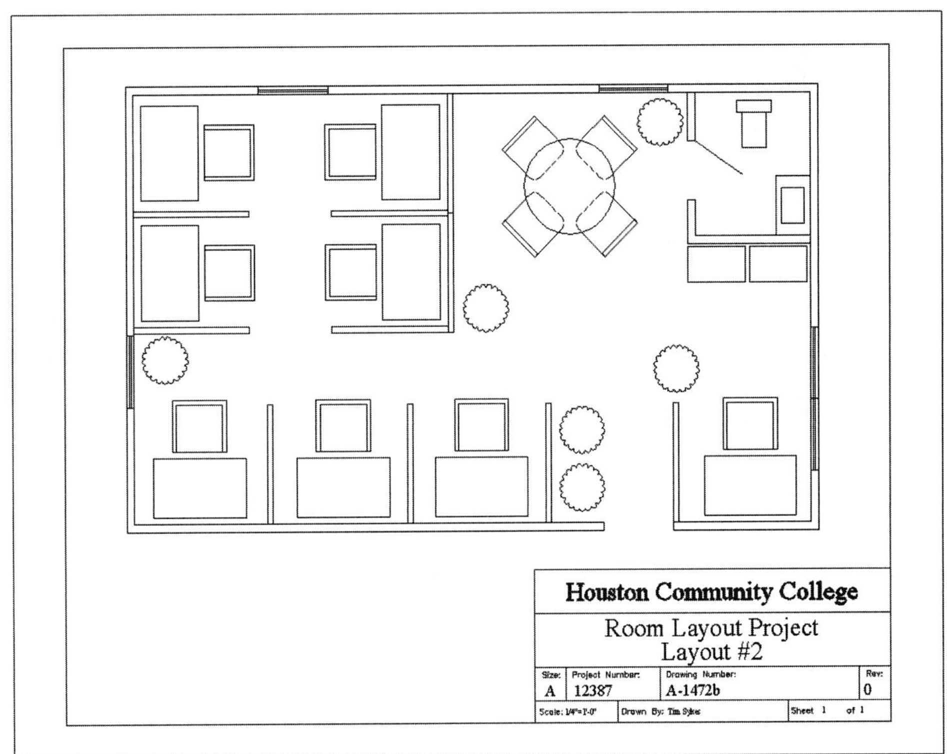

FIG. 14.7.3a *Floor Plan Layout1.dwg*

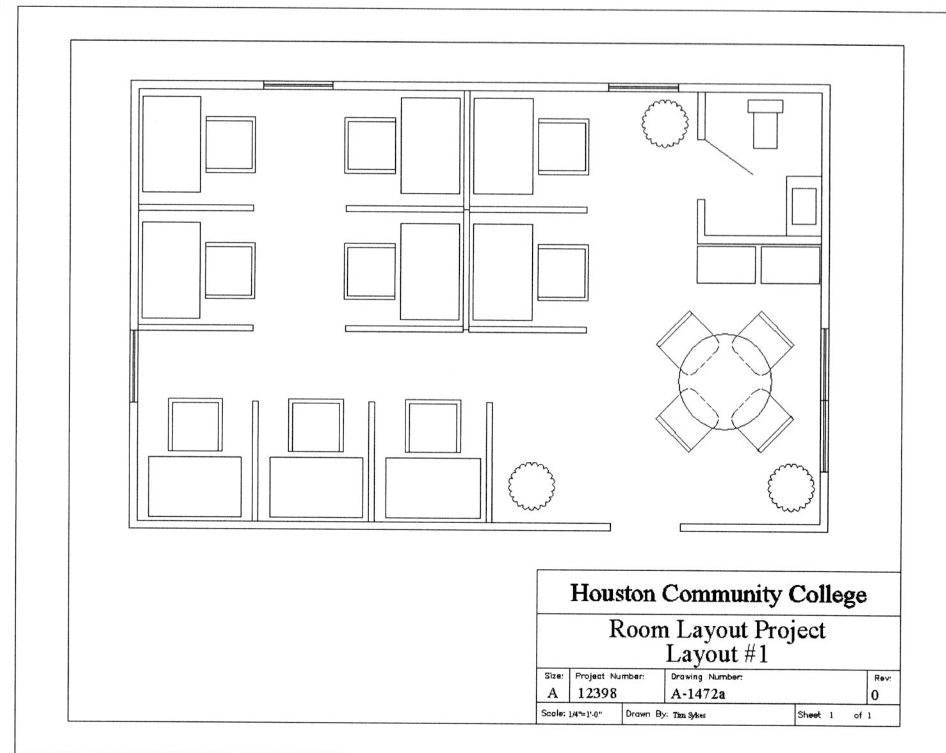

FIG. 14.7.3b *Floor Plan Layout2.dwg*

4. Open the *cutting table.dwg* file in the C:\Steps3D\Lesson14 folder. Create the 11" × 17" layout shown in Figure 14.7.4.
   - Xref the *ANSI B* title block from AutoCAD's template folder.
   - Create appropriate layers, text styles, linetypes, and so forth.
   - Use the title *info.dwg* attributed block in the C:\Steps3D\Lesson14 folder to fill in the title block information.

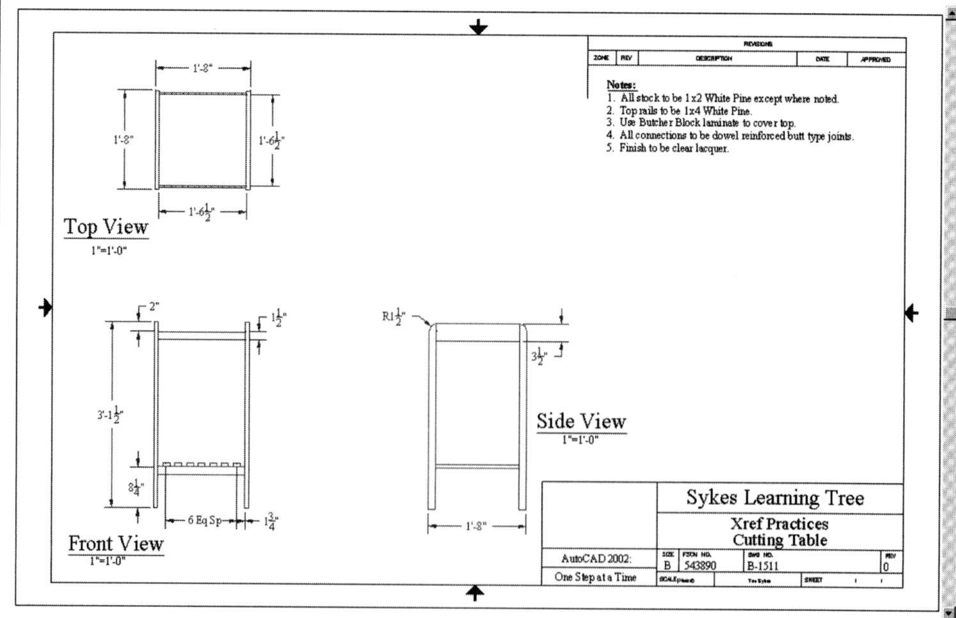

FIG. 14.7.4 Cutting Table

5. Open the *Wheel.dwg* file in the C:\Steps3D\Lesson14 folder. Create the $8\frac{1}{2}$" × 11" layout shown in Figure 14.7.5.
   - Xref the *ANSI A* title block from AutoCAD's template folder.
   - Create appropriate layers, text styles, linetypes, and so forth.
   - Use the title *info.dwg* attributed block in the C:\Steps3D\Lesson14 folder to fill in the title block information.

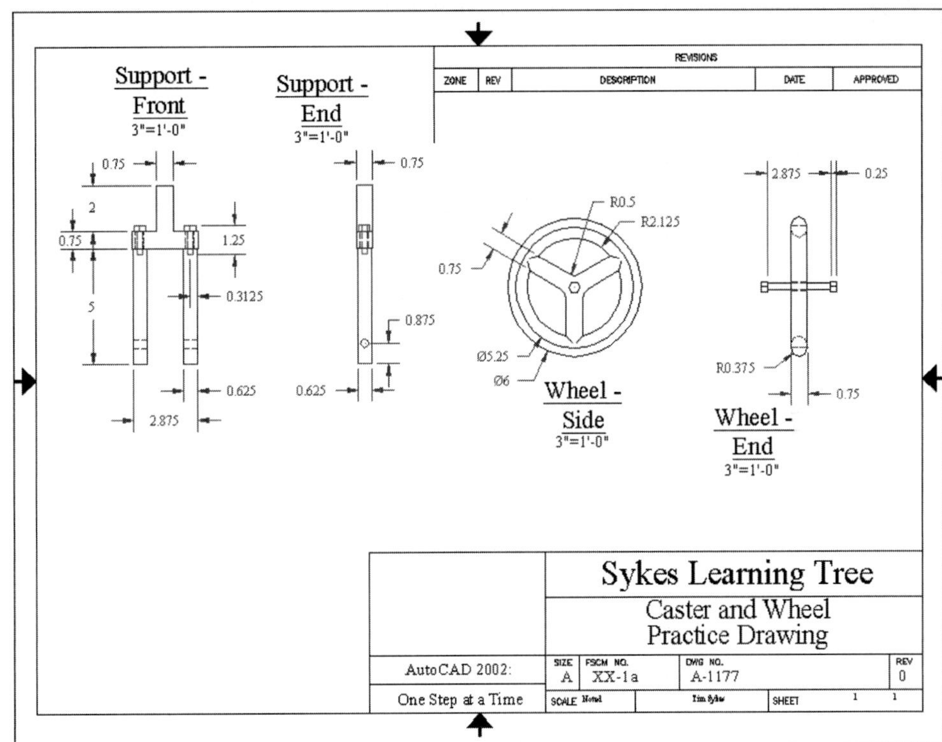

FIG. 14.7.5 *Wheel.dwg*

6. Open the *table lamp.dwg* file in the C:\Steps3D\Lesson14 folder. Create the $8\frac{1}{2}$" × 11" layout shown in Figure 14.7.6.
   - Xref the *ANSI A* title block from AutoCAD's template folder.
   - Create appropriate layers, text styles, linetypes, and so forth.
   - Use the title *info.dwg* attributed block in the C:\Steps3D\Lesson14 folder to fill in the title block information.

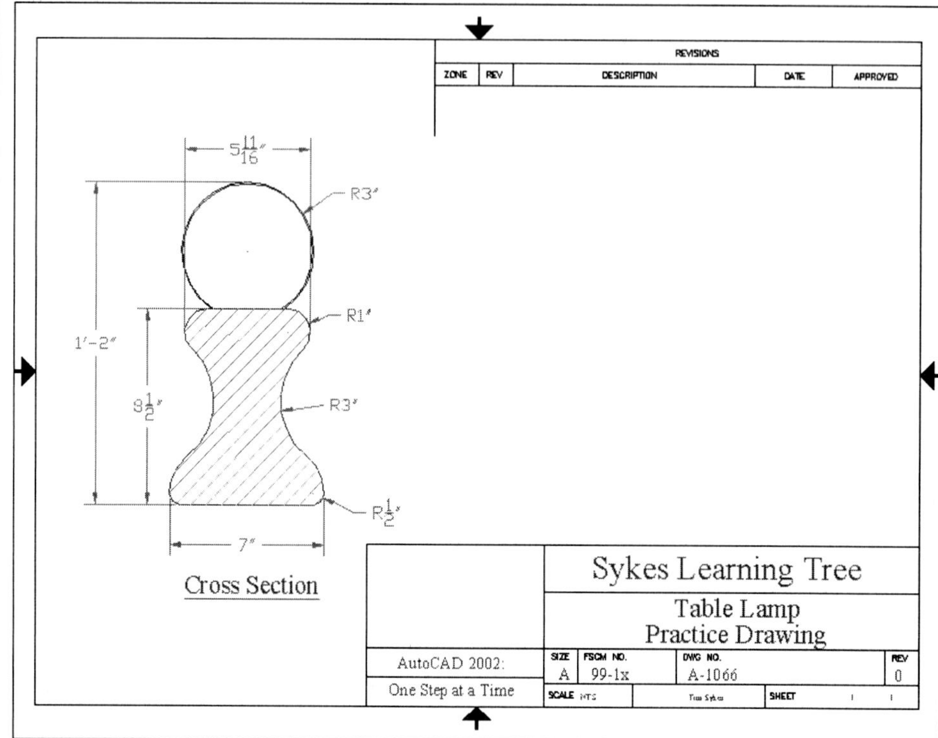

FIG. 14.7.6 Table Lamp

7. Open the *planter.dwg* file in the C:\Steps3D\Lesson14 folder. Create the $8\frac{1}{2}$" × 11" layout shown in Figure 14.7.7.
   - Xref the *ANSI A* title block from AutoCAD's template folder.
   - Create appropriate layers, text styles, linetypes, and so forth.
   - Use the title *info.dwg* attributed block in the C:\Steps3D\Lesson14 folder to fill in the title block information.

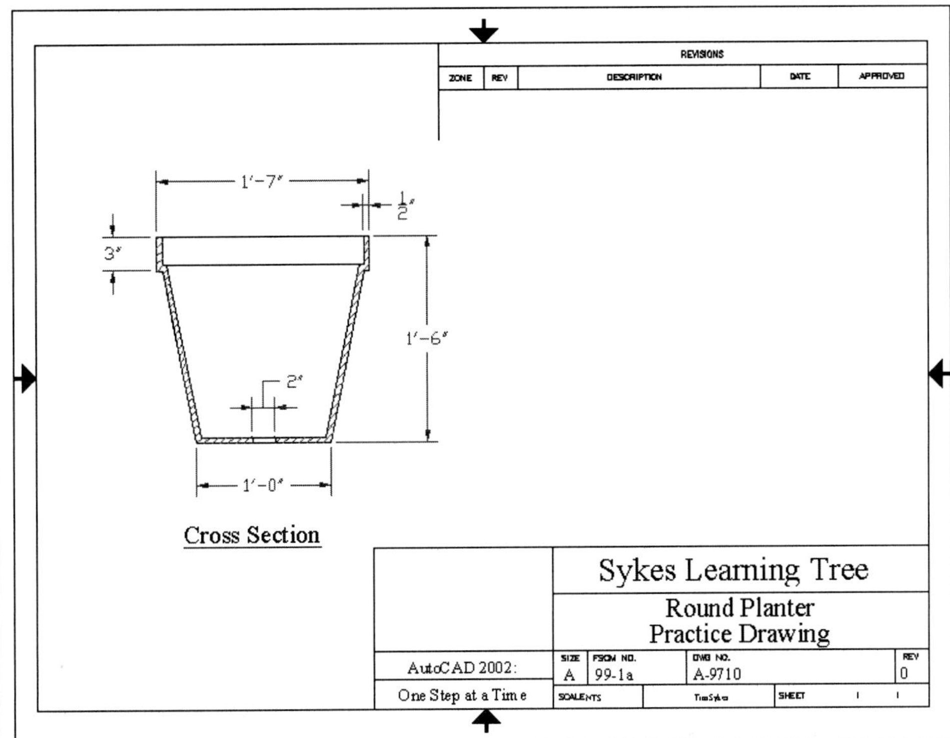

FIG. 14.7.7 Round Planter

8. Open the *patio planter.dwg* file in the C:\Steps3D\Lesson14 folder. Create the $8\frac{1}{2}$" × 11" layout shown in Figure 14.7.8.
   - Xref the *ANSI A* title block from AutoCAD's template folder.
   - Create appropriate layers, text styles, linetypes, and so forth.
   - Use the title *info.dwg* attributed block in the C:\Steps3D\Lesson14 folder to fill in the title block information.

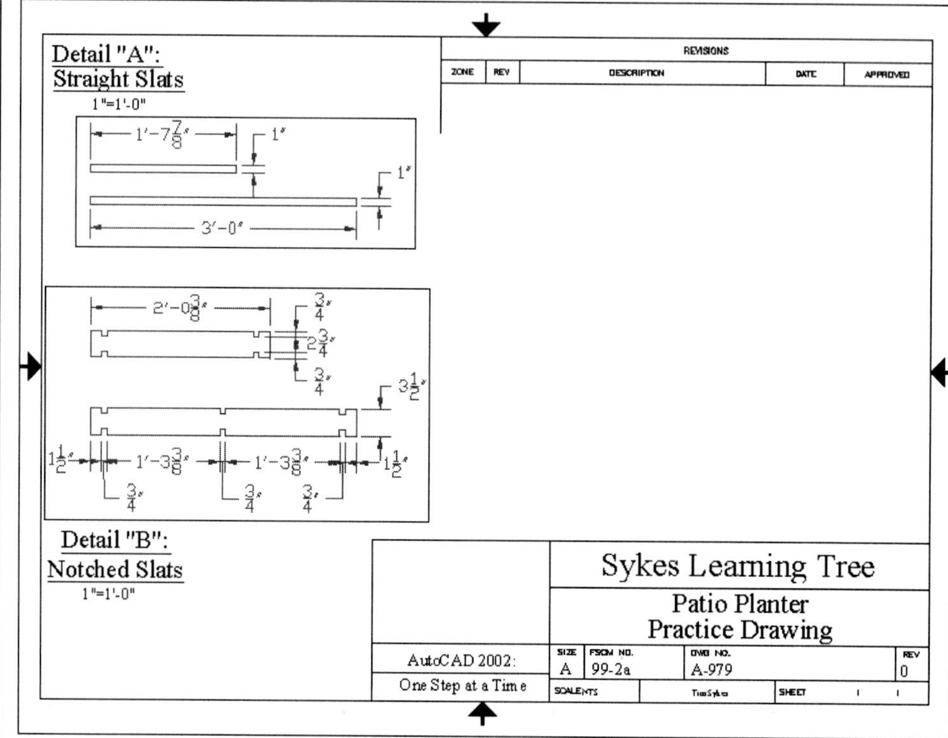

FIG. 14.7.8 Patio Planter

9. Open the *OnArtesia.dwg* file in the C:\Steps3D\Lesson14 folder. Create the 17" × 23" layout shown in Figure 14.7.9b.
   - Xref the *ANSI C* title block from AutoCAD's template folder.
   - Create appropriate layers, text styles, linetypes, and so forth.
   - Use the title *info.dwg* attributed block in the C:\Steps3D\Lesson14 folder to fill in the title block information. Use the information in Figure 14.7.9a to help you.

	Sykes Learning Tree				
	Artesian House Proposed Retaining Wall				
AutoCAD 2002:	SIZE C	FSCM NO. 2379	DWG NO. C-2379a		REV 0
One Step at a Time	SCALE 3/32"=1'-0"	Tim Sykes	SHEET	1	1

FIG. 14.7.9a Title Block

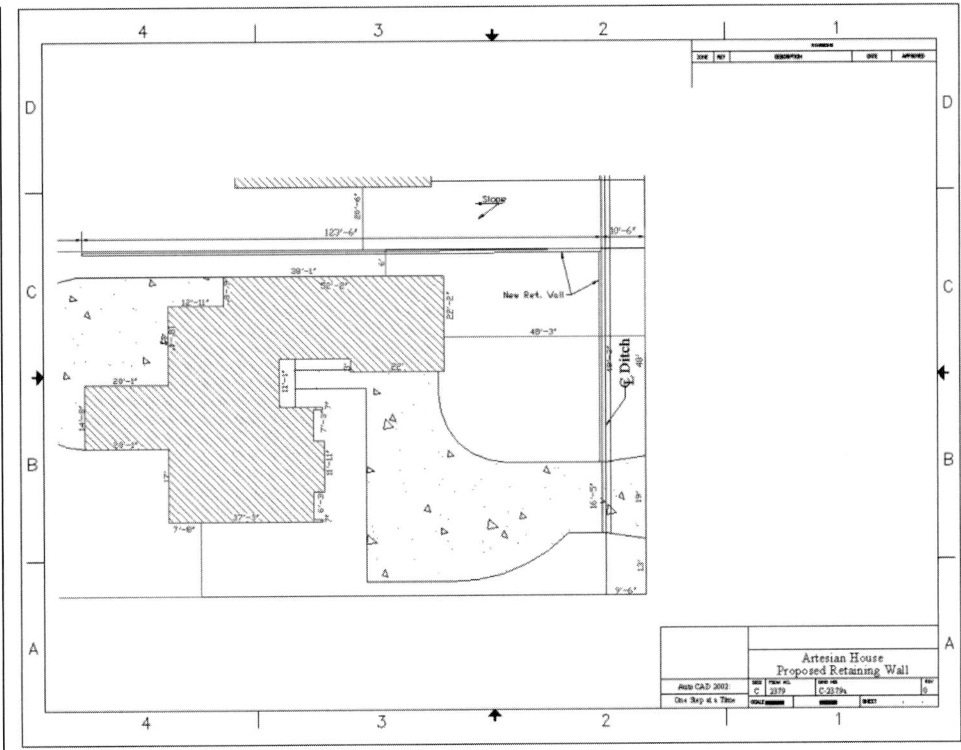

FIG. 14.7.9b Artesian House

14.8 REVIEW QUESTIONS

Please write your answers on a separate sheet of paper.

1. Xref stands for __________ __________ drawing.

2. (T or F) You cannot access attribute information from a referenced drawing.

3. (T or F) The primary drawing automatically reloads the referenced drawing whenever the primary drawing is accessed.

4. The tutorial demonstrating how to set up a Project File Search Path is found in the __________.

5. Use the Xref command to access the __________.

6. through 12. List and explain the seven statuses that may apply to a referenced drawing:

a.

b.

c.

d.

e.

f.

g.

13. If you cannot see references that should be attached to a drawing that you have referenced (nested references), the nested references might be __________ on the drawing you have referenced.

14. (T or F) The Saved Path column of the XRef Manager tells you where the reference was found.

15. If a copy of the referenced drawing exists both in the Saved Path location and the folder in which the current drawing resides, which will AutoCAD use?

16. and 17. Use the __________ button on the XRef Manager or the __________ command to attach a new reference to your drawing.

18. (T or F) If a referenced drawing (ref. "A") has a reference to another drawing (ref. "B") that you do not wish to include in your primary drawing, you should detach the second reference (ref. "B").

19. Which of the following layers has been bound to my drawing?

a. board | slots

b. board0slots

20. We refer to layers, blocks, text styles, dimension styles, and linetypes of a referenced drawing as __________.

21. When I bind by insertion a reference called *MyBoard*, it becomes a block. What is the name of the block?

22. (T or F) To use a referenced layer, simply make it current.

23. Use the __________ command to modify the view of a referenced drawing.

24. If the Clipdepth option returns this statement on the command line: *Xref must contain a clip boundary before specifying a clipdepth,* what does it mean?

25. (T or F) You can define a clipping boundary using an existing circle or polygon.

26. To see a clipping boundary even if it is not a polyline, set the __________ system variable to 1.

27. Use the __________ command to permanently attach only one or two dependent symbols from a referenced drawing to the primary drawing.

28. __________ on the reference type in the XRef Manager to change it from attach to overlay.

29. (T or F) Editing a referenced drawing will affect how it appears in all the drawings that reference it.

30. When adding an object to the Refedit working set via the ***Refset*** command, objects are added as __________ and must be treated as a whole (you cannot modify part of the added object).

31. How does binding references affect the size of the primary drawing?

32. Use the __________ command to examine the properties of the current drawing.

33. To bind a nested reference, bind __________.

Afterword

I learned to keep my balance
    And then I learned to walk.
I learned my ABCs
    Before I learned to talk.

I studied throughout high school
    And learned I had to grow.
I studied throughout college
    And still had far to go.

I trained while on the job
    And learned to make ends meet.
I trained myself to know
    Just how to beat the heat.

I've tried to rest upon the beach
    But studied every wave.
I have no doubt I'll end my life
    A-studying in the grave!

Anonymous

As a child (and later as an adult), I was always impressed by my father. Whenever I saw him—whenever he was not delivering babies or saving lives—he was always studying about new or better ways to deliver babies or save lives. Today, he is in his seventies—still saving lives . . . still studying! (He'd no doubt still deliver babies if he could find the time and energy!)

Since my mother suffers the same learning obsession, it is no wonder that I do, too. And it is an obsession I'd like to pass on to you—my readers and students.

You have completed a difficult course of study—basic and advanced AutoCAD. You can draft with the best of them. Given some experience, you'll surpass many of your co-workers because you have built a solid foundation through your studies. ***But never allow yourself to believe that your studies are over!*** **When that happens, you stagnate and others pass you by.**

Where Do You Go from Here?

The next course of AutoCAD study is Customizing AutoCAD. This includes topics like Creating Menus, Creating Linetypes, and Scripts and Slides.

Parallel to that course, you might want to look into courses in AutoLisp and/or Visual Basic (VB). AutoCAD recognizes and incorporates both of these programming languages into its operations. Many of the commands you have studied in the basic and advanced texts began as Lisp programs, and some of the newer additions (like the Object Properties Manager and the Batch Plotting Utility) are actually VB programs working with or within AutoCAD. A CAD operator who has mastered these becomes a guru (a CAD coordinator) for projects. This position generally straddles the border between worker and management. [Houston Community College (the Autodesk Training Center where I teach) even offers a class in AutoCAD Management.]

Other courses/subjects that will increase your knowledge of CAD (and your value as an employee) include

- **3D Studio Max**. This Autodesk application often works with AutoCAD files (but can create its own). **Max** animations have become quite popular in the motion picture industry.
- **Mechanical Desktop**. **Desktop** works within AutoCAD as an add-on. You can't ask for a better, simpler tool for creating parametric 3D Objects. This tool has become a necessity for mechanical parts designers.
- **Architectural Desktop**. **Architectural** is a new addition to the Autodesk stable. It simplifies architectural design.
- The **Pro series** (ProPipe, ProPlant, ProISO, etc.). These are third-party add-ons designed to work within AutoCAD to make design in a specific discipline faster and easier.

  Other Autodesk applications include **Map**, **CAD Overlay**, **3D Studio Vis**, and others.

I'd like to provide a final piece of advice. Speaking as a guru and an instructor (and all-around nice guy), let me remind you that nothing takes the place of experience. Training, studying, and testing provide an excellent foundation for any job, but "real-world" experience has no substitute. Therefore, the best suggestion I can make to you at this point is to go to work.

Even if you continue your studies (as I hope you will), the job will provide insights into what you will need as a professional that no amount of classroom training can offer. Bring those insights (and the endless questions that will arise on the job) to class with you.

If you're not in class, never be afraid to ask someone (your boss, your buddy, the guru, . . .). If they don't know, ask someone else. If no one knows, *explore, examine, experiment* until you find the answer.

Remember: *Knowledge is the only thing in the world that you can sell over and over again.*

Thank you for your time, and good luck in your endeavors.

Sincerely,

Tim

Appendix A Drawing Scales

Scale	Scale Factor	Dimensions of Drawing When Final Plot Size Is:				
(= 1′)		$8\frac{1}{2}$″ × 11″	11″ × 17″	17″ × 22″	22″ × 34″	24″ × 36″
$\frac{1}{16}$″	192	136′ × 176′	176′ × 272′	272′ × 352′	352′ × 544′	384′ × 576′
$\frac{3}{32}$″	128	90′8 × 117′4	117′4 × 181′4	181′4 × 234′8	234′8 × 362′8	256′ × 384′
$\frac{1}{8}$″	96	68′ × 88′	88′ × 136′	136′ × 176′	176′ × 272′	192′ × 288′
$\frac{3}{16}$″	64	45′4 × 58′8	58′8 × 90′8	90′8 × 117′4	117′4 × 181′4	128′ × 192′
$\frac{1}{4}$″	48	34′ × 44′	44′ × 68′	68′ × 88′	88′ × 136′	96′ × 144′
$\frac{3}{8}$″	32	22′8 × 29′4	29′4 × 45′4	45′4 × 58′8	58′8 × 90′8	64′ × 96′
$\frac{1}{2}$″	24	17′ × 22′	22′ × 34′	34′ × 44′	44′ × 68′	48′ × 72′
$\frac{3}{4}$″	16	11′4 × 14′8	14′8 × 22′8	22′8 × 29′4	29′4 × 45′4	32′ × 48′
1″	12	8′ × 6′11	11′ × 17′	17′ × 22′	22′ × 34′	24′ × 36′
$1\frac{1}{2}$″	8	5′8 × 7′4	7′4 × 11′4	11′4 × 14′8	14′8 × 22′8	16′ × 24′
3″	4	34″ × 44″	3′8 × 5′8	8′ × 6′11	7′4 × 11′4	8′ × 12′
(1″ =)						
10′	120	85′ × 110′	110′ × 170′	170′ × 220′	220′ × 340′	240′ × 360′
20′	240	170′ × 220′	220′ × 340′	340′ × 440′	440′ × 680′	480′ × 720′
25′	300	212′6 × 275′	275′ × 425′	425′ × 550′	550′ × 850′	600′ × 900′
30′	360	255′ × 330′	330′ × 510′	510′ × 660′	660′ × 1020′	720′ × 1080′
40′	480	340′ × 440′	440′ × 680′	680′ × 880′	880′ × 1360′	960′ × 1440′
50′	600	425′ × 550′	550′ × 850′	850′ × 1100′	1100′ × 1700′	1200′ × 1800′
60′	720	510′ × 660′	660′ × 1020′	1020′ × 1320′	1320′ × 2040′	1440′ × 2160′
80′	960	680′ × 880′	880′ × 1360′	1360′ × 1760′	1760′ × 2720′	1920′ × 2880′
100′	1200	850′ × 1100′	1100′ × 1700′	1700′ × 2200′	2200′ × 3400′	2400′ × 3600′
200′	2400	1700′ × 2200′	2200′ × 3400′	3400′ × 4400′	4400′ × 6800′	4800′ × 7200′

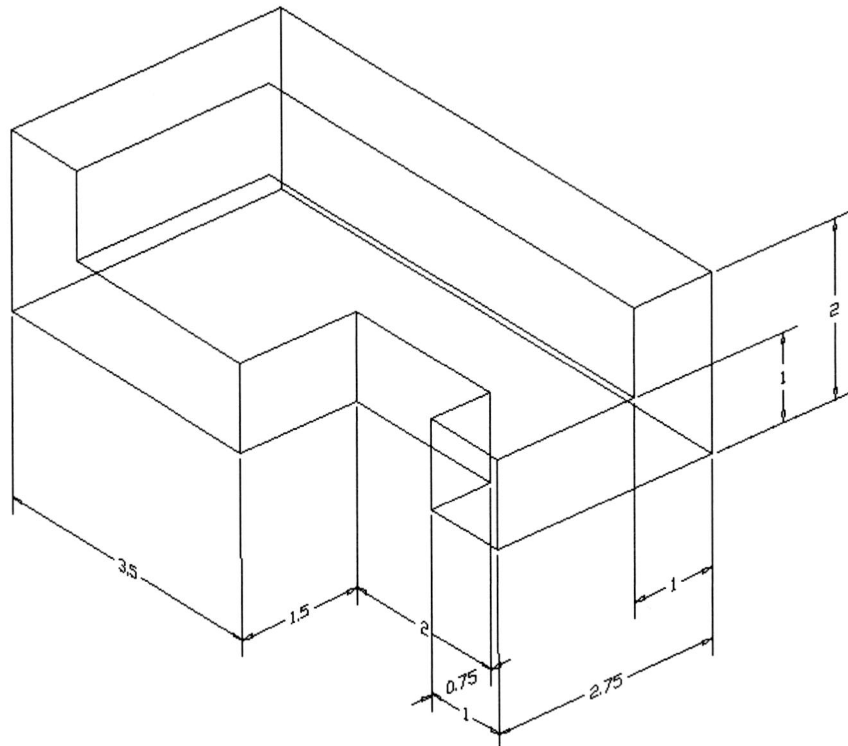

FIG. B-1w

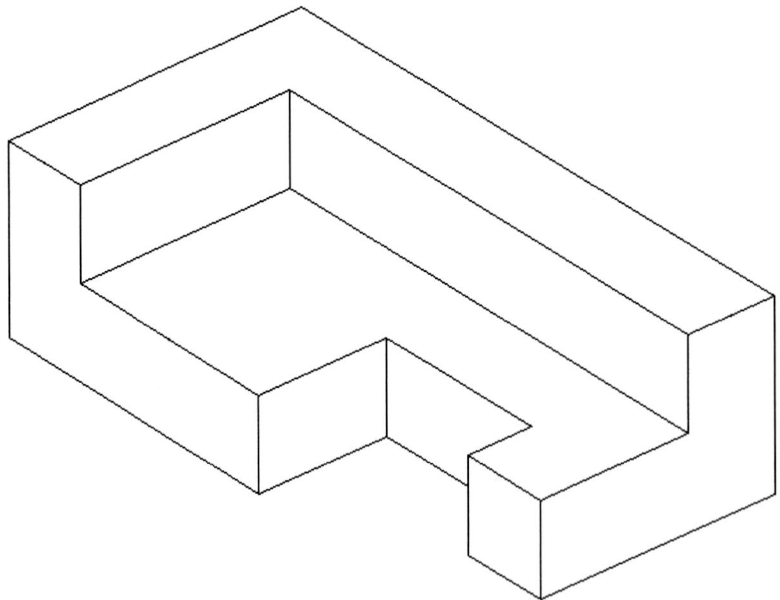

FIG. B-1su

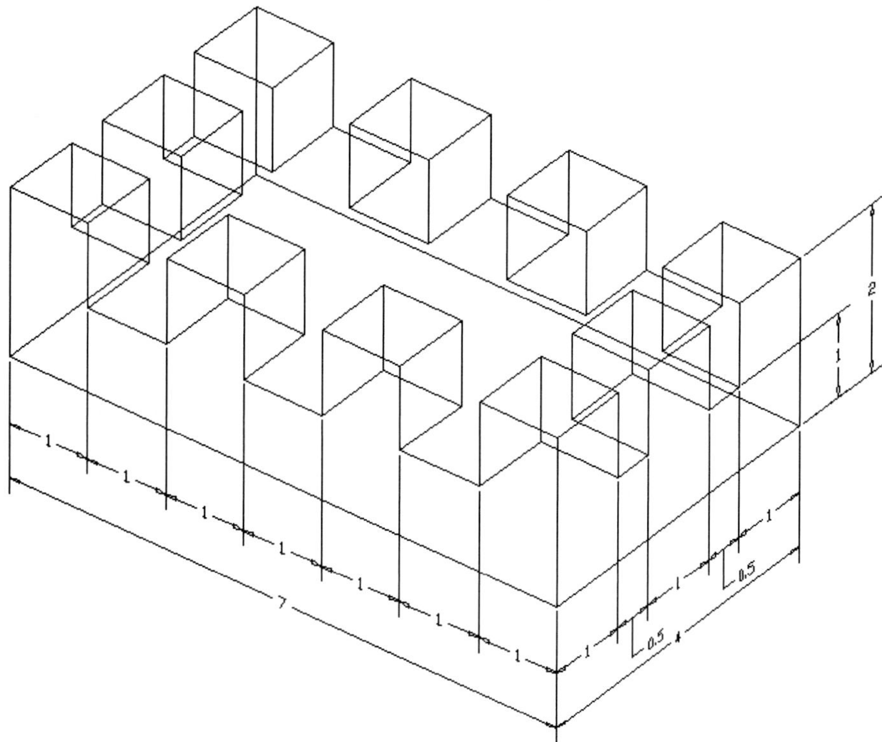

FIG. B-2w

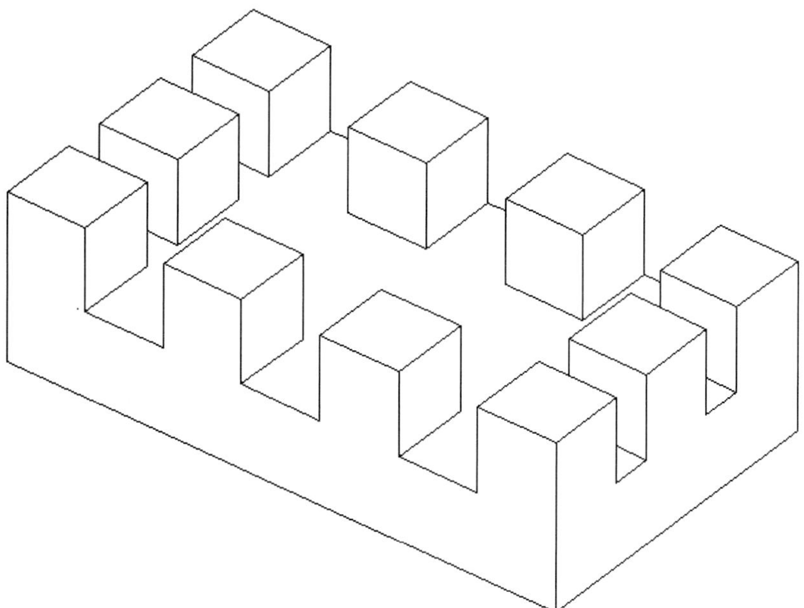

FIG. B-2su

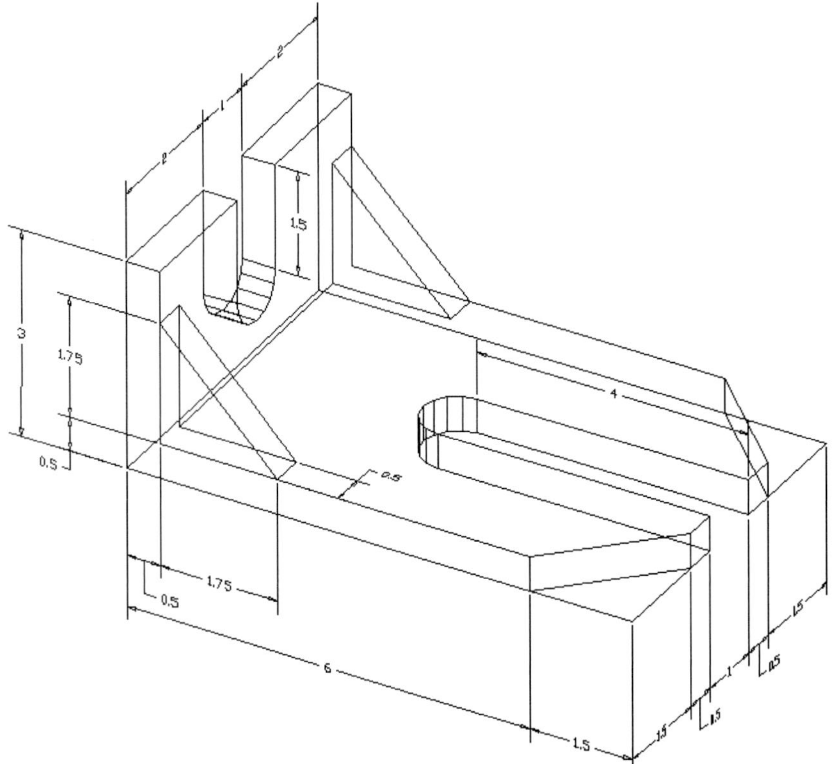

FIG. B-3w

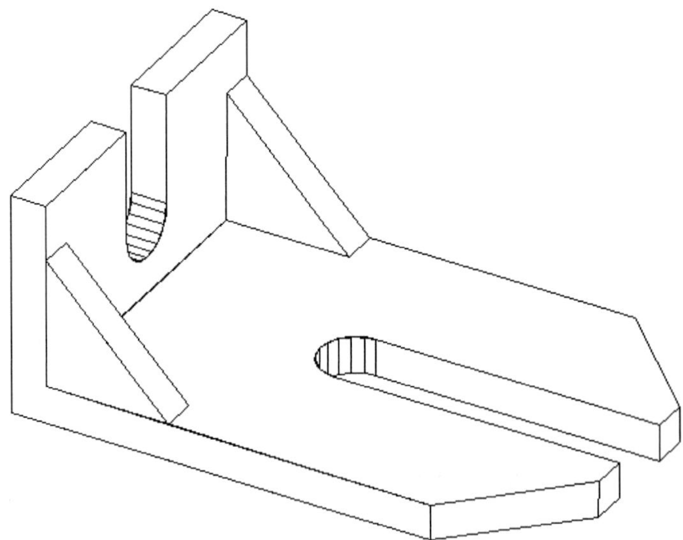

FIG. B-3su

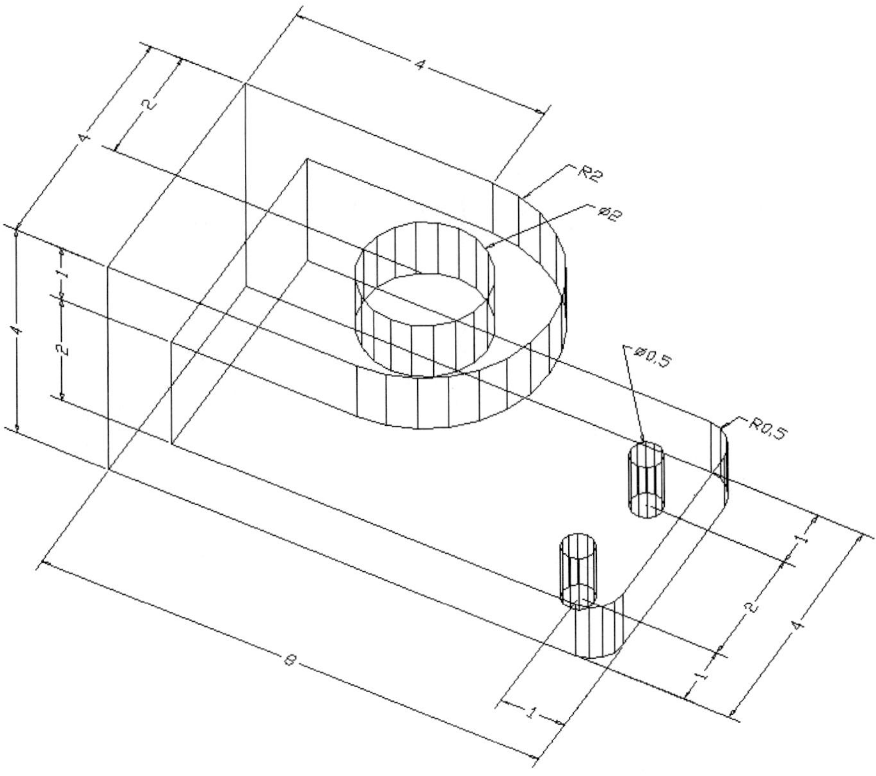

FIG. B-4w

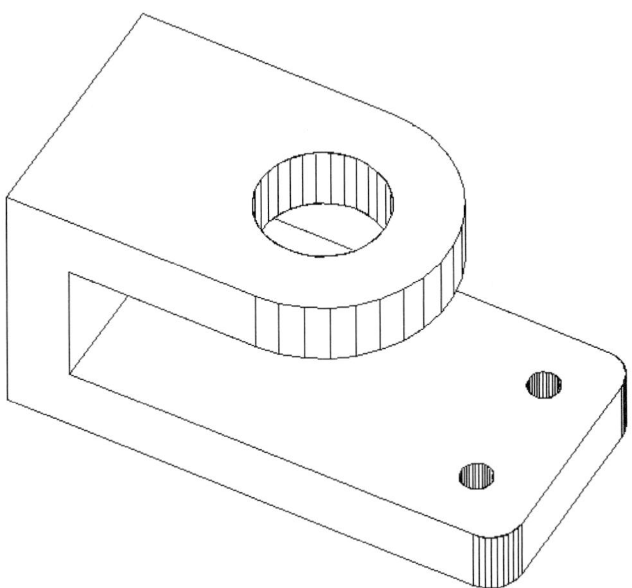

FIG. B-4su

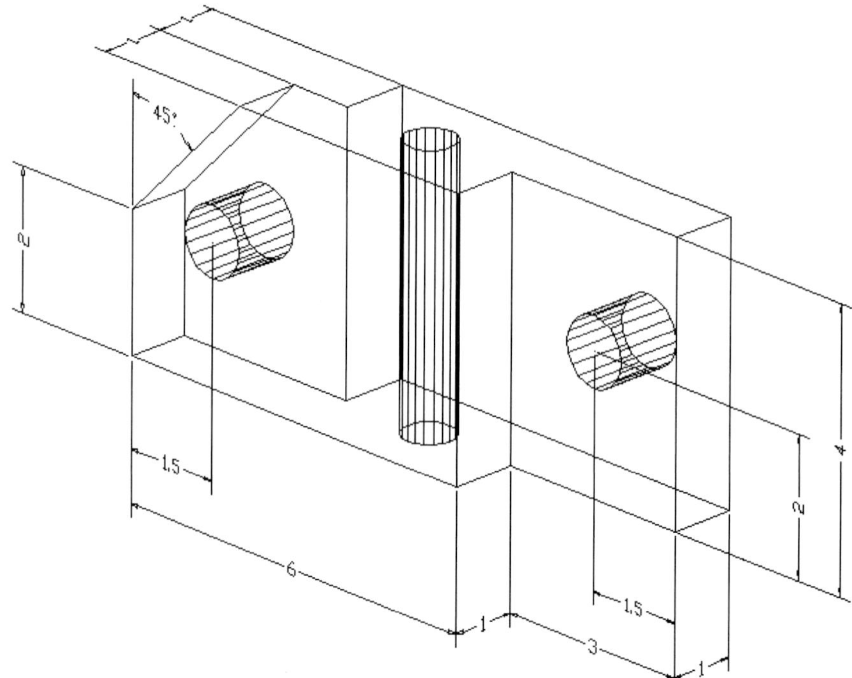

FIG. B-5w

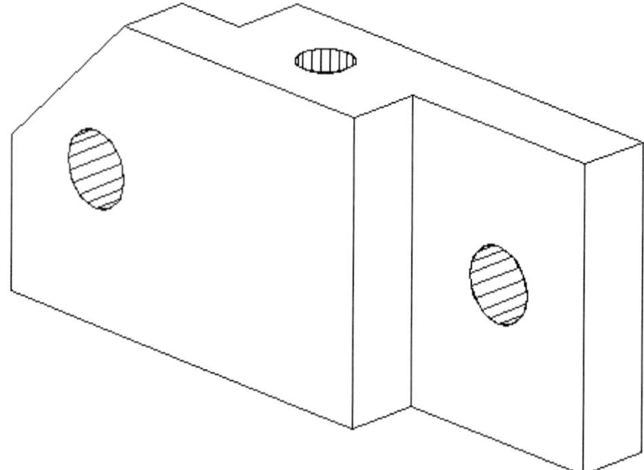
FIG. B-5su

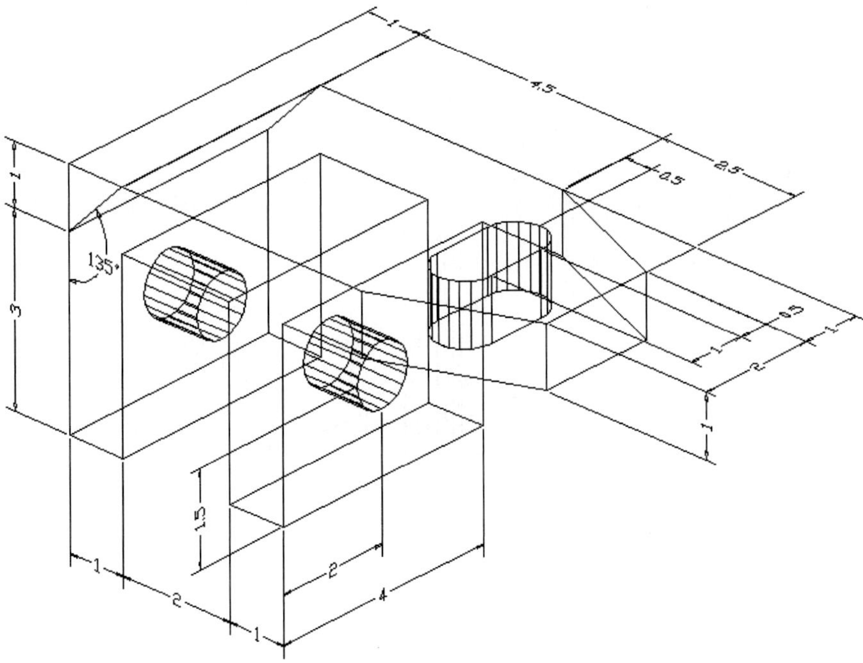

FIG. B-6w

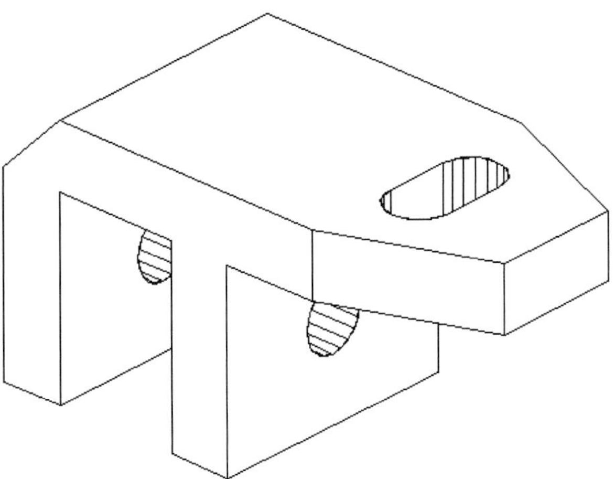

FIG. B-6su

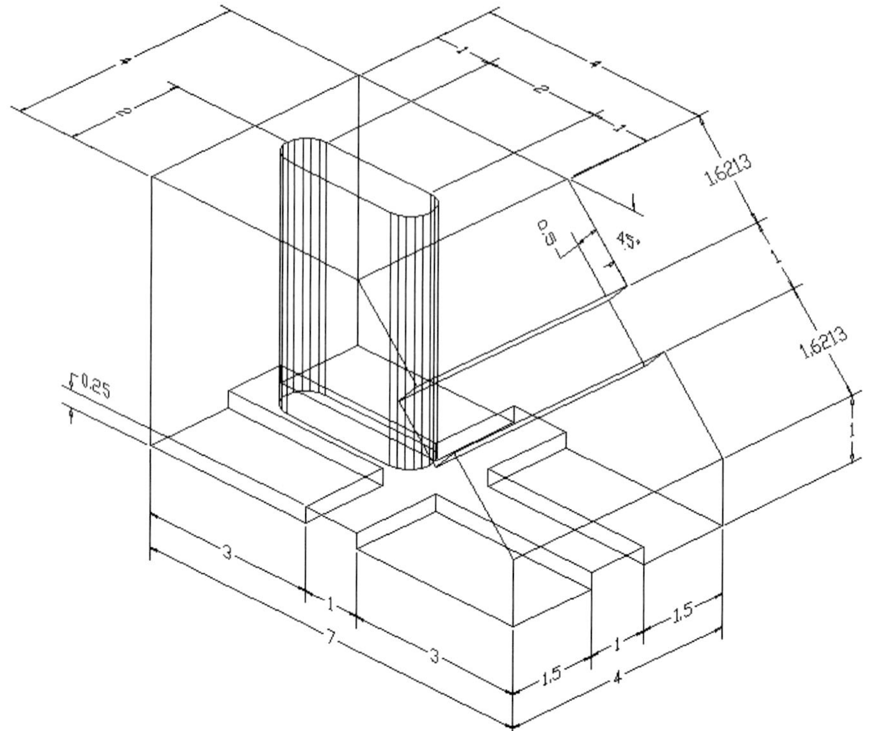

FIG. B-7w

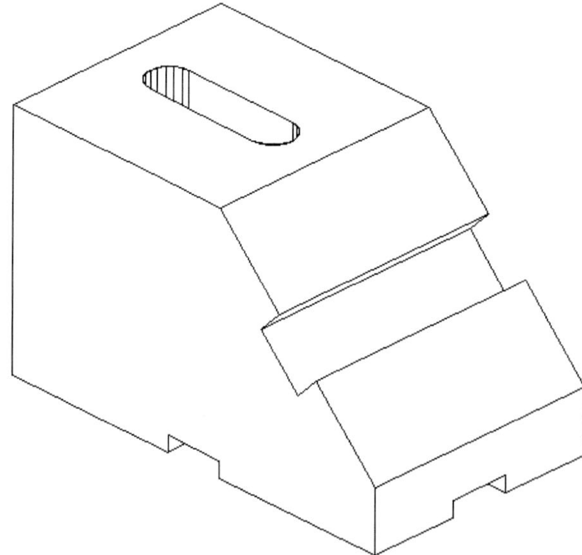

FIG. B-7su

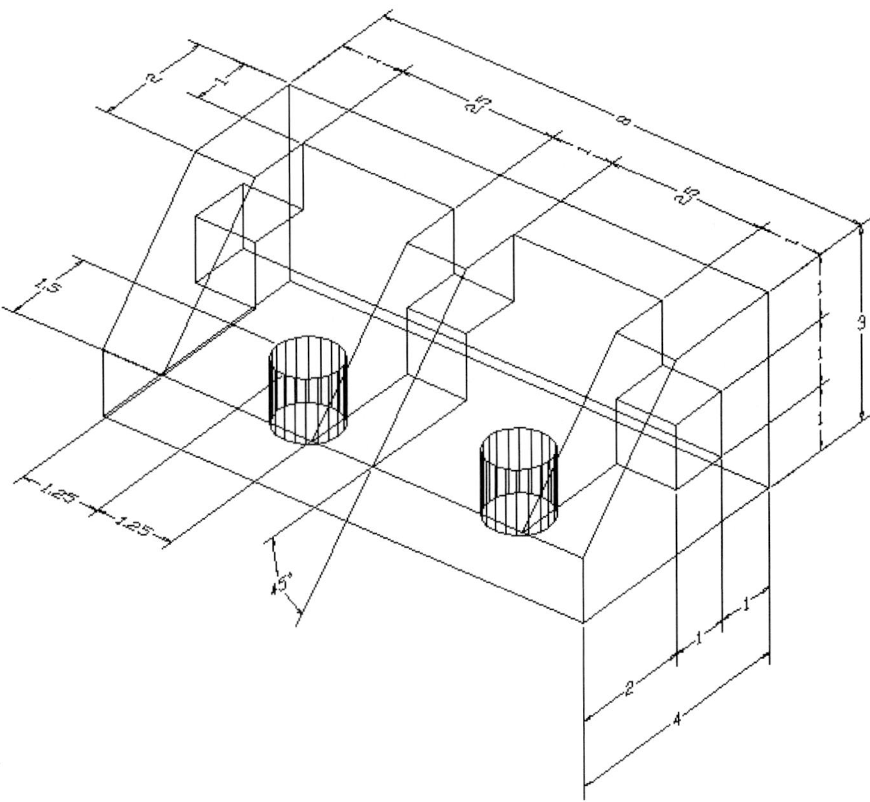

FIG. B-8w

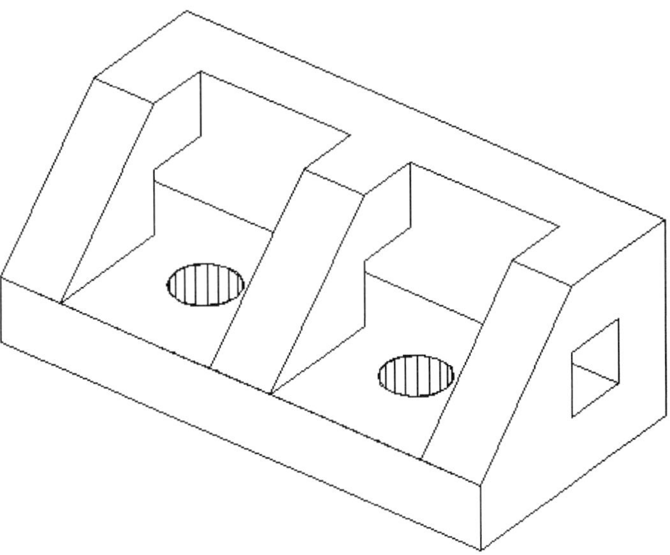

FIG. B-8su

Appendix C Review Question Answers

Lesson 1

1. Viewport
2. Tiled
3. Floating
4. Ucsicon
5. Space Tab
6. Mspace
7. Pspace
8. Tiled
9. Viewports
10. T
11. Crosshairs
12. Cursor arrow
13. Left mouse button
14. F
15. Universally
16. Pagesetup
17. T
18. 1:1
19. Triangle
20. Floating
21. F
22. F
23. T
24. Mview
25. Mview
26. F
27. Zoom
28. Scale control box

Lesson 2

1. (see Section 1.1, paragraph 1)
2. Model Space
3. Paper
4. VPLayer
5. Vpvisdflt
6. VPLayer
7. Relative to Paper Space
8. Boundary Hatch
9. It is part of the model.
10. 1=1
11. Plot
12. F
13. T
14. Modifying
15. T
16. Refreshall
17. Regenall
18. Pedit
19. VPClip

Lesson 3

1. Cartoon professor who helped Tennessee Tuxedo
2. Z-Space
3. Ucs
4. Orogin
5. Ucsicon
6. All
7. (see Figure 3.1.1a)
8. right-hand rule
9. VPoint
10. Isometric
11. Dimetric
12. 0,0,1
13. 0,1,0
14. Broken Pencil Icon
15. command line
16. compass
17. dialog box
18. tripod

19.–31. (see Figure 3.2.2b)

32. plan
33. @dist<Xyangle <Zangle
34. @dist<Xyangle,X-dist
35. T
36. T
37. F
38. thickness
39. elev.
40. property
41. F
42. Shademode
43. Over the left shoulder
44. 2D wireframe

Lesson 4

1. UCS
2. UCS
3. 3point UCS
4. UCS
5. 3DOrbit
6. 3DOrbit or Standard
7. 3DCOrbit
8. 3DOrbit
9. Previous UCS
10. UCS
11. UCS
12. Zaxis
13. 3point
14. Move
15. Orthographic
16. World
17. UCS Icon
18. Origin
19. F
20. Viewpoints
21. Viewports
22. UCS
23. View
24. T
25. UCS Manager
26. Details button of the UCS Manager
27. T
28. T
29. Layers
30. 3DOrbit
31. 3DOrbit

32.–39. (see Section 4.3.1)

40. Reset View
41. 3DCOrbit
42. A

Lesson 5

1. Wireframe
2. Surface
3. 3dpoly
4. T
5. Spline
6. Point Projection
7. PDMode
8. T
9. Regions
10. Solids
11. 3D Faces
12. Region
13. Region
14. 3D Face
15. Invisible
16. Edge
17. F
18. Display
19. SPLFrame
20. Solid
21. Solid
22. Region
23. 3D Solid
24. Region
25. Region
26. 3D Face
27. Boundary
28. Zero coordinate
29. Region
30. Subtract
31. Union
32. Intersect
33. (Refer to Section 5.3.4)

Lesson 6

1. Box
2. Wedge
3. Pyramid
4. Cone
5. Sphere
6. Dome
7. Dish
8. Torus
9. 3D meshes
10. 3D Face
11. AI_
12. AI_Box
13. Cube
14. UCS
15. Pyramid
16. Ridge
17. Tetrahedron
18. Flat Top
19. Tetrahedron
20. Polyhedrons
21. Apex
23. Ridge
24. T
25. F
26. F
27. Dome
28. Dish
29. Torus
30. F
31. F
32. T
33. T

Lesson 7

1. Surftab1
2. Surftab2
3. T
4. Tabsurf
5. Edgesurf
6. Rulesurf
7. Revsurf
8. Basic shape
9. Path
10. 60
11. F
12. Current layer
13. T
14. T
15. Single object
16. Revsurf
17. Edgesurf
18. Revsurf
19. F
20. 3D Mesh
21. PFace
22. T
23. T
24. M
25. 6
26. PFace
27. Edge
28. 3D Mesh
29. Revolved Surface
30. Tabulated Surface
31. Ruled Surface
32. Edge Surface

Lesson 8

1. Projmode
2. Project
3. 0
4. 2
5. T
6. T
7. F
8. T
9. F
10. OPM
11. Edge command
12. OPM—Edge option
13. Pedit
14. OPM
15. Grips
16. Smooth Surface
17. Quadratic B-Spline
18. Cubic B-Spline
19. Bezier
20. Surftype
21. F
22. Axes
23. An imaginary axis drawn perpendicular to your monitor's screen

Lesson 9

1. Cylinder
2. Extrude
3. Solid Modeling Building Blocks
4. Isolines
5. Taper for extrusion
6. F
7. T
8. T
9. the X-, Y-, and Z-axes
10. Specify first corner
11. Command
12. Cylinder
13. T
14. T
15. Distance from the center to the outer edge
16. Distance from the center to the center of the tube
17. Revsurf
18. Must
19. Closed
20. F
21. Extrude

Lesson 10

1. Union
2. Subtract
3. B
4. Slice
5. "Up" if you are standing on the slicing plane
6. MassProp
7. Interfere
8. F
9. T
10. F
11. T
12. Section
13. Region

Lesson 11

1. Face
2. Edge
3. Body
4. Face
5. Extrude
6. Move
7. Rotate3d
8. A positive or negative number
9. Volume of a 3D Solid
10. Taper
11. Delete
12. Regions or bodies
13. Edge
14. Imprint
15. Body
16. Figure 11.8.16b
17. Clean
18. Extrude (face)
19. Move (face)
20. Rotate (face)
21. Offset (face)
22. Taper (face)
23. Delete (face)
24. Copy (face)
25. Color (face)
26. Color (edge)
27. Copy (edge)
28. Imprint (body)
29. Clean (body)
30. Separate (body)
31. Shell (body)

Lesson 12

1. T
2. Axis
3. 1
4. Solview
5. Soldraw
6. Solprof
7. Solview
8. Soldraw
9. Solprof
10. UCS
11. Ortho
12. Auxiliary
13. Section
14. Visible lines
15. Hidden lines
16. Dimensions
17. Hatching
18. UCS
19. Soldraw
20. T
21. Profile
22. Solprof
23. A different

Lesson 13

1. Rendering
2. Render
3. Render
4. Photo Real
5. Photo Raytrace
6. T
7. RPref
8. F
9. Smoothing angle
10. Show materials
11. T
12. Phong
13. Anti-aliasing
14. High
15. 10
16. An image projected onto an object
17. Current viewport
18. Render window
19. File
20. .BMP
21. .PCX
22. PostScript
23. .TGA
24. .TIF
25. 4:1
26. Gradiant
27. Fog/Depth Cue
28. Regen
29. Appload
30. ACRender
31. Standard
32. Granite
33. Marble
34. Wood
35. RMat
36. Cube
37. Sphere
38. Select
39. Attach
40. T
41. Landscaping
42. Ambient
43. Point Light
44. Spotlight
45. Distant Light
46. Ambient
47. Point
48. Attenuation
49. Sun Angle Calculator
50. Scene

Lesson 14

1. Externally Referenced
2. F
3. T
4. AutoCAD Learning Assistant
5. XRef Manager

6.–12. (See Section 14.1.1)

13. Overlaid
14. F
15. The one in the Saved Path location
16. Attach
17. XAttach
18. F
19. board0slots
20. Dependent Symbols
21. MyBoard
22. F
23. Xclip
24. You must have a two-dimensional boundary defined before using the clipdepth option.
25. F
26. XClipFrame
27. Xbind
28. Double-click
29. T
30. Blocks
31. Increases it
32. Dwgprops
33. Its primary drawing

Appendix D Additional Projects

Here are some drawings that might challenge you.

1. The pieces for Aloysius' Cabin can be found at our Web site—www.prenhall.com/divisions/esm/app/sykes/autocad2000_advanced. They include
   - **1.1.** *longlog.dwg*
   - **1.2.** *medlog.dwg*
   - **1.3.** *shortlog.dwg*
   - **1.4.** *longhalflog.dwg*
   - **1.5.** *medhalflog.dwg*
   - **1.6.** *roof.dwg*
   - **1.7.** *gable.dwg*
   - **1.8.** *HS_Logo.bmp*

2. The bookshelves are 7′ − 6″ square × $11\frac{1}{2}$″ deep, with a $\frac{1}{2}$″-plywood back inserted into rabbets on the sides. Use your own spacing for the internal shelves.

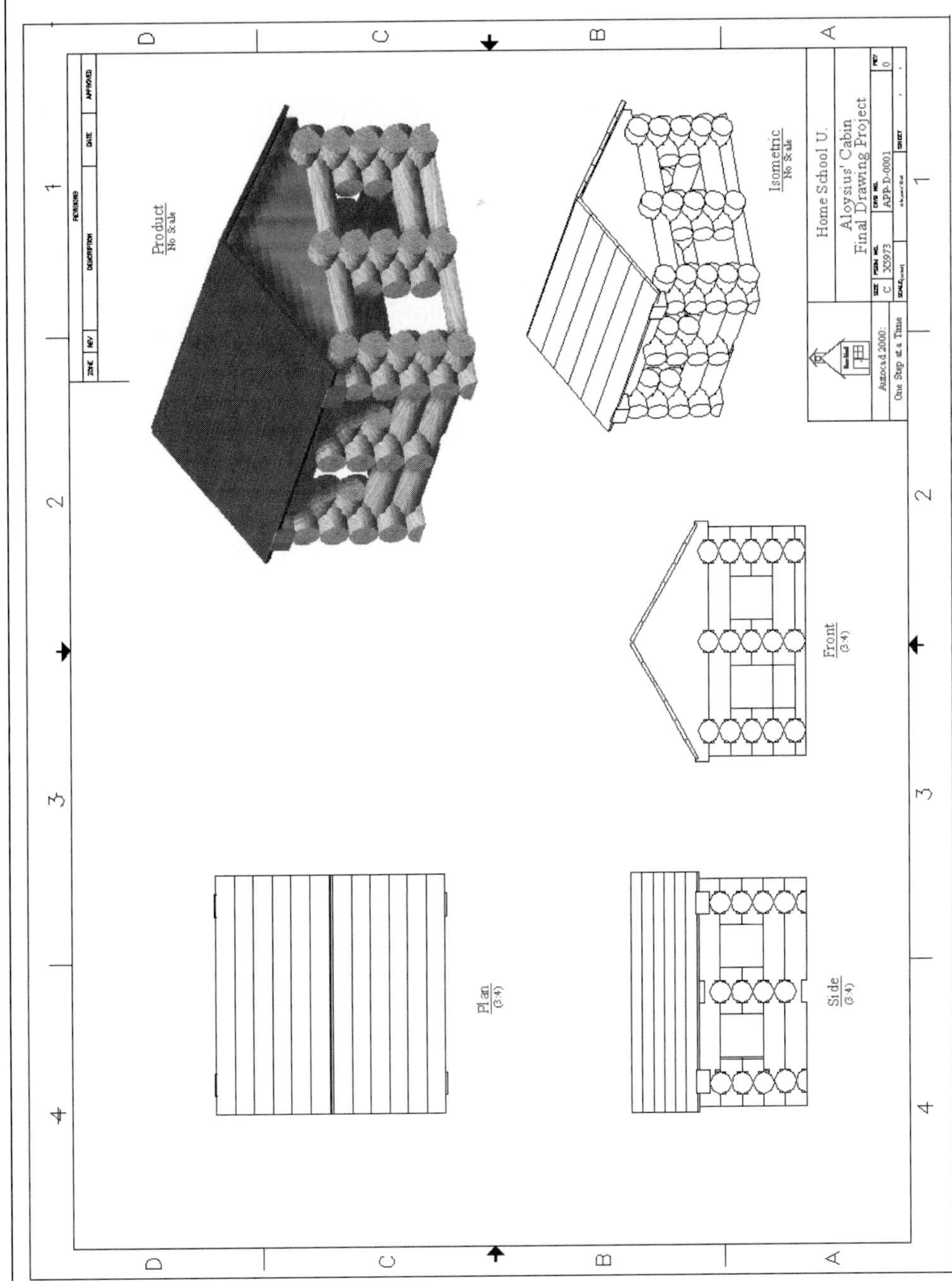

FIG. D1

3. Search the Web for additional projects. Try to draw some of them. I used keywords like "3D render" and "solid model" and found these:
   3.1. www.blackline.com/drafting/drawings/buildings.htm. (This is a good site to see some .dwf files.)
   3.2. www.pleione.com/pithouse/. (This site has some cool renderings.)
   3.3. www.powerup.com.au/~bkhcg/. (More really good rendering.)
   3.4. www.gsmmedia.com/cad/renderings.html. (Fair renderings.)

FIG. D2

4. See if you can create Figure D3. It is the metric drawing of a steel angle. Use the image (*logo-mini.gif*) in C:\Steps3D\Lesson03 in the title block.

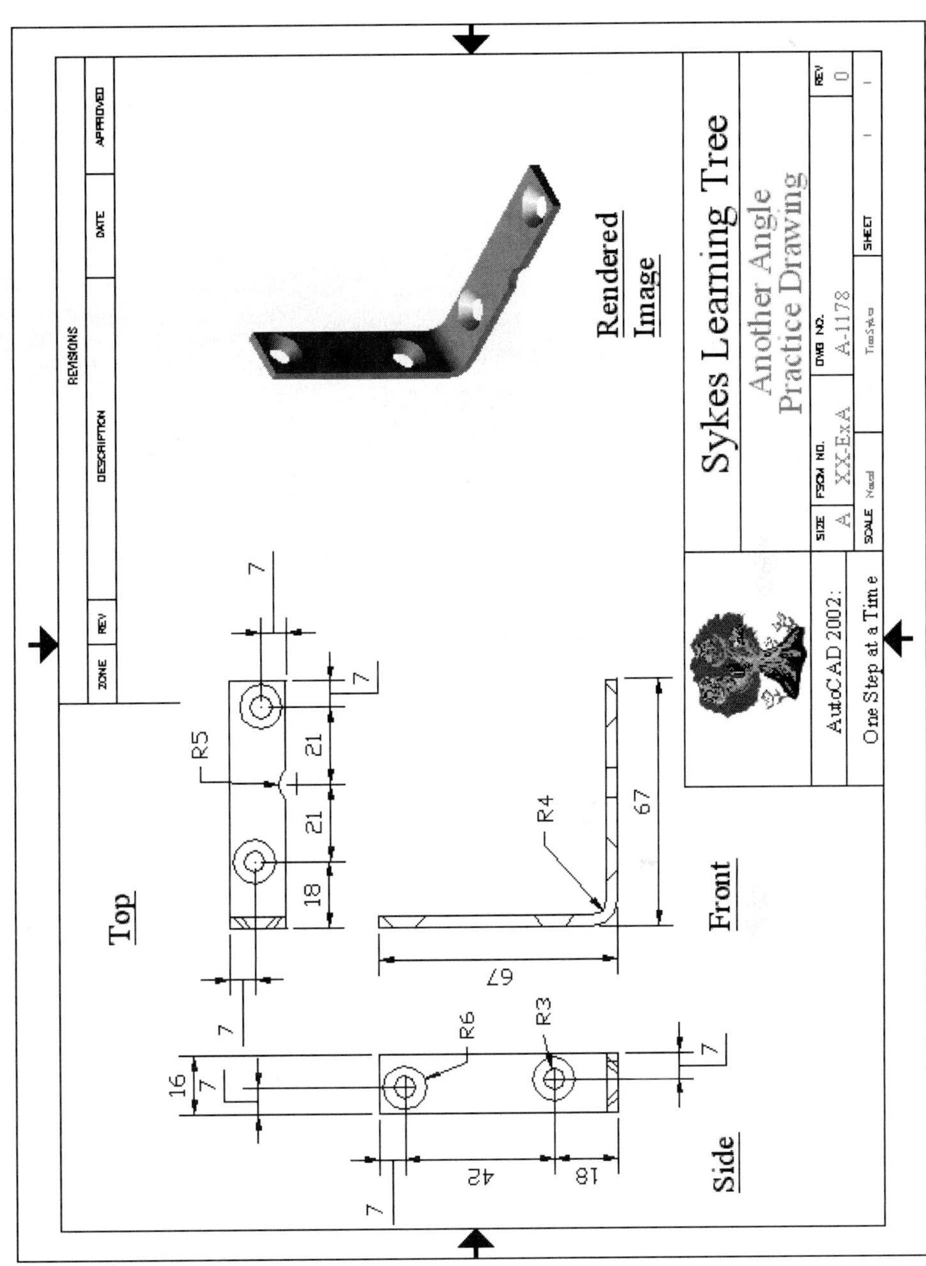

FIG. D3

5. This is a tricky one. The plates are 154mm square with an overlapping arc in the cutout. The plates rotate on a series of 4.5mm diameter bearings (spheres). Good luck!

FIG. D4

6. See if you can create Figure D5. It is the metric drawing of a steel angle. Use the image (*logo-mini.gif*) in C:\Steps3D\Lesson03 in the title block. Instead of shading the 3d view, try rendering it.

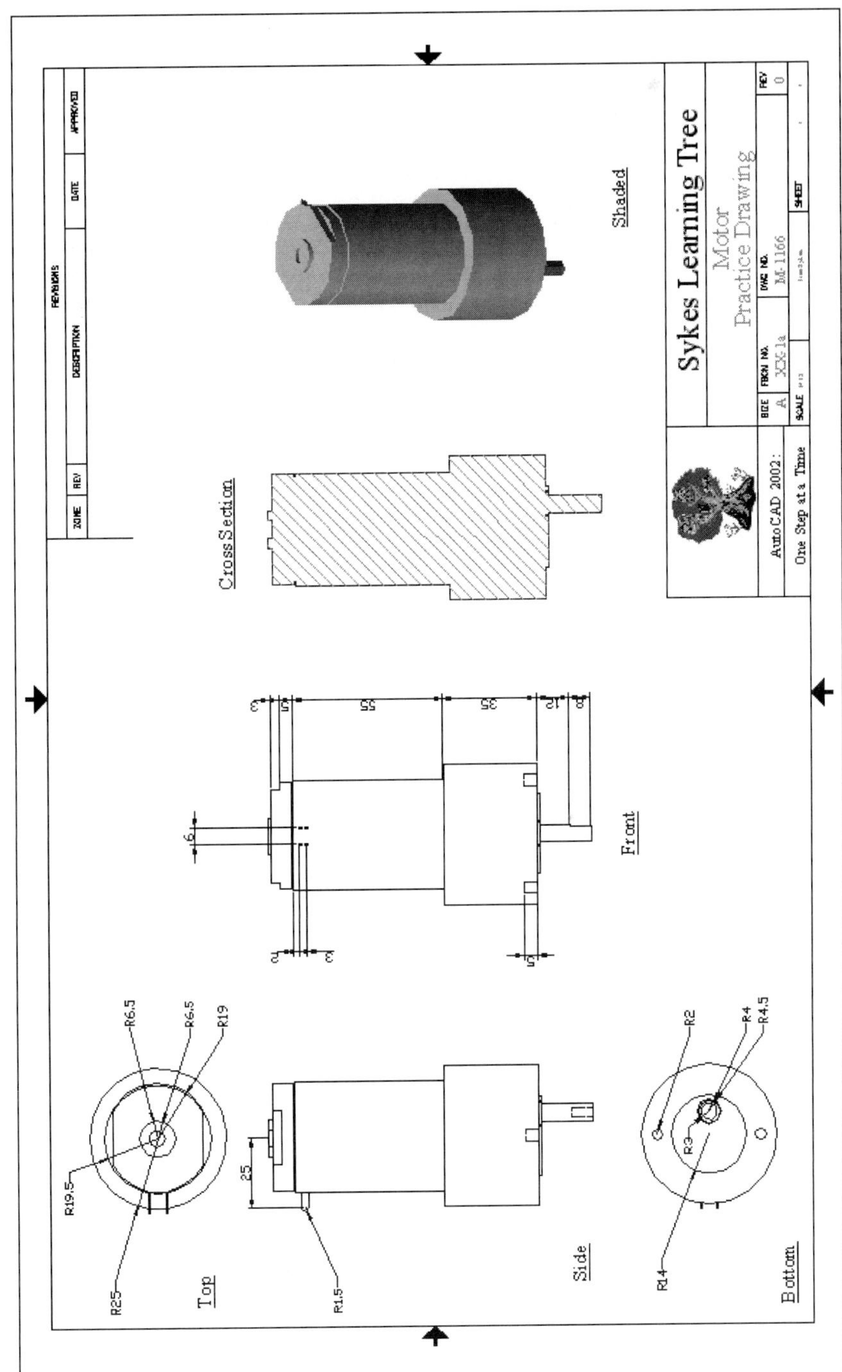

FIG. D5

INDEX